DATE DUE

MY 27 '97			
SE 24 '97			
NO 5 '97			
AP 10 '98			
MY 30 '98			
OC 15 '98			
NO 5 '08			
MY 19 '99			
NO 17 '00			
FE 1 '00			
FE 7 '02			
AP 2 '02			
DE 4 '05			
FE 11 '10			

DEMCO 38-296

Companion to Medieval and Renaissance Music

Companion to Medieval and Renaissance Music

Edited by Tess Knighton
and David Fallows

SCHIRMER BOOKS
An Imprint of Macmillan Publishing Company
New York

Maxwell Macmillan International
New York Oxford Singapore Sydney

Copyright © 1992 by Tess Knighton and David Fallows

First American edition published in 1992 by Schirmer Books, An Imprint of Macmillan
Publishing Company

Schirmer Books
An Imprint of Macmillan   Publishing Company
866 Third Avenue
New York, NY 10022

Maxwell Macmillan Canada, Inc.
1200 Eglinton Avenue East
Suite 200
Don Mills, Ontario M3C 3N1

First published in Great Britain by
The Orion Publishing Group Ltd.
Orion House
5 Upper St. Martin's Lane
London WC2H 9EA

Macmillan Publishing Company is part of the Maxwell Communication Group of Companies.

Library of Congress Catalog Card Number: 92-32213

PRINTED IN THE UNITED STATES OF AMERICA

Printing number
1 2 3 4 5 6 7 8 9 10

Musical examples set by Tabitha Collingbourne

Frontispiece: Lorenz Geddon, bronze cast of Wagner, 1880-83.

Library of Congress Cataloging-in-Publication Data

Companion to medieval and renaissance music / edited by Tess Knighton and David Fallows. —
1st American ed.
p. cm.
"First published in Great Britain by The Orion Pub. Group, Ltd."—Verso t.p.
Includes bibliographical references and index.
ISBN 0-02-871221-8
1. Music—500-1400—History and criticism. 2. Music—15th
century—History and criticism. 3. Music—16th century—History and criticism. I. Knighton,
Tess. II. Fallows, David. III. Title.
ML172.C65 1992
780'.9'02—dc20
92-32213
CIP
MN

The paper used in this publication meets the minimum requirements of American National
Standard for Information Sciences—Permanence of Paper for Printed Library Materials. ANSI
Z39.48-1984™

Contents

Contents

vi

Illustrations

Music examples

Music examples

Abbreviations

Add. MS	Additional manuscript
anon.	anonymous
b.	born
Bib. Nat.	Bibliothèque Nationale, Paris
c.	*circa*
CMM	*Corpus Mensurabilis Musicae*
d.	died
ed.	editor, edited by
edn	edition
Eng.	English
esp.	especially
fl.	*floruit* (flourished)
Fr.	French
Gr.	Greek
It.	Italian
JAMS	*Journal of the American Musicological Society*
Lat.	Latin
lit.	literally
MM	Maelzel's Metronome
MS(S)	manuscript(s)
New Grove	*The New Grove Dictionary of Music and Musicians*
orig.	original, originally
r	recto
RMA	Royal Musical Association
repr.	reprinted
rev.	revised
Sp.	Spanish
trans.	translation, translated by
v	verso
vol(s).	volume(s)

Letters indicating pitch

C' — B'   C — B   c — b   c' — b'   c'' — b''   c''' — b'''

Introduction

It should be said at once that this book makes no attempt at yet another methodical survey of medieval and Renaissance music. We felt the time was right for a much more informal approach, outlining some of the ideas that are alive at the moment for performers, researchers and particularly listeners.

The chronological approach that the French call *histoire événementielle* does conceal certain important issues: one is the vast range of types of music that existed and continued to exist through many centuries; another is the variety of ideas and disciplines that have their direct impact on the way we hear music – or rather, the *ways*, because each listener reacts differently. These matters are legion. A comprehensive or formal coverage would have duplicated much fine work that can be seen in any public library with a music section. (Some of this is listed on p.375.) More important, though, there are ways in which such formality is contrary to the very essence of a performing art.

So we also make no attempt to emulate the methods of modern historiography. Rather, this is a group of essays, many of them by young writers or by performers whose views have rarely appeared in print. The more established contributors write here mainly on subjects rather apart from their normal territory.

The initial invitations were sent out in very broad terms, mostly asking contributors to write on something that interested them but on which they had not previously published. When their suggestions were received, some were modified a little, and a plan for the volume was evolved. When its shape was beginning to come clear, a few more contributions were invited in rather more specific terms. In general the principle was that if a particular subject was of no special interest to any of the contributors, then perhaps it was not something that needed covering. Moreover, a few of the more obvious gaps in the coverage here may well give the reader some sense of angles that could be investigated in future.

What we have here, then, is a group of thoughts by a range of musicians and researchers from both sides of the Atlantic and both sides of the Channel. They are united by a fascination with the sounds of medieval and Renaissance Europe; they are also united by a sense of excitement at the way this music is coming more and more into focus as an artistic reality. The changes in sound and attitude over the past decades have been constantly astonishing and invigorating for everyone concerned, even if they have often also been perplexing. Almost every year, new kinds of performance, new research and new approaches have seemed to broaden and deepen understanding; and it looks very much as though the recovery of that music over the next decades will continue to surprise and enlighten us in ways yet to be imagined. That's fun. And it's culturally fulfilling. It may also be the main thread that unites these writers with our readers.

David Fallows

Anyone who has come into contact with medieval and Renaissance music will be immediately aware of the bewildering amount of terminology that has inevitably evolved in the study of such a wide and varied subject. This welter of terms, the meaning of which may in any case change over a period of time, can be daunting, even off-putting to the non-specialist and almost as confusing for the student. For the reader's convenience, therefore, I have compiled a Glossary that includes brief definitions of the terms used in the book as well as biographical sketches of the main musical personalities involved. This is intended as a basic on-the-spot guide so that readers will not have to interrupt their perusal of the *Companion* to consult a reference book. Similarly, the Chronology is presented as a guideline to some idea of the broad sweep of history and of where the individual personalities and sources discussed in the *Companion* fit into such an overview. The short bibliographies at the end of each article have been supplied by the contributors as suggestions for further reading.

Tess Knighton

The editors wish to thank all those who have been involved in this book, particularly Malcolm Gerratt who initiated the project and Julia Kellerman who saw the text through to publication. Thanks, too, to Elisabeth Agate who advised on picture research and Tabitha Collingbourne who set the musical examples. Above all, our thanks go to all those who responded so imaginatively to the invitation to contribute to the *Companion*.

Contributors

Margaret Bent studied at Cambridge with Thurston Dart. She has worked on English, French and Italian music of the fourteenth and fifteenth centuries, including editions of the Old Hall MS, English Masses, Dunstable and Ciconia, as well as studies of notation, musica ficta, text-setting and other performance-related issues, and a monograph, *Dunstaple*. She is a Dent Medallist of the RMA (1979), has held professorships at Brandeis University and at Princeton and served as President of the American Musicological Society. In 1992 she will take up a Fellowship at All Souls College, Oxford.

Katherine Bergeron teaches at Tufts University. She is editor, with Philip Bohlman, of *Disciplining music: musicology and its canons* (University of Chicago Press), and is currently completing a book on the nineteenth-century reform of Gregorian chant.

Thomas Binkley is director of the Early Music Institute at Indiana University. His earlier career included study at the University of Illinois, many years as director of the Studio der frühen Musik and teaching at the Schola Cantorum Basiliensis and Stanford University. He is editor of *Music Scholarship and Performance* and *Publications of the Early Music Institute* for Indiana University Press.

Ardis Butterfield is a Research Fellow in English at Downing College, Cambridge. She has contributed several articles on medieval music and poetry to journals such as *Medium Aevum* and the *Journal of the Royal Musical Association*, and is writing a book on song and narrative in thirteenth- and fourteenth-century France and England entitled *Medieval mixed genres*.

Irena Cholij is a lecturer in music at the University of Birmingham. She studied as an undergraduate at Cambridge University, and later at King's College, London. She is now researching music of the eighteenth century and is completing a doctoral thesis on music in eighteenth-century Shakespeare productions.

Randall Cook is currently on the Medieval-Renaissance Faculty of the Schola Cantorum Basiliensis. He is founder and director of the Ensemble Este and is one of the founding members of the Ferrara Ensemble. He plays and records regularly with the Ensemble Binchois, with Dominique Vellard and with Project Ars Nova from the USA.

Rogers Covey-Crump began his singing career as a boy chorister at New College, Oxford, later becoming a lay-clerk at St Alban's Abbey and graduating in music from London University. He has sung with many early music ensembles, notably with The Hilliard Ensemble and Gothic Voices, and has appeared as a soloist with other leading groups in concerts and recordings all over the world. During his years as a singer he has developed a special interest in tuning.

Gareth Curtis is Staff Tutor in Music in the Department of Extra-Mural Studies at the University of Manchester. He has written articles on and compiled editions of fifteenth-century Mass music.

Liane Curtis studied at the University of North Carolina, with a dissertation on Cambrai Cathedral in the fifteenth century. She has taught at Dartmouth College, and is currently Lecturer in Music at the Ohio State University.

Keith Falconer took his PhD in musicology at Princeton University in 1989 with a dissertation on the tropes to the Gloria. He was Visiting Assistant Professor at Duke University in Durham, North Carolina, and is at present engaged in writing a book about chromaticism and musica ficta.

David Fallows, who teaches at the University of Manchester, is the author of *Dufay* (London, 1982), and is preparing a study of the fifteenth-century song repertories. He is a Dent Medallist of the Royal Musical Association (1982), general editor of the RMA Monographs, and Books and Music Reviews Editor of *Early Music*.

Iain Fenlon worked at the Harvard Center for Italian Renaissance Studies in Florence and in 1975 became a Fellow of King's College, Cambridge. An advisory editor to *The New Grove Dictionary of Music and Musicians*, and Dent Medallist of the Royal Musical Association (1984), he has published studies of music at the Mantuan court during the Renaissance and (with James Haar) of the madrigal. He is also founder and editor of *Early Music History*.

James Haar has taught at Harvard, the University of Pennsylvania, and New York University and is currently Professor of Music at the University of North Carolina at Chapel Hill. His main interests are the sixteenth-century madrigal, the history of music theory and humanism and music. His publications include *Essays on Italian poetry and music in the Renaissance* (Berkeley, 1986) and (with Iain Fenlon) *The Italian madrigal in the early 16th century: sources and interpretation* (Cambridge, 1988).

Barbara Haggh is Assistant Professor at the University of Maryland, Baltimore County, and has published articles on music in the Low Countries and assisted with two recordings of a work she discovered by Guillaume Dufay, the *Recollectio Festorum Beatae Mariae Virginis*.

Frederick Hammond teaches at the University of California, Los Angeles, and at Bard College. He is the author of *Girolamo Frescobaldi* (Harvard, 1983) and *Girolamo Frescobaldi: a guide to research* (New York, 1988), as well as numerous articles on archival materials. He is also active as a professional harpsichordist and organist.

Paul Hillier, formerly musical director of The Hilliard Ensemble, now lives in California where he directs the Theatre of Voices and is Assistant Professor of Music at the University of California, Davis. His interests range from medieval lyrics to the music of Arvo Pärt and composers in the American experimental tradition. He is General Editor of a new series of early music editions from Fazer Music (Finland) and has published several anthologies of vocal music. He records for ECM, EMI, Harmonia Mundi and Hyperion, and is active as a singer and choral conductor in the USA, Japan and Europe.

Philip T. Jackson studied at the University of Richmond, Virginia, and at the University of North Carolina, Chapel Hill. He has taught at Occidental and Oberlin Colleges and currently serves as Head of Music History and Musicology at Ball State University. His main interest is the sixteenth-century Mass in Italy and the music of Jacquet of Mantua, which he is editing (with George Nugent) for the American Institute of Musicology.

Lewis Jones teaches medieval and Renaissance music at the Royal College of Music, London, and is Senior Lecturer in the Department of Music Technology of the City of London Polytechnic, where he also directs instrument research. He divides his time between performing, research, instrument-making and teaching.

Tess Knighton is a temporary lecturer in music history at Cambridge University. She has worked for the BBC and as Assistant Editor to *Early Music*, is co-founder and Artistic Director of the Lufthansa Festival of Baroque Music and writes as the early music critic for *The Independent*. She has published various articles on Renaissance Spanish music and is currently writing a book on music at the courts of Ferdinand and Isabella.

Kenneth Kreitner took his PhD from Duke University with a dissertation on ceremonial music in late-medieval Barcelona. He is the author of *Robert Ward: a bio-bibliography*, *Discoursing sweet music: brass bands and community life in turn-of-the-century Pennsylvania* and various articles. He is Assistant Professor of Music of Memphis State University.

Andrew Lawrence-King is a harpist and continuo-player, performing and recording with such Renaissance music groups as The Hilliard Ensemble, Gothic Voices and Tragicomedia. As well as researching the repertories and techniques of the pre-Classical harp, he is particularly interested in the role of improvisation in early music. He teaches at the Akademie für alte Musik (Bremen, Germany) and at the Sibelius Academy, Finland.

Daniel Leech-Wilkinson is a lecturer at Southampton University and specializes in the music of fourteenth-century France. Other publications include *Machaut's Mass: An introduction* (Oxford, 1990) and *Compositional techniques in the four-part isorhythmic motets of Philippe de Vitry and his contemporaries* (New York, 1989).

Margaret Mabbett studied music and Italian at Victoria University of Wellington, New Zealand, and in 1989 obtained her PhD from King's College, London, with a thesis on the Italian madrigal, 1620–55. Other research projects have included the life and works of the New Zealand composer Larry Pruden, Italian musicians in

Restoration England, and the Italian *mascherata* and related vocal forms of the late sixteenth century.

Laura W. Macy holds a PhD from the University of North Carolina and is on the music faculty at Pennsylvania State University. She has presented papers in the United States and Great Britain on aspects of sixteenth- and early seventeenth-century vocal music, and is preparing a monograph on Petrarchism and the late Italian madrigal.

Honey Meconi is Assistant Professor of Music at Rice University. She has published articles on Pierre de La Rue and the Basevi Codex and is currently writing a book on artsong reworkings.

Michael Noone is a Music Researcher for the Australian Broadcasting Corporation. He is also a choral director and lectures at Sydney University. His recent major study of music and musicians at El Escorial, based on his PhD thesis for Cambridge University, won the Spanish Musicological Society's 1990 prize for music research.

Jan Nuchelmans studied musicology in Utrecht and has played in various early music ensembles; he also teaches at the conservatories at The Hague and Amsterdam. In 1982 he was one of the founders of the Utrecht Early Music Festival of which he is Artistic Director.

Christopher Page is a Fellow of Sidney Sussex College, Cambridge, a Dent Medallist of the RMA (1990) and a Lecturer in Middle English Literature at Cambridge University. He is also director of the group Gothic Voices who have made many recordings for Hyperion. His publications include *Voices and instruments of the Middle Ages* (London, 1987) and *The owl and the nightingale* (London, 1989).

Peter Phillips was Organ Scholar at St John's College, Oxford, and is Director of The Tallis Scholars with whom he has toured the world and made many recordings on the Gimell label. He contributes a regular column to *The Spectator* and is the author of *English sacred music 1549–1649* (Gimell, 1991).

Philip Pickett is a recorder player and director of the New London Consort. In 1972 he was appointed Professor of Recorder and Performance Practice at the Guildhall School of Music and Drama in London, becoming a Fellow there in 1985. The New London Consort's many recordings for the Decca L'Oiseau-Lyre label range from the *Carmina Burana* to Monteverdi's *Orfeo*.

John Potter is a member of The Hilliard Ensemble with whom he has toured extensively and made many recordings. He also performs regularly with Tragicomedia and Redbyrd. He teaches singing at the Akademie für alte Musik, Bremen.

Anthony Rooley has an established reputation in several related fields: as a lutenist discovering forgotten masterpieces from the Renaissance; as director of the Consort of Musicke, renowned for its dedication to the research and performance of music for voices and instruments from the sixteenth and seventeenth centuries; and as a producer of music-theatre of that period. He is also the author of *Performance: revealing the Orpheus within* (Element Books, 1990).

Ephraim Segerman was born in New York, trained as a physicist-crystallographer and settled in England in 1964. Since the early 1970s he has concentrated on the history, design and technology of stringed instruments and various aspects of performance practice. He is proprietor of Northern Renaissance Instruments (which makes and sells strings, varnish and reproduction early instruments) and Editor of the quarterly journal of the Fellowship of Makers and Researchers of Historical Instruments. He also lectures on acoustics in the Music Department of Manchester University.

Richard Sherr is Professor of Music at Smith College, Northampton, MA. He has published numerous articles and is currently writing a history of the papal choir in the sixteenth century.

Hopkinson Smith, a New Yorker by birth, has performed and recorded extensively on all major early plucked instruments. He lives with his wife and three children in Basel, Switzerland, and teaches at the Schola Cantorum Basiliensis.

Reinhard Strohm studied in Munich and Berlin, has held teaching posts at London University and Yale, and is a Dent medallist of the Royal Musical Association (1977). His publications include books on Wagner, Handel and Vivaldi as well as *Music in late medieval Bruges* (London, 1985) and *The rise of European music, 1380–1500* (forthcoming).

Elizabeth C. Teviotdale is a Visiting Assistant Professor at Davidson College (Davidson, North Carolina). Her field of specialization is Western medieval manuscript painting.

Bernard Thomas is Managing Editor of London Pro Musica which specializes in performing editions of Renaissance and early Baroque music, including a series entitled *Ricercata e passaggi* . . .

Bruno Turner has had a varied musical career alongside his activities as the Managing Director of the family business, Turner Wallcoverings. He is perhaps best known as the co-founder (1977) and General Editor of Mapa Mundi performing editions, for his performances and recordings with Pro Cantione Antiqua and, since 1958, for his many broadcasts on music and the liturgy. He is a great enthusiast for and champion of Hispanic Renaissance music.

Hendrik van der Werf studied in Utrecht and later at Columbia University, New York. Formerly Professor of Musicology at the Eastman School of Music of the University of Rochester, he now holds that position in an honorary capacity and is Senior Research Associate in the Office of the Provost. His publications include

The chansons of the troubadours and trouvères: a study of the melodies and their relation to the poems (Utrecht, 1972), *The emergence of Gregorian chant* (Rochester, NY, 1983) and *The oldest extant part music and the origin of Western polyphony* (Rochester, NY, 1992).

Rob C. Wegman studied at the universities of Amsterdam and Manchester before becoming a Junior Research Fellow at New College, Oxford. He has published on various subjects in late fifteenth-century music, and is currently preparing a dissertation on the Masses of Jacob Obrecht.

Lorenz Welker studied medicine in Munich and musicology and psychology in Basel and Zurich. He was a research assistant at the Schola Cantorum Basiliensis and the Musikwissenschaftliches Institut, University of Basel. Currently Assistant Lecturer at the Musikwissenschaftliches Seminar, University of Heidelberg, he has published articles on medieval German song, Renaissance wind bands and Baroque instrumental music.

Stevie Wishart is a performer involved in medieval, traditional, and avant-garde improvisatory repertories. Formerly holder of the Vicente Cañada Blanche Fellowship, she researched bowed string instruments at Oxford Univeristy and is founder-director of Sinfonye, with whom she performs medieval music and, in particular, repertories by and about women. She also performs original music for violin and hurdy-gurdy with contemporary groups, and records for Acta, Split Records, and Hyperion.

Alison Wray is a linguist and a solo singer. Formerly a Leverhulme Research Fellow on the Singers' Language Project at the University of York, she is currently a lecturer in the Department of English Language and Linguistics at the University College of Ripon and York St John, York. She is pronunciation adviser for a number of consorts and solo singers specializing in music from the Middle Ages and Renaissance.

Crawford Young has taught plectrum lute and pre-sixteenth-century music history and performance at the Schola Cantorum in Basel since 1982. An active performer and recording artist, he has published several articles on medieval plucked instruments and their iconography. In addition to his work at the Schola, he also teaches lute at the Conservatoire National Supérieur de Lyon. He records for Deutsche Harmonia Mundi and New Albion, USA.

I The music of the past and the modern ear

1 The good, the bad and the boring

Daniel Leech-Wilkinson

Considering how readily musicologists criticize one another – witness the merciless footnotes (and reviews) of so many books and articles – the innocent bystander must find it strange that they remain unwilling to venture judgments about the quality of the music around which they work. The explanation for the anomaly lies partly in fear of contradiction (which is why scholars feel safer pointing to evidently good pieces than to bad); partly in the view of surviving compositions as 'documents', and thus sacrosanct, unsuitable to be engaged at an interpretative level; and partly (and quite properly) in the difficulty of understanding enough of the technical basis of medieval styles to enable valid judgments to be made. If only the last of these is fully justifiable, all are understandable concerns. But it is hard to see what can be the purpose of musicology if not to advise people on what to hear and how to hear it. Separating out the good, the bad and the indifferent, and helping listeners enjoy the best, is surely the least we can offer society in return for our keep.

Certainly there are any number of reasons for avoiding the problem. By whose standards are we to judge quality? How can we take account of period views without written authority for them? What evidence is there for medieval musical aesthetics? And yet, on closer inspection not all these difficulties appear insuperable.

Is it really the case, for example, that quality is 'period-dependent'; or, to put it another way, that only those alive around the time a piece of music was composed were capable of arriving at a valid judgment of its quality? If we can leave to one side the insidious moral slant to this question (do we have any right to criticize the work of other cultures?) then there seems good reason to doubt that music is meaningless beyond its own time and place. Even a brief acquaintance with medieval polyphony reveals that its forward motion is generated by juxtapositions of dissonance and consonance: melodic lines start in a consonant relationship (for example, a fifth or an octave apart), then move up or down by different amounts to produce a more dissonant sonority (say a third and a sixth above the lowest note), the tension in which then seems to require resolution into another consonance (in this case, outwards to the nearest fifth and octave). That this was the experience of medieval listeners is amply confirmed by their own theories of counterpoint; and for us the principle is clearly comparable to that which underlies most music of subsequent centuries.

Similarly, a hierarchical relationship of structure and decoration, such as has been laboriously if incontrovertibly demonstrated for eighteenth- and nineteenth-century repertories, is equally apparent in medieval music. Notre Dame organum and the fourteenth-century motet (to take only the simplest examples) are clearly nothing but decorations of an evident structure (their chant and the consonances strategically placed around it). Again, the observation can be confirmed as valid for the music's contemporaries by their manuals on composition and improvisation.

The counterpoint treatises offer such crucial evidence that it is worth pausing for a moment to look at some examples. The early (?) thirteenth-century Vatican

Organum Treatise[1] provides in its text instructions for making well-formed progressions over any likely pair of adjacent chant notes, using two voices. The result of applying these rules would be a sequence of two-voice chords – a harmonization of the chant. But what the accompanying music examples illustrate is a range of elaborations, in the added voice, of the simple progressions described in the text. Thus the reader is instructed verbally in those matters which can be expressed simply in words – the basic principles of good voice-leading – but by example in those aspects which allowed an almost infinite variety of possibilities, namely the possible decorations of those basic progressions.

We find exactly the same dual approach in the fourteenth-century counterpoint treatise of Petrus frater dictus palma ociosa (Brother Peter of the Withered Palm?).[2] The text outlines the essential principles of good progression, but, explaining that 'of innumerability it is impossible to have certainty', Peter leaves his music examples to demonstrate what can be done with counterpoint when (in his delightful phrase) it is 'adorned with flowers'. And just as the Vatican examples illustrated patterning typical of contemporary organum, so Brother Peter's show how a simple harmonization of a Mass chant may expand into a setting typical of the fourteenth-century motet. Clearly, composition was taught in terms of structure and decoration. And therefore an essential assumption (perhaps the essential assumption) about the way music 'works' is common to them and to us.

We can say that evidence of period taste exists, then; at least in so far as it can be deduced from writings designed to aid medieval teachers of music. In addition a certain amount can be deduced by examining composers' priorities during the composition process. Examples have to be very detailed to be worthwhile,[3] but essentially it is possible in certain types of strictly ordered compositions (mostly isorhythmic) to see composers being forced into choices between the competing demands of melodic writing, rhythmic schemes and good counterpoint; and from their eventual choices some indication of each composer's priorities is available to us. Such study is in its infancy; but there seems good reason to suppose that in time we will find that the music is a richer source of evidence about itself than any surviving documentation.

We do also have qualitative judgments of specific works surviving from the period. The English writer known as Anonymous IV tells us that Master Perotinus was a better composer of discant clausulae than his predecessor Leoninus, but implies that Leoninus was the better composer of organum – a remark that would be more use today if we knew what Leoninus wrote. Johannes Boen, writing on notation in about 1350,[4] cites as an example 'that most excellent motet *Virtutibus*' – the four-voice *Impudenter/Virtutibus/Alma/CT* (probably) by Philippe de Vitry – and it would be a brave scholar who disagreed with him, for the piece is clearly a virtuoso display of four-part isorhythmic writing. There are also the fascinating

---

[1] I. Godt and B. Rivera, 'The Vatican Organum Treatise – A colour reproduction, transcription and translation into English', *Gordon Athol Anderson: In Memoriam*, Musicological Studies Vol. ixl/2 (Henryville, Institute of Mediaeval Music, 1984), pp.264₁–345₁₁.

[2] J. Wolf, 'Ein Beitrag zur Diskantlehre des 14. Jahrhunderts', *Sammelbände der Internationalen Musikgesellschaft*, xv (1913–14), pp.504–34.

[3] See D. Leech-Wilkinson, *Compositional techniques in the four-part isorhythmic motets of Philippe de Vitry and his contemporaries* (New York, 1989) and *Machaut's Mass: An introduction* (Oxford, 1990).

[4] *Johannes Boen: Ars (Musicae)*, ed. F. A. Gallo, Corpus Scriptorum de Musica, xix (American Institute of Musicology, 1972), p.26.

remarks of Guillaume de Machaut about some of his own songs, recorded in his narrative poem *Le Voir Dit* in 1363–4. The music for his ballade 'Ploures, dames' 'pleases me very much'; that for 'Nes qu'on porroit' 'seems to me very strange and very novel', and 'it's a long time since I made anything as good, in my opinion', 'the lower parts are as sweet as unsalted gruel'. An unnamed rondeau, possibly 'Puis qu'en oubli', 'seems to me good'; while 'Dix et sept' is 'one of the best things I've made for seven years past, in my opinion'.5 Yet despite the rarity value of Machaut's remarks their interpretation is not easy. Was unsalted gruel sweet, or is this a joke? Is Machaut saying that to him the piece sounds sweet or sour? How did he rank his last seven years' work in relation to 'Dix et sept'? We have so few such remarks that we are almost bound to read too much into them.

We need to be wary, too, of relying on a single view of a piece. There will always be maverick opinions, and a surviving view may be one of them. How might the twenty-fifth century approach Romantic opera if the only surviving contemporary view were Nietzsche's, that *Carmen* was 'the best opera in existence'6? ('This view is especially valuable since we know that Nietzsche was a close associate of Wagner. We must surely conclude that even those closest to the composer were in no doubt that Bizet was the greater figure . . . ') It need hardly be said, in the light of such a possibility, that period views need confirmation from study of the music, not vice versa.

The wider field of medieval aesthetics has relatively little to offer. Medieval writing about musical beauty tends to be abstract (concerned with the power of music in the ancient world) rather than specific (this is a good piece because . . .). In the rare cases where examples of musical effects are offered, they tend to be drawn from the repertory of ecclesiastical chant – a reflection partly of the clerical background of author and audience, but also of the fact that while chant was heard on a daily basis – was, in fact, the primary musical experience of most literate people – polyphony was relatively rare, confined for the most part to festal occasions in a few of the wealthiest institutions. Despite providing the main area of compositional activity it played too insignificant a part in the lives of the writing classes to stimulate detailed speculation. Its higher mechanisms were taught verbally and by example. Although composed polyphony required literacy for its practice, there was little need for high level speculation about compositional technique, still less for a generalized theory of musical perception.

As a consequence, it has sometimes been assumed that medieval composition is better thought of as a craft than an art – the application of rules rather than the creation of beauty7– and, therefore, that discussion of medieval music should be limited to description of its evident form. Such a distinction is meaningless. Unless he is composing by numbers (an option which treatises do offer to the inexpert), a composer cannot help writing what to him sounds good: it is, after all, his only way of achieving job satisfaction.

---

5 These remarks are considered in greater depth in my forthcoming study of *Le Voir Dit*. A good (and available) introduction is S. J. Williams, 'The lady, the lyrics and the letters', *Early Music*, v (1977), pp.462–8.
6 Letter to Heinrich Köselitz, 8 December 1881, published in G. Colli and M. Montinari (eds), *Nietzsche Briefwechsel*, Abt. 3, Bd. 1: *Januar 1880-Dezember 1884* (Berlin, 1981), p.147.
7 See, for example, E. E. Lowinsky, 'Musical genius: evolution and origins of a concept', *Musical Quarterly*, (1964), esp. pp.476–8 and 489–90; repr. in Lowinsky, *Music in the culture of the Renaissance and other essays* (Chicago, 1989) pp.49–50 and 55.

There is a limit, then, to how much of a 'medieval view' of musical values can be recovered. Documentary evidence is rare, and very difficult to interpret. On the other hand, we do have a great deal of music; we know a lot about the grammatical principles on which it rests; and the music itself is a rich source of evidence for the way these principles were built upon in practice. There must be a good case to be made for judging a piece on its success in applying medieval compositional techniques. At the very least, that should provide a firm basis for a wider ranging consideration of quality. To what extent might this already be possible?

Some contrasts are obvious. Few would disagree that, for instance, Machaut's *Messe de Nostre Dame* is a far finer achievement than the Mass of Tournai. It is not hard to isolate the towering monuments. We need to be able to deal with less striking contrasts, to distinguish, for example, between better and worse songs and motets. It would be unrealistic to expect, at this stage, to be able to compare between repertories; but we should be able to get somewhere in sorting pieces within each. We should surely be able to offer some indication of which are the best Machaut motets, even if, because of its wider chronological span, it is too early to point to the best pieces in the Montpellier manuscript, for example.

Some basic steps are self-evident. It seems very likely that, through a process of natural selection, the manuscripts offer a high proportion of competent to good pieces. Ascriptions in the manuscripts of pieces to composers may imply fame, and so quality, provided that the composers so named are not local to the copying of the manuscript or, if they are, that their works also occur elsewhere. On these grounds we need to be wary of, for instance, Matteo da Perugia, whose relatively large output is confined to the Modena manuscript. He is a prime example of a composer whose greatness has been assumed on the basis of the large number of pieces surviving and the complexity of their notation. But the quality of his work remains to be demonstrated.

Similarly, the appearance of a piece in many different manuscripts clearly indicates its popularity; but again we need to be wary of converting that into evidence of perceived quality. The anonymous 'Jour a jour la vie' survives, in one form or another, in ten manuscripts; but it has yet to be shown that it owes its popularity to anything more than its amusing metrical contrasts. It may be fun to perform, but is it a good piece?

On the other hand, it may be that really bad pieces – the contrapuntally inept – offer valuable clues as to the way ordinary musicians composed. Isolating them should at least enable us to narrow the field of music worth hearing and studying. But if we are to approach the repertory from this end we need to be careful to distinguish between those pieces which are simply incompetent and those which look odd but which, on closer inspection, prove to be extending the language in ways which work. The latter will be applying principles consistently, albeit principles which differ to some extent from those which are conventionally followed, whereas the incompetent works are more likely to behave irregularly, correctly in some contexts but with evident contrapuntal errors in similar contexts elsewhere within the piece.

There must also be works which, though contrapuntally correct, are simply dull. This is a group particularly susceptible to enlargement through prejudice. It is dangerously easy to assume that anonymous pieces are of less interest than those with composers' names attached, or that two-voice works are of less interest in repertories where three parts are the norm, or that certain forms stimulate greater compositional sophistication than others (ballade than virelai, for example, or organum than motet). Likewise monophony tends to lose out at the hands of scholars primarily interested in polyphony, and vice versa. But where such prejudices can be overcome, or at least allowed for, it should be possible to begin to identify pieces which do nothing out of the ordinary, or which fail to do the ordinary in an interesting way, monotonously using and reusing a few hackneyed melodic shapes, rhythmic figures and contrapuntal progressions.

In none of the categories so far outlined should we overlook the possibility that a piece which looks odd, or just boring, may succeed in performance. This must be a valid criterion, particularly when so much of our aural knowledge of these early repertories has still to be acquired at the piano or the desk, in either case working (literally or in the imagination) with equally tempered scales. Performances using Pythagorean tuning, period pronunciation, and appropriate voices, can often make sense of sonorities which on paper looked incomprehensible. Equally, bad performances, particularly on record, can do great damage.

It is clear that the kinds of judgments these various categories require must be analytically based. 'Contrapuntal ineptitude', 'extensions of the language', 'monotony' and so on have to be demonstrated, not simply alleged. The critic must convince his audience that his judgment is fair. Of course, analysis cannot prove that a piece is good. What it can do is to point out how a piece functions (or fails in part to function); and appreciation of that may suggest a particular view of the piece and of its composer's achievement. It will certainly affect the way it is heard. For in the end, any estimate of quality depends on a judgment of how a piece sounds. Bias, often of one or more of the varieties outlined above, may prejudice the analyst in advance but, if he is doing his job adequately, should be erased by contact with the facts of the piece.

Principles are no use without example, though the following illustrations of the categories just outlined are no more than objects for debate. If eventually each is shown to be a masterpiece, musicology will at least have acquired a point of view.

Prevalet simplicitas (ex.1), a three-voice song with a Latin text from the early fifteenth century, seems clearly inept. Its tenor is probably a popular song, and above it the composer has written an acceptable if undistinguished cantus line. The second cantus, on the other hand, seems to have been composed separately against

Ex. 1
Ar. de Ructis, *Prevalet simplicitas*

Daniel Leech-Wilkinson

(Oxford, Bodleian Library, Canonici misc. 213, ff. 128v - 9r; Bologna, Civico Museo Bibliografico Musicale, Q15,

ff. 291v - 2r (= cclxijv - iijr))

the tenor, after the first was complete and without the first cantus being altered to accommodate it. This explains its lack of melodic logic (see for example the leaps in bars 8 and 32, and its tiresome attraction to figures cadencing around *c'*, and the parallel unisons and seconds with Cantus I. It is hard to attribute any of these problems to copying mistakes by the scribes of the surviving (or previous) manuscripts – there are no simple changes of pitch level or note lengths which would produce better sense – and one has to conclude, therefore, that the composer was inexpert.

If *Prevalet simplicitas* is a relatively straightforward case of a bad piece, that is largely because its inadequacies are occasional and are recognizable against a background of conventional contrapuntal progressions. The composer is trying to write conventionally, but is not always succeeding. But there are surviving pieces in which this may not be so. A work such as Martinus Fabri's 'Or se depart', (ex. 2) which survives uniquely in the Leiden University manuscript,[8] makes imperfect sense in terms of the general style of its period. Both of the intended combinations of voices (Triplum – Cantus – Tenor and Cantus – Tenor – Contratenor) contain intervals and progressions which would conventionally be considered poor,[9] but these recur often enough for their use to seem consistent and intentional, so that

[8] Published in J. van Biezen and J. P. Gumbert (eds), *Two chansonniers from the Low Countries*, Monumenta Musica Neerlandica xv (Amsterdam, 1985), no.L19, pp.66–9. (This edition is much preferable to that in G. K. Greene (ed.), *French Secular Music: Rondeaux and miscellaneous pieces*, Polyphonic Music of the Fourteenth Century, xxii (Monaco 1989), no.7, pp.12–14.)

[9] For example: in Tr-C-T, 8–6 chords (bars 2, 7, 18), 8–3 chords on *b* (bar 6, 17), fourths over the lowest pitch (bars 4, 5, 8, 13, 16), unconventionally resolving seconds and sevenths (bars 4, 5, 17, 25, 29); in C-T-CT, unresolved 6–4 (bar 28), unconventionally resolved 7th (bar 20), seconds (bars 13, 47), fourths (bars 16, 33, 35, 39, 60).

9

the song cannot simply be dismissed as incompetent. (It is worth remembering, in looking at such a piece, that if Machaut were not famous for other reasons, and if as a result we had only those works of his which survive outside the 'Machaut

Ex. 2
Martinus Fabri, 'Or se depart'

³ the ligature orig. in red

(Leiden Universeitsbibliotheek, B.P.L. 2720, ff.8*v* - 9*r*), © Monumenta Musica Neerlandica

manuscripts', it is probable that there would be some doubt about their excellence: it is only because Machaut's very individual approach to dissonance is consistent over a great many pieces that we can recognize in him a brilliantly original composer, and not simply a crank.) Although there are relatively few pieces as awkward as 'Or se depart', so that its context is not obvious, similar examples do occur in the Leiden manuscript.[10] This is not the place to mount a detailed study of these songs, but such an investigation should be able to determine whether this is a collection of rubbish, or the work of 'primitives' – composers deliberately ignoring mainstream compositional principles in favour of something equally consistent but less refined. Consistently odd pieces, then, need very cautious treatment.

Compositions which look odd on the page but which work in performance are potentially the most difficult category, since there are as yet few objective criteria by which the success of a performance may be judged. An absolutely clear example, nevertheless, is provided by the three- and four-voice conductus of the later-twelfth and early-thirteenth centuries. This is a repertory which on paper looks more wildly dissonant than either theory or practice (in the shape of contemporary organum) could possibly explain. And yet, as Christopher Page has demonstrated,[11] when sung in the Pythagorean tuning for which it was conceived, with the fifths (which fix the shape of almost every chord) tuned pure, a piece like *Novus miles sequitur* (ex. 3) takes on a richness and a logic which the modern reader would be hard put to extract from the printed page.

[10] See, for example, 'Tsinghen van der nachtegale', 'Des vasten avonts' and 'Eer ende lof' (van Biezen and Gumbert, op. cit., nos. L16, L17 and L20). 'Des vasten avonts', in particular, is a piece which for all its peculiarities is arguably rather beautiful.
[11] In many concerts but outstandingly in the disc *Music for the Lion-Hearted King*, Gothic Voices, directed by Christopher Page (Hyperion, CDA66336, 1989).

Ex. 3
Anonymous, *Novus miles sequitur*

- ti - tur   pro   sa - lu - te   gre - gis,
- ni - co   pa - sto - re   pru - den - ti,
- pu - li   pa - stor   spi - ri - ta - lis,

(Florence, Biblioteca Mediceo - Laurenziana, Pluteo 29, 1, ff. 230r - v; Madrid, Biblioteca Nacional, 20486, f. 139r)

It is not impossible that several of the pieces one might wish to include in the category 'Dull compositions' could be rescued by fine performances, but there must also be a fair number which could not; and the finer judgments at which musicologists should be aiming ought to enable us to identify some of those with reasonable conviction. One such might be Johannes de Lymburgia's setting of *Pulcra es, amica mea* (ex. 4) preserved, like almost all his surviving work, only in the manuscript Bologna Q15.[12] While Lymburgia knows how to avoid dissonance (though not how to do it gracefully), his rate of chord-change is monotonously

[12] Published in A. Lewis (ed.), *Johannes de Lymburgia: Four Motets* (Newton Abbot, Antico, 1985), pp. 2–6.

Ex. 4
Johannes de Lymburgia, *Pulcra es, amica mea*

om - nes ge - mel - lis fe - ti - bus, et ste - ri - lis non est in ____

[Contratenor]

[om - nes ge - mel - lis fe - ti - bus, et ste - ri - lis non est in

om nos ge mel lis fe - ti - bus, et ste - ri - lis non est in ____

e - is.   Si - cut cor - tex ma - li pu - ni -

e - is. ____ Si - cut cor - tex ma - li pu - ni

e - is.   [Si - cut cor - tex ma - li pu - ni -

consistent, he has little sense of the possibilities of directing progressions and no significant sense of melodic shape. The piece lacks form at any level. Though rarely 'incorrect', in terms of contemporary theory or models, it is agonisingly dull.

What, then, is good? A good piece is one which engages the mind of the listener until it is over, which is fundamentally consistent in itself though interestingly unpredictable in matters of detail, which makes logical use of directed counterpoint, has well shaped melodic lines, and subjects the resultant phrase shapes to the underlying pattern of metre. It stretches established notions of good style just far enough to be recognizably new, without going so far beyond the norm as to alienate the listener. One of the pleasures of working with medieval music is that so many pieces are this good. And it may be that the really difficult task facing scholars of the future will not be to choose between the good and the bad, but between the good and the marvellous. In that case scholars, performers, publishers and listeners have nothing to fear from criticism. While most of this music remains to be studied, we have everything valuable to look forward to, and nothing worthwhile to lose.

2 Value judgments in music of the Renaissance

James Haar

> It is not long ago that certain verses were presented here as being Sannazaro's, and they seemed most excellent to everyone and were praised with exclamations and marvel; then when it was known for certain that the verses were by someone else, they at once sank in reputation and were found to be less than mediocre. And a certain motet that was sung before the Duchess [Elisabetta Gonzaga] pleased no one and was not thought good until it was known to be by Josquin des Prez.

Castiglione's *The book of the courtier* (1528), cited above, gives evidence that even in the High Renaissance people made value judgments based on snobbery. Other remarks by fifteenth- and sixteenth-century writers could be quoted to demonstrate that composers were admired solely because they were countrymen – by birth or employment – teachers, or personal acquaintances of the author. But before dismissing commentators of the period as of no help in a quest for criteria on which to form value judgments about the music of the Renaissance, we might look for some more helpful contemporary testimony.

The name of Josquin had evidently become a byword for excellence early in the sixteenth century. A letter to Duke Ercole I of Ferrara, written in 1501, states that Josquin 'composes better' than his great contemporary Isaac. Petrucci certainly counted on the composer's reputation in choosing Josquin as the first composer to have printed volumes (the first appearing in 1502) devoted entirely to his music. The Tuscan humanist Paolo Cortese (d.1510) thought, or had heard it said, that Josquin excelled all other musicians in the knowledge and skill (*doctrina*) he brought to the composition of polyphonic Masses. Luther said that Josquin's mastery was so great as to defy comparison with other musicians' efforts. For the Florentine Cosimo Bartoli, writing near mid-century, Josquin was of a stature equivalent to that of Michelangelo in sculpture.

Somewhat more informative than these scattered accolades is the judgment of the Swiss humanist and theorist Heinrich Glarean, in whose *Dodecachordon* of 1547 there is an encomium of Josquin and discussion, less full than one could wish, of several of his works. Here is the central passage of Glarean's judgment:

In this . . . great crowd of talented men, there stands out particularly in talent, conscientiousness, and industry . . . Jodocus a Prato, whom in his native Belgian language the ordinary people endearingly call Josquin . . . His talent was so versatile in every way, so equipped by a natural acumen and vigour, that there was nothing in this field which he could not do . . . No one has expressed more effectively in songs the moods of the heart than this *symphonetes* [polyphonist], no one has been able to vie with him on an equal plane in grace and fluency of expression, just as no one of the Romans is superior to Maro [Vergil] in the epic. For just as Maro, with the felicity of a natural talent, was accustomed to make a poem equal to the subject matter . . . so also Josquin sometimes moves with light, accelerating notes where the subject demands it, sometimes sings the songs with slow, moving tones; and to say finally, has never brought forth anything which was not pleasant to the ears, and which the learned did not approve as superior in talent, which in short, even if it should seem less erudite, would not be agreeable and acceptable to discerning listeners.

Here is value judgment; indeed it is a kind of text on which the rest of my sermon may be preached. Like Cortese, Glarean admired Josquin's technical command; he also found the composer's versatility and deftness in matching words to music worthy of praise. Writers of Glarean's generation were more and more inclined to stress this latter side of a musician's art; indeed they began to describe older composers as 'mathematici' in contrast to what they saw as the more humanistically inspired art of 'poetici' who achieved a correct and rhetorically affective union of words and music. For Glarean, Josquin was the first composer to excel in this way; later writers extolled Willaert, Rore, and others as pioneers in the composition of 'poetic' music. No one had told Renaissance writers that cultural evolutionism was a sin. They very naturally found the music of their own generation to be not only the most advanced but the most expressive; older music was not merely simpler but more neutral in character. Theorists occasionally deprecated a current fad or excess, but not until the last quarter of the sixteenth century did the sort of academic quarrelling over style and genre that plagued sixteenth-century literary criticism – Vincenzo Galilei damning contrapuntal music as a betrayal of humanistic goals, G. M. Artusi faulting Monteverdi for his transgressions of established rules of musical syntax – begin to disturb the self-satisfaction of music lovers. On the whole Renaissance men and women seemed to like contemporary music a lot.

Whether they liked the same things we do about this music may be questioned. Whether their ears were more alert to individual, regional, or chronological differences of sound and gesture – because they were blessedly free from the distracting influence of four centuries of music yet to come – or whether they were unable to make more than naively superficial comment – because they lacked the intellectual equipment of modern musical theory – may also be questioned. We are of course entitled to judge early music through use of any and every modern analytical and critical method, just so long as we avoid condescension or partiality (nineteenth-century theorists tended toward the former, seeing early music as tonal thinking *manqué*, while Romantic critics and amateurs stressed the latter, praising early music as a lost Golden Age of religious sincerity and secular innocence). But we should not underestimate the depth of knowledge, fund of good sense, and refinement of ear of Renaissance musical thinkers because they did not express themselves as we would choose them to do. It would be odd if we continued to find the music of the fifteenth and sixteenth centuries an artistic marvel and yet belittled the reactions to it of the society for which this music was written.

Praise of individual musicians, chiefly performers, may be found in ancient, particularly in Hellenistic writings; it was taken up as a regular topic in Renaissance literature. Discussion of music as an art tended in antiquity to be twofold: encomia, illustrated through use of anecdote, on the 'power' of music on the one hand, and technical accounts of the science of harmonics – the nature and measurement of musical sound – on the other. In Renaissance writings one sees the same two strands of thought, sometimes within works of a single author. Theorists lay stress on systems of tuning, on precise measurement of rhythmic values; 'philosophers' of music repeat the ancient praises of its near-magical powers, sometimes mixing modern and antique illustration. Of course there are new elements, including technical as well as 'ethical' description of melodic mode (here some antique lore remains); principles and details of contrapuntal technique; the art of fitting words to melody. What was missing in ancient writing on music, description and evaluation of individual works, is still for the most part absent in the Renaissance. Plenty of single pieces are cited; but the discussion is nearly always in purely technical terms, and is concentrated on detail rather than on structural procedure. On the rare occasions when aesthetic aim is mentioned, the language chosen is one in which critical evaluation is absent.

The territory thus seems unpromising. There was no tradition for evaluating musical compositions as works of art. And while the science of harmonics was both tangible and ever demonstrable, music itself was thought of as evanescent, delightful in the hearing but not graspable as a thing to contemplate. The extraordinary development of musical notation from the ninth through the fifteenth centuries should have changed all this. But written music, apart from plainchant, was for a long time seen by few people and was the product and the property of a tiny élite.

For a sign that in the later fifteenth century this situation was beginning to change, we may turn to a celebrated remark made by the theorist-composer Johannes Tinctoris in the dedication of his *Liber de arte contrapuncti* (1477):

Further, although it seems beyond belief, there does not exist a single piece of music, not composed within the last forty years, that is regarded by the learned as worth hearing. Yet at this present time . . . there flourish . . . countless composers, among them Jean Okeghem, Jean Regis, Antoine Busnoys, Firmin Caron, and Guillaume Faugues, who glory in having studied under John Dunstable, Gilles Binchoys, and Guillaume Dufay, recently deceased. Nearly all the works of these men exhale such sweetness that . . . I never hear them, I never examine them, without coming away happier and more enlightened.

The French-trained Tinctoris, who elsewhere credits the beginning of this musical renaissance to the English under Dunstable's lead but says that of late the English have foundered in provincial conservatism while French musicians have forged ahead to write 'in the newest manner for the new times', did indeed study the work of mid-fifteenth-century musicians closely. His counterpoint treatise is not only a reflection of this music but, in its examples, shows a very careful control of dissonance, offering models of stylistic purity and consistency that the composers themselves, or perhaps their scribal redactors, rarely attained.

The concerns of Tinctoris with this music were technical (elsewhere he writes in humanistic-anecdotal vein about the invention and powers of music), not aesthetic. Still, he plainly admired the music of his great contemporaries and immediate forebears. His position that 'newest is best', to become, as we have seen, a watchword among Renaissance writers, may be noted. But his claim that the art of music had only recently reawakened from a long sleep, so convenient for historians looking for a date to 'start the Renaissance', seems rather to indicate that polyphonic music, cultivated with great refinement in the thirteenth and fourteenth centuries, had in his own century become much more broadly practised and widely circulated, in written form. I would thus suggest that Tinctoris is making as much a sociological point as an aesthetic judgment. If a sizeable body of artistic polyphony could not only be heard but seen and studied by musically literate professionals and amateurs, real grounds for development of critical and comparative evaluation of individual compositions – studied like paintings or poems – were being laid. Colin Slim has recently observed that Leonardo da Vinci, who thought music inferior to painting because of the evanescence of sound, admitted that 'music becomes eternal when it is written down'. Music as a subject for serious critical study had in other words to be seen as well as heard.

The development of a successful, if labour-intensive, method of printing part-music at the beginning of the sixteenth century was, of course, of great importance in this regard. How widely the prints of Ottaviano dei Petrucci and Andrea Antico circulated among performers we do not know; and indeed the real 'explosion' of music into print came only in the late 1520s (in France) and *c.*1540 (in Italy, Germany, and the Netherlands). But these early prints were studied as well as sung from; the theorist Pietro Aaron, writing in the 1520s and '30s, based much of his work on examination of their content, and Petrucci's publications were still in the hands of theorists (among them, in the late sixteenth century, Lodovico Zacconi), when they had long since ceased to be of use to performers.

There is no doubt that the increasing commercial success of music printing in the mid- and late-sixteenth century was a spur to compositional activity on the part of amateurs and professionals alike. Madrigals and chansons, even motets, by an extraordinary number of musicians, not by any means all of whom had professional ties to music, appeared in print, perhaps more often than we know subsidized by the composer or his friends. Here, by the way, there should be ample material for modern scholars to undertake useful if not very inviting studies of dilettantism in Renaissance music. Rore, Palestrina, and Lassus had skilled, professional followers; composers such as Arcadelt or Claudin de Sermisy, who worked in a somewhat 'easier' vein, had both professional and amateur epigones, much as did Mendelssohn in the mid-nineteenth century.

Writers on music, who through much of the fifteenth century aimed primarily at a small readership of Church musicians, now directed their work at a much larger audience of educated amateurs. This can already be seen in some of the theoretical output of the early sixteenth century; it is certainly the case with humanistic musicians of mid-century, such as the Swiss Glarean and the Venetian Gioseffo Zarlino. The dialogue, beloved form for Renaissance writers wishing to instruct and even to entertain a mixed audience, was increasingly used in musical treatises, the most familiar example being Thomas Morley's *Plaine and easie introduction to practicall musicke* (1597).

Here, we might think, should be the beginnings of a critical literature on music as an expressive art. Beginnings there are, indeed, some of them fascinating. Quickelberg's description (1559) of Lassus's music for the Penitential Psalms as so vivid that it set the content of the text in images 'almost as if before one's eyes' is a promising bit. Cosimo Bartoli's praise (*c.*1540) of his friend Verdelot as a worthy successor to Josquin, a composer whose music shows wondrous flexibility of character in adapting to the words it set, is another. These and others like them remain generalizations, testimony to the wide acceptance of music as a rhetorical art capable of giving heightened utterance to the imagery and 'affections' of words.

Remarks in the cooler vein of stylistic description can also be found. An example is Hermann Finck's statement (1556) that the music of Gombert was in a new style because of its richness of texture and density of imitative counterpoint, placed in contrast to the 'spareness' of Josquin's polyphony. The same Cosimo Bartoli who gushed over Verdelot wrote an account of the composers of his time which distinguishes between a simpler Florentine style and a more complex polyphony practised by Willaert in Venice and by Imperial composers in the Netherlands.

Something more than this is found in Lodovico Zacconi's *Practica di musica* (in two parts, published in 1592 and 1622 respectively), which contains an account of a conversation on musical topics said to have been held in Venice in 1584, in the presence of Zarlino. In this passage seven aspects of music, labelled with rhetorical or quasi-rhetorical terms, are given. They include inventiveness, artifice, melodic grace, contrapuntal skill, ability to weave a good musical texture, skill in arrangement of tonal materials, and the power to please. A half-dozen prominent composers of the day are then compared in their possession of these qualities – from Zarlino's modest gift of artifice and maintenance of a regular texture to Palestrina's happy blend of artifice and contrapuntal skill, pre-eminent ability to arrange materials well, and command of flowing melody. Zacconi adds that experienced listeners can distinguish the work of one composer from another through their individual blends of these qualities.

Sixteenth-century music lovers could, then, hear individual composers' voices; Zacconi tells us they did recognize the grace of Palestrina's melody as opposed to the 'judicious disposition' of material in Willaert; they applauded Lassus's 'outstanding inventiveness' as contrasted with the more predictable regularity of Costanzo Porta's art. The only thing that should surprise us about this is to find it said by a contemporary musician.

Further than this they seem not to have gone. The fullest Renaissance discussion of a single piece known to me, Joachim Burmeister's analysis (1606) of Lassus's motet *In me transierunt*, in terms of its hypothesized rhetorical structure and use of rhetorical figures, is despite twentieth-century scholarly interest in rhetoric a somewhat remote and artificial – not in the best sense of the word – exercise. Not that later generations did all that much better; for a satisfying if inevitably dated mix of factual information and sensitive evaluation of individual compositions one really has to wait for the work of the great nineteenth-century musicologist A. W. Ambros.

Zacconi's account suggests that Renaissance musicians were indeed able to talk well about the music of their time; they simply did not systematize this talk into critical theory. Experienced musicians must also have been able to comment critically on the compositional efforts of students or friends. A nice bit of evidence that this was so is supplied in a group of letters from Palestrina to someone as much his inferior as a musician as he was superior in social status: Guglielmo Gonzaga, Duke of Mantua.

After the building of the new ducal chapel of Santa Barbara in the 1560s, the Duke set about furnishing the chapel with a new musical repertory. Palestrina was commissioned to write some polyphonic Masses, a task he dutifully fulfilled. Most of the other new music was by local composers, among them the Duke himself. Guglielmo, a musical enthusiast with somewhat conservative tastes, favoured contrapuntally rigorous music of the sort he had known in his youth (the work of Giaches of Mantua, for example). In 1570 he sent Palestrina some music of his own, asking for criticism. Here is part of the composer's reply:

Having let me hear a motet and a madrigal by your excellency, you have asked me to give you my frank opinion of your music . . . In order to study it more fully, I scored the motet, and have seen the *bello artificio* far from common, and the lively expression given the text. I have marked a few spots where it seems to me that the music could have a better sound, especially where you proceed from sixth to unison or use a series of ascending or descending fifth-sixth progressions. Similarly, there are places where the fugal procedure results in too many unisons, and the strict interweaving of imitative parts sometimes obscures the text so that hearers cannot enjoy it as in less strictly written music (*musica comune*).

Other letters comment in less detail but similar vein. And in a letter of 1578 Palestrina informs the Duke that he himself, in composing a Mass, took the liberty of transposing its chant cantus firmus by a fifth and elsewhere by an octave so that the result might be brighter (*più allegra*) than would otherwise be the case.

What Palestrina, amid many expressions of admiration for ducal musical skills, is saying is that the sound of the music is more important than scholastic rigidity of technique. The full harmonic texture and bright sound of Palestrina's music, undimmed by the passage of time, are testimony to his aesthetic creed: contrapuntal technique alone does not produce really good music; the sound must satisfy the ear, the words must speak with clarity and affective force in the music. This is perhaps more valuable than any theoretical treatise, and it should encourage us to consider Renaissance polyphony as musical substance in the fullest sense, not just as successions of points of imitation varied by chordal patter.

Examples of Renaissance music that follow the rules but amount to little more than spinning of contrapuntal wheels are not hard to find, though much of the mass of second-rate sacred and secular polyphony printed in the sixteenth century has mercifully remained unedited in modern times. One piece might be cited. In his *Dodecachordon* Glarean included about one hundred compositions or sections of music as illustration, chiefly of modal procedure. His taste was conservative but on the whole good; Josquin, Isaac, Pierre de La Rue, Obrecht are all well represented. Music by lesser-known composers may also be found. One such work is a three-voice *Ne laeteris, inimica mea* by one Damian à Goes, described as a 'Portuguese knight, nobleman, and distinguished composer of the time', who had visited both Erasmus and Glarean and had become a friend of the latter. The piece, introduced as an example (no.43 in the modern edition of the *Dodecachordon*) of the Aeolian

Ex. 1
Damian à Goes, *Ne laeteris, inimica mea* (Example of the Aeolian mode from Glarean's *Dodecachordon*)

mode, is not otherwise described, nor is it praised for its beauty; one must try to be fair to Glarean. It is a singularly dull, aimless, indeed monotonous piece of music; consistently imitative in procedure, the work is led by the notes rather than leading them – to paraphrase Luther's comparison of Josquin with other musicians (see ex. 1). Its parts are clearly visible and audible, articulated by all-too-obvious seams in the texture. It might comfort twentieth-century students of 'modal' counterpoint to find that one of their sixteenth-century forebears did no better than they at capturing the live spirit of polyphonic music.

If it seems self-evident to say that Renaissance music should be judged by how it sounds, we might recall that most discussion of fifteenth- and sixteenth-century polyphony, whether contemporaneous or modern, has emphasized its technique almost to the exclusion of its sound. The latter is surely what we love, however much we may admire technical ingenuity. Or perhaps we should try, as did Zacconi, to think of sound (his *buona dispositione*) and melody as partners with artifice in the creation of works at once artistically skilled and aesthetically

James Haar

satisfying. No set of rules, no critical slide-rule can be given for this; if we are to try to evaluate this music, we must simply and honestly try to judge it whole, seeing and hearing its technical elements as in the service of genuine musical statement.

Select bibliography

H. GLAREAN, *Dodecachordon*, trans., transcription and commentary by C. A. Miller, 2 vols. (American Institute of Musicology, 1965)

J. HAAR, 'The courtier as musician: Castiglione's view of the science and art of music', in R. W. Hanning and D. Rosand (eds), *Castiglione: the ideal and the real in Renaissance culture* (New Haven and London, 1983), pp.165–89; and J. Haar, 'A sixteenth-century attempt at music criticism', *Journal of the American Musicological Society*, xxxvi (1983), pp.191–209

K. JEPPESEN, 'Pierluigi da Palestrina, Herzog Guglielmo Gonzaga und die neugefundenen Mantovaner-Messen Palestrinas: ein ergänzender Bericht', *Acta musicologica*, xxv (1973), pp.132–79

C. PALISCA, '*Ut oratoria musica*: the rhetorical basis of musical mannerism', in F. W. Robinson and S. G. Nichols, jr. (eds), *The meaning of mannerism* New Haven, 1973), pp.37–65

H. C. SLIM, 'Dosso Dossi's allegory of music at Florence', *Journal of the American Musicological Society*, xliii (1990), pp.43–98

J. TINCTORIS, *Liber de arte contrapuncti* in *Opera theoretica*, A. Seay (ed.), American Institute of Musicology, 1975; trans. A. Seay, American Institute of Musicology, 1961

3 The English *a cappella* heresy

Christopher Page

'The English *a cappella* heresy' is the name given by Howard Mayer Brown to the theory that a great deal of medieval secular music was originally performed by voices only and not by voices and instruments. As a name it is cunningly chosen. There are those who do indeed regard the *a cappella* theory as an ill-founded and subversive challenge to accepted views, and therefore as a heresy, while in its most extreme form the theory argues for the complete elimination of instruments from modern performances of medieval music on both historical and artistic grounds. The theory is English in the sense that it has been explored to most effect in the articles, reviews and recordings of certain English scholars and musicians, and it owes some of its credibility to the exceptional quality of the *a cappella* performances which English singers, trained in chapels and cathedrals, are currently able to give of much pre-Baroque music. In retrospect, this heresy will probably be interpreted as more than an academic quarrel, for it is partly the result of complex changes in the English early music scene since 1975.

Between 1960 and 1975 the performance of medieval music was dominated by some miraculous individuals: Noah Greenberg in America, Thomas Binkley in Munich and Michael Morrow and David Munrow in England. 'A miracle', said George Bernard Shaw, 'is anything that creates faith', and the ensembles which these men founded did much to create faith in the orthodox view of medieval performance practice. Without exception The New York Pro Musica, Studio der frühen Musik, Musica Reservata and The Early Music Consort of London used fiddles, rebecs, crumhorns and shawms in the works of composers such as Machaut and Dufay. They played textless parts, sometimes doubled voices (a practice which soon lost favour) and occasionally performed purely instrumental versions of vocal originals. As the scholars of the day recommended, this was all done in a flexible fashion, and most performances pursued a linear rather than a harmonic ideal, each part possessing a distinct colour. The results were often flamboyant, very appealing to audiences and so deeply individual that it is a heresy of a different sort to speak of Greenberg, Binkley, Morrow and Munrow as if they shared some manifesto of style. But whatever their differences may have been, these ensembles had one thing in common: nearly all their performances of medieval music were accomplished with copies of Renaissance instruments.

For many years the performance traditions of the Middle Ages have been viewed through a Renaissance optic. With the establishment of presses in the late-fifteenth century, Europe was gradually papered over with anthologies of chansons 'appropriate for the human voice as for playing upon all kinds of musical instruments'. Such claims, dear to the hearts of printers angling for every kind of customer, are familiar – perhaps too familiar – and it seems reasonable to ask whether the same flexibility existed in the lifetimes of Perotinus, of Machaut or even of Dufay.

For early writers on medieval performance practice, this question did not arise. The enormous wealth of musical instruments shown in medieval art and listed in contemporary literature encouraged them to imagine a flexible, multi-instrumental practice along Renaissance lines. The prospect was as exciting to the imagination as the wealth of iconography was enticing to the eye. In 1929, for example, Rudolf Ficker evoked the sound-picture of Machaut's motets in these terms:

Now let your mind conceive how the metallic boy-voices were mingled with all the gentle tintinnabulation of the glockenspiel, cymbals, triangle etc. then in use, together with the dulcet tones of the viols, while the long-sustained notes of the lower parts were sung by smooth tenor voices supported by manifold wind instruments, and you will get a fair idea of the dazzling tone-magic of such motets.

This impressive sentence – leisurely in construction but urgent in tone – forms the rhetorical climax of Ficker's article; it calls every imaginative reader to the beauty of medieval music. The call was duly heeded, and many times during many years, for Konrad Ruhland's Capella Antiqua of Munich was recording Ars nova motets in exactly the way described by Ficker until at least the late 1960s. For a project of 1967, Ruhland scored a three-part motet by Vitry for soprano, tenor, recorder, fiddle, crumhorn and tenor trombone, and other scorings of Vitry pieces on the same record introduce cornetto, positive organ and shawm.

Fashions in musical taste, as in scholarship, can change swiftly, and records of medieval music are soon out of date. What seemed fresh and authoritative a moment ago can suddenly be seen as a response to a particular set of personalities and persuasions. Twenty years after Ruhland's work with Vitry, and half a century after Ficker, it now seems plain that their view of Machaut's music as an art of bright colour and nervous energy is an interpretation, in miniature, of the late Middle Ages, and one that owes much to Huizinga's masterpiece, *The waning of the Middle Ages*. The first chapter of Huizinga's book, entitled 'The Violent Tenor of Life', is surely one of the most eloquent historical essays ever written, and in his article Ficker accepts it all: the luxuriant decay; the instability of feeling; the child- like love of primary colours. The 'dazzling tone-magic' of medieval instruments seemed to Ficker to capture the very spirit of what Huizinga called 'the world when it was half a thousand years younger, [when] the outlines of things seemed more clearly marked than to us . . . [and when] all experience had yet to the minds of men the directness and the absoluteness of the pleasure and pain of child-life'.

The waning of the Middle Ages will always be revered, but there are some historians today who believe that Huizinga underestimates the wit and the intelligence – in a word, the sophistication – of men in the fourteenth and fifteenth centuries. Whether this new emphasis can help to define a fresh understanding of medieval sound-pictures will remain to be seen; what is certain is that Ficker was an aural visionary, and that his article was one of the earliest and most passionate attempts to imagine the sound of medieval music.

A few years later, another and much more influential scholar was reaching similar conclusions: Arnold Schering. In 1931, when all was still silence (for even the first recordings in the pioneering *Anthologie Sonore* series lay in the future), Schering published his treatise on early performance practice entitled *Aufführungspraxis alter Musik*. Throughout the book he draws a sharp distinction between what he regards as inherently 'vocal' and 'instrumental' styles, and he concludes that a great deal of medieval polyphony with its wide, supposedly awkward leaps and florid runs, is instrumental in character. The music that he characterizes in this way includes Machaut's ballades and much of the Italian trecento repertory. Schering's claims are now generally regarded as exaggerated, and they were most ably challenged by Lloyd Hibberd as long ago as 1946; none the less, the idea that medieval polyphony contains melodic lines which are not appropriate for voices is one that has proved remarkably durable. In an article entitled 'Voices and instruments in the music of Guillaume de Machaut', a heroic effort for the mid-1950s, Gilbert Reaney rejects the tintinnabulation of Ficker, but is still convinced that some of Machaut's textless parts could never have been intended for singers. He accordingly devotes much of his article to a review of the musical instruments known in fourteenth-century France.

This conception of medieval polyphony as instrumental in many respects was most welcome to the successful medieval ensembles of the 1950s and 1960s. Almost without exception, these groups were formed of virtuoso instrumentalists. Singers tended to be an appendage. This was the pattern of Noah Greenberg's New York Pro Musica, founded in 1952, and in Greenberg's Machaut recording of 1967, for example, it is apparent that the singers do not match the stylishness and bravado of the players. The instrumentalists of these ensembles were not usually content to sit idle. In rehearsal, pieces were arranged and scored according to a process of trial and error whose results characteristically tended to keep most of the instrumentalists occupied. The result was a generously instrumented sound and an approach to programming which favoured relatively short pieces with abrupt changes of scoring.

By 1975 some musicians and scholars had already begun to wonder whether the so-called boom in 'early music' was really a *musical* revival, or whether it was an international fad for exotic instruments. These reflections found a musical voice in the Medieval Ensemble of London, a group whose work can be interpreted in retrospect as a decisive rejection of what had been done in the years between 1960 and 1975. The founders of the Ensemble, Peter and Timothy Davies, favoured instrumental sounds of a pastel kind and therefore used a small palette of instrumental colours, sometimes only four or five per concert. Their sense that the performance of medieval music in Britain lacked a certain high seriousness was reflected in their choice of tails for concert dress so that the four members might give the appearance of a conservative chamber ensemble. By choosing to specialize in some of the most demanding repertory available (the Ars subtilior), and by concentrating on a few composers in each programme (sometimes, indeed, upon a single one), they succeeded in creating for themselves the kind of audience reception associated with serious chamber music. The course of medieval performance in England during the 1980s owes an enormous amount to them.

By 1977, the year of the Machaut centenary, there was a certain sense of pause. It was in that year that an *a cappella* performance of Guillaume de Machaut's *Messe de Nostre Dame* was given in York Minster by Andrew Parrot's Taverner Choir singing one voice to a part. It was by no means the first all-vocal performance of the Mass to be attempted, but it was heard on this occasion by many of the country's professional musicians and scholars committed to medieval music and is unlikely to be forgotten by those who were present. The dignity of the conception, and the complete absence of triviality, gimmickry and undue haste, left a profound impression. Many devotees of medieval music discovered voices on that day.

In the next year, 1978, an English vocal group called the Hilliard Ensemble embarked upon a series of recordings which set new standards for the performance of medieval and Renaissance vocal music. The quality is already there in their anthology entitled *Songs for a Tudor King* (1978). Using a basic team of four male singers, all products of the English choral tradition as nurtured in cathedral and chapel, the Hilliards went on to make pioneering records of music by Leonel Power and John Dunstable. Since then they have gone from strength to strength, and with the success of other British vocal ensembles, including the Tallis Scholars and The Sixteen, French record reviewers now speak in admiring terms of an 'école nouvelle anglaise de chant'. The paradox there, of course, is that in the last decade England has merely diverted the performance of early vocal music back towards its ancient source of musical strength: the choral tradition.

The ascendancy of the new vocal ensembles coincided with two important developments. One was the virtual demise, at least in England, of the old type of medieval group: multi-instrumental, versatile and based upon essentially Renaissance instruments. The second development was the emergence of the *a cappella* heresy. In 1977 Craig Wright in America and myself in England independently argued in favour of the theory that medieval secular music was often performed by voices alone (Wright's arguments were not published until 1981). In both cases the evidence adduced was taken from literary sources. In 1982 I wrote another article presenting what I interpreted as fresh literary support in favour of the *a cappella* theory, and by this time was beginning to explore these findings with a new ensemble, Gothic Voices. Events now gathered apace. In 1982 David Fallows published a comprehensive survey of all the known literary testimony relating to the performance of the song repertory, and he concluded (perhaps to his own surprise) that all-vocal performance was much more common than had hitherto been supposed. As the American critic Richard Taruskin wrote in a review of the English *a cappella* heresy on record, this was becoming serious. At about this time the Medieval Ensemble of London began to record *a cappella* versions of fourteenth and fifteenth century chansons to much acclaim, while various younger scholars writing for the journal *Early Music* expressed the anxiety – and even the distaste – which they were made to feel by recordings of medieval music in the older manner, combining voices with an assertive instrumental presence.

The English *a cappella* heresy is founded upon evidence which is all literary in the broadest sense of the word. It includes extracts from Middle French romances, vernacular chronicles and a treatise on poetry. Virtually none of it is new in the sense of being newly-discovered; the statement by Machaut's nephew, Eustache Deschamps, that a 'threefold voice' ('triplicité des voix') is the best means of performing a polyphonic chanson has been known for many years (Gilbert Reaney mentions it in his article of 1956), and it is doubtful whether any of the excerpts from French and Burgundian chronicles listed by Fallows were entirely unknown to earlier musicological literature. However, it seems that the cumulative force of this evidence was simply never recognized.

The interpretation of these sources turns upon the meaning of individual words (as, for example, 'voix' in the excerpt from Deschamps mentioned above), and as a result the evidence will never be regarded as definitive. In some cases there is real ambiguity, while in others the *a cappella* theory rests upon an argument from silence: a text does not mention the use of instruments, or does not appear to. Such evidence can easily fall victim to forced or partisan interpretations, and no doubt it has done so in the past. None the less, it is possible to make the opposite mistake and to regard the literary evidence with an exaggerated scepticism; although it contains ambiguities and uncertainties, it scarcely differs in this regard from countless other kinds of written evidence which historians habitually employ, and it is revealing that the most implacable opponents of the English *a cappella* heresy have sometimes expressed their doubts about the validity of the theory by questioning the whole enterprise of writing history with its presumption that we can ascertain things about the past.

In addition to the evidence, however we may judge it, the English *a cappella* heresy gains strength – or at least gains colour – from several supplementary considerations that are in themselves invigorating and challenging.

One of these antedates the current debate about the use of musical instruments in secular polyphony by a considerable margin and concerns the performance of liturgical music. In recent years, it has become increasingly apparent that a great deal of ecclesiastical music, both monophonic and polyphonic, the fundamental experience of all literate musicians in those centuries, involved instruments other than the organ very little or not at all. There is now general agreement (at least among Anglophone scholars) that musical instruments participated in liturgical services only on the most rare and solemn occasions, and even then it is not certain that they doubled or supplied lines in polyphonic compositions; they may simply have accompanied certain ritual actions such as offerings made to shrines and processions (when outside the church). This aspect of the problem is fraught with difficulties; concepts such as 'liturgical' and 'para-liturgical' are slippery ones, and a medieval cleric would surely have been surprised to learn that there was a special context where something called 'liturgy' was done. None the less, there is no solid evidence for regular or significant instrumental participation in plainchant nor in any composed liturgical polyphony from the large repertory of Notre Dame organum through to the Masses of the fifteenth century. Virtually the entire repertory of medieval English polyphony, for example, mostly devotional in character, passes before our eyes without the question of instrumental participation raising its head, save perhaps in relation to the performance of some motets in the 'secular' contexts of hall or refectory.

In the present context the importance of this new perspective on medieval sacred polyphony is that there are sacred pieces in the French, English and Italian repertories which borrow their musical style directly from contemporary secular music. If, as now seems assured, the users of the English Old Hall MS almost invariably sang unaccompanied, then around 1410 Mass compositions in styles modelled upon the contemporary French chanson were being sung in England with voices on all parts, and apparently without there being any possibility of the lower voices bearing the full text. Similar comparisons of style might be drawn from the French and Italian repertories and it is needless to multiply examples; such resemblances show that there is little in medieval polyphony, whether French, English or Italian, that can be confidently described as 'unvocal'. There were vocal solutions for these textures, in other words, and singers must often have been content simply to vocalize their part. The equation 'lack of text = instrumental performance' seems to have been proved false.

These deductions look more plausible in the 1990s than they could have done in the 1950s because it is now customary to take a broader view of what is 'vocal' and 'unvocal' – a change that owes much to the systematic exploration of non-Western music by European and American scholars. There are no absolute standards governing what can be sung and what cannot; judgments in these matters vary according to the individual's taste, background and ability, and in relation to the prevailing emphasis of the musical environment in which he or she is raised. We have seen that in 1956 Gilbert Reaney spoke with some confidence of the 'unvocal' character of some tenor and contratenor lines in Machaut's polyphony; it is a confidence that can no longer be shared.

As our knowledge of medieval instruments has gradually advanced, the uncertainties about their role in the performance of contemporary written music have been multiplied rather than reduced. It is no discredit to the reputation of a great musician to repeat that David Munrow's performances of medieval polyphony were usually accomplished with Renaissance instruments and some-times Baroque accessories (covered strings, for example). The point of this observation is that genuine medieval instruments, insofar as we can reconstruct their properties, may not have served such vocal/instrumental performances as Munrow's in quite the same way. Covered strings enable a bowed instrument of a given size to achieve significantly lower pitches, with more satisfactory tone, than would be possible with gut strings over the same string length. The bass rebec, for example, a Renaissance instrument, has been a major workhorse in countless modern performances of Machaut and Dufay where, with its large size, round bridge and covered strings, it is ideal for the textless tenors and contratenors lying below the vocal part in pitch. However, many (perhaps most) medieval bowed instruments appear to have been quite small in size; they often had flat bridges and did not use covered strings. It remains uncertain in the present state of our knowledge whether such instruments could ever have been used in the way the bass rebec has been.

Any consideration of medieval instruments eventually brings us back to the problem of vanished repertories. To musicians of Ficker's generation this did not seem a pressing problem; they saw that a wealth of medieval music had survived, and that medieval art was full of representations of musical instruments. The one body of material was matched to the other, no doubt with sixteenth-century practice in mind. In recent years, however, the study of medieval music has been increasingly opened out to include the evidence of literary sources, and it is from them that the signs of a vanished instrumental repertory principally emerge. One example must suffice. In a thirteenth-century poem entitled the *Dit des taboureurs* a spokesman for players of the fiddle – the classic instrument of the medieval minstrel and of court culture in that period – describes the repertory which, in his view, is the foundation of every good fiddler's claim to respect. The repertory concerned is not the motet, nor the conductus, nor even the trouvère chanson. Indeed, it is nothing that makes an appearance in the musical sources. It is the narrative epic, or *chanson de geste*, in which stories of heroes such as Roland and Oliver were chanted to instrumental accompaniment. Apart from a few scraps of melody, we have virtually no musical remains of these epics (although the literary remains are abundant). The later we go, the more complex the issue of unwritten instrumental repertory becomes.

Richard Taruskin, reviewing a recording of fifteenth-century song performed *a cappella*, writes that the recording 'has lately shown the skeptics among us, to our astonishment, to what extent our conceptions of this repertoire had been formed by unwitting prejudice'. Those are generous but also telling words. The English *a cappella* heresy is not, in the final analysis, a partisan defence of a few ambiguous sources designed to discredit some orthodoxy. It is not, in short, a heresy. It is a way of exploring a musical repertory too fine and extensive for narrow allegiances to have any meaning.

Select bibliography

R. FICKER, 'Polyphonic music of the Gothic period', *Musical Quarterly*, xv (1929), pp.483–505.

J. HUIZINGA, *The waning of the Middle Ages* (London, 1919)

G. REANEY, 'Voices and instruments in the music of Guillaume de Machaut', *Revue Belge de Musicologie*, x (1956), pp.3–17.

A. SCHERING, *Aufführungspraxis alter Musik* (Leipzig, 1931; 1969).

4 Going down on record

Tess Knighton

In many ways the medieval world was not so dissimilar to our own: true, there were no cars or aeroplanes, but people could, and did, travel, if at a rather slower pace; there was no electricity, but they did have wax and fire; there were no word processors, but they could write, and paper and the printing press were already an integral part of daily life by the end of the fifteenth century. The mind of a genius such a Leonardo da Vinci could imagine, and design, all kinds of machines, including some for flying or going under water. But it would seem that one thing that did not occur even to da Vinci, whose musical knowledge was also quite extraordinary, was the idea of reproducing sound. Recording is, of course, a relatively recent phenomenon, but already it is hard to imagine what life – especially musical life – must have been like without it.

The recording of music from the centuries before our own has undoubtedly enriched our appreciation of our musical heritage in a totally unprecedented way and has stirred up the quest for 'authenticity', for the truthful reproduction of the musical sounds of the past. Indeed, it is doubtful that the so-called 'authentic movement' could have got off the ground at all without the greater accessibility afforded by recordings, let alone the financial backing of the record companies. Yet the whole concept of recording is at odds with that quest: the recording process – including the preparation, rehearsal, studio setting, the switching on and off of the red light, and the splicing of tape – is a deeply inauthentic one as far as any musician living before the twentieth century would have been concerned.

This needs to be borne in mind in any discussion of the recording of 'early music' and therefore in our modern perception of it – particularly so in the case of music composed before 1600, when often we have little idea of how that music must have sounded in terms of instrumental and vocal colours, tempo and the details of phrasing and dynamics. If new evidence or reinterpretation of old evidence over the last ten years can so radically alter our perception of, say, Bach's B minor Mass (a work that in any case may never have been performed in its entirety in its own day), the questions of how to perform Machaut's *Messe de Nostre Dame* are still even further from being resolved, and the trouble is that recordings can close doors as well as open them. A recording quickly and stealthily – almost without our realizing it – becomes a document, one all the more potent and influential for being perceived by the senses as well as by the intellect. In this way evidence for performance that on paper may give pause for thought makes far greater impact when realized in sound. A recording makes the music accessible, but it is all too easy to accept that sound world as being a just and accurate reflection of how Machaut might have heard his Mass, either in his mind's ear or in actual performance. I would not go so far as to suggest that we adopt the extremist stance once expressed by a university lecturer that if we cannot know how, say, a Dufay chanson would have sounded around 1460, then it would be better not to hear it performed now; but it would seem sensible to bear in mind what we are actually hearing (and enjoying) while listening to a recording of music from before 1600.

Any recording is essentially an audio-sculpture: the end result has been shaped, finely chiselled and honed so that it is gratifying to the ear in terms of sound quality and balance and so that it can bear repeated hearings. In short, a recording is – or at least it can be if it is a successful one – a work of art in itself. David Munrow is reputed to have said that 'the essence of recording this type of repertory is a good programme and a good producer'. He should probably have added 'and a good sound engineer', but he was basically right in his recognition of the importance of a level of creativity beyond that of the music-making itself: a creative area much influenced by modern technology. In addition to the interpretation or pre-performance decisions (as some would rather have it) reached by the performers themselves there is that, presumably well informed, pair of ears constantly assessing and adjusting – sometimes blatantly manipulating – the overall effect. There is little doubt that recordings have shaped not only our appreciation of 'early music', but also our whole experience of it; our ears are prejudiced in deeply-rooted and complex ways, and not just because of the musical experience of the intervening centuries. In addition, the ear is fickle, constantly flattered and distracted by the new, growing quickly accustomed to one sound world whose former delights begin to pall as time passes. When music from before 1600 first began to be recorded, there was an underlying assumption that the repertory needed to be made attractive to the modern ear by those means that had come to be deemed as being 'good' in any music: dramatic contrast, imaginative 'orchestration', a directional sense of structure. Many years later these assumed pre-requisites have come to be questioned, or at least put into perspective, according to the repertory that is being recorded.

To go back to the beginning. Before Noah Greenberg founded the New York Pro Musica (or Pro Musica Antiqua as it was then called) in 1952, Michael Morrow his Musica Reservata in the mid-1950s, Thomas Binkley the Studio der frühen Musik in 1960 and David Munrow the Early Music Consort of London in 1967, hardly anyone had the opportunity to experience pre-1600 music at first hand, save, perhaps, those who sang in cathedral or college choirs or those who under the influence of Arnold Dolmetsch had taken up the recorder, the viol or possibly the lute. With their concerts, but more especially with their recordings, these professional groups began to spread the word. Quite suddenly a whole new area was opened up: even if you couldn't get to a concert, you could hear the Play of Daniel or music from the time of the Crusades or Italian trecento madrigals in your own home. The enthusiasm and excitement generated by these discoveries is reflected in the presentation of their early recordings which almost always adopted an anthology format: a selection of pieces from a wide repertory that might be broadly divided into medieval or Renaissance. These groups, because they were the 'first' and although each enjoyed a highly individual approach, could feel free to roam over what was basically uncharted territory, the Studio der frühen Musik and the Early Music Consort of London presenting, for example, a number of recordings that could then be gathered into boxed sets of music from the fourteenth to the sixteenth centuries from every European tradition, all performed with various combinations of voices and instruments, some of which provided entirely novel sounds.

Their performances were lively and colourful, the kaleidoscopic coincided with the encyclopedic in an aesthetically pleasing and intellectually stimulating way.

Contrast was at the heart of Huizinga's vision of medieval culture in his highly influential socio-historic study entitled *The waning of the Middle Ages*, and here was musical contrast brought back to life for all to hear: different types of pieces presented in contrasting colours. The fact that the 'early music' movement, in this country at least, grew out of the arts-and-craft revival at the turn of the century brought a close association with instrument-makers fascinated by the iconography and craft skills of the period. Those instruments existed (well, some of them anyway) and must have been played, so why not 'orchestrate' the music? And who, after experiencing the *Ring* cycle, would not emphasize those aspects that brought out a larger-scale structure that progressed from beginning to end in a harmonically and motivically logical and unified way? These early recording artists and producers sought, whether consciously or unconsciously, to accommodate or overcome these obstacles to a retrospective understanding of music from before 1600, and because they were the first, they were extremely influential. Sequences of short pieces (or, at least, short musical units, for often the original texts were cut out of a fear that the simple repetition schemes – on which most songs pre-1500 were based – would be unacceptable to modern ears) tended to be strung together to form larger structures, even though these resulted in anachronisms; for greater contrast no two songs, even by the same composer, were 'scored' in the same way, so that the ear was distracted from some of the more subtle qualities of the music in favour of instrumental colour. Compromise was glossed over or more easily accepted when the excitement of the new understandably swept all before it.

This is not to say that the earlier groups were frivolous or in any way set out to deceive: they were experimenting to the best of their knowledge and ability, but decisions had to be made, and once the results were fixed by the process of recording these tended to take on an evidential life of their own. This is how medieval music sounded, proclaimed the black vinyl witnesses, but Morrow and his colleagues were ever aware of the pitfalls of aiming at the true or authentic reproduction of the original sounds. They were not to know that the very concept of 'authenticity' that spurred them on to their finest achievements would become such a highly effective advertising slogan for the commercial side of the recording industry and thus become a loaded word endowed with black-and-white meanings they as performer-researchers had never intended.

The recording of 'early music' brought with it other concomitants, many of them common to the recording of music of any period, and some – like the general raising of technical performing standards (an out-of-tune note, a fluffed run being so much less acceptable on disc than in the concert hall, although this in itself creates an artificial perfection that is deeply inauthentic) – almost immediately positive and rewarding. Others – such as the manipulation of the market for 'early music' – had less obvious, more far-reaching consequences. The more 'artistic' side of the recording industry relates to the emphasis on the recreation of sound in as vital and beautiful way as possible; we all demand this, but it is not necessarily 'authentic'. At the same time, the more commercial aspects of the recording industry rely heavily on the identity of the performers for the marketing of a particular repertory. This has been no less true for the 'early music' recordings of Munrow than for Herbert von Karajan's multiple versions of the Beethoven symphonies.

The two are interconnected: it is not just a question of personality (though that helps), but of an identifiable sound. It was the sound of the London Early Music

Consort, with its emphasis on virtuoso instrumental playing, that was appealing, almost irrespective of the repertory that was being played. And it was this quality – the creation of a clearly recognizable 'sound print' – that was picked up and developed by the next generation of 'early music' groups to land recording contracts, even though they could afford to abandon the concept of covering the whole field – that had more or less been done – and begin to home in on certain repertories.

Thus, with the Medieval Ensemble of London directed by the brothers Peter and Timothy Davies, box sets were dedicated to the complete secular works of Dufay or Okeghem (at the expense of a fine repertory of anonymous works), while Jordi Savall's Hespèrion XX concentrated, initially at least, on the early Hispanic repertory cultivating an unmistakable, quasi-exotic character for their 'sound-print' matched by the surreal sleeve designs adopted for their EMI Reflexe recordings. In slightly later repertory, Anthony Rooley's Consort of Musicke brought their individual stamp to bear on the songs of Dowland and the madrigals of Monteverdi and even, as recently as 1980, to the mostly anonymous music of a particular fifteenth-century collection, *Le Chansonnier Cordiforme*. All these groups created a readily identifiable 'sound-print' that is closely linked with their leading musical personalities, notably James Bowman, Montserrat Figueras or Emma Kirkby. As they produced more records, the record companies could rely more and more on those musical personalities to 'sell', irrespective of the repertory they presented. This had its positive side: some of the more obscure repertory would almost certainly never have been recorded if this was not so.

To describe groups such as the Medieval Ensemble of London or their successors, the New London Consort and most recently the Dufay Collective, and their non-British counterparts such as the Boston Camerata or Sequentia, as all-purpose 'early music' ensembles might seem to be derogatory: it is not intended to be, for they reflect a modern performing tradition that goes back to Greenberg and that still provides an outlet for those talented instrumentalists whose imaginations have been captured by the sounds of old instruments. Yet, at the same time, the notion of 'all-purpose' has become outdated; specialization in repertory – the direction already heralded by those recordings of 'complete works' – has become more and more the norm. In addition, the 'early music' groups who are now making records are tending to concentrate on a particular area of the repertory in combination with a 'sound-print' unique to them and their interpretation of the music. Thus, if we were to look at a score of a fourteenth-century chanson or a Palestrina Mass it might be the 'sound-prints' of Gothic Voices or the Tallis Scholars that sprang to mind, these being the groups who have most consistently recorded those repertories in recent years.

Specialization of this kind occurred almost naturally with those vocal or choral groups dedicated to performing sacred music, where the issue of 'orchestration' was clearly less pertinent. This did not mean that choirs never used instruments, at least at first: on occasion, Pro Cantione Antiqua combined men's voices with ensembles of cornetts and sackbuts in Renaissance sacred music. With counter-tenors on the top line, their choral sound was as distinctive as any, and is one that has been curiously little developed since, the preference going almost entirely in favour of the mixed choir (with the notable exception of the Westminster Cathedral Choir's recent impressive recordings). It was perhaps David Wulstan's Clerkes of Oxenford, who recorded (for the excellent budget label Classics for Pleasure) some of the masterpieces of English Renaissance polyphony loved by those familiar with the cathedral tradition, who most influenced this trend. Wulstan's theories on transposition meant that he needed singers who could cope with high, not to say stratospheric, treble lines, and, given the difficulty of assembling a boys' choir outside the cathedral or Oxbridge choir schools, it was logical for women with pure treble-like voices to be brought in. The groups who followed in the Clerkes' footsteps widened out this approach to embrace other repertory, particularly, in the case of The Tallis Scholars, the Masses of Palestrina. This group has aimed at and achieved such a degree of accuracy of intonation and sheer beauty of sound on their own Gimell label, that the efforts of the earlier recordings now seem comparatively unrefined. The sound is undeniably beautiful (and presents new challenges for any group recording this repertory in the future), but it cannot represent the 'authentic' sound of Palestrina's choir. Nor is it 'authentic' to present his Masses as continuous, self-contained five-movement pieces, though this does not impair our enjoyment of The Tallis Scholars' performances, only our vision of the original context for the music. Other groups such as Andrew Parrott's Taverner Consort, the Gabrieli Consort and The Sixteen have sought to reconstruct on disc particular musico-liturgical occasions from the past. This concept has been an especially exciting one, with the recordings making use of a sense of space for a moving procession or items sung from different positions according to ritualistic demands and extra-musical sound effects such as firecrackers or even mini-cannons.

The seamless welding of chant and polyphony makes once again a persuasive argument for the contrast within a unified whole that is very appealing to the modern ear. (Technology has also helped here: reviews of such recordings have drawn attention to the possibility of 'programming out' the chant tracks on CDs of such reconstructions. Reconstructions can represent something of the 'authentic' flavour of these occasions, and while it is again crucial to bear in mind the limitations, this is a direction which future recordings of sacred music will surely continue to explore over the next decade. Some more recent experimentation with larger-scale structures is also taking place in the field of secular music, as with Joel Cohen's compilation in sound of the legend of *Tristan et Iseult* with the Boston Camerata. This certainly makes for interesting listening, but does not relate to any known performing tradition of the time.

Developing in parallel to these choral recordings have been those of the smaller – usually single voice, but often still *a cappella* – vocal groups. Single voices give a far greater degree of flexibility of repertory – both secular and sacred – as well as of approach. The Hilliard Ensemble, one of the most recorded of all 'early music' groups, is the epitome of that flexibility, encompassing sacred and secular repertories from a wide time-span from Machaut to Lassus and beyond to nineteenth-century partsongs and contemporary music. Their sound is distinctive (again characterized by individual voices, notably that of the countertenor David James) and instantly recognizable, and the sheer professionalism of their music-making is a reflection of the high standards demanded by the art of recording.

The Hilliard Ensemble is clearly a specialist group but they are by no means as specialized in their choice of repertory as still current developments would seem to suggest will be the way forward. More recent *a cappella* groups such as Marcel Pérès's Organum or the Ensemble Clément Janequin have so far restricted themselves to recording a much more limited range of material, both groups bringing a highly individual approach to specialist repertories built respectively around chant and French Renaissance music. The very highly specialized versus the more flexible is an issue that can pose problems for the 'early music' group and their record company. In a recent interview, Christopher Page admitted that he used to think that 'a group should be like a kind of hoover – you could clip on appliances according to the job', but that he now realizes through his experiences with Gothic Voices that any reshuffling of personnel or musical forces brings with it its own problems. With a group of people working regularly together it is easier to get down to the kind of detail of musical performance (phrasing, unanimity of vowel sounds, tuning) that characterize the recordings of Gothic Voices: Page has proved that you can take away the superficial contrast of instrumentation and still bring out variety of texture, rhythm and melody in medieval music. At the same time, should he or any other director wish to bring a different approach to a different repertory, there are the pressures exerted by record companies: first, if the company has found and promoted a successful combination, it is more likely to want to stick with it; and second, it would almost certainly be unwilling to invest in the extra time in rehearsal and other costs that an alteration in a line-up would inevitably mean if the same standards and specialness of quality were to be achieved.

Experimentation is not cost-effective, especially where a successful end result is less easily guaranteed, but it may be what is needed. There are, of course, some groups who continue to fluctuate in numbers and constitution according to the occasion, Andrew Parrott's Taverner Consort and Singers being a notable exception to the fixed-personnel concept. From their small-scale, all-vocal recording of Machaut's Mass to the vast array of instruments and voices used in the Florentine Intermedi, some of the personnel remain the same, but inevitably each project demands that in terms of ensemble and response to the performing context the group must start from scratch. It is not impossible in this way to achieve very fine results, as the Taverner 'collective' has proved, but the pressures are far greater than, for example, for a group like the Tallis Scholars whose constancy of personnel must make a consistent quality of recorded sound far easier to achieve. Experimentation with other aspects of 'early music', such as the improvisatory approach of groups like the Dufay Collective and Sinfonie (who also draw on non-Western performing techniques), will, I hope, find an increased outlet on disc, despite the added difficulties of improvising to the red light. A successful recording of music from before 1600 certainly presupposes an imaginative, sympathetic and flexible producer, as well as a record company prepared to take risks.

Perhaps the crux of the issue as far as recording music from before 1600 is concerned remains how to find the balance between an attractive mode of presentation (in a sense that remains faithful to the music yet accords with modern tastes) and the realization in sound of the concept of authenticity. As long as the listener is aware that the one is achievable in a variety of ways while the other will never really be attained (although it should still be striven for), then all that matters is that the recording should make the music live again, should make it move and cheer us as it did our predecessors all those centuries ago. The irony is, of course, that if Machaut or Josquin had been able to record their music, there would be no need for an article, or, indeed, a book of this kind – or would there? The period-instrument revival has yet to grapple with the thorny problems posed by, for example, Stravinsky's own recordings.

5 The work is not the performance

Thomas Binkley

Early music flows, as any music does, from practice to practice with modest changes from time and place to time and place. What applies to one kind of music may easily apply to another; what I write below about medieval music surely has bearing upon most other music as well.

Roman Ingarden justifies the distinction between the work and its performance by saying that a performance is temporal, while a score is a persisting object.[1] Performance is a process in time, one event following another, while a score is not a process, all of it existing at the same time.[2]

Very different performances of the same work occur. This not only draws our attention to the differences between performances as versions of works, but also invites the observation that the work and the performance are two quite different things. The relationship between the two is experienced in different contexts: improvisatory deviation from the score, use of good and bad sources, adequate or inadequate presentation of style or, in the case of historical performance, of historical information, and so on.

Just as a work may receive multiple performances, it may have multiple exemplars. Each manuscript version of a piece of music, no matter how much at variance with other versions, is usually equally valid as a representation of that piece, and each performance is a valid event in itself, separate and apart from the notes in the manuscript.[3] Differing manuscripts often do present quite different musical details, not necessarily of equal quality but each with a separate claim to validity. Thus we might legitimately encounter multiple different and valid performances of the same work. This is perhaps more likely in some repertories than in others, depending upon the level of control by the composer over details in the 'score', as well as the accidents of transmission.

It is fundamental to the establishment of sensible performance priorities that the written work was often really nothing more than a model for the performance.[4] There are philological priorities for analysis of a work and there are performance-determined priorities appropriate for its performance. These priorities are not at all the same.

Traditional philology focuses on *Quellenkritik* and *Textkritik*, that is, the evaluation of sources and of texts. Explaining a piece is in a certain sense musical hermeneutics. To paraphrase Friedrich Schleiermacher, musical hermeneutics

[1] R. Ingarden, *Das literarische Kunstwerk: eine Untersuchung aus dem Grenzgebiet der Ontologie, Logik und Literaturwissenschaft* (Halle, 1931), chapters 1 and 4.

[2] R. Ingarden, *The work of music and the problem of identity*, trans. A. Czerniawki, ed. J. G. Harrell (Berkeley, 1986). See also the review by Karol Berger in *JAMS*, xli (1988), pp.558–65.

[3] There is an opposite view: that an ideal version of a work exists, even if that version happens not to survive in manuscript or print, in which case all existing versions would be in need of 'correction'.

[4] Wulf Arlt raises this issue in connection with the Prologue of Monteverdi's *Orfeo* (and many other works) in 'Der Prolog des "Orfeo" als Lehrstück der Aufführungspraxis', in L. Finscher, ed., *Claudio Monteverdi: Festschrift Reinhold Hammerstein zum 70. Geburtstag* (Laaber, 1986), pp.35–51. The importance of the work as a model is perhaps most poignant in the vernacular monophonic repertory of the Middle Ages, in which the role of the work is crucial to an understanding of performance modes.

consists of an imitation of the compositional process.5 Accordingly, analysis serves to reveal the compositional tactics, problems and solutions; it searches for accuracy and clarity. The philologist (theorist) stands back from his analyses and sees a family of related members joined by describable characteristics which were observed in and derived from the musical score. The 'understanding' of the work is guided by the process itself and, I do not hesitate to add, limited to its objects, all of which were captured because they were philological events. The goal is to locate a place for the work in the 'history of music', creating an exegetical account of a composition as a link in an historical Markov chain. The links in that chain are forged of notational mannerisms or transmission characteristics that represent some sounds, but do not represent the sound picture of performance, the sound received by the listener. The score is a guide or at least a point of departure for interpretation. This ultimately leads to a sounding event, a transformation of the visual event or perhaps in many cases a sounding paraphrase of the visual document. The document is not the sound.

It is evident that performance-determined priorities are quite different from philological priorities because analysis based upon those priorities examines communication, with paradigms more closely related to those of rhetoric or (since World War II) information theory than etymological analysis. Analysis that is performance-driven is not at all what Bukofzer called 'composition backwards'.6 The performance process places the 'score' in the context of a larger environment which includes elements very much external to it. The composition itself is seen as a part of a complex event occurring within an immediate and limited time. It may not be clear at all at what point the composition actually begins or ends.7 This is not an uncommon experience in ritual music, for example. Of the thousands of Masses performed during the Middle Ages, there is not a single score, only bits and pieces for the liturgist to assemble. There never was such a score because the event was not considered a work, an opus.

Much of the discussion of performance practices today would profit from considering the composition in its performance environment, imagining a performance that can be analysed, rather than isolating the work from even a theoretical performance model. In a discussion of interpretation, we must go beyond seeing and recognizing the component parts of a musical work and relating them to a model derived from the study of historical theoretical works. We must create paradigms that permit a work to appear in vastly different performances. Interpretation requires context. The philological aspects of the work alone do not reveal the work in an interpreted dimension because they are measurable, objective and lacking context. In understanding an interpretation of a musical work we must include the general, accidental and subjective elements in its reception. Georg Feder, writing of 'Syntagma und Paradigma', describes the compositional process.8 Traditional stereotypical events incorporate repetition, transformation,

5 See G. Feder, 'Musikphilologie: eine Einführung in die musikalische Textkritik, Hermeneutik und Editionstechnik', in *Die Musikwissenschaft* (Darmstadt, 1987), p.81.
6 M.F. Bukofzer, *The place of music in American institutions of higher learning* (New York, 1957).
7 See A. J. Minnis, *Medieval theory of authorship: scholastic literary attitudes in the later Middle Ages* (London, 1984).
8 Feder, op. cit.

omission, etc., and result in an action of the mind (which is the composition). This he compares with the process of understanding, in which an aural impression leads to traditional stereotypical responses in the imagination, stimulating a comparative view. Understanding is seen as comparative, and the comparative view is the result of the interpretation of stereotypical events. This is an acceptable paradigm but we must step much closer to the event itself for detail.

Such terms as form, structure, modality, compositional process, tonality and so forth are the stereotypical components that reveal the *least* about the specific event. To understand performed music we must shift our attention away from the compositional process towards a collective process of the event, the performance in its surroundings.9 In doing so we might challenge many of the currently accepted priorities widely under discussion.

What we know of early music is limited to a large degree to the documents reflecting the compositional process (the manuscript containing the notes), but not the performance. Performance must be reconstructed theoretically from many sorts of documents and respecting the need to hypothesize well-founded but not provable performance situations.

The degree to which the composer controls the work is important here because the contribution of the performer to the creative process of performance has declined constantly since the Middle Ages, while that of the composer has increased. This is reflected in the vocabulary of the period. The modest term 'trovar' was once the verb which indicated the act of creating a poem or a melody, a term wholly inappropriate for, say, Handel's *Messiah*. There was some discussion in the Middle Ages of the relative contribution of performer and poet, for example the interesting interchange between Alfonso X and the troubadour Guiraut Riquier. In his *Declaración del sénher rey N'Amfos de Castela*, from 1275, Riquier represents a serious discussion with the King, in which the King explains the Spanish usage of some terms: 'joglar' refers to those who play instruments; 'remedadores' are those who act or imitate ('contrahacen o imiten'); the 'trovadores' are called 'segrieres'; and finally those who have vulgar manners and who recite without feeling and who practise their art in the streets are called 'cazurros'. All these are included in the word 'juglar' in Provence, but not in Spain. Those who are able to combine 'cortesia' (style) with 'ciencia', know how to interact with cultivated people, play instruments, tell stories ('contar novas'), recite poems, sing 'versos y canciones' written by others, and may be given the title of 'juglar'. Those who know how to create poems, and melodies ('saben trovar verso y tonada'), and who 'saben hacer danzas, coblas, baladas, albadas, y sirventesivos' can be called 'trovadores'; and among them, those who can compose perfect verses, 'y de buen enseñamiento y muestra los caminos del honor, de la cortesia y del deber, declarando los casos dudiosos', these can be called, 'don doctor de trobar'.10 The distribution of creative activity varied, separating the invention of the work from its presentation. According to one model, winters were spent in study and writing, summers in the presentation of the poetry. Social distinctions were made according to accomplishment, but not according to aristocratic station.11 A troubadour might be of noble or common birth, but he/she must be

9 See F. Reckow, 'Zwischen Ontologie und Rhetorik' (forthcoming).
10 M. Menéndez Pelayo, *Antología de poetas líricos castellanos*, ix (Santander, 1944), p. 27.
11 Christopher Page sees history differently in *Voices and instruments of the Middle Ages* (London, 1987).

able to write poetry. Some, like Giraut de Bornelh, were of low estate, who progressed from *joglar* to *trobar* through, one supposes, application, study and talent. While the station of a troubadour was considered higher than that of a joglar (minstrel), both were in the business of entertainment.

Not long ago one scholar suggested that we should add nothing in the performance of monophonic vernacular song that is not in the score, for 'these [notes] at least we know were sung'. I think we need not be so suspicious of performance done convincingly and appealingly. To limit performance to the sketches that have been preserved would be to limit the performance to a rendition of only the model. The one thing we can say for certain about the performance of that music is that the notes as we see them did not constitute the performance. To find out what did, we must examine the elements of performance, working back, I suggest, from an imagined performance that is historically plausible. These elements can be isolated as follows:

Elements that define genre and environment

Every musical performance contains elements of definition. The performance may direct the listener's attention to elements that are characteristic of one genre but not characteristic of another. Often the surround-structure of a performance reveals important elements of definition: liturgy or other ritual, dance, drama, literary entertainment, lament, social criticism, etc.

Elements that denote structure

There are rational or denotative elements, which are tangible and which sustain analysis. These elements thrive on consistency, they have clear borders and impart clear information. Examples are formal schemes, treatment of consonance and dissonance or cadence structure. These are philological events which can be studied, learned and reproduced in the compositional process. They are easily transmitted literary elements.

Elements that connote quality and method of communication

These differ markedly. They might be termed irrational because they are connotative elements which have contextual properties and conditions: beauty, function, perception, deception, reception, conception, *Gestalt* are all examples of these irrational elements. (I am tempted to refer here to the left and the right sides of the brain, the rational area and the mystical or irrational area.) These are not simply referential or non-referential. Surely we are deceived when we ignore the irrational elements of performance in our analysis of music.

Thomas Binkley

Elements of reception

A performance includes, beyond the rational and irrational elements, its contextual properties – the given conditions, the expectations, the knowledge and experience. These are brought to the performance by the listener and by the performer as a sort of baggage. Receptive elements are not elective and not composed into the music, but are always present.

Balance of orality and literacy

A performance always contains some degree of orality. A *primary orality* is found in any completely unwritten (non-literate) practice while a *secondary orality* consists in performance in some way based upon a written 'score', even when it is not identical with it. Just as we may speak of a primary and secondary orality, we may speak of primary and secondary literacy. As we move from primary orality (completely oral) to primary literacy (complete dependence upon the written score), there are three levels to consider. The first level of literacy reflects the model with variations attributed to some secondary writing – 'variants'. The next level introduces in the writing unnecessary difficulties, obstacles such as puzzles or notational curiosities which require solution, and which create a class of insiders (who understand) and outsiders (who do not). The boundaries of the third level are fixed by the idea that what is not contained in the notation is not part of the work, and presumably must not be done. No one today would seriously suggest that the troubadour repertory is an example of either the second or the third levels of literacy.

It is probably fair to suggest that twelfth- and thirteenth-century monophonic vernacular song (troubadours, trouvères, Minnesang, etc.) is far more oral (level one) than the polyphonic song of the following century, and that the polyphonic songs of Lescurel and Adam de la Halle reflect more orality than those of Machaut. This is seen in the unsystematic, pragmatic notation of the earlier models as opposed to the (relatively) systematic practice of Machaut and later composers.

But no serious performer today expects to find in manuscripts and early prints all that he needs to know in order to perform correctly even the pitches and rhythms of any of this music (let alone the articulation, phrasing, tempo, instrumentation and so forth). The oral tradition supplied the missing information that is now lost. The information that was considered important and necessary to identify a composition in terms of its musical literacy was written down; the information that concerned practices shared between pieces and that falls outside the world of literacy, was imperfectly transmitted.

The solution to this apparent dilemma must be looked for in period-specific practices. We will hardly profit much more in the performance of Renaissance and Baroque music by consulting still more manuals on diminution, ornamentation or articulation (presuming of course that well-known sources have indeed been consulted). We will profit immensely if we consult literary theory. (Doni has been on the tip of the tongue for a few years now.) I suggest we try to connect our performance priorities with those of earlier times.

Take the case of 'rhetoric', a term today much abused in the Baroque context. 'Grammar' and 'rhetoric' appear in the Middle Ages within the *artes liberales* of the universities as two somewhat competitive fields derived directly from classical learning. In a very general sense, these fields formed a vehicle of discourse so that the structure and content of an event might lead to successful, convincing communication. While the bare roots of the art remained for centuries much the same – extending from the *Ad herennium* and Cicero's *De inventione* to the close of the Middle Ages – they were advanced, recast, augmented and renewed to satisfy many needs, among them the need to understand or at least guide effective communication. This included communication in the creative arts, especially composing letters and poetry, and perhaps music as well.[12]

Rhetoric, the art of convincing discourse, provided the only compositional method in the fine arts; behind the pedantic and sterile side of the rhetorical method was a potent and creative force which guided eloquence in many fields for centuries. The endless figures with Greek names, with forced analysis of passages in literature (and if we think of Burmeister, music too), winding back to the figures themselves, camouflage the contribution that field made in shaping the presentation of art.

The rhetorical process functioned in many areas other than speech: Curtius wrote about 'rhetorical landscape representations' while Serpieris speaks of 'la retorica al teatro' (the rhetorical use of theatrical space),[13] and music historians have learned that the language and approach of musical theory in the Middle Ages were borrowed directly from medieval grammar and rhetoric.[14]

While the art of rhetoric certainly played an important, even direct role in the *musica theoretica*, it surely played an important, perhaps subliminal role in the composition and performance in the realm of *musica practica* as well, because the *ars poetica* contained the only analytical vocabulary for the planning and executing of musical works.

Geoffrey of Vinsauf's *Poetria Nova*[15] (written in the early thirteenth century, still copied out in manuscript in the fifteenth century, and freshly printed as late as 1721) provided an elaboration on the Ciceronian rhetoric by focusing on the writing of poetry (and its spoken delivery) rather than on speech. By focusing on the devices of communication, it provides an invaluable reference work for performers. According to Geoffrey, there are three elements necessary for learning to write poetry: *ars*, a knowledge of the immutable laws; *imitatio*, the imitation of models; and *usus*, practice.

The first step (in composition) is the ordering of the materials. There are two paths, the path of Nature is to present events as they are presented in Nature – begin your story at the beginning. A more artful way, however, the path of Art, is to begin at some other point or with some material taken not from the beginning, and to proceed from there to the beginning. Donatus had written, 'Let the beginning contain the whole', in other words permit a prelude to prepare the work. A work may proceed from its opening in a hurried or

---

[12] Machaut's *Voir dit* provides an ample illustration of poetry and letter-writing in which the rhetorical flowers are in full bloom.
[13] E. R. Curtius, 'Rhetorische Naturschilderung im Mittelalter', *Romanische Forschungen*, lvi (1942), pp.219–56. A. Serpieris, 'La retorica al teatro', in G. Ferroni, *La semiotica e il doppio teatrale* (Naples, 1981).
[14] F. Reckow, '*Vitium* oder *color rhetoricus*? Thesen zur Bedeutung der Modelldisziplinen der grammatica, rhetorica und poetica für das Musikverständnis', *Forum musicologicum*, iii (1982), p.307. J. Yudkin, *De musica mensurata: the Anonymous of St Emmeram* (Bloomington, 1990).
[15] Text printed in E. Faral, *Les arts poétiques du XIIe et XIIIe siècle* (Paris, 1924). A fine translation into English is M. F. Nims, *Poetria nova of Geoffrey of Vinsauf* (Toronto, 1967).

leisurely manner, leaping ahead to a conclusion or tarrying here and there along the path. Methods of amplification and delay are employed to achieve this, the longer route. Following are a few of the techniques of amplification that were employed, dwelling on this or that to delay the arrival at the conclusion:

Repetition – present the material in different clothes, concealed in multiple forms, the same varied in multiple garb.

Periphrase – suggest rather than say, encircle the material but do not reveal it all at once, move by a devious route, thus retarding the tempo.

Digression – go outside the bounds of the material, draw away, but not so far as to lose the way back.

Opposition – let the negative or the opposite join with the positive to form a single harmonious meaning – if one is fast, one is not slow.

However, if the shorter route is selected, then techniques of abbreviation are to be employed. These consist essentially of avoiding the techniques of amplification such as those above, with at least one other:

Implication – effect a fusion of material so that what is said may say the unsaid, and do not enshroud the material in a mist, but let sunlight penetrate to reveal clarity; emphasis is a useful tool.

Whether the selected path be short or long, the material must be appropriately adorned. Examine the mind of the material rather than just its face and be sure there is harmony between the adornment and the path. If the material has dignity, let it not be debased by vulgarity. Permit an old word to regain its youth by giving it a home in another situation where it can be a novel guest, giving pleasure by its strangeness. Material can be adorned as an object is painted, and many an object can be adorned with the same paint. Attribute to the cause what the effect claims as its own.

Rhetorical colours are more readily understood in terms of words than tone. There are difficult ornaments and there are easy ornaments, appropriate for a dignified or a simple style. Consider a few: *repetitio* (restatement for emphasis); *traductio* (multiple forms of the same material); *exclamatio*; and ambiguity (multiple meaning of the same material).

There are faults to avoid: Art tolerates a sequence but forbids a concentrated sequence. Graceless and excessive repetition or incongruous sequencing of the material is to be avoided. Judge the material to be sure that what wins the mind's approval also charms the ear and withstands repeated reflection. Memory must be trained actively. The mind craves what is delightful, not what is boring. Do not burden the mind, but gratify it. In delivery let three tongues speak: that of the mouth, that of countenance and that of gesture. Each has its own laws. Vinsauf offers us a textbook for the delivery of vernacular medieval lyric. He reveals both the considerations and the tactics employed in artistic communication, and for performers today this gives us a matrix for our performance priorities.

Against the background of the above, many disagreements concerning performance practice might be placed in a new perspective. The questions such as whether this or that instrument played a tenor line or accompanied a troubadour song are clearly philological considerations that do not materially bear on the sound of the performance or on the interpretation of the work. Such issues as whether there is a prelude, digressive interludes or gestures are of a higher order, because they are oral elements of definition and connotation that have a material bearing on the performance, both in terms of its total sound picture and its reception.

Thus, while the philological elements of a work are analysable, they must be placed alongside – and perhaps slightly below – the performance elements which determine what we hear and what we play. The music is the sound, not the written document. We must consider first the whole composition-performance process and not merely that part of the process that found written expression. A general anthropological and sociological context of the specific performance allows us to determine important priorities, especially the goals of the performance and what it is trying to communicate. If we examine music with these points in mind, we will be better equipped to consider interpretation in a medieval context.

6 Beyond authenticity

Peter Phillips

We have learnt recently that revolutions have a second phase: there is the revolt itself, and afterwards there are the repercussions of the revolt. The repercussions may not be quite what those doing the revolting had expected or hoped for, and they may even call for measures which seem to return to pre-revolutionary practice, after all the effort and the slogan-mongering.

The second phase of the 'authenticity' revolution is the desire to make the music expressive again. We have overthrown the autocratic hegemony of the nineteenth-century symphony orchestra and its vibratoful pronouncements, and for some years now have been enjoying the freedom which has been won. Yet as 'authentic' recordings of the greatest masterpieces begin to proliferate and to vie with each other for critical attention, a new pressure is being felt by performers to make their version the most attractive. They are finding that the old battle-cries are no longer enough and the old dogmas, enshrined in those battle-cries, too restrictive. *All* the new recordings, as a matter of course, claim to be historically as accurate as possible: no one, for instance, would dream of using that unreliable old edition which we all grew up with, published perhaps fifty years ago; the instruments are as near as practically possible of the same epoch as the composer; the number of performers taking part is modelled where possible on a documented performance actually directed by the composer. These things are now taken for granted; and although there may be discrepancies between one scholar's view of what constitutes strict accuracy as against another's, the public does not follow the small print, since they know the essential struggle to be over. What they are looking for now are performances which bring the music to life for them: techniques and methods from the past, of course, but put to the service of modern, post-Romantic ways of thinking and reacting.

The question which I believe will dominate the next decade is: to what extent does a personal interpretation of early music represent an affront to historical accuracy? Twentieth-century directors have twentieth-century perceptions and there would be no point, even if it could be done, of trying to recreate, say, Palestrina's own interpretation of the *Missa Papae Marcelli* since it could have only a partial meaning to us. For many people it would be fascinating to know what Palestrina did actually make of it, but having heard it, the musicians in favour of the strictest historical accuracy would be most terribly stuck, since they would be obliged to perform the piece like Palestrina every time, and the music would come exactly to resemble a painting, the finished and unalterable work of its creator.

Away from this extreme are the bulk of directors, who want to put the insights gained by recent research towards their understanding of the music, which will then in turn contribute to their interpretation of it. This seems reasonable until one goes into detail; and then it may be found that not only do scholars disagree about fundamental issues (as for example in Renaissance music, pitch), but that there are directors who are prepared to float their own questionably documented theories to support a practicality in performance which they find attractive, and yet others who simply get on and do what they think the music requires without comment. They all, overtly or covertly, lay claim to the principle of historical accuracy, and many increasingly take licence with the strictest interpretation of those principles.

This debate takes on new dimensions when it is applied to pre-Baroque music, since there is so much more to argue about than in the later repertories. By about 1650 the sources are relatively forthcoming about some of the fundamental aspects of performance practice, and the surrounding source material incontrovertibly clears up some of the others (most people seem happy with $a' = 415$, and would not dare these days formulate a personal vision around a' being anything else); but there is far greater scope for doubt in music from before that date, and the earlier one looks, the greater the problems become. In much medieval music, the questioning has to embrace pitch, scoring (not just what timbre of voices and how many of them on each part, but also whether instruments should be involved), the notes themselves (via *musica ficta* and scribal error) and sometimes, even, whether there are missing parts or parts which were not part of the composer's original conception. There are no holographs, so the performer is always at least one stage – more often several stages – removed from the composer. It is therefore not uncommon to find two performances of what is said to be the same piece sounding so different that they are not identifiable as such. In these circumstances it is extremely dangerous to criticize one version as being of greater historical accuracy than another: the acid test must be which version brings the music most effectively to life. The revolution has touched this repertory only relatively, since very little of it was performed before the revival of interest in early music. Both now and in the future it will be uniquely free of pre-conceived ideas, putting its advocates in the paradoxical position of needing to consider and justify every performing decision while in practice having greater freedom than any of us.

Specialists in Renaissance music can neither be so certain about the fundamental questions governing historical accuracy as their Classical counterparts, nor so uncertain as those involved with medieval music. Furthermore, the performance of sacred music from the High Renaissance, at least, is still indebted to influences from pre-revolutionary times. We sense the freedom to experiment with the exceptional sonorities which underlie the polyphonic technique of this repertory, but are constantly being brought up short either by scholars who have just enough evidence to tell us that in a certain year in a certain place the choir consisted of a combination of voices quite other than the one we are planning to use; or, on the other hand, by the evidence of the continuing choral traditions of several countries, but especially England, which are very widely recorded and against whom it is hard to level the charge of inauthenticity since they have been singing Renaissance sacred music with just about the same distribution and the same number of voices from the composer's day to our own. One of the most blatant contraventions of the ground rules of historical accuracy is perpetrated by modern chamber choirs who claim, while using female sopranos and even altos, to come nearer to what the composer had in mind than our cathedral choirs, which consist entirely of male singers.

The apparent freedom of decision in practical matters of those who perform *a cappella* Renaissance music derives from the fact that no vocal sounds have come down to us over the centuries. Unlike Baroque and Classical instruments, there are no Renaissance voice-boxes for us to re-animate, and words are not equal to the task of describing pure sound, even where contemporary commentators tried to use them, which they did very infrequently. We may look into the question of vocal scoring (for instance, whether a countertenor sang the top, second or third vocal part in a piece of English music of the period), but any attempt to fix the sound as a result of such research is immediately foiled by the fact that we do not know, and can never know, what the difference between a modern countertenor and his Tudor equivalent really was; not even if the problem of whether he was a falsettist or not is solved. Any speculation as to what boys sounded like in the sixteenth century is rendered futile by the evidence which shows that their voices broke years later than voices break now, perhaps as late as eighteen. It is curious, though, to be told that they must have sounded like thirty-year-old, twentieth-century women.

Yet the drive towards historical accuracy in its earlier days seemed to require absolute statements. David Wulstan (to whose theories I am in many ways indebted) has consistently maintained that pitch in England in the sixteenth century was a minor third higher than it is now and that modern performers should transpose the music up by that amount in order to achieve the necessary accuracy. I do not say he is wrong; but experience taught me early that that pitch is too high, at least when the music contains a treble part, to give convincing performances in present conditions. Perhaps in the future a breed of super-trebles will develop who can show us how splendid the music sounds up a full minor third or more; though I can only doubt it. In any case, these singers will still not represent sixteenth-century boys. Wulstan's theory has promoted a fascinating change in perception of the sonorities of Tudor music, yet strict adherence to it has deprived many directors, on disc and in concert, of the kind of freedom which would have encouraged them to analyse the sound their choir was making, and consider whether that sound was able to express the music effectively. To espouse upward transposition of the music by only a tone (which I prefer) would have been considered inadequate on a number of counts ten years ago.

There will be further theories about performance practice which will no doubt be forcefully proposed. The current ones in the Renaissance field concern: the correct pronunciation of the words, including Latin; the case for believing in written pitch after all; and whether the falsetto voice existed at that time. These are fascinating issues which, however relevant to historical verisimilitude, may add nothing to the expressive power of the music and may quite easily detract from a performance if the musicians taking part are not at ease with them. For this reason I await with trepidation the advocates of what may be called manuscript authenticity in Renaissance music: those who will claim that since there are no tempo and dynamic markings in the sources, every piece should be founded on the same basic speed (determined by the heart-beat or 'pulse') and that a deliberately contrasted use of dynamics is not appropriate. In fact, I believe that sixteenth-century composers would have expected far greater unanimity between pieces in performance than we give them; but I repeat that what was acceptable to sixteenth-century ears is probably not so to twentieth-century ones. To have to sit through a concert of Renaissance polyphony undertaken on these principles would be to understand why the early Baroque composers reacted so strongly against it.

Similarly, the present trend for performing sacred music in its liturgical context, with the correct chant and order of pieces should never take the place of a carefully-planned concert programme, since modern audiences deal in concerts not church services. Although these reconstructions are enjoyable and occasionally revealing as regards the relationship between chant and polyphony, they encourage a bloodless, museum-like attitude to an activity which is supposed to create something fresh at each performance. They also distract from the essential and simple task of finding first-rate music and singing or playing it as well as possible. If, in the excitement of making discoveries about historical accuracy, we have strayed from this elementary position, we should return to it, because therein lies the best chance of making the music expressive to our public. Practising musicians should not be frightened of not having a special theory of their own, as if their occupancy of a stage requires one as a *raison d'être*. They may find it hard to explain themselves in words; but the only real abiding issue at stake is the strength of their musical vision.

7 Hard-sell, scholarship and silly titles

Philip Pickett

Why, in this enlightened time of mass-market classical CD buying and concert-going, should really early music remain almost a specialist interest, while 'authentic' Baroque and Classical recordings and concerts continue to enjoy spectacular popular success? For there can be no doubt that much medieval and some areas of Renaissance music have experienced yet again their own dark age over the past fifteen years or so, though it was actually with such music that the popular revival of interest began in the late 1960s, when Musica Reservata and David Munrow first began attracting new audiences with strange and wonderful sounds. But since those early days, the period-performance bandwagon – undoubtedly aided by the record companies – has moved inexorably on through the centuries, with ensembles, choirs and orchestras competing ever more desperately to present 'first' modern performances and recordings of standard works such as the Monteverdi Vespers, the Bach Passions, Mozart and Haydn symphonies and now Beethoven, Berlioz, Weber and Wagner, through the seemingly almost mandatory media of period instruments and supposedly historical performance practice.

It was, of course, inevitable that it should become commercially more desirable for early music organizations to 'rediscover' familiar works rather than to uncover the rich treasures of the Renaissance and medieval periods. After all, unusual sounds and new styles of performance applied to familiar music are not only controversial and attractive, they are also far easier to market than even the most stunningly virtuoso and emotionally-charged performances of unknown works by Johannes Ciconia or Bartolino da Padova, however exciting, fresh and illuminating they may be. But there must be more to it, and it must be worth examining the problem in more depth. What did happen to the crowds who flocked to those early performances, who were so captivated by the strange squeaks, squawks and buzzes and the little man with the red face who epitomized early music at that time?

I believe that many of those who attended Munrow's concerts have never been to an early music concert since: to them the vital elements of energy, enthusiasm and personality cult have been missing. In part this was due to the fact that, for more than a decade following Munrow's death, a number of small, low-profile ensembles (often devoting themselves to one short period in music history) vanished into their garrets to discover what the music itself was all about rather than developing the personalities to project it. If they appeared in public at all, they often presented programmes of little to interest the layman. One and a half hours of Burgundian chansons, all performed with roughly the same scoring and all at about the same tempo might prove useful to a musicologist attempting to delve deeply into the subtleties of that particular style – and it must be pointed out that many critics applauded the dedication and scholarship displayed, and the praiseworthy turning-away from commercialism and the what might be called 'toyshop' approach – but it did very little for the audiences.

Academic debates and wrangles that had begun during the last period of

Munrow's activities now assumed such importance that many serious and questioning performers, editors and arrangers felt obliged to avoid completely certain areas of repertory due to their feelings of unease. The loss, while all this was going on, was of the wider public awareness that here was music worth hearing. But there were important gains, too: a dramatic improvement in performers' awareness of credible performance practice, and then in performance standards – a change that coincided with a move away from jack-of-all-trades multi-instrumentalists to virtuoso specialists.

With hindsight, the aftermath of the Munrow phenomenon displayed clearly that good scholarship and musical competence were not enough to retain the interest of either the 1960s sensation seekers or the general audience at large, and too narrowly focused programmes and dull performances must bear some responsibility. Once the novelty of unfamiliar sounds, music and instruments had worn off, the fringe departed in search of the latest stimulus while the ordinary music lover returned to the classics, leaving behind a dedicated but small audience who loved the music for itself.

A natural communicator, Munrow, like other English scholar-performers before him, had taken the fruits of his researches and vivid imagination not only to the publishers but to the concert hall, the recording studio, the radio and television, thus consolidating and continuing an important principle which was to give British musicology greater vigour than America's – an emphasis on performance as the end-product (indeed, the *raison d'être*) of research, with the researchers themselves often being foremost among the performers, and a feeling that early music was fun, and too entertaining to be reserved for academics. Building on and refining the pioneering work of such groups as the New York Pro Musica, the Studio der frühen Musik and Musica Reservata, Munrow showed exactly how the earliest of music could be a commercial success. Perhaps his time as a member of the Royal Shakespeare Company's wind band had given him a useful insight into the theatrical possibilities of concert-giving, not to mention the attractiveness to any audience of a slick production. Whatever, he showed how fragmentary dance and song tunes could be organized into cohesive programmes under the attractive umbrella of a catch-all title which meant more to an audience than any number of erudite programme notes. In fact, after his own effervescent personality, perhaps the second most important ingredient in all his success was his intuitive grasp of effective programme planning.

After deciding on the overall programme subject, and choosing and perhaps editing a number of 'good' or 'interesting' or even 'educational' pieces from the sometimes enormous surviving repertories, one of the greatest difficulties faced by the programme planner is to order all the material for concert performance, often in venues not suited to or far removed from the music's original acoustic setting or function. Concert giving, formal or informal, is a relatively recent development, and the idea of sitting in the rather unevocative environment of most modern concert halls to listen for hours to large-scale musical compositions comparable to works from the opera house or church did not really take root until the Baroque period. Amateur and professional performances, often informal, sometimes highly organized, but forming a regular part of medieval and Renaissance courtly and domestic life, came nearest to our modern concert situation. For the rest of the time music formed a natural part of religious and secular ceremonial.

Another problem is the lack of large-scale musical constructions, though there has certainly been a rediscovery of the sacred and Latin works which formed the bedrock of medieval musical composition, and a trend towards the performance of lengthy works from the period – motets, Masses, the long and passionate French lais and Latin lyrics, and the compelling laments for the dead. But while Mass settings can be substantial, the effect of separating the individual movements by the original chant and other suitable interpolations leads to an experience vastly different from the normally-accepted concept of a complete work, as does a programme of carefully chosen and varied troubadour chansons – even when given without cuts. For a performance of secular music, where the programme may have to consist of between fifteen and thirty short pieces, the problem is even greater, and has led some programme planners into often arcane realms of imagination and invention. The sheer range of themes adopted is simply staggering.

The most common disadvantages of all this are that musicians often find it difficult to settle in as they would in a traditional recital; pieces, however short, have to establish their individuality and content instantly, and too many sharp contrasts in vocal and instrumental colour and texture can work against the cumulative effects so necessary in captivating an audience. Yet there is a greater danger here, often leading critics, academics and even the general public to wish that programmes be more concentrated and less glibly titled: the catch-all label is attractive, and the handbill speaks of wild mirth, debauchery, chivalry, minstrelsy (in fact, almost anything which the promoter feels to be attractive to the uninitiated concert-goer), but the concert is just another medley from four or five centuries of Western European music. The diversity of pieces and national styles presented encourages the audience to pay more attention to the strange sonorities than to the qualities of particular composers and their works, and the miscellany often leaves nothing more than an impression of bittiness, the sheer variety of music presented becoming in the end rather tiring.

While concerts of pre-Classical music can still too easily degenerate into obscurity and academicism for their own sake on the one hand, and the productions of the 'hard-sell and silly title fraternity' on the other, it is perfectly possible to present even fairly obscure corners of the repertory with elegance and wit through well-planned programmes where related – or even seemingly unrelated and varied – items add up to a comprehensive, comprehensible and entertaining picture, and where the performances are carried off with the precision, showmanship and sheer personality expected by today's concert-goer. And it has to be pointed out that it is again entirely acceptable to critics and audiences alike that one of the most highly regarded and iconoclastic of scholars now producing concerts and recordings of medieval music should be perhaps the most creative and fanciful when it comes to the 'silly title'.

One of the most successful trends in programming has been the attempted musical reconstruction of actual historical events, or specific medieval and Renaissance festivals and ceremonies. Others have related music to pilgrimages, battles and even paintings. In fact, anything which focuses the attention of the general public onto an aspect of history already familiar to them while promoting an awareness of the social, historical and cultural background to the music of different periods seems to draw at least some of the crowds.

Even problems of emotional 'build-up' in the programme can be solved through experience and the application of such well-known organizational principles as the Golden Section or the rhetorical format. Forms and devices such as these have long been known to and used by composers to influence and control the listener's response to music – ordering the material in such a way as to elicit just the right variety and sequence of feelings – of excitement, of repose, of climax. If these principles work so well within reasonably large-scale musical structures, then there is no reason why the overall shape of concert programmes should not be guided by them and collections of small-scale works organized with the same manipulative end in view.

There are other solutions, too, many of them reflecting the flexibility of the various organizers and artistic directors of early music groups, and a testimony to the seemingly bottomless well of invention present in the minds of the stalwarts of the early music movement. A constant search for new and exciting ways of presenting this music, together with an astute awareness of the general trends and changes of direction in concert-going will slowly bring the music to a larger audience. Why not introduce a theatrical element into the concerts? Why not try presenting early lyrics in more immediate modern English translations? Why not combine music with dance, or with mime? Why not juxtapose earlier music with contemporary music, or ethnic music, or even classical music if the contrast makes a point? And if the music had a particular function, then why not try to represent that function in some credible way?

All these and many more have again begun to bring in the crowds, gently combining education with excitement, and concert-goers are slowly learning that the music itself is worth a second hearing in its own right. If some new approach will reach a wider audience, then we should grasp it with alacrity, and not be fearful of the wrath which will inevitably fall from some less imaginative quarters. For a performer should never forget that he is an entertainer, however scholarly, and that the future of earlier music depends to a great extent on the general public's awareness of its real value and its ability to enchant alongside better-known and better-understood masterpieces.

II Aspects of music and society

8 Centre and periphery: mainstream and provincial music

Reinhard Strohm

It seems clear that communications were more difficult in the Middle Ages than they are today, that travel took longer and that ideas were disseminated at a much slower pace. We also know that Europe was inhabited by far fewer people, of whom only a tiny élite were in a position to take an interest in the arts or literature. Before the fifteenth century, written information reaches us generally only from urban or courtly centres, monasteries or universities. It may be inevitable, therefore, that our picture of medieval musical life is all about 'centres'. Thirteenth-century music is all about Paris, the home of the Ars antiqua or Notre Dame polyphony; the Burgundian court of the fifteenth century or the Tudor court of the sixteenth were the places where anything of musical significance happened, to the exclusion of the provinces. For most of the time between 800 and 1600, music history took place, if we are to believe the textbooks, in exactly three European countries.

'Significance' is the keyword: only what is 'central' is significant to us. Even if we can rarely prove (for a lack of proper criteria) that music originating outside the centres was less skilfully composed or more conservative, music history has in any case adopted the model of centres and peripheries, at least for convenience's sake. The historiographer does not need scientific proof to find something 'significant'.

Sometimes, however, historians get fascinated by the peripheral and provincial. Jacques Handschin was one of the medievalists who, since the 1920s, maintained that around the rather extraordinary phenomenon of the Notre Dame organum and motet, there were immense areas of 'peripheral organum' practice, partly connected with the centre, partly, perhaps, more independent. In evidence of this, he could muster large, elaborate codices containing the Parisian mainstream music but apparently used in outposts such as the Spanish Las Huelgas monastery or the cathedral of St Andrews in Scotland as well as countless smaller witnesses for musical practices that seemed to emulate Parisian tastes only as best they could. This 'primitive' or 'simple' polyphony, based on compositional or extemporising techniques which the 'centre' had abandoned by the thirteenth century, was to flourish for several hundred years longer in other countries (central Europe, Italy) or in rural areas. In sixteeth-century manuscripts of Le Puy (Auvergne), Wulf Arlt has identified sacred pieces of drastically different ages, some stemming from the fourteenth and some even from the twelfth century. Music seems to have aged more slowly in some areas – an observation which can also be made in folk-art and folklore. The stylistic yardstick for the music of those outposts is not necessarily always that of the centre. This music does not remain the same through the ages, but has its own kind of development which it may share, sometimes surprisingly, with other 'peripheries' in quite distant places.

The underlying value judgment implied in the model centre-periphery (the same for which nowadays any shop in the high street calls itself a 'centre' of something) is the essential problem, and one that has often been discussed. The research of primitive polyphony aims, of course, at a revaluation of the music involved. The 'historicist' school of thought argues that every tradition is worth studying in its own right. It is clear that hindsight evaluation from a modern point of view easily errs in according significance to those traditions that have led more directly to us. Also, people have destroyed the achievements of entire cultures, thus making them insignificant – to us. History is always written by the winning team, and that is as true for papal dogmas when 'defended' against heretics as it is for Notre Dame motets when compared with provincial organum. Against this 'survival of the fittest' syndrome, music historians have pitted the scientific interest of remote or closed cultural circles, which innovation failed to penetrate for centuries; the real beauty of some of their music, for example 'primitive' two-part pieces mostly in parallel fifths; and, last but not least, the evaluation of the contemporaries themselves, who may have looked upon music not as a dynamic and developing art but as a vehicle to praise God in the most traditional ways. The role of plainsong in medieval society, and that of the cantus firmus principle in composition even until the eighteenth century, can be cited to argue the case of artistic conservatism, simplicity and even provinciality. To some, the model of centre and periphery is altogether misleading in art: J. S. Bach was in many ways *not* a mainstream composer – Telemann was.

On the other hand, there is no use in pretending that history is not right in rewarding innovation. Those circles which, in the fourteenth century, shared the reservations of Pope John XXII's 'Docta Sanctorum' Bull against any kind of mensural music were going to miss out on a very good thing. Where have, after all, the provincial or peripheral alternatives led? They remained ever more behind the times or were finally absorbed into the main stream anyway.

What shall we make, then, of the tempting but perhaps unfair classification into mainstream and central, provincial and peripheral phenomena? Differentiation is necessary, and the model should be used preferably where it explains something other models cannot explain. Let us see how it holds up to selected aspects of early European music history.

The introduction of 'Gregorian' chant into the Frankish empire under Charlemagne was a major cultural event, contrived by a small centrally-placed group of churchmen and administrators working for the king. They skilfully merged various Roman, Frankish and Gallican style elements and created a unified chant repertory; also an abundance of newer melodies was added. The result proved successful in the sense that it came to be adopted by the Roman Church itself; this was also due to Charlemagne's political alliance with the Roman pontiff. Nevertheless, many other repertories and 'uses' of Latin plainsong survived outside the realm, and some even inside it. None of them could truly be called 'peripheral', since their users would not have wanted to take their cue from the Franks anyway. By the time of the Council of Trent in the sixteenth century, however, what was now the chant of the Roman Church was imposed with little exception on all the churches of Christendom, wiping out most of what had remained of 'peripheral', 'provincial' or simply 'local' practice. The story of Latin plainsong is, then, a story of progressive centralization imposed onto a 'free' artistic development for mostly political ends. From the viewpoint of the losers, it is a story of emargination.

The cultivation of chant and early polyphony in medieval Britain seems remarkably uncentralized. The great abbeys and monastic cathedrals (later also the other cathedrals as well as colleges and friaries) seem to have constituted a flexible network of musical practice, with shifting emphasis from century to century but never admitting an overall 'centre'. The network was disturbed, however, with the growing influence of secular powers and the accumulation of cultural eminence at the Royal courts. The centralization of English music from the later fourteenth century onwards also implied growing international influence. A result was that the music of, say, Exeter Cathedral, had by c.1500 become truly provincial, which it had never been in preceding centuries.

For some centres we do not really know the peripheries, and vice versa. It would be good in some cases to scrutinize our model for its geographic implications. Socio-economic patterns in the later Middle Ages have been interpreted in such a way as to form geographic 'regions' of about 100–200 miles in diameter, dominated by major cities and sprinkled with smaller provincial centres. Very approximately, these economic regions coincided with the ecclesiastical administration (in archdioceses). We could experimentally apply this model to musical practice as well. Music in the region of Florence, for example, would be oriented towards the practice in the leading city, allowing for provincial variants. North of the Appennines, however, provincial practice would gravitate towards Venice or Milan instead, and south of Rome towards Naples or Palermo. This model has the merit of displaying the competition of regional centres and the claim over 'their' peripheries, which does accord with certain aspects of medieval music. The stylistic divisions of Italian trecento music, for example, have been described in just the way indicated here. But in other ages and other parts of Europe, the model of 'regions' is well out of focus as regards music. Socio-economically speaking, other centres of European regions included Cologne, Toledo, Magdeburg, Vienna, Ghent – some of which were the largest cities of Europe after Paris. But what was their musical significance, or rather, what do we know about their musical significance? As the centuries pass, it is also increasingly difficult to reconcile the concept of regions with the importance of dynasties and courts for artistic life. We should ask: what was the periphery belonging to these centres? The cultural influence of the court of Burgundy (its 'outer periphery', so to speak) reached well beyond one or two socio-economic regions. Nevertheless, this court could be said to have had its 'inner periphery' in the local churches, cities and baronial castles of Northern France and the Low Countries, and in that respect, it coincided with a 'region'.

In some cases it is interesting to ask what centre belonged to a given periphery. Manuscript discoveries in central Italy have recently formed a strange pattern, suggesting that small towns in the Abruzzi area participated, around 1400, in a strikingly international musical repertory. Fragmentary sources containing Ars nova motets, Mass music and even chansons, partly of French or even English provenance, have been found in places such as Todi, Grottaferrata, Atri, Guardiagrele, Foligno and Cortona. Did they form an 'outer periphery' of Paris or Avignon? Of course not, but they were all then subject to the (schismatic) popes of Rome, who around 1400 could not afford to hire as many chapel singers from France or the Netherlands as they used to have at all other times. Thus, they employed musicians from the nearby provinces (among whom was the important composer Antonius Zacharius of Teramo), and those chaplains must have brought the international music of the papal chapel back home, where it has been preserved until today.

The example also demonstrates the duple function of the Roman chapel as a 'centre' for its own region, as well as a 'periphery' at that time for the main-stream music of the French-dominated Ars nova. It must be admitted, however, that music then composed by the chaplain Antonius Zacharius was also distri-buted in the opposite direction, reaching northern Italy, central Europe and even England before 1420. Relationships such as 'creation-reception' or 'in-novation-conservation' obtain on many different levels, often simultaneously and in conflict.

The 'mainstream music of the French-dominated Ars nova' is a phrase not everyone would subscribe to, and we have to dwell on it a little longer. French Ars nova music of the fourteenth century, and its influence, can very well be described with our model. The term 'Ars nova' itself, coined as the title of a treatise allegedly by Philippe de Vitry, is justified for the music of French courtly intellectuals, among them the great composers Vitry and Machaut. The European distribution of their most distinguished works is in no doubt: they are actually found in sources from Britain to Poland, from northern Germany to central Italy – often in somewhat reduced or simplified or incorrect versions. The depth of the influence varied, but in central Europe, for example, there was hardly any polyphonic technique by 1400 that was not either primitive or French-influenced. With most of these countries, the relationship may be characterized by the 'centre-periphery' model; in some cases we could perhaps speak of 'satellites'. Machaut's first employer, Duke John of Luxembourg, was also King of Bohemia, and his city of Prague may have harboured, for a short time, the musical practice of the Ars nova like any other French court.

The music of the Vitry-Machaut generation was continued by two subsequent generations of French musicians, who somehow managed to outdo their masters without ousting their basic precepts. In the late fourteenth century, a tradition was formed which turned more and more onto itself in further refinement, commentary and referentiality – the so-called 'Ars subtilior' ('more subtle art'). This happened in a rather limited geographical area in southern France, northern Spain and. northern Italy, with dynastic outposts or satellites in Cyprus and apparently Hungary. This post-Machaut tradition could still be called a 'central' tradition, as it was firmly based on the Ars nova and did not undergo significant external influences.

In contrast with this, musicians in England, the Low Countries, Germany and Italy – all of whom had been at first on a 'periphery' with respect to the Ars nova – now found their own ways and goals in musical style, very much by way of a 'lateral' exchange between their respective countries. Some parts of their repertory indeed travelled all along the outer edges of France, for example from England to Italy, without entering the 'centre'. This 'lateral' tradition had older elements in common with French Ars nova music, but combined them with regional, often simpler but original ideas. A political catalyst for this development was the papal schism (1378–1417), in which France and, partly, Spain (Aragon, Navarra, Castile) adhered to the popes of Avignon, most other nations to those of Rome. By the second decade of the fifteenth century, as the demise of the Avignon papacy and the re-unification of the Catholic Church under the Roman pope in 1417 would suggest, the 'central tradition' was extinct, whereas the 'lateral traditions' had consolidated.

There was now a network, not a new centre. Somehow the 'peripheral' nations in music had managed to turn the tables on the central tradition. The artistic polyphony of the fifteenth century as practised first in England and the Low Countries became a general European musical culture, enhanced by an increase in musical production and communication which a modern spectator would find unbelievable. There was a 'mainstream' type of music, yes: it was first defined in the secular songs and sacred music of Dufay, Binchois, and their English and French counterparts – a combination later misleadingly called the 'Art of the Netherlanders'. But regional and vernacular forms were also coming into the open during this period: Czech and Moravian protestant songs; Spanish *romances* and *villancicos*; English carols; German organ preludes; Italian *frottole*, and so forth. Local centres and their orbits did survive, often pocket-like. Many local idiosyncrasies enriched the mainstream tradition, for example in the works of the Franco-Netherlanders working in Italy (Josquin, Obrecht, Isaac, etc.).

It could be said that the Renaissance was in essence a culture which benefitted music by bringing out the individuality of various European idioms, but loosely integrating them into a mainstream type of compositional language, whose masters were the Franco-Netherlanders, then also the Italians. There was a certain balance between unification – which concerned the level of craftsmanship – and diversification – which concerned the level of ideas. And with regard to ideas, each country was, in some sense, the other's periphery. This meant, as we know, a lot of strife, but in artistic matters it meant progress.

Select bibliography

G. CORSI and P. PETROBELLI (eds.), *Le polifonie primitive in Friuli e in Europa* (Rome, 1989)

J. RUSSELL, *Medieval regions and their cities* (Newton Abbot, 1972)

R. STROHM, *Music in late medieval Bruges* (Oxford, 1985)

R. STROHM, *The rise of European Music, 1380–1500* (Cambridge, 1992), Part III, 2

9 The meeting of sacred ritual and secular piety: endowments for music

Barbara Haggh

A letter sent in 1176 from the Benedictine, Nicholas of Saint Albans, to the Cistercian, Peter of Celle, uses the noun *purgatorium* to describe a place one passes through before joining the Lord. One of the earliest documents to mention purgatory, it signalled a change in Christian dogma which was to have a profound effect on worship – and on music – in succeeding centuries. No longer could confession alone redeem sinners, who would pass through purgatory before meeting with their judgment; from then on only good works as a form of penance could shorten the stay in purgatory and lead to the true absolution of sin.

Medieval documents testify that endowments (donations made to churches by clerics and laymen alike) were such good works, made primarily to benefit the souls of the donors, their friends or relatives. The proliferation of endowments in the late Middle Ages has not received the attention given to the sale of indulgences as a catalyst for the Reformation. Yet it was the endowments that created the controversial wealth and power of the church, as well as substantial changes in the content and interpretation of the liturgy, and even the flourishing of elaborate sacred polyphony, all objects of the reformers' zeal in the sixteenth century. Because endowments afforded the laity a means of participation, sacred ritual and secular piety were joined together.

Endowments were donations of land or money to a church or convent. Sometimes they were gifts with no associated requests, but usually they had a specific purpose. They established benefices, provided for the construction of chapels and altars, or paid for 'perpetual' services requested by the donor. Endowments introducing new rituals were known as foundations. Other endowments added ceremony to existing rituals by providing for candles, music or additional distributions. Some simply increased the 'trust' associated with an established foundation. Only endowments for rituals associated with the rise of sacred polyphony are considered here: the evidence is drawn from the archives of secular rather than monastic establishments.[1]

Most endowments were formal bequests, but some were made well before death, such as those associated with the acquisition of new relics or icons or the construction of new chapels. However, not all were made willingly: many churches required clerics to endow commemorative services known as obits as part of their initiation. Endowments could be made by any parishioner, or even by those with no other association with the church, although most people endowed the most elaborate services at the churches where they would be buried. For this reason, churches sought a monopoly on funeral and burial rights, because these automatically ensured a steady flow of income from endowments. Most endow-

---

[1] On endowments and private Masses in monasteries, see A. Häussling, *Mönchskonvent und Eucharistiefeier*, Liturgiewissenschaftliche Quellen und Forschungen, lviii (Münster-Westfalen, 1973), and O. Nussbaum, *Kloster, Priestermönch und Privatmesse*, Theophaneia, xiv (Bonn, 1961).

ments were made by noblemen, clerics or wealthy burghers. Those with lesser means could contribute to a collective endowment.

Procedures for endowment are found in church statutes. Once the endowment was approved by the chapter, the transaction was recorded in a charter. This document named the donor and witnesses and described the property or money to be given, the manner in which it was to be received and distributed, the services rendered in return, and other administrative details or qualifying rules. The charters usually provide only the briefest descriptions of endowed services, but exceptionally they name liturgical items, performers, and even composers. Copies of these charters appear in cartularies, and other references to endowments can be found in wills, in the records of the chapels where the services were performed (if this was the case) and in obituaries, confraternity records, and account books.

The earliest endowments for liturgical services were those for the *opus Dei* or for obits. Next were those for votive offices and Masses or other devotional services centred around the performance of an antiphon. Individual liturgical items were also endowed: Elevation motets, sequences, processional chants, prayers and readings following offices, antiphons, and motets. Of great significance for our understanding of the medieval liturgy is the fact that endowments could introduce new feasts and the rituals associated with them, or raise the rank of existing feasts. (New feasts added to the Sanctorale seem to have been endowed only by clerics. Perhaps only clerics could afford them, and there was no bias against laymen. More likely, such endowments by laymen were considered inappropriate.) This is one reason why the liturgies of churches in the same diocese could vary greatly in content and ceremony.

Endowed services (feasts celebrated in the choir or chapels, votive Masses, some suffrages, the liturgy for the dead) were copied into liturgical books; but some were probably copied into smaller manuscripts, such as processionals, or into fascicles and survive less often (devotional services such as the *Salve*, prayers, and processional chants, hymns, or sequences). Liturgists often ignore endowment records as an aid for dating liturgical books, but they can establish the dates when feasts were introduced, thereby providing a *terminus ante quem* for their inclusion in a book, and they help to explain the great diversity in content and format of pre-Tridentine liturgical books, often compendia of inserted or removed fascicles, marginalia, additions or erasures.

Endowed feasts differed from the rest of the liturgy because individual donors benefited from them as much as the community of believers. A definition of 'liturgy' as the ritual of the Church is thus misleading and oversimplified. The appearance of words such as 'paraliturgical' in modern writings on medieval music reflect our misunderstanding of the nature of medieval ritual. The term 'liturgy' originally meant any service done for the common welfare of the people. Christian antiquity applied the term to prayer in general; writers of the patristic period applied it to public rather than private devotions directed by a priest. In the East, the word was restricted to the Eucharistic sacrifice and, later, to the Mass. The Renaissance adopted the word in the titles of collections describing the Church's worship, but by the late Middle Ages distinctions between communal and private rituals were blurred, and some services were held without priests. Many essentially private services, such as those for confraternities or individual donors, were held in the church, yet portable altars permitted the celebration of Masses in secular or private buildings: in city halls or palace oratories. Seemingly communal rituals, such as the Mass, were endowed to benefit private individuals, and as chapels were built and new services endowed, a new distinction reflecting the location of the ritual emerged. Endowed rituals were usually held in side chapels; long-established rituals for the congregation in the main choir. But these were tendencies, not rules. In the context of medieval ritual, the word 'liturgy' should best be understood as a formal expression of faith, either public or private, communal or individual.

Which services were endowed to benefit the souls of the donors? To ensure salvation, selection of services was as important as their endowment, since some were considered more efficacious than others. The most frequent endowments were for obits, yearly commemorations for the deceased. They were usually held on the day of death, with provisions for removal to following or preceding days if feasts conflicted, or, less often on the feast of a patron saint (though this day was usually reserved for endowed Masses associated with the obit). In the later Middle Ages, obits were also held in conjunction with Marian and Eucharistic devotions, and obits or commemorations for the deceased were held at all confraternity and chapter meetings. They could be collective, for the souls of many, or individual; they could benefit the donor or another.

The origins of the obit are found in the recitation of names of living and departed Christians as part of the intercessory prayers of the Canon of the Mass. Copied on diptychs or tablets, these lists became so long that separate commemorations were instituted. Those who endowed commemorations or obits had the privilege of having their name, together with the date of their obit and sometimes a summary description of the associated services inscribed in a necrology or obituary organized as a calendar. Lists of names continued to survive in late medieval documents such as confraternity statutes, which are organized in the same way as the combined martyrologies and obituaries of the earlier Middle Ages, the statutes or Rule being followed by lists of living and deceased members. Similar lists also occur in many later polyphonic compositions asking for intercession on behalf of musicians: Compère's motet *Omnium bonorum plena* is perhaps the best known example.

The obit used the liturgy for the Office and Mass for the Dead. The vigil began with Vespers and Matins; then Commendations, a series of psalms and prayers, were read, usually at dawn. A procession to the grave sometimes preceded the Requiem Mass, the final service. With slight changes, this liturgy was also used on the first, third, seventh and thirtieth day after burial, on All Souls' Day, a feast introduced by St Odilo of Cluny to be celebrated on 2 November, and as part of the weekly cycle of votive offices (on Mondays it was common to complement the ferial office with the Office of the Dead).

The simplest services, for parishioners who could not afford a separate endowment, were collective obits often read by a single priest. But most obits were endowed separately for differing degrees of solemnity indicated by the number of lessons for Matins (three, six or nine), and, perhaps also, by the length and manner of performance of the last responsory for Matins, usually the *Libera me*. Especially solemn obits even had octaves, while special performances of the sequence and offertory of the Requiem Mass were also endowed.

Documents give evidence that polyphony was sung at obit Requiems by the mid-fifteenth century, but there is little surviving polyphony for the Office of the

1 Funeral Mass with Souls released from Purgatory; by the Coëtivy Master (Henri de Vulcop?) (France, Angers?, 1460s)

Dead. Dufay composed a polyphonic Requiem Mass and also an Office for the Dead, but it has not been ascertained whether this office was polyphonic. Polyphonic settings of the Office of the Dead were composed by Morales and Victoria, and there are many examples of polyphony using chant from the Office of the Dead, especially the medieval invitatory *Circumdederunt* and the responsory *Libera me*, as cantus firmi. The earliest surviving polyphonic Requiem is Okeghem's; those by La Rue, Brumel, Févin, and others soon followed. It may be significant that the tradition of setting polyphonic Requiems originated and flourished in the Franco-Burgundian and later Habsburg territories among composers who also composed the *L'Homme armé* Masses that William Prizer has linked with the Order of the Golden Fleece. One could propose Dufay as the originator of this tradition since his lost Requiem and Office, the earliest settings attributed to a specific composer in the documents, were taken over by the Order after his funeral. It seems likely that the obits held at every meeting of the Order provided an occasion for the performance of the other Requiems as well.

As is explained in *The Golden Legend*: 'The sacrifice of the Host has been found to be of the greatest profit not only to the dead, but also to the living.' In their early history, diptychs listed the living as well as the dead, and the dual manifestation of this plea for intercession continued in the celebration of votive Masses. First mentioned in the third letter of Eugene of Toledo, the Leonine and Gelasian sacramentaries contain votive formulae, and Charlemagne allowed votive Masses to be added to the Roman Mass books, many of which were by Alcuin. But votive Masses reached the height of their popularity only in the late Middle Ages when extraordinary salutary powers were attributed to them. Votive Masses for Mary and for the Holy Spirit, in particular, were endowed to be celebrated for the living, to be replaced by obits after they had died.

It is well known that much medieval polyphony was composed in honour of the Virgin Mary, but why did Mary become a principal object of late medieval veneration? Purgatory did more than encourage endowments supporting polyphony, it coloured medieval interpretations of the Bible and the liturgy, and of the role of the Virgin Mary. Before the twelfth century she was worshipped as the mother of Christ, but the fear of unabsolved sin and of purgatory led to an emphasis on Mary's sinlessness – her immaculate conception and virginity – and on the intercessory powers she held as mediatrice between Man and God. The need for salvation, so keenly felt once purgatory became a conceptual reality after the twelfth century, made Mary's new role as mediatrice very appealing and brought her to the centre of public and private worship.

After obits, Marian votive services were the earliest and most numerous of the endowed services. Often they were endowed to be celebrated for the living and replaced later with an obit. Indeed, many early Mass Ordinary cycles end with the Mass for the Dead followed by the Marian votive Mass, and new archival evidence has supported the theory that Machaut's *Messe de Nostre Dame* was celebrated for his soul before he died and was later replaced by an obit.

Marian texts and chant could be added to the liturgy for the dead to strengthen the intercessory plea or vice versa. Evidence that the two liturgies were closely associated has been discovered in an early Aquitanian manuscript containing the Marian antiphon *Salve Regina* with a responsory found elsewhere with the *Libera me*. The Dominicans used the *Salve Regina* as a prayer for the dying after 1230, and the texts *O intemerata* and *Obsecro te* became especially popular, since it was believed that they would ensure a vision of the Virgin upon death.

The Office of the Dead and Marian services were also combined in Books of Hours, where they appear with other devotional texts. Books of Hours were produced in record numbers in the fourteenth and fifteenth centuries, especially in the Low Countries and in France, since they contained precisely those texts considered to be most efficacious in the saving of souls. Papal supplications contain numerous requests for permission to say Hours according to a particular usage, and medieval clerics were often admonished against reading Hours during the Office and Mass – further evidence of the importance attached to these private intercessory devotions.

Marian devotions, including the *Salve* and votive Masses endowed and celebrated independently of services for the dead, also included polyphony after the mid-fourteenth century. This is confirmed by the many surviving Marian Masses and motets from later centuries.

2 Okeghem's *Missa Ecce ancilla domini*; opening (Vatican City, Biblioteca Apostolica Vaticana, MS Chigi C VIII 234, f. 19*v*)

Another votive Mass celebrated for the living and replaced by an obit was the Mass of the Holy Spirit. One such endowment was made by Duke Charles the Bold of Burgundy who requested the prior and monks of the abbey of Groenendael near Brussels to hold a solemn Mass of the Holy Spirit in chant and polyphony on Pentecost. After his death, this Mass would be replaced by an obit held on his death date. The Carmelite convent in Brussels celebrated a similar obit for Duke Philip the Good of Burgundy in order to regain his favour which they had lost upon giving asylum to a scheming priest pretending to be a knight.

On some occasions, both the Marian and Holy Spirit Masses were combined with the liturgy for the dead. Meetings of the Order of the Golden Fleece added only the Mass for Andrew, their patron saint, to the three Masses. Funerals for the King of Aragon and the Duke of Brittany held in 1458 at the abbey of St Jakob in Brussels were accompanied by two high solemn Masses – of the Virgin and Holy Spirit. The same year, at the funeral for the Countess of Charolais, two solemn Masses were sung, perhaps those for the Virgin and Holy Spirit, though the documents do not specify this. Two unspecified solemn Masses were also celebrated at St Jakob for the funeral of Isabelle of Bourbon in 1465. Petrus de Domarto's well-known *Missa Spiritus almus* is based on a part of the Marian responsory *Stirps Jesse*, the text of which emphasizes the 'nourishing spirit'.

An annual Holy Cross Mass was celebrated for Charles the Bold before his death at the Franciscan and Carmelite monasteries in Brussels. After he died, it was replaced by an obit. A *Missa Crucis* by Johannes Regis was copied into the choirbooks of Cambrai Cathedral. Of the best known votive Masses, only those for the Holy Sacrament and Holy Trinity remain absent from the list of Masses sung for the living and subsequently replaced by obits.

Of the endowed votive Masses, the Masses for the Holy Sacrament followed those for Mary in frequency of celebration: they were only later associated with the liturgy for the dead. A shift of emphasis from communion to consecration is already evident in the twelfth century Mass, but the emphasis on personal redemption through the Eucharist is not fully apparent until the fourteenth century, when it is manifested in the texts of prayers associated with Eucharistic devotions now using the first person singular. By the end of the fourteenth century obits were celebrated with Eucharistic services, a combination which became more frequent in the later centuries. The many *O salutaris hostia* motets and Josquin's *Missa Di dadi* are among the extant polyphonic works with Eucharistic associations.

Masses for patron saints also contributed to salvation, and many polyphonic settings survive, including Dufay's Mass for St Anthony of Padua, Masses for St Livinus by La Rue and Pipelare, and for St Donatian by Obrecht. Examples of manuscripts containing polyphony for the patronal feasts of confraternities also survive, such as Brussels, Bibliothèque Royale, MS 215–216, with compositions for the feast of the Seven Sorrows of Mary.

Other parts of the liturgy remained independent of endowments. The ferial Office and Mass (which, following initial foundations and unlike the votive services, were supported by common church funds), retained their original function, with some exceptions. The Mass had become longer, and readings were often appended to the Hours. The Temporale seems to have remained untouched, although Christmas, Epiphany, Easter, Pentecost, the Ascension, Trinity Sunday and the new feast of Corpus Christi were all enhanced with endowments.

The ambivalence of the Church towards the intercessory liturgy had its counterpart in the medieval view of polyphonic music. Music and light were characteristic of the highest heaven, but Satan could also entice with the magic of music. Thus polyphony embellished high feasts in some churches, but was banned on all but a few occasions in others. Objections to endowments could be overruled, since the incomes to be gained were substantial, and even the content of private Masses was rarely regulated. The logistics of scheduling overlapping Masses and of finding clerics to perform the chapel services must have proved difficult. It seems likely that even polyphony considered inappropriate could have been introduced by endowments that were not regulated, since sacred polyphony was sometimes used out of context in commemorative services: the obits endowed for Dufay in Cambrai Cathedral included liturgies and polyphony for feasts that were not part of the cathedral ritual, the feasts of St Anthony of Padua and Mary of Snows.

The evidence presented above has emphasized the relationship between endowed services (for the dead and for the Virgin, Holy Spirit, Holy Sacrament, Holy Cross, and patron saints) and the composition of sacred polyphony. Since all of these endowments were made by donors seeking salvation, it seems very likely that, on the surface, the purpose of the associated polyphony was always the same.

Examples of this polyphony date back to the organum maintained by endowments at Notre Dame in Paris. Marian Masses and motets are the earliest polyphonic compositions recorded in the Low Countries in the fourteenth century, and they are invariably associated with endowed votive devotions. Endowed elevation motets were common, as were cantus firmus Masses on Marian plainchant; to them can be added the many surviving polyphonic Requiem settings of the sixteenth century. The earliest surviving Mass Ordinary settings are also associated with votive services or obits: the Mass of Tournai, like the Machaut Mass, was also a Marian votive Mass.

The private intentions of endowed services explain why some sacred compositions were personal statements rather than works composed to serve an impersonal Church – statements which used the established liturgy as a means rather than an end. This is even suggested by compositional procedures. Polyphonic settings of the Lamentations, the Magnificat, Benedicamus and of some hymns, compositions for the Mass and Office held in the choir of a church, tend to have transparent textures or to use simple alternatim techniques, in this way emphasizing the texts rather than the manipulation of musical material found in many cantus firmus works. Sacred polyphony with emblematic cantus firmi, numerical structures, quotations from sacred and secular polyphony in homage to other composers, and embedded pleas for intercession bear personal stamps far more compatible with late medieval piety.

In the fourteenth century, confraternities supported the most elaborate sacred polyphony, but in the fifteenth and sixteenth centuries, the performance of polyphonic Masses and motets was concentrated at the courts, where there was wealth to support such music and the intellectual demand for it. The polyphony, which had been supported by endowments at the outset and had received its themes and messages with the birth of purgatory, no longer needed endowments or a Church to bring salvation once the secular world had control. Yet endowments continued to influence the performance of polyphony in the churches: the widespread incorporations of endowments made in the late fifteenth century provided the support for professional salaried singers, organists, and musically-trained choirboys.

Endowments permitted the secular to influence the sacred; education reversed the process. The Church's monopoly on education was absolute until the fourteenth century, when other schools made their first appearance, but even in the sixteenth century most schools came under the direction of clerics. The secular music known from manuscripts could only have been composed by those able to use musical notation, namely those with a clerical education. To what extent some ostensibly secular medieval music reflects truly secular interests remains to be discovered.

The changes wrought by the Reformation and the Council of Trent altered the course of sacred music. Without purgatory and endowments, a supplicatory liturgy seeking intercession was no longer necessary. Obits continued to be celebrated in some churches until the French Revolution, and Marian polyphony and motets were composed and sung as they had been formerly, though in diminishing numbers. By the seventeenth century, the impoverished Catholic church could no longer attract the most skilled composers, and sacred music became increasingly more conservative as innovation passed to the Protestants. By contrast, secular music, now freed from the confines of the Church with the changes in dogma and in education, also freed itself from sacred compositional techniques and from its formerly restricted audience. A marriage had ended in divorce.

Select bibliography

A. FRANZ, *Die Messe im deutschen Mittelalter* (Freiburg im Breisgau, 1902; repr. Darmstadt, 1963)

A. KREIDER, *English chantries: the road to Dissolution*, Harvard Historical Studies xcvii (Cambridge, Mass., 1979)

J. LE GOFF, *The birth of purgatory*, trans. A. Goldhammer (Chicago, 1984)

A. MOLINIER, *Les obituaires français au moyen âge* (Paris, 1890)

J. DE VORAGINE, 'The commemoration of All Souls', in *The Golden Legend*, trans. G. Ryan and H. Ripperger (New York, 1941; repr. 1948), pp.648–57

10 Ritual reflections

Keith Falconer

Liturgy in its most general sense consists of the various ingredients, verbal, musical and gestural, that make up the meetings of a religious community. How these meetings are conducted will necessarily vary according to place and time and, especially, religious conviction. But liturgies are often governed by rule or custom established over a long period, and they will normally make provision for music. Thus liturgical music is not merely devotional in character but is closely bound to the requirements of liturgy. And how the music is bound to the rest of the liturgy is a vital question for anyone interested in medieval and Renaissance music.

It makes a great difference to our understanding of liturgical music if we can find out for what time of the year it was composed, for which service on what day and the exact part of the service. This is information that cannot always be drawn directly from the music, or its text, and may require a great deal of leg-work in a library. It can also be very difficult to draw a clear line between liturgical music for use in church and non-liturgical music for private devotions in the home, or at private ceremonies – and even these are liturgical in a way. Again, only external evidence will settle the question.

Liturgical music in the western world, at least before the Reformation, had as its centre the traditional melodies known as Gregorian chant. First introduced in the late eighth and early ninth centuries, Gregorian chant quickly became a repertory of unparalleled richness, with special chants for almost every occasion of the Church year. Composers based all sorts of new music on the traditional melodies, from the new chants of the tenth and eleventh centuries, to the Parisian clausulae of the thirteenth century, and the cantus firmus Masses of the fifteenth. Most of the earliest works of polyphonic music were in effect embellishments of the chants on which they were based. The chant was complete in one voice, the text was the same as the chant, and only the additional voices were new. Compositions of this sort were substitutes for the chant, equivalent in the sense that they occupied the same position in the liturgy; substitution was the means by which polyphony made its way into the liturgy of the medieval Church. Early manuscripts of polyphonic music from the eleventh and twelfth centuries include numerous settings of chant, particularly those parts sung by a soloist: the responsory and antiphon verses for the Office, the alleluia and gradual for the Mass, and others besides. Later settings include hymns, the Proper of the Mass, and above all the Ordinary of the Mass: the familiar Kyrie, Gloria, Credo, Sanctus and Agnus Dei.

The practice of substitution is still evident in settings of chant from the fifteenth century. Various new chants, particularly votive antiphons, also appear in polyphonic settings. Thus many compositions previously identified only as motets in the broadest sense have been recognized as votive antiphons, responsories, and other chant substitutes. The opposite case is represented in some early Protestant works, such as Martin Luther's *Deutsche Messe*, which set the old melodies to a new text in the vernacular.

Substitution is only one of many difficulties that affect the place of medieval and

Renaissance music in the liturgy. Gregorian chant was a central tradition in the history of polyphonic music but not the only one, and numerous works survive that are based on very different melodies. Settings of tropes, sequences and conductus are known from the eleventh century onwards, and though these are certainly chants, they are not in any sense Gregorian. Scholars exploring this area have preferred to relegate these melodies to the rubbish heap of 'paraliturgy', as if they were not liturgical at all. But there is little trace of this notion in the ordinals and other documents that mention them or the compositions based on them (see Costa). I think we must assume for the sake of consistency that any music can be liturgical if performed in a church.

A further problem with substitution is that the conventional categories of Gregorian chant are not always suitable for polyphony, and were not so even in the Middle Ages. We cannot assume that a work in polyphony was always performed at exactly the same place (or places) in the liturgy as an equivalent chant. A musical or textual correspondence is often not enough to establish its position. This becomes increasingly evident when we shift our attention from the regular services of Mass and Office to the entire range of services a church or chapel might wish to hold.

During the Middle Ages, numerous additional services were established in the churches of western Europe. These included the Lady Mass and Masses for the Dead, most of which were held in side-chapels, and various memorials at the end of Lauds and Vespers. Further Masses in addition to these were held for the many guilds and confraternities that marked so much of life in medieval cities. All of these services made provision for music, and where it was provided it was often in chant or improvised polyphony. How often the polyphony was composed is unfortunately very hard to judge, but the chant for these newer services was almost always borrowed from elsewhere, usually from the Mass or Office that was held in the nave of the church. Sometimes the borrowing was so extensive that some chants, the votive antiphons in particular, seem to have travelled aimlessly from one type of service to another.

Under such circumstances chant and polyphony might, in theory, have been interchangeable, but the evidence available to us shows that this was not true in practice (see Harrison). Churches reserved polyphonic performance for certain services, such as Vespers or the more handsomely endowed Masses, and the remainder were presumably done in chant. The decisive factors here were local custom and the presence of suitably qualified singers. By comparison, the liturgical categories of Gregorian chant were of only secondary importance.

Liturgical polyphony had achieved at least a partial independence from chant by the beginning of the fifteenth century, and this increasingly affected its significance in all parts of the liturgy. An appropriate choice of polyphony could introduce new layers of meaning far beyond the limits of traditional practice.

Central to all these developments was the motet of the fourteenth century, with its contrast of texted voices and liturgical cantus firmus. The works of Philippe de Vitry, Guillaume de Machaut, Johannes Ciconia and their contemporaries represent not one but several traditions of the form. In the disposition of voices, the type of rhythmic artifice, and above all in the handling of text, the motet changed quickly in the course of the century: motets were always a mixture of things from a liturgical point of view. They were often required for votive Masses, both for the Virgin and other intentions. Some were composed for civic and political occasions:

a royal wedding, a coronation, the baptism of an heir. Others, perhaps from a later date, were sung in the nave of the church at the Elevation of the Host, or as a substitute for the offertory. Music and text were always carefully suited to the occasion, and where there was a liturgical tenor, as there usually was, that too was carefully chosen.

Similar techniques appear in Mass movements of the early fifteenth century. English composers seem to have been the first to cultivate the cantus firmus Mass, a complete cycle in which every movement is based on a single cantus firmus in the tenor voice. Among the leading practitioners of the form were John Dunstable, Leonel Power, Walter Frye and John Bedyngham, all of whom seem to have composed at least one complete Mass. From England the form was quick to spread to the continent, and it was widely adopted there, most notably by Guillaume Dufay. Its ready acceptance was most likely the result of a larger movement to adopt English practices on the continent, but the popularity of the form continued throughout the fifteenth and into the sixteenth centuries, and attracted some of the finest composers of the day.

And yet, though the importance of the cantus firmus Mass is not in doubt, its liturgical significance has attracted far too little comment. Each movement was performed at its appointed place in the Mass, of course; but the cantus firmus, if it was taken from chant, always belonged somewhere else. The cantus firmus could also be taken from a secular song, from solmization syllables and other patterns, or even, in the case of Johannes Martini's Mass *Cucu*, from birdsong. Often it was taken from an Office chant such as an antiphon or responsory. At least one fine scholar has criticized the latter practice in particular for apparently disregarding 'liturgical propriety' (Bukofzer, p.225). I find it difficult to believe, however, that this was a common complaint among the clergy of the fifteenth century, let alone composers and their patrons. Even the Council of Trent, that bastion of liturgical propriety, only banned Masses based on popular songs. If the music was liturgical, the cantus firmus was too.

Most scholars have tried to explain the problem retrospectively in artistic terms. This has seemed particularly appropriate in the case of Masses based on a pre-existing composition, the so-called parody Masses, in which the voices of the old work could be smoothly blended into the new. The parallels with Bach, Handel and other composers who borrowed are all too tempting. But the cantus firmus Mass is different because of the clear contrast between the cantus firmus and the surrounding voices. At the very least the tenor moved in longer note values and was sung by a specialist in tenor parts; it may also occasionally have been performed on an instrument such as the organ. It was prominent enough to be heard, and to be identified in numerous manuscripts (see Planchart). I agree that composers may sometimes have chosen cantus firmi for technical reasons, for purposes of inversion and retroversion, for instance, or for canonic imitation. But whatever its technical significance the cantus firmus was always a part of the liturgy.

We have already seen that polyphony was often required for Lady Mass at major festivals. It seems likely that polyphonic Masses were composed especially for these, as were motets, since many survive with cantus firmi on Marian subjects. One possible example is the anonymous English Mass *Salve sancta parens*, which has a cantus firmus taken from the introit for Lady Mass from the Purification to Advent (see Bent). In the Low Countries this Mass was known as the *Missa de*

Salve, and at some churches, such as St Donatian's in Bruges, it was performed daily in polyphony. But at St Donatian's the polyphony was probably improvised or assembled from disparate Mass movements, and not from a complete cycle (see Strohm, pp.22–3). This service was presumably the starting-point for the numerous Masses *De beata virgine* by Josquin, Morales, Kerle and others that were so popular in the sixteenth century.

Votive services like these were normally supported by private endowment and performed in the side-chapels of a church or cathedral. Settings of the Requiem Mass and Masses of the Holy Spirit may also have been votive, since these too were often well funded. Normally the endowment would pay a fee to the celebrant and a group of singers each time they sang the Mass, but it may also have paid for – or at least encouraged – the composition of polyphony.

Some evidence survives to indicate that a church might require the composition of polyphonic Masses as a condition of employment. In 1487 Durham Cathedral required Alexander Bell, the recently appointed cantor and master of the Lady Chapel choir, to compose a new Mass each year in four or five parts in honour of God, St Mary and St Cuthbert (see Bowers, p.11). And from 1475 or 1476 the succentors of St Donatian's were required to compose a new Mass each year, in polyphony, for the 'feast of cripples' in the nearby town of Aardenburg (see Strohm, p.35). These are interesting and unusual instances of a church encouraging the composition of polyphonic music. Most interesting of all is that the Masses required were of a particular kind: for a local saint in the former case, for a local festival in the latter. These are liturgical requirements, and they would presumably have had a substantial effect on the finished composition.

Too often we can only guess at the reasons why polyphonic Masses were composed. We cannot always be sure of finding an answer even for a Mass with an identifiable cantus firmus taken from chant. A Mass for St John might just as well have been composed for the patron saint of a church, a side-chapel or a prince, or for several other occasions too, and the problems are even greater for works with secular models, such as a Mass on a polyphonic song. The difficulty is to find circumstances that would have justified the meeting of sacred and secular.

Among the first places to look are the court chapels of the nobility, which served the interests of the state as much as they did the Church. These were often lavishly provided with music, and attracted some of the finest composers of the day. Some courts also employed musicians to give music lessons or for other purposes, and these too were often composers. The courtly milieu was free of the restrictions imposed by churches and cathedrals, even as they imposed restrictions of their own. Here it was appropriate to allude to secular music in the liturgy, provided only that the allusions were fitting. A revealing example is the Mass *Io ne tengo quanto te* by Johannes Martini composed for the court of Ercole I d'Este of Ferrara, perhaps in the 1470s. The Mass is based on a popular song that refers to the cutting of May branches, a tradition that belonged to the May Day celebrations at the court. A chronicler of the time describes Ercole riding out after Mass to cut the branches, and afterwards galloping joyfully through the piazza with members of the court. Martini's Mass is surely both appropriate and fitting for the occasion (see Lockwood, pp.233–8).

A work of this sort extends the boundaries of what constitutes the liturgical in church music. It establishes ties of its own to events outside the church, and above all it poses a challenge to the inherited traditions of liturgical music, which were largely defined by Gregorian chant. This is music that can think for itself. The alliance of chant and polyphony, however, was never simple. Composers took the chant and made of it what they wished, or they chose other materials, secular music and polyphony, as models for composition. What came out was not so much a substitute for the model – though the model was often clearly audible – but new music that made its own demands on the resources and customs of a church. Liturgy has always made demands on the form of music sung in church; but when the music changes, the liturgy may also have to change.

Select bibliography

General

A. HUGHES, *Medieval manuscripts for Mass and Office: a guide to their organization and terminology* (Toronto, 1982)

C. JONES, G. WAINWRIGHT and E. YARNOLD (eds), *The study of liturgy* (London, 1978)

T. KLAUSER, *A short history of Western liturgy*, trans. J. Halliburton (London, 1969)

R. W. PFAFF, *Medieval Latin liturgy: a select bibliography* (Toronto, 1982)

R. TAFT, *The liturgy of the Hours in East and West* (Collegeville, Minnesota, 1986)

C. VOGEL, *Medieval liturgy: an introduction to the sources*, rev. and trans. W. G. Storey and N. K. Rasmussen (Washington, DC, 1986)

Liturgico-musical studies

M. BENT (ed.), *Fifteenth-century liturgical music, 2: Four anonymous Masses, Early English Church Music*, xxii (London, 1979)

R. BOWERS, 'Obligation, agency and *laissez-faire*: the promotion of polyphonic composition for the church in fifteenth-century England', in I. Fenlon (ed.), *Music in medieval and early modern Europe: patronage, sources and texts* (Cambridge, 1981), pp.1–19

M. F. BUKOFZER, '*Caput*: a liturgico-musical study', in *Studies in medieval and Renaissance music* (New York, 1950), pp.217–310

E. COSTA, 'Tropes et séquences dans le cadre de la vie liturgique au Moyen Age', *Ephemerides Liturgicae*, xcii (1987), pp.261–322 and 440–71

R. L. CROCKER, 'Matins antiphons at St. Denis', *Journal of the American Musicological Society*, xxxix (1986), pp.441–90

F. LL. HARRISON, *Music in medieval Britain*, 4th ed. (Buren, 1980), pp.156–219

L. LOCKWOOD, *Music in Renaissance Ferrara 1400–1505: the creation of a musical center in the fifteenth century* (Oxford, 1984)

A. E. PLANCHART, 'Parts with words and without words: the evidence for multiple texts in fifteenth-century Masses', in S. Boorman (ed.), *Studies in the performance of late mediaeval music* (Cambridge, 1983), pp.227–51

R. STROHM, *Music in late medieval Bruges* (Oxford, 1985)

11 Musicus and cantor

Christopher Page

There is something alarming about music. The more we care for it the less we want to hear it. John Keats understood this paradox: 'Heard melodies are sweet, but those unheard are sweeter'. This is a reminder that when we love music, we love the idea of it better. Beautiful and yet intangible, existing in time and therefore perishable like ourselves, musical sound is absent from our lives more often than it is present; it principally lives in our memory and imagination as an ideal, freed from the contingencies, failures and compromises of actual music-making. In comparison with that ideal, the mechanical business of performance can sometimes appear a very unreliable, mundane and mercenary affair.

So it appeared to Boethius (d. 524), the man who taught the clerics of the Middle Ages virtually everything they knew about the music theory of Antiquity. He came from a distinguished Roman line, and it is Boethius the father of consuls whom we should see behind every page of the work which became the prime textbook of medieval musicians: the *De institutione musica*. To a Roman gentleman of the sixth century, it seemed becoming in a great man than that he should long for the quiet of his rural estates; there he could read and study to the end of his days. Why should he seek public office? To put the question in terms that Boethius would have recognized: why should he prefer business, *negotium*, to studious ease, *otium*? The State might have public honours to confer upon its officers – and, indeed, the family of Boethius received many of them – but Roman aristocrats had no doubt that Man's true dignity lay in the power of his mind. Practical skills like playing upon a musical instrument were manual and therefore essentially vulgar; requiring a strong right arm or a sharp eye, they were left to slaves or to artisans of servile status. The heard melodies of lyre-players might be sweet, but it was judged far better for a gentleman to contemplate unheard melodies by studying the mathematical exactitudes of music-theory. He dealt with practical music to the extent that he presided over it like an aedile, judging good from bad, wholesome from unwholesome.

So it was that Boethius came to formulate his definition of the true musician, the *musicus*. In contrast to singers and instrumentalists, whom Boethius regarded as servile and 'entirely exiled from the true understanding of music', the true *musicus* lives the life of the mind:

How much more admirable, then, is the science of music in apprehending by reason than in accomplishing by word and deed . . . He . . . is a *musicus* who has taken to himself the art of music not by the servitude of work but by the rule of contemplation . . . He is a *musicus* who assumes the skill of judging, weighing rhythms, melodies and the whole of music.

Written at a time when there was a Goth, not a Roman, sitting on the Imperial Throne, this is an austere definition and perhaps a rather self-conscious gesture of obeisance to the traditions of the ancients whose legacy Boethius sought to preserve. How did it fare in the centuries after his death?

In some respects the churchmen of the Middle Ages were well placed to relish this portrait of the *musicus*. Boethius's disdain for string-players and other instrumentalists was easily redirected against one of the Church's most persistent enemies, the professional minstrel (the *joculator, histrio, scurra*, and so on); this patrician scorn, mixed with the much more bitter gall of Christian moral outrage, proved a powerful poison during the Middle Ages and one that brought some writers to the verge of hysteria in their hatred of *joculatores*. Boethius and the monks, therefore, shared a sense of distance from the professional secular entertainer. Furthermore Boethius and the monks shared a belief in Grammar and Rhetoric: the arts of writing and speaking the Latin language. For Boethius, theory was superior to practice because theory matured in authorship; it presented the studious man with an opportunity to address an audience, the greatest responsibility and challenge which Roman civic life could present. This conception of learning thrived upon a disdain for technology (surviving until the 1970s in the 'Grammar' schools and 'Technical' colleges of England), and for the monk a somewhat changed but none the less powerful conception of Grammar and Rhetoric was the foundation of a contemplative life. In the cloister, texts were read and elucidated with techniques borrowed from the Roman schools, and novices were set to learn with Latin grammars of antique shape. In some respects the monks were the heirs of the Roman aristocracy with their secluded villas and rolls of the poets. 'I desire at least a modicum of solitary life', wrote the celebrated theorist Guido of Arezzo around 1000, professing the same longing for studious quiet, and the same disinterest in official responsibility, as the Roman gentlemen of late antiquity.

And yet there were other forces at work which made Boethius's voice seem weak and strange. Above all, there was a profound change in the conception of musical performance. For men like Boethius – for aristocrats, that is, with country estates and a staff of slaves to adminster them – practical music was offered as a delicacy for the ear in much the same way as olives were offered as a delicacy for the palate. No doubt the music of these *tibicines* and *citharoedi* was often consumed in a careless or listless manner, but none the less we may regard Boethius and his fellows as 'listeners', just as each servile singer or instrumentalist, living by his art, was a 'performer'.

It was otherwise in the monasteries. Assembled in the choir, monastic singers heard, but they did not exactly listen; they sang, but they did not exactly perform. Furthermore, the clear distinction between master and servant, so familiar to Boethius and essential to his notion of the patrician *musicus*, was profoundly modified in the monastic context. Between 700 and 1000, for example, differences of social class were not always as clear in the cloister as they had been on the Capitol, and when the monks were gathered together, sharing a common rule as they shared a common bench, the distance between the free man and the slave was not the same as in the public world of Rome or Ravenna. The life of the monks could be as levelling as the habits on their backs, and the central document of Western monasticism, the *Rule of St Benedict*, contains measures designed to obliterate class distinctions within the monastery in a systematic way.

These developments softened the contempt for manual skill which is apparent in Boethius's notion of the *musicus*. His disdain for the practical musician, a mere artisan, was not easily translated into cloistered communities where the concept of labour, physical as well as spiritual, was central to the routine of life and where the liturgy was the work of God, the *opus Dei*. This *opus* was a labour of practical music-making to which the monk was summoned many times each day.

A monk's sense of what the monastic life meant was deeply influenced by the experience of standing with his brothers and making music. A vast amount of plainsong takes its words directly from the Vulgate Bible or rhapsodizes upon Biblical words to produce new texts. Plainsong was therefore an intense form of prayer, returning to God (as prayer was supposed to do in its purest form) the words that He Himself had spoken. At the same time, plainchant offered an experience of the Word that was even more intense than *lectio divina*, rumination upon Scripture. The ideal of monastic devotion was a meditative quiet in which eyes, ears, body and mind were thoroughly occupied, then becalmed and eventually stilled, so that a monk could hear the voice of his Creator. The experience of plainsong, where the eyes saw the neumes, the mind reflected upon the meaning of the text, the voice produced the chant and the ears heard the result, was what monastic writers understood by the 'whole machine of the body' labouring to praise and to comprehend God.

There was no place here for the idea that music-making of this kind might be menial or degrading. It was still possible for the monks to scorn the activities of secular minstrels in Boethian language ('they are exiled from all true understanding of music'), but plainchant was a repertory whose excellence of purpose, dignity of pedigree and sublimity of means distinguished it from all the other music which Man had known since Eden; in relation to that, Boethius's disdain for practical music could only have meaning in the narrowed context of polemic against secular musicians, the minstrels. Nor could the monk share Boethius's nostalgia for a vanished Golden Age when music was invariably sober and uplifting; in the monasteries plainchant was a treasure for the here and now, the end of an evolutionary process which had begun with the reed-pipes of shepherds 'around the beginning of the world'; hastened by the achievements of Jubal, Orpheus and Amphion it had finally come, via Ambrose and Gregory, to the perfection of the present. The Golden Age was now.

Every monk, therefore, was a singer, a *cantor*; but not every monk was equally learned in the theory of chant, and it is here that the pairing of *musicus* and *cantor* begins to assume its familiar outline. Around 800 a massive effort was made in the Carolingian realm to record the Latin texts used in liturgical chant, followed soon after by an attempt to devise ways of recording the music. Plainchant became a field of study, or to use contemporary terminology, a *disciplina*: something which possessed its own technical terminology and textbooks to place beside the works of the Fathers. The labour of producing a body of plainchant theory was immeasurably lightened by what was probably a chance discovery. Boethius never finished his *De institutione musica*, and nobody knows what happened to the rolls containing the text after his execution in 524. After that, the book is enveloped in profound silence for more than two centuries. Before 800, however, some fortunate monk or pilgrim discovered it, probably in Italy. It almost immediately became established as the major textbook on music,

As the new monastic and Christian readership began to absorb Boethius's book, the term *musicus* came to mean the monastic singer who had studied the theory of his art. How could it have been otherwise when the *opus Dei* was waiting to be sung every day? The monk who knew about the plainchant modes, for example, could list their finals or explain the meanings of terms like diapente and diatessaron – he was a *musicus* now. Such men had made the effort to elevate the performance of chant into something that was intellectually comparable to the study of grammar or the positions of stars. Exploring music theory in this way was an intoxicating experience for men of the right spirit; it offered a chance to approach mystery in the deliberate and even pedantic way which the Middle Ages found so satisfying. Chant, as we have said, was in effect an enormous repertory of prayer and an anticipation of the angelic song around the Throne. Any monk who had spent some time in his library could cite miracles in which the clouds had opened to reveal angels singing with some monastic community or other, and when the angels appeared to mortals they respected the liturgical customs of the world, mixing antiphons and responsories in the correct way, and they sang as earthly singers did. To ponder the rational basis of chant, therefore, to contemplate the 'precepts' of its 'science' as devised by the great 'philosophers' of the past, was to set one's foot upon a ladder of reason that ended in Glory. Each cleric could ascend as far as his ability and conscience would take him.

We have a portrait of a monastic *musicus* in the person of Tuotilo (d. 915), a monk of St Gall. Described as a distinguished *musicus* by a later chronicler, Tuotilo was a composer of chants, a fine singer, a gifted performer upon the organ and so skilled with stringed instruments that he taught the sons of local noblemen to play them in a room set aside for the purpose by the abbot. It is in the last detail, perhaps, that we can judge the full distance which separates Tuotilo from the *musicus* of the Boethian sort with his airy disdain for string-players. The case of Tuotilo is a reminder that fragments of lyres have been excavated from Anglo-Saxon and Frankish aristocratic warrior graves of the sixth, seventh and eighth centuries in Britain and Northern Europe; medieval civilization absorbed an esteem for string-playing which Germanic barbarians carried with them as they rode over the ruins of Rome.

Tuotilo had made the effort to study his art. What of the singers who had not? They were simply singers: *cantores*. These were the men who, in contemporary phrase, replied to any question about music with the reply 'because it is so', and who never attempted to prove anything with 'therefore'. Thus it was that a term which originally denoted the essential occupation of every monk, *cantor*, sank until it became almost a term of abuse. It was an insult to be thought of as a mere *cantor* or 'singer', one who did not have the intellectual power or curiosity to understand the theory of chant. In the words of a famous maxim first encountered around 1000, a *cantor* who knew nothing of the rational basis of his art was no better than a beast; as medieval readers knew from their bestiaries, the owl, the lark, the swallow and many other birds could sing, and sing beautifully, but without any rational understanding of what they accomplished.

There is a full discussion of the *musicus* and the *cantor* in a treatise which has often been cited but rarely read – so rarely, indeed, that the authorship of the work has remained a mystery for five hundred years, even though the author names himself in the text three times. He is Perseus, otherwise unknown, and he appears to have collaborated with a certain Petrus. Their book is entitled the *Summa musice*. Dutifully, and in a mixture of prose and verse so that the text does not become prosaic in any sense of the word, Perseus and Petrus lay out all the information that turns a boy or novice into a *musicus*.

77

Like many writers before them, they emphasize that a *musicus* is a *cantor* – every man who has learned the rational basis and terminology of chant is still a singer – but that the equation cannot be reversed for not every *cantor* is a *musicus*; that requires special study. On page after page the two authors express a characteristic medieval revulsion for everything which can be deemed irrational or arbitrary, and the *cantor*, who only knows how to sing, 'is like a drunken man trying to get home', or better still, 'is like a blind man trying to beat a dog'. The *musicus* will be one who knows why music was first instituted in the service of the Church and who accomplished it ('Ignatius and Ambrose were the first, and after them Gregory . . .'). The *musicus* will know the etymology of the word *musica* ('derived from a certain very simple instrument, invented by shepherds, and called the *musa*'). Beyond that the *musicus* will know the names of all the plainchant modes and their characteristic ranges; he will also be familiar with the 'Guidonian' Hand and be able to plot the solmization syllables on his left palm with ease (providing, of course, that 'Nature has not erred in forming his hand and he does not have too many fingers or too few'). Next, the *musicus* will know how to inflect the lesser doxology (the *Gloria patri*) and how to sing psalm verses matching the mode of an antiphon. He will also be able to compose new chants, making sure, if he is commissioned to compose, that the mode of the chant matches the temperament and character of the cleric who has asked for the new composition, 'for just as all men do not delight in one dish, but some in sweet things and some in bitter, so it is with chants'. Finally, the *musicus* as envisaged by Perseus and Petrus will perhaps wish to know something about polyphony in up to four parts, although that is far from essential.

A *cantor*, in contrast, does not know any of these things, and, most important of all, he cannot read musical notation. Indeed, the *cantor* is unable to learn a chant unless it is repeatedly sung to him first by one who knows it already. He is, in short, a fool: the kind of hopeless cleric that is often to be encountered in Visitation records where bishops report on what they find in their dioceses: 'an idiot who cannot sing'; 'an imbecile who can neither sing nor read'. Boethius would not have dismissed a man because he could not sing; such a man could certainly become a *musicus* of the Antique sort. In the Middle Ages, however, the striving to hear the unheard melodies of the angels made every responsible cleric a well-informed and practising musician: *musicus et cantor*.

12 A day in the life of Francisco de Peñalosa (*c.* 1470–1528)

Tess Knighton

Introduction

Singer-composer of the Aragonese royal chapel, favourite of Pope Leo X and contemporary of Josquin Desprez, Francisco de Peñalosa was perhaps the most important and influential musician active in the Spanish kingdoms at the beginning of the sixteenth century. The half a dozen Masses, almost thirty motets, six Magnificats and other liturgical settings (hymns, Lamentations etc.), as well as the ten songs attributed to him in surviving Hispanic sources, reveal him to have been instrumental in the formulation of a native polyphonic idiom that owed much to mainstream Franco-Flemish developments yet which retained the highly distinct-ive stylistic traits also found in the works of his fellow composers in the chapels of Ferdinand and Isabella: Juan de Anchieta, Pedro de Escobar, Alonso de Alba, Tordesillas and many others. His influence on the next generation of Spanish composers, notably on Cristóbal de Morales, was considerable: indeed, he may have come into direct contact with the young Morales while a canon at Seville cathedral.

This imaginary day in the life of Peñalosa is set in Seville during Ferdinand's visit there at the beginning of 1511. It would have differed little in broad terms from the day of any other singer-chaplain in the service of a prince or magnate throughout late medieval Europe. All the facts on which this account is based have been gleaned from the works cited in the bibliography. The letter itself follows the style and content of the correspondence of the Sicilian humanist Lucas Marineus, who also served in the Aragonese royal chapel where he was responsible for the Latin education of its members: an exchange of letters with Peñalosa survives in his epistolary.

Francisco de Peñalosa royal singer to my nephew Luis. Greetings.[1]

The great Hercules, having swept the Augean stables, could have been no more exhausted than I. We arrived here after nearly a month on the road and today is the eve of the Purification of Our Lady, one of the most important feasts of the year in our chapel with a sermon preached at Mass, processions at Mass and Vespers and sweet music as harmonious as that of the heavenly choirs. Tomorrow my Mass on the Marian salutation will be sung, our singers joining forces with the cathedral choir in an angelic hymn of praise. As the Philosopher has said, Art imitates Nature and I think my Mass will be pleasing to those ears on which it falls, especially those of the *maestro de capilla* here, Pedro de Escobar whom I first met when I joined the royal chapel some thirteen years ago: so dear do I hold him that our two souls are as

---

[1] Peñalosa's nephew became a canon of Seville cathedral on 2 April 1527.

but one. Indeed, with Vespers over I await him while he attends to the choirboys' supper and moral welfare: these duties are inextricably linked as you will understand if I tell you that those boys caught laughing while serving at the altar this evening go to bed hungry. When maestro Pedro has finished, we shall make our way to the tavern round the corner, where no doubt the others have already hailed Bacchus many times over, the sackbut-players faster than the rest – playing during the procession is thirsty work, they would maintain. Would you believe that the chapelmaster's house here, behind the consistory of the new cathedral, used to be a tavern? It is said that Pedro keeps the cellar fit for a Canaanite wedding, but that for want of guests other than choirboys he drinks it himself as if it were indeed water.

Seville is pleasantly cool at this time of the year and it would appear that this will prove a long sojourn, for his royal highness, indefatigible crusader against the Infidel that he is, plans to take Tunis this spring and is come to oversee the preparations for the armada. That will suit me well. Boethius may have been right when he said that in things that do not move there is no music, but all this travelling is very wearisome, even though the king granted me a new mule last year. It may be an evil-natured creature but it can carry a ton, which is just as well given those choirbooks I had to bring back for the cathedral chapter. It must be one of the worst aspects of being a member of the royal chapel: hardly have you found a decent billet when the court is on the move and the whole procedure has to be borne once more.

Perhaps while I am here I shall purchase a house: now that my canonry seems secure it would make sense. It would not be unpleasant to live here and, in any case the king is sixty next year and the whiteness of his hair is beginning to take its toll: he seems to be obsessed with killing Moors and stags in equal measure. When his illustrious soul departs this life anything could happen. It is quite possible that his highness will make me chapelmaster to his second grandson, the Infante Ferdinand at the monastery of San Pedro outside Burgos, but Charles, the first-born, will succeed – and what of your uncle then? The Flemish prince is skilful in music according to Anchieta, who taught him in Flanders a few years ago, but he already has his own chapel choir and, truth to tell, there are not many of us can rival those northerners. Perhaps I stand a chance in Rome; but if not, Seville would do quite well.

Enough of these worldly concerns: as Horace says, 'I labour to be brief but I make myself obscure'. You asked me what it was like to be a singer in the royal chapel and how you might get a place in the choir school. As regards the last, that should not be impossible: influence is the key, and given my position at court I should be able to find a place for my nephew. You will have to work, though: not only learning to follow the Guidonian Hand, but also counterpoint, organ, Latin and grammar and theology, and that will be be the beginning of your Apollonian trials. But your career prospects will be good: many of our chapelboys have gone to study at Salamanca with the support of the king or queen, graduated and had a good job waiting for them here in the chapel even if they fail to enter the choir. Some also become theologians, lawyers, royal secretaries, that kind of thing, but it is certainly worth trying to keep that voice. Singers in the royal chapel are generally paid much more than the ordinary chaplains and rewarded with many more extras: clothing allowances, mules, and favours of all kinds, especially when it comes to benefices. Our singers are rewarded better than any throughout the kingdoms of

Aragon and Castile, though we have never been as paid as much as the Flemish choir was a few years ago by the poor mad queen – I mean his highness's daughter Juana. And musically the royal chapel choir is currently the best in all of Spain; at the moment, the stellar composers among us include the Tordesillas brothers Pedro and Alfonso, Alonso de Mondéjar, Juan Ponce, and many others. Rumour has it that Anchieta hopes to rejoin the king's chapel: at one time he is said to have hated the good Ferdinand as much as if he had been denied the Archbishopric of Toledo! Then, of course, we met those Flemish singers several times while they were still in Spain and they can teach you much about canons and other refinements of counterpoint. La Rue weaves counterpoint as effortlessly as Penelope in Ulysses's absence, and you should have heard some of the pieces they had by the peerless Josquin. 'Distance lends enchantment' is how Tacitus expressed it, but if my memory serves me well there is a pile of their music gathering dust in Tordesillas. I believe Anchieta has attempted to gather some of it together for posterity, but I have heard the cathedral chapter in Segovia are after it now. Cathedrals from Cádiz to Santiago are crying out for polyphonic music in these lustrous times: which is why the chapter of Seville are demanding my choirbooks.

But I digress. I shall seek an audience with his highness and speak to the sacristan don Alfonso Cortes to see if a place cannot be found for you amongst the chapelboys. Should that fail, Escobar would doubtless enrol you at the cathedral here: you would receive a good training in counterpoint and organ, and they are beginning to build up the choir. Pedro tells me that at the moment there is an outstanding young lad about your age called Cristóbal de Morales, a beacon, according to him, shining out amongst the others.

Let me tell you a little more about life in the choir of the royal chapel. It is not so bad – even allowing for the travelling – and as his highness gets older there may be less of that. Perhaps the court will settle into some agreeable place like the Castelnuovo in Naples; they even had special music rooms there – much more conducive for composing than some drafty vestry in some isolated church on the way to somewhere else. I had rather hoped we would stay in Naples; we might have been there now but for the sudden death of Philip, the one they called the Fair, and the total incapacity on his widow's part to sign anything other than the pay chits for his singers. That was a nice irony; the affairs of Castile might have fallen into total disarray but at least the singers were paid. In all madness there lies some sanity.

My own duties afford little opportunity for rest. Not that I have ever had to spend the siesta singing polyphonic songs with my royal employer as Anchieta did with the ill-fated prince Juan. The main services we have to sing are as follows: Mass and Vespers every Sunday and on all the major feasts of the year as well as Mass on Saturday morning. Christmas and Holy Week are by far the busiest times: it is customary to perform a shepherd play at Matins on Christmas morning, and throughout Lent we have to chant all the hours as if we were members of a monastic order. Otherwise we take it in turns with the other royal chaplains to be present at the daily Mass, wherever that might be. Sometimes, depending on where we are in the court's itinerary, Mass is celebrated in his highness's chambers (our kings have a special dispensation from the Pope allowing them to set up an altar wherever they might be), but more often his highness attends the local church. When we settle for more than a few days in one place, the vergers unload all the adornments for the chapel and hang it with a wealth of tapestries and silks – especially on major feast days.

If his highness is away on a hunting trip, just a few chaplains will go with him; there is a strict rota for that worked out by the head sacristan, the illustrious don Alfonso Cortes. In fact, one's turn comes round seldom enough – there are almost two hundred paid-up members of the chapel, though many of them are honorary or absent or retired. It is customary to serve for a week, but you can arrange to exchange your week – with permission from the sacristan – if you are absent or if during that time your services are required at the lectern to sing polyphony. All decisions of this kind are taken at a weekly meeting held on Fridays, similar to a chapter meeting in a cathedral. The sacristan keeps a falcon eye on everything: even as a chapelboy you have to make sure that your surplice is clean and that you are suitably attired for serving in the chapel. Cortes has become one of the most powerful men at court – and one of the richest through all the benefices he has accumulated – and he began his career as a tenorist in the choir. With enough ambition you can soar as high as Icarus: his highness has always rewarded administrative talent regardless of station.

The chapelmaster is responsible for the musical training of the boys, just like a cathedral *maestro*, but there are others who teach them Latin and grammar like the Sicilian Lucas Marineus and another Italian, Pietro Martire, and in Queen Isabella's day there was a master of chant as well. It was Queen Isabella (may she rest in heaven) who insisted that all the members of the royal chapels be instructed in Latin so that we might know what we sing about in our daily services. Her highness's reverence for God extended to the details of ritual; if anyone made a mistake in pronunciation or misplaced a syllable she would come round afterwards and point it out. Our Marineus is a grumpy old soul – I doubt he will ever recover from being overshadowed at Salamanca by that prince of Latin elegance Antonio de Nebrija. According to our teacher, all the young men at court are barbarians taken up with warlike pursuits with little or no interest in the delights of letters. Still, should I meet him in the chapel I thought I might ask him if he would help me with a poetic gloss on the Ave Maria – an idea I had for a motet for Our Lady.

Before I go on to further musical matters, I should perhaps explain about benefices because they take up so much of our time: first in obtaining them and then in keeping hold of them. They are also one of the main reasons why such a number of us are absent from court from time to time. Most members of the royal chapel supplement their salaries at court by seeking benefices or posts of one kind or another at the cathedrals and churches throughout both the kingdoms of Castile and Aragon. This practice has been in force for some time, but recently it seems to have reached almost epidemic proportions. The prestige is one thing – a title gives you more importance at court even as regards where you sit in chapel – but important too are the income and security they bring. Expenses at court are high, despite the occasional bonus from the royal coffers, and some of these benefices are worth a lot – even if you have to give some of it to the person collecting or serving it on your behalf. Basically what happens is this. About once a year his highness and the royal counsellors allow members of the chapel to petition for either specific or non-specific benefices: you might want one in your home town or you might not be too worried where it was and be ready to accept anything that fell vacant. You must make sure you are present at court at that time, though, if you are to have any hope of securing what you want, and even then it is by no means certain that what you ask for will be yours. His highness has a number of benefices under royal patronage, mostly in chapels founded by his royal ancestors, and these are not usually contested. He also has a good deal of control over the presentations in the new churches in the kingdom of Granada: well, the Pope had to honour him somehow for his victories over the Infidel.

When it comes to canonries in other cathedrals (generally the most lucrative, but also the most problematic), the chapter there can easily refuse to accept the royal candidate on the grounds that if a chaplain is serving at court he cannot possibly fulfil his duties at a cathedral perhaps hundreds of leagues away. So it is a question of whether the bishop is wanting to please the king, or perhaps representation will be made to the papal see through our ambassador in Rome and the chapter will have no option. The struggles that ensue have to be seen to be believed. Virgil talks of 'war the horror of mothers', but these are battles that can leave many chaplains bereft. My canonry here in Seville, for example, was hard won indeed; my opponent was an Italian cardinal, if you please, and a few years back my father had to come to Seville to protect my interests while I was at court. In the end, with his help, I held on to it, but I still encounter some opposition amongst the clergy here. It is a strange system, I must admit, and one that is constantly abused: and all in the name of the service of God.

But let us sing unto the Lord a new song and return to musical matters. There are currently about forty singers paid in the royal chapel, although, as I have said, we may not all be here at any one time. On very special occasions – as, for instance, tomorrow – we join forces with the local cathedral choir for the Mass. When King Philip of glorious memory came to Spain about ten years ago, there was a tremendous occasion in Toledo cathedral when we must have numbered about eighty: the Flemish choir singing some parts of the Mass and we other parts, and with the cathedral singers as well, that day heard three of the nine angelic choirs. On such occasions we sing in polyphony those parts of the Office of Vespers that are usually sung in counterpoint – the hymns, Magnificat and probably a motet or two, and at the main Mass at least the texts of the Ordinary. All the rest is generally chanted: you learn all the chants by heart as a boy, but we still gather round the lectern and read from the huge choirbooks. In the case of something unfamiliar being short-sighted can prove a problem.

Sometimes one of us will compose a new setting for the particular occasion; other times we draw on a piece already in the chapel repertory, again usually by one of us, although we might sing something by, say, one of the Flemish singers, if we can get hold of a copy. As I mentioned, Holy Week is a particularly important time, and I recently composed a set of Lamentations for each of the *triduum sacrum*. Most of our liturgical works are built round the appropriate plainchant – or at least sometimes it is not so appropriate – overtly at least. Some of those Flemish composers are very clever at seeing the possibilities in a melody – it might be a chant or even a secular song – for the structure and they achieve impossible feats of counterpoint with canons in forward, retrograde and even crab-like motion. Actually, I had a lot of fun in the final Agnus Dei of my *Ave Maria* Mass – the one we are to sing tomorrow: the last Agnus provides a good opportunity to end with something especially impressive. I had been looking at a chanson by one Flemish composer, Ghizeghem by name, when I realized how well the tenor would fit – if you sang it backwards – with the chant for the *Salve Regina* and how there were all sorts of canonic possibilities too. Not even all the singers have yet guessed its hidden secrets, and I think La Rue would have been proud of me. But I am forgetting my Ovid: 'True art conceals the means by which it is achieved'.

Not all the music we compose is for the chapel services. We also write songs: love songs, humorous songs (Ponce once devised a drinking song, in Latin, that was a parody of the Marian salutation – it was well received), ballads telling of heroes of chivalry or the feats of his highness in the campaigns against the Moors, devotional songs: any kind of song you can think of, but love songs most of all. It is irrelevant that most of us are dedicated to the priesthood – you have to be at least in minor orders if you want to get on in the ecclesiastical hierarchy, though there are some lay members of the chapel too: music is our craft. There are songs we sing on special occasions and songs for a good evening's entertainment, and there are other kinds of music, too, for dancing and to accompany meals and so on. The new queen is French and likes to enjoy herself with banquets and music and dancing, though she has failed to produce the son who would seal the unification of these kingdoms, and things are not what they were in the days of Queen Isabella. Well, young Luis, here comes my friend Pedro now and I distinctly heard the lowing of a sackbut across the square: hardly the summons of Roland but a call to pressing matters none the less. Have I spoken too much of myself? I have shown the pride of Nero: *qualis artifex pereo* – what an artist here dies in me! Farewell. Written in Seville on the first day of February in the year of our Lord 1511.

Fran. de penyalosa

Select bibliography

H. ANGLÈS. *La música en la corte de los Reyes Católicos, Monumentos de la Música Española* I (Barcelona, 2nd edn 1945), and *MME*, v and x (Barcelona, 1947 & 1951)

J. E. AYARRA JARNE, 'La música en el culto catedralicio hispalense', *La catedral de Sevilla* (Seville, 1984)

M. K. DUGGAN, 'Queen Joanna and her musicians', *Musica Disciplina*, xxx (1976), pp.73–96

T. KNIGHTON, *Music and musicians at the court of Fernando of Aragon, 1474–1516*, PhD. diss., Cambridge, 1983

C. LYNN, *A college professor of the Renaissance: Lucio Marineo Siculo among the Spanish humanists* (Chicago, 1937)

L. MARINEUS SICULUS, *De las cosas memorables de España* (Alcalá de Henares, 1539)

L. MARINEUS SICULUS, *Epistolarum* (Valladolid, 1514)

P. MARTIR DE ANGLERÍA, *Epistolario*, trans. J. López de Toro, *Documentos Inéditos de la Historia de España* ix–xii (Madrid, 1953–7)

A. RUMEU DE ARMAS, *Itinerario de los Reyes Católicos, 1474–1516* (Madrid, 1974)

R. STEVENSON, *La música en la catedral de Sevilla 1478–1606: documentos para su estudio* (Madrid, repr. 1985)

R. STEVENSON, *Spanish music in the age of Columbus* (The Hague, 1960)

13 A portrait of Sir Henry Unton

Anthony Rooley

Here is a brief miniature, intended to encapsulate the Elizabethan 'Golden Age' by focusing on the life of one of its minor players: Sir Henry Unton. He, and others like him, such as Henry Noel and Sir Henry Lee, were true Renaissance men; gifted courtiers who straddled the arts, both martial and venereal, who exercised their love of poetry and music directly and who left a sufficient legacy of interesting data on which to build modest portraits. In the light of this information, we perceive the Elizabethan time to be really rather odd, so very different from our own, and yet tantalizingly close too – our forefathers' conceptual frame is wonderfully strange and invigorating.

Sir Henry Unton (or Umpton) died after a bout of fever at around the age of forty in 1596 whilst fulfilling his duties as Ambassador for Queen Elizabeth I in France. His voluminous correspondence shows him to be a man of integrity, adoring of the Queen even though frustrated by her indecisions, a close friend of Henri IV of France, and a firm believer in the Protestant cause. Some of his actions had shown him to be occasionally headstrong when on the battlefield – examples of misplaced chivalry no doubt – and had caused the Queen to lose her temper. He also raised her ire with some scathing comments he made in parliament during his representation of Berkshire. But essentially the character that comes across to us is one of sanguine cheerfulness and sound principles.

His death was therefore an occasion of real grief, felt by all who had known him, for yet another 'flower of English chivalry' was cut down in his prime. The loss brought forth a series of laments in a variety of media from a wide circle of contributors. Unton died with the French King virtually at his side, and the first written lament was a letter from Henri to Elizabeth, a letter of true personal grief, for the King held Unton to be a dear friend. Henry's body was returned to England in accordance with his last wishes and was buried in the family tomb at All Saints Church, Faringdon, Berkshire. Thus he was returned from whence he began, for though his work abroad had been considerable, he had maintained ties with his birthplace throughout his life.

He had studied at Oriel College in Oxford; and since his home, Wadley Manor, was only twelve miles distant, he had maintained close connections with Oxford scholarly life. That he was held in high esteem there was made clear when, as a token of respect and love, a volume of memorial verses was published in the year of his death. The *Funebria Nobilissima* contained verses by more than fifty Oxford dons, lecturers and students, providing an impressive literary monument to the English knight. Though the content is uneven in quality (some of the encomia are trite in the extreme and written, one suspects, by people to whom Unton was only a name), the tenor is one of marked respect and a genuine love shines through even in this most formal of literary expressions.

The fullest expression of grief was understandably that of his wife Dorothy. She appears to have been single-minded in her devotion to him, and behind the formal expressions of grief allowed by convention one is moved by the tenderness that comes from her. Despite her re-marriage within two years of his death, she regarded Henry Unton as her real partner, and when she died in 1633 her body was laid beside his in Faringdon Church.

Dudley Carleton, who was with Sir Henry Unton at his death, gives us this description of Dorothy five months later:

She has very well beautified her sorrow with all the ornaments of an honourable widow. Her black velvet bed, her Cyprus veil, her voice tuned with a mournful accent, and her cupboard (instead of casting bottles) adorned with prayer books, and epitaphs do make her chamber look like the house of sorrow.

Several of the 'mementi mori' Dorothy made still survive today, and the west wing of Faringdon Church is given over to the effigies and tomb-stones of the Unton family. The Unton line died with Henry, for he had no male heir, and no doubt this intensified the loss for Dorothy. But she served his memory well in having an

1 *The Life of Sir Henry Unton* (London, National Portrait Gallery)

elaborate monument constructed. Only part of it remains today. The church received considerable damage in the Civil War, with the loss of its wooden spire and part of the Unton monument; but even so, the surviving work is impressive.

One of the most famous paintings of the period was also commissioned by Dorothy to be a permanent record of her husband's life. This memorial picture, now hanging in the National Portrait Gallery, is an extraordinary visual document. The kindly sagacious gaze of Sir Henry Unton dominates and oversees, as it were, scenes from his life. His face is painted to reveal the healthy complexion of a sanguine temperament, thought at that time most nearly to approach perfection in the human condition.

A viewer reading the picture from right to left passes through the important phases of his life and sees the activities held dearest to Sir Henry. His face appears no fewer than twelve times, discounting the large inset of him writing at a desk. The inset shows him at work as ambassador, penning a letter to Burghley or Henri no doubt, and before him in a pendant is the image of his Queen whose honour he was once prepared to defend in a duel. This was how Dorothy wished him to be

remembered: capable, vital, faithful and, I think we must agree, handsome. The other twelve appearances show him as an infant in his mother's arms; as a student in his study at Oriel College; on his youthful travels in Italy; on manoeuvres in the Low Countries where he received his knighthood for bravery; then in a series of scenes in his own house, Wadley Manor. At the top of the house he is in isolation praying; below he entertains a select company, presumably of his many friends or relations; to his right he plays the bass viol in a viol consort; in a room below he attends a meeting, planning matters of state perhaps; in the foreground he plays the lute in the mixed consort which accompanies a masque. Back in France, he rides on horseback to meet Henri IV, during the fatal visit where he contracted 'the purple fever'. We then see him ill in bed with physicians around him, just before death claims him. The shrouded coffin is shown returning to Wadley Manor and then being carried by bearers with a train of mourners behind. The last time we see his face is just before the entrance to the family tomb, appearing to be half lying, half floating and holding a banner in each hand. He is about to rest, beneath his effigy, for the final time.

In commissioning this picture Lady Dorothy prepared a fitting memorial for her fine husband, and also left us an immensely rich social document. The painting is of special value to musicians since it gives the only contemporary depictions of those two very English ensembles of the high Renaissance: the viol consort, and the mixed consort. In approving the programme for the painting, Dorothy chose to show her husband's interest in music, which not only included patronage but extended to direct involvement as well. No doubt he developed his skill as a bass viol player and lutenist whilst a student at Oriel, and he was probably active in the music-making in and around Oxford. The largest manuscript collection of viol consort songs was compiled in the 1580s by an Oxford don, Robert Dow, and it would be no surprise to discover that this same repertory was heard at Wadley Manor.

Sir Henry Unton's ability on the bass viol and lute probably encouraged Lady Dorothy to organize what appears to be the only musical lament relating to his

Ex.1
John Dowland, *Sir Henry Umpton's Funerall* from *Lachrimae or Seven Teares* (1604): first strain

death. John Dowland's solemn pavan 'Sir Henry Umpton's Funerall' was not published until 1604 in his *Lachrimae or Seven Teares*, but it is very likely that the pavan was composed some years before that, as were a number of the dances in that collection. The instrumentation Dowland calls for is five viols (or violins) and lute, the same instruments as in the painting. We have no record of Dorothy commissioning this work nor any record of its time and place of use, though the solemnity of the work would make it a suitable accompaniment for the funeral cortège as depicted in the painting. It is more likely that psalms would have been used for the procession itself, rather like the settings Dowland made for the death of another courtier in 1596, Sir Henry Noel. Perhaps the 'Funerall' pavan was heard back home in Wadley Manor to maintain the atmosphere of grief and mourning. The Elizabethan and Jacobean age did undoubtedly make the most of the opportunity provided by death for a particularly solemn and 'monumental' use of music. There were death-songs in plays as well as funeral elegies for real people. Music's ability to move the soul and elevate it helped not only ease the grief of those remaining but also helped send the soul of the newly-departed heavenward.

Dowland's pavan is a fine work of extraordinary breadth and seems to transcend the limits imposed by the pavan form with its three sections, each repeated. He achieves this elevated stature immediately by the stillness of the part-writing, by slow but powerful suspensions, by a soaring cantus line and especially by the unusual and unexpected fermata in all parts at the end of bar three. All the movement is held, made to hover and to defy the very law of tactus, increasing the tension to bursting point. The work then proceeds at this heightened state of awareness with a bold plan of utterly simple harmonic progressions with suspensions held by turn in every part.

It comes as something of a surprise, then, to discover that a work of such artistic integrity and skill from the hand of one of England's masters should be almost identical with another pavan by one of Dowland's fellow composers. 'The Countess of Pembroke's Funerall' by Antony Holborne, published in 1599 for five viols, or other instruments, and available as a lute solo in several contemporary

Ex.2
Antony Holborne, *The Countess of Pembroke's Funerall* (1599): first strain

manuscripts, is without question fundamentally the same piece as the Dowland pavan. Is it a question of mistaken ascription? No, for both composers saw to it that the printed books contained what they really wanted. Is it a question of plagiarism? Again, no, how could it be that these two friends should unashamedly steal from one another? Since the similarity of the two works has remained hitherto unnoticed, it is worth analysing the features of each to see how closely they are modelled on each other (see exx.1 and 2). We can then take up the question again as to why there are so many points of comparison.

Both works are in pavan form, *AA, BB, CC,* and in their ensemble versions have no written-out decorated repeats. Both are in slow duple measure, as would be expected for a pavan, and both are in G minor. The second section begins on the dominant, D, and closes on the same; the third section begins on the mediant B and closes on G. Thus the broad harmonic outline is exactly the same. Taking the tactus unit as a semibreve in the transcriptions, the Holborne pavan has a total of twenty-seven bars, whilst the Dowland has twenty-six. This difference works out in section lengths as follows (with the Holborne first): section *A,* 10: 8; *B,* 8: 8; *C,* 9: 10. None of these general similarities causes much surprise, for the standard Elizabethan pavan would automatically share some of them. Just how much they have in common can be seen by comparing the two *A* sections in detail. Holborne's half-way cadence is at bar 4 whilst Dowland's is at bar 3, though the harmonic movement (seen most clearly in the bass) is the same in both for the first four bars. Holborne makes a bigger feature of the emotive E flat, which Dowland touches (in bar 5) then departs quickly to return to the dominant ready for the cadence. The only difference in this section from a harmonic point of view is that Dowland drops an E flat bar and a D bar, but since his section is eight instead of ten bars, this is a logical difference. Dowland's cantus begins more simply than Holborne's but then proceeds with increasing activity, playing much on the variant rhythms around ♩ ♫♩ (his 'Lachrimae' rhythm), though this rhythm, an obvious one for 'bating' a work with syncopation, is found in the tenor part of Holborne's piece. The tolling of the death knell is clearly heard in both works, expressed in the reiterated D chord, but Holborne is more expansive and more fluid, whereas Dowland has a distilled simplicity over which is laid a surface agitation.

The *B* sections of both compositions have almost as much in common as we have seen for the *A* sections. The harmonic outline in the first two bars is the same, then the following two bars differ radically; but at bar 15 in Holborne and halfway through bar 12 in Dowland the closeness is remarkable. Not only the bass and harmony follow the same direction, but the cantus has the same melodic contour, though different rhythmic values. The inner parts are quite independent in the two pieces and contain only passing and fortuitous resemblances to each other.

The final sections have greater independence. Apart from starting on the mediant, B, very few points can be shown to be in common. The harmonic sketch is very roughly the same, but no more than might be expected from two works composed independently but in the same mood, key and form. However, the closing cantus phrase, a delayed descent from *d* to *g,* is unmistakeably similar in both cases, each bringing with the final cadence an evocation of the other pavan.

We must conclude that both works have been designed on the same harmonic plan, with many directly quoted features in the bassus and an unusual number of adapted quotations in the cantus. The two works permeate each other in general plan and in points of detail. One is, in the best sense, a parody of the other. Which came first? Did Holborne parody Dowland, or the other way around? Date of publication gives very little real guide as to chronology because we know that for both composers their collection was retrospective. An obvious lead to follow is the information regarding the two dedicatees, Sir Henry Unton and the Countess of Pembroke, and an obvious question is did they have anything in common, death aside?

Since we have discussed Dowland's dedicatee in some depth, let us consider the identity of Antony Holborne's. No Countess of Pembroke died within the dates reasonable to assume for this composition. The second Earl of Pembroke was married three times; the first marriage was dissolved, the second wife died in 1576, and his third wife, Mary Sidney, died in 1622. It is highly unlikely that Holborne's collection of 1599 could be retrospective by as much as nearly a quarter of a century and relate to the death of Pembroke's second wife, and it can therefore only refer to Mary Sidney, the third Countess, and have been composed for her while she was still very much alive. It does not appear to have been common practice (as it was at the end of the seventeenth century) to have one's funeral music or 'tombeau' composed while one was still alive. This idea would have been unthinkable in Elizabethan England and quite against accepted decorum. The dedication must have quite other implications. We know of Holborne's closeness to the literary circle around the Sidney family and his love of emblematic titles for his dances, several of which have links with works by Edmund Spenser, and can therefore assume that the dedication has some very specific literary reference.

The only events in Mary Sidney's life that could relate to the composition of such a funeral pavan were the series of tragedies she experienced in 1586, one of the most public mourning periods of the time, for Mary lost not only her father and mother in that year but also her internationally admired brother, Sir Philip Sidney. After his death, Mary shouldered the responsibility for continuing the artistic patronage of her brother, and for ordering his poetic works for publication.

This 'flower of chivalry' was mourned throughout the nation and was the subject of an unprecedented number of elegies and musical laments. The sad event was raised to a position of symbolic significance, being an example of 'cursed fate' removing one of the most gifted minds of the time. A number of the laments were written as personal expressions of Mary, some of which may have been penned by her, but the idea of a gifted sister grieving for a gifted brother became a conventional 'type', of which the Holborne pavan is probably one, written shortly after 1586 and circulating widely in manuscript.

In less than ten years, a second victim is claimed by fate in circumstances of some similarity. And not only that: Henry Unton had his moment of greatest valour in 1586 at the side of Sir Philip Sidney when the latter received his mortal wound at the Battle of Zutphen. After the battle, the Earl of Leicester knighted Henry for his bravery, whilst the whole army mourned the death of Sidney. Unton may be seen as carrying the torch of chivalry from that moment therefore, and there is no doubt that his distraught wife, Dorothy, on hearing the news of his death saw history repeating itself.

In all the encomia and 'mementi mori', the theme of Unton's death being an echo of Sidney's is well to the fore. On the monument inscription, Dorothy takes care to mention the Battle of Zutphen specifically, picking it out from all the events of his life for special mention. In the memorial picture the scene is portrayed, as we might expect, in that context. In particular, we see the parallel with Sidney drawn in the Oxford *Funebria*, where in the preface the editor of the volume, Robert Wright, who was Unton's chaplain, claims that only Sir Philip Sidney had previously had the similar honour of a memorial collection of verse. No fewer than twelve of the verses specifically recall Sidney or associations with him and make parallels with Unton's untimely death. It was most unfortunate that Unton died of fever or plague rather than from a battle wound as Sidney had, for this robbed the verse writers of a much richer poetic vein.

Presumably, then, Lady Dorothy Unton, in memory of her husband's love of music in general and the viol and lute in particular, commissioned Dowland to compose a funeral pavan. We will never know whether the idea of taking the well-known and much-loved Sidney lament, 'The Countess of Pembroke's Funerall', was Dorothy's or John Dowland's. But certainly the subtle and artistic reworking makes a moving link with the earlier knight's memory and confirms that to Dorothy's mind, at least, her husband was a flower of equal chivalry. Court society seems not to have taken up the parallel with the same belief as Lady Dorothy and the Oxford circle. An overwhelming connection with Sidney was made in 1612 at the death of Prince Henry when all society grieved and wept. It would appear that Henry Unton was not quite influential enough to warrant that treatment and outside a few Oxford dons, Wadley Manor and his faithful Lady Unton, his death was lamented but quickly forgotten. We may muse on how many of his contemporaries noticed the subtle compliment Dowland paid to him in his pavan. Perhaps it was a subtle parody enjoyed only by the inner circle of musicians who had played with Sir Henry in his musical gatherings, and, of course, his wife who so faithfully wished to perpetuate his memory.

Select bibliography

M. C. BOYD, *Elizabethan music and music criticism* (Philadelphia, 1974)

E. DOUGHTIE (ed.), *Lyrics from English airs 1596–1622* (Cambridge, MA, 1970)

J. GODWIN, *Harmonies of Heaven and Earth* (London, 1987)

W. MAYNARD, *Elizabethan lyric poetry and its music* (Oxford, 1986)

B. PATTINSON, *Music and poetry of the English Renaissance* (London, 1970)

D. POULTON, *John Dowland* (London, 1972)

A. ROOLEY, '"I saw my lady weepe": the first five songs of John Dowland's *Second Book of Songs*', *Temenos*, ii (1982), pp.6–21

O. STRUNK (ed.), *Source readings in music history: the Renaissance*, 2nd edn (London, 1985)

J. M. WARD, 'A Dowland miscellany', *Journal of the Lute Society of America* (1977), pp.5–153

P. WARLOCK, *The English ayre* (London, 1970)

M. VALE, *The gentleman's recreations* (Cambridge, 1977)

14 Women's history and early music

Laura W. Macy

Women's history seeks, in the words of Joan Kelly-Gadol, to 'restore women to history and to restore our history to women'. Historians of music have taken up this challenge only recently. The definition of 'feminist musicology' is not yet clear – its role is uncertain. My purpose here is twofold: to locate feminist musicology in the broader context of feminist historiography, and to propose some ways in which a feminist viewpoint can enrich the study of early music.

Women's history is less a field of its own than a part of all humane disciplines. Its justification lies in the premise that women have traditionally been excluded from the historical narrative. In her important article 'Women's History and the Rewriting of History', Joan Scott delineated three types of feminist historical research. Her categories are not completely separate and distinct, but they offer a useful framework for a discussion of the methodology of feminist musicology. In Scott's first category, women become the focus of scholarship, much as men traditionally have been. This can amount to a kind of 'Herstory' to be placed alongside History: influential women are given the attention hitherto reserved for their male counterparts.

The second category includes studies in which the history of women is used to challenge traditional historical 'facts'. As an example, Scott cites Kelly-Gadol's feminist study 'Did women have a Renaissance?' in which, by looking at changing patterns of women's autonomy and power, she argued that there was no renaissance for women – at least not during the Renaissance. If Scott's first category adds a companion women's history to be placed next to that of men, this second one uses the former to challenge the latter, identifying and confronting points of conflict between the two.

Scott's third category is the least explored: it consists, in essence, in a rewriting of history, which seeks to make sex a 'fundamental classification alongside class and race'. In such an approach, women become agents of the historical narrative, as well as its subjects.

Studies of women in music, and early music in particular, have dwelt primarily in Scott's first category. By bringing forward important and previously neglected female composers, patrons, and performers and assessing their contribution to music history, we are gradually etching out a Herstory to be placed alongside or ideally to be incorporated into the existing History. One especially fruitful approach has been to research institutions rather than individual women. Various studies of musical life in convents, for example, have added a new dimension to our once male-dominated picture of religious music. Such investigations not only increase our understanding of fifteenth- and sixteenth-century women, but broaden and deepen our knowledge of music-making in these centuries as well.

Some scholars have ventured into the realm of Scott's second category: the challenge. Paula Higgins has shown that women played an active creative role – as poets and perhaps even composers – in the fifteenth-century chanson. Her study challenges our image of women's role in the courtly-love tradition as purely passive.

This work is all vitally important, for it tells a story that needs telling. But I would like to explore here the possibilities offered by Scott's third category, involving the rewriting of history. For music history, this would mean treating the female musical experience as a vantage point from which any and all musical questions could be asked. To see what such an approach might reveal, we can look at a subject that has received a relatively large amount of attention: the rise of the professional female singer in sixteenth-century Italy.

In many ways the sixteenth-century Italian musical world was a liberating one for women. The Italian court system seems to have nurtured and encouraged female patronage of music. More important, the course of the sixteenth century saw an increasing demand for female performers. Correspondence relating to the important Italian courts attests to a growing interest in the female voice, and this interest was reflected in the music itself – most especially in the madrigal.

Concentrating on the musical establishment at Ferrara in the last quarter of the sixteenth century, Anthony Newcomb has discussed the rise of professional female singing in Italy, and its implications for women's history. Musical ability was cited as a desirable attribute of the 'courtly lady' in Castiglione's influential manual of manners, *The book of the courtier* (1528). The importance of musical skills for both sexes among the upper classes and the resulting rise, during the course of the sixteenth century, of amateur music-making among these classes contributed to the development of the madrigal – possibly the first musical genre in modern history to which the female voice is crucial.

Not all madrigals were written for amateurs; at Ferrara, in the last quarter of the century, there arose a new style of virtuoso madrigal that required highly sophisticated female singing. In order to accommodate this style, a group of noblewomen, ladies-in-waiting to the Duchess, formed the famous *Concerto delle donne* – an ensemble that was to become a model for musical establishments all over Italy. As the group improved, and their repertory grew and developed, a subtle but important shift took place. Noblewomen who happened to sing were gradually replaced in the ensemble by gifted singers who happened to be noblewomen. From there it was a short step to the admission of singers of the untitled classes – the upper bourgeoisie. By the end of the century, imitations of the Ferrarese *Concerto* had sprung up in all of the Italian courts, creating a widespread demand for female singers. Young girls began to be trained in music not just as one of many social graces, but with an eye towards a career; the professional female singer was born.

Newcomb and others have stressed the opportunities that professionalism offered women. And our modern belief that employment leads to greater independence and hence self-esteem, leads us to conclude that, in the musical world, women's circumstances improved during the course of the sixteenth century – that, at least in this limited arena, women did have a renaissance.

But what if we view this whole complex of evidence from the point of view of the women themselves? We will want to ask some different questions. What was the hierarchy of power in the families to which female singers belonged – in other words, who actually handled their careers and incomes? What was the social position of these women? And what was the relationship between the patron and employee – specifically, what were the acceptable relationships between males of the nobility and respectable females of the bourgeoisie? Such questions force us to revise our view about the 'renaissance' of women's musical life, to one of limited freedom at best, exploitation at worst.

We might begin by looking at salaries, for which Newcomb and others have accumulated a fair amount of information. Renaissance musicians were compensated for their services in various ways: salaries were often supplemented by room and board, and augmented by expensive gifts. Even a cursory look at the Ferrarese singers discussed by Newcomb reveals that they were handsomely rewarded, often with combinations that exceeded, in pure monetary values, those of their male counterparts. But the detail of this remuneration tells a different story. Laura Peverara, the Ferrarese singer and a founding member of the *Concerto delle donne*, earned an annual salary of 300 *scudi* over and above lodgings in the ducal palace for herself, her husband, and her mother. In addition, the duke provided her with a dowry of 10,000 *scudi* upon her marriage in 1583. Peverara's female colleagues received similar awards. Tarquinia Molza, a widow who Newcomb observes 'did not need to be provided with husband and dowry', also received 300 *scudi* per year and rooms in the palace.

As evidence of the value of these incomes, Newcomb contrasts that of the Ferrarese court composer, Luzzasco Luzzaschi, whose salary was a meagre (by comparison) 125–35 *scudi*. Luzzaschi also had rooms in the palace; but among the Duke's gifts to the composer was a house in the country. Likewise the bass Cesare Brancaccio was granted a house in town in addition to 400 *scudi* per year and other benefits. Exact values of houses and so forth are difficult to assess; but while the value of the women's total income was perhaps equal to or even greater than many of their male counterparts, these few examples point up a significant difference in kind. While the women received high salaries, gifts, and dowries, the men were granted independent dwellings – a kind of autonomy noticeably absent from the documents pertaining to women.

We might further ask whether a woman's income was indeed her own. Many singers were married, often to fellow musicians, and there is evidence that women's careers were often managed by their husbands or fathers. The Caccini family, perhaps one of the most successful musical families of the period, is a good example. Its success was due, at least in part, to the amazing gift for self-propaganda of Giulio Caccini, the family's patriarch. Giulio was a singer, composer, intellectual dilettante and, according to one letter written on his behalf, an excellent gardener. He was married twice, both times to singers, and had three musical children, a son and two daughters. The most famous of his offspring was his daughter Francesca, herself a gifted composer – arguably a better one than her father.

Caccini is credited as the vocal teacher of both of his wives as well as his two daughters. But his role went beyond that of teacher: he acted as a kind of impresario who controlled the careers of all of the members of his family. Caccini arranged the premières of both of his daughters at the age of thirteen, and his correspondence shows him constantly negotiating positions for his family, often using them to further his own career.

The story of the Caccini family suggests that female singers, far from being self-determining professionals, were frequently pawns in the musical power-play of their husbands and fathers. One final example underscores this point and raises another vital issue: the social position of the female singer.

Caterina Martinelli is famous today as the Mantuan court singer originally meant to sing the title role in Monteverdi's *L'Arianna* in 1608. Monteverdi wrote the part for Martinelli, but the young singer died, apparently of smallpox, shortly before the work's première. At the time of her death, at seventeen, she was already a famous singer. In a recent article on Martinelli, Edmond Strainchamps reconstructs her biography from the beginning of her career at Mantua. The earliest documents are a series of letters from the year 1603, negotiating her employment at Mantua. Martinelli, a Roman, was to be brought to Mantua by way of Florence where she was originally intended to stay and study with Caccini. This plan was later abandoned in favour of bringing the girl directly to Mantua to be housed with Monteverdi and trained by his wife, Claudia Catteneo, a Mantuan court singer.

A subject of heated exchange in the correspondence is that of an examination, ordered by Duke Vincenzo I of Mantua, to confirm the thirteen-year-old singer's virginity. Her father acquiesced, but not without protesting vigorously this slight to his daughter's honour. The Duke's request, and its apparent acceptance by all involved, gives one pause for thought. Why did it matter, we might be inclined to ask; and given that it did, what reason was there to doubt that the girl was a virgin? These questions bring us to the issue of the probable social status of female professionals.

Many women who excelled in artistic endeavours – in literature especially, but in theatre and music as well – were courtesans. These high-class prostitutes were expected to excel, much like 'courtly ladies', in the arts and humanities. But their marginal position in society allowed them to pursue artistic interests with a professionalism that would have been considered inappropriate for a lady of social standing. The Venetian courtesan Veronica Franco, for example, used her connections in literary circles to further her career as a poet.

As a class of 'legitimate' female singers began to emerge, the line between singer and courtesan must, at times, have been difficult to draw. Given this uncertainty, we might read Duke Vincenzo's request in one of two ways. Assuming that the Duke was interested in Martinelli purely for her vocal ability, he may have been trying to protect his court musical establishment from the taint of impropriety. On the other hand, we cannot dismiss the possibility that Martinelli was in fact being hired as a singer/courtesan; in this case, the girl's virginity may have been considered one of her selling points. Whichever the case, it is hard to see Caterina Martinelli as anything but a pawn in the hands of an ambitious father and an acquisitive Duke.

None of the issues raised here is easily resolved. But if we want to know where women fit into the picture we are painting of musical life in early modern Europe, we must have the courage to ask the women themselves: not their husbands, not their fathers, nor their patrons, admirers, or lovers.

Feminism challenges the very criteria on which we construct history. We have seen that simple salary comparison gives an incomplete picture of the status of women singers. On a larger level, since women have so often been barred from traditional musical careers, women's history seeks alternatives to the traditional musico-historical narrative that amounts to a parade of 'great composers'.

Like women, 'early music' has been marginalized by traditional historical methods. Just as women suffer from being valued according to a history developed by and for men, 'early music' is inadequately served by criteria and methods developed for later music on the one hand, and other disciplines (especially literature, art and architecture) on the other. In both cases the subjects are distorted to fit the procrustean bed of authoritative criteria.

To draw upon an example already mentioned: Kelly-Gadol, using feminist methodology, has shown that the standard periodization of history is based on categories exclusive of women. Among the assumptions that crumble under Kelly-Gadol's challenge is the notion of 'the Renaissance'. Although nobody likes to admit it outright, the Renaissance has been a real thorn in the flesh of musicology. Formulated primarily to describe developments in the visual arts and the birth of modern systems of government, the concept of the Renaissance is Italocentric and deeply rooted in the idea of a rebirth of ancient culture. These criteria simply do not work well for music, and efforts to apply them have resulted in such incongruities as the so-called 'segreto del quattrocento' – our consternation over the nearly total absence of written music by native Italian composers between roughly 1420 and 1490. Similarly, the musical ascendancy of Northern Europe during this period has fuelled the dispute over whether the great fifteenth-century northern composers should be considered as part of the medieval or Renaissance tradition. Finally, when clear 'Renaissance' traits do appear, they are out of step with the other arts: hence the continuing, if apologetic, characterization of the rise of opera at the turn of the seventeenth century as a Renaissance phenomenon.

We are uncomfortable with these contradictions, and we work hard to explain them away – to make music fit the existing historical model. What we seem unable to do is to challenge – as feminism has – the validity of the model itself; we are unwilling to abandon a system of periodization that marginalizes (indeed, ignores) our subject, and replace it with one sensitive to music's own unique characteristics. If we are to weave 'early music' into the historical tapestry, we must unravel and redesign that tapestry. This is precisely the challenge to which feminist historians have been addressing themselves with increasingly rich results; we could do worse than to follow their lead.

Select bibliography

General

J. KELLY-GADOL, 'Did women have a renaissance?' in R. Bridenthal, C. Koonz and S. Stuard (eds), *Becoming visible: women in European history* (Boston, 1987); and 'The social relation of the sexes: methodological implications of women's history', *Signs* i (1976), p.809

S. MCCLARY, *Feminine Endings: Music, gender and sexuality* (Minneapolis, 1991)

L. NOCHLIN, 'Why have there been no great women artists?', *Arts News*, lxix/9 (1971), pp.22–67

J. W. SCOTT, 'Women's history and the rewriting of history', in C. Farnham (ed.), *The impact of feminist research on the academy* (Bloomington, 1987)

Women and 'early music'

S. C. COOK, *Virtuose in Italy, 1600–1640: a reference guide* (New York, 1984)

P. HIGGINS, 'Parisian nobles, a Scottish princess, and the woman's voice in late medieval song', *Early Music History*, x (1991), pp. 145–200

A. NEWCOMB, 'Courtesans, muses or musicians? Professional women musicians in sixteenth-century Italy', in J. Bowers and J. Tick (eds), *Women making music: the Western art tradition, 1150–1950* (Urbana, 1986)

E. STRAINCHAMPS, 'The life and death of Caterina Martinelli: new light on Monteverdi's *Arianna*', *Early Music History*, v (1985), pp.155–86

III Questions of form and style

Genres: vocal

15 Chant, or the politics of inscription

Katherine Bergeron

In the study of medieval and Renaissance music, chant is typically regarded as a kind of Ur-repertory, a practice that both precedes and gives rise to more complex, or 'developed' musical types. Within an extended sense of the term 'repertory' (referring to those works available for performance), one might also consider chant a musical 'genre', distinct in form, content and style from other forms of music issuing from the Middle Ages and Renaissance. Yet such categorization may be problematic, especially if one attempts to look beyond forms and styles. For despite apparent musical qualities, chant ultimately stands apart from other types of medieval music – a condition that becomes immediately evident to anyone who has attempted to penetrate the complexities of the ritual practice from which it emerges. Indeed, it may be well to ask from the start whether chant can properly be considered 'music' at all.

If what is thought to be music in any culture is a socially negotiated phenomenon, then it must be recognized that chant occupies a radically different social space from the motet, or the secular song, or the instrumental music performed either solo or in ensembles for the pleasure of listeners. Chant, we could say, refers less to a body of compositions (in the conventional sense) than to a set of specialized, or ritualized, vocal habits. Belonging to the sacred liturgy of the most important institution of medieval culture, the Roman Church, it presupposes a large and complex body of sacred words, hierarchically ordered through the principal rituals of Mass and Office, and repeatedly given 'voice' – often in a highly stylized and symbolic manner – by means of formulaic tones or elaborate melodies. This melodic aspect may in fact be musical, but it also serves an eminently practical purpose: to make ritual words audible, memorable, powerful. Through chant the 'living' word becomes material, set in motion. It is this special vocalization that gives words their power, the symbolic force that causes them to achieve a desired effect. In this sense a particular chant is hardly different from a spell or incantation, a set of specially pronounced words designed to bring about a certain magical result. Given such conditions, particularly this aspect of ritual efficacy, I think it is safe to say that chant operates at some distance from other so-called genres of vocal or instrumental music to be found before 1600.

The earliest manuscripts that contain chant give some indication of this special status. For the most part the manuscripts reflect a ritual – not a musical – logic, with pieces arranged in separate books according to their function: in one type we find chants for the Mass the texts for which change from day to day; in another, readings; in another, psalms to be chanted at the Offices; in another, prayers intoned by the priest at Mass; in still another, general rules for the production of liturgy or other special ceremonies. The books devoted to chants are but one type among a diverse body of texts serving various ends. Indeed it is not much before the tenth century (that is, many centuries into the practice) that we find consistent attempts within the manuscripts to represent the 'musical' aspects of the chant with notation – in this case, a very elemental symbolic system of diacritical marks indicating upward and downward vocal inflection. This historical fact in itself would seem to diminish, if not completely marginalize, the status of such manuscripts for performance: in the centuries before writing, cantors obviously learned to chant without the aid of notation.

These written documents, however, give some insight into the importance of the practices they aim to represent. It has been suggested that the earliest efforts to write down local rituals resulted from political pressure in Rome, beginning in the eighth century, to codify or standardize Christian worship throughout the West. Yet when by the tenth century such writing contains more and more precise information about chanting – actual notated performance directions – these manuscripts may begin to appear in a different light. For if we regard writing as something of a powerful new technology in the early Middle Ages, a technology owned principally by the Church (much like the database technologies that today maintain vast stores of information for world powers), then the writing down of words and melodies at different monastic centres suggests the attempt to invest individual practices with that power. Certainly, the written records from the tenth century and after can be read as a response to Roman decree, a demonstrated attempt to participate in the liturgical reforms, but they also can be seen as efforts graphically to empower local centres – principally in Gaul, Italy, and the Iberian peninsula – in the face of such standardization. Indeed, as Jacques Attali has indicated, we should view such records as 'a means of social control, a stake in politics, regardless of the available technologies . . . [For] stockpiling memory, retaining history or time, distributing speech, and manipulating information have always been an attribute of civil and priestly power.' (See Attali, p.87)

Through the technology of writing, the manuscripts distribute a unified or 'normalized' practice at the same time that they bear witness to the presence of separate, local traditions. Yet the whole notion of a chant 'tradition', as a set of practices maintained through collective memory, is clearly complicated by such writing. In a largely pre-literate culture an act of writing serves not so much to preserve or maintain as simply to make the tradition visible, material – to make recognizable that which is already known. The manuscript thus functions as a powerful sign, a graphic representation linking memory, and hence Tradition itself, to those who have the power to inscribe it.

The political implications of such inscription are just as apparent today, where a certain practice of singing plainchant has been around for as long as most of us can remember. The Benedictine monks of Solesmes, France, were primarily respons-ible for the invention of this modern chant tradition over a century ago, through their daily activities at the Abbey of St Peter: studying, compiling and, most importantly, singing all those melodies forgotten through centuries of modification or neglect. Their singing is what we now remember most, since it was as early as 1904 that the monks began to inscribe their performances on gramophone cylinders, a marvellous technology that made their authentic voices available to all who might listen. Today more advanced forms of sound recording (stereophonic

LPs, pristine compact discs) keep alive our memory of their performances – of the tradition known as the 'Solesmes method' that issued from those who had originally laid claim to the technology. This very beautiful, very Romantic, and somehow very French tradition of singing has never ceased to dominate our notion of Gregorian chant, despite whatever else we may know about other repertories of medieval or Renaissance music.

Select bibliography

W. APEL, *Gregorian chant* (Bloomington, 1958)

J. ATTALI, *Noise: the political economy of music*, trans. B. Massumi (Minneapolis, 1985)

K. BERGERON, 'Representation, reproduction, and the revival of Gregorian chant at Solesmes', PhD. diss., Cornell, 1989

G. DUBY and P. ARIÈS (eds), *A history of private life*, Vol. II: *Revelations of the medieval world*, trans. A. Goldhammer. (Cambridge, MA, and London, 1988)

W. ONG, *Interfaces of the word: studies in the evolution of consciousness and culture* (Ithaca 1977)

C. PAGE, *The owl and the nightingale: musical life and ideas in France 1100–1300* (London, 1989)

L. TREITLER, 'The early history of music writing in the west', *Journal of the American Musicological Society*, xxxv/2 (1982), pp.237–79

16 Monophonic song: questions of category

Ardis Butterfield

'Monophony' is one of the primary terms in medieval music, not only because it is the dominant mode of the European vernacular genres as well as of Latin song, but because, even in polyphonic works, it remains a central compositional principle. None the less, the term remains difficult to define precisely because the distinction between monophony and polyphony is often hard to maintain. Countless examples of medieval polyphony are built up from originally independent monophonic songs existing in a variety of contexts. But this common ground between monophony and polyphony also reveals one of the most striking and distinctive aspects of medieval music: the constant tendency of composers to elaborate single lines by all kinds of interpolation, juxtaposition or superimposition. For this reason, medieval monophony is not strictly a single subject, but often an exploration of the kinds of strain and attraction in the relationship between one line and another.

Monophonic melody survives in the Middle Ages in a highly disparate range of language-cultures, genres and forms. There are three main Latin repertories: two are associated with chant and comprise on the one hand, tropes, sequences, rhymed offices, liturgical conductus and, on the other, liturgical drama. The third is non-liturgical, and includes planctus and lais as well as secular sequences and conductus, love songs and drinking songs. This distinction between liturgical and non-liturgical, though superficially convenient, can often seem forced: ecclesiastical life permeated so many aspects of musical and verbal composition that it seems unlikely that composers (who must have been largely clerical in the case of the Latin repertories) perceived a hard edge between the two. Songs in the vernacular survive from all over Europe, including Italy (the *laude spirituali*), Spain (the *Cantigas de Santa María*), Germany (the Minnesang), and England (though in a scattered and fragmented state); but the two largest, and most influential groups of vernacular song were composed in Provençal (the *langue d'oc*) and French (the *langue d'oïl*) by the troubadours and trouvères respectively. The earliest known troubadour was Guillaume d'Aquitaine (1071–1127), the first trouvère Chrétien de Troyes (*fl.* 1160s–80s): flourishing throughout the twelfth century, the southern style passed north and was imitated prolifically by thirteenth-century poets and composers.

It should already be clear that 'monophonic song' is not a straightforward category: indeed, a closer look at the Provençal and French songs reveals that questions about category are some of the most interesting raised by monophony. For example, it is arguable whether vernacular songs are best discussed on their own terms, separately from the Latin repertories, and this issue, in turn, cannot be disengaged from the question of how sacred and secular are distinguished in the medieval period. In musical terms, as the many examples of contrafacta show, melodies constantly cross these (perhaps anachronistically) created boundaries by being sung to pious Latin words in one context and frivolously amorous French rhymes in another. But it would be rash to assume that medieval music does not have powerful, and powerfully different generic associations; the question is not whether distinctions exist, but where they are made, and how clearly they are drawn.

In the case of the troubadour and trouvère songs, certain social and stylistic conventions are clearly signalled: many composers, though not all, are high born, and many songs are highly-wrought, with both music and words cast in an elevated, intricately patterned, sometimes deliberately obscure style, concerned with examining a refined, ideal experience of love. However, the tone of these *grands chants* is not always straightforwardly 'courtly' or ennobling: their texts can reveal subtly ironic, even obscene uses of language. Moreover, other kinds of song survive, such as the *rondet de carole*, which present a different aesthetic again: that is, their register is not 'aristocratisant' but 'popularisant'. Musically, and formally, the *rondet de carole* (which is often associated with dance) is characterized by short, simple and regularly repeated phrases, which alternate (textually) with brief pastoral sketches describing girls washing their clothes, or dancing by the river. But since these phrases or 'refrains' occur in large numbers, not just in *rondets*, but in all the lyric genres (and in numerous narrative contexts too), they often put 'courtly' and 'popular' registers into a surprisingly awkward relationship.

Most modern attempts to comprehend the diversity of monophonic song have also had to admit to the existence of genres such as the *pastourelle*, the *chanson de toile*, or the *aube/alba* which conform to neither the 'courtly' nor the 'popular' model. Furthermore, by presenting conflicting or ambiguous registral signs, such as the use of learned alongside 'popular' elements, these genres raise doubt as to whether the 'popular' in the folkloric sense, has survived at all except in a form heavily mediated by courtly or by clerical assumptions.

The additional presence throughout monophonic song of numerous 'irregularities' of notation, metre, form and style, formerly regarded as an irritating but, given enough editorial ingenuity, removable idiosyncrasy of manuscript transmission, could be described more sympathetically as part of a general cultural concern with presenting tension and contrast. In this view, the clashes just described between registers (as in a *pastourelle* with a courtly refrain), between regular and irregular form (as in the *descort*), or between languages (as in macaronic songs), might reveal significant clues to the kinds of expectation about notation, form and style current among medieval composers themselves.

Appreciating rather than discounting such instances of dislocation leads, in turn, to different ways of interpreting the melodies. It is possible, for example, that some of the more puzzlingly divergent ways in which melodies have been transcribed by medieval copyists are a sign not of error, but of a deliberate attempt to create new and unexpected liaisons between unmensural and mensural rhythms by placing one kind of generic expectation against another. Modern arguments about the nature of the rhythm of troubadour and trouvère song (which have raged even to the point of death) have paradoxically not taken irregularity (the kinds of conflicting evidence which create unruly scholarly disagreements) seriously enough as a principle of discrimination; making sense of the evidence requires paying respect to features which do not 'fit', being alert to what they imply not only about the differences between socio-cultural groupings, manuscripts, authors and individual compositions, but to the potentially conflicting expectations operating within a single piece, or in the presentation of that piece.

In this sense, many of the aspects of medieval monophonic song currently perceived to be problematic (how the melodies and words relate, what kind(s) of rhythm the music possesses, the origin and formation of genres, how social and intellectual registers apply to musical style) are perhaps a sign less of the confusion of evidence than of the subtlety of medieval explorations of discontinuity.

Select bibliography

P. BEC, *La lyrique française au moyen-âge (XIIe-XIIIe siècles)*, 2 vols. (Paris, 1977)

P. DRONKE, *The medieval lyric*, 2nd edn (London, 1978); and *Medieval Latin and the rise of European love-lyric*, 2 vols., 2nd edn (Oxford, 1968)

B. STÄBLEIN, *Schriftbild der einstimmigen Musik*, in *Musikgeschichte in Bildern*, iii/4 (Leipzig, 1975)

J. STEVENS, *Words and music in the Middle Ages* (Cambridge, 1986)

H. VAN DER WERF, *The chansons of the troubadours and trouvères: a study of the melodies and their relation to the poems* (Utrecht, 1972)

17 Early Western polyphony

Hendrik van der Werf

A pair of treatises dating from *c.* 900 contain what usually are considered the earliest specimens of Western part-music, but it is by no means certain that they represent the very origin of polyphony in general or of Western polyphony in particular. The manner in which the author of the oldest treatise introduces his first piece gives us ample reason to doubt that his short snatches for two, three, or four voices were ever performed outside the classroom: they are based upon excerpts from pre-existing melodies; they are in strict note-against-note style; and the voices move primarily in parallel octaves, fifths, and fourths. Almost all of the pieces in these treatises probably served to illustrate the sound of the chords discussed in a chapter or, more likely, a lecture on acoustics. The polyphonic style presented in these and some other didactic sources differs sharply from what we find in the earliest decipherable practical collections, that is, manuscripts containing polyphony that almost certainly was performed, or at least was intended to be performed, 'in public'.

Two manuscripts known as the 'Winchester Tropers' contain a wide variety of monophonic and polyphonic pieces; they are the oldest extant practical sources for the latter (see Holschneider). The earlier one, compiled near the turn of the millennium, is now in Oxford; the more recent one, dating from the early or mid-eleventh century, is in Cambridge. For students of medieval culture they represent both a treasure and a tragedy. For the history of script, they are a treasure; they are beautifully executed, the parchment is in excellent condition, and the Oxford source still has its original binding. For the history of music notation, the Winchester Tropers are a mixed blessing. The neumes are finely traced, they are a pleasure to behold, but they indicate neither intervals nor pitch levels. Many of the monophonic pieces also occur in sources with precisely heighted neumes; they show that many of the chants sung in Winchester were performed elsewhere in essentially the same version. However, a medieval melody rarely occurs in an identical state in two or more sources and we thus have little or no chance of reconstructing the precise pitches for any melody in the Winchester Tropers.

For students of Western polyphony, the manner in which the melodies are copied is extremely vexing. In the more recent source, it is implicitly indicated that certain groups of seemingly monophonic tunes are countermelodies to pre-existing chants appearing either elsewhere in the same book or somewhere in the earlier manuscript. Potentially, the Winchester Troper is a great treasure because it is the largest single source of early practical polyphony. In reality, it is a great tragedy since the pitches for the 160 to 170 pieces for two voices cannot be deciphered. At the present stage of research, we cannot even give a vague and general description of the polyphonic repertory because we have insufficient knowledge of the style of early Western part-music and, I fear, we are far from knowing how and when human beings came to produce something upon which we are willing to bestow the lofty term 'polyphony'.

The next earliest group of sources for practical polyphony was compiled during the twelfth century in Aquitaine, in the southern part of what now is France (see Fuller and Gillingham). The part-songs, all of them for two voices, in these sources vary rather widely in style. At one extreme are a few pieces in strictly pitch-against-pitch style; at the opposite end of the spectrum are several pieces in which one voice has far fewer pitches than the other, and it seems safe to assume that the former sustained its pitches while the other sang melismas of varying lengths. In still other compositions, these two styles occur side by side. Most of the texts are religious poems; very few of them are likely to have been sung during the Mass or the Office so that we do not know their precise function in medieval culture. Where its date of origin and polyphonic repertory are concerned, the Codex Calixtinus, now in Santiago de Compostela but not necessarily compiled in that city, may be seen as belonging to that group (see López-Calo). Most of its texts explicitly honour the Apostle James, and several of them were intended to perform a specific liturgical function in the Mass or the Office. It shares two specific pieces and its polyphonic styles with the Aquitanian collections. As well as many monophonic pieces, these manuscripts contain close to a hundred compositions for two voices. In addition, they have the enormous advantage of yielding multiple versions for some twenty complete pieces.

Although these continental sources are approximately a century more recent than the Winchester Tropers, their notation still leaves much to be desired. For some pieces we know which neumes in the manuscript represent simultaneously sounding pitches, but we do not know their precise level because the neumes are imprecisely heighted. For other pieces, the scribes indicated the level very precisely, but the vertical alignment of the neumes is imprecise so that we cannot figure out which pitches were sounded against one another. In fact, we have only a few compositions that can accurately be transcribed in their entirety, while substantial passages of many other pieces are notated with sufficient precision to allow meaningful transcription.

Putting together all the information we can glean from these transcribable passages, we can form a surprisingly good, although not complete, picture of the repertory in general. The most pervasive feature may well be the obvious preference for contrary motion. In textbook discussions on early polyphony, much attention is given to parallel and oblique motion, but little is said about the many instances in which one voice remains stationary while the other moves. Due to our incomplete knowledge, it would be unwise to present statistics of the ways in which the voices behave towards one another. Yet I can safely say that contrary motion by far outnumbers the combined total of the other three options. On the other hand, I would not want to guess which of the other three occurs most frequently.

In most pitch-against-pitch passages, the voices move in essentially the same range and cross each other frequently so that the labels 'higher' and 'lower' are meaningless unless they merely refer to the staff a given voice occupies in the notational system. In sustained-pitch passages, the slower moving voice tends to stay below its partner, but when it comes near the summit of its range, it may briefly ascend above the faster moving one,

Almost invariably, a composition starts and ends on an octave, a fifth, or a unison, regardless of whether it is primarily in sustained-pitch or pitch-against-pitch style. The same holds true for major subdivisions of longer compositions, such as individual strophes of sequences. Again, it would be unwise to give precise numbers of the frequency with which specific chords occur, but one can say that throughout a composition, the octave, the unison, and the fifth are the preferred chords. Other chords occur, at least in part, because there does not seem to have been any rule or tradition against using them. Some of them occur because a certain chord can perform a certain function in a certain situation, although there do not seem to have been any hard and fast rules as to how and when a specific chord was to be used. For example, the seventh and especially the second often perform a 'harmonic' function at a cadence; but they also occur in other situations. The third occurs very frequently as a natural 'passing' tone when the voices move from a fifth to a unison and vice versa. Thus there are numerous instances in which one voice sings five contiguous pitches, for example *defga*, while the other sings the same pitches in reverse order, *agfed*, yielding the chord sequence fifth, third, unison, third, fifth. It must be stressed that the fourth is not the equal of the fifth, the unison, and the octave: it clearly is not the equal of the third in harmonic function; it is often unclear whether its occurrence is prompted by melodic or by harmonic considerations; and it is difficult to determine whether it occurs as frequently as the third.

For some of the compositions we know that one voice is earlier than the other. For instance, one of the Aquitanian sources contains a setting of the well-known Easter sequence *Victime paschali laudes*. We know not only that its lower voice is much earlier than the Aquitanian collections, but it also seems to have been conceived for monophonic performance. A similar situation pertains to the melody used by Notker of St Gall for his poem 'Sancti spiritus adsit nobis gratia'. In either case, the lower voice not only occurs as a monophonic tune in many other sources, but it also has all the melodic characteristics of its genre, while the upper voice differs considerably from the style of monophonic song in general. Someone made up a new tune to be sung simultaneously with a melody that had been in existence for decades.

The two-part setting of the text 'Benedicamus domino' (ex.1) presents a diametrically opposed situation. Neither voice occurs anywhere else, and neither voice makes much sense as a monophonic tune. The two voices together, however, have many of the characteristics found in the decipherable pitch-against-pitch music of this period. Most of our textbooks would have us believe that medieval composers were not capable of conceiving two voices simultaneously. We may not be able to reconstruct the precise sequence of events for the origin of this specific piece, but it is difficult to imagine that either voice was composed without any conception of what was going to be sung simultaneously. There is no question in my mind that in addition to producing successively composed pieces, such as the *Victime paschali laudes*, medieval singers were perfectly capable of inventing two voices simultaneously.

This evaluation leads to some intriguing questions which we should pose even though they cannot be answered here and now, if they ever can be. Was a simultaneously composed piece literally 'written' by someone with a pen in his hand or is it a remembered improvisation, that is, a piece slowly built up in the course of one or more practice sessions? If it originated by the latter procedure, was it invented by one or by two people? It is relatively easy to imagine how one person might invent two voices without being able to write them down. We only need to

Ex.1

Anonymous two-part setting of 'Benedicamus domino'.
The vertical lines in the upper voice represent short slanting lines in the manuscript; they have been interpreted as reflecting the position of the syllables '[Be]nedicamus do[mino]'

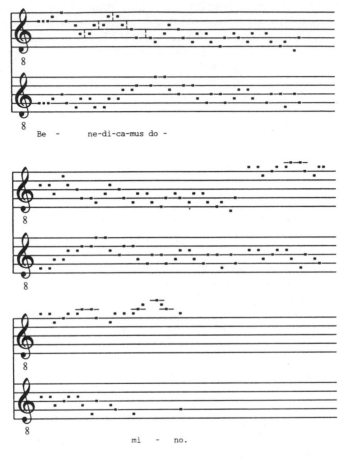

Paris, Bibliothèque Nationale, Latin 3719, f.46

admit that medieval singers who were experienced in performing two-part music, were as capable as we are to 'hear' two voices without producing any audible sounds. Simultaneous composition by two people may seem strange at first glance, but even a passing acquaintance with the 'jam' sessions of jazz musicians, or with the composition of four-part settings for the American barbershop quartet, should counteract whatever prejudice we may have against simultaneous invention by two or more musicians acquainted with the style concerned.

When considering the possibilities and implications of notationless composition by more than one participant, we cannot ignore the sequential patterns that occur in the practical compositions. Most of these patterns are descending; some cover an entire octave but most descend only a third, a fourth, or a fifth. A given pattern may comprise only two pitches in each voice, and it may include as many as half-a-dozen pitches. If my present evaluation is correct, most are either strictly or essentially in pitch-against-pitch style, but some involve sustained pitches of moderate length. In most cases, moreover, both voices are involved in the sequential movement. Sequential patterns may be the most obvious, but they are not the only stock phrases, formulae, or clichés for two voices to be found in the extant music. As anthropological research has shown, stock phrases and formulae are among the most common elements of epics in scriptless cultures.

At this point, we must face up to what may well be our greatest problem in exploring the history of Western polyphony. We know that many more medieval manuscripts were intentionally or accidentally destroyed than were preserved.

Ex. 2

Thus, it is possible, perhaps even probable, that more collections of polyphony have been lost than have come down to us. In the first two centuries of our millennium there must have been a large number of people who could sing. We know that there were even many 'professional' singers, now generally referred to as cantors and members of the *schola* in cathedrals and abbeys. We do not know how many of these singers could read music, but it is likely that for most of them it was much easier to learn a piece by hearing it performed than by laboriously deciphering it from one of the very few music books that existed. For that reason it is quite possible, perhaps even probable, that far fewer part-songs were ever written down than were performed. All in all, we can be fairly certain that we do not have all the polyphonic pieces that once existed, but we still have no idea whether the decipherable extant music represents all the styles that once were in existence. Our uncertainty on the last issue has risky consequences. On the basis of music presumed lost, we can defend any theory we choose to espouse. Conversely, we may reach woefully incomplete evaluations if we take for granted the fact that the extant music adequately represents all there once was.

The setting of 'Benedicamus domino' (ex. 1) almost cries out for some brief remarks about duration in early Western part songs. For a while, it was rather widely accepted that pitches in a polyphonic piece must have been precisely measured so as to enable the performers to stay together. However, it is far from certain that medieval singers wanted to 'stay together' in our meaning of that term. In this respect, there may have been considerable differences of execution between passages with sustained pitches and those in pitch-against-pitch style. I am afraid that we will never be able to reconstruct the medieval performance of a piece in the former style, but we may be in a slightly better position for a piece like ex. 1 because the two voices are likely to have moved in precisely or at least approximately simultaneous motion. The medieval neumes almost certainly were developed for the notation of Gregorian chant. It now is fairly well accepted that duration in chant was not precisely measured and that double or triple notes (that is, two or three successive notes at the same level over one syllable) represent pitches that were held longer than pitches represented by single notes (see van der Werf). Our ex. 1 comprises more double notes than any other piece of similar size. In order to draw attention to them, ex. 2 restates the second staff of ex. 1 so that single and double notes have been replaced by modern notes in a ratio of 1:2. We have no reason to assume that all notes in a medieval manuscript represent pitches that were precisely measured and exactly equal in duration but in the piece under scrutiny it is probable that they represent pitches of more or less equal duration. In this specific case, the almost regular alternation of single and double notes extends over a longer passage than is typical for the repertory as a whole, but it is not the only piece in which double notes occur, suggesting that some pitches were held more or less twice as long as those of average duration. I must stress, however, that we know little about the degree of more or less equal, more or less double, and average duration.

For a number of reasons, researchers and authors of textbooks have paid much less attention to the music briefly described above than to the polyphony of the thirteenth century. Sarah Ann Fuller's dissertation (1970), easily the best and most extensive study of the Aquitanian polyphony, has been virtually ignored. Even Peter Wagner's transcriptions from the Codex Calixtinus (1931) have not had much impact. This one-sided research has resulted not only in inadequate discussions of polyphony from before 1200, but also in some serious distortions of early thirteenth-century polyphony. Until recently, moreover, belief in the omnipresence of modal rhythm was a major characteristic of scholars working on the so-called Notre Dame polyphony. This belief is now waning, and soon it will be accepted that, for example, there is considerably less difference between the Aquitanian versus and the Notre Dame conductus than is suggested by the unfortunate distinction in terms. We also cannot avoid concluding that, in general, thirteenth-century passages in sustained-pitch style were not intended to be performed in modal rhythm. A consequence of this change of heart will be the realization that there is little difference between twelfth- and thirteenth-century passages in that style. We may also find that almost the only innovation in the discant (that is the almost-note-against-note) style is a pervasive alternation of long and short durational units. However, even this alternation was not as systematic and rigorous as our textbook discussions of modal rhythm suggest. Moreover, as ex. 2 and similar passages in other pieces show, alternation of long and short units was not unknown to musicians of the eleventh and twelfth centuries.

We still need to examine whether the attitude towards the fourth as a chord underwent a change, albeit a temporary one, in the late twelfth or early thirteenth century. But future comparison of medieval polyphony, in general, may well reveal that reliance upon notation in the compositional process is the most important new characteristic of the clausulae, motets, and discant passages attributed to the

'Notre Dame School'. This change from improvising to writing music is likely to have been a slow and gradual one; it probably started well before the thirteenth century. Nevertheless, it was a momentous evolution in the history of Western music, and thirteenth-century musicians deserve great credit for their contributions in this area. If that innovation had occurred much later, or if it had progressed even more slowly, such great composers as Guillaume Dufay and Josquin Desprez might not have been able to conceive their most beautiful creations.

The data and observations in this article, as well as exx. 1 and 2, are taken from my forthcoming book The oldest extant part music and the origin of Western polyphony (Rochester, NY, 1992).

Select bibliography

S. A. FULLER, 'Aquitanian polyphony of the eleventh and twelfth centuries' (Ph.D. diss., University of California at Berkeley, 1970)
B. GILLINGHAM, *Saint-Martial polyphony*, in *Musicological Studies*, xliv (Henryville, 1984)
A. HOLSCHNEIDER, *Die Organa von Winchester: Studien zum ältesten Repertoire polyphoner Musik* (Hildesheim, 1968)
J. LÓPEZ-CALO, *La música medieval en Galicia* (La Coruña, 1982)
H. VAN DER WERF, *The emergence of Gregorian chant: a comparative study of Ambrosian, Roman and Gregorian chant* (Rochester, NY, 1983), pp.22–42
P. WAGNER, *Die Gesänge der Jacobusliturgie zu Santiago de Compostel* (Freiburg, 1931)

18 The late-medieval motet

Margaret Bent

'A piece of music in several parts with words' is as precise a definition of the motet as will serve from the thirteenth to the late sixteenth century and beyond. This is actually very close to one of the earliest descriptions we have, that of the late thirteenth-century theorist Johannes de Grocheio. He attached the motet to the learned, who cultivate and appreciate subtle art, and removed it from the vulgar, who neither like nor understand it. He thereby added the dimension of ingenuity that survives at least through the sixteenth century, when it calls forth the finest-wrought imitative contrapuntal art of the polyphonic *a cappella* tradition. To concur with Besseler's astonishingly dismissive proposition that the motet was 'not intended for aesthetic effect but for the faithful while they watch and pray', or to evade the motet's unfashionably subtle sophistries, is both to align ourselves with Grocheio's vulgarians and to ignore the aesthetic power of richly clever combinations of symbol, number, and allusion.

The motet was born in the thirteenth century out of the more tightly measured discant sections of organum, by the addition to their upper part(s) of words unrelated or newly related to the parent composition. Not only did the discant (clausula) sections differ in musical style from the melismatic organum that surrounded them; the added words were often different in language (French) and subject matter (secular love) from the sacred Latin chants on which they were built, and where there were two or more texts, different from each other.

OAMM nos.43–5 illustrate how whole families of related and mutually referential compositions were spawned. No.43 shows the clausula motet embedded in the organum; the tenor is organized in repeating rhythmic groups, and the two added parts have the same text. The same tenor, identically arranged, becomes the basis for textually and musically new upper parts in no.44 (the texts of which take a homiletic and critical stance that became common in the fourteenth century), and no.45, now first with an amorous French text coupled with a new Latin text that refers back elliptically to the 'orphan' idea of the parent organum from which it is now itself orphaned, *Non vos relinquam orphanos*, and then a version with two amorous French texts that in turn gives newly subverted meaning to the original tenor text 'and your heart shall rejoice'.

Although from the beginning rooted in sacred material, satirical, social, amorous, exegetical and topical themes soon outweighed sacred subjects. Celebratory pieces predominate in Italy, sacred subjects in England. By the sixteenth century, motets were more often sacred than secular. Starting with diversity of texture, contrasting lines and different texts, motets came to have homogeneously imitative textures with all parts singing the same text.

The motet provided for the first time a vehicle that could present different musical, textual and symbolic ideas truly simultaneously. It wraps counterpointed texts and music artfully together for aural, visual, numerical, symbolic and other forms of intellectual contemplation that go beyond the real time needed for musical performance. The contrasting musical time-planes of the motet's simultaneously projected rhythmic hierarchies are sometimes paralleled in the textual combination of contemporary events and people with those of antiquity, and further reflected in the expanded fourteenth-century notational system. Spatially, some texts combine terrestrial place with celestial space, just as the proportioned monochord is grandly mirrored in the music of the spheres.

The early fourteenth century developed new notational levels which opened up in different ways for France, England and Italy a spectrum of note shapes and values from long to short, and corresponding principles of organization that were hitherto inconceivable. The extended potential of the notation was fully realized in motets such as those exemplified in *OAMM* nos. 58–60. Ideas of diversity (*varietas*) were played out most conspicuously in the arena of rhythm, which is to say, number. Art further consisted in devising clever (and often cleverly concealed) symbolic relationships (both verbally allusive and numerically musical) between the tenor and the parts added to it. One motettish Credo boldly explores a full range of mensural and proportional permutations; its tenor is punningly crafted from two segments of a chant both with the words 'all time' (*Omni tempore*). The internationally-disseminated sound of ancient and contemporary musicians is celebrated in a group of fourteenth-century motets, two of which have the same tenor text, 'their sound is gone out into all lands', while another related piece develops for its singers the missionary message of the Apocalypse, further sealing its links to the 'parent' motet in shared overall lengths of 144 breves. The added texts may prescribe a unique canonic or proportional performance of the cryptic tenor (for example, 'twice by hemiola' for the 9:6:4 proportion; 'precursor' to signal both John the Baptist as the forerunner of Christ and the canonic *dux* of the tenor going ahead); numerical references – to twelve Zodiac signs, twelve musicians, seven stars, seven names – may be closely mirrored in local and long-term aspects of musical design.

While a saint petitioned in the text could determine the choice of a liturgical tenor, there are also incongruous or even blasphemous juxtapositions: *eros* and *caritas* are blended in amorous counterpoint over the Song of Songs tenor *Quia amore langueo* ('For I am sick from love') in Machaut's motet no. 14. Alliteration and puns often yoke texts together: *Ade finit perpete, Ade finite misere, A definement d'este* (*PMFC* xv/4); *Ianuam quam clauserat, Iacintus in saltibus/Iacet granum* (*PMFC* xv/1). An English motet combines a Latin text on St Lawrence with a French song about cuckoldry (*Triumphat hodie, Trop est fol: PMFC* xv/17).

The possibilities for clever treatment of old and new material, both verbal and musical, go well beyond that most commonly celebrated in the primary dimension of cleverness known to us as isorhythm. Coined early this century to denote the results of the dominant organizing principle for melodic and rhythmic restatements, the term came to be used synonymously with fourteenth-century motet composition, particularly when the upper parts also had rhythmic repeats, or when the tenor was repeated at increasing speeds. Since the criteria for 'isorhythm' are premised on sameness of results rather than sameness of notation, the net fails to catch all the fish.

Whether proportional restatements result in the same or different rhythms will depend on the kind of proportion used, any implied mensural change associated with that proportion, whether the tenor is notated in the values of its first or last statement, and the range of note values selected. Whether mensural restatements

Ex. 1

Tenor patterns in *Inter densas* (*a* = alteration, usually double a note's normal length preceding one of the next higher value)

result in different rhythms will depend on opportunities contrived for alteration and imperfection. If any of the permutations of twos and threes differ, and especially if values smaller than the breve are introduced, a single notated segment can yield spectacularly differing results from the ground rules that govern their evaluation, as in ex. 1 (*Inter densas*), a beautiful encapsulation of diversity within identity.

Color (melodic) and *talea* (rhythmic) repetitions can always be described in terms of a proportional relationship or of a mensural re-reading. If the results *are* identical, it may not be possible to distinguish their causes. These categories of proportional and mensural adjustment to a tenor have exact parallels in the use of red notation to achieve either proportional or mensural change of notated values, likewise not always distinguishable. Their presence side by side elegantly extends the analogy between motet composition and notational expansion.

Treatises on arithmetic and on music, following Boethius, distinguish various proportional relationships. The list is headed by proportion of equality, which results in non-reducing successive tenor statements. Other relevant proportions are arithmetic (3:2:1), geometric (9:6:4), harmonic (6:4:3), and the proportion of extreme and mean ratio or Golden Section (0.618). These different proportions have different mensural consequences which are sometimes in practice displayed and sometimes camouflaged; all are used.

To see equality as the first of a series of proportional possibilities softens Ursula Günther's distinction between non-reducing (unipartite) and reducing (bipartite) motets. Categories of mensuration and proportion permit finer distinctions within isorhythm, and extend the spectrum of which isorhythm can now be viewed as an artificially segregated portion. The starting point is an isomorphically notated tenor, subjected to one or more kinds of manipulation; these further include retrograde, inversion, canon, and other operations.

Having now suggested that the qualifying technical criteria for the late-medieval motet are more broadly-based than modern scholarship has sometimes allowed, what are we to make of Besseler's disqualification of the grand four-part motet *Ave regina celorum* in which Dufay embedded a personal petition and which he wished to have sung on his deathbed? Or of Harrison's exclusion of an equally ambitious, long, four-part, five-section St Katherine motet *Rota versatilis*, composed in England 150 years earlier? Besseler's Dufay edition opens with motets as Volume I. But we have to go to Volume V ('Minor Liturgical Compositions') for the *Ave regina celorum*, presumably because it uses a liturgical text and is not isorhythmic. Thus liturgical definition for a *text* can exclude a piece while liturgical definition for a *tenor* melody can qualify it. These criteria make no sense for the Italian motet repertory, where chant tenors are the exception; their tenors were free accompanying voices added to a primary upper-voice duet. They apply even less to the English repertory, where a basis in chant was a secondary consideration, and where other building methods were applied to large-scale compositions. One of these techniques was *rondellus*, in which voices exchanged material in succeeding, paired sections. *Rota versatilis* is constructed in this way, with proportioned and mensurally varied sections but without common thematic material. Harrison discounted it, while including a similar *rondellus* (*Salve cleri speculum/Sospitati*) that happens to use a chant tenor, linked alliteratively and by subject to the upper-voice text. Our primary standard for the fourteenth-century motet has been French and isorhythmic. Harrison required of a motet either two or more different texts and/or a pre-existent cantus firmus. Hence, the new identification of a chant or of a liturgical placement for a text could affect the status of a piece as a motet for reasons that do not touch its musical substance or structure.

By the fifteenth century, the two upper parts often did have the same text. But a thirteenth-century precedent for a single text exists already in *OAMM* no.43, and is common for Italian and English motets in the fourteenth century. The motets of Ciconia and Dufay blend French and Italian techniques, having sometimes one, sometimes two texts, pre-existing or newly written. A setting of the same text, let us say *Ave regina* or *Salve regina*, might be labelled a motet if set by Josquin, an antiphon as edited by Harrison from the English Eton Choirbook, a 'minor liturgical composition' in Besseler's Dufay edition, and a chant setting or cantilena by other editors. Yet the manuscripts do not make these distinctions, and we should rather see the increasing use of liturgical texts in fifteenth-century motets (by Dunstable, for example, whose motets have not been disqualified) as an extension of a tradition that had some continuity in England, and not as a new departure. Dufay's song-like setting of Petrarch's Italian canzona 'Vergene bella' is found alongside early fifteenth-century motets that also include civic and sacred pieces; the surviving index of a lost manuscript of 1376 includes chaces and Mass Ordinaries under the heading motets. The evidence suggests that genre boundaries were broader than we have allowed them to become.

So long as modern scholarship has defined the motet as French, isorhythmic, chant-tenor-based, and with different upper-voice texts, border disputes hardly arose. Ludwig and Besseler were fully occupied with charting the body of complete, relatively cleanly transmitted French motets. It was left to the next generations to discover and decipher the much more fragmentary English and Italian repertories – which are still only partly represend in *PMFC*. Distinctively English and Italian motets circulated alongside French pieces, prompting us to investigate influence in both directions. The French motet is normally built from the tenor up; the English, often, from the middle out; the Italian, from the top down. Criteria derived loosely from the motet's beginnings did not necessarily survive as consistent or universal features through even a generation of travel and creative development. We should set aside German historiographical models of the 1920s and redraw the boundaries more broadly, in accordance with – no doubt equally conditioned – late twentieth-century correctives. Marginalized, hybrid, minority and unusual pieces return to centre-stage and challenge some of the traditional confining and tidy definitions.

Tinctoris, writing in the 1470s, arranged musical forms in a hierarchy headed by the Mass (which had not existed as a musically unified cyclic form a century – or even half a century – earlier), followed by the motet and then by the cantilena. His criterion was *varietas* (demonstrated in quantity, perfection, proportion, conjunction, syncopes, imitations, rests, ornamentation), of which devices it was fitting for a Mass to have more than a motet, a motet more than a song. At the very end of an era dominated by techniques of tenor repetition, the weight of responsibility borne by the motet as the primary outlet for musical ingenuity and cleverness of combination had shifted to the large-scale Mass cycle, just as it later shifted to the contrapuntal ricercar-fantasia and the fugue, and even later to the symphony and string quartet. Works such as Josquin's large six-part motets with canonic scaffolding have venerable precedents in late-medieval motets, as do other large proportioned motet structures even after the abandonment of the literal repetitions associated with isorhythm. To blend isorhythm into a broader view of motet traditions is to bring out continuities where they have been pushed aside.

Select bibliography

U. GÜNTHER, 'The fourteenth-century motet and its development', *Musica Disciplina*, xii (1958), pp.27–58

F. LL. HARRISON, *Music in medieval Britain*, 2nd edn (London, 1963)

W. T. MARROCCO and N. SANDON (eds), *Oxford Anthology of Music: Medieval music* (Oxford, 1977) = *OAMM*

Polyphonic Music of the Fourteenth Century i, v, xv = *PMFC*

E. H. SANDERS, 'Motet' I, *New Grove*; and 'The medieval motet', in W. Arlt (ed.), *Gattungen der Musik in Einzeldarstellungen: Gedenkschrift für Leo Schrade*, i (Berne and Munich, 1973), pp.497–573

G. DE VAN and H. BESSELER (eds.), *G. Dufay: Opera omnia, Corpus Mensurabilis Musicae* i/1-6 (1947–9, 1951–66)

19 Mass polyphony

Philip T. Jackson

It may seem glib to say so, but the growth of polyphonic music for the Mass can be seen as a direct reflection of the ambitious building programmes in the great European cathedrals. In the entire history of European culture there are few projects as grand as the one credited to Leoninus, the creation of a relatively unified cycle of two-voice polyphony on Mass and Office chants across the entire church year. Another such project, confined to Mass chants, arose around the middle of the fifteenth-century and may even be the work of Dufay; the most famous later cycles are those in Isaac's *Choralis Constantinus* and Byrd's *Gradualia*. All are breathtaking in their ambition.

In these, the settings were of Mass Proper movements, which were different for each major feast: Introit, Gradual, Alleluia (or Tract), Sequence, Offertory and Communion. What we normally think of as the polyphonic Mass is a setting of the five Ordinary movements: Kyrie, Gloria, Credo, Sanctus, and Agnus Dei. These had generally much simpler chant and therefore offered a less obvious basis for a grand conception, which may help to explain why the idea of a group of stylistically coherent settings grew so much more slowly. Although there are settings of individual movements from the earliest days of Western polyphony, it was not until the fourteenth century that the notion of a cycle arose.

Given the sparsity of sources, it is hard to trace the early history of the five-movement Ordinary cycle with any confidence. Among the apparent cycles from the fourteenth century, there is now only one that has the unified scoring, style and voice-ranges that suggest conception as a unit: Machaut's four-voice *Messe de Nostre Dame*, perhaps composed soon after 1360. Here the Kyrie, Sanctus, Agnus Dei and Ite Missa Est are based on their respective chants in isorhythm; the Gloria and Credo are bound to no chant, but move through their long texts quickly and in simultaneous style. In one of the ironies of music history, there is no evidence that Machaut's unparalleled work had any direct influence on future developments, though it is thought possible that a copy came into the hands of Leonel Power who composed a very differently constituted cycle some sixty years later.

In the first half of the fifteenth century there are many examples of paired Mass movements (Gloria-Credo; Sanctus-Agnus); and there are many isolated settings. But history tends to focus on the relatively few complete cycles: however much one is aware of the Darwinian assumptions involved, it is hard to resist the knowledge that these led to the wonderful stream of cycles that began with Dufay, Domarto and Okeghem around 1450 and continued through Josquin and Obrecht to the cycles that in so many ways dominate the music of the entire sixteenth century.

Several kinds of unification technique appear in these cycles from the 1420s by composers including Arnold de Lantins, Dufay, and Grossin on the continent as well as Power and perhaps Dunstable in England. They include elements of motto-opening, tenors in similar style, possible parody, repeated material, and so on. But it looks as though the most decisive influence on the future was in the English cycles that used the same chant in the tenor through all movements, often including consistent 'motto' openings and techniques borrowed from the isorhythmic motet. All are present in the four grand four-voice cycles that crown the career of Guillaume Dufay (d. 1474). Too little is yet known about the musical chronology of the years around 1450 that saw this first coherent flowering of the cyclic Mass. But it is notable that two of Dufay's late Masses are based on secular songs. One of them, the *L'homme armé* Mass, may be the first of an astonishing series of interrelated works on the same tune; at least twenty-five from the fifteenth century and fifteen from the next (including two by Palestrina).

Okeghem based five of his fourteen Masses on chansons, one of them being *L'homme armé*. Factors that gave rise to his reputation as founder of the Franco-Flemish School are his novel non-imitative texture with its emphasis on accelerating 'drives to the cadence' and the complexity of his settings. His *Missa prolationum* has achieved fame as the first Mass to be based wholly on canonic writing. In his *Missa cujusvis toni*, he achieved a rare catholicon, a piece designed for performance in any of the four authentic modes.

The next generation of composers who, with Okeghem, dominated the second half of the fifteenth century and the beginning of the sixteenth included an extraordinary number of distinguished composers of Masses: Josquin Desprez, Jacob Obrecht, Pierre de La Rue, Jean Mouton, Loyset Compère, Heinrich Isaac and Antoine Brumel. Their combined works represent a major peak in Mass history. Josquin clearly set the standard for his generation: no fewer than three books of his Masses were published by Petrucci between 1504 and 1514. There are several types of Masses among his works: cantus firmus or tenor, canonic, imitative paraphrase, an early prototype of the parody Mass, and *soggetto cavato dalle parole* (*Missa Hercules dux Ferrariae*) where he derives the subject by matching the vowels of the title with those of the solmization syllables (*Ut re mi fa sol la*). What distinguished the new parody Mass from the older cantus firmus Mass was the borrowing of not just a melody but sections of the model's polyphonic web which could be used at various junctures in a new Mass to bring it unity and cohesion. The imitative parody Mass gradually replaced the tenor Mass to become the leading Mass-type of the sixteenth century.

Few important composers of the Ordinary can be identified in fifteenth-century Germany. A notable exception is Heinrich Isaac, who is best known today for his monumental *Choralis Constantinus*, a series of Proper settings so vast in scope that it would be matched only once in music history, by William Byrd in his *Gradualia*, printed in 1605–7.

In Italy such foreign composers as Willaert and Morales dominated the musical scene until about 1550 when native Italians gradually began to replace them as the leading musical force on the peninsula. Soon their Masses and other sacred music became drastically affected by the Council of Trent. It named Carlo Borromeo to head a Commission of Cardinals in 1562 to purify church music by making the text intelligible, *a cappella* if possible, and free of secular influences, in particular, the chansons and madrigals which had served as sources for tenor and parody Masses.

The reformed style, as established by Vincenzo Ruffo, Palestrina, and others, resembled the French Mass style from the first half of the sixteenth century with its emphasis on homophonic writing mixed with simple rather than more sophisticated polyphony. The Borromean mandates made most previous music obsolete; composers and publishers rushed to replace it with musical settings of all sacred texts, the Ordinary included, in the new intelligible style. (The notion of Palestrina's nineteenth-century biographer Giuseppe Baini that his *Missa Papae Marcelli* 'saved' Catholic church music single-handedly has long been rejected.) An indication of the amount of new music can be seen in the numbers of Masses printed in Italy before and after 1570. Prior to that date, only 200 Masses had been published in Italy; between 1570 and 1610, over 750 new Masses appeared in print there. With few exceptions, almost all of them were written by the now dominant Italians.

Over 100 of those Masses were Ordinary settings by Palestrina. As one of the last great masters of the Renaissance Mass, his output stands comparison with Josquin's. He reveals his conservative roots by his five canonic and seven tenor Masses more typical of the first decades of the century. Thirty-five Masses are paraphrase works, with the largest group of fifty-one being parody works, most often based on his own motets or works by composers with Roman connections before 1550. Palestrina's important pupils, Victoria, Soriano, and Giovanelli, continued his style past 1600. While Orlande de Lassus wrote fifty-three Masses, they are less admired today than his motets and secular works.

Select bibliography

D. FALLOWS, *Dufay* (London, 1982)

P. GOSSETT, 'Techniques of unification in early cyclic Masses and Mass pairs', *Journal of the American Musicological Society*, xix (1966), pp.205–31

R. HOPPIN, *Medieval Music* (New York, 1978)

L. LOCKWOOD, *The Counter-Reformation and the Masses of Vincenzo Ruffo* (Venice, 1970); 'Aspects of the *L'homme armé* tradition', *Proceedings of the Royal Musical Association*, c (1973–4), pp.97–122; and 'On parody as term and concept in 16th-century music' in *Aspects of medieval and Renaissance Music: a birthday offering to Gustave Reese* (New York, 1966), pp.560–75

E. SPARKS, *Cantus firmus in Mass and motet, 1420–1520* (Berkeley & Los Angeles, 1963)

H. STÄBLEIN-HARDER, *Fourteenth-century Mass music in France* (1962)

R. STROHM, 'Einheit und Funktion früher Messzyklen', in *Festschrift Rudolf Bockholdt* (Pfaffenhofen, 1990), pp.141–60; and *The rise of European music, 1380–1500* (forthcoming)

R. TARUSKIN, 'Antoine Busnoys and the *L'homme armé* tradition', *Journal of the American Musicological Society* xxxiv (1986), pp.255–93

P. WAGNER, *Geschichte der Messe, I: bis 1600* (Leipzig, 1913; repr. 1963)

20 Polyphonic song

David Fallows

Polyphonic songs that were through-composed or in plain strophic form were extremely rare between about 1300 and the early sixteenth century. Composers preferred to use a relatively small number of fixed forms, all with a fairly intricate internal design. They are the dominant feature of the courtly song traditions of the fourteenth and fifteenth centuries; and they are what makes these songs fundamentally different from anything before or after in European song. One early writer states that Philippe de Vitry soon after 1300 was the first composer to cultivate them extensively; but none of his *forme-fixe* works has been identified. Their earliest coherent appearance comes just a little later in the works of Guillaume de Machaut.

Of these, the ballade had the longest roots, because it was essentially just an *AAB* form, common in the music of the troubadour generation as well as many earlier poets back to classical antiquity. But in the *forme-fixe* generation it had two further characteristics: a musical 'rhyme' between middle and end (thus *AArBr*); and three stanzas. Quite often the later stanzas do not now survive; but the available poetic sources consistently give three stanzas, sometimes followed by an *envoi* (a shorter final dedication stanza, characteristically naming the dedicatee and applied to the last section of the music). After Machaut (who composed forty-two ballades), the form was increasingly used to mark grand public occasions; but by the middle of the fifteenth century it had all but disappeared from the French musical tradition, though it lived on in English and German music.

Of all the *formes fixes*, the rondeau has the most astonishing career, since by the fifteenth century it had come almost entirely to dominate the French song tradition, accounting for some eighty per cent of the repertory, including not only most of the known songs of Dufay and Okeghem but also virtually everything of Binchois and Hayne van Ghizeghem. It was the strictest of these forms and remained a vital part of musical life for some 200 years. Like sonata form (which has a similar career), it derives its strength mainly from an underlying simplicity that gives the aural effect of inevitability. The line-numbering in most modern editions tends to hide the pattern, which is most easily seen from a full rondeau text by Machaut:

I	A	*Ce qui soustient moy, m'onneur et ma vie*
	B	*Aveuc Amours, c'estes vous, douce dame.*
II	a	*Long, pres, toudis serez, quoi que nulz die.*
	A	*Ce qui soustient moy, m'onneur et ma vie.*
III	a	*Et quant je vif par vous, douce anemie,*
	b	*Qu'ains mieus que moy, bien dire doy, par m'ame:*
IV	A	*Ce qui soustient moy, m'onneur et ma vie*
	B	*Aveuc Amours, c'estes vous, douce dame.*

In this diagram, *A* and *B* represent the two halves of the music; *a* and *b* have the same music but different text. Essentially there are four two-line stanzas here: the first and last are identical; the third is musically identical, though with new text; and the second is more complicated in that it incorporates the first half of the refrain stanza. (In the fifteenth century the stanzas are usually of four or five lines, but the principle is the same). The resulting musical design *abaaabab* offers an elegant irregularity to the ear. By witholding the *b* section for so long after its first statement, it creates a mounting musical tension, aided by the half-close at the end of *a* and by the habit of putting a particularly memorable gesture at the beginning of the *b* section: the eventual return of *b* (at III*b*, and remarkably often close to the Golden Section of the work) thereby often creates a sense of momentum that carries the ear through to the end of the last stanza.

Machaut's poem shows two further characteristic devices of the rondeau. Because *A* has no main verb (it comes only at 'c'estes' in the next line), it must in stanza II derive its main verb from the preceding line, adding to the coherence of the pattern. And the syntax of stanza III leads directly in to stanza IV, so the returning refrain acts as a kind of motto for the whole song. If those few comments hint at the ways in which the form works, they perhaps also stress that a performance needs to begin from a clear view of the four-stanza pattern.

By contrast with this, the virelai has a much looser form and a wider distribution. It appears in Italian as the ballata, in Spanish as the cançion and the villancico, and in English as the carol. Its clearest ancestry is in the monophonic thirteenth-century Gallo-Portuguese *Cantigas de Santa María*. In all of these, the main principle is that the song begins and ends with a refrain, which can also come between the stanzas. A subsidiary principle is that the stanza (related formally to the ballade stanza) ends with the music of the refrain. So the form is generally *AbbaA bbaA*, etc. Machaut has three-stanza virelais, but otherwise the number is not at all fixed: there are many with two stanzas; the most common of all is a single stanza (sometimes called the bergerette in France); while in the English fifteenth-century carol and the Italian frottola of the years around 1500 there can be any number of stanzas.

The other forms used in the polyphonic song of the fourteenth and fifteenth centuries are less widespread and less rigid, apart from the fourteenth-century Italian *madrigale* (*aab, aabb,* or *aaabb*), the related sonnet (*aabb*) and, in late fifteenth-century Italy, the *strambotto* (8 lines with music: *ababababab*).

Most of this music sets lyric texts in a relatively bland courtly-love mode (like the Machaut example shown above), though there are isolated songs in a more Rabelaisian mood. Generally the settings are in three voices, even though composers increasingly prefer the richness of four voices or more for their motets and Mass music, which is to say that there is a certain emphasis on re-straint and refinement. Moreover, it is usually possible to fit the music of a song onto a single page, although the sounding length can vary from one to seven minutes.

Those longest examples come particularly at two moments in history, and both those moments show pieces that seem to collapse under their own weight. One was at the end of the fourteenth century, when the songs were additionally often very complex, a situation resolved by the return to simplicity in the early works of Dufay and Binchois. The other occasion was in the 1470–80s, particularly with the works of Compère and Agricola: this time the reaction was to abandon the *forme-fixe* tradition in French music. Although the principle was to continue for a few more years in the Spanish villancico and the Italian frottola, again with simpler and briefer forms, the idea had run its course.

The future lay in several different directions, all of which reflect composed polyphony reaching out to a far wider audience, not only in terms of listeners and amateurs able to purchase the music-books, but also in terms of performers. Where the fifteenth-century chansonniers presuppose a highly skilled and probably professional group of performers, every detail of the notation and texting in the sixteenth-century sources is directed towards accessibility to musicians at many different levels.

Of these new genres the madrigal now seems the most important, if one takes the word to denote a through-composed song genre with a characteristically imitative style not unlike that of the motet. Here there was considerable scope for composers to dwell on a phrase, vary the texture, allow free play to the imagination and surprise the listener at every turn – features that were hardly possible or desired in the *formes fixes* and not usually appropriate in the motet. Obviously the Italian tradition is the largest and most famous, stretching from the first examples by Arcadelt and Verdelot in the 1520s, via Willaert, Rore, Wert and Marenzio through to the astonishing run of books by Monteverdi. If it was in some respects an intimate medium suitable for home recreation, it was also a style that allowed room for vocal virtuosity and the display of brilliant technique exploited initially by Wert and Luzzaschi. But the madrigal had a massive impact throughout Europe, not only in the late flowering of the English madrigalists but also in most other languages.

At the same time, the imitative style in five and six voices was never the perfect medium for projecting a text, and it was surely in line with the spirit of the Reformation that many composers felt drawn to a simpler and clearer presentation. One symptom was in what is generally called the 'Parisian chanson', as found in the earliest printed partbooks of Pierre Attaingnant (1528 onwards). At its purest, particularly in the almost homophonic four-voice songs of Claudin de Sermisy, this is one of the most controlled, economical and balanced forms in the history of music; but similar styles are found in all European languages as well as in much music of the Reformed Church.

Another reaction was in the rise of solo songs with lute or vihuela accompaniment and generally strophic in design. There may be a long prehistory to this in the unwritten musics of the fifteenth century; and in some of the earliest examples (the Bossinensis lutebooks of 1509 and 1511, for example) the lute plays what is essentially just a reduction of the lower voices from existing polyphony. However, in the vihuela books of Luis Milán (1536), Luys de Narváez (1538) or Alonso Mudarra (1546), there is a move away from dogged polyphony and towards clear declamation, particularly in the narrative *romances*. They seem to have codified the tradition that reached a later flowering in the French and English lute songs of the years around 1600, most spectacularly in the songbooks of John Dowland (1597 onwards).

Yet another strand in the story was confined mainly to Germany: the *Tenorlied*, in which the sung line (or at least the leading voice) was not on the top of the texture but buried within it. Whether as cause or effect, the text and melody were often borrowed material from the folk realm, with results that contrast strikingly with the Petrarchan courtliness and refinement of the full-dress Italian madrigal. In the hands of a genius like Senfl, the genre could blend the popular with the sophisticated, with the clear syllabic declamation of the vocal line embedded in polyphony of considerable complexity. How far this can have influenced the English consort song of Byrd and his successors, it is impossible to say; but throughout Europe the new styles of the seventeenth century seem to have taken their lead from the kind of direct communication most tellingly exploited in the German *Tenorlied*.

Select bibliography

All the music of the fourteenth-century song repertories is now published in L. SCHRADE, *et al.* (eds), *Polyphonic music of the fourteenth century*, 24 vols. (Monaco, 1951–90); see especially vols. ii–iv, vi–xi, xviii–xxii and xxiv. Much from the fifteenth and sixteenth centuries is among the several hundred volumes of *Corpus Mensurabilis Musicae* (American Institute of Musicology). A fine introduction to the fifteenth-century repertories appears in H. M. BROWN (ed.), *A Florentine chansonnier from the time of Lorenzo the Magnificent*, 2 vols. (Chicago, 1983) (Monuments of Renaissance Music, vii). For the madrigal, the classic study remains A. EINSTEIN's three-volume *The Italian madrigal* (Princeton, 1949), which can now be supplemented for the earlier period by I. FENLON and J. HAAR, *The Italian madrigal in the early sixteenth century* (Cambridge, 1988). Despite (or perhaps because of) the enormous body of important and stimulating detailed work on the other repertories, none of them is yet the subject of a comprehensive study.

21 Genre and function

Some thoughts on Italian secular vocal music in the sixteenth century

Margaret Mabbett

There are various ways of defining form and genre. Whether it is appropriate to adopt a general grouping or a strictly-defined form as a genre will depend on what we wish to define and why. Each of the sources of information which help us to define genre has its own strengths and weaknesses. In addition, some types of music belong to a much wider context than we are likely to appreciate from the form in which they have come down to us.

Two of the most important genres in this period, the madrigal and the villanella or *canzone villanesca alla napolitana*, are among the forms most readily identifiable on technical criteria. The apparently 'formless' madrigal can be defined by analogy to the sixteenth-century verse-form of that name, a free concatenation of fluid seven- and eleven-syllable lines with no set length and no predetermined scheme of rhyme or metre. In contrast, the villanella's form is strict: usually, a strophic setting, with repeats at the end of each line, of a text of four *ABB* strophes where the third line serves as a refrain and the same rhymes are maintained throughout the poem.

Of the many other musical forms and labels circulating in this period, most are either resistant to such technical definition or little studied as genres in their own right because of their limited application. The non-strophic forms are usually tucked into a discussion of the madrigal, while strophic forms are considered alongside the villanella. Until the mid-sixteenth century it was common for a variety of genres to be gathered in one publication without distinction, and as some forms such as the madrigal and villanella became more clearly defined, others, such as the canzone, either changed their meanings or were applied ambiguously to several different types of work. One solution has been to treat as one genre all the forms found in a particular context and period: for example, the use of 'frottola' to denote a wide range of music to Italian texts published before the emergence of the madrigal around 1530. Such treatment has the advantage of considering music of that particular period in context, but proves cumbersome in discussions which seek to trace in the frottola the origins of a later form.

Until recently, even the distinctive villanella was discussed largely as a fringe manifestation of the madrigal. The advantage of Alfred Einstein's approach, regarding everything else only as 'lighter forms' of the madrigal, was that he could devote three volumes to a form which he never defined. Although the formal criteria underlying the madrigal actually remained consistent for its entire life-span in Italy, major changes in its musical style and social function have made most writers reluctant to adopt a formal, rather than a stylistic, definition. Modern writers need to decide why they wish to define a genre in the first place, and which factors – stylistic, technical, poetic, functional – are the most important for their purpose.

There are a number of possible sources for genre definition. That which tends to be accorded the greatest respect is contemporary literature, especially theory. Even in an age of humanism, however, theoretical works tended to retain the influence of the medieval world-view that as all knowledge has been revealed to us, the writer's duty is simply to codify the works of earlier authors. The retrospective nature of such theory means that there may be no reference to the phenomenon being researched: even if there is, it may be framed according to underlying conventions which can mislead the modern reader. A good illustration of this problem is Agostino Agazzari's treatise on continuo playing (1607), which contains a reclassification of all known continuo instruments, the apparent practicality of which has misled many scholars and performers into believing that he was writing about combinations of instruments used together in performance.

Useful, if sporadic, information regarding current practices is often found in polemical writings and memoirs. Giambattista Basile's and Tommaso Costo's contemporary discussions of the villanella's actual and ideal roles in society have helped us to trace its origins in Neapolitan folk music (see E. Ferrari Barassi and G. M. Monti respectively).

Perhaps the most useful and certainly the most comprehensive source of definitions is the study of contemporary terminology as it was applied to works with particular structures of music and text. Even this type of evidence, however, is incomplete in terms of the repertory to which it relates and is bound by conventions which limit its usefulness.

To define genre by examining surviving music narrows our perspective. Nearly all of the music concerned comes from contemporary publications: of the few manuscript sources of sixteenth-century Italian secular music, most are themselves copies or arrangements from publications. As such, they tell us much about the uses to which printed music was put and how it may have been performed without greatly expanding the repertory. Publication is also no guarantee of survival: in studying the seventeenth-century madrigal I found inventory references to one vanished print for every two which survived. If a similar proportion of sixteenth-century prints has also disappeared, it is difficult to judge the extent to which the music now in our possession reflects what was then available.

If the representation of published music may be skewed, the problems in trying to understand largely unpublished repertories, such as occasional music, stage music or folk music, are almost unimaginable. Many printed collections may in fact contain such works, which we often fail to recognize because they are presented stripped of their original context and dressed up in publishing conventions. We tend to think that madrigals were normally performed with one voice to a part, because this is how they appear in print: but some madrigal-books are now known to consist largely of occasional works which may have been performed by more voices and/or with additional instruments.

Looking beyond the published source, the villanella and its equivalents from other regions appear to have played an important part in the *commedia dell'arte*. The evidence lies partly in the number of musicians who performed in stage plays: indeed, the first *commedia*-type performance of which a detailed record survives was hastily assembled and performed for the Duke of Bavaria in 1568 by the composers Lassus and Massimo Troiano, both of whom published villanellas (Lassus's *Villanelle, moresche et altre canzoni* of 1582, dedicated to the Duke of

Bavaria, culminates in 'Zanni, dov'estu?', a madrigalian setting for eight voices of what might well be an excerpt from his original dialogue). Illustrations of musicians participating in the *commedia dell'arte* (for example, those reproduced by Nino Pirrotta) often show three characters singing together: one does not even have to accept, therefore, that these works, published in three vocal parts, were in fact commonly performed by one singer with an instrument to believe that the villanella was often used in stage performances. It is also worth noting that the madrigal comedies by Adriano Banchieri which use a *commedia*-type plot are also set for the three-voice texture generally associated with the villanella.

Among the forms of music-making represented in the printed repertory but difficult to pin down in terms of genre are the parlour entertainment and the masquerade. Both of these overlap with the villanella in Serafino Candido's *Delle mascherate musicali* of 1571, which contains humorous masking pieces, most of which adopt the villanella form and texture; examples of the villanella proper; and several pieces which are closely related to parlour games of the sort set by Vecchi in his *Veglie di Siena* (1604), especially the Hunt for Love, where the participants espy Cupid in each others' features. In a contemporary manuscript copy of the bass partbook, an amorous couple have filled in any blank spaces with their own literary games.

That the villanella was a form of Neapolitan folksong which was taken up and refined as an art form is clear from the comments of Giambattista Basile and Tommaso Costo. Its suitability for the *commedia*, in which dialects form a major part of the characterization, was enhanced by the existence of similar forms in other local dialects which, however, somehow lacked the durability of the villanella when brought into the art-music world. Before the Neapolitan villanella became widespread in northern Italy, for example, there were twenty years (*c.* 1520–40) when the northern *villotta* was cultivated and published as an art-music form for four voices, often in dialect and sometimes with a folk-tune in one of the middle voices: it shares with the still surviving folk *villotta* strophes of four eleven-syllable lines and vocable refrains. Other points of contact between the folk and art traditions which might prove rewarding to researchers are the continuing presence in the Emilian folk violin repertory of the *ballo di Mantova* and the *Ruggiero* and, indeed, of *cantastorie* who sing epics such as Ariosto's *Orlando furioso* to standard formulae, a practice recorded at the sixteenth-century Italian courts and related to the publication, especially in the frottola repertory, of harmonized formulae to which certain fixed verse-forms such as the octave or sonnet could be sung. The villanella is relatively well-documented largely because of local interest in dialect literature. It would be a pity if other links between sixteenth-century art music and folk music remained unexplored because of invisible walls between historical musicology, ethnomusicology and literary history.

Until recently, the madrigal has dominated our understanding of Italian music of this period. We are just beginning to appreciate the richness and diversity of other contemporary genres and their social and cultural importance. While some genres are easily defined on the technical level, membership of others must be decided on the basis of context. However rewarding it is to trace developments within a single clearly-defined form, for example in following the madrigal through the stylistic changes of the seventeenth century, we should ensure that we do not lose in this process those genres which depend upon context. We should also remind ourselves that even a piece whose genre may be obvious may have its origins in quite different surroundings.

Select bibliography

E. FERRARI BARASSI, 'La villanella napoletana nella testimonianza di un letterato', *Nuova Rivista Musicale Italiana*, ii (1968), pp. 1064–87

G. BARGAGLI, *Dialogo de' giuochi che nelle vegghie sanesi si usano da fare* (Siena, 1572)

D. G. CARDAMONE, *The canzone villanesca alla napolitana and related forms, 1537–1570*, 2 vols., (Ann Arbor, 1981)

A. EINSTEIN, *The Italian madrigal*, 3 vols. (Princeton, 1949)

J. HAAR (ed.), *Chanson and madrigal, 1480–1530* (Cambridge, Mass., 1964)

D. HARRÁN, 'Verse types in the early madrigal', *Journal of the American Musicological Society*, xxii (1969), pp. 27–53

K. M. LEA, *Italian popular comedy, a study in the commedia dell'arte, 1560–1620* (New York, 1962).

G. M. MONTI, *Le villanelle alla napolitana e l'antica lirica dialettale a Napoli* (Castello, 1925)

N. PIRROTTA, 'Commedia dell'arte and opera', *The Musical Quarterly*, xli (1955), pp. 305–24

J. ROCHE, *The madrigal* (London, 1972)

Genres: instrumental

22 Fourteenth- and fifteenth-century keyboard music

Lewis Jones

The organ stands apart from other instruments in medieval Europe in that it was accepted – more or less – in church. Since it is likely, from Carolingian times, to have been in the hands of musically-literate players, who could attach letter names or solmization syllables to its notes, it is not surprising to find that the earliest specifically instrumental notations appear to be for keyboard instruments. The small amount of instrumental music that survives from the thirteenth and fourteenth centuries mostly consists of monophonic dances. Their notation resembles that of the vocal music which makes up the bulk of the manuscripts in which they are found. The keyboard sources, in contrast, use a variety of types of score and tablature to dispose two or more parts for the convenience of a single player. They often use bar-lines to clarify vertical alignment and to describe regular units of time, and their notation of rhythm tends to be primitive and conservative.

The earliest known keyboard source is a pair of leaves, probably of mid-fourteenth-century origin, bound at the end of a register from Robertsbridge Abbey, Sussex (London, British Library, Add. 28550, known as the Robertsbridge Codex). It contains three *estampies*, and intabulations of two motets (probably by Philippe de Vitry) from the *Roman de Fauvel*, and of a hymn, 'Flos vernalis'. As the leaves are a fragment of a larger manuscript, one of the *estampies* and the hymn are incomplete. Even in this earliest source, we can distinguish between the two main sorts of instrumental music which extend throughout the Renaissance; pieces which stem from a vocal model, and others which do not, being either dances or, as the fifteenth century progresses, preludes and, later, ricercars, toccatas and other free forms.

The Robertsbridge *estampies* are essentially in two parts, just occasionally enriched by a third. In the two motets the intabulator has mostly kept the three original parts, occasionally dropping or adding one, as at the start of the second motet, *Tribum quem*, where the solo entry of the *triplum* (the highest voice) gains an accompaniment. The intabulator's technique demonstrates many of the practices which became firmly established in the following century. He decorates the highest part (in the motets in a swift triplet rhythm), mostly using unaccented neighbouring pitches, but sometimes alternating with the note a fourth below, or creating a momentary dissonance by approaching the written note from the step above. Some accidentals are added, though not as comprehensively as in a lute tablature, which must always specify where the player is to put his finger.

A range of seventeen notes is used, from *c* to *e″*, including all the accidentals from *f♯* upwards. There are no low *e♭*s, and if the keyboard intended had lacked that note (like many later instruments which are diatonic in the bass) that might explain why *Tribum quem* (which would otherwise call for it) is transposed up a tone, whereas the other motet is copied at its original pitch.

A simple letter notation, long used in theory and associated with the monochord, might have been employed to record the earliest, monophonic organ music, which presumably derived from chant. Something of the sort may be indicated by the theorist Anonymous IV in the late thirteenth century. In the Robertsbridge fragment, letters giving the names of the notes of the lower, tenor part are combined with a single five-line stave (an early instance of simultaneous ruling with a rastrum) which carries the upper part (or parts) in a post-Petronian notation, with dots of division at intervals of a breve. This combined notation is commonly known as old German keyboard tablature, but since it appears here almost a century before the earliest surviving German sources, it probably is not of German origin.

The most curious aspect of the Robertsbridge notation is its inclusion of a text below the stave of the three vocally-derived pieces. The motets originally have three texts, that in the tablature being a composite, usually drawing upon the highest sounding voice. The tablature is inadequate for a full vocal rendition, and the text may be merely an acknowledgment of the origins of the piece, but could it have been put there for the organist to sing? In a similar way, late sixteenth-century lutenists sometimes sang only the bass part of a madrigal or motet to the accompaniment of an intabulation of all the parts.

The Faenza MS (Faenza, Biblioteca Comunale, 117), from the Carmelite friary in Ferrara, dates from the early years of the fifteenth century. It preserves some forty-eight pieces in a score of two six-line staves, all in two parts which just occasionally blossom into three. More than half of these are intabulations of existing polyphonic compositions, mostly by composers of the fourteenth century, including Machaut, Jacopo da Bologna, P. des Molins, Landini and Bartolino da Padova. Although most of these pieces are in three parts, the keyboard settings present only the tenor and a decorated upper part. The remaining pieces comprise several based upon liturgical tenors, including two Kyrie-Gloria pairs on the plainsong *Cunctipotens genitor Deus* (apparently intended for liturgical use, *alternatim*, with choral plainchant), a few dance-related pieces (two recently identified as *istampite* by John Caldwell) and some pieces based on tenors of unknown origin. All have a florid upper part, a setting of 'Benedicamus Domino' (no. 25) being particularly virtuosic. Pythagorean tuning was normal at this time, and several of the pieces seem to exploit the just thirds on D, A and E which result from placing the wolf fifth between G♭ (F♯) and B; indeed, one 'Benedicamus te' section closes, unprecedentedly, with a full E major triad.

For what instruments was this music intended? It all calls for the use of both hands, and must therefore have been played on the positive organ, winded by an assistant, rather than on the portative. Since one hand was busy with the bellows, the music of the portative must have been monophonic, or may have extended only to such polyphony as could be encompassed by the other hand. Most portatives had a single bellows, so playing must also have been subject to pauses, like a wind player's breathing, allowing for their reinflation. In Simone Prudenzani's early fifteenth-century poem *Il Saporetto*, the musician Sollazzo uses the mysterious *organi framegni* to perform *El molin de Paris* (by P. des Molins?).

Stringed keyboard instruments were also available. The clavichord was probably invented in the first half of the fourteenth century, and plucked types in the second half. Certainly in 1360 King Edward III of England gave his captive, John the Good of France, an *eschequier*, a term which was used for the clavichord, and seems to have extended to other types. In about 1440, Henri Arnaut of Zwolle was able to describe the construction not only of organs and clavichords, but of harpsichord- and virginal-shaped instruments, with a range of four possible plucking and striking actions. Much of this music suits the harp also, and a good player could probably have coaxed a similar texture from the psaltery.

There are two early fifteenth-century English sources in the Bodleian Library, Oxford, which broaden our view of the range of styles played on keyboard instruments. Bodley MS 842 has a textless, two-part, ballade-like piece, perhaps of *c.*1370, extraordinarily adventurous in its use of accidentals. The parts are written separately, not in score, but an accompanying rubric seems to indicate that it can be played on the clavichord. Douce MS 381 has a two-part *Felix namque* in a distinctive English discant style, with lilting 6/8 rhythms.

The majority of fifteenth-century tablatures are of German origin. Adam Ileborgh's tablature (Philadelphia, Curtis Institute of Music) of 1448 includes five preludes in which an animated upper part is supported by sustained two-part chords. The lower parts are notated in a single line of letters, grouped in pairs, each pair to be played simultaneously. A direction *pedaliter sive manualiter* (with pedals or with manuals alone), elsewhere in the manuscript, is the first evidence of the use of pedals. A large positive, like the one surviving from Norrlanda, or the mitre-shaped church instrument is presumably envisaged, and the paired letters may reflect double pedalling. Ileborgh presents other pieces in score, with two parts on a single large staff. In a slightly later example in score (Vienna, Österreichische Nationalbibliothek, Cod. Vindob. 5094), the three parts of Dufay's 'Ce jour le doibt' are presented on two staves, the tenor and contra being void and black notes respectively.

The most celebrated organist of the time was Conrad Paumann (*c.*1410–73), for many years attached to the court of Duke Albrecht III of Bavaria. He played to Philip the Good of Burgundy, and in 1470 travelled to Mantua where he was lauded as the 'miraculous blind one'. His *Fundamentum organisandi* (Berlin, Staatsbibliothek, 40613) of 1452 is the first of several demonstrations of the art of decoration, of adding a florid part above a tenor, and of other aspects of keyboard composition. It includes a collection of preludes and pieces by several composers based upon songs and borrowed tenors. The *Fundamentum* shows the German notation in its mature state. Where in the earlier sources the rhythm of the lower parts is dependent upon their alignment with the more explicit notation of the top part, separate rhythm signs are now placed above the letters of the lower parts, giving them much greater independence.

By far the largest collection of fifteenth-century keyboard music is the Buxheim Organ Book (Munich, Bayerische Staatsbibliothek, Cim. 352b), copied between about 1452 and 1470. It incorporates Paumann's *Fundamentum*, and it is assumed that many of its 256 items originated with him or his associates. The main part of the manuscript, up to f. 124, is in a single hand, and encompasses a wide range of compositions of the first half of the century, including pieces by Binchois and Dufay. Some are sparsely decorated, but most are richly embellished, often displaying great delight in rhythmic variety and syncopation. Several pieces display much greater freedom, borrowing only the tenor of a composition, and adding two new parts. As might be expected, the range of styles is wide, including, in addition to intabulations, liturgical pieces, basse-danse settings and preludes, some of them developed to considerable length. Towards the end of the collection, more modern chansons in the manner of the 1460s are included.

There remains much that we may never know about the early use of keyboard instruments; when and how they participated in ensembles; whether, and if so how, the organ accompanied singing in church; but the tablatures provide evidence of a vigorous tradition of playing, which encompassed the most advanced compositions of the day.

Select bibliography

W. APEL (ed.), *Keyboard music of the fourteenth & fifteenth centuries*, *Corpus of Early Keyboard Music*, i (American Institute of Musicology, 1963)

J. CALDWELL, 'Two polyphonic *istampite* from the 14th century', *Early Music*, xviii/3 (1990), pp. 371–80

D. PLAMENAC (ed.), *Keyboard music of the late Middle Ages in Codex Faenza 117*, *Corpus Mensurabilis Musicae*, lvii (American Institute of Musicology, 1972)

E. SOUTHERN, *The Buxheim Organ Book* (New York, 1963)

B. A. WALLNER (ed.), *Das Buxheimer Orgelbuch*, 3 vols., *Das Erbe deutscher Musik*, xxxvii–xxxix (Kassel, 1958–9)

23 Plucked instruments: silver tones of a golden age

Hopkinson Smith

> [Francesco da Milano] played with such ravishing skill that
> little by little, making the strings languish under his fingers in a
> sublime way, he transported all those who were listening with
> so pleasurable a melancholy that . . . it was as if the listeners
> were ecstatically carried away by some divine frenzy.[1]

The great lutenists of the Renaissance were performer-improvisers whose musical magnetism was legendary. The power of the lute has, of course, nothing to do with its volume: it has always been a relatively quiet instrument, and its power is rather that of persuasion, taking the listener into a dimension of sensitivities and subtelties rarely reached by other instruments. No intermediary object such as a bow or keyboard comes between the performer and the strings, and the 'touch' of the lutenist – the control of colour, warmth, intensity and purity of sound – is therefore all-important.

One might think that the ideal instrument for the polyphonic music of the period would be the organ, where all the voices could be sustained for their full duration and a texture could be maintained as it appears in a modern score. From this objective point of view, a plucked string instrument with its lack of sustaining power would appear to be the least appropriate instrument. In fact, the opposite is true. The degree of subtlety that the lute can bring to the varied voices of the polyphonic music (far more than is possible on the organ) assured its revered position in the hierarchy of Renaissance instruments. Almost all the sixteenth-century music for the lute (and related instruments such as the vihuela and the four-course guitar) is polyphonic.

The earliest significant lute music that has come down to us was written around 1500. A large variety of styles of fantasias or ricercars (terms which were used interchangeably at that time) is evident. The degrees of organization within these pieces ranged from sections arbitrarily strung together and varying in texture (chords, two- or three-voice passages, sequences, bursts of single-line activity as in, for example, the works of Vicenzo Capirola) to pieces which are constructed with relatively few melodic and rhythmic elements and developed into extraordinarily refined and mathematically proportioned compositions (as in certain pieces by Francesco da Milano or Luys de Narváez). More loosely structured contrapuntal meanderings also exist and reach fascinating proportions in the works of Albertus da Ripa.

Almost all instrumental music is conceived with the particular capabilities of a specific instrument in mind. Some musical ideas seem to have been born on an instrument, while others are clearly brought in from elsewhere. Elements of vocal polyphony were used in lute music from the beginning, and were so well

[1]Pontus de Tyard, *Solitaire second en prose de la musique* (Lyons, 1555), cited in A. J. Ness (ed.), *The lute music of Francesco Canova da Milano (1497–1543)* (Cambridge, Mass., 1970)

assimilated that the vocal ideal remained an essential part of the instrument's language throughout the Renaissance. Elements of vocal style even represented the building blocks of a lutenist's technique. The lute was learnt to a large extent by ear through duplicating one-, two- or three-voice passages, and eventually elaborating on them with diminutions in the master's style. Instrumental technique, contrapuntal practice, and intuition for improvisation were learnt and developed simultaneously. Eventually, even the most sophisticated part-writing existed not only on paper, but also resided in the capabilities of the hands of a skilled improvising lutenist. Contemporary descriptions (as, for example, that of Francesco da Milano cited above) testify to the extraordinary creative power of the lutenist to bring about an unforgettable musical event.

More than half of the continental repertory for the lute and vihuela is made up of arrangements of vocal pieces. These are referred to as intabulations – that is, settings in tablature, the system of notation for almost all lute music throughout the instrument's history. Individual chansons, motets, parts of Mass movements, even entire Masses were arranged for plucked instruments. Some intabulations remain very close to the vocal originals; others are profusely ornamented with diminutions running between different registers of the instrument and elaborating more on the harmonic texture of the original than on the individual polyphonic lines.

After fantasias and intabulations, the third important musical genre for the Renaissance lute, and one which through constant evolution and development in different countries was to partner the lute through to the eighteenth century, is music inspired by and adapted for the dance. The styles differ in character from drone-accompanied melodies (as in the works of Joan Ambrosio Dalza) to pieces with section upon section of driving diminutions (Pietro Borrono) and to the better known English lute repertory from the end of the sixteenth century and the beginning of the seventeenth (Dowland, Holborne, Cutting, etc.). The English gift for melody invited the lute into a realm of lyric subtlety which produced a unique moment in the instrument's history. Pavans and galliards are the most common forms to be found in English scores. The pavans are essentially polyphonic pieces whose slow melodic pacing requires enormous sensitivity of touch and intensity of line. The varied reprises of their three repeated sections are often so elaborate and rhythmically intricate that one could hardly consider actually dancing to them. This is, in fact, pure instrumental music.

Stravinsky referred to the lute as 'perhaps the most perfect and certainly the most personal instrument of all',[2] and this statement accurately summarizes the Renaissance ideal of the instrument. The sixteenth century was clearly the first Golden Age of the lute, as witnessed by the vast surviving repertory and reams of eulogistic literature. Documenting its role in the musical societies of earlier periods is considerably more difficult. The lute was common as an ensemble instrument in polyphonic works, dance music and for accompanying the voice – functions which carried on into the sixteenth century and beyond – but how and what the great lute soloists of earlier eras played makes for fascinating conjecture. The evidence points to single-line extemporisations as one of the lute's main roles in the fifteenth century, but still earlier centuries remain mute as to its specific contributions to music-making.

[2] R. Craft (ed.), *Conversations with Igor Stravinsky* (Berkeley and Los Angeles, 1958)

Modern music histories often state that the lute was introduced into Europe through Spain during the Moorish occupation. This hypothesis ignores the wider European contacts with the southern and eastern Mediterranean that date back to Phoenician times. Italy or the southern coast of modern France represent more credible points of entry for the assimilation of the lute into European cultural life. From the earliest period up until the mid-fifteenth century, the four or five ranks of strings were plucked almost exclusively with a plectrum, as is still the case with the lute's Arabic ancestor the *'ud*. In the second half of the fifteenth century, lutenists began to favour plucking the strings with the fingertips. There were certain definite parallels to the earlier technique: for single-line work the plectrum's down-stroke was relegated to the thumb and the up-stroke to the index finger, a technique which, as playing with a plectrum, required relatively wide spacing between the courses at the lute's bridge.

Throughout most of the sixteenth century, the lute had five courses of double strings and a single top course. By the early seventeenth century, with the introduction of continuo accompaniment, up to four more bass courses were added with a resulting change in lute technique. The thumb was now assigned to the strings lowest in pitch, leaving all the melodic activity to the fingers, a technique better suited to an instrument with necessarily closer spacing (due to the greater number of strings) at the bridge. The right hand, which was held with fingers almost parallel to the strings during the fifteenth and sixteenth centuries, now moved round so that the fingers were essentially parallel to the bridge – a position which continued to be used into the eighteenth century and has been carried over into modern guitar technique.

Select bibliography

o. GOMBOSI (ed.), *Compositione di Meser Vincenzo Capirola: lute book (circa 1517)* (Neuilly-sur-Seine, 1955)

J. JACQUOT (ed.), *Le luth et sa musique* (Paris, 1958; 2nd edn, 1976)

D. POULTON, *John Dowland* (London, 1972)

J. M. VACCARO, *La musique de luth en France au XVIe siècle* (Paris, 1981)

24 The medieval fiddle: reflections of a performer

Randall Cook

What can one say about bowed string instruments and early music performance practice, especially when concerned with medieval music? The information we have is, at best, minimal, and it would seem that up to and including the fifteenth century, instrumental music was, for the most part based on an oral, and/or improvised tradition.

Fortunately, there are some references to the medieval fiddle in contemporary literature, by people such as Johannes de Grocheio and Jerome of Moravia who talk about tunings and give some information about what life must have been like for Parisian musicians in the thirteenth century. It is important to read what various theoreticians of the period have to say, but it does not make for easy reading, nor are there any clear-cut answers.

So what can we do? The answer is simple: study the existing material as closely as we can, and stay in contact with musicologists. We should know the sources, how to find and use them, and search for a musicologist with whom to collaborate. We go to a doctor for advice, either for regular check-ups or when something is wrong. It might take some time to find the right one, but it's better to react than ignore danger signals: consultation sessions can cause no harm. It seems to me that performers and scholars should have a similar interreaction.

Something else that anyone can do on his or her own is to delve into the world of musical iconography, especially today when a professional musician is also a traveller. To have a pet subject to search for in museums and churches can give new excitement to what can often turn into just another tour of concert halls, dining rooms and hotels.

For all periods, and perhaps especially for the fifteenth century, paintings, sculptures, reliefs and miniatures can be a perpetual source of information. The question is, can we take pictorial evidence at face value? Since there are very few existing instruments from the medieval period and indeed up to the end of the sixteenth century, we really have no other choice as to exactly what instruments could have been played. Isolated examples of fiddles and rebecs have turned up in obscure places: the most recent in a tomb in Poland. However, we should never take one source completely at face value, whether dealing with a painting, sculpture, or even an existing instrument. We must always be aware of the possibility of a false impression due to aging, bad restoration, or even fraud. With depictions of instruments we must always ask, is this based on an existing instrument, an artist's model, pure imagination, or symbolism? Repetition of an instrument, or of a certain characteristic or playing technique are important things to look for.

By way of an example of the challenges raised by such considerations, I shall take up a subject which has already provoked a good deal of discussion: whether fiddles up to and including the 1480s had flat or arched bridges. With the assumption that fiddles did not exist with arched bridges comes the theory that these instruments were not used in polyphony. To Howard Mayer Brown's most recent information to the contrary, I would like to add a couple of observations of my own gained from actual performance.

In my possession is a fiddle based on an instrument portrayed in a painting of *c.*1500 from the Museo Nazionale, Cagliari (illus. 1). It is supplied with a completely flat, lute-like bridge, and is tuned strictly to Gs and Ds. I have at present a fairly substantial repertory of pieces and improvisations upon which to draw, but it is still at best quite limited as an instrument. Depictions of a tailpiece sitting on top of a bridge are often found, and my instrument also has such a device. It is ever so slightly curved – in a way that is barely discernible to the naked eye – but nevertheless enough to enable single lines to be played. Yet I would not relish having to play a particularly difficult contratenor line with such an instrument.

1a Fiddle *c.* 1500 (Sardinia, Museo Nazionale)

b Author's copy

2a Fiddle, Chartres Cathedral (Photo, P. Lefèvre)   b Author's copy

Another of my fiddles is based on a sculpture from Chartres Cathedral (illus. 2). Due to aging it is almost impossible to tell what sort of bridge the instrument has, but we will assume that it looks flat. My instrument, like the sculpture, has no raised fingerboard, and has what looks like a flat, lute-like neck. The bridge is low and is also flat in appearance, but both the fingerboard and the bridge are slightly arched. The grooves for the outer strings are a little deeper, while the inner strings have almost no grooves, and this gives quite a bit of leeway, enough to allow any contratenor line to be played. How exact were the medieval artists? Would this slight arch be noticed, and, if so, be considered important enough to be portrayed? In that case would the artist possibly even exaggerate the arching? It seems unlikely that fiddle players and makers over a number of centuries would have imposed the limitations of a completely flat bridge on their instruments.

A number of artists apparently chose to give certain fiddles what appears to be a second bridge, and this has given rise to a fair amount of speculation as to its purpose. The second bridge is up by the fingerboard, or, more important, half-way along the vibrating string-length. Crawford Young, Richard Earle and I have been experimenting with my various fiddles, and I would have to agree with Bernard

Ravenel's observation that when more force or bowspeed is used, a percussive sound not unlike that of the hurdy-gurdy is achieved.

Both Christopher Page and Howard Mayer Brown agree that Jerome of Moravia's tuning system was based on intervallic relations rather than actual pitches, and that most probably the lowest notes were the low *c* of a modern viola, or *g* of a violin. I would like to agree, since I have tried and not been successful in finding a plain gut or catline *G* below the *c* of a viola that comes even remotely close to responding. Most of the modern players who have not reached the same conclusion have covered lower strings, which is certainly unacceptable. With *c* as the lowest string, many people use a *c, g, d', g'* tuning. I have always found a strict tuning with *c*s and *g*s more accommodating, especially for the *estampie* repertory.

My work as a performer of medieval fiddle can be divided into basically two categories: as an accompanist to a singer or another instrument, or as a melody instrument, with or without accompaniment. The surviving medieval repertory that can strictly be considered instrumental is basically limited to dance music, and three-part hockets. In addition, there are extant examples of instrumental versions of vocal works from the fourteenth and fifteenth centuries, but unfortunately these are probably keyboard works. Nevertheless, they are invaluable tools for study: they could be adapted to my own instrument, or, after careful analysis and experience, I could compose my own versions of existing vocal works. The next step would be to add appropriate spontaneous diminutions, first aiming for cadential figures, and gradually growing more courageous. As an accompanying and a melody instrument for the monophonic repertory, the fiddle will need to be equipped with drone strings. Drones were one of the first devices used in accompaniment, and their addition to a melody is often effective. Again, careful analysis of the original melody with a knowledge of mode should lead in the right directions.

Since a large part of the medieval instrumental repertory is lost (mainly because of its origins as an oral/improvised tradition), these same basic rules can be applied to any or all styles: study and analysis of the extant works, and practice in composing, with the aim of being able to improvise. When it comes to reading music, it is not too difficult to find and use facsimiles of monophonic music from the thirteenth century onwards. As regards polyphonic music, it is important to have copies of the original to hand, but it is not easy, until perhaps the fifteenth century and later, to read and play from the original. That is not to say that you shouldn't try! It's certainly not impossible. A new dimension of understanding is added to music-making when you play from original notation; it can also be quite thrilling.

One final thought: it is far more acceptable to use a slightly antiquated instrument for a particular style or ensemble than to use an instrument or instruments that did not even exist at the time. Playing early Renaissance consort music with Baroque seven-string gambas with late Baroque or early Classical bows should now be considered a part of performance practice of the 1960s and '70s.

Select bibliography

w. ARLT, 'Instrumentalmusik im Mittelalter: Fragen der Rekonstruktion einer schriftlosen Praxis', *Basler Jahrbuch für historische Musikpraxis*, vii (1983), pp. 32–64

M. BAXANDALL, *Painting and experience in fifteenth-century Italy* (Oxford, 1972)

E. A. BOWLES, *La pratique musicale au Moyen Âge* (Geneva, 1983)

H. M. BROWN, 'The trecento fiddle and its bridges', *Early Music*, xvii/3 (1989), pp. 307–29

E. CARLI, *Sienese painting* (New York, 1983)

C. PAGE, *Voices and instruments of the Middle Ages* (London, 1987)

B. RAVENEL, 'Rebec und Fiedel-Ikonographie und Spielweise', *Basler Jahrbuch für historische Musikpraxis*, viii (1984), pp. 105–30

M. REMNANT, *English bowed instruments* (Oxford, 1986)

K. VELLEKOOP, 'Die Estampie: ihre Besetzung und Funktion', *Basler Jahrbuch für historische Musikpraxis*, viii (1984), pp. 51–65

E. WINTERNITZ, *Musical instruments and their symbolism in Western art*, 2nd edn (New Haven, 1979)

I. WOODFIELD, *The early history of the viol* (Cambridge, 1984)

25 On the trail of ensemble music in the fifteenth century

Crawford Young

To discuss the history of ensemble music is to confront two inseparable yet separate areas of study: the nature of groups of musicians playing together and the music that such groups played. Information for the former can be culled from literary accounts, archival material such as payment records, and the visual arts, whereas for the latter we have manuscripts and prints containing music. The music, however, does not necessarily 'speak for itself' as regards any intention of the way in which it might have been performed.

The modern view of musical notation embraces the concept that music is written down in a way that specifically indicates for which instrument(s) and/or voice(s) the composition was originally intended. To what extent is pre-Baroque notation unlike its modern counterpart? It was often used to preserve a generic version of a piece of music – similar perhaps to a jazz musician's 'fake book'. The advent of printed music around 1500 resulted in an increase in specific indications for performance, in part because the new accessibility of music books for amateurs meant that the writer or copyist no longer knew exactly who would be using the book. Music historians, therefore, have substantially more information concerning ensemble music of the sixteenth century than that of the fifteenth, the focus of this brief essay.

'Ensemble' within the present context denotes two or more musicians making music, especially in certain configurations whose repeated occurrence seems to indicate a major role within a tradition of performance: for example, the wind band of the fifteenth century and the so-called mixed consort of the Elizabethan period. Due to its importance in providing music for numerous social rituals, the *alta capella* is perhaps the best-documented ensemble of the late Middle Ages, yet despite payment records dating from as early as the late fourteenth century, precise information concerning what this ubiquitous ensemble played remains all too scarce. It is also clear, for example, that string instruments such as the lute and harp often performed in pairs, and the extensive surviving documentation confirms a well-established tradition of such discantor-tenorista duos from the first quarter of the fifteenth century.

Is it possible to make a direct connection between the performing ensembles indicated by the documents and the music preserved in the manuscripts? An attempt to do so might be made bearing in mind the following points: (1) textless voices in manuscripts point to traditions of musical notation rather than to those of actual performance; (2) 'instrumental style' *per se* was not recognized or discussed by theorists in the fifteenth century, and even as 'instrumental' a repertory as dance accompaniment was not limited to instruments; and (3) strict, either-or classifications such as loud/soft have their place in medieval theoretical writings, but in practice variety seems to have been the rule. Here the case of Arnaut de Zwolle's lute construction plan serves as an example: in theory, the form of the instrument is perfectly Pythagorean, being derived exclusively from a circle and based on simple proportions, whereas in contemporary visual representations we find a rich variety of lute shapes, always however with the recognizable Pythagorean model in the background. Theory was often thus tempered in practice.

Manuscript sources containing music which can clearly be associated with specific instruments (excluding the organ) or ensembles cannot be identified until the last quarter of the fifteenth century: these relatively few sources include the so-called Casanatense Chansonnier (which may have had a connection with a wind band in Ferrara), basse danse manuscripts (also likely for wind band) and the earliest lute tablatures. A few earlier manuscripts do have limited sections of possible instrumental accompaniment or dance-related music: examples include the Mondsee-Wiener Mönch von Salzburg MS with elaborated *bordun*, that is, simplified accompaniment voices labelled 'gut zu blasen' ('works well on a wind instrument'), as well as the manuscript fragment of the Nuremberg Stadtbibliothek containing the 'Bobik blasen' rubric.

By focusing on the 'problem' of instrumentation, we tend to place a false emphasis on one aspect of performance invariably at the expense of other important features, such as the technical and musical function of a voice within an ensemble texture, and the broader context of the social role of the performance. For example, rather than trying to establish whether a contratenor voice in a polyphonic chanson *c.*1450 is inherently 'instrumental' in style and best served by being played on the lute, or whether it could in fact be sung, equally essential to a responsible interpretation is understanding that the contratenor is the most flexible, often-replaced voice with the most 'choices' for controlling the strength of cadences, levels of dissonance and phrase-binding. It is often the most 'improvised' voice of a composition and one that ranges from the non-obligatory triplum parts of Machaut songs (parts that frequently double the contratenor at the octave) to the *si placet* altus parts in the Petrucci collections, or from the early fifteenth-century 'contratenor trompette' to the (for lack of a better term) 'contratenor bassus diminutus' genre of various 'Le serviteur', 'Tandernacken' and 'J'ay pris amours' settings of the last quarter of the fifteenth century. These kinds of voice parts, with their special functions and vocabulary of clichés, were provided by a musician trained as a *tenorista*.

One school of musicological thought holds that instrumental music is indicated in manuscripts by a voice that: (1) has been notated without text; (2) is partially or entirely without rests; (3) has 'difficult' or 'non-vocal' leaps (rather hard to define); (4) has an excessively wide range; (5) has a high density of florid passages; and (6) has a certain kind of title such as 'La martinella' or 'Pfauenschwanz'. Evidence that contradicts such a list is not hard to find: the composition which closes Tinctoris's solmization treatise *Expositio manus* features a texted superius voice with a range of two and a half octaves; texted superius parts from the Cypriot manuscript Torino, Biblioteca Nazionale, J.II.9, contain passages which make the most excessively florid untexted superius parts in the highly-ornamented keyboard pieces in the Faenza MS (Biblioteca Comunale 117) look tame; untexted, angular, leap-filled contratenor parts in Chantilly, Musée Condé 564 (*olim* 1047) suddenly have an exclamation of one or two words of text, followed by no more. There are, on the other hand, textless cantus firmus settings which clearly foreshadow sixteenth-century diminution pieces, just as some textless late fifteenth-century motet-style compositions seem to foreshadow early fantasias of the following century.

Certain nuances of ensemble practice become visible only when the glare of what is theoretically the 'strongest' evidence is removed and hints begin to assert themselves more clearly against the backdrop of simple practical experience. Who, without being a lutenist, would ever realize that a hand holding a plectrum is perfectly capable of plucking not one but up to three, even four notes simultaneously? Indeed, what historical source confirms the oft-encountered remark that the plectrum lute was strictly a monophonic instrument? Who can know how a double-bridged fiddle functioned in an ensemble, or whether instruments with buzzing devices are really more percussive and penetrating than those without if they never play them? As Gaffurius put it in his *Practica musicae* (1496): 'Nor could I be considered free from blame if I were to teach the art of music and disclose its innermost secrets, as it were, but would pass over in silence this part of music which is called practical and which consists of and is completed by the performance of music.'

Select bibliography

H. M. BROWN, *Instrumental music printed before 1600: a bibliography* (Cambridge, Mass., 1967)
W. EDWARDS, 'Sources of instrumental music to 1630', *New Grove*; and 'Songs without words by Josquin and his contemporaries', in I. Fenlon (ed.), *Music in medieval and early modern Europe* (Cambridge, 1981), pp. 79–92
F. GAFFURIUS, *Practica musicae*, trans. C. Miller, Musicological Studies and Documents, xx (American Institute of Musicology: Rome, 1968)
D. KÄMPER, 'Studien zur instrumentalen Ensemblemusik des 16. Jahrhunderts in Italien', *Analecta Musicologica*, x (Köln, 1970)
L. LITTERICK, 'On Italian instrumental ensemble music in the late fifteenth century', in I. Fenlon (ed.), *Music in medieval and early modern Europe*, pp. 117–30.

26 Wind ensembles in the Renaissance

Lorenz Welker

> Modernis etenim temporibus tibie ac tube altitone fidulas
> morigeras a conviviis communiter fugant, et altisono strepitu
> certatim iuvencule saliunt . . .
>   Indeed, in modern times loud shawms and trumpets
> generally banish the sober fiddles from the feasts and the young
> girls dance eagerly to the loud noise . . .

This quotation is a moralist's view of wind band performances around 1350, written by the Parisian *magister* Konrad of Megenberg in his instruction book for young princes, *Yconomica* (his full comment on musical instruments can be found in Page, 1982). The group of shawms and trumpets, which was newly in vogue for banquets and dance in Konrad's time, had an incredible career in the following century. No prince and no wealthy town could successfully display their significance without the services of the wind band, and the many instances of its employment are documented not only in countless archives, but also in paintings, drawings and miniatures which give a vivid picture of musical life and how it was represented in the early Renaissance (see, for example, illus. 1).

The theorist Johannes Tinctoris commented on the wind band in his treatise *De inventione et usu musicae*, printed around 1480. He praised the wonderful sound of the ensemble ('melodiosissime clangunt'), and he mentioned the term *alta* to describe an assembly of loud wind instruments. What he actually did, was to revive the traditional classification of 'loud' and 'soft' instruments, a classification which implied that both categories were kept strictly apart from one another. In other words, shawms and trumpets were never allowed to play together with strings, flutes and voices. *Alta* (i.e. *instrumenta*) being the Latin equivalent for 'loud instruments' was taken by twentieth-century musicologists to create a name for the fifteenth-century wind band: *alta* or *alta capella*. Although the term is useful, it should be clear that fifteenth-century documents never mention such a name. The wind band was usually referred to as (loud) minstrels in England, (*hauts*) *ménéstrels* in France, *ministriles altos* in Spain, *piffari* in Italy and *Pfeifer* in Germany.

The *alta* ensemble did not disappear after Tinctoris's statement. It was still widely used during the sixteenth century, and even in the seventeenth and eighteenth centuries it was occasionally heard. The great Goethe experienced *alta* performances in his youth: in his autobiographical *Dichtung und Wahrheit*, he reports that the music for the opening ceremony of the Frankfurt fair was played by shawm, bombard and trombone, an instrument combination not much different to that described by Konrad von Megenberg and Tinctoris. At this point we should turn to the instruments which constituted the core of the wind band from the fourteenth to the eighteenth centuries.

The shawm (*chalemie, chirimía, ciaramella, Schalmei*) depicted in fourteenth-century illustrations shows essentially the same external characteristics as the few specimens that survive from the sixteenth and seventeenth centuries in instrument collections: a double reed woodwind instrument with seven fingerholes (and an

1 Cristoforo de' Predis (or school of), Garden of Delights (before 1470), showing an *alta capella* on the right, behind the fountain (Modena, Biblioteca Estense)

alternative fingerhold for the little finger), no keys, a long flared bell and *d'* as its bottom note (albeit at a higher pitch than ours). The conical bore of extant museum instruments, of course, cannot be seen in pictures. A second, slightly larger reed instrument accompanied the shawm from the time of Konrad: the bombarde. It is pitched a fifth lower and has one key hidden under a wooden barrel (*fontanelle*). This is the alto bombarde described by Michael Practorius in his *Syntagma musicum* (Wolfenbüttel, 1619). Some surviving instruments can be found in the collections of Brussels and Vienna, and a fine late specimen, built around 1700 by Johann Christoph Denner of Nuremberg (the inventor of the clarinet) for the Frankfurt town band, is preserved in the Frankfurt Historisches Museum. Finally, a trumpet joined the reeds, bringing an element of variation into an otherwise constant and conservative context. Trumpet shapes changed from place to place and from decade to decade; Konrad probably had straight *buisines* in mind when he commented on wind music. Around 1400, S-shaped and other folded trumpets of various sizes replaced the straight instrument: shortly before 1500 a trombonist took over the duties of the trumpeter.

In organological terms, the trombone is still a trumpet, but in contrast to the *natural* trumpet which is restricted to the fanfares of the harmonic series, the U-shaped movable slide gives the trombone a fully chromatic scale (something that was achieved for the rest of the trumpet family only around 1800 by the invention of valves). It is possible that an immediate precursor of the trombone existed among the various trumpet types which played together with shawm and bombarde. This mysterious instrument is generally referred to as a slide-trumpet: it looked like a trumpet, but a moveable mouthpipe allowed diatonic as well as chromatic playing within a more restricted range than that of the trombone. Slide trumpets are documented in court inventories of the sixteenth century as survivors of an old-fashioned technology in more conservative areas of central Europe. Circumstantial evidence points to probable employment of this proto-trombone during several decades in the middle of the fifteenth century: long mouthpipes and certain particular hand positions can be observed in pictures, while some mid- to late-century documents mention a *trompone*, a *tuba ductilis*, a *trompette saicqueboute* long before the modern, U-slide trombone can be found in paintings. The slide-trumpet hypothesis is widely accepted although it has recently come under attack mainly for the lack of any hard evidence.

Experiments with slide-trumpet replicas demonstrate the musical and mechan-ical characteristics of the instrument. After some practising, considerable agility can be achieved (comparable to that of a bass trombone – the extension of the player's arm is about the same). The movement of the whole trumpet body on the mouthpipe is unfortunately not extremely beneficial to the stability of the instrument and might even prove dangerous to the player's teeth. Also, the player's arm length is the decisive factor for the low end of the diatonic range of a slide-trumpet. Thus, an instrument in *d* (a very comfortable size) yields approximately the same range as the alto bombarde. The use of bigger instruments does not affect the bottom register, since the maximum arm extension has to remain the same. One conclusion from these physiological facts is that three-part polyphony up to the age of Dufay and Binchois works well with a combination of shawm, bombarde and slide trumpet. Later compositions in many cases (and whenever a low contratenor is present) require a trombone. This might in fact be one reason why the trombone had to be invented at a certain point: as soon as composed polyphony generally required a contratenor bassus, one instrument of the wind band had to cross the until then accepted limit in the low register.

It is an interesting question – not only for instrument historians, but more generally for historians of science and the mechanical arts – why the trumpet was chosen to undergo the transformation and not the alto bombard. Two factors need to be considered here: the above-mentioned mechanical problems of the slide trumpet, and the rapid progress in metal technology, especially in places such as Nuremberg (the centre of trombone and trumpet making from 1500 to 1800). The development of a tenor bombarde, which would have answered the same purpose, took place only later, and this instrument, as Anthony Baines has shown, never enjoyed much popularity.

In the fourteenth and fifteenth centuries the *alta* ensemble usually consisted of three players (an additional musician is often found in pictures, apparently as a replacement for a tired shawm player). The years around 1500 saw an increase in size of the wind band. In order to accommodate the needs of the new four-voice norm in composed polyphony, a second bombarde player was added: the trombone (or sackbut – a tenor trombone in modern terms) took the bass; tenor and alto lines were given to the bombardes; and the shawm player performed his virtuoso diminutions on the top line, the treble voice. But the turn of the century was also marked by experimentation with other woodwind instruments, mostly descendants of the shawm family: loud, ringing wind-cap shawms enhanced the brilliance of the ensemble's outdoor performances; and crumhorns (also windcap reed instruments, but with a conical instead of a cylindrical bore) added different colours to the warm timbre of trombones and bombardes in indoor events.

The most successful addition to the shawm band, however, was a hybrid between woodwind and brass: the cornett. It was either straight and turned from a single piece of fruit wood, or it was curved and made in two halves that were glued together and sealed by a cover of leather or parchment. The sound was produced using a cup mouthpiece, similar to that of a trumpet or trombone. This kind of sound production forces the organologist to hesitate to classify the cornett as woodwind, while the material prevents the classification among brass instruments. The combination of cup mouthpiece, short tube and fingerholes results in many difficulties of intonation and embouchure. Once mastered, however, the sound quality of the cornett is superior to any other Renaissance wind instrument, the agility is immense and the range of dynamics and expression span between brassy trumpet sounds to incredibly sweet flute-like tones. Small wonder, then, that we know the names of virtuoso cornett players from the beginning of the sixteenth century to the end, from Augustin Schubinger at the court of Emperor Maximilian to Girolamo Dalla Casa at St Mark's in Venice.

In the latter part of the sixteenth century a true bass was needed (the lowest instrument was still the tenor trombone). Instrument makers started to construct bass trombones and bass bombardes. These instruments produced a beautiful sound, but were not particularly handy for outdoor performances. Better suited for the needs of town bands and princely minstrels was a new development: the bassoon (curtal). Its origins are still shrouded in darkness, but it appears regularly in inventories and instrumentation lists from the middle of the century. The total length of its bore was the same as that of the bass bombarde, but since the bore was folded, the instrument could easily be carried from the market place to the minstrel gallery and back.

It should be clear from this that these various new instruments were still additions to the basic shawm/bombarde/trombone group: the standard wind band of the Renaissance was a mixed woodwind/brass ensemble. 'Pure' ensembles of crumhorns or trombones were rare, and they were employed mainly for special effects (in theatre productions, for example). Pure shawm bands existed in the earlier fifteenth century, but then gave way to the more common woodwind/brass combination: they do not reappear after 1500.

One alternative standard combination existed concurrently with the mixed shawm/trombone ensemble, and this was a very influential one: the cornett/trombone ensemble without reeds. The remarkable sound quality of the cornett has already been noted. The trombone apparently lost its trumpet characteristics shortly after the invention of the U-slide and acquired an enormous flexibility in sound and dynamics, albeit without the virtuoso potential of the cornett. The sound quality of this formation paved the way for all kinds of artful and sophisticated wind music, which reached its climax in the instrumental canzonas of the Gabrielis in Venice. The mixed shawm band was soon excluded from these impressive performances, at least in Italy and at Italianate courts north of the Alps, but more conservative town bands and princely chapels in England, France and Germany continued to play motets and dance music with shawms and trombones, occasionally with the inclusion of crumhorns.

Shortly after 1500 we find the cornett and trombone performing together with human voices, not only in secular feasts and in the theatre, but also during the Mass. Just a few decades earlier, the combination of (loud) winds and voices must have been almost inconceivable: this was dictated by the rules of separation of *haut* and *bas*, and applied particularly to the strictly regulated use of music in church. Wind bands were not generally excluded from church before 1500, but their performances were restricted to those parts of the Holy Service in which the choir was silent: at the beginning of the Mass, at the Offertory, during the Elevation and at the end of the service. This is all we can learn from the few extant documents specifying the place of instrumental performances during the Mass. The fact that singers and instrumentalists were both employed by the Church has led to some misconceptions about mixed vocal-instrumental performance. Collaboration between singers and wind instruments earlier in the fifteenth century was further suggested by Mass movements that have parts designated 'trompette', 'trompetta' or similar. Yet, at least at the current state of knowledge, it is clear that there was no place for wind instrumentalists in performances of the Mass Ordinary before the introduction of the trombone and cornett. Trompetta parts were not intended for a trumpet player, but for a singer who had to imitate trumpet fanfares in a vocal context.

Finally, we should consider the possible repertory of the *alta* ensemble. A few fifteenth-century compositions have been discussed as possible instrumental ensemble music (for example, an 'Alta' ascribed to Francisco de La Torre in the *Cancionero Musical de Palacio*, textless settings in the lost Strasbourg MS, 222 c.22, and in the Trent Codex 87, as well as a complete chansonnier (Rome, Biblioteca Casanatense, MS 2856). The criteria for identifying such pieces include: absence of text, 'instrumental' formulae; and florid upper voices above slowly-moving tenor lines. Unfortunately, the significance of these criteria can be questioned: many sources transmit untexted chansons, 'instrumental' formulae are also found in undoubtedly vocal compositions, and florid top lines with slow tenors are not unusual in song settings. Thus, the identification of instrumental ensemble music is not without its problems, and the assignment of ensemble music to the wind band offers even more difficulties. In the reconstruction of a fifteenth-century wind band repertory, it is probably better to be content with arrangements of vocal music than to rely on doubtful instrumental settings.

From pictures and archival documents it is clear that dance music made up a large part of the repertory. Unfortunately, almost no polyphonic dance settings are extant. Music for the most famous of all fifteenth century dances, the basse danse, is available only in dance tutors, and there only in the form of monophonic melodies without rhythmic differentiation. The near absence of polyphonic elaborations of these melodies (only a few settings of the famous *Spagna*-tune survive from the fifteenth-century, and those might be compositional studies rather than actual dance music) have given rise to a number of hypotheses on instrumental improvisation on the dance tunes: either bombarde or slide trumpet/trombone could have played the dance melody in long note values while the other two instruments improvised; or slide trumpet and bombarde performed some sort of 'chordal' framework, to which the shawm player added a virtuoso top line. But the nature of *ad hoc* performances is still a subject for speculation. The 'free' improvisation of basse-danse music on slowly moving tenors was not the only possible way to construct dance music in the fifteenth century: instrumental adaptations of existing chanson settings could have been used as well. The appearance of chanson tenors in the dance tutors lends the second solution greater probability.

In the early sixteenth century it was common for chansons to be arranged as polyphonic dance settings. Many of the then popular Parisian chansons reappear in printed dance collections by Attaingnant, Moderne, Susato *et al*, with only a little reworking to accommodate the needs of the dancers. However, as in the fifteenth century, the playing of dance music was not the only task for the wind musician: a few manuscript collections prepared by court instrumentalists (such as the Copenhagen MS Gl.Kgl.Sml.1872–4° of about 1540) as well as contemporary descriptions of performances demonstrate that adaptations of vocal music were still the wind musician's daily diet.

Although a considerable amount of original instrumental ensemble music exists from the sixteenth century, most of the printed collections were aimed at the well-educated amateur. Loud wind instruments, however, were excluded from the music-making of noble and bourgeois circles in the Renaissance, as Baldassare Castiglione pointed out in his *Il cortegiano* (1528). Therefore, most collections of fantasias and ricercars are of little value in the assessment of the wind band repertory. Compositions actually intended for wind bands appeared only late in the century and in most cases required special forces, as in the case for the polychoral canzonas of Andrea and Giovanni Gabrieli and their Venetian colleagues. These highly sophisticated works were not to be played by the then already old-fashioned *alta* ensemble with shawm and bombardes, but by the brilliant cornett and sackbut players of St Mark's.

Although the *alta* ensemble continued to exist for more than a century, its performances were more and more restricted to dance and outdoor music. Thus, the wind band ended with the same tasks with which it started its career in Konrad of Megenberg's time.

Ex.1
Francisco de La Torre, *Alta*

(Madrid, Palacio Real, MS 1335, f. 223), © Tess Knighton

Select bibliography

A. C. BAINES, *Woodwind instruments and their history*, 3rd edn (London, 1967); and 'Shawm', *New Grove*

E. A. BOWLES, *La pratique musicale au Moyen Age* (Geneva, 1983)

C. PAGE, 'German musicians and their instruments, a 14th-century account by Konrad of Megenberg', *Early Music*, x (1982), pp. 192–200

Techniques of composition

27 Musical design and the rise of the cyclic Mass

Gareth Curtis

Even the most basic contact with Mass music of the late medieval and early Renaissance periods suggests that it cannot be listened to in the same way as, say, a Classical symphony. This is not merely a function of their different purposes, that Mass music is strictly an adjunct to liturgy, whereas a symphony is to be listened to as music for its own sake. It is also because sonata form, like most other forms of the seventeenth, eighteenth and nineteenth centuries, is dynamic: it has within it a sense of progress, and it is the logic of this progress which gives aural coherence. By contrast, the music with which we are concerned here is essentially decorative. Hence, the sort of coherence it has and the means by which it attains it – in effect, the principles behind its design – are correspondingly different.

The decorative function of medieval and early Renaissance Mass music follows, of course, from the broader ethos of sacred polyphony and its place in the liturgy of the day. At root, liturgy is a form of words which can be decorated to different degrees of complexity with ritual action and music. So far as the latter is concerned, the most basic application is plainsong – though even this varies considerably, with the grander liturgical occasions being reflected in a more florid style of melody. At a still higher level of adornment, liturgy may then be decorated by the use of polyphony – often itself a decoration of plainsong – and this in turn may be relatively simple or may draw on all the ingenuity at the disposal of its composer.

Clearly, the interaction between text and musical form lies between two possible extremes. At the one end, musical form may be generated almost entirely by the text; in other words, the composer more or less sets the words as they come until he reaches the end. Conversely, it may be generated quite independently; the composer erects a musical edifice upon which he then hangs the text and the details of the polyphony.

In the medieval and early Renaissance Mass repertory, the most strictly text-based music usually tends to be the simplest in style. An obvious example is the discant repertory from the Old Hall MS, much of which moves in little more than block chords. Subsequent manifestations of the same basic approach might be seen in the various so-called *Playn Song* Masses from late fifteenth- and early sixteenth-century England, and later still in simple block-chord settings written by such composers as Lassus and Ruffo.

Yet, for all the austere dignity of many of these pieces, one is forced to conclude that the level of liturgical adornment remains modest. Later in the sixteenth century, this was undoubtedly a response to the ideals of the Counter-Reformation, in particular to a perceived need for clear word-setting. In the fourteenth century, on the other hand, such technical 'innocence' probably reflects more the lowly regard in which Mass music was still held, at least by comparison with the then prestigious isorhythmic motet.

Clearly, more composerly music involved more conspicuous musical structuring, a fact especially evident once early fifteenth-century composers began to group movements into pairs and whole cycles. In particular, such movements came to be linked by quite a range of features such as similar scoring and modal character, and often by structural parallels like identical mensuration schemes and patterns of alternating duets and fully-scored sections.

This is perhaps most obvious in the early English cantus firmus Masses, notably in those where the underlying chant is rhythmicized in the same way in each movement. In the anonymous *Missa Fuit homo missus*, by no means an extreme case for its time (late 1420s or 1430s?), it appears that the anonymous composer started by laying out a basic musical template which controlled the rhythm of the cantus firmus, its disposition between passages of reduced scoring, and the overall mensural scheme; only then did he fill in the details of the polyphony and the words (see Table 1).

Table 1

Mensuration	Kyrie*	Gloria	Credo	Scoring	Chant
3-time	[Kyrie 1]	Et in terra	Patrem	reduced	–
	[Kyrie 2]	Gratias	Et in unum	full	A
2-time	[Christe 3]	Qui tollis	Et incarnatus	reduced	–
	[Kyrie 4]	Qui sedes	Crucifixus	full	B
3-time	[Kyrie 6]	Cum Sancto	Et exspecto	full	C

Mensuration	Sanctus	Agnus Dei	Scoring	Chant
3-time	Sanctus	Agnus 1	full	A
	Pleni	Agnus 2	reduced	–
2-time	Osanna 1	Agnus 3	full	B
	Benedictus	–	reduced	–
3-time	Osanna 2	Dona nobis	full	C

(*Texting reconstructed as the source is corrupt)

Demonstrated here are a number of structural points which were, in fact, treated as conventional by most English composers of the immediate post-Old Hall period. For example, each movement has a major division near the centre, this being reinforced by a mensuration change from triple to duple time; the second 'half' may then end, as here, with a brief return to triple time. The placing of these divisions in relation to the text was also largely conventional: in the Gloria, for example, the main division was normally made before the first 'Qui tollis', and any second division at 'Cum Sancto Spiritu'.

The importance attached to musical form for its own sake brings about some curious anomalies between the musical structure and that of the text. In order to place the major musical division as near as possible to the mid-point of the text, English composers usually split the Kyrie, not into three groups of three prosulae, but after the fourth or fifth prosula and perhaps again before the final one. As we see from the *Missa Fuit homo missus*, the Sanctus could be divided immediately before rather than after the first Osanna; the Agnus Dei was almost invariably divided, not between each of its three invocations, but before the third, and perhaps again before 'Dona nobis pacem'. The one significant link between musical and textual structure which became conventional (though by no means universally so) was the placing of reduced scoring at the Benedictus and the second Agnus Dei. As will be seen, the ground plan of the *Missa Fuit homo missus* has been modified accordingly.

Such conventions are typical also of English Masses that make freer use of a cantus firmus; in practice, for example, it became more common for a cantus firmus to be further divided by the addition of extra reduced-scoring sections. Neither was it vital that a chant should be rhythmicized in the same way in each movement (see, for example, the *Missa Rex seculorum*, with conflicting ascriptions to Leonel Power and John Dunstable), or indeed that it should be stated literally and unadorned. The same norms even apply, if less strictly, to those Masses nowadays termed 'freely' composed (no doubt in many cases merely because we have not yet discovered the basis of their composition). Indeed, many of the main conventions were so readily accepted that they still survive into the early Tudor festal Mass repertory. Taverner's *Missa Corona spinea*, for example, is organized as in Table 2.

It is, perhaps, unusual to find the main division of the Agnus before the second rather than the third invocation; presumably this is simply another solution to the problem of dividing a tripartite text over a bipartite musical structure. Obviously, too, one has to admit that the structural method is treated with a little more freedom than would be typical in the English repertory of the early to middle fifteenth century. Nevertheless, it would appear that, from its beginnings in the 1420s until its demise some 130 years later, the mainstream English Mass cycle treated purely musical structure as the first consideration, and it was over the bones of a pre-existing and largely conventional edifice that the glories of its polyphony were spread. What we would regard as the rational projection of text was barely an issue.

For a period around the middle of the fifteenth century, the English style of writing cyclic Masses became a critical influence on Western European sacred music generally. There survive, for example, a large number of mid-century continental Masses which were so closely modelled on the English style that they took over many of its structural conventions – including the pre-eminence of musical form – apparently without question. Even in early fifteenth-century works such as Dufay's *Missa Sancti Jacobi* (late 1420s?), one finds obvious parallels between movement groups: the Kyrie, Gloria and Credo, for example, are all in the Dorian mode and scored for the same vocal layout consisting of a three-part chorus (marked as such) and a duetting (solo?) pair of high voices. Furthermore, the

Table 2

Mensuration	Gloria	Credo	Scoring*
3-time	Et in terra	Patrem	reduced
	Gratias	Et ex Patre	full
	Domine Deus	Genitum	reduced
	Filius Patris	Qui propter	full
2-time	Qui tollis	Et incarnatus	reduced
	Qui sedes	Et resurrcxit	full
	Quoniam	–	reduced
	Jesu Christe	–	full
3-time	Cum Sancto	Et exspecto	full

Mensuration	Sanctus	Agnus Dei	Scoring
3-time	Sanctus	Agnus 1	reduced
	Dominus Deus	Miserere	full
	Pleni	–	reduced
	Osanna 1	–	full
2-time	Benedictus	Agnus 2	reduced
	Osanna 2	Agnus 3	full
3-time	–	Dona nobis	reduced

(*The arrangement of the cantus firmus has been omitted since it varies from movement to movement.)

structure of each of these movements is built from blocks of three contrasting panels (see Table 3).

Taking the wider perspective, it looks as if the continental Mass tradition may normally have favoured a rather closer relationship between music and text. True, one might wonder about the logic of the breaks made in Dufay's Gloria and Credo (though equally one might wonder where the most logical divisions do, in fact, lie). However, as in other early continental cycles, the tripartite shape of the Kyrie is respected, as also is that of the Agnus Dei. Incidentally, apart from being a plenary Mass, complete with Proper as well as Ordinary settings, the *Missa Sancti Jacobi* differs from the typical English cycle in having not one but several ground plans, each of which affects its own particular group of movements.

After the mid-century, Dufay was one of a number of continentals who adopted the idea of the English cantus firmus Mass, but without following its traditions as literally as the pure imitators mentioned above. In particular, their treatment of the genre was free enough both to take account of the varying forms of the texts, and to allow a considerable measure of structural differentiation between movements.

Table 3

Mensuration	Kyrie	Gloria	Credo	Scoring
2(₵)-time	Kyrie 1	Et in terra	Patrem	Chorus
3-time	Kyrie 2	Domine Deus, rex	Et ex Patre	Duo
2(C)-time	Kyrie 3	Qui tollis	Genitum	Chorus
2(₵)-time	Christe 1	Qui sedes	Qui propter	Chorus
3-time	Christe 2	Cum Sancto	Crucifixus	Duo
2(C)-time	Christe 3	Amen	Et ascendit	Chorus
2(₵)-time	Kyrie 4	–	Et in Spiritum	Chorus
3-time	Kyrie 5	–	Qui cum Patre	Duo
2(C)-time	Kyrie 6	–	Et unam sanctam	Chorus
2(₵)-time			Amen*	Chorus
3-time				

(*One source only has a section in ₵ time.)

Consider, for example, the layout of Dufay's *Missa Ave regina celorum*, probably written in the early 1470s (see Table 4).

Here, the only substantial parallels lie between the two long-text movements; elsewhere, much as the care of the underlying musical planning is clear enough, it looks pragmatic, depending to a great extent on the shape of the text.

Table 4

Mensuration	Kyrie	Scoring*	Chant
3-time	Kyrie 1	full	A
	Kyrie 2	full	B
	Kyrie 3 (=1)	full	A
2-time	Christe 1	full	C
	Christe 2	reduced	–
	Christe 3 (=1)	full	C
3-time	Kyrie 4	full	D
	Kyrie 5	reduced	–
	Kyrie 6	full	E

Mensuration	Gloria	Credo	Scoring	Chant
3-time	Et in terra	Patrem	full	A
	–	Et ex Patre	reduced	–
	Gratias (reduced)	Genitum (full)		B
	–	Qui propter	reduced	–
	Domine Deus, rex	Et incarnatus	full	C
2-time	Domine Deus, agnus	Et ascendit	reduced	–
	Qui tollis	Et in Spiritum	full	D
	Qui sedes	Et unam sanctam	full	E¹
	Tu solus altissimus	–	reduced	–
	Cum Sancto Spiritu	Et exspecto	full	E²

Mensuration	Sanctus	Scoring	Chant
3-time	Sanctus	full	AB
	Pleni	reduced	–
	Gloria tua	full	C
	Osanna 1	full	D
2-time	Benedictus	reduced	–
	Osanna 2	full	E

Mensuration	Agnus dei	Scoring	Chant
3-time	Agnus 1	full	AB
2-time	Agnus 2	reduced	C
	Agnus 3	full	DE

(*Fully-scored sections may include short duos etc.)

With this greater differentiation between movements came new musical opportunities. Some composers undoubtedly used it to exhibit the sheer range of techniques at their command. In each of the movements of his *Missa Prolationum*, for example, Okeghem embeds mensuration canons at different intervals. Then again, there is the remarkable sub-tradition of Masses based on the secular melody *L'homme armé*, which drew forth a prodigal display of canonic and other self-consciously ingenious techniques. Thus, in his *Missa L'homme armé super voces musicales*, Josquin begins the cantus firmus on different solmization syllables in each movement, and adds a number of mensuration canons for good measure.

Compositional virtuosity aside, greater structural flexibility fitted in conveniently with a move towards kinds of Mass cycle other than the standard cantus firmus type. It gave particular impetus to, for example, the parody Mass, whose origins may go back some way into the fifteenth-century, but which continued to flourish well into the period of Palestrina. We see, too, the rise of a new type of chant-based Mass, in which the underlying plainsong is divided into convenient segments formed into imitative points; these then articulate the musical structure into miniature fugal expositions. This, again, is a technique with a history – Josquin's *Missa Pange lingua* is an early example – but, as the sixteenth century wears on, it becomes central to the mainstream continental tradition. Clearly, both of these are methods which thrive where movements are structured on a more individual basis; parallel structuring simply imposes too many constraints.

So far, our discussion has concentrated on features which are clearly visible from the written page, and which are, in many cases, audible to the experienced listener. It is clear, however, that many medieval and early Renaissance composers, especially English ones, were not entirely concerned with what was heard, any more than the craftsmen of the great Gothic cathedrals cared whether the ordinary mortal could see all their finest workmanship. In order to understand some of the more closely-guarded secrets of the composers' work, it is necessary to delve further into what they regarded music to be.

Perceived at its highest level, music was a component of the quadrivium, the basis of all medieval and Renaissance learning. Its study stretched from the philosophical *musica mundana* (the harmony of the universe) and *musica humana* (the harmony of the ideally attuned human being) down to the audible type of music (*musica instrumentalis*) which was, in turn, divided into higher and lower levels, respectively *musica speculativa* (musical theory) and *musica practica* (music as composed and performed). Nan C. Carpenter has suggested that medieval universities saw '*musica speculativa* as a mathematical discipline, one of the encyclopedic liberal arts forming the basis of philosophy and pre-requisite to the study of theology; and *musica practica* as a living art, cultivated *ad majoram gloriam Dei*' (p. 89). The extent to which music was viewed as a mathematical discipline is well attested by the amount of material in 'high' musical theory which is concerned with the relationship between intervals and the proportions of string lengths. Yet these simple proportions did not merely explain consonance: they also partook of the perfection of the higher musics, in that they too reflected the harmonious nature of God's creation. It follows, almost certainly, that even the modestly regarded *musica practica* might raise itself within the wider philosophical framework if it could in some way emulate this perfection.

It is not surprising, then, to find that the use of proportions in the construction of Mass settings is commonplace, if apparently not universal. Even in the fourteenth century, when the isorhythmic motet rather than the Mass was the normal vehicle for a composer's highest endeavours, proportions are not unusual. In the French repertory, for instance, it is quite common, even in stylistically modest pieces, for sections to have the same lengths or to be in simple proportion to each other. For example, the largely block-chord Kyrie setting by Chipre (Ivrea and Apt MSS) consists of three sections containing respectively 30, 30 and 36 breves. (This count includes the final notes of each section; very often, and increasingly so as time goes on, it is necessary to exclude end-of-section longs from such counts.)

Proportions could also be more intricately organized, as in the main part of the Gloria of the Sorbonne Mass:

$$\text{breves} \quad 63\ / \quad 91\ / \quad 39$$
$$\text{i.e.} \qquad\quad 9:\quad 13 \qquad\quad \times\ 7$$
$$\qquad\qquad\qquad 7:\quad 3\times 13$$

There follows an Amen whose two sections are respectively 16 perfect and 16 imperfect longs in length.

In fifteenth-century England, as the Mass cycle became the most prestigious form, there is considerable evidence for the use of proportions. In fact, it seems that John Dunstable based virtually all his surviving music on proportional schemes; he, of course, represents the learned musician *par excellence*, famed also in his day as a mathematician and astronomer.

As an example of mid-century English practice, we may take that most majestic of all Masses of the period, the *Missa Caput*, whose whole structure seems to be permeated by an extraordinary series of proportional relationships (see Table 5).

Table 5

Semibreve beats:		in 3-time bars		in 2-time bars	
		C.F.*	non-C.F.	C.F.	non-C.F.
Kyrie	I:	252	63		
	II:			216	80
Gloria	I:	222	48		
	II:			180	76
Credo	I:	228	57		
	II:			212	112
Sanctus	I:	229	51		
	II:			192	48
Agnus Dei	I:	234	48		
	II:			132	40
		1165		932	
			267		356

(*Short rests in the middle of statements on the cantus firmus are counted as part of those statements.)

Most obviously, if we separate the duets from the cantus firmus sections, and then compare the number of semibreve beats in the triple- and duple-time 'halves' of each movement, the following exact proportions emerge:

$$\text{C.F.} - 1165{:}932 = 5{:}4 \qquad \times\ 233$$
$$\text{Non-C.F.} - 267{:}356 = 3{:}4 \qquad \times\ 89$$

Again, totalling all the beats respectively in the triple- and duple-time sections, we find the following almost exact proportion.

$$
\begin{aligned}
1165 + 267 &= 1432 & 932 + 356 &= 1288 \\
&= 179 : & & 161 & \times 8 \\
\text{i.e. almost} &= 180 : & & 162 \\
&= 10 : & & 9
\end{aligned}
$$

Many other internal proportions are evident: for example, in the Sanctus we find:

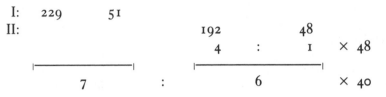

$$
\begin{array}{llll}
\text{I:} & 229 & 51 & \\
\text{II:} & & 192 & 48 \\
& & 4 \;\; : \;\; 1 & \times 48 \\
& \overline{\qquad\quad 7 \qquad\quad} & : & \overline{\qquad\quad 6 \qquad\quad} \quad \times 40
\end{array}
$$

Adding beats in certain groups of movement sections is also suggestive:

Gloria I C.F. + Credo I C.F.   (222 + 228)   = 450
Kyrie II C.F. + Sanctus II C.F.
+ Agnus II C.F.   (216 + 192 + 132)   = 540
                        i.e. 5:6 × 90

Gloria I non-C.F. + Credo I non-C.F.   (48 + 57)   =105
Kyrie II non-C.F. + Sanctus II non-C.F.
+ Agnus II non-C.F.   (80 + 48 + 40)   = 168
                        i.e. 5:8 × 21

However, all this probably raises at least as many questions as it solves. The problem is not so much whether the proportions exist – clearly they do. But what special significance did they have (if indeed any), why were these particular numbers chosen, and why, at the internal level, do they seem to have been applied in such an apparently haphazard manner? Why, for example, are there internal proportions in the 3-time sections of the Kyrie and Credo, but not in the other movements?

It is also difficult to say whether the inexact proportion between the total number of beats in the 3-time and 2-time sections is of any significance – though it is perfectly possible that exactitude here would merely have spoiled the figures elsewhere. It is, in fact, surprising how many pieces seem gratuitously to use almost but not quite exact proportions; one might even speculate that their composers deliberately built in these imperfections as a sign of humility. A representative example is one of Leonel Power's Credo settings from the Old Hall MS (no. 73), in which changes of scoring divide the music into four sections as follows:

	à2	à3	à2	à3
semibreve beats	28	34	36	45

Were the second section 35 semibreves long, the following elegant proportions would appear:

	à2	à3	à2	à3
	28	35	36	45

i.e.

$$4 \ : \ 5 \ [\times 7] \qquad 4 \ : \ 5 \ [\times 9]$$

and

$$7 \ : \ 9 \quad [\times 9]$$

It would be pointless to attempt any definitive statement about the use of proportion in medieval and Renaissance music. As yet, the extent of its use is too uncertain, though we have sufficient evidence to suggest that numerical relationships were regularly employed by English composers up to the Reformation, and by various continentals including Okeghem, Busnois, Obrecht and Josquin. Even where no proportions have been found, it may in many cases be that no one has yet counted in the correct way. That said, it is all too easy to imagine that proportions exist where they probably do not.

The other respect in which numbers may be used is for their symbolic connotations. In the medieval and Renaissance periods, the symbolism of number was a crucial part of theological exposition, and the study of numerology according to the principles of Pythagoreanism, Neo-Platonism and gematria held an important place in medieval study. Given the extent to which number association pervades the art and literature of the period, one would hardly expect it to be absent from the music.

Some Mass music undeniably does make use of symbolic numbers: Trowell has pointed out, for example, that Qweldryk's Credo from the Old Hall MS contains 888 minims, signifying *Iesous* in Greek gematria, and that Dunstable's Gloria *Spiritus et alme* contains 801 minims, the number by which the Gnostics equated Christ the Alpha-and-Omega with Christ the Dove.

Less esoteric numbers also appear regularly, even as early as the fourteenth century; for example in the Sanctus of the so-called Toulouse Mass

$$\text{breves} \quad 27 \, / \, 23 \, / \, 23 \, / \, 26 \, / \ 33$$
$$\longmapsto 99 \longmapsto 33$$
$$3 \ : \ 1 \ \times \ 33$$

where 33 stands for the number of years Christ is thought to have spent on earth.

Again, it is clear that numbers were often chosen for their elegance or arithmetical interest. Dunstable's large-scale paired Gloria and Credo for four voices are respectively 28×36 and 36×36 minims long: 36 is, among other things, a perfect square, and 28 is both the second perfect number (i.e. the product of its factors, viz. $1 + 2 + 4 + 7 + 14$) and the seventh triangular number ($28 = 1 + 2 + 3 + 4 + 5 + 6 + 7$). The combined length of the two movements is, of course, 64×36, i.e. $8^2 \times 6^2$. All this can hardly have happened by accident; it has to be planned into a work from the most basic stages of the compositional process. Also, for what it is worth, those rather unlikely looking factors at the heart of the *Caput*

Mass – 89 and 233 – both lie on the Fibonacci series, a set of numbers which had been known for at least two hundred years.

The trouble is that, as with the use of proportion, limits on current knowledge prevent us from generalizing with any degree of safety. Not least of the problems is that a little determination and ingenuity can provide significance for virtually any number. Besides, we all too rarely know the sort of preoccupations which might have impinged on a particular composer in a particular situation, and which might have led him to use a particular set of symbols.

In the last resort, no tidy pattern should be imposed upon such a wide range of traditions and available techniques; besides, given the limits of a relatively short article, many important considerations have necessarily been omitted here. If we are to extract any general principle at all, we must return to the original proposition – that music for the medieval and early Renaissance Mass has a largely decorative function, which probably only gives way to more self-conscious edification well into the High Renaissance. At its most elevated level, then, musical design seems to have meant the creation of an architecturally satisfying edifice which in turn provided a firm framework for the polyphony. And if, as clearly happened in a significant number of cases, composers chose to build those edifices in accordance with mathematical principles, this should not be thought of as contriving mere perfection in numbers. Rather, it was an attempt to achieve a higher spiritual perfection – indeed, a musical parable for the universal truths of philosophy and theology – and hence the more richly conceived *ad majorem gloriam Dei*.

Select bibliography

General

N. C. CARPENTER, *Music in the medieval and Renaissance universities* (Norman, Oklahoma, 1958)

T. GÖLLNER and L. LOCKWOOD, 'Mass: II Polyphony to 1600', *New Grove*

P. GOSSETT, 'Techniques of unification in early cyclic Masses and Mass pairs', *Journal of the American Musicological Society*, xix (1966), pp. 205–31

E. H. SPARKS, *Cantus firmus in Mass and motet, 1420–1520* (Berkeley and Los Angeles, 1963)

B. TROWELL, 'Proportion in the Music of Dunstable', *Proceedings of the Royal Musical Association*, cv (1978–9), pp. 100–40

Music

Most of the relevant music can be found in volumes from the series *Musica Britannica* (especially vol. viii); *Early English Church Music* (especially vols. xx and xxii); and *Corpus Mensurabilis Musicae* (especially series i, xi, xvii, xxix and xlvi).

28 Borrowed music
'Allez regrets' and the use of pre-existent material

Irena Cholij

During the Middle Ages and Renaissance composers often built their music around pre-existent compositions. The original composition could be a polyphonic work, such as a motet or chanson, or it could be a single melodic line, such as a monophonic song or a plainchant melody. (Indeed, polyphony arose from the simple practice of different voices singing plainchant melodies at parallel pitches.) Sometimes the composition employed was relevant to the final product; increasingly, however, it became more of an abstract starting point.

Far from being a restrictive practice, the use of pre-existent material was seen as a compositional and intellectual challenge. This was clearly the case when a number of composers chose to base their works on the same composition. The most popular 'borrowed melody' was the monophonic song *L'homme armé*. From the earliest settings by composers in the third quarter of the fifteenth century (including Masses by Okeghem and Dufay) to a somewhat anachronistic seventeenth-century twelve-voice setting attributed to Carissimi, the 'L'homme armé' melody served as the basis for over thirty Masses, as well as for a number of chansons and instrumental pieces.

An illuminating way of studying approaches to composition is to compare works based on the same pre-existent work. A fascinating group, from this standpoint, is the one built around the chanson 'Allez regrets', by the Franco-Flemish composer Hayne van Ghizeghem. We know little about the life of Hayne, who was born some time around 1445. His extant output is small: a mere seventeen chansons are definitely attributable to him. Yet the chansons were well known and widely disseminated. Testimony to the popularity of 'Allez regrets' is the fact that it has come down to us in no fewer than twenty-seven manuscript or early printed sources. (This is a greater number even than the sources for Hayne's best known chanson 'De tous biens plaine' on which a very large number of compositions are based.) Its text, a rondeau *cinquain*, was written by Jean II, Duke of Bourbon (d.1488).

Among works based on 'Allez regrets' during the last two decades of the fifteenth century and during the first part of the sixteenth century are three intabulations, several chansons and six Masses. Between them they exhibit a rich variety in compositional approaches. Of these pieces, the intabulations are the most straightforward. An intabulation was essentially an arrangement of a vocal piece for an instrument such as a lute or organ, transcribed into a system of musical notation for instrumentalists. Ornamentation was often added, using figures idiosyncratic to the instrument for which the intabulation was intended, thus transforming the original composition.

The earliest of the three extant intabulations of 'Allez regrets' is in the very ornate manuscript of the famous Vicenzo Capirola in Venice (*c.*1517). Of its forty-two compositions about half use vocal pieces. A second lute intabulation is found in a volume of arrangements made by Hans Gerle (1533). The third is also in a German source, this time a volume of keyboard music compiled by Leonhard Kleber between 1521 and 1524. A comparison of the opening bars of these three intabulations appears in Ex. 1.

Capirola's is the simplest, with the lightest degree of ornamentation. As with other intabulations, most of the ornamentation takes the form of passing notes, neighbouring notes, scales to fill in larger intervals and written out turns. Not surprisingly, these occur most where previously there was relative inactivity. Where there is more movement in the original the intabulation is often literal.

Capirola ornaments each of the vocal lines to some degree, though the top part

Ex. 1

Bars 1–4 of 'Allez regrets' in three different intabulations
(a) Hayne van Ghizeghem, 'Allez regrets'; (b) Vicenzo Capirola, 'A les regres'; (c) Hans Gerle, 'Ales regres'; (d) Leonhard Kleber, 'Ales regres'

((b) Chicago, Newberry Library, Vicenzo Capirola's Lute Book, ff. 37v-8 ; (c) (*Tablatur auff die Laudten*. ff. 43v-4);

(d) Berlin, Staatsbibliothek Preussischer Kulturbesitz, Musikabteilung MS 40026, ff. 21-2v) has most of the faster movement. Gerle, on the other hand, aims for a more even distribution of quicker notes and obtains a degree of dialoguing between parts. Unlike Capirola, he also adopts one or two figures which he uses more frequently than others. The figures [♩♩] and [♩♩] (and minor variants) are often used imitatively or sequentially, lending some cohesion to the piece without making it too monotonous.

Kleber's intabulation is more uniform than the other two. He uses a clear-cut texture of a quite heavily ornamented top part supported by a simple two-part bass

Ex. 2
Bars 1–4 of 'Allez regrets' in four different chanson versions
(a) Hayne van Ghizeghem, 'Allez regrets'; (b) Alexander Agricola; (c) Anonymous;
(d) Bartolomeo; (e) Ludwig Senfl

((b) Rome, Cappella Giulia, C.G.XIII 27,ff.78v–9; (c) Bologna, Civico Museo
Bibliografico Musicale Q17, ff.50v–1; (d) Bologna, Civico Museo Bibliografico
Musicale Q17, ff.23v–4; (e) Munich, Universitäitsbibliothek 326–31, ff.20v–1,
3–3v, 57v–8, 12v–13)

– though the lower parts do have moments of more interest. Like Gerle, Kleber
favours one figure above others: ♩ ♬♬ and its retrograde version ♬♬ ♩ .

All three intabulations carefully follow their model, decorating the chanson bar
by bar. The only significant departures from this pattern are the opening flourish,
by way of an anacrusis, added by Capirola and an extension by Kleber of three bars
to the important central cadence.

In terms of the chronology of compositions based on 'Allez regrets' the
intabulations are all rather late. A much earlier group, and one using freer
treatment of Hayne's composition, is represented by five chansons. With the
exception of the one by Senfl these were probably composed in the final two
decades of the fifteenth century. Four are cantus firmus settings. In each case one
voice of the Hayne chanson is transferred into one voice of the new chanson and
the remaining voices are newly composed. Thus these chansons embody far more
free composition than the intabulations, as well as greater experimentation with
ideas from the original Hayne setting. They all display different compositional
approaches, but they share one characteristic: each begins with a quotation from
the opening bars of the Hayne superius and tenor parts (see Ex. 2).

The four cantus firmus 'Allez regrets' chansons are by Alexander Agricola, anon., Bartolomeo degli Organi and Ludwig Senfl. The earliest is probably the one by Agricola. He uses Hayne's tenor as his tenor, but since his contratenor uses the same tessitura as his superius, his tenor is actually the lowest sounding voice. Agricola's piece is exactly the same length as its model. Here, however, the structural similarities end. Hayne's chanson is constructed from a well-balanced duet between an equally lyrical tenor and superius, supported by a surprisingly melodic bass. Each of the voices moves in similar note values and within its own particular pitch range – though there are instances of voice crossing. Agricola's piece has the superius and contratenor constantly weaving in and out of each other's paths – and not infrequently crossing the tenor's domain – in a fairly restless contrapuntal tapestry, featuring many scalic figures. He observes Hayne's first major cadence and begins the next phrase with the only instance of imitation in this piece (Hayne uses no imitation in his chanson). From here, however, the voices unfold in continuous threads, scarcely acknowledging the cadences – not even the important central one. In general, the piece displays density and complexity as opposed to Hayne's simplicity and clarity.

Hayne's tenor also serves as the bass for the anonymous 'Allez regrets' setting found in a manuscript in Bologna. Here, however, it has been transposed down a fifth into the bass register, though the signature of a single flat has been retained, as has the mode of the piece. This causes problems with musica ficta and some awkward cadences (see Ex. 3).

Ex. 3
Anonymous, 'Allez regrets'

The bass note in the final cadence of the piece is altered, however, so that the work ends happily in the correct mode. Texturally, this setting is much closer to its model. The individual voices behave in much the same way as in the Hayne chanson, with very little voice crossing and with equal rhythmic activity in each voice. None the less, the lines lack the grace and shape of their model. This setting is four bars longer than the Hayne chanson as the cantus firmus voice first enters in the fourth bar of the opening superius-tenor duet, and an extra bar is interpolated at the central cadence (this setting, as with all except Agricola's, carefully observes Hayne's two-part division of the chanson). It also differs from the Hayne chanson in that there are a few instances of imitation.

Bartolomeo degli Organi's 'Allez regrets' setting displays a very imaginative mind. He exploits the two-part division of the model by exploring different techniques in each part. First he uses Hayne's superius, transposed down a fifth, as his tenor. Unlike the anonymous setting, a number of E♭s are indicated in Bartolomeo's piece, clarifying the musica ficta situation. The mode, which as in the anonymous setting remains unchanged, presents no problems; the transposed voice is not the bass, which allows Bartolomeo considerably more harmonic freedom. The most striking feature of this first section, however, concerns the relationship between the voices. The superius and tenor here are very closely related, with the superius deriving almost all its material from the tenor by skilful imitation at the fifth or unison. Where the imitation is at the fifth, the superius ends up quoting sections of Hayne's superius at its correct pitch. In contrast, the bass part is quite independent.

Barolomeo's tenor in the second section abandons Hayne's superius and uses instead Hayne's tenor. The texture is altered as bass and superius voices unite in frequent parallel tenths or sixths around the slightly slower-moving tenor voice (where the tenor does move more quickly it is usually joined in parallel motion by one of the other two voices). Although the section tries to open sequentially, imitation plays no real part, and thus the section as a whole differs considerably from that preceding it.

Senfl's 'Allez regrets', the last of this group, is a straightforward setting, and is the only one for four voices. Hayne's tenor is used as a cantus firmus, but is transposed up a fifth and placed in the altus part. Unlike the other settings with transpositions, Senfl transposes the whole mode of the piece up a fifth. The cantus firmus voice enters in the fourth bar – the same entrance point as in the anonymous setting (Bartolomeo and Agricola begin with all the voices together). Around the tenor are constructed three independent voices, and the resulting texture is similar to that in the anonymous setting. Imitation plays no role, though there are incidental occurrences. Cadences are passed quickly by (except those at the end of each major section) as the voices unfold in long, almost shapeless lines, scarcely pausing for rests. The continuous motion right up to the last cadence is such that the voices require an additional four bars at the end in order finally to run their course.

The remaining chanson not so far mentioned is Loyset Compère's 'Venes regretz', a work that could loosely be described as a parody setting. Many 'regrets' chansons, from the last quarter of the fifteenth century onwards, have texts and sentiments that seem to owe something to Jean's poem 'Allez regrets'. They include: 'Sourdes regrets', 'Va-t-en regret', 'Les grans regres', 'Plusieurs regretz', 'Aprez regrets', 'Tous les regretz', and others. Compère's 'Venes regretz', however, parodies not simply the text, but more importantly, the music of Hayne's 'Allez regrets'.

The prime difference between the Compère chanson and the four cantus firmus settings is that Compère chooses not to quote the model slavishly bar by bar. Instead, although he bases his work very closely on material derived from Hayne's chanson, he often departs from the model. 'Venes regretz' is just five bars longer in each section than Hayne's chanson, and it cadences on the same degree of the scale as its model in both cases. It opens with Hayne's superius-tenor duet. But Compère has realized that the duet is written in invertible counterpoint, and he

Ex. 4
Loyset Compère, 'Venes regretz'

gives the opening superius phrase an octave lower to his contratenor, while leaving the tenor phrase, at pitch, in his tenor (see Ex. 4).

The technique Compère then uses resembles that used by Bartolomeo in his first section. Almost all of Compère's first half is built around a loose canon between his tenor and superius, where both paraphrase Hayne's tenor. Unlike Bartolomeo's chanson, the imitation is at the octave throughout. The contratenor is freely composed (except the first four bars) and joins in the imitation in only one place.

Compère changes his approach for the second half of the chanson. He opens with another quotation from his model – the first two and a half bars of the second half of Hayne's tenor and contratenor, both at their proper pitch. First by altering and extending the end of the tenor phrase, Compère then creates a passage built entirely on sequential and imitative treatment of two figures given as examples 5a and 5b.

Ex. 5
Compère, 'Venes regretz

(a) Tenor

(b) Bassus

For eight and a half bars the superius is in strict canon at the fifth with the tenor, and during this section the contratenor moves in parallel motion with whichever voice has the figure 5b. Compère ends the piece with some fourteen bars of freely-composed material, which nevertheless resembles its model in spirit. Despite the lack of slavish adherence to the bar by bar unfolding of Hayne's chanson, of the five 'Allez regrets'-based chansons examined this one most closely approaches its model in two aspects; in its clear-cut structure and its lyricism.

The final, and largest, group of compositions which remains to be discussed are the Masses based on 'Allez regrets'. There are six extant Masses that use Hayne's

'Allez regrets' as their basis, all probably composed between 1480 and 1520. Five of these, by Prioris, Compère, 'Scompianus', anonymous and one attributed to Josquin, are all essentially cantus firmus settings. The sixth Mass, by Bruhier, although also in a sense a cantus firmus Mass, uses the chanson in an unusual and remarkably abstract way.

Antoine Bruhier's *Missa Carminum* employs a number of chansons throughout the Mass, with Hayne's just in the final movement. The Mass is a four-voice composition, except for the last Agnus Dei, which has an additional Bassus II part. This part, headed 'Alles regret', is none other than the contratenor (surprisingly) of Hayne's chanson, written out in full. (This is unusual since the tenor, and sometimes the superius, were the normal voices to be quoted). Beneath this part, however, is a canon instructing the bass to sing only the breves and longs, missing out the faster- moving notes. Also, since the part is written in C time, where the others are in $\mathbb{C}$ time, these notes are to sound at double their length, in relation to the other voices.

Bruhier's use of Hayne's chanson is unusual. The presence of the chanson is aurally (and visually) apparent in the other Masses, but here, despite the visual impression in the source, Hayne's chanson is used in an abstract and aurally unidentifiable manner. Nor are motifs of the chanson really to be found in the other voices of this movement, except for two brief allusions.

A much more straightforward approach is present in the anonymous *Allez regrets* Mass found in a manuscript in Cambrai. The tenor part quotes Hayne's tenor throughout, though during the 'Domini fili' section of the Gloria, where the tenor is silent, the contratenor carries the cantus firmus. Unlike the other Mass composers, this one presents the cantus firmus at different degrees of uniform augmentation in each of the movements, with progressively longer and longer statements. These, however, are interspersed with statements at *integer valor*. With one small exception, each statement is literal and unadorned. Like so many composers of cantus firmus Masses in the years around 1500, the composer is concerned simply with using Hayne's tenor part as a structural foundation; he does not exploit other aspects of the chanson.

In striking contrast is the Mass, probably the earliest of the group, by Johannes Prioris. Its voices are saturated with material from Hayne's original chanson. A cantus firmus seems to be present in each of the Mass movements, though at times, owing to paraphrasing, it is hard to detect. During the four-voice sections it is normally carried in the tenor. During the frequent duos and trios, however, the cantus firmus migrates to the other voices (often moving mid-phrase).

Like Compère (see below), Prioris is concerned with contrapuntal reworking of material that was not designed for imitative treatment. Thus, he is very flexible with the rhythm of the cantus firmus and also interpolates additional notes where he feels them necessary. But he seems often to paraphrase his cantus firmus simply for contrast and variety. For the final Agnus Dei the cantus firmus is transposed down a fifth and placed in the bass, with the necessary additional flat in the key signature.

Compère's Mass, like that of Prioris, displays an unusual and almost eccentric degree of experimentation and impregnation with material from its model. Yet Compère seems obsessed with the contrapuntal possibilities of Hayne's voices, and his Mass reveals a very different imaginative approach. Unlike the other 'Allez regrets' Mass composers, Compère casts each movement of the Mass in duple metre, as in the original chanson. Hayne's tenor receives six unadorned, literal statements, one for each of the main Mass movements and an additional one for the final Agnus Dei. But Compère subjects it to different rhythmic alterations in each movement, by the use of different mensuration signs – that is maintaining the same appearance in its note values as in the chanson sources.

The variety of manner and ways in which Compère manipulates Hayne's material around the cantus firmus is much greater than in Prioris, and can be listed as follows:

1 Direct quotation of two or three voices from the chanson, either on their own or, more usually, with an added third and/or fourth voice. These direct quotations most often occur at the beginnings of sections or in cadential passages, and when the tenor voice is at *integer valor*.

2 Direct quotation of two or three voices (with or without added voices) but with inverted counterpoint (as Compère used in his chanson 'Venes regretz').

3 Quotation of simultaneous voices, but at speeds different to the original, resulting in new contrapuntal relationships between the voices.

4 Simultaneous quotation of a single motif, at different speeds, in different voices.

5 Related to 4, canonic treatment of a motif, at pitch or at the fourth or fifth, with or without rhythmic alteration.

6 Simultaneous sounding of two motifs from different parts of the chanson.

7 Motifs from the chanson appearing in a sequence different from their original.

8 Imitative 'previews' of cantus firmus motifs, often far more extensive than was common practice.

9 Situations as above, but where the material in the non-cantus firmus voices is derived from a different part of the chanson from that about to be stated in the cantus firmus voice.

10 Use of a motif as an ostinato.

All the Masses discussed so far use Hayne's tenor for their cantus firmus. The *Allez regrets* Mass attributed to Josquin, however, uses Hayne's superius as the cantus firmus in most of the movements, where it is usually quoted in the superius voice. Only in the Credo and Hosanna movements is Hayne's tenor used instead, and it is then presented in the tenor voice.

Imitation and quotation of other chanson voices play a limited role here. When they do occur, however, it is usually in intriguing ways and for significant reasons. For example, the second Kyrie opens with the tenor quoting the opening bars of the tenor part of Hayne's chanson (hinting at its future role) against which, a bar later, the contratenor sings the superius part of the opening of the *second* half of the chanson (temporarily taking over the superius's role). Of more concern to the composer, however, is the exploration of a simple pattern of a rising fifth, starting on *f*, followed by a step up to *d* then descending in a mirror image through *c* and *f* (see Ex. 6).

Ex. 6

Tenor

The fundamental use of this pattern, and particularly the perfect fifth, emphasizes the common presence of these key notes in many of the motifs of Hayne's tenor part, and of one motif in the superius part (see Ex. 7).

Ex. 7

Furthermore, these key intervals can be found in the opening superius parts if it is transposed up a fourth (see Ex. 8).

Ex. 8

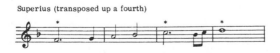

Each major movement of this Mass begins with some form of paraphrase of this transposed opening superius idea. The climax of all this is reached in the first

Agnus Dei where a version of this figure is used as an ostinato and replaces the cantus firmus. The figure is sounded in parallel fourths throughout in the two inner voices (starting on *c* and *f*), and in retrograde from the mid-point of the movement.

Of the Mass by Nicolaus Scompianus, only the altus and bassus part books survive. Nevertheless, a certain amount of reconstruction suggests that it is a straightforward cantus firmus setting, based on Hayne's tenor. Cantus firmus statements were probably literal, unparaphrased and at either *integer valor* or half speed. As in several of the other 'Allez regrets' Masses, the Agnus Dei II movement contains a sort of ostinato: a motif from the tenor appears four times in the four different mensurations. As in the Josquin Mass, the motif has been transposed down a fourth, which emphasizes its relationship to the opening superius phrase, which is the 'usual' ostinato figure in these Masses (see Ex. 9).

Ex. 9
Hayne van Ghizeghem, 'Allez regrets' compared to (b) Scompianus, Agnus Dei II

(Scompianus, Agnus Dei II: Kraków, Biblioteka Jagiellońska [olim Berlin, Deutsche Staatsbibliothek 40634], ff. 50–54)

A final point worth noting about this Mass is that it is the only one of the group to have a real head motif (though the Mass attributed to Josquin approaches it). Each of the major movements of the Mass opens with the altus voice quoting the opening tenor statement of the chanson unparaphrased (except rhythmically altered in the Credo) and at *integer valor*.

Evidently, Hayne's chanson 'Allez regrets' proved a very fertile starting point for several composers. What is almost surprising is the wealth of different approaches used by these composers, as well as the similarities in approach. Whether or not they knew each other's works is hard to prove. But the potential for such an exciting variety of compositions lies mainly in the nature of the pre-existent work. Of particular importance in Hayne's chanson 'Allez regrets' is the lyrical and thus memorable nature of its tenor and superius parts, together with its lack of imitation, resulting in three independent musical lines.

Select bibliography

I. CHOLIJ, 'Fifteenth- and sixteenth-century settings of "Allez regrets"' (M. Mus. diss., King's College, London University, 1984)

L. FINSCHER, *Loyset Compère (c.1450–1518): life and works* (American Institute of Musicology, 1964); *Loyset Compère: Missa Alles Regrets, Das Chorwerk*, lv (1955); and *Loyset Compère: Opera omnia*, 5 vols., *CMM*, xv (American Institute of Musicology, 1958–72)

A. GEERIN ɜ and W. ALTWEGG (eds), *Ludwig Senfl: Sämtliche Werke*, vi (Wolfenbüttel and Zurich, 1961)

H. GERLE, *Tablature pour les luths, Nuremberg, Formschneider 1533*, 5 vols. (Paris, 1975)

O. GOMBOSI (ed.), *Compositione di Meser Vincenzo Capirola: lute-book (circa 1517)* (Neuilly-sur-Seine, 1955)

B. HUDSON (ed.), *Hayne van Ghizeghem: Opera omnia*, *CMM*, lxxiv (American Institute of Musicology, 1977)

N. S. JOSEPHSON and A. K. LAIRD (eds), *Antoine Bruhier: Missa Carminum, Das Chorwerk*, cxxvii (Wolfenbüttel, 1979)

T. H. KEAHEY and C. DOUGLAS (eds), *Johannes Prioris: Opera omnia, CMM*, xc (American Institute of Musicology, 1982–5)

E. R. LERNER (ed.), *Alexander Agricola: Opera omnia*, 5 vols., *CMM*, xxii (American Institute of Musicology, 1970)

M. PICKER, *The chanson albums of Marguerite of Austria. MSS.228 and 11239 of the Bibliothèque Royale de Belgique, Brussels. A critical edition and commentary* (Berkeley and Los Angeles, 1965)

R. WEXLER, 'The complete works of Johannes Prioris' (Ph.D. diss., New York University, 1974)

IV Using the evidence

29 Music and pictures in the Middle Ages

Elizabeth C. Teviotdale

Musical iconography, the description and study of the visual arts in the interest of elucidating the musical thought and practice of a remote culture, was first explored by artists of the Italian Renaissance. These painter-scholars were primarily interested in accuracy of detail in the rendition of scenes and themes from classical mythology. They might study Greek and Roman depictions of musical instruments in the hope of ascertaining the appearance of instruments that had gone out of use by their own time, or they might replicate in their own compositions dance poses found in ancient scenes of Bacchic revelry.

Although the figurative arts have been exploited since the Renaissance for what they might reveal about ancient Greek and Roman musical life, it has been only within the last century or so that scholars have systematically studied the painting and sculpture of the Middle Ages in the hope of learning more about medieval musical culture. This enterprise was initiated by the Romantic interest in all things medieval, and has been encouraged by developments and refinements in photographic reproduction in the late nineteenth century, by the early music boom of the mid-twentieth century, and by recent developments and refinements in computer technology and data base management. The artists of the Italian Renaissance perceived a gap between their culture and the classical culture they sought to emulate. We similarly recognize a distance between our culture and that of the Middle Ages, a gulf wide enough to have seen the destruction of all but a few musical instruments and the discontinuation of many performance practices.

Research in the visual arts has contributed most conspicuously to the study of musical instruments and to the history of secular performance practice, the very fields in which we have a dearth of archaeological and written evidence. But scholars interested in sacred performance practice, in music theory, and in the history of ideas have also turned to the figurative arts, and within the past generation few scholars of medieval music would dare to ignore pictorial evidence. At the same time, music scholars have become much more sophisticated in the study of the visual arts, and the discipline of musical iconography has undergone a genuine reform in recent years, reflected above all in the writings of James McKinnon.

Works of art emphatically were not created in order to provide documentation for future generations of historians. Whatever a painting or sculpture may reveal about the musical culture of its time, it will do so within a context shaped by a myriad of extra-musical factors including authorship, patronage, style, medium, genre, and pictorial tradition. We have come to recognize that a proper grounding in art historical methodology is essential to the practice of musical iconography and that works of art ultimately reveal more about the history of art than about ancillary issues such as the history of music.

The most plentiful artistic survivals of the medieval period are paintings in manuscripts. Architectural stone sculpture might be subject to weathering, metalwork was often melted down so that its material might be reused, and wall paintings were particularly susceptible to damage from damp conditions, but manuscript art was generally protected from sun and abrasion by a padding of animal skins and a pair of wooden boards. The medium of manuscript illumination offers the most fertile ground for musical iconography not only because of its survival rate but also because a consideration of the text of a given manuscript may help us better to appreciate its pictures. For this reason, the examples discussed here will be drawn from that medium.

In the early medieval period, the psalms directly or indirectly provided the chief inspiration for pictures with musical subject matter. Not only are the psalms rich in allusion to music and musical instruments, but King David, to whom many of the psalms are attributed, is described in the Old Testament historical books as a musician. An eighth-century manuscript of Cassiodorus' commentary on the psalms from northern England (now in the Durham Cathedral Library) is one of our earliest witnesses to a long tradition of pictures of David as king and musician in manuscripts containing the psalms. He is shown seated on an immense high-backed throne, and he holds or plays a chordophone of the lyre type, which appears to be propped on his left knee.

We are told in the Old Testament that as a youth David played the kithara before Saul, and that as king he was responsible for various musical practices in connection with the translation of the Ark of the Covenant. He and all Israel are reported to have played musical instruments and he to have danced in celebration of the installation of the Ark in the Temple. But the picture in the Durham Cassiodorus does not illustrate an episode in the life of David; rather it serves as a kind of author portrait (see illus. 1). The chordophone, therefore, need not represent one of the instruments specifically associated with David in the Old Testament. Nevertheless, the painter might have been concerned to show an old-fashioned instrument, one appropriate for an Old Testament king and prophet. On the other hand, the painter might not have been interested in such historicism, and he may have depicted a musical instrument of his own time. In fact, he can hardly be said to have done either. His rendition of David's instrument shows the overall shape and distinguishing features (strings and tuning pegs) of a type of musical instrument without representing any particular instrument, real or imagined, just as his rendition of the throne conveys the rectilinear outlines and animal head terminals of a generic throne.

The portrait is constructed according to a carefully balanced scheme character-istic of insular art of this period and is dominated in certain respects by its frame of interlace panels. The figure is given special emphasis through the articulation of drapery and the halo; the bold concentric arcs and zig-zag hem of David's outer garment contrast with the delicate interlace decoration of the frame and the throne, and the halo is the only element of the picture painted blue. The tilt of the musical instrument counterbalances the sweep of drapery over David's left shoulder; at the same time its shape mirrors that of the definition of his left leg. Finally, the figure envelopes the instrument much as the throne brackets the figure. The size, shape, and position of David's instrument, therefore, can be seen to have followed directly from the artist's concern to create a tightly-constructed picture.

This is not to say that the shape of the musical instrument here depicted might

1 Cassiodorus, *In psalterium*; first third of the eighth century, Jarrow (Durham, Cathedral Library, MS B. II.30, f. 81*v*)

not be found among contemporary instruments. The few physical remains we have of early medieval chordophones suggest that there were instruments of this configuration, and it is perhaps not unwarranted that this picture has partially informed the most recent (1970) reconstruction of the chordophone found in the Sutton Hoo ship burial (seventh century). It is unlikely, however, that there was ever an instrument of this type with only five strings, as the archaeological evidence (including the instrument from Sutton Hoo) overwhelmingly points to six. And this picture can tell us extremely little about contemporary performance practice. David's outer garment is arranged so that his right arm is free, as is customary with garments of this kind, but his right hand is not engaged in playing the instrument, and his left is held over the strings in a way inappropriate to the task of plucking them.

Portraits of David as king and musician are featured in hundreds of medieval psalters. These include liturgical psalters used in the daily recitation of the psalms, bilingual (Latin and vernacular) psalters used perhaps in the teaching of Latin, and patristic commentaries on the psalms. In the high Middle Ages, illustrated psalters were made for layman and churchman alike, and most would have included an author portrait. The theme was subject to variation both in detail and in overall conception. The shape of David's crown changed over the centuries, as did the shape of his musical instrument. David might appear alone or accompanied by the four Levite musicians described in the historical books of the Old Testament. He might be depicted as an elderly bearded figure or as a youth. Through all of the variations on the author portrait, David is virtually always shown with a chordophone (although he is depicted playing other instruments in other contexts), which may well ultimately reflect the ancient *topos* of the poet accompanying himself on a stringed instrument.

During the fourteenth century, the Book of Hours eclipsed the psalter as the favoured book of private devotion. The central text of a Book of Hours is the Office of the Virgin, and the penitential psalms are almost invariably included. In illustrated manuscripts, these psalms were frequently introduced by a picture of the penitent David at prayer. In the Hastings Hours, a Flemish manuscript of the fifteenth century preserved in the British Library, David is shown kneeling, with his hat on the ground and his harp placed on a shelf or bench; he recoils from the Lord above (see illus. 2).

The traditional association of David with the psalms certainly contributed to the use of a picture of David at prayer to introduce the penitential psalms in Books of Hours, but a series of events in the life of David also inspired this choice. We learn from the Old Testament that after David's adultery with Bathsheba, he was rebuked by the prophet Nathan and repented. The pool visible in the middle ground of the miniature in the Hastings Hours is undoubtedly meant to remind the viewer of David's first glimpse of Bathsheba while she was bathing, and the architectural surroundings may also be meant to invoke the circumstances of his encounter with her.

There is no reason why the penitent David should have a musical instrument at his side, except that a long pictorial tradition dictated that David should appear with this attribute. The instrument in the Hastings Hours is a frame harp with six strings. Its depiction here tells us virtually nothing about the physical character-istics of this late medieval harp that we do not know better from archaeological remains. Indeed, both archaeological and literary evidence speak strongly against the existence of instruments of this type with as few as six strings.

The presence of this instrument here does, however, inform us of the artist's willingness, and perhaps desire, to incorporate a modern instrument into his picture of the historical David, and this is consistent with his treatment of costume and architecture. Furthermore, it indicates that the painter considered the harp an instrument appropriate to royalty. Unfortunately, we cannot discern from the painting alone whether the artist considered this chordophone analogous to one of the instruments mentioned in the Old Testament, whether, for example, he thought the kithara of David to have been something like the instrument he depicted.

As central as the psalter was for the depiction of music in medieval manuscript

2 Book of Hours, known as the 'Hastings Hours'; before 1483, Ghent or Bruges (London, British Library, Add. MS 54782, f. 150*v*)

illumination, another portion of the Bible, the Apocalypse, also provided an important impetus for musical illustration. Many manuscripts of the Apocalypse contain extensive picture cycles which include illustrations of musical subject matter (for example, the seven angels blowing seven *tubae*). And it was not only the Bible that provided the subjects for pictures in the Middle Ages: secular texts also might inspire pictures, and these too include references to music.

One of the most famous manuscripts of German secular poetry is the lavishly illustrated Codex Manesse in the University Library at Heidelberg (see illus. 3). This fourteenth-century manuscript includes nearly 150 full-page paintings that appear to provide a fascinating glimpse into contemporary court life, but these pictures are not straightforward representations of courtly activities. They are a series of 'author portraits', often showing the poet engaged in an activity described in one of his poems. The portrait of Herr Hiltbolt von Schwangau is an illustration of the refrain to his dance-song: 'Elle and Else dance in such a way that one should be thankful to them both'. Hiltbolt is depicted wearing chainmail and helmet with a full complement of heraldic devices. He holds the hands of Elle and Else on either side of him. At the right, a man plays a fiddle. The four figures appear to stand in a straight line under a Gothic arcade, but we cannot be certain whether the dance depicted would necessarily have been conducted in a straight line (indeed, scholars have identified this as a round dance). Figures are virtually always shown close to the picture plane in this manuscript, and it would lie outside the prevailing stylistic conventions to depict the dancers in any other way. Nor can we infer from the picture alone that dances involving one man and two women were practised in this period, for we can be reasonably certain that this illustration is a direct response to the conceit of the poem. On the other hand, the gesture of the woman on the left, pulling a portion of her garment up to her hip, might well have been incorporated into the picture from a familiarity with contemporary dancing. The arcade neatly fills the upper portion of the picture space, while its individual arches correspond visually to the figures below. It was probably also meant to suggest an interior location for the dance, even though the ground line might suggest an exterior setting.

Heraldry plays a central role in the Codex Manesse. Usually the shield of the poet is included in the picture but is not integrated into it (as it is here). It might be imagined, therefore, that Hiltbolt is shown in armour because it is appropriate to dancing (however unlikely this may seem on a practical level). The artist certainly would have welcomed the opportunity afforded by this choice of costume to include Hiltbolt's device (the swan) no less than five times, but the principal motivation for depicting Hiltbolt in armour was to make a play on the meaning of his name ('fearless in battle'). The pun is successful precisely because his garb is inappropriate to the scene.

The dancers are shown accompanied by a single instrumentalist playing a fiddle, and this could well reflect contemporary practice. This is the sort of performance practice question that is best explored by examining a wide range of pictorial and literary sources. This picture, if it were one of an overwhelming majority of broadly contemporary dance scenes showing a single fiddler, could support a contention that courtly dance music was performed on the fiddle. It should be said, however, that the inclusion of a solo musician in this picture can be accounted for on artistic grounds alone. His presence serves chiefly to identify the activity of the others, and

3 'Codex Manesse';
c. 1304, Zurich
(Heidelberg, Uni-
versitätsbibliothek,
Codex Palatinus
Germanicus 848,
f. 146*r*)

only one instrumentalist would be required to accomplish this end. The painting does allow us to conclude with reasonable assurance, however, that this sort of bowed, necked chordophone was considered appropriate to a courtly setting.

The instrument in the painting may well display the salient features of the outward appearance of a contemporary fiddle, but the painter's manifest preference for bold simple forms would have precluded a detailed rendering of such a small object. The playing stance of the fiddler would have been occasioned as much by space constraints as by contemporary practice. This painter rarely allows elements of the picture to extend beyond the frame, and he may well have compensated for a lack of lateral space by adjusting the position of the fiddle. Furthermore, the painter has presented the surface of the instrument that conveys the most information (because of the presence of strings and sound holes) parallel to the picture plane, as is consistent with the conventions of his style; his picture, therefore, may not tell us much about the playing posture of a contemporary fiddler.

The Codex Manesse contains a collection of poetry that was created by Minnesingers, courtly poets who performed their verses in song, but the manuscript preserves only the texts and not the melodies of their songs. Only a tiny percentage of extant manuscript art with musical subject matter is contained in music manuscripts. This is not to say that these were never illustrated, but their production involved the services of specially trained scribes, and they were not made in nearly the numbers that psalters or Books of Hours were.

The corpus of manuscripts of music theory texts provides another fruitful source for pictures with musical subject matter. The frontispiece to Boethius' treatise on music in a twelfth-century Canterbury manuscript now in the Cambridge University Library is a unique document of the medieval conception of the music theory inherited from classical antiquity (see illus. 4). Its subject might be described as the authority of the ancients as the basis for medieval musical theory and practice.

Boethius, who wrote in the early sixth century, considers only peripherally the practice of music. He concentrates instead on the investigation of the quantitative nature of sound as a preparation to the study of philosophy. The frontispiece is divided into three sections. Above are Boethius (who is labelled) at the left and Pythagoras at the right. Below, Plato (seated on an orb) and Nicomachus, a Greek arithmetician, are engaged in discussion, their hands raised in gestures of speech. The drawing is accompanied by Latin hexameters that paraphrase portions of Boethius' text relevant to the picture.

Boethius is shown seated with the monochord in his lap. This emphasizes the aspect of his treatise that was crucial for the development of the more practical music theory of the Middle Ages, for the division of the monochord allowed for the explanation of the modes, and it was through the modes that medieval theorists attempted to reconcile the melodies of plainchant with the inherited tradition of ancient music theory. It is not entirely clear why Boethius should be pictured crowned and enthroned. He was a Roman senator, a fact that was well known in the Middle Ages, and is described as *consul* in the inscription. In medieval art he is usually depicted with some sort of headgear, which may allude to his political status. On the other hand, the regal trappings in the Cambridge manuscript may point to a reliance, direct or indirect, on traditional David imagery.

Pythagorean ideas about consonance lie at the root of much of Boethius' treatise, and Boethius relates the story of Pythagoras' initial discovery of the importance of proportion to the understanding of consonance. Happening upon a blacksmith's shop, Pythagoras is reported to have weighed the hammers being used and to have found that the four that sounded well together were of comparative weights of simple proportion (1:2, 2:3, 3:4) but that a fifth hammer, which was discordant, did not share these simple ratios. The artist has shown the four blacksmith's hammers that produced consonances in the balance held aloft by Pythagoras and the fifth discordant one discarded at his feet. Pythagoras directs his attention to the bells overhead, but the bells are an intrusion into the philosopher's world. These eight bells are not the subjects of Pythagoras' experiments (he would have needed only four), but a medieval musical instrument. Once again, the artist has introduced an allusion to the contemporary practice of music into his picture of the ancient theorists.

Boethius reports Plato's theory of consonance and Nicomachus' refutation of it.

The artist has conceived this as a disputation between the two characters. The inclusion of the books held by Plato and Nicomachus may indicate that the artist knew that the philosophers were not contemporaries and that their 'debate' was carried out in their writings. The orb on which Plato sits may allude to his notion of cosmic music, although Boethius only barely associates this idea with the name of Plato. Or the orb may have been borrowed from sacred imagery to indicate that Plato held a special authority not shared by the others. Within the picture as a whole, however, Boethius and Pythagoras are given pride of place. Each inhabits his own portion of the drawing and each has his own set of hexameters. This probably reflects the medieval view that the work of these two constituted the substance of music theory inherited from antiquity. The inclusion of the monochord and the octave of bells may also indicate that they were particularly appreciated for their ultimate contribution to the practice of music.

Each of the four pictures discussed here affords a glimpse into medieval musical culture. The portrait of David in the Durham Cassiodorus may tell us something

4 Boethius, *De arithmetica* and *De musica*; twelfth century, Canterbury (Cambridge, University Library, MS Ii.3.12, f. 61v)

about the configuration of chordophones in a period for which we have very little archaeological evidence. The painting of David at prayer in the Hastings Hours indicates the appropriateness of the frame harp to an aristocratic setting in fifteenth-century Flanders. The portrait of Hiltbolt in the Codex Manesse provides clues to performance practice in a fourteenth-century courtly milieu. The frontispiece in the Cambridge Boethius documents a twelfth-century English view of Boethius' treatise as preparatory not exclusively to the study of philosophy, but also to the practice of music.

The pictures discussed here are worthy of study chiefly because of their quality as works of art; they would be of little interest if they were poorly conceived and badly executed. Because they are works of art, their study is essentially an art historical enterprise. Their evidential value for the history of music cannot begin to be judged until their integrity as pictures is considered. The creators of medieval works of art with musical content were principally concerned with making good pictures, and musical iconographers should be fundamentally concerned with appreciating them as such.

Select bibliography

H. M. BROWN, 'Iconography', *New Grove*

J. MCKINNON, 'Iconography', in D. K. Holoman and C. Palisca (eds), *Musicology in the 1980s: methods, goals, opportunities*, (New York, 1982), pp. 79–93

E. WINTERNITZ, 'The visual arts as a source for the historian of music', *International Musicological Society Congress Report, New York, 1961* (Kassel, 1961), pp. 109–20; repr. in E. Winternitz, *Musical instruments and their symbolism in Western art*, 2nd edn (New Haven, 1979), pp. 25–42

30 Music in Italian Renaissance paintings

Iain Fenlon

Visual representations of musicians and the instruments that they played can lead us into the sound-worlds of the past, but the path of interpretation is littered with pitfalls. All too often, musicologists have taken pictures at face value, without careful discrimination between real and imaginary objects; without an awareness of the political or theological ideas which might determine the content; without sufficient regard for pictorial conventions, individual artistic mannerisms, and changing styles. For organologists the principal interest of images lies in what they may reveal about the instruments themselves, how they were constructed, sounded and arranged in ensembles. Here a complex of difficulties immediately intrudes. Artists may not have been principally concerned with accurate depiction, and indeed may often have had good reason to invent instruments or to modify an acknowledged type for allegorical, stylistic or compositional reasons. And even in cases where fidelity might seem to be a high priority, an instrument might be copied not from life but from another image, or even from an image of another image, producing in the process a chain of transformations that can lead back several centuries. Raphael, for example, employed draughtsmen to make drawings of works of art from classical antiquity some of which he then used in his own paintings; a number of the instruments in his *Parnassus* fresco (*c.*1509–11) in the Stanza della Segnatura in the Vatican (see illus. 1a) are taken from the famous third-century Asiatic Sarcophagus of the Muses from the Mattei collection, then in S Paolo fuori le Mura and now in the Museo Nazionale delle Terme in Rome (see illus. 1b). A further though intermediate twist to the line of descent is provided by Marcantonio Raimondi's engraving of the *Parnassus* project, which records a fully worked out earlier version in which Apollo plays the lyre rather than the lira da braccio. This might seem surprising (it is a point we shall return to), since all the other alterations made to the musical instruments and other attributes between print and painting are in the direction of that greater archaeological accuracy which seems to have been one of Raphael's concerns in his depiction of instruments in the fresco. In the case of the trumpet held by Euterpe for example, archaeological ambition has produced an instrument with the typical protruberances of the ancient Roman tibia, but with the mouthpiece and bell of the trumpet traditionally associated with Fama, an arrangement that is clearly taken from a detail of the Mattei Sarcophagus. In this way two separate mythological traditions are united to father an acoustical impossibility; the priorities here are the allegorical significance of the merged instruments (which thus fuse Euterpe with Calliope, whose traditional attribute was the trumpet) and faithfulness to an antique model.

This sort of procedure was common among Renaissance artists with strong archaeological interests; Filippino Lippi, for example, in his fresco on the window wall of the Strozzi Chapel in S Maria Novella in Florence, has apparently copied two Muses with a kithara from a second-century Roman sarcophagus showing the Muses with Apollo and Minerva, then in S Maria Maggiore in Rome and now in

1a Raphael, *Parnassus* (Rome, Vatican Palace)

the Kunsthistorisches Museum, Vienna. In the process the artist has transformed the traditional kithara into a monumental pedestal lyre, an instrument certainly known to the Renaissance through representations on sarcophagi, but in doing so he has omitted several details that are essential for it to be functional. Once again, the acoustical construction of instruments is not a matter of concern, and the result is that the instruments shown in the Strozzi Chapel fresco are a mixture of the real and the imaginary. This is a general pattern. Many Italian Renaissance paintings, particularly large angel concerts, similarly include a mixture of actual instruments (sometimes embellished with Renaissance decor) and invented ones that are without historical or indeed acoustical justification; both types occur in Gaudenzio Ferrari's fresco in the cupola of the Santuario in Saronno (*c.*1535) which includes, among the fifty-six instruments depicted, a number showing the basic character-istics, at a surprisingly early date, of the nascent violin.

The authority and appeal of classical antiquity frequently led Renaissance artists in the direction of allegory and invention rather than that of archaeological fidelity. Common themes such as the musical contests between Apollo and Marsyas, Apollo and Pan, or between the Muses and the Sirens, often inspired the depiction of fantastic instruments for which there is no archaeological evidence and which, in some cases, are acoustically impossible. In Filippino Lippi's *Worship of the Egyptian Bull God, Apis* (see illus. 2), a picture previously misidentified as the *Worship of the Golden Calf*, the narrative content is taken from a story familiar from Petrus Comestor's *Historia scholastica*, the textbook from which many derived their knowledge of biblical history in the Middle Ages. Filippino's picture represents the

1b Sarcophagus of the Muses (Rome, Museo Nazionale delle Terme)

2 Filippino Lippi, *Worship of the Egyptian Bull God, Apis* (London, National Gallery)

annual levitation of the Egyptian bull-god Apis, a lunar divinity identified by means of the crescent moon on his shoulder. According to legend he used to emerge from a river, and would rise into the air when the Egyptians gathered around him singing and dancing. Filippino has imagined Egypt as a half-classical, half-oriental world, and it is these two elements which have in turn determined the kinds of instruments, in effect a strange mixture of contemporary and ancient shapes, that

are played by members of this bucolic crowd. The small 'Turkish' kettledrums (*nacchere*), the S-shaped trumpet and the tambourine (or, more correctly, jingle drum) are quite realistically represented, as is the Roman *buccina* (probably copied from a classical relief) to the right of the picture. The kithara, on the other hand, is rendered with considerable freedom, merging classical models with Renaissance ornament, and the complex brass instrument played by the third figure from the left in the painting is without precedent and is clearly invented. Bizarre instruments *all'antica* may also reflect the artist's engagement with intermedi and other staged entertainments, as with the implausible instruments shown in Piero di Cosimo's *cassone* painting of *The Liberation of Andromeda* (Florence, Uffizi). Vasari tells us that Piero was actively involved in works for the stage, and it is clear from printed descriptions and engravings of later Italian *intermedi* that mythological characters in such scenes were often required to carry papier-maché instruments freely-invented after imagined classical models.

At a more straightforward level, it might seem that a pair of *flauti dolci*, arranged in aulos fashion, are merely intended to evoke the instruments of the classical past, but at the same time there is often a powerful sexual symbolism at work; the two instruments held by the girl in Titian's Giorgionesque *Three Ages of Man* of *c.*1509 (see illus. 3) may signify the harmony of souls through the simultaneity of their sounds, but their more powerful message is sexual. The point is made clear by Titian's famous *Fête champêtre* (Paris, Louvre) painted at about the same time, where the participants are playing contemporary rather than antique instruments or modern instruments with classical resonances. Here two youths, richly dressed, are sitting on the grass engaged in conversation while two naked girls, one of whom is holding a recorder, are to right and left. Neither this instrument, nor the lute which one of the young men is holding, are being sounded. There have been many ingenious explanations of the meaning of this scene, but a basic reading via the common theory of decorum which relates to wind and string instruments in the period makes the overt sexual message inescapable. The erotic symbolism of musical instruments, particularly wind instruments and idiophones, pervades all cultures, but the Dionysiac connotations of woodwind instruments such as reed pipes and vertical flutes are particularly prominent in Renaissance art as in the woodcuts from the *Hypnerotomachia Polyphili*, numerous *trionfi* including Mantegna's *Triumphs of Caesar* (Hampton Court Palace), and Francesco del Cossa's celebrated frescoes in the Palazzo Schifanoia in Ferrara. Such symbolism is based on both shape and sound, and is reinforced by antiquity, the *locus classicus* being Plato's warning against the use of the aulos in education. Similar ambiguities surround pictures of women lutenists, of which Bartolommeo Veneto's much-copied portrait (see illus. 4) provides an early example of the type. Here a modestly-dressed woman invites the viewer, via the open and legible part-book turned to face us, to participate in her music-making, offered as part of the process of seduction. These pictures are presumably to be read as portraits of a courtesan; certainly it is suggestive that in two copies of the painting (in Milan and Boston), a later hand has added a halo in an attempt to transform the sitter into Saint Cecilia. A direct line of descent leads from pictures of this kind to paintings such as Parrasio Micheli's *Venus and Cupid* (Budapest, Szepmuveszeti Muzeum), Bernardo Strozzi's portrait of a female musician (Dresden, Gemäldegalerie), and to the innumerable lessons on the lute and theorbo in Italian Baroque genre paintings.

Despite the interpretational difficulties particularly of those pictures with a high archaeological content, there are plenty of Italian examples of the period where contemporary musical instruments are painted with considerable care and attention to detail. The important instance of Ferrari's frescoes at Saronno have already been mentioned (this artist's interest in the accurate depiction of musical instruments is also evident from some of his other works such as the *Madonna degli aranci* in the church of S Cristoforo in Vercelli), and there are also many examples among the *sacre conversazioni* by Giovanni Bellini and his contemporaries working

3 Titian, *The Three
Ages of Man*
(Edinburgh, National
Gallery of Scotland)

4 Bartolommeo
Veneto, *The Lute
Player* (Boston,
Isabella Stewart
Gardner Museum)

Iain Fenlon

5 Giovanni Bellini, *Sacra conversazione* (Venice, S Zaccaria)

in Venice and the Veneto (see illus. 5), though it should be borne in mind that the almost traditional incorporation of angel musicians in the foreground is often done for compositional reasons. A very particular class of images where faithful and detailed representation of real objects is a priority is that of *intarsia*, or marquetry, most of the surviving examples of which are to be found in churches and the private rooms (*studioli*) of princely palaces. Inspired by refinements in the theoretical study of perspective, and in some later cases by the treatises of Piero della Francesca and Luca Pacioli and their imitators, *intarsie* were often designed as virtuosic perspectival explorations of the possibilities of the new technique of geometrical projection, and as such they aimed at precision. The accurate depiction of curved surfaces was a major concern of perspective treatises throughout the Renaissance; Lorenzo Sirigatti's *La pratica di prospettiva* (Venice, 1596), for example, stresses the ingenuity needed to portray difficult shapes such as those found in certain musical instruments: 'It is held a most difficult thing to put into foreshortening regular bodies and above all those composed of curved lines such as the viola and the lute'. In the ducal palace at Urbino, the principal residence of Federigo da Montefeltro, musical instruments are shown in the *intarsia* in his *studiolo* alongside books, a quadrant, a celestial globe and armour – the accoutrements of a true Renaissance prince, learned in both the arts and the sciences while still retaining the virtues of a

6 Studiolo of Federigo da
Montefeltro, *intarsia*
(Urbino, Palazzo Ducale)

man-of-arms. Prominent among the musical instruments is a clavichord with forty-seven keys (see illus. 6); the earliest surviving instrument, dated 1537 and now in New York, has only thirty-six keys and is constructed with a much more primitive arrangement of bridges. In view of the accuracy inherent in the medium, this record of a real instrument must be taken seriously. There is no special symbolism attached to the jumble of trivia and quadrivia in which these musical instruments are usually found, but the presence of instruments in the company of the other paraphernalia of the ideal princely type of man-of-arms *cum* scholar is an indication of the new status of the art of music in Italian Renaissance thought.

   This wider issue of the social status of the composer, the performer (and in some cases the audience), and also of music itself is reflected in the increasing frequency with which musicians are shown in portraits (or, alternatively, that members of the portrait-commissioning classes now wished to advertise themselves as musically accomplished), the perceptible development of the concert scene as a genre (though it was not acknowledged as such in the theoretical literature until later), and the new presence of legible musical inscriptions in paintings (and occasionally on artifacts such as ceramics). All these are indicative of the position which music had come to occupy in Italian intellectual and cultural life by the first half of the sixteenth century. The importance of the courts for the patronage of music, the impact of music printing (particularly after the adoption of the single-impression method in the 1530s), the rise of the bourgeoisie, and improvements in the technology of instrument-building were all important factors in this development, but a key element in this web of related phenomena was the dissemination and influence of humanistic thinking about music. Humanism, while not the only intellectual current of the Italian Renaissance, was nevertheless the most characteristic and pervasive trend of the period. Strictly speaking, the *studia humanitatis* consisted of grammar, rhetoric, poetry, history and moral philosophy, but the revival of classical learning that lay at the core of humanistic study slowly spread to other branches of philosophy, to mathematics, natural science, and eventually to music itself. It was precisely because the study of music did not belong to the traditional core of humanistic studies that so little attention was paid to it in the earliest, fourteenth-century, phase of Italian humanism; neither Petrarch nor Boccaccio for example offer any evidence that they considered it as a proper subject of enquiry. In effect, it was not until the second quarter of the fifteenth century that there are any significant indications that music should be recognized as a serious discipline worthy of scholarly attention. Here the first event of any real historical significance was the inclusion of music in the curriculum of the school founded by the humanist educator Vittorino da Feltre at the court of Gian Francesco Gonzaga II in Mantua in 1424. According to Vittorino's fifteenth-century biographer Bartolomeo Plantina, '[Vittorino] affirmed an education which rendered a man able, according to the time and the needs, to treat of nature, of morals, of the stars, of geometry, of harmony, of numbering and measuring'. From this point forward both the theoretical study and practical execution of music gradually acquired a new and increasingly important significance in Italian culture, above all in courtly society.

Some sense of the development is shown in the way that musicians are portrayed in late fifteenth-century images. A revealing example is the portrait medallion of Pietrobono, a famed Ferrarese singer and lute player praised by a long line of humanist writers including Tinctoris. From literary descriptions it is clear that he was particularly admired for his performance of narrative verse in which he accompanied himself on a string instrument, and it is both ironic and characteristic of these *maestri* of the improvised tradition that more is known about Pietrobono's appearance than about the sound of his art. The instrument most commonly associated with this largely lost tradition of improvised singing of which Pietrobono was such a master was the lira da braccio, and it is this that is often shown in depictions of gods, heroes, poets and humanists from the last decades of the quattrocento onwards, largely because of its association with the lyre of classical antiquity. A small number of actual instruments has survived (the oldest, by Giovanni d'Andrea da Verona and now in the Kunsthistorisches Museum in Vienna, is dated 1511), and the lira was often depicted in the late fifteenth and throughout the sixteenth centuries in woodcuts, *intarsie* and paintings. The instrument is frequently shown in the hands of musicians in angel concerts and in *sacre conversazioni*; in Giovanni Bellini's San Zaccaria altarpiece a lone angel sits in front of the Madonna's throne playing the lira da braccio, a clear indication of the status of the instrument (see illus. 5). It is a lira da braccio that Apollo plays in Giovanni Bellini's painting *The Feast of the Gods* (1514) orginally painted for Duke Alfonso I d'Este (Washington, National Gallery) and, as we have seen, in the final version of Raphael's *Parnassus* (*c*.1509–11), where it was substituted for the classical lyre at a late stage in the evolution of the work (see illus. 1a). The apparent curiosity of this substitution has already been remarked on, but a clue to the explanation lies in the fact that in Raphael's fresco Apollo's instrument has nine strings (seven stopped plus two open) instead of the customary seven (five plus two); in the context of the picture it is clear that the artist's primary intention was to allude to Apollo's traditional role as the leader of the nine Muses rather than to represent a real instrument. Number frequently plays an important role in allegorical depictions, as in the numerous representations of the nine angel choirs which typically show each of the choirs singing or playing the same type of instrument. Even in cases where contemporary instruments are depicted, there is no information here about ensemble groupings.

Throughout the fifteenth and sixteenth centuries, courtly society acted as a behavioural model, not only for the diplomats, ecclesiastics and administrators who served it, but also for the upper reaches of the wider world. The rise of the middle

middle classes was already a feature of life in the fifteenth century, and by the sixteenth it had become a phenomenon. An accompanying growth in musical literacy, stimulated by the development of music printing, is reflected in the increased popularity of certain kinds of paintings with a musical content, notably portraits showing the musical interests of the sitter, through association with open music books, instruments or musical inscriptions, as in Piero di Cosimo's profile head of Francesco Giamberti (Amsterdam, Rijksmuseum), the right hand wing of a diptych whose left hand side shows Giamberti's son, the architect Giuliano da Sangallo, his profession identified by a sharpened quill and a pair of calipers. In keeping with the enhanced status of practical music, composers themselves are sometimes the subjects of portraits; an early example is Sebastiano del Piombo's much-discussed double-portrait of Verdelot and a mysterious singer called Ubretto described by Vasari in the second edition of the *Vite*, a picture which can no longer be securely identified. By the middle of the sixteenth century portraits of composers are not unusual; that of Giovanni Nasco still hangs in the rooms of the Accademia filarmonica in Verona where he was *maestro*; and in Giuseppe Belli's portrait of Gasparo Alberti, the sitter is identified not only through an inscription but also by a clearly legible extract from one of his sacred compositions (see illus. 7).

7 Giuseppe Belli,
*Portrait of Gasparo
Alberti* (Bergamo,
Accademia Carrara)

8 Bachiacca (Francesco d'Umbertino), *A Youth Playing a Lute* (New Orleans Museum of Art: Kress Collection)

9 Giovanni Cariani, *The Lutenist* (Strasbourg, Musée des Beaux-Arts)

The incorporation of music into a complex of humanistic interests conferred upon it a new authority and status; alongside other skills, both practical and theoretical, music now formed part of an aristocratic ideal the essence of which was taken up later by a number of writers concerned with formulating models of correct behaviour. The most vivid picture of Italian court life during the early decades of the sixteenth century occurs in the pages of Baldassare Castiglione's classic text *Il libro del cortegiano*, a manual of behaviour and practice for the Renaissance courtier. The role that music plays in the conversations of Castiglione's courtiers is an interesting reflection of progressive thinking about its function in contemporary courtly society, based not merely upon an idealized conception, but also upon experience. And in turn, this enhanced status of practical musical skills as a necessary part of the accomplished courtier's social equipment is reflected in the frequency with which the upper echelons of Italian society are now depicted as practitioners.

The conventions for portraying solo musicians go back at least to the fifteenth century; an early and fine example is the depiction of a lutenist in the *intarsia* choir-stalls orginally commissioned for the chapel of S Giovanni in Siena Cathedral, and now in the Collegiata at S Quirico d'Orcia. A hundred years later a similar formula is still followed by Bartolomeo Passerotti in his portrait, dated 1576, of an unknown gentleman playing the lute (Boston, Museum of Fine Arts). The sitter is shown three-quarter length, leaning against a table and gently touching the strings of his instrument. Behind him on the table there is a folded sheet of paper, but neither the inscription nor the music written on it is legible. This would have presumably provided an identification, but from the style of his dress (as well as from the very existence of this portrait, painted by the foremost Bolognese portraitist at the height of his career), it is clear that the sitter was a man of means. Since music also possessed considerable symbolic power, not all portraits, however iconographically simple they may at first appear, can be taken at face value. In *A Youth Playing a Lute* by Bachiacca (Francesco d'Ubertino) (see illus. 8), a gentleman holding a lute is seated on a ledge together with a vase of flowers and an hourglass, both symbols of transience. This theme is brought into a sharper focus by two scenes in the background of the picture; Apollo kneeling before Daphne transformed into a tree (love denied), and Delilah cutting Samson's hair in front of a chariot carrying Cupid (love betrayed). In this context the lute itself reinforces the central notion through its association with transitory pleasures, and above all with love. Another set of contemporary ideas about music are present in the apparently uncomplicated portrait of an unknown gentleman playing a lute with, in the background, a stormy scene opening out beyond a leafy screen, by the North Italian painter Giovanni Cariani (*c*.1485–1547) (see illus. 9), one of a number of musical pieces by this artist. Its thematic content, clearly derived from Giorgione, presupposes an allegorical and intellectualized conception of music as a dream-like interlude in reality, a moment of reverie reserved only for a small circle of *cognoscenti*. It was precisely through its association with this idealization of music, through references to its legendary power to move the minds and hearts of men, that practical involvement in music was elevated to the status of a serious enterprise.

Group-portraits of musicians can also be allegorical. Often described as 'Concerts', they are usually no such thing since one of the distinguishing features of these ensembles is that they seem to play for themselves and not for an audience. Characteristically placed behind a ledge or sill that distances them from the real world, these small and intimate groups cohere around some sort of overt music activity; instruments are often shown, as are partbooks and single sheets of music which sometimes display authentic and legible notation, messages which are themselves part of the meaning of the picture. The meaning of the group may ramify, but the central tenet common to all of them is that of 'harmony', with all that this meant to Renaissance humanists. For the humanist music operated through the upper senses, via the ears (audible sounds), the eyes (musical notation and diagrams in treatises), and through touch (performance). Pictures showing groups engaged in using these senses in common musical activity thus make an implied reference to the laws governing harmonic intervals in time and space: concord between high and low, measure between slow and fast. Beyond this, Platonic thought emphasizes the ability of music to bring together any group, political, social or otherwise, into concord, a concord which can be equated with universal law.

'Concert' scenes were a peculiarly north Italian-Venetian genre. One of the earliest and most familiar (it dates from the 1480s) is Lorenzo Costa's *Concert* (see illus. 10) which shows a woman and two men singing to the accompaniment of a lute with, before them on a marble parapet, two part-books (one open), a recorder, and a rebec. The main theme of the London picture is harmony, and in a number of sixteenth-century pictures showing several generations of a single family, the performance of music serves as a metaphor for familial harmony. For this reason music-playing groups often appear in ceiling paintings and frescoes in palaces and villas, as in the ceiling painting of the Aula Costabiliana in the Palazzo di Ludovico Moro (già Costabili) in Ferrara by Benvenuto Tisi *detto* Garofalo, Giovanni Antonio Fasolo's frescoes in the *salone* of the Villa Caldogno near Vicenza, and Veronese's more famous cycle at the Villa Maser, all of which are presumably intended to depict the domestic music-making which actually took place. Pictures such as these can be valuable for the organologist, showing instruments, the way in which they were played, and sometimes how ensembles were constituted. At the same time they are often difficult to interpret since the artist's primary intention was not necessarily to represent the details of the musical elements in the picture exactly and, more importantly, the primary purpose of the picture was often allegorical rather than realistic.

What at first might seem to be an amiably harmonious bourgeois ensemble is the circle of close friends, some performing, others listening, that inhabits Sebastiano Florigerio's *Musical Conversation* (see illus. 11). Yet despite its traditional title, this is far from being a simple concert scene. In the first place, it is unlikely that any performance is taking place; notwithstanding their finger gestures which would appear to be marking the tactus, only two of the nine figures in the painting are actually singing, and the open part-book held by the central female figure contains only the alto part, faithfully copied from the *Motetti e canzone. Libro primo* (Rome, 1520), of Michele Pesenti's setting of an anonymous poem 'Alma gentil, s'en voi fusse equalmente'. Around her bodice, this same elegantly-turbaned young woman carries the motto MAL STA ASCOSTO UN BEL SERENO ('It is wrong to hide a beautiful face'); these details, in the context of a picture in which the central action is overlooked by a veiled old woman suggests that, at one level, Florigerio's painting is intended at the least as an allegory of the passing of time, but more

10 Lorenzo Costa,
Concert (London, National Gallery)

precisely evokes the world of the brothel with the older woman acting as procuress. This central idea may also explain the fact that two of the figures are both singing and marking the tactus, thus referring not only to temporal but also to musical time. Even Titian's strange and mysteriously tense *Concert* of *c.*1515 (Florence, Palazzo Pitti), while clearly in the tradition of concert scenes, makes symbolic reference to the Three Ages of Man, perhaps in an attempt to stress the importance of music in all phases of civilized life. This theme is found elsewhere in 'Concert' scenes beginning with Pinturicchio's late fifteenth-century fresco lunette personifying Musica in the room of the Liberal Arts in the Borgia Apartments in the Vatican, in Titian's painting in Edinburgh (see illus. 3) and also in the well-known picture in the Pitti Palace in Florence sometimes attributed to Morto da Feltre (see illus. 12). In the Pitti picture the whole composition is dependent upon the subject of music, represented by the notated sheet held by the central figure of a boy. The equation of music with measured time is evident from the figure of the mature man to the right who is marking the tactus, while the old man is, symbolically, looking away. In a second version, at Hampton Court, the group is joined by a girl who is associated with the mature man, thus uniting the Three Ages of Man in temporal harmony enriched by the reference to love.

11 Sebastiano Florigerio, *Musical Conversation* (Munich, Alte Pinakothek)

12 Morto da Feltre, *The Three Ages of Man* (Florence, Pitti Palace)

The changing attitudes towards music which are characteristic of the early Renaissance period in Italy are powerfully evident in works executed for the major centres where the art was encouraged: Florence, Venice, Rome and, above all, the North Italian courts of Mantua and Ferrara where music was patronized, as a permanent feature of courtly life, on an unprecedented scale. A good if complex example is provided by the cycle of paintings commissioned by Isabella d'Este for her rooms in the Gonzaga palace at Mantua. Nearly all these canvasses rely on some sort of musical imagery to convey their message, if only on the ubiquitous opposition of string and wind instruments as symbols of good and evil respectively. More complicated allusions to the power of music are present in Mantegna's *Parnassus* of *c.*1497 (see illus. 13) and in one of the later paintings in the group, Lorenzo Costa's *Allegory of the Court of Isabella d'Este* completed *c.*1505–6 (see illus. 14). In the *Parnassus*, the centre of the stage is occupied by the nine Muses (some singing but all dancing), while to the left is the lyre-playing Apollo (or Orpheus), and to the right Mercury (inventor of the lyre and the syrinx) and Pegasus (the horse of the Muses). In the middle plane to the left, Vulcan (who can be equated with Tubal Cain who participated in Jubal's discovery of the laws of harmony) is stimulated by Amor who according to Plato was 'a composer so accomplished that he is the cause of composing in others'. In this way it is possible to relate all the mythological characters to the theme of musical activity or invention. Finally, Amor

13 Andrea Mantegna, *Parnassus* (Paris, Musée du Louvre)

14 Lorenzo Costa,
Allegory of the Court
of Isabella d'Este
(Paris, Musée du
Louvre)

15 Jacopo Sansovino, Loggetta, St Mark's Square, Venice.

in his more familiar role unites the figures of Mars and Venus who stand above the scene, thus ensuring the peace in which the arts (and particularly the art of music) symbolized beneath may flourish. Mars and Venus are in turn allusions to Isabella and her *condottiere* husband Marchese Francesco Gonzaga, clearly implying that the central theme of musical harmony is to be read as a symbol of the earthly harmony and peace over which they preside in the Duchy of Mantua. The same overall message is also present in Costa's *Court of Isabella d'Este* which shows scenes of violence, brutality and vice in the middle distance to the left and right of the picture. In the centre is a separate area fenced off and guarded by Cadmus and Diana. This is the Garden of Harmony where a figure usually taken to be Isabella herself, surrounded by musicians and artists including Pythagoras, is about to be crowned as Queen. Here again the Garden is probably intended to be seen as a symbol for Mantua where, isolated from earthly afflictions and failings, the arts flourish and harmony reigns under Isabella's protection. (This is presumably the picture that Vasari describes as a depiction of Isabella d'Este and members of her court 'who, singing variously, make sweet harmony'.)

These are later interpretations for which there is no evidence beyond the paintings themselves and an understanding of conventions and traditions, but in the case of the new Loggetta, designed by Jacopo Sansovino in 1537 for the base of the old campanile in St Mark's square in Venice (see illus. 15), the artist's explanation of the iconographical scheme has survived. The previous structure had been used by the Venetian nobility when they came to the square on government business. Sansovino's replacement, ornamented with precious materials and rich sculptural decoration based on classical allegory and mythology, imposed a different dimension. In architectural terms its forms and colours complement those of the nearby ducal palace, while the facade, with its obvious overtones of a triumphal arch, is an essay in a classicizing style which is primarily associated with state buildings of the period. In political terms, the structure was conceived as a visual representation of the myth of Venice, that specifically Venetian view of their own state as the perfect republic, and as such the Loggetta served to impress that mythology not only upon foreign visitors but also upon the Venetian population. At the centre of the decorative scheme are four bronze statues representing Minerva, Apollo, Mercury and Peace, which occupy niches in the facade. Recalling his father's explanation of the significance of Apollo, Francesco Sansovino wrote:

the statue of Apollo is the sun, which is singular and unique, just as this Republic, for its constituted laws, its unity, and uncorrupted liberty, is a sun in the world, regulated with justice and wisdom; furthermore, it is known how this nation takes a more than ordinary delight in music, and Apollo signifies music. Moreover, from the union of the magistracies, combined with equable temperament, there arises an unusual harmony, which perpetuates this admirable government: for these reasons was Apollo represented.

There could hardly be a better demonstration of the way in which the powerfully evocative image of music, bolstered with humanistic justifications, could be deployed for symbolic, and in this instance propagandistic purposes. At the same time we should not forget that behind the conceits and allegories lay a rich musical reality without which those same musical images, for all their theoretical underpinning, would have lost much of their potency.

Select bibliography

P. EGAN, '"Concert" scenes in musical paintings of the Italian Renaissance', *Journal of the American Musicological Society*, xiv (1961), pp. 184–95

G. KINSKY, *Geschichte der Musik in Bildern* (Leipzig, 1929)

K. KOMMA, *Musikgeschichte in Bildern* (Stuttgart, 1961)

P. W. LEHMANN, 'The sources and meaning of Mantegna's *Parnassus*', in P. W. Lehmann and K. Lehmann (eds), *Samothracian reflections. Aspects of the revival of the antique* (Princeton, 1973)

B. W. MEIJER, 'Harmony and satire in the works of Niccolo Frangipane: problems in the depiction of music', *Simiolus*, vi (1962–3), pp. 94–112

V. SCHERLIESS, *Musikalische Noten auf Kunstwerken der italienischen Renaissance bis zum Anfang des 17. Jahrhunderts* (Hamburg, 1972)

H. C. SLIM, 'Two paintings of "concert scenes" from the Veneto and the Morgan Library's unique music print of 1520', in F. della Seta and F. Piperno (eds), *In cantu et in sermone. For Nino Pirrotta on his 80th birthday* (Florence, 1988), pp. 155–74

E. WINTERNITZ, *Musical instruments and their symbolism in Western art* (London, 1967)

31 Echoes of the past in the present

Surviving traditional instruments and performance practices as a source for performers of medieval secular monody

Stevie Wishart

The recent studies by John Stevens (*Words and Music in the Middle Ages*) and Christopher Page (*Voices and Instruments of the Middle Ages*) offer performers an inspiring and practicable analysis of the secular monophonic repertories; they present much of the most informative early literature relevant to its performance. Page also fleetingly opens the door on another avenue of enquiry when he draws an analogy between Jerome of Moravia's first tuning for the fiddle and 'non-Western' (in this case classical southern Indian) playing traditions. It is through a brief exploration of non-Western, or more specifically semi-notational and oral musical traditions, that I hope to suggest to performers, and in particular fiddle-players, ways in which to recreate the extra-notational aspects of our surviving manuscript sources.

From the instrumentalist's point of view, there is one rather serious handicap to be overcome; there are no surviving medieval instruments in anything approaching playing condition and we are thus unable to try out an instrument's musical potential or make reconstructions from actual models of the time. All we have are representations from the visual arts, and but for these, we would be ignorant of the very existence of many instruments, and of their various designs. In the case of medieval fiddles, they were impressively varied in comparison to our current meagre diet of the violin family.

Musical iconography can provide us with only a limited amount of the information needed to reconstruct instruments of the time; all too often the gaps in the story are supplied from constructional features and playing techniques familiar from Renaissance instruments. In a few specific cases outlined below, iconographical evidence can be substantiated, or expanded upon, through comparisons with surviving traditional instruments which bear morphological similarities to their medieval ancestors. Furthermore, these instruments are played exclusively within more-or-less orally based, monophonic or heterophonic musical cultures.

Visual correspondences between traditional instruments and medieval representations

One of the most publicized and colourful musical traditions which still shares points of correspondence with medieval times survives among various Arabic-speaking musical communities of North Africa, in particular Algeria, Tunisia and Morocco where the so-called Andalusian court ensembles can still be heard. As their name suggests, these ensembles preserve vestiges of the musical heritage of Al-Andalūs, a highly sophisticated musical heritage which flourished during the

Muslim occupation of Spain, and has subsequently survived in towns settled by Spanish exiles; from Seville to Tunis, Córdoba to Tlemcan (Algeria), Valencia to Fez during the tenth to twelfth centuries, and finally, in the fifteenth century, from Granada to Fez and Tetuán. Depending on the political climate of the time, non-Christian minorities were tolerated at various Christian courts in Aragon and Castile and this provided opportunities for Islamic musical traditions to be transmitted to northern Europe, and for northern Spanish, and particularly Occitan musical traditions to travel south and subsequently to Morocco and West Islam. The courts of Alfonso el Sabio (1221–84) at Toledo and Seville were particularly lively centres of acculturation; in Alfonso's collection of *Cantigas de Santa María* (Escorial, MS j.b.2, *c*.1280), we find Christian musicans playing the *rabāb* and the *'ūd*, while a Moor appears alongside a Provençal styled Christian at the head of Cantiga 120. Each is playing an identical oval guitar. The possibility that Andalusian classical music of the Maghreb may shed some light on the former musical traditions of medieval Spain becomes all the more alluring when a comparison is made between the *rabāb* (which, with regard to its medieval antecedent, will be described as 'lintaform') and the most highly esteemed instrument of the Arab world, the *'ūd*.

Well-defined late 13th-century examples of the *'ūd* include those in the *Cantigas* (particularly the more carefully delineated lute at the head of Cantiga 170, which is paired with a piriform, or pear-shaped, fiddle), and in León Cathedral (south door and north rose window). Subsequently they appear played by angel musicians in Aragonese altar screens from the mid- to late-fourteenth century. Modern *'ūds* share the same general outlines, with a tapering piriform or round resonator, short neck and reverse pegholder fitted with lateral pegs, as well as some of the same components such as a fixed string holder, richly ornamented soundholes, and the application of a plectrum. Likewise, the most commonly illustrated string arrangement is from eight to ten strings, and in the most detailed examples, such as in a painted panel by the workshop of Jaime Serras in Perpignan, they are clearly paired as courses. This string grouping is characteristic of the Andalusian *'ūd*, while the four-course *'ūd* survives in Morocco as the *'ūd 'arbī*. There are rarely frets, but marquetry along the neck guides the placement of the stopping hand, a feature which is also suggested on the lute (and a fiddle) in the *Cantigas*.

While the *'ūd* is the principal accompanying sonority, it is the bowed *rabāb* which has the most soloistic role, improvising preludes and leading the ensemble through the various movements of the *nawba*, the main classical form of the Andalusian tradition. A multitude of fiddles are known as the *rabāb* – the term may signify nothing more than a skin table – but it is the Maghribi *rabāb* which bears a remarkable resemblance to lintaform fiddles depicted in Spain from the thirteenth century onwards, and which subsequently features in Italian as well as Aragonese angel consorts. The lintaform fiddle decorating a corbel in the cloister of Vich Cathedral (see illus. 1) is virtually the same as the modern *rabāb* (see illus. 2) with its distinctive lintaform resonator, slightly concave along its length, a bipartite table which is also gently concave, and a reverse pegholder terminating in a scroll, a feature also found on a *rabāb* depicted in the north rose window at León.

The *rabāb*'s components, as well as its shape, can also be traced back to thirteenth- and fourteenth-century representations. Common features include the two strings attached directly to an endblock on the underside, the pair of

1 Corbel with fiddler (early fourteenth century, Catalonia) (Vich Cathedral cloister)

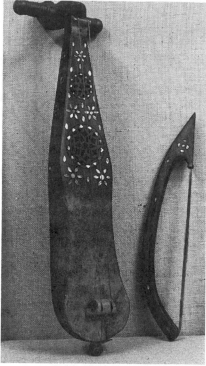

2 Moroccan rabāb (? nineteenth century) (Oxford, Bate Collection)

soundholes towards the proximal end (the end where the instrument is held), the various bridge designs, and both are bowed. Medieval bridges are usually in the form of simple bridge-bars (particularly well-defined on the famous reliquary chest from San Piedra de Arroya, now in the Academia de Historia, Madrid), a design found on nineteenth-century Moroccan *rabābs* in the Museo Municipal de Música, Barcelona. The other type of bridge consists of a cylinder or semi-cylinder, and it is the latter form that is found on the exceptionally detailed Vich corbel.

Having established a visual continuity between medieval iconographical sources and the Moroccan *rabāb*, it seems justifiable to go one step further and fill in the missing parts of the jigsaw with constructional features adopted on extant instruments, always looking toward the most conservative models available. The construction of the *'ūd*, or medieval lute, is described in Arabic treatises from the tenth century onwards, and has been well documented by modern organologists, but the bowed instruments have enjoyed less attention.

The modern Andalusian *rabāb*, like its medieval predecessors, varies from a very narrow, almost parallel-sided instrument, to those with wider resonators which taper towards the pegholder. It varies in length, and therefore pitch, but a typical tuning is *g* and *d'*, matching the lower two strings of the modern violin. A unique feature is a hollow neck; the entire body up to the pegholder is hollowed out, and the entire upper surface forms the table. The proximal section is wood (or sometimes copper plate in the case of Algerian and Tunisian models), and the distal part (that furthest from the player's hand) is skin-covered – materials suggested in a number of Aragonese paintings. There is a high nut which raises the two gut strings well clear of the table up to the point where they pass over the bridge, often made from a section of a reed.

Another group of fiddles more frequently compared to medieval models are those common to countries around the Aegean, that is, the *kemençe*, or piriform, trichordic fiddle of western Turkish classical music. It is better known in Greek folk music as the *lira*, and is similar to the Bulgarian *gadulka*. Bachmann, in particular, has made a detailed comparison between their tunings and use of drones. Features in common with semi-necked medieval representations (see illus. 3) include a convex-backed resonator tapering to form the neck; a flat, leaf-shaped pegholder with posterial pegs; D-shaped soundholes; and the most detailed examples are usually trichordic. These are all features common to the piriform fiddles, known as *gudoks*, excavated at the site of a medieval house in Novgorod in Russia. They date from *c.*1055 to 1368, a time span coinciding with the main body of iconographical evidence. The *gudok*, like the *kemençe*, is carved from the solid, with the resonator hollowed out and covered by a wooden table. On the *kemençe*, the table is slightly convex along both axes and is thickest in the middle, where it supports the bridge and measures about 3mm, rapidly thinning out to about 1.5mm around the perimeter. If adopted on medieval reconstructions, these features help strengthen the table without the use of barring or a soundpost, as well increasing its volume. However, there is much variation in the finer details among medieval examples, and nothing like the level of continuity linking the lintaform design to the *rabāb*. In the handful of highly

3 Elders with piriform fiddles (Soria, west door, Santo Domingo)

detailed representations of piriform fiddles there is no suggestion of the combined bridge and soundpost arrangement characteristic of the *kemençe* and south eastern European folk fiddles. Medieval models tend to conform to the *gudoks* with the soundholes towards the centre of the resonator, and the bridge standing further towards the endblock.

Moving closer to the heart of medieval Europe, there are also a number of surviving folk instruments to be found in northern Spain, some of which can be traced back to iconographical sources from at least as early as the last quarter of the twelfth century. They include the Galician *pandeiro*, and the guitar-shaped *zanfona* or hurdy-gurdy, an instrument which is also enjoying a lively revival in the Auvergne region of France, and to a lesser extent in Hungary and England. The least documented, and yet the most important in view of the popularity of the fiddle in the Middle Ages, is the *rabel*, now found mainly in the isolated villages in the province of Santander, but formerly played in other provinces. Some fiddles that are referred to as the *rabel* are in fact rustic violins with a soundpost, fingerboard, arched table, and S-shaped soundholes. The Cantabrian *rabel*, on the other hand, is morphologically distinct from the violin, but exhibits features familiar from medieval fiddles. Among the earliest surviving examples (dated to the seventeenth century), are those now owned by the Museo Etnográfico y Folklórico de Cantabria, and by Francisco Sobaler, a *rabelista* from the village of Espinilla. Later instruments have survived up to the 1950s, but in recent times the *rabel* would have died out completely except for a few makers and players intent on maintaining their local folk traditions. The following description of extant models is drawn from a survey by Fernando Gomarín, published in Santander in 1970, and from recent discussions with Fernando, and other *rabelistas* still living in Cantabria today.

Like medieval fiddles, models of the *rabel* display little standardization in size, and vary from small treble fiddles (of about 45.5cm in length) to alto instruments measuring between 53 and 59cms. Larger fiddles, measuring up to 64cms in length, are usually held vertically and supported between the knees, and therefore sometimes called *rabé morisco* (the term cited in Juan Ruiz's *Libro de Buen Amor* of 1330), although a nineteenth-century *rabel* of some 62.5cm in the Museo Etnográfico appears to have been played on the shoulder (see illus. 4b). Similarly, the number of strings varies from one to four, although in recent times players prefer to use only two strings, even when playing on archaic instruments originally designed to be fitted with four strings.

There are various morphological types: octoform, with single or double waists (see illus. 4a-b); bottle-shaped; piriform (see illus. 5a); or with C-shaped waists, with and without corners (see illus. 5a-b). The seventeenth-century *rabel* in the Museo Etnográfico has a double-indented octoform resonator and is carved from the solid without a fingerboard (see illus. 4b) and this construction is most common today (see illus. 4a, 9a-b). Another incomplete seventeenth-century *rabel* is of a different construction: only the sides, neck and pegholder are carved from the solid, the back and front being separate. In Cantabria, as in the Maghreb, a metal-plate table is interchangeable with the skin one, although traditional makers today seem to prefer to use skin. Wooden tables are much rarer, but are adopted by less conservative makers.

These resonator designs echo medieval forms as depicted from the front. Well-defined portal reliefs of octoform fiddles include those at the Cathedrals of

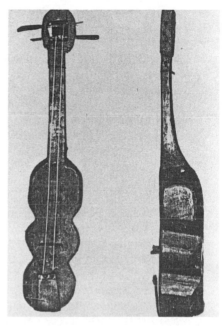

4a Modern *rabel* by Antonio Martínez (Cabuérniga)

b Seventeenth-century *rabel* from Las Costeras, after Fernando Gomarín (Museo Etnográfico y Folklórico de Cantabria)

5a Bottle-shaped, waisted and piriform *rabels* (Santillana del Mar, Museo de las Comarcas de Cantabria)

b Waisted *rabel* from the Campoó valley (Museo Etnográfico y Folklórico de Cantabria)

Santiago de Compostela, Orense and Chartres, and in the collegiate church in Toro (see illus. 7a-b). C-shaped waists are in evidence by the later twelfth century (illus. 7a), but become more numerous by late fourteenth-century representations, initially in Italy, and subsequently in Aragon (see Woodfield, pls. 27–9) where, as on the *rabel*, the neck is more elongated. There is little standardization regarding the shape of the back, which may be either slightly convex and rounded into the sides, or occasionally completely flat (see illus. 6b). Makers also use a variety of woods such as pine, oak and elder, and the above-mentioned seventeenth-century instruments are made from cherry and walnut respectively. In common with medieval practice, strings are traditionally made from black horse-hair taken from the mane or tail, or from gut. *Rabelistas* such as Pedro Madrid use modern metal-wound strings, but some suggested this was due to the unavailability of gut strings and, on seeing my fiddles strung with gut, they excitedly requested supplies of similar strings for their own instruments. As on medieval models, the strings extend from lateral, frontal or posterial pegs and over a simple yoke-like bridge which on taller examples is pierced with one or two apertures (see illus. 5b). There is invariably a tailpiece, which on conservative instruments is leather and pinned to the base (see illus. 8), and on the piriform model is looped to a large endpin (see illus. 5a). Occasionally, as on a nineteenth-century model with horse-hair strings, these are attached directly to endpins. Fernando Gomarín's survey also includes a *rabel* from Silio which resembles a small bowed guitar, with a fixed stringholder and metal strings (see illus. 9). Ian Woodfield's important study illustrates the

6a,b Modern *rabels* by Pedro Madrid (Santa Eulalia de Polaciones)

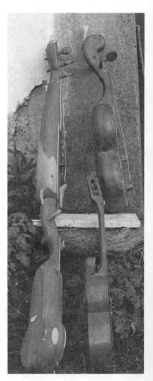

7a Elder with waisted fiddle,
c. 1170–1200 (Toro, Collegiate Church,
archivolt over north door)

b Elder with waisted fiddle, *c.* 1240
(Toro, Collegiate Church, archivolt over
west door)

significance of this design with respect to the origins of the viol, and a minority of late fifteenth-century Spanish representations feature similar instruments such as the one played by Salome in a panel by the Quiteria Master.

As well as providing morphological comparisons with medieval models, the *rabel*'s finer constructional details may also throw some light on the nature of corresponding details in medieval depictions where crucial information for players, such as the bridge design and string-stopping surface, are often unclear. On many instruments the top of the neck is flush with the level of the table (see illus. 4a-b, 5a-b), on others there is slight change in level (see illus. 6a-b). If a fingerboard (or raised stopping surface) is adopted, the simplest approach is to carve the fiddle from the solid, slice off the table and hollow out the resonator. If the table is then shaved down to an acoustically desirable thickness (around 2mm), it will be stepped down from the level of the neck when it is glued or nailed onto the resonator (this method was explained to me by Alan Crumpler). A few instruments (both medieval and modern) have a long fingerboard extending over the table. In contrast to the violin, where the angle of the fingerboard tilts up towards the bridge so that the strings remain more-or-less parallel with the stopping surface, the fingerboard on the *rabel* is only slightly incremented (if at all), and the neck is not angled back to compensate for the height of the bridge (see illus. 6b). Consequently, the bridge must be significantly lower, and therefore flatter (see illus. 8), than on a violin, and this would probably have been the arrangement on medieval models with

8 Detail of waisted fiddle (illus. 5a)

9a,b Antonio Martínez making a *rabel* at his house in Cabuérniga

fingerboards, such as those depicted in the famous Pórtico de la Gloria at Santiago where in similar fashion the neck and flat table lie along the same plane, and the bridges are also low. This appears to have been the usual arrangement up to the mid-fifteenth century, when, as Mary Remnant has shown, fingerboards with wedges begin to appear.

It is interesting to note how a single structural detail, such as keeping the neck and table along the same plane, indicates the nature of a succession of other components, such as the design of the bridge and the convexity of the table on which it sits (aspects which are invariably unclear from iconographical sources), and these in turn define crucial parameters for the player: the method of string-stopping, the upper limit of stopped pitches available on each string, and the drone-based monophonic, as opposed to polyphonic, potentials of the instrument in relation to its number of strings.

Extant performance practices pertinent to the medieval fiddle

Descriptions of tunings and rudiments of performance noted down by Jerome of Moravia and his contemporaries become much more meaningfl if we can also hear players adopting comparable practices, just as a static representation of a musical instrument tells us so much more if we can compare it to a real one.

Cantabrian *rabelistas* make varying use of the drone depending on the local style adopted from village to village. Some play purely melodically, while those from the valley of Polaciones sound a more continuous drone with the upper string, tuned to the tonic, taking most of the melody but occasionally sounding as an intermittent open drone when the melody falls to the lower (drone) string, tuned a fourth below. Very occasionally two strings are stopped simultaneously in parallel motion. In Polaciones, players tend to hold their *rabels* in their lap (see illus. 10), while those from Campóo play on the shoulder, and this position is also preferred for accompanying dancers. As a self-accompanying instrument associated with simple dance music or in combination with the solo voice, the *rabel* strikes resonances with descriptions of medieval performance practice. Its principal repertory is the *jota* in the 'pesao' or 'bajo' duple metre, or the 'ligero' triple metre. Occasionally, a player would recall a more elaborate, less metrical *romance, tornado,* or *marza.* The *rabelista* usually shadows the vocal melody and improvises interludes between the stanzas, often embellishing with turns, bow articulations, and, more rarely, with trills, but without vibrato. Sometimes the melodic movement is interspersed with a drone-based rhythmic one, and these simple ornamentation patterns sustain the fairly limited musical ideas.

Classical non-Western string instruments tend to sound intermittent drones, even with a consonant tuning, as adopted by players of the Turkish *kemençe*, the Turkish *rebab*, and its Persian counterpart, the *kamānche*, a spike fiddle which was formerly strung with silk strings, but latterly with three or four metal ones. Tuned in combinations of perfect fourths and fifths (i.e. A-E-A or G-C-G), their practice of bowing one or more strings as occasional open drones when sounding in consonance with the melody (although they may also be stopped at other times) is strikingly reminiscent of Pierre de Limoge's interpretation of Jerome's advanced fiddle technique. Christopher Page's interpretation of fifthing is certainly

10 Pedro Madrid Gómez playing outside his house in Santa Eulalia

plausible, but Pierre may well be describing another musical practice familiar to him. An intermittent use of drones falls logically midway between the initial development of a bowing technique limited to sounding continuous drones with the melody to one that in combination with a more graduated string span, adopted a less arbitrary use of drones. Cantabrian *rabelistas* occasionally adopt more sophisticated techniques such as fifthing and playing a fragmented polyphonic line against the melody, techniques which become more sustained on the more violinistic Hardanger fiddle with its gently arched bridge and adoption of consonant tunings.

The classical *kemençe* and *Maghribi rabāb* are usually played purely melodically and have a far more elaborate and subtle vocabulary of ornamentation in comparison to the northern European viol and violin families. Their tone and much of their technique have evolved from, and aspire towards, the sonorities of the human voice and it is no coincidence that at the Istanbul Conservatorium of Music a respected vocal professor, İshan Özgen, is also responsible for teaching the *kemençe*. Both the *kemençe*'s construction, repertory and playing techniques are well codified and nurtured within a dogmatic teaching tradition. Students can study courses specializing in the *kemençe*, and although these courses are aimed toward exponents of the Turkish classical repertory, there are many aspects pertinent to medieval string instruments.

Both the *rabāb* and *kemençe* are held downwards, usually more-or-less vertically, with the endblock resting on the left knee, although the *rabāb* may also be held more obliquely on the right knee with the pegholder coming to rest against the left shoulder. Both playing positions can be seen in the illustration in the *Cantigas* (MS b.j.2., f. 118r). Sometimes the *lira* is supported between the knees, in a similar manner to the piriform fiddles in Soria. As is the case with the majority of traditional fiddles that can be traced back to before the eighteenth century, the strings are stopped laterally or pulled sideways by the terminal phalanges of the left hand, rather than being pressed against a solid string-stopping surface, as on instruments with a raised fingerboard. Such a technique is implicit on the fourteenth-century *gudok*, and on medieval representations of the *rabāb*, where, as on modern models, the presence of soundholes towards the proximal end would inhibit the strings being stopped by downward pressure against them. This stopping technique emphasizes the upper partials, accentuating the vocal quality of the bowed string, and facilitates a rapid, highly embellished melodic style with a considerable degree of timbral and pitch fluctuation within each note of the melody.

The art of controlled improvisation, in the form of instrumental preludes in which various sections explore the mode, is perhaps the most highly-prized aspect of Islamic musical aesthetics. The melodic movement defining a particular mode (Turkish *makam*; Arabic *Maqām*) is strictly structured at the intermediary and final resting points. These points often form consonances with the drone which, on three- and four-string instruments, is consequently sounded, emphasizing the melodic hiatus. Each successive phrase is developed around axial notes of the mode with the tonic and so-called predominant note (often the fifth) being the most axiomatic. The skill of the performer depends on the pacing of each phrase up to the points of greatest tension when the highest pitch is reached. These melodic treatments are well-suited to the modal monodies of the twelfth to early fourteenth centuries, either as preludes, interludes or postludes to strophic songs, or in the interpretation and improvised extensions of additive forms, namely the *estampie* and lai. Perhaps these correspondences spring from a common tendency for the song texts to be written down and for the music to be orally transmitted.

This discussion has focused on correspondences between past and present musical traditions, but we must be equally aware of divergences. Microtonal subtleties characteristic of many modal systems do not require modifications in technique, and the discerning listener can concentrate on the diatonic modes common to medieval monodies. Other differences such as the widespread practice of holding traditional bowed instruments downwards in contrast to medieval fiddlers, who apparently were equally at home supporting their fiddles on the shoulder, may point to divergent techniques. In this respect, the Cantabrian *rabelistas* are all the more intriguing since, like their medieval forebears, they too adopt vertical and horizontal playing positions. Furthermore, in accordance with medieval Spanish representations, they invariably use an over-hand bow grip in both playing positions (see illus. 10), whereas the medieval and the modern *rabāb*, as well as numerous fiddles held vertically in northern European iconography, are bowed under-hand.

A circumspect study of those musical traditions still accessible to players today and which seem to preserve echoes of our medieval past, may provide tangible guidelines to compensate for aspects of performance practice left unanswered by the notational, iconographical, theoretical and literary sources available. At the very least our ears will be opened to levels of virtuosity and musicality which are rarely attained in concert performances based on historical reconstruction, for we will be drawing on a level of musicianship acquired through contact with a relatively limited time and place, a background familiar to the musicians of the Middle Ages but foreign to the urbanized musical contexts of professional Western musicians today. At most, we can more fully comprehend and even expand upon medieval evidence. But the global village is upon us, making it possible to hear the musics of the Moroccan *rabāb*, the Turkish *kemençe* and *rebab*, the Persian *kamānche*, the Spanish *rabelista*, while at the same time undermining the isolation and anachronisms of these very traditions. The oldest *rabelistas* remember playing on gut or horsehair strings, but now many prefer wire strings originally made from the metal core of bicycle brake-leads.

I am indebted to İhsan Özgen of Istanbul; the Cantabrian folklorists and musicans Kate Goff, Marcos Barcena Borrajo and Roberto Diego; Jesús García Preciados of Radio Nacional de España (Santander); Alfonso Garciaoliva, curator of the Bagpipe Museum of Gijón; Fernando Gomarín Guirado, director of the Aula Etnografía, University of Cantabria, and curator of the Museo de las Comarcas de Cantabria; and also to the rabelistas Pedro Madrid Gómez and Carlos Fernández Calderón, and the rabel-maker Antonio Martínez. This project was partially funded by a Vicente Cañada Blanch Fellowship and an Arts Council of Great Britain award.

Select bibliography

AL FARABI, *Kitab al-musiqi al-kabir* (Great Book on Music), R. d'Erlanger (ed.), *La musique arabe* (Paris, 1930–59)

W. BACHMANN, *The origins of bowing*, trans. N. Deane (London, 1969)

F. CRANE, *Extant medieval instruments: a provisional catalogue by type* (Iowa, 1972)

J. LÓPEZ-CALO, *La música medieval en Galicia* (Santiago de Compostela, 1982)

C. PAGE, 'Jerome of Moravia on the *rubeba* and *viella*', *Galpin Society Journal*, xxxii (1979), pp. 77–95; and *Voices and instruments of the Middle Ages* (London, 1987)

D. RANDEL, 'Al-Farabi and the role of Arabic music theory in the Middle Ages', *Journal of the American Musicological Society*, xxix (1976), pp. 173–88

M. REMNANT, 'The diversity of medieval fiddles', *Early Music*, iii (1975), pp. 47–51

K. SIGNELL, *Makam, modal practice in Turkish art music* (Seattle, 1977)

J. STEVENS, *Words and music in the Middle Ages* (Cambridge, 1986)

H. H. TOUMA, 'The maqām phenomenon: an improvisation technique in the music of the Middle East', *Ethnomusicology*, xv (1971), pp. 38–48

I. WOODFIELD, *The early history of the viol* (Cambridge, 1984)

O. WRIGHT, *The modal system of Arab and Persian music AD 1250–1300* (London, 1978)

Select discography

Los últimos tañedores del rabel (Saga, VPC–251, 1988)

Modal music and improvisation–Arabian music: maqam, Unesco Collected Musical Sources (Philips, 6586 006)

A musical anthology of the Orient: Turkey II, Unesco (BM 30 L2020) and *Tunisia* (BM 30 L2008)

32 Surviving instruments

Lewis Jones

Instruments occupy an anomalous and uncomfortable position in our present understanding of the music of the Middle Ages and Renaissance. To many scholars, interested chiefly in the study of musical sources – their transmission and interpretation – they are irrelevant, or at best peripheral. To many amateurs, captivated by the instrument-dominated performances of the 1960s and '70s, they remain the very stuff of 'early music'. Amongst professional performers of late medieval music, attitudes are equally polarized, some favouring the exclusively vocal approach (historically well-founded in many repertories) discussed by Christopher Page in chapter 3, above, while others clothe simple songs in an elaborate fabric of instrumental sound whose pattern may hail as much from Morocco or San Francisco as from Europe. Often, moreover, quite apart from the question of what they might play, neither the instruments used nor the playing techniques adopted stand up to scrutiny in the light of the wealth of contemporary evidence available to us.

Have modern players and makers of these instruments lost their way? Is there any point in concerning ourselves with the earlier instruments if it can be demonstrated that their role in the surviving repertories of music was slight? What, then, is their significance?

This is not the place to chronicle in detail the evolution of instrumental practice, but between about 1300 and 1600 we can observe a process whereby instruments were gradually assimilated into, and themselves gradually adapted to, the originally ecclesiastical tradition of notated polyphonic music. Though the details are often difficult to piece together, and to reconcile with the music we know, this trend is reflected in theoretical writings and accounts of music-making. At the start of this period, most instruments were small in size, and were used singly or sometimes in pairs. During the fifteenth century, instruments capable of playing only a single, quasi-vocal line were enlarged to give a range of sizes which could be played in families, initially of two or, by the sixteenth century, of three or more sizes at once. For example, two sizes of shawm playing together are identifiable early in the fifteenth century, while late fifteenth-century paintings show three recorders together, sometimes two of one size and one smaller, probably a fifth higher, which would ideally suit the ranges of much mid-century polyphony. Instruments of modest polyphonic capacity (harps, lutes, keyboards, etc.) were changed, and their playing techniques developed, to enable a single player to sustain counterpoint in the current vocal manner in four or more parts. Other instruments, less immediately adaptable to either of these ends (horns, trumpets, tabor pipes, psalteries, hurdy-gurdies, etc.) either became confined to ceremonial or folk uses, or faded from view, in some cases to wait until the seventeenth or eighteenth centuries before gaining acceptance in a new role in the orchestra.

Thus an ostensibly vocal tradition shaped the instrumental music of the Renaissance, but the influence was not all in one direction. By the later sixteenth and early seventeenth centuries, with the growing independence of instrumental activity and the increasingly routine use of instruments to accompany voices, instruments, the idiomatic styles they evolved and the concepts of pitch associated with them, exerted a powerful influence upon vocal music and upon musical thought in general.

The further back we go in time, the more central instruments become to our understanding of what music there was. From prehistory, they are the only traces of music we have, and though by the Middle Ages we have both notated music and writings on music, instruments are still the only guide we have to the actual *sound* of music. Indeed, they remain so until the invention of recording late in the nineteenth century. It may be argued, of course, that voices also existed in the Middle Ages, and that they can be assumed to have changed little; but the infinitude of vocal productions, the sheer variety of vocal sounds accepted as musical the world over, must place them relatively low in the hierarchy of evidence.

What instrumental sounds survive from the Middle Ages? Of the hundreds of extant instruments from before 1500 catalogued by Frederick Crane (and his list can now be added to), most are whistles, bone flutes, rattles and signalling instruments, which, though they broaden our view of the medieval soundscape, tell us little about learned music. A few fifteenth-century string instruments, though too frail to be played, are well enough preserved to be copied as they stand, but the resulting sound depends upon many unknowns in respect of stringing, tuning, setting up, playing technique and so forth. Most valuable as sound guides are the organs, many of which survive with fifteenth-century pipework, even if most instruments of that date have been retuned and rebuilt more than once.

The visitor to Bologna, where past and present co-exist so stimulatingly, will find several pointers. The organ of 1470–4 by Lorenzo di Giacomo da Prato in the vast Church of San Petronio, though moved within the church and rebuilt, preserves most of its original pipework in good order. In spite of a downward transposition by a tone of the pipes in relation to the keyboard, it must speak with essentially the same voice as it did five centuries ago. The *principale* and *ottava* of this instrument have a quality of extraordinary calm and stability, noticeably different from the more assertive speech of the 1596 Malamini organ which now faces it on the opposite side of the choir. To play music of the period on the earlier instrument, or to sing chant or a Josquin motet with it in the unchanged acoustic, is to witness something of fifteenth-century music which no description or recording can convey.

Nearby, in the Chiesa del Corpus Domini, is preserved a mid-fifteenth-century *violeta*, a four-stringed fiddle said to have been played by S Caterina de' Vigri (1413–63), and now mounted on her shrine. Preserved with it are apparently original fittings (including a slightly curved bridge) and a bow. Like most bowed instruments of the previous centuries, it is strikingly small, the strings shorter than those of a violin and sounding – whatever their precise tuning – in the soprano register. Apart from the fact that the bridge is now clearly lodged in the wrong place, it is quite convincing as a fifteenth-century relic, as are a gittern by Hans Ott, and a twenty-six stringed harp, both at the Wartburg, Eisenach.

String instruments may also be reconstructed from pictures or technical descriptions. An uncritical attitude on the part of several makers, however, sometimes led astray by the expectations of players, has produced some extraordinary hybrid and enlarged instruments, which can be misleading in musical use. Only by assembling a large collection of pictures and analysing them in the light of all the other available evidence (including the constructional methods used in the few surviving instruments) is progress towards a probable medieval sound likely to be made. An idea of pitch and perhaps something of the general character of the sound may be gained from the size and shape of an instrument, but the playing properties of a string instrument depend to a large extent upon details which may not be visible in even a relatively detailed painting. Such factors as the height and possible curvature of the bridge, the relationship of the strings to the fingerboard, their grouping into courses, and their thickness and stress, together contribute to the quality of sound and determine what can be played on the instrument. The distribution and role of tone-modifiers such as brays on harps and comparable buzzing devices on fingerboard instruments is still little studied. Amongst the most dependable representations of instruments are the geometrically precise *intarsie* which decorate north Italian rooms and choirstalls. From those in the *studiolo* of Federigo da Montefeltro at Urbino, for example, it is possible to trace the curvature of the bridge of a *lira da braccio*, or the spacing of the tangents of a clavichord.

A little earlier than the instruments already considered is the organ of the church of Notre-Dame de Valère, Sion, in Switzerland. Though the original four-foot pipes have been replaced and lower-pitched pipes have been added, three high ranks, their metal cast on sand, seem to date from *c*.1390, and offer a vivid impression of the sort of sound that might have given life to the music of the Faenza Codex.

An instrument may also illuminate contemporary musical theory, since it is the static embodiment of aspects of the musical system it is built to serve. This is clearly the case with clavichords, the disposition of whose tangents corresponds to the sizes of the semitone steps of the scale, and with the sole surviving instrument by the celebrated Lorenzo da Pavia, his paper-piped organ of 1494, now in the Museo Correr, Venice. Made at the time when Pythagorean tunings were giving way to new temperaments, it has two alternative ranks of pipes (sharing the same pitch standard by having one pipe in common per octave). To judge from the surviving pipes, one rank was Pythagorean while the other was in a form of meantone temperament. Though the instrument is unplayable (it now has a dummy keyboard), the one pipe sampled produced a sound of remarkable sweetness and purity, and enough survives of the instrument for a working replica to be built. This has been done recently with another multiple-pitched keyboard instrument, the *clavemusicum omnitonum* of Vito Trasuntino (1606), now in the Museo Civico, Bologna. A late masterpiece by one of the greatest Venetian harpsichord makers of the sixteenth century, it has thirty-one pitches per octave, and was intended to be tuned in a similar way to that described by Nicola Vicentino in his *L'antica musica* (1555). A sophisticated tetrachord (four-stringed monochord) is provided to help with tuning, and this has the microtonal intervals built into it, like the fretted neck of a guitar. The instrument's chromatic and enharmonic possibilities are scarcely hinted at in the mainstream of sixteenth-century publications, but it allows one to probe some of the outer limits of late Renaissance music in the enharmonic madrigals of Vicentino and the experimental compositions of the Neapolitan school of *c*.1600.

Instruments are also our chief repository of evidence concerning early pitch standards. It is noteworthy that several of the fifteenth- and sixteenth-century organs seem originally to have been close to one or other of the paired pitches, a fourth or fifth apart, first recommended by Arnolt Schlick in 1511 (approximately a tone below and a minor third above $a' = 440$ hertz). Many later sixteenth-century instruments are about a semitone above 440, and it is clear that when these emerging pitch standards were established in major organs, they exerted a strong influence upon the pitch of other instruments made in the same region.

Regional preferences in sonority can also be observed. Italian instruments in the sixteenth century tend to be sweet and bold, simple in harmonic make-up, often, one imagines, softened by spacious and reverberant acoustics; Northerners, by contrast, produced keen sounds, harmonically more complex and incisive, in keeping with the nasal and gutteral character of their languages. To take three examples from around 1600, the organ built by Claudio Merulo in his retirement in his native Parma (now in the Conservatorio di Musica Arrigo Boito, Parma), the anonymous English organ at Knole, Kent, and the Compenius organ at Fredericksborg Castle, Hillerød, Denmark, each have highly individual sounds, in some respects reflecting the prevailing sonorities of their maker's native tongues.

From the time of Silvestro Ganassi's *Fontegara* (Venice, 1535), devoted to the art of recorder playing, we are told that instruments are inferior to the voice, and that they should imitate it as closely as possible. Instrumental performance depends upon the player having a particular rapport with the instrument. In this, the instrument takes on a role beyond that of mere voice substitute; it tends to be given, or assumes, an identity – one might almost say a life – of its own. Quite apart from its sound, the instrument influences the least tangible aspects of performance, beyond the quantifiable elements of pitch, tempo, articulation and ornamentation, which impart energy and grace to the line. This brings us close to the analogy which exists between singing and instrumental playing. In a given culture, there usually exist close stylistic parallels between singing and the best instrumental playing. If, for example, we compare several recordings of singers and string players made in about 1910, 1950 and 1990, it becomes clear that each era has its own approach to the shaping of line, to vibrato, to the presence or absence of portamento, and so forth. To compare *sarangi* or *rabāb* playing with singing from the same Indian or Javanese culture is to find a common vocabulary of sound and inflection.

It follows that our understanding of instruments, of their sonority and capabilities, should inform the way we sing the music of earlier centuries. This is not to advocate a 'sing it like crumhorns' approach in Renaissance music. We know, after all, that the best chamber singers sang in a supple and affective manner, responsive to the text in ways that the least flexible instruments cannot hope to emulate. Just as we can approach the sound worlds of the past by studying their instruments, producing successively closer approximations to instruments needing reconstruction, so it should be possible to develop styles of singing and playing which are truly complementary.

Select bibliography

W. BACHMANN, *The origins of bowing and the development of bowed instruments up to the thirteenth century*, trans. N. Deane (London, 1969)

K. BORMANN, *Die gotische orgel zu Halberstadt* (Berlin, 1966)

F. CRANE, *Extant medieval musical instruments: a provisional catalogue by type* (Iowa City, 1972)

G. LE CERF and E.-R. LABANDE (eds), *Les traités d'Henri-Arnaut de Zwolle et de divers anonymes (ms. B. N. Latin 7295)* (Paris, 1932; repr. Kasel, 1972)

M. REMNANT and R. MARKS, 'A medieval "gittern"', in *Music and civilisation*, The British Museum Yearbook, iv (London, 1980)

M. REMNANT, *English bowed instruments from Anglo-Saxon to Tudor times* (Oxford, 1986)

M. TIELLA, 'The violeta of S Caterina de' Vigri', *Galpin Society Journal*, xxviii (1975), pp. 60–70

M. TIELLA, 'The positive organ of Lorenzo da Pavia (1494)', *Organ Yearbook*, vii (1976), pp. 4–15

33 Unwritten and written music

Reinhard Strohm

Past ages have left more riddles than evidence: the one-way communication between them and us, which we call 'history', is interrupted by silences. This much the historian can gladly accept. It only irritates him when he does not even know whether or not there was any message in place of these silences.

Usually, lack of evidence does not threaten to overturn our picture of the past. When, of the oeuvre of a minor Renaissance composer, only the 'First' and 'Third Book of Madrigals' are extant, we can cope with the resulting uncertainties. We believe that the 'Second Book' must have existed, and may even speculate why it got lost and what it was like. The agents of Henry VIII who ripped out the pages dedicated to St Thomas of Canterbury in the Sarum plainsong books have done so in vain. Modern scholarship has uncovered sources containing the missing chants that were overlooked. It is hard to erase the memory of anything people once cared to write down.

Music that has never been written down constitutes a bigger challenge. According to legend, Pope Gregory the Great (590–604) notated all the music of the Roman Mass and Office in books – the 'archetypes' of Gregorian chant. Nobody has ever seen these books. Centuries of research were needed to replace legend with fact, and to start facing the actual silence of the documents. It is no mean success for scholarship to have at least established that Latin plainsong had been orally transmitted for centuries before musical notation was first introduced in the West in the realm of Charlemagne. Another ocean of silence for us, with very few islands, is secular song in the modern European ('vernacular') languages before the twelfth century. We have no idea how much of it there was. In contrast with the Latin chant repertories, we even lack written texts. The new languages, and their tunes, were just growing up: 'writing' and 'writing Latin' were almost synonymous concepts for the earlier Middle Ages.

The most tantalizing questions, however, are those where we cannot be sure that there is a question at all. For example, no extant European music manuscripts before c.1450 seem to be intended for polyphonic solo-playing on the lute. This could, then, be a performance technique which (a) was not written down because musical notation had not developed sufficiently to cope with it; (b) was written down but the documents are lost; (c) was not written down because it did not exist at all. And how, if we were to discover one, would we recognize a polyphonic lute piece of that period?

This kind of problem has to be approached, like other historical questions, by drawing inferences from the closest related evidence. For example, it would help to know what the earliest sources for polyphonic lute after 1450 looked like, enabling us to extrapolate back in time. We would also have to explore what non-musical sources tell us about lute-playing: chronicles and similar literary or documentary witnesses, on the one hand, and pictorial sources on the other. Now these sources say that lutenists usually played with a plectrum, that is they produced essentially only one line, and that they usually played without written music. And, when the first written source admits to being suitable for polyphonic lute-playing (a piece in the so-called Buxheim Organ Book, *c.*1460), it is also intended for the keyboard, suggesting that an independent notation for the solo lute was not yet available or necessary. Thus the combined evidence seems to support conclusions (a) or (c).

It is approximate evidence, however. Since we are told that lutenists usually played only one line, and without written music, we might also conclude that someone, exceptionally, could have done the opposite, as indeed happened more often later. With that assumption, it is possible to reach conclusion (b) instead: it is precisely because the practice was rare, that documents for polyphonic playing from a written score are lost. It may seem paradoxical, but it is historically correct to make deductions from nothing to something, *ex silentio in sonum* as it were.

The three conclusions, mutually exclusive under the laws of logic, are reconcilable under the rules of history. We can quite simply construct the following pattern: at first, there was nobody who played more than one line on the lute, then there were a few lutenists who played with fingers and arranged their pieces polyphonically by ear, and then somebody even wrote some arrangements down in keyboard notation – perhaps because the technique was still new and in need of a memory aid.

The question of oral versus written traditions is the daily bread of the student of some non-European musical traditions, and of much European literary history as well. In the field of European music, the debate gets periodically overheated when newcomers to the scholarly scene 'discover' how much their predecessors seem to have overlooked or neglected. Especially in the performance of medieval music, where creativity expects to be rewarded, it is tempting to jump right into the middle of these huge areas of silence and invent the kinds of sound the sources deny us. This is a good thing as long as the path to the truth is not obstructed by wishful thinking or mystification – perhaps the biggest mystification would be to define 'unwritten music' as a specific kind of music at all.

In almost any kind of music, certain elements are not usually written down: at the beginning of Western musical notation it was pitch, and today it is voice production or text pronunciation. Many other elements of the musically-organized sound exist which were not always granted written codification – think not only of rhythm but also tempo, dynamics, embellishments, musica ficta, instrumentation, absolute pitch or tuning. Some of these elements were, accordingly, left quite undecided by the composer. It was not 'the piece' that remained unwritten, but very important aspects of it.

Furthermore, in most popular traditions, and in artistic traditions such as troubadour song or the Latin conductus (twelfth-thirteenth centuries), 'the piece' and 'the transcription' are clearly not the same. The effect of so-called 'improvisation' makes sure that many variant versions existed of these songs, only some of which were recorded in script. Which of them is 'the piece'? Oral transmission was so strong that the version written down in a book could occasionally have been the only one that was never sung. But since nobody can prevent music from being written down at some stage, even if that was not the intention of its creator, strictly speaking, 'unwritten music' cannot exist as a category at all.

On the other hand, we all know how written music can exist in the mind without ever appearing on paper – it can be composed, rehearsed, performed, taught and transmitted all by memory, whether the piece resembles a Josquin motet or a Mozart sonata. It is not thereby orally transmitted music, of course: its structure presupposes the existence of a fairly sophisticated notational code. The structure of music and what people do with it are thus two different things, and history is generally more interested in what people do: thus the question is not so much 'written or unwritten music' as 'to write or not to write music'.

We should not assume that all the gaps in our knowledge of old music are results of its 'unwrittenness'. Furthermore, much ignorance is due to incomplete knowledge of the extant documents, and even more to incorrect understanding of the written messages that have come down to us. Nino Pirrotta, a great scholar and specialist of unwritten traditions in Italian secular music, believes that secular musicians in fifteenth-century Italy shunned the complex written polyphony of the North, and that they 'reverted entirely to kinds of music which were mainly committed to oral tradition'. It is possible, on the contrary, that these Italian musicians did 'commit to oral tradition' quite a lot of the allegedly shunned polyphony of the North – even that they used manuscripts of it, although perhaps not in public performances. It was natural for a professional singer or player (a minstrel) to perform without written music in public; this is the situation all the chroniclers and painters record. A professional musician who plays and improvises by ear can, of course, also learn by ear, either a piece of written polyphony or a famous tenor (the equivalent then of the later 'ground bass') on which to improvise. But he and his companions can learn new pieces from manuscript just as well, or even more quickly, and can arrange them for performance according to their needs. In that case, what would have come down to us in history is not their unwritten arrangements, but the original written versions of the compositions. This is exactly what has happened: Italy abounds with fifteenth-century copies of French polyphonic songs and other complex polyphony. Was this music all copied – and often expensively illuminated – never to be used again? Of course, we must doubt whether the musicians were always allowed to lay their hands on courtly chansonniers, but it would surely be erroneous to claim that, because they 'improvised' in public, they never had anything to do with the wealth of written music available to their patrons.

This case may serve, once more, to re-direct our enquiry from types of music to types of human activity. It also implies that there was a great historical difference between the age of the troubadours and fifteenth-century Italy: a difference consisting in the growth of musical literacy and use of script. This development is what we need to investigate, in order to gauge what written transmission can tell us about early music and what lies beyond its scope. The following is an extremely brief survey of what happened with musical literacy in the Middle Ages.

As I have mentioned, musical notation was introduced in the Western tradition in the Carolingian era, exclusively for the benefit of church musicians in their day-to-day work which by that time already included the teaching of music theory and polyphonic singing. The mainstream element, however, was the transcription and performance of liturgical plainsong: the 'neumes' were a code which the choir director could decipher when rehearsing the chants with a full choir of monks, all literate men. Important musical aspects such as pitch (relative and absolute) were left to transmission by memory for the first few centuries. But we must not forget that the texts of Latin plainsong were written, that they belonged to many musically differentiated genres, and that above all the system of the eight church modes helped to identify the traditional melodies and their styles by way of classification. Even tonal reference works were at hand ('tonaries'), where you could look up the mode of a plainsong the text of which suddenly appeared in your Mass or Office book.

This oral practice survived within a strongly literate community. By the time Guido of Arezzo (eleventh century) codified an excellent means of recording pitch as well – staff notation – the practice of music writing had spread from the area of the old Carolingian Empire all over Europe. It also began to spread beyond liturgical practice. A more discontinuous, socially disrupted environment, the feudal society of western Europe, was the first to take up the practice of musical notation outside the church. People used it to record the troubadour and trouvère songs, and the sacred and increasingly secular polyphonic music of clerics and scholars. By the thirteenth century, the growth of musical literacy had produced new genres (conductus, organum, motet), reached new social groups (secular performers) and geographic areas (eastern and northern Europe). At the same time, the availability of notation transformed musical production itself: actual polyphonic composition was, in a sense, helped along by pitch and rhythm codes which could not only be designed according to a composer's flexible imagination, but also be learnt by performers who were not in touch with the composer. Musical literacy grew in interaction with musical invention.

We must not forget what was 'left behind' in purely oral traditions: all folksong; most art-song in countries other than France; almost all instrumental music (although it is fair to argue that instrumentalists played mostly vocal music anyway); and much traditional polyphony which was often improvised in the manner of the catch and glee. Written music was still very much the business of an élite in élitist forms; 'unwritten music' at that time was any music at all, for most people.

In the later Middle Ages, a steep increase in general literacy took place, fostered mainly by town life and commerce, by centralist administrations and, above all, by the improvement of paper production. Paper was considerably cheaper than parchment and, around 1400, most larger institutions adopted paper for their day-to-day business. Just as the more modern forms of music (polyphonic Mass settings, motet, polyphonic secular song) had already presupposed the use of notation, they were now stimulated by the expanded scope of general literacy, which, with little educational effort, could be turned into musical literacy (for example, in the cathedral schools). In other words, in that period the most 'advanced' types of music benefited most from the growth factor. For that reason, the forms of music-making which had gained the privilege of usually being written down started to become everybody's music, for example mensural (rhythmically-codified) polyphony. About ten times more music of this kind survives from the fifteenth century than from the fourteenth, and the number probably decupled once more in the sixteenth century with the introduction of music printing.

There is an anecdote claiming that in a Corpus Christi procession at Munich in the sixteenth century, when motets by Orlande de Lassus were performed in the streets, the common people, having never heard such mixture of melodies before, thought the devil had possessed the court singers. Yet it is quite certain that in the cities of western, southern and central Europe, mensural polyphony written by professional composers was well known since the later fifteenth century. Western music took the road of counterpoint and harmony because that happened to be its most advanced form when general literacy was advancing by leaps and bounds.

Characteristically, in this dynamic of growth and progress, the more traditional attitudes had to join the queue. It is exciting to see how, in the course of the Middle Ages and beyond, dignified old traditions such as folksong and related repertories take their first tentative steps into literacy. Popular 'refrains' and even street-cries are quoted in thirteenth-century motets, although surely not out of respect. Later, in the fifteenth century, polyphonic elaborations of European folksongs became significant sources for those songs; the 'unwritten' tradition enters the realm of script under the umbrella of a more sophisticated style.

Instrumental music gradually entered musical notation in its own right in the fourteenth to sixteenth centuries, one species after the other. For 'polyphonic instruments' (keyboard and eventually lute) new forms of notation were quickly developed, whereas the chivalric harp, traditionally serving composers and performers of secular vocal music, declined in status. Probably, keyboard notation was first introduced because the organ and other keyboard instruments were the domain of university-trained musicians. By the fifteenth century, however, minstrels, too, must have started to learn musical notation, particularly in more affluent areas. By the end of that century, wind bands, at least in Flanders and northern Italy, were able to perform (by heart, of course) polyphonic motets.

In England, improvised forms of polyphonic liturgical chanting ('English discant') were widespread in the fourteenth century. Whenever there were more than two independent lines, they were soon written down. In the next century the style of these written specimens of English discant influenced the stylistic vocabulary of the greatest composers. Two of the simplest unwritten practices of chanting, the English 'faburden' and French 'fauxbourdon', did not escape sophistication and stylization in written versions over the course of the fifteenth century. At the same time, techniques of extemporising additional voices to a plainsong read from the chant book survived in many parts of Europe, and were even encouraged by the authorities and described by theorists. 'Conservationist' attitudes were popular in the Middle Ages.

Moreover, those oral traditions which were absorbed into script were allowed to survive as unwritten practices. What we call 'folksong' has led this double life for centuries: a type of music which is available in innumerable printed versions, but yet is practised in a few places without direct reference to the books. The fact that folksong is now usually taught in schools by teachers who learn it from books – Granny doesn't sing anymore – does not destroy its status as a traditionally oral practice.

One of the most promising exercises in the recovery of unwritten or 'lost' traditions can be the study of early, primitive forms of their notation. We are on the right track towards a reconstruction of these repertories if we investigate the frontiers of the written tradition itself.

Early written sources of traditionally improvised church polyphony, for example, are rhythmically indifferent and thus tell us that the rhythmic element was often optional in this music. Pieces travelled widely, but a specific two-part Kyrie might have been sung in one cathedral in triple metre, in another in duple, in the third without any measured rhythm. Melodic variants existed as well, of course. Whatever was missing in the notation might have been added from memory, possibly following rigid local conventions. Other primitive musical notations, mostly adopted for styles and forms which had no established place among the written genres as yet, can tell us much about the social environment of such practices (for example when scribbled on the last page of a monastic prayer-book). Within the mainstream repertory of mensural polyphony, scholars such as Nino Pirrotta have detected traces of improvisational or 'unwritten' vocal practices – identifiable because their structure required modification of or exception to the notational code.

Music stemming from oral tradition is often, once written down, surprisingly sophisticated. No wonder: the most compelling reason for such music to be written down is precisely because it has become too complex to be remembered with ease. The musically literate minstrel codified not his weekday exercises but his Sunday pieces.

It goes without saying that growth and progress of musical literacy are not equivalent to increases in artistic or human value. Some people might give all the musical codices of the Middle Ages for the recovery of a single eighth-century 'Alleluia' melody. It is human to like best what is farthest removed. But let us not forget that the written copies of old music are silent in many respects. The task of interpreting them, and of turning their silence into sound, is by no means yet complete.

Select bibliography

N. PIRROTTA, 'Italy: 1, 3', *New Grove*

R. STROHM, *The rise of European music, 1380–1500* (Cambridge, 1992), Part III, 2

34 Researching the past: archival studies

Frederick Hammond

Archival studies have long occupied an important place in the history of medieval and Renaissance music. Gustave Reese's pioneering book, *Music in the Renaissance* (1954), devoted more space to biographical and bibliographical accounts of a greater number of composers than any other comparable study. Where earlier interest in archival materials was largely centred on biographical material, scholars have now widened their focus: 'The recent spate of musicological activity based on the archives of institutions and cities arises from an awareness that too much is missed if research is confined to big names and prominent manuscripts. Musical life grows from a complex interaction between innumerable musicians and their employers; the compositions grow not only from the minds of creative geniuses but from a context' (David Fallows, review of the recent books by Lockwood and Strohm, *Early Music History*, vi (1986), p. 279).

Archival studies are important to several fields of current musicological interest. In the spirit of the French *annales* scholars, many musicologists now present music history not solely as a series of biographical narratives and major artistic creations at the controlling level of society, but as a non-linear web of daily life in which music forms a part and in which the artillery salvos and trumpet-fanfares on the piazza have their place as well as the Masses of the great composers in the cathedral. In patronage studies, the major artists and their works are considered in the context of the tastes and requirements for which they were created. *Rezeptionsgeschichte*, the study of the afterlife of works of art, which has a strong archival component, has grown into an independent field. Finally, the information gathered from archival studies is increasingly being put to good use in the field of performing medieval and Renaissance music, with scholars – including the most distinguished – becoming more involved in historical performance, either as advisors or as directors.

The creative employment of archival studies can be demonstrated by the history of three recent works on Dufay. Machaut and Dufay, the most notable composers of their respective eras, are also the first Western composers for whom we have sufficient information to construct some kind of biography (although in the case of Machaut some of the juiciest episodes, such as his liaison with Péronne d'Armentières, may be fictitious). It would seem likely that little more remains to be discovered about composers of such visibility. In 1975, however, Craig Wright published his article 'Dufay at Cambrai: Discoveries and Revisions' based on new archival research which illustrates well the links between research, stylistic analysis, and performance practice. By proving Dufay's presence in Cambrai from 1439 to 1450, Wright re-dated the motet *Juvenis qui puellam* to c.1428, not 1441–6 as had previously been thought, and thus challenged our previous understanding of Dufay's stylistic development. One of the steps in his argument is the identification of an acrostic dedication in another Dufay motet. Wright's researches further revealed that the cathedral of Cambrai, for which Dufay's later Masses were written, had no organ, unlike most churches of the period. This presumably lays to rest the idea of any instrumental participation in 'authentic' performances of these works. That new discoveries always await the inquiring archivist was demonstrated by David Fallows, whose *Dufay* (1982) presented a full portrait of the composer and his music with additional archival material (including a re-dating of *Juvenis* to the Council of Basle in 1438). After the publication of Fallows's book Barbara Haggh added, on the basis of archival research, nearly fifty monophonic chants to the catalogue of Dufay's works. Finally, Alejandro Planchart's researches (1988) illuminated the important period in Dufay's life and work 1440–50, to which he assigns a cycle of six polyphonic Masses, the survivors of a monumental cycle setting the Cambrai liturgy *per circulum anni*.

The archivally-oriented scholar of medieval and Renaissance music must control a wide variety of materials. The archivist for later periods – seventeenth-century Italy, for example – often has simply the task of reading intelligently through a mass of material, such as a family archive, the form of which has not changed much from its original assembly. Since most of the identifiable singers and composers of the Middle Ages and Renaissance had some connection with the Church, their traces are to be sought mainly in ecclesiastical archives. Owing to the anticlericalism of the French Revolution and much of the nineteenth century, the disestablishment of the Church in various parts of Europe, and the wholesale dissolution and destruction of religious houses, this material may be widely scattered. Of the two books of *actes capitulaires* from the cathedral of Cambrai that Wright uses to establish Dufay's whereabouts, for example, one remains at Cambrai, but in the Médiathèque municipale, while the other is found in the Archives départementales du Nord at Lille. Much archival material has been published in one form or another (often in out-of-print books and unobtainable periodicals, the consultation of which becomes in itself a form of archival research). Monographs dealing with music in a specific place or institution require a horizontal cross-section of various kinds of material (see Prizer). Much of the effort of the best archival historians in patronage studies is expended in giving a sense of context, and this requires an especially wide net (see Lockwood). Familiarity with liturgical material in its various dialects, for some scholars a career in itself, is merely an indispensable tool for the dating and attribution of sacred works by the archivist (see Planchart).

In the field of performance practice, archival studies offer their most obvious service in the reconstruction of performing organizations. The payment records of churches and secular musical establishments establish at least a maximum number of performers and possibilities. Clearly, more detailed research is necessary to determine how many and which musicians performed at any given time. Archival research has changed ideas about the use of instruments in certain kinds of vocal performance and about vocal performance itself; it can be proved from written sources that Dufay did not intend instruments to participate in his late Masses, nor did Gesualdo in his madrigals. It seems likely that in certain areas polyphony was sung more frequently by solo voices than we previously believed; close analysis of manuscripts has largely demolished the idea that melismas in vocal music were performed instrumentally. It is always the task of responsible scholarship, of course, to make clear how far its conclusions obtain. The Sistine Chapel in Rome, for example, seems to have had so peculiar a tradition of performance practice that it is valid only for itself unless otherwise substantiated.

Archival materials exist in many types. Musical archives include such collections as the Trent codices, the Düben manuscripts in Uppsala, the scattered manuscripts copied and collected by the Tregian family, the great medieval manuscripts of the Biblioteca Laurenziana in Florence, the collections of Modena, Turin, Oxford and Cambridge or the Santini collection in Münster. Ecclesiastical archives include liturgical books, music, and financial records, such as expenses for food and wine, for the fabric of the building, income and expenses for church property, the chapter acts of a cathedral or collegiate church, records of trials for disciplinary purposes. The Vatican archives contain material relating to the benefices with which musicians were often rewarded. Archives of important families contain financial records, such as salary-lists and lists of alms, household inventories, letters and diaries, bills, orders for payment, and account-books. Diplomatic archives preserve instructions to envoys, letters to princes, replies from envoys and others. Municipal archives often preserve documents requiring the services of a notary, such as the sale, rent, lease of property, marriage settlements, wills and testamentary inventories, and the acts of city governments. (These may be catalogued only by the name of the notary, which increases the difficulties of consultation.) University archives can provide material on the whereabouts of composers and musicians as students, graduates, and associates of those institutions. Legal records can be unexpectedly revealing. Since testimony in trials was taken down *verbatim*, this is one of the few instances in which we can hear the voices of the common people of history, as in the works of Emmanuel Le Roy Ladurie and Carlo Ginsburg.

Laws and customs vary from country to country and with the type of archive involved, but access to archives is usually controlled by a government office and/or the institution or family holding the archive. In Italy, for example, the administration of archives involves two ministries, a general council, a central archive in Rome, ninety-two state archives in provincial capitals, as well as sub-archives in various towns. Eighteen regional superintendancies oversee other public records and significant private archives. (This does not include the Vatican archives, the property of the Vatican state.) In order to confront such bureaucracies, in addition to personal identification a reference from one's own government and/or academic institution may be necessary. In the case of some private archives, only personal contact and influence can procure access for the researcher.

The first step in consulting an archive is to find some specific reference to useful material contained therein. Although published catalogues of musical research materials are obvious starting places, other disciplines such as art history can provide important references. The next step is to obtain the address and schedule of the institution (see Benton), the requirements for its consultation, and its policies regarding such services as xeroxing and microfilms. Printed catalogues of its holdings may be available, or it may be necessary to write for further information. In most cases a personal visit will be required; this will be facilitated by writing beforehand to make an appointment and to request specific materials.

In order to employ archival materials it is necessary to be able to read them, which demands a working knowledge of the relevant musical notations and languages (including the changing meanings of words) and may also require special training in paleography for dealing with difficult scripts. A knowledge of such things as abbreviations, cryptography, acrostics, currencies, Latin place-names, historical weights and measures, paper watermarks, systems of dating, double-entry bookkeeping, liturgies, and systems of indicating time is also necessary. Texts on such subjects are available, but serious archivists learn much of their craft simply by reading, transcribing, and interpreting documents.

Archival researchers cultivate two complementary skills: reading comprehensively, both for establishing context and on the chance of discovering material previously overlooked; and the utmost economy of effort. This requires understanding the organization of each archive, so that as little time as possible is wasted in false starts. Once one has some feeling for the kind of material each source presents, it also encourages the ability to skim and extract pertinent information.

Beyond these elementary beginnings, archival work demands an inquiring mind and imaginative detective work. Take the simplest case possible – a personal letter, whose salient points would seem to be sender, recipient, and message. Where, when, and how was the paper made? What are its watermarks, and how closely can they be identified and dated? How was the paper stored, cut, sold, and by whom? How, where, and when was the ink made? What kind of pen was employed? Who wrote the letter – the signatory, some other person, a secretary or professional scribe? What does the calligraphy tell about the writer? How was the letter folded, sealed, addressed, transported and delivered, and preserved? Does the seal give any additional information about the writer? Is the foliation original and correct? Has the letter suffered alteration (removal of sheets or seals, loss of pages or enclosures), and has it been filed or stored in more than one manner? What is its state of conservation? Has it been damaged by *Tintenfraß* (the chemical action of the ink on the paper), humidity, fire, water, insects? How can these conditions be remedied, and how can lost or illegible parts of the text be recovered (grid analysis, infra-red rays, etc.)? By what steps did it pass from the original recipient to its present location? All of these questions form part of the archival research possible before considering such matters as who wrote the letter to whom, and what its explicit content is. In the pursuit of such answers, archival studies combine the satisfactions of solving puzzles and historical detective-work with the excitement of direct contact with the past.

Select bibliography

General guides

R. BENTON, *Directory of music research libraries:* I Canada and the United States; II Thirteen European countries; III Spain, France, Italy, Portugal; IV Australia, Israel, Japan, New Zealand (Iowa City, 1967–72)

V. DUCKLES, *Music reference and research materials: an annotated bibliography*, 3rd edn (New York, 1974)

D. THOMAS and L. CASE (eds), *The new guide to the diplomatic archives of Western Europe* (u.p., 1975)

Frederick Hammond

Selected research tools

Abbreviations   A. CAPPELLI, *Dizionario di abbreviature latine ed italiane* (Milan, 1961)
Chronology and dates   A. CAPPELLI, *Cronologia, cronografia e calendario perpetuo* (Milan, 1969)
General   F. HAMMOND, *Girolamo Frescobaldi: a guide to research* (New York, 1988)
Weights and measures   R. E. ZUPKO, *Italian weights and measures from the Middle Ages to the nineteenth century* (Philadelphia, 1981)
Catalogues   *Répertoire International des Sources Musicales (RISM)*
Guida generale degli archivi di stato italiani, Ministero per i beni culturali e ambientali (Florence, 1981–)

Archival studies

Biography   D. FALLOWS, *Dufay* (London 1982; rev. 1988)
A. E. PLANCHART, 'Guillaume Dufay's benefices and his relationship to the court of Burgundy', *Early Music History*, viii (1988), pp. 117–71
C. WRIGHT, 'Dufay at Cambrai: discoveries and revisions', *Journal of the American Musicological Society*, xxviii (1975), pp. 175–229
Inventories   F. WALDNER, 'Zwei Inventarien aus dem XVI. und XVII. Jahrhundert über hinterlassene Musikinstrumente und Musikalien am Innsbrucker Hofe', *Studien zur Musikwissenschaft*, iv (1916), pp. 128–47
Musical life of a city   R. STROHM, *Music in late medieval Bruges* (Oxford, 1985)
Musical life of a country   F. LL. HARRISON, *Music in medieval Britain* (London, 1958)
Musical life of an institution   J. J. DEAN, 'The repertory of the Cappella Giulia in the 1560s', *Journal of the American Musicological Society*, xli (1988), pp. 465–90
W. PRIZER, 'Music and ceremonial in the Low Countries: Philip the Fair and the Order of the Golden Fleece', *Early Music History*, v (1985), pp. 113–53
Organology   H. M. BROWN, 'The trecento fiddle and its bridges', *Early Music*, xvii/3 (1989), pp. 311–29
Patronage   L. LOCKWOOD, *Music in Renaissance Ferrara 1400–1505* (Oxford, 1984)
Performance   C. PAGE, *Voices and instruments of the Middle Ages* (London, 1987)

35 A manuscript case-study

The compilation of a polyphonic choirbook

Michael Noone

Like the printed book, a manuscript transmits a text across geographical and temporal boundaries. Unlike its mass-produced cousin, however, the hand-made article is unique. Because music manuscripts were commissioned and copied to fulfil a specific purpose within a particular set of circumstances, they are an important source of evidence for both music historians and performers. Manuscripts interest us not only because of the repertory which they preserve, but also because of what they tell us about the individuals or institutions which cultivated, maintained and performed that repertory. They are also often executed with such expertise and beauty that they are regarded as works of art in their own right.

As a major repository of the works of Josquin, Morales and over sixty other peninsular, Franco-Flemish and Italian composers, the manuscript choirbooks of the Spanish primatial cathedral in Toledo are among the most important extant sources of Renaissance music in Spain. In their *New Grove* article 'Sources', Hamm and Call described the manuscripts as 'the largest and most handsome set' copied in sixteenth-century Spain. Stevenson, whose research brought the number of Josquin Masses preserved in this set of manuscripts to eleven, writes that 'the Toledo choirbooks also rank highest among surviving Spanish manuscript sources for Josquin's motets'. In 1957, Lenaerts observed that 'among seven Spanish archives still holding Netherlandish musical treasure, the Toledo Cathedral chapter library takes first rank'. In addition to 'Netherlandish musical treasure', the choirbooks also preserve, often uniquely, the works of such Spanish masters as Boluda, Ceballos, Escobar, Escobedo, Guerrero, Lobo, Morales, Navarro, Pastrana, Peñalosa, Quevedo, Ribera, Santa María, Torrentes and Victoria. Despite some recognition of their significance, however, the Toledo manuscripts, either individually or as a set, have received surprisingly little detailed attention from scholars and a comprehensive study of them is overdue. In this article I shall describe the first of the Toledo choirbooks to be completed and show, by reference to newly uncovered archival documents, how this relatively straightforward manuscript was compiled and produced.

The manuscript *ToleBC16* comprises 107 numbered parchment folios and three guard-sheets bound between original covers. The folios, which were trimmed at the top before binding, measure 715×498mm. The covers, which measure 758×554mm, are of brown leather-covered wooden boards and bear markings that show that they once supported two brass clasps. The front cover bears the manuscript's current *siglum* ('16') within an iron badge. A parchment folio of a liturgical manuscript whose folios are found as guard-sheets in other manuscripts of the Toledan polyphonic set is pasted, upside-down, to the inside front cover. It bears its original folio number ('xcv') and is followed by another folio of the same manuscript, also upside-down, which bears the folio number 'xc'. Then follow the 107 folios of polyphony, which retain their original, red-inked Roman numeral foliation. This foliation runs correctly and continuously from i to cvii. A folio of the same liturgical manuscript which was used to provide guard-sheets at the beginning of the manuscript is pasted, upside-down, to the inside back cover. *ToleBC*16 is made up of thirteen eight-leaf gatherings. Folios 105 and 106 constitute a gathering of their own, being secured in the middle, and folio 107 is secured to the guard-sheet which is pasted to the inside back cover. An inscription found on the guard-sheet pasted to the back cover of *ToleBC*16 and dated 1603 is irrelevant to the dating of the manuscript, although it does tell us that the choirbook was still at Toledo Cathedral, and probably still in use, in that year.

The original index, which is found on fol.1, is complete and accurate except for its omission of a folio number for Mouton's *Missa dictes moy toutes voz pensees*. A diplomatic transcription of the index follows:

Josquin	Missa de beata v[ir]gine	fo. i
Josquin	Missa sup[er] pa[n]ge lingua	fo. xxi
Joannes mouton	Missa dictes moy toutes vox penses	
ToRe[n]tes	Missa sup[er] nisi d[omi]n[u]s	fo. lxiii
Noe valdovin	Missa in diapason	fo. lxxxv
Morales	Et incarnatus	fo. cvii

The four four-voice Masses are grouped together, beginning with the two popular Josquin Masses, and the five-voice works (those of Bauldeweyn and Morales) are placed at the end. The repertory consists of five complete Mass settings by Josquin, Jean Mouton, Andrés de Torrentes and Noel Bauldeweyn and an *Et Incarnatus* by Cristóbal de Morales. The works of the two Toledan chapelmasters, Torrentes and Morales, are *unica*.

The illumination of this choirbook, with the exception of ff.106v–107, is stylistically uniform throughout. The most telling clue to the identity of the illuminator of this and, indeed, the entire set of Toledan choirbooks, is found on fol.51, where the letters 'F.D.B.' have been inscribed within the alto inked initial (see illus. 1). The illuminator also inscribed the date '1542' within both the *tiple* initial of fol.9v and the alto initial of fol.91 (see illus. 2). The elaborate illumination of fol.1v depicts the now faded coat of arms of Cardinal Juan Tavera flanked on either side by two cherubs, in pink, mauve, green, blue, red and gold inks.

1 Toledo Biblioteca Capitular MS 16, f. 51: inked initial, alto voice

2 Toledo Biblioteca Capitular MS 16, f. 91: inked initial, alto voice

Thanks to a series of recently uncovered documents held in Toledo Cathedral's Archivo de Obra y Fábrica, it is now possible to trace the copying of each of the Toledo polyphonic manuscripts in some detail. As primary sources, the documents of the Archivo de Obra y Fábrica complement the cathedral's *Actas capitulares* which record the proceedings of chapter meetings and run uninterrupted from 1466. The sixteenth-century Obra y Fábrica account books are of special interest because they offer all sorts of valuable information about the musical life of, at that time, one of Spain's most active and well-endowed musical foundations. They provide such information about the musical manuscripts as the names of the scribes and illuminators who worked on them; they offer itemized accounts of the work as it was completed; they give the sources of parchment and leather and the prices of these materials together with details about repertory which was copied into choirbooks, but which no longer survives, in addition to information about the binding and re-binding of choirbooks.

The true princes of Renaissance Toledo were its archbishops, whose liberal and enlightened patronage was not seriously rivalled within the peninsula until Philip II began work on the Escorial in 1563. Juan Tavera's term as archbishop (1534–45), for example, saw the completion of such important works in the cathedral as the Vigarni and Berruguete choir stalls, the interior façade of the Puerta de los Leones and the doorway of the Capilla de San Juan. It was also in the last years of his term that the magnificent series of polyphonic choirbooks was begun. The day to day overseeing of all such projects was the responsibility of the *obrero*, an important and powerful cathedral post which was occupied throughout the pontificates of Alfonso II of Fonseca (1524–34), Cardinal Juan Tavera (1534–45) and Cardinal Juan Martínez Siliceo (1546–57) by Diego López de Ayala (d.1560). López de Ayala was a man of erudition and learning who had translated works of Boccaccio and Sannazaro into Castilian. His coat of arms, two black wolves on a silver background with a border of golden saltires, is a familiar sight throughout the cathedral and is found at least twice in the manuscript choirbooks: once in *ToleBC33* on fol.1v and again in the alto initial of *ToleBC34* on fol.1 (second foliation).

Once the decision to commission a series of polyphonic choirbooks for the use of the cathedral musicians had been made, Diego López de Ayala initiated negotiations for the copying of the manuscripts with the scribe Martín Pérez. Little is known of Pérez, whose name figures frequently in the documents until 1558, when the last notice, dated 5 August, records a final payment to his widow. Although Pérez worked on some non-musical copying (for example, late editions to the sumptuous *Libro de los prefacios*), the large bulk of his work was music copying, particularly the new set of polyphonic choirbooks. From the agreement which was eventually drawn up between them, we know that Pérez furnished López de Ayala with a sample of his work on paper. On 13 February 1542, as a result of his negotiations with the cathedral chapter, Pérez signed, before the public notary Juan Mudarra, an agreement 'to write and point in polyphony the books which were necessary for the service of the choir of the holy church of Toledo' (see Casares, I, p. 375). In the agreement, Pérez insisted upon using well-prepared, high-quality parchment from Segovia which he himself would purchase. Throughout the fifteenth and sixteenth centuries, Segovia monopolized the Spanish parchment market. That the Toledo scriptorium regularly bought its parchment there is attested to by a number of archival documents. Pérez also agreed to copy the manuscripts in gatherings of eight folios with nine staves to a page, and he sought assurances that the exemplar from which he would make his copy would first be corrected and signed by the cathedral chapelmaster, at that time Andrés de Torrentes. Pérez charged 816 *maravedís* for copying each gathering of eight folios, contracting for an initial payment of 11,250 *maravedís* in order to procure parchment and a T-square, to be followed by regular payments of 11,250 *maravedís* until the completion of the work. The agreement was signed by Diego López de Ayala on 12 March 1542.

It seems certain that an account dated 12 September 1542, which records Pérez's copying of 'books corrected by the *racionero* [prebendary] Torrentes, chapelmaster' refers to our manuscript (see document 1). There can be no doubt that the correction of *ToleBC*16 was the work of Torrentes since at the foot of fol.106*v* the following signed inscription is found: 'I, Andrés de Torrentes, chapelmaster of this holy church of Toledo, say that this complete book has been corrected by my hand and because it is true I sign it with my name' (see document 2 and illus. 3). Pérez was at work on this manuscript, then, for no longer than six months.

A document of 8 February 1544 (see document 3, reproduced as illus. 4) records the payment of 58,650 *maravedís* to Pérez for the copying of five polyphonic choirbooks. This cumulative account undoubtedly includes *ToleBC*16, the others being *ToleBC*33 (1543), the manuscript which is now bound as the second section of *ToleBC*18 (1543), *ToleBC*19 (1543) and very probably *ToleBC*32. No other polyphonic choirbooks of the Toledan set can be dated 1543 or earlier. The sum of 58,650 *maravedís* paid to Pérez for his work may be compared with the salary of 43,500 *maravedís* with which Andrés de Torrentes was installed at the beginning of his second term as cathedral chapelmaster in 1547.

It is clear from an examination of the manuscript that it was illuminated after the music and text had been entered. Frequently, for instance, the border of an illuminated initial avoids note stems and texts when the scribe has been obliged to trespass onto the space usually reserved for illumination. It seems reasonable to suppose that Pérez would pass to the illuminator each gathering as it was completed. A document of 29 October 1542 (see document 4), which records the payment of 14,763 *maravedís* to Buitrago for his illumination of 'the first book of polyphony which is newly made', seems definitely to refer to *ToleBC*16. Certainly the name Francisco de Buitrago explains the presence of the initials 'F.D.B.' which we have noted in one of the manuscript's initials. The following table lists the items of this account in the left column and gives the number of illuminations surviving in *ToleBC*16 in the right column:

371	letters of ink	367
19	letters of gold	19
1	coat of arms	1
5	titles	4
28	inked labels	25

All of the Toledo choirbooks have been mutilated, many of their fine illuminations having been cut out. This vandalism, as well as the possible loss of a few folios, is sufficient to explain the discrepancy between the number of illuminations for which Buitrago was paid, and the number surviving in the manuscript today.

The earliest reference to Francisco de Buitrago in the documents is dated 1536, and the latest is dated 1559. During these years he was responsible for a good deal of the illumination work carried out in the prolific cathedral scriptorium, including the exquisitely illuminated *Libro de los prefacios*, and it is probable that at first he worked in this scriptorium as an assistant to the master illuminator Diego de Arroyo.

After Buitrago had finished his illumination, the thirteen gatherings of *ToleBC16* were ready for binding. A document of 23 March 1543 records the payment of 900 *maravedís* to the book merchant Diego López for binding 'the first book of polyphony' (see document 5). After cropping the folios at the top, López bound them between wooden boards which were covered with deer hide, of which the nearby Montes de Toledo furnished a plentiful supply. The deer hide was lightly tooled and two brass clasps were added to secure the covers. The total cost of the manuscript was 26,271 *maravedís*, calculated as follows:

13 gatherings (@ 816 *maravedís* cach):	10,608 *maravedís*
Illumination:	14,763 *maravedís*
Binding:	900 *maravedís*
Total:	26,271 *maravedís*

ToleBC16, then, was copied by the scribe Martín Pérez, illuminated by the miniaturist Francisco de Buitrago and corrected by the chapelmaster Andrés de Torrentes in 1542. In the following year the manuscript was bound by Diego López and went into the service of one of the most active and well-endowed musical centres of the Renaissance. Thus, the first of the lavish set of manuscript choirbooks commissioned by Diego López de Ayala on behalf of the cathedral chapter under Cardinal Juan Tavera was completed.

The present case-study demonstrates the application of a methodology which seeks to correlate the diverse primary source documents comprising the rich archival legacy of Toledo Cathedral. The case of *ToleBC16* is, in fact, relatively straightforward because the manuscript is well preserved, because it has not been divided and rebound and because it has not suffered the vandalism to which other manuscripts of the set have been subjected. In a forthcoming study, the copying and compilation of each of the Toledo polyphonic manuscript choirbooks is traced through a similar correlation of the payment documents and the choirbooks to which they refer. Such a study not only throws light upon the manuscripts as documents in their own right, but also enhances our understanding of the role which they played in the service of one of the most active and well-endowed musical centres of the Renaissance.

Document 1[1]

[Heading:] Escreuir libros
[Margin:] m[art]yn p[ere]z

En doze [12] dias d[e]l mes d[e] setiembre d[e]l dicho año [1542] di çedu[l]a que diese al dicho m[art]yn pérez onze mill y d[o]sc[iento]s y cinquenta m[a]r[avedí]s [11,250] los

243

quales se le dan p[ar]a escrivyr y puntar los libros d[e] canto d[e] organo y tiene los p[un]tados cuerpos los cuales estan corregidos d[e]l rraçion[ero] torrentes maestro d[e] capilla.

XIMCCL [11,250]

(Toledo, Catedral Metropolitana, Archivo de Obra y Fábrica, MS 836, f.81*r*)

[1] *Note on the transcription of documents*:
The original orthography and punctuation of the documents have been retained. Some marks of punctuation have been silently introduced and all abbreviations have been realized. The Arabic numeral equivalents of all numerals and dates which in the sources are either written out in full or expressed in Roman numerals, are given within square brackets in the transcriptions.

Document 2

Digo yo, Andres de Torrentes, maes[tr]o de capilla de esta santa iglesia de Toledo que este cuaderno está corregido por mi mano y porque es verdad lo firme de mi nombre digo este cuerpo del libro todo.
[signed] Andres de Torrentes
(*ToleBC*16, f.106*v*)

3 Toledo Biblioteca Capitular MS 16, f. 106*v*: signed inscription of Andrés de Torrentes attesting to his correction of the first completed choirbook of the Toledan set

Document 3

[Heading:] Escrivyr libros
[Margin:] m[art]yn perez [?] de cuenta d[e] los cinco cuerpos d[e] Canto d[e] organo

En ocho [8] dia d[e]l mes d[e] febrero d[e] 1544 años di çedu[l]a que diese el rraçionero fern[an]do d[e] lunar receptor d[e] la obra al dicho martín pérez dos mill y quatro m[a]r[avedí]s [2,004] con los quales y con cinquenta y seys mill y dosc[iento]s y cinquenta m[a]r[avedí]s [56,250] q[ue] le a sido librados por cinco partidas en el libro d[e] quinientos y quarenta y dos annos [1542] se le acaban d[e] pagar los cinco cuerpos d[e] libros que escribio y punto d[e] Canto d[e] organo para el Choro que tiene todos quatroc[ientos] setenta y cinco [475] hojas q[ue] se le da por virtud del asiento q[ue] con el dicho m[art]yn pérez se tomo d[e] cada hoja d[e]l pergamino y escrivyr y puntar y pautar y zolfar a tres reales la hoja, que montó cinq[uen]ta y ocho myll y seyscientos y cinquenta m[a]r[avedí]s.
(Toledo, Catedral Metropolitana, Archivo de Obra y Fábrica, MS 837, f.113*r*)

4 Toledo Cathedral Obra y Fábrica MS 837, f. 113r.

Document 4

[Heading:] Ill[u]minar libros
[Margin:] buytrago

En veynte y nueve [29] dias d[e]l mes de octubre de mill y quinientos y quarenta y dos años [1542] di çedu[ll]a que diese a buytrago yllumynador catorze mill y setecientos y sesenta y tres m[a]r[avedí]s [14,763] los quales hubo de aver d[e] tres[cient]as y setenta y una [371] letras d[e] tinta que ylumino p[ar]a el primero cuerpo d[el] libro que nuevam[ent]e se hizo d[e] canto d[e] organo cada una p[or] conveniençia a real y diez y nueve [19] lettras doradas a dos reales y los estorias d[e] oro y armas de la prym[er]a hoja setenta y qui[nien]tos [570] m[a]r[avedí]s y cinco [5] titulos dorados a m[edi]o real cada uno y veynte y ocho [28] titulos d[e] ti[n]ta y yluminaçión d[e]lla a quartillo cada uno.

XIIIIMDCCLXIII [14,763]

(Toledo, Catedral Metropolitana, Archivo de Obra y Fábrica, MS 836, f.82r)

Document 5

[Margin:] Enquadern[ac]ion del libro primero de canto de organo

En veynte y tres [23] dias del mes de marzo del dicho año [1543] di çedula que diese a diego lopez librero novecientos m[a]r[avedí]s los quales hubo de aver los trescientos y quarenta [340] m[a]r[avedí]s de la guarnicion de laton y los quinientos sesenta m[a]r[avedí]s del enquadernacion del dicho libro acabado en cuero de venado y tablas que le dio al dicho obra.

(Toledo, Catedral Metropolitana, Archivo de Obra y Fábrica, MS 837, f.105v)

I should like to thank the Dean and Chapter of Toledo Cathedral for permission to consult documents held in the Archivo de Obra y Fábrica, the cathedral archivist Don Ramón Gonzálvez and Don Pablo Oliveros. I am also indebted to Javier Huidobro Pérez-Villamil, Professor Sir Peter Platt and His Excellency Dr José Luis Pardos for their advice and support. I gratefully acknowledge the assistance of a Research Fellowship awarded by the Spanish Ministry of Foreign Affairs for my work in the Toledo Cathedral archive in 1989.

Michael Noone

Select bibliography

E. CASARES (ed.), *Francisco Asenjo Barbieri – Biografías y documentos sobre música y músicos españoles (Legado Barbieri)*, 2 vols. (Madrid, 1986, 1988)

Census-catalogue of manuscript sources of polyphonic music 1400–1550, Renaissance Manuscript Studies I, 5 vols. (Neuhausen-Stuttgart, 1979–88)

R. GONZÁLVEZ, 'El arte del libro en el renacimiento: el libro de los prefacios', *V-Simposio Toledo Renacentista III* (Toledo, 1980), pp. 55–95

R. GONZÁLVEZ and J. JANINI, *Catálogo de los manuscritos litúrgicos de la catedral de Toledo* (Toledo, 1977)

R. B. LENAERTS, 'Les manuscrits polyphoniques de la Bibliothèque Capitulaire de Tolède', *Internationale Gesellschaft für Musikwissenschaft. V. Kongress Utrecht 3–7 Juli 1952 Kongressbericht* (Amsterdam, 1953), pp. 276–81

F. RUBIO PIQUERAS, 'El archivo musical de la catedral de Toledo', *Tesoro Sacro Musical* (1927), pp. 90–2; (1928), pp. 1–2, 18–20, 35–6, 46–7, 53, 60–1, 68–9, 77–9, 84–5; (1929), 12–14, 92; *Códices polifónicos toledanos* (Toledo, 1923); and *Música y músicos toledanos* (Toledo, 1923)

R. STEVENSON, 'Josquin in the music of Spain and Portugal', in E. E. Lowinsky (ed.), *Josquin des Prez* (New York, 1971), pp. 217–46; and 'The Toledo manuscript polyphonic choirbooks and some other lost or little known Flemish sources', *Fontes Artis Musicae*, xx (1973), pp. 87–107

M. R. ZARCO DEL VALLE, *Datos documentales para la historia del arte español. Documentos de la catedral de Toledo*, 2 vols. (Madrid, 1916)

V Pre-performance decisions

36 The editor: diplomat or dictator?

Bruno Turner

> If the text be left uncorrupt, it will purge herself of all manner
> false glosses, how subtle soever they be feigned, as a seething
> pot casteth up her scum.
>
> *William Tyndale (1534)*

The notation is not the music. Yet, in Western art music, notation is not simply a means of transmission of something fully conceived in advance; it is inextricably bound up in the process of creation that we call the composition of music. Equally inseparable is the highly variable nature of performance and its ever-changing bonds with the notation of composed music. However objective his intentions may be, the editor's influence will be subjective on personal and on public levels, being as subject to current fashions as the composers were and the performers are and will be.

In the last two hundred years the evolution of the editor's task has been based on a rapidly increasing fund of knowledge and experience in scholarship and in revived performance of earlier music, tempered by fashion and pragmatism, occasionally fired by idealism and sometimes limited by that arrogance which is the scourge of scholars, curbed by the harsh truth that increased knowledge brings neither increased wisdom nor better judgement.

The function of the editor is to enable the truest transmission of the substance of the music, letter and spirit, by means of critical and exacting standards of scholarship to a re-notation and fully comprehensible representation of the remains of the original work. The degree of re-notation that may be required is the most contentious aspect of the editorial process.

It was R. R. Terry, not the most scrupulous scholar but the boldest of performing pioneers, who described the 'mere scoring' of late Renaissance music as well within the capability of 'an intelligent plumber or gas fitter'. At the same time he noted the rarity of artistic grasp of the true significance of the music that emerged from transcription. He went on to vilify the academic absorption in technicalities and 'correlative matter'. Nearly sixty years later it is easy to scoff at Terry's naive simplification, but his priority was right. All too often dissertations and studies appear obsessed by trivia, lacking in artistic discernment, rich in facts and poor in judgement of value.

The true editor, not the casual transcriber who merely scores the parts, must have an intimate knowledge of his subject in all its multifarious aspects, not least, and rather obviously, the notation of the period, its earlier history and subsequent development. Nothing can be judged or adequately worked upon in isolation. If you study Palestrina's precursors you will understand him better. You will not understand fifteenth- or sixteenth-century church music properly if you are not intimately acquainted with its liturgy and its plainchant. A legitimate complaint against editors and performers is their woeful ignorance of the proper chant melodies of the appropriate time and place, of their notation, of their probable manner of performance and even of the proper Latin texts. That the necessary complaints are rarely raised is itself due to this widespread ignorance. That editors should be well qualified ought to be obvious, rather like the frequent medieval statements that the most important thing for a good singer is to have a good voice.

The best modern summary of the editor's tasks, duties and techniques is John Caldwell's *Editing early music*. It is full of information and clear advice, most of it very good. Here we will not attempt to distill that wisdom nor pick away at a very few points of disagreement. What is of great concern is the danger that modern transcription and editing may to some degree be as much a strait jacket as a liberator.

The editor and his edition should free old music from its museum status, covered, as it were, in the dust sheet of an obsolete notation, and prepare it for re-creation in modern performance. The editor changes the shapes and usually the values of the notes, changes the clefs and puts the parts in score. These and all his other alterations and injunctions bring new implications of pitch and intervals, of tempo and tempo relationships, of phrasing, of text underlay, spelling, pronunciation and punctuation. There are innumerable ways in which the editor intervenes. He means to do so constructively. He means to be the music's liberator who prepares it for a new life, but he may inhibit that very freedom that was truly at the heart of music in the Middle Ages and Renaissance. The composer and his wishes were not then so paramount as in our immediate post-Classical past.

The performer and composer were then closer together than they have ever been since. At the end of this chapter we shall turn to a possible escape from the strait jacket of modern fixity. Certainly the desire for conformity and standardization is not entirely new, but it is a twentieth-century obsession. 'Someone ought to stop all this diversity over pitch and voicing, someone ought to call a conference to agree about tuning, about musica ficta, about . . . someone ought to . . .' It is not long since an early music association's committee heard a proposal that authenticity certificates could be granted to approved performers to reassure the public.

Editorial intervention between the surviving sources of old music and the studied assessment and performance of that music has produced within the ranks of scholars its own parties, moderates wandering at their peril between the extremes. The very diplomatic school, on the one hand, purports to intervene little; on the other, the radicals intervene strongly. The editor, the latter cry, is there to edit, to be bold with his opinions and virtually force the performer to agree. Yet such boldness can be punished by time and the fickleness of fashion. The diplomat is punished by his guilt, his feeling deep down being that he should not have done it at all.

Editors and performers share in the desire to have their work published, in printed volumes or as recordings, to have it declared definitive or at least received as very good. They share equally in the certainty that their work will be superseded, not necessarily in quality of execution but in the manner of it and the objectives of it. It is not that standards always improve, but that fashion changes, the goal is shifted. There are no absolutes except to closed minds.

It may be laudable to sing contrapuntal music with an emphasis on clarity, but if that is won at the expense of feeling or flexibility of phrasing, lacking warmth or dramatic contrast, another period of fashion only a few years later may judge the priorities to have been wrong. If, for instance, the music of the Roman liturgy had continued to flourish in practice, in church, 'live', its use and performance evolved not revived, and if that living tradition had coincided with the 'early music' movement's commitment to the revival of historical performance practice, then a collision of claims to validity would have occurred. The fitful survival of the pre-1960s vigour in Roman liturgical music places on the sidelines a once majestic tradition sadly dwindled. Yet it had a very genuine authenticity of its own: that of evolved continuity.

To give a specific pair of questioning examples: is it more proper to try to perform La Torre's *Libera me* in what we might research as the way it was sung in Toledo Cathedral in 1549, or to accept as very proper the fact that the piece was sung at the funerals of prelates of that cathedral throughout some four centuries to at least 1925 by a continuous succession of singers in the manner of their own times? Is it really so wrong, as some would have it, that the scholarship of the monks of Solesmes resulted not in a scientific edition but in service books for a living liturgy (at least until the 1960s) within which historical performance would have been unthinkable, unpractical and, indeed, undesirable?

The century of Roman Latin liturgical revival which brought with it revived interest in and fully contextual use of plainsong and polyphony came to an end, maimed and executed by its custodians, in the 1960s just as the 'early music' movement blossomed and flourished. The collision between living tradition, evolved and hallowed, and the brash new goddess Authenticitas never really took place as history's timing might have ordained. But if it had, then tradition would have been modified by becoming historically informed and authenticity would have been mellowed if not sanctified in the true contextuality of the liturgy.

That digression has the purpose of calling into question the assumption that all performances should in some way be obliged to attempt historical accuracy. Such attempts are to be encouraged by the efforts of editors and by performers, but that is because the evolved and evolving traditions have now been largely broken. That means that we must at present go back to the surviving foundations of traditions, and that means a return to the notation of the sources. Must we, then, as editors of those sources re-erect a complete superstructure of later paraphernalia submerging once again our one and only important survival from the very past we are trying to re-create?

Even the most diplomatic of editions uses barlines in one form or another. With modern clefs they wittingly or unwittingly fix the pitch in one way or another. They introduce quite modern forms like the beaming together of quavers and the smaller values. They unbind the old ligatures and apologize with ugly new signs for them. We, the editors, shiftily put our suggested accidentals with feigned conviction over the notes; we fear our colleagues as the performers fear offending Authenticity's latest edicts. We have convinced ourselves that musicians cannot read long notes nor learn old mensuration signs. And so, for all the good we think we do, we multiply our restrictive practices, air superior knowledge and continue, despite working closely with them, to obscure our only bedrock: the sources.

Sources of medieval and Renaissance music are, like their literary counterparts, notable for their orthographic waywardness. Latin or vernacular texts are largely unpunctuated and even in liturgical books spelling is extremely variable. Notation is equally inconsistent, not least in plainsong. The editors of past times, as now, were quite as capable of obscuring as of clarifying, of destroying whilst attempting to improve or to explain. Yet this imperfect process is as much a part of changing fashions as every other aspect of music. It is the reader who recreates the book, the player or singer the music. The editor should be recognized as the translator and arbiter who, when needed, must 'transmute boldly' (Belloc on translation). But, despite the difficulties, the old forms, however obsolete, can teach in verbal text and musical notation lessons of the greatest importance in the quest for the truest re-creation.

Plainsong in the sixteenth century and beyond became subjected to drastic changes, to editing that amounted to transformation. That there were different traditions from place to place and that all of them changed during that period are facts that cannot be passed by in the preparation of modern editions. It is bad that the problem has been ignored so often in editions which simply omit the plainsong verses – text and music – of polyphonic hymns, Magnificats, responsories and other liturgical works in which the plainsong was an integral part. It remains disgraceful that anachronistic use is made of plainchant from the modern Roman service books (for example, the ubiquitous *Liber Usualis*). Using stemless black note heads instead of true plainsong notation of the correct period and place cries out for abolition if not vengeance; for it obscures the essential link with performance practice of its time.

Some of our present most notable choirs have been accused of producing manicured polyphony, and one authority has now castigated 'note-head' editions of plainsong as sanitized. Perhaps it is sadly true that in our age of perfected recordings and scientific editing the baby has gone out with the bath water.

The notation of plainsong in the sixteenth century exhibits three concurrent uses of black notation, not all of it quadratic in the sense of the modern Solesmes books. The tradition of strict mensural values usually producing a swinging triple time persists, mostly for hymns, for at least another two hundred years and is indisputable. The tradition of free but equalist interpretation of the main stream of quadratic notation is by no means to be accepted as eschewing at least three different note values. There is a distinct third class of notation which is designed to approximate the stresses not only of accent but also duration in recitation, mainly syllabic chants and psalmody. To obscure all these notational distinctions and to ignore the numerous chant instructors of the time is reprehensible and editors (most of us, myself included) should be made to sing *Emendemus in melius* in penance and to mend our ways.

The moral is that good editing should aim at liberating what seems locked up in 'difficult' sources, not imprisoning it anew *in obscura tenebrarum loca* (from which the unrevised Requiem Mass begged for us to be delivered). That, too, is a reminder that editors should not impose by carelessness, nor by design without good note, those revised Latin texts of 1568 and 1570 (imposed by Pius V), the revised Vulgate Bible (1592) and the liturgical hymns so much changed under the Popes of the ensuing generation. It is a temptation to go on taking swipes at Aunt Sallies specially set up for knocking down: let us succumb.

The modern editor's greatest single problem is pitch. It is taken by many scholars as obvious that editorial transposition is a dangerous and unsound practice. The opponents of notated transposition claim that choirs should surely transpose at sight to the most convenient pitch. Other scholars, notably David Wulstan, maintain that the music should be presented 'at the pitch at which the music is to sound'. The article in *New Grove* on 'Editing' summarizes by saying that it seems inevitable that unsatisfactory compromises must be made between scholarly idealism and pragmatic realism. Thus it is that most (but not all) library editions, collected works and the great scholarly publications of specific early repertories are presented at the original notated pitch. Many performing editions offer transpositions of the music, some without any consistent policy except simple pragmatism in terms of modern performers (usually choirs), others with complete consistency in keeping with a particular editor's pitch theories.

Now all this presupposes a general agreement that our modern notation implies a pitch of $a' = 440$ hertz, or very close. The defenders of pragmatic transposition claim that it is unrealistic to expect choirmasters to buy works (or even to consider them) if they appear to be at a pitch and for a combination of voices that does not suit the standard modern mixed (SATB) choir. The opponents of printed transposition claim that choirs should surely transpose to the most convenient pitch. It should not escape notice that some famous professional groups regularly go to great trouble and expense in having music, already well edited and published, written out again at another pitch for their performances. One is tempted to speculate that there could be other reasons.

My considered advice is that editors of practical performing editions should accept as fact that most performers expect the music before them to indicate the performing pitch in terms of $a' = 440$. Few will object and most will find it quite acceptable if the music is then rendered at a slightly higher or lower pitch standard, a semitone either way. If the general need is for a greater transposition in performance, then the editor should transpose by a fourth or fifth or by one tone. Thus in medieval and Renaissance music the editor does not normally need to use modern key signatures of more than two sharps or three flats. Even in the most scholarly publications there is a strong argument for printing certain kinds of music transposed by a fourth or fifth. To go into more detail here would be to trespass on the ground of another chapter.

Editorial choice of pitch is inextricably bound up with the fear that our modern vocal score notation (with just two clefs) and its implied anchorage to a pitch of $a' = 440$ constitutes a strait jacket. It is widely assumed that it is too late now to revive the old clefs and with them a reading technique based on relative pitch alone. The whole subject will remain controversial, and unavoidably so. The scholar and instrument maker Ian Harwood prefaced his contribution to a Pitch Conference with this Biblical quotation (*Ecclesiastes*, 13:1): 'He that toucheth pitch shall be defiled with it.'

We have seen how the extremes of diplomatic and of radical editing have ebbed and flowed in the great tide of the 'early music' revival in the past one hundred years and that the apparently opposing forces can and may have to co-exist in a balance between idealism and realism. Yet there has always remained a way out for at least the most dedicated performing groups, vocal, instrumental or both.

It may well be that the next major step the 'early music' movement must make is a widespread return to the original notation, not only in facsimile reproduction but also – perhaps more often – in scrupulously edited reprints of original choirbooks, part books, tablatures and the various other forms of notational transmission that have survived from the past. The different clefs, the general differences of appearance and the re-learning processes would themselves be conducive to accepting old notation as not being definitive of absolute pitch. Why not move the performers towards the notation instead of modifying the notation for the moving target of fashion-fickle modern performers?

Let us consider this proposal. Some would argue that it is nothing new. It is not. Not only are facsimile reproductions being published in increasing numbers, but a few pioneers are printing 'old notation' parts together with a modern score for reference and assessment – a highly commendable compromise. What is needed so badly is a breakthrough into the general musical world outside the sphere of 'early music' specialists. If instrumentalists are taught from childhood to play from parts, why should there not be a return to singing from parts? If children can be taught the notation and the playing of modern transposing instruments and the use of C clefs, why not return to reading by relative pitch from voice parts in various clefs? Plainsong was taught in most British Catholic schools until around 1960 – quadratic notation, relative pitch, variable clefs, tetragram (four-line) staves and all. For most of this century the old Breitkopf Palestrina editions in separate parts and various clefs were used at Westminster Cathedral and elsewhere.

There are two simultaneous ways to achieve this goal. One is to encourage publishers to bring out facsimiles or reprinted versions of choirbooks and of sets of part books – with edited scores. The other way is to convince choirmasters, teachers and their institutions of the improvements in understanding and of performance standards that would result. Simply, the 'early music' movement must create and increase both the demand and the supply for this changed approach to editing.

The proposal in no way invalidates the modern score of old music for study, for reference and assessment. But it will be a significant achievement when the finest professional groups regularly give their concerts at their favoured pitch and in their favoured voicing from a full size reproduction choirbook on a great lectern in the midst of the singers.

The role of the scholar and editor is not to be diminished. 'Editing is a mug's game' said an American academic to Philip Brett (recalled in his chapter in *Authenticity and early music*). Well, if it seemed like that to him, he was either in the wrong profession or he had lost touch with reality. Editing at its best is the means by which music is transmitted from its sources and original notation to a state in which it may be best comprehended and interpreted by the students and performers of later times. The requirements of successive generations will keep changing; so also must the editorial means of transmission. That may entail conscious and voluntary changes in attitudes and methods by the scholars and editors, the teachers and the taught, by musicians of all sorts and the performers above all.

Select bibliography

J. CALDWELL, *Editing early music* (Oxford, 1985)
N. KENYON (ed.), *Authenticity and early music* (Oxford, 1988)

37 Mode

Liane Curtis

For the nature, melody, and solmization of every song is learned from the mode of that song. Therefore we cannot perform any song skilfully without knowing its mode in advance.[1]

Definition

In music of the Middle Ages and Renaissance, the modal system provides sets of pitches with a designated primary pitch, or final, with other pitches organized around and prioritized by that final. The mode of a piece suggests ranges, melodic content, and where cadences occur; and these features affect other musical characteristics as well. This article investigates the nature of the modal system, and the importance of its consideration to modern listeners and performers.

From the eleventh century to the end of the Middle Ages, descriptions of mode by music theorists were fairly stable. Presentation of the final and sets of pitches of the modes are frequently found, both in the Middle Ages and in modern discussions of mode (see ex. 1). They illustrate an aspect of the modal system, but the modes should not be equated with scales: principles of melodic organization, placement of cadences, and emotional affect are essential parts of modal content.

Ex. 1
The eight modes

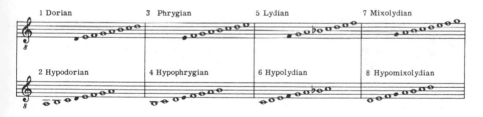

Each mode contains a particular fourth and fifth. The modes sharing the same final are a closely related pair. Odd-numbered modes, those with both their constituent fifth and fourth above the final, are called authentic, while even-numbered modes, with the fourth falling below the final, are plagal. While the final is generally the most frequent cadential pitch in a particular mode, as well as the usual ending pitch, the confinal is also suitable for ending a piece, as well as an important cadential point. The confinal is a fifth above the final in authentic modes, and a third above in plagal modes. The exceptions are the places where the confinal

---

[1]Georg Rhau, *Enchiridion utriusque musicae practicae* (Wittenberg, 1538), cited by Meier, *The Modes*, p. 27.

would fall on *b*, which, because it could be either soft (flat) or hard (natural), was not accepted as a confinal (or final).

Because of the desire to avoid the F – B♮ tritone, the use of B♭ in the fifth and sixth modes was commonplace from the eleventh century onwards. The use of a flat signature in other modes usually indicates the transposition of the mode upwards by a fourth.

All eight modes developed together, but the plagal modes are traditionally considered subsidiary to the authentic. The ancient Greeks gave their modes the names of particular tribes. The medieval use of the ancient Greek names illustrates the derived status of the plagal modes, since each is a 'hypo' (Greek for 'under' or 'beneath') version of its related authentic. Since medieval understanding of these ancient modes was flawed, today it is more consistent and practical to use the traditional designation of the modes with the numbers one to eight.

Classifying function

The modal system was used as a means of classifying medieval and Renaissance music, both chant and polyphony, and this function is frequently emphasized in scholarly literature today. The steps taken to assess the modal content of a piece are in themselves significant analytical approaches.

The use of distinct species of fourth and fifths (tetrachords and pentachords) provides each mode with unique melodic content. Marchetto da Padova and Johannes Tinctoris are among the late-medieval theorists who present these species as fundamental melodic building blocks (see ex. 2).

Ex. 2

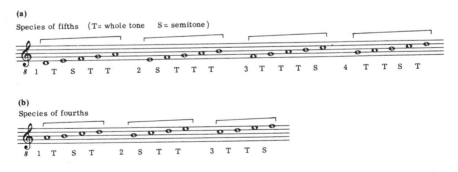

The choice of mode determines which set of species will dominate the melodic content of a piece. Since fifth and sixth modes traditionally use B♭, they appropriate the intervals of the fourth species of fifth. The seventh and eighth modes share the intervals of the first species of fourth with modes one and two. The use of fourths or fifths from modes other than the main mode of a piece is called commixture, which can be considered as the modal equivalent of modulation. In his treatise on modes, Tinctoris presents his own composed examples of commixture: the use of monophonic examples demonstrates the importance of the

Ex. 3
Johannes Tinctoris, *Liber de natura et proprietate tonorum*, chapter 13

1st mode   7th mode   1st mode

melodic use of mode, while the central role of mode in the compositional process is illustrated by his having written his own examples, rather than analysing commixture in a pre-existent melody (see ex. 3).

The mode of a piece, then, can be classified by observing the use of the final, confinal, ranges, and species of fourths and fifths. That there are a few pieces that defy unambiguous categorization illustrates the flexibility of the modal system: the guidelines served composers as a stimulus and resource rather than as rigid and narrow rules. While medieval theorists discuss mode in terms of melody, we must remember that this melodic aspect is essential to every voice of a polyphonic piece, and moreover, melody is inseparable from other aspects of musical content. The whole character, mood, or affect of a piece of music – what Rhau refers to as 'nature' – is generated by the composers response to and use of mode.

Affect

The concept of modal affect – the idea that particular modes evoke specific emotions and responses – originated with the ancient Greeks. Some modern scholars dismiss modal affect because of the divergent qualities which are attributed to various modes, and because theorists rely in differing degrees on the ancient descriptions of modal ethos. Rather than brushing the concept of modal affect aside because of certain inconsistencies, we should find the widespread interest in the subject remarkable and significant. Musicians – those who wrote about music, at any rate – clearly express a commitment to the concept of modal affect, and signify that this was an important aspect of mode. The sixteenth-century theorist Gioseffo Zarlino observes the variety of views on modal affect expressed by ancient writers, which he sees as corresponding to actual differences in the musical content of the modes in different geographic areas and times:

I think that this variety may have originated from changes in the customs of a province; these customs changed in time, and thus gave rise to changes in the modes . . . if a change in customs comes into being from variations in harmonies, . . . it is not impossible that variations in harmonies and modes can come into being from changes in customs. (Gioseffo Zarlino, *On the Modes*, part iv of *Le istitutioni harmoniche*, 1558.)

Bernhard Meier notes that a general pattern of mode and affect was widespread and common knowledge from at least the fourteenth century. The authentic modes were known as cheerful and bright, while plagal modes were dark and sombre. He cites a range of theorists from a medieval Carthusian monk concerned with the composition of new chant, to Orazio Vecchi, a madrigalist of the late sixteenth century.

Composers were aware of the general affects of mode but they also felt that they could, for certain reasons, work around these standard affects. In many cases, it was a challenge to compose in ways contradicting the usual affect of the mode, a challenge that could be taken 'provided', as Heinrich Glarean says, 'that the happy genius of such as Josquin Desprez . . . is present'.

Meier has extensively discussed the link between mode and text, particularly the sixteenth-century flexibility in using mode to express the meaning of specific words and phrases in an intense and concentrated manner. While little attempt has been made to identify mode as linked to character and affect in music of the late Middle Ages, it seems that such an association was often present. Today, performers in particular can benefit from observing the consistencies in compositional approach and musical character and that are often associated with certain modes. The manifestations of mode varied in different periods, genres, or regions: a group of pieces unified in function and geographic origin can often be found to share musical traits that correspond to their modal orientation. For some repertories, features that are aligned with mode are not readily apparent, and thus mode, while still an underlying element, was probably not a primary compositional consideration. On the other hand, when features of character correspond with the mode, it seems likely that it played an important role in the compositional process.

Mode as a compositional tool

In the late fifteenth and sixteenth centuries, theorists discussed the application of the modal system to polyphony in increasing detail. These more self-conscious explanations result from both a humanistic desire to explain music with approaches grounded in ancient theory and from a willingness to depart more readily from medieval traditions and to give their treatises a more practical value.

To the music theorists of the Middle Ages, the viability of the modal system for all music, both monophony and polyphony, was part of a set of underlying givens. Evidence that this was the case is found in the denial, by a few theorists, that this was so, as well as in a number of theoretical statements that are based on such an assumption, or that state it explicitly.

The anonymous author of the Berkeley treatise (1375) is one of those theorists who provide positive evidence for an underlying assumption that what was described for chant was applicable to polyphony. This theorist states that any song, including motets and chansons, can be evaluated in terms of modal content. In another passage, the composing of chant is contrasted with polyphony. For both, the choice of mode controls the ranges, the ascents and descents, but in chant, the plagal modes have a more restricted range, while in polyphony, the plagal modes can have as wide a range as the authentic modes. It is also advised that the tenor line in polyphony ought to 'follow the nature of ecclesiastical song' (*The Berkeley Manuscript*, Ellsworth translation, p. 75). This emphasis of the tenor foreshadows Tinctoris's statement, a century later, that the mode of the tenor is the mode of the piece.

In this passage, the Berkeley theorist is concerned with the compositional process, revealing that mode may be considered a compositional factor for both monophony and polyphony, and not merely as a tool of classification. Furthermore, the author mentions polyphony in order to contrast it with monophony. The vague term 'cantus' is used throughout the treatise; only in this one passage does the author need to distinguish 'ecclesiastical song' from polyphony. Were it not for this passage, we might assume that 'cantus' referred only to chant, but because of this reference, it is clear that 'cantus' means both chant and polyphony.

The introduction to the Berkeley manuscript clearly states that the subsequent material is applicable to all kinds of music:

Since in past times diverse authors have said so much . . . about songs – ecclesiastical as well as other types (such as motets, ballades, rondeaux, virelais, and others) – I intend to proceed . . . presenting some other things concerning the practice of all the aforesaid songs, treating briefly: first, the tones or modes of all of them . . . (*The Berkeley Manuscript*, Ellsworth trans., pp. 30–1.)

This theorist, then, considers the material applicable to both polyphony and monophony. It seems likely that this attitude may inform many medieval treatises on mode that do not specifically mention polyphony. Further, it can be noted that a parallel to this attitude can be found in other theoretical topics as well: intervals and solmization, for instance, are discussed only in reference to monophony. This material did not have to be repeated in sections on polyphony, nor was there any need to mention its relevance to polyphony: it was common knowledge, an underlying given.

Tinctoris's *Liber de natura et proprietate tonorum* (1476) is usually considered the first treatise to discuss the use of the modal system in polyphony. He is indeed explicit that he is writing about mode because it is so useful and important to polyphony. This self-conscious outspokenness concerning the role of polyphony reflects the influence on him of new humanistic trends. But the fact that Tinctoris gives few examples that actually concern polyphony, and that he, to a great extent, follows the medieval pattern for explaining mode, is because he was still working within the medieval framework: a melodic, monophonic discussion of mode was considered sufficient for polyphony. Although Tinctoris's discussion and explanations on the modal system in polyphony might seem inadequate to some scholars today (as it probably did in the fifteenth century), it was written as part of a tradition where the consideration of mode in the context of monophonic lines was necessary to the understanding of combining lines in a polyphonic texture.

In order to comprehend the importance of the modal system to composers, we must turn to their music, and examine it closely. Consistent associations of certain modes with aspects of musical character and compositional technique indicate the presence of common systems of applying mode, systems which might vary for different genres and periods. An understanding of this use of mode can only be achieved through detailed analyses of individual pieces.

An expanded and multi-dimensional view of mode suggests that it not only influenced the basic melodic material but affected other aspects of musical content, such as mensuration, harmonic content, and phrasing. The principles described by Tinctoris and other theorists, defining modal content by means of finals, ranges, and the species of fourths and fifths, can be used to assess the basic modal orientation of the pieces in question.

Case study 1

If we examine two groups of freely-composed Mass movements from the early part of the fifteenth century, one Franco-Netherlandish, the other English, we find that some traits are specific to certain modes. Mode is indeed a melodic feature, and the mode of a piece can be identified through ranges and the melodic emphasis of the inherent species of fourth and fifth. Furthermore, the significant characteristics are frequently linked to the character, the range of emotions that a certain mode expresses, and the gestures that are associated with a particular mode.

The freely composed Mass movements from the early fifteenth century, by the continental composers Dufay, Grossin, Velut, Johannes Franchois, Hugo de Lantins, Loqueville and Tapissier demonstrate an association of mode and mensuration. The pieces beginning in Ꞝ (*tempus imperfectum, prolatio major*, transcribed as 6/8 time) are almost all in first mode. Fifth mode is used exclusively in *tempus perfectum, prolatio minor* (usually transcribed as 3/4 time).

A number of other features are distinct to each mode. The first-mode pieces all begin with clear modal *exordia* – a demarcated initial phrase that presents the modal orientation. While such *exordia* are often used in other modes, in this mode they are especially consistent and clear (see ex. 4). The first-mode pieces also have a narrower range of harmonic motion than the other pieces; the control of the final is more pervasive.

The pieces in Ꞝ mensuration (*tempus imperfectum, prolatio minor*, 2/4 or 4/4) employ a variety of modes, so the choice of mode cannot be linked with mensuration. However, mode does play an important role in organizing the harmony and cadential structure of these works: each mode has a different set of structural pitches, pitches that serve as the basis of cadences or other uses of the important 8–5 sonorities.

Although in every case the final of the mode is the most important structural pitch, the plagal modes two and eight, for instance, have a pattern of structural pitches very different from each other. Those in mode eight use the third below the final and not the degree above the final; this is in contrast to those pieces in mode two. Certainly this kind of underlying harmonic structure is a more subtle ingredient to the overall character of a piece, but it is a significant element to understanding compositional choices and processes.

The group of English Mass movements is found in the Old Hall MS, whose earlier layer dates from the first two decades of the fifteenth century. Here we find no apparent association of mode with mensuration, but we do find consistencies in character and musical language that seem to be generated by mode. The first-mode pieces in Ꞝ mensuration (transcribed as 6/8 time) have a step-wise melodic quality, with concise phrases and narrow ranges. They have clear initial gestures that unambiguously present the modal orientation. Thus the melodic traits of these pieces differ markedly from what is often described as typical of English music of the period: there are few triadic figures or leaps of a third; instead the melodic character is smooth, animated by the bouncy rhythms of Ꞝ time. The melodic directness and modal straightforwardness of these pieces is comparable to that of the continental settings in this mensuration.

Ex. 4

Exordia of ℂ pieces in the first mode

First mode on D

(a) Tapissier, Sanctus

San - - - - - ctus San -

- - - - - - ctus

(b) Loqueville, Gloria

Et   in   ter - ra   pax ho - mi - ni - bus

bo - ne   vo - lun - ta - tis

(c) Dufay, Gloria iv/ 21, Cantus

Et   in   ter - - ra   pax

ho - mi - ni - bus   bo - nae   vo - lun - ta - - tis

First mode on G

(d) Dufay, Kyrie, Missa sine nomine, Cantus

Ky - - ri - e   e - lei -

- - son   Ky - ri - - e

We find the English pieces in fifth mode have the melodic traits that have so often been described as typically English: triadic figures, frequent use of thirds (often sequentially), and long, sometimes meandering melodic lines. These pieces also employ distinctive rhythmic patterns, such as syncopations formed by the use of offset semibreves in all voices.

Thus in the English pieces, melodic character and other aspects of musical style have particular tendencies according to the modal orientation. In the continental movements, some combinations of mode and mensuration were conventional, while in both groups, mode is one of a number of musical features that interdependently make up the musical style.

Liane Curtis

Case study 2

It should be no surprise that mode was associated with mensuration, since both are obvious features producing the character of a piece. A composer's sensitivity to modal character resulted in an alignment of the features of mode and mensuration, combining them so that they worked together in producing the desired affect within a certain range of conventions. In the later fifteenth century, this association of fifth and sixth modes with ○ mensuration recurs. While I do not know how widespread this tendency was throughout the century, it is present in the mid-century chanson repertory.

Several modern scholars have pointed out that the melodic lines of the chanson repertory are constructed using the species of fourths and fifths characteristic for their mode. These features of melodic writing are clear evidence that the modal system was a guiding fa.tor in the compositional process, although, of course, melody is inseparable from a number of other musical components, notably the overall character of a work and its mensural organization. Again in this repertory we find that the fifth, and also the closely related sixth modes, are closely associated with the use of *tempus perfectum* (○).

A survey of two central chansonniers reveals that the vast majority of their fifth or sixth mode pieces employ *tempus perfectum* (○) rather than either *tempus imperfectum* (C) or *tempus imperfectum diminutum* (₵ – a faster version of *tempus imperfectum*). In the Mellon chansonnier, the figures are arresting: six out of seven of the fifth or sixth mode pieces are in ○ time (86 per cent). Since this is a small number of pieces, it is possible that this alignment of mode and mensuration was a chance occurence. In the Dijon chansonnier, the larger number of ○ pieces provides a better basis for evaluation. If we begin with the strictest criterion, of the pieces in fifth or sixth mode that begin in with all three voices in *tempus perfectum*, the results are not overwhelming: 21 of 36 (58 per cent). (The four-voice pieces have not been considered.) This figure, however, is not really accurate, since it is drawn from such a narrow interpretation of *tempus perfectum*. A closer inspection of some pieces reveals that the link between fifth and sixth mode and *tempus perfectum* is actually much more prevalent.

In two cases, the scribal indication of C (*tempus imperfectum*) in the Dijon chansonnier is misleading. Robert Morton's *Le souvenir de vous me tue* is a particularly obvious case. Its triple metre organization is clear, but the Dijon scribe was not alone in marking it C. In this case, the use of fifth mode is an additional indication that the mensuration given by the scribe is incongruous with the metrical organization of the piece.

Both pieces beginning in C but then having a second section in ○ (or ϕ) mensuration are written in the fifth and sixth modal pair. This unusual change of mensuration (the other way around – ○ followed by C – is much more common) was another way of associating ○ mensuration with these modes; these pieces can be added to our statistics. Similarly, both pieces that use ○ and C simultaneously employ fifth mode. In Dufay's *Les douleurs*, a mensural canon is employed: Cantus I is in ○, while Cantus II has the same material as Cantus I but organized in C mensuration. Yet even the parts that are read in *tempus imperfectum* can easily be barred in triple metre. These observations on the use of mensuration signs by scribes should remind us that these often served to indicate how the musical notation was to be read – most significantly, whether or not alteration was operative – rather than how the material was metrically organized.

Thus, by broadening our view of the use of ○ mensuration, we observe that 27 of the 36 fifth or sixth mode chansons make use of triple metre in some form, a striking 75 per cent. While ○ is widely used in every mode (it occurs in 58 per cent of the Dijon three-voice pieces), this alone does not account for the link with fifth and sixth mode and *tempus perfectum*.

Mode in the sixteenth century

In the sixteenth century, numerous manifestations of the importance of mode are present, and should be considered by performers. These include:

1 Patterns in the use of commixture, the use of another mode besides the main mode of a piece. For instance, in the motets from the period of Josquin, the use of the eighth mode in a third-mode piece is common, while commixture with the first mode in a third-mode piece is not only rare, but usually of special significance when it is employed. Glarean's discussion of Josquin's use of first mode within his third-mode setting of *De profundis* is extraordinarily detailed.

2 The close associations of certain genres of texts with particular modes. In the early sixteenth century, the second mode was generally chosen to set lamentation texts. The practice of using standardized types of melodic *exordia* for each mode meant that these phrases not only signalled the mode of the piece, but also indicated the text content. The importance of modal affect in this respect is obvious.

3 The modal ordering of pieces in printed collections suggests that modal content should be considered in organizing programmes. Pieces could be arranged into sets with related or complementary ranges and affect, and the surrounding pieces in the original sources might be considered for performance as well.

4 The many ways mode is used to heighten the meaning of the text being set. One of the most obvious ways is when an abrupt commixture (change of mode) accompanies a sudden shift in the text; for instance, a shift in voice from narrator to first person. Changes of mode can also emphasize individual words and phrases. Patterns in these kinds of relationships are in need of further investigation by scholars.

Conclusions

An attempt to understand and interpret early music should include a consideration of contemporary theoretical material. Mode is a part of this theoretical background to compositional practice, but the theorists do not tell the entire story. After beginning with their discussions, we must then turn to the music itself, and look for ways in which use of certain modes meant the consideration of certain styles, characters, textures, and metre. Performers should compare pieces in the same mode, as well as pieces sharing mode and mensuration, in order to examine the emotional range, and musical gestures of such pieces, since the areas of overlap may indicate a shared concept of modal affect. Mode serves as a part of this musical language, not just as sets of theoretical rules, but as part of the stylistic value system that provided compositional vocabulary and guidelines.

Select bibliography

Medieval and Renaissance references

P. AARON, *Trattato della natura et cognitione di tutti gli tuoni di canto figurato non da altrui piu scritti* [1525, facsimile] (Utrecht, 1966); Chapters 1–7 trans. O. Strunk, *Source readings in music history: the Renaissance*, 2nd edn. (New York, 1965), pp. 15–28

O. B. ELLSWORTH (ed. and trans.), *The Berkeley Manuscript* (Lincoln, Nebraska, 1984)

H. GLAREAN, *Dodecachordon*, trans. C. A. Miller (American Institute of Musicology, 1965)

J. W. HERLINGER (ed. and trans.), *The Lucidarium of Marchetto of Padua* (Chicago, 1985)

J. TINCTORIS, *Liber de natura et proprietate tonorum*, in A. Seay (ed.), *Johannes Tinctoris: Opera Theoretica* (American Institute of Musicology, 1975), pp. 59–104; and (trans.) A. Seay, *On the nature and propriety of tones*, 2nd edn (Colorado Springs, 1976)

G. ZARLINO, *On the modes*, trans. V. Cohen (New Haven, 1983)

General

S. HERMELINK, *Dispositiones modorum: die Tonarten in der Musik Palestrinas und seiner Zeitgenossen* (Tutzing, 1960)

D. HILEY, 'Mode', in *The New Oxford Companion to Music* (Oxford, 1983), pp. 1183–9

B. MEIER, *The modes of classical vocal polyphony*, trans. E. S. Beebe (New York, 1988)

L. L. PERKINS, 'Mode and structure of the Masses of Josquin des Pres', *Journal of the American Musicological Society*, xxvi (1973), pp. 189–239

H. POWERS, 'Mode', *New Grove*; and 'Tonal types and modal categories', *Journal of the American Musicological Society*, xxxiv (1981), pp. 428–70

L. TREITLER, 'Tone system in the secular works of Dufay', *Journal of the American Musicological Society*, xxviii (1965), pp. 131–69

38 Musica ficta

Rob C. Wegman

The term 'musica ficta' has two meanings, which are only partly related. In medieval and Renaissance music theory, the term applied to transgressions of what was considered the 'proper' tonal vocabulary. Study of musica ficta in this sense can help us to understand how medieval and Renaissance musicians conceived and visualized notions of pitch, step, and scale, and how their understanding of these notions developed in response to changing musical practices. In current musicological usage, musica ficta applies to the performers' and editors' application of accidentals not specified in practical sources. The identification of situations that demand such application is still an issue of debate, and involves criteria of contrapuntal propriety rather than the definition of musica ficta in its authentic sense. The original and present-day definitions of musica ficta overlap only in a minority of practical situations: they are therefore best discussed separately.

Medieval theorists defined the range and nature of the tonal material in a system called the Hand (*manus*). Music whose tonal material remained within that definition was described as 'true' or 'proper' (*musica vera* or *recta*). Music whose tonal material exceeded that definition was called 'false' or 'feigned' (*musica falsa* or *ficta*).

The system of the Hand comprised a nearly diatonic scale spanning two octaves plus a sixth (*G* to *e″*). That scale was formed by the conjunction of two sub-systems. The first of these defined the order of the available steps, and indicated the rank of each step by a serial letter. These letters were, in ascending order:

Γ A B C D E F G a b c d e f g aa bb cc dd ee

The second sub-system determined the intervals separating each step from the ones around it, by fitting a fixed pattern of tones and semitones to the series of steps. This pattern, the hexachord, consisted of a central semitone (S) with two whole tones (T) on either side. Together, the five intervals of the hexachord spanned a major sixth; they connected six steps, which were indicated by the following syllables:

syllables	ut	re	mi	fa	sol	la
intervals		T	T	S	T	T

If there were no restrictions to the ways in which hexachords could be fitted to the series of steps, each of these syllables could be identified with any of the serial letters. Consequently the *mi–fa* semitone progression could occur between every two consecutive steps, and the resulting scale would be fully chromatic. However, beginning with Guido of Arezzo (*c.* 990–after 1033), theorists allowed the *mi–fa* progression to occur only at three places in each octave: B–C, E–F, and A–B♭. The number of hexachords that could be fitted to the above series of steps was thereby reduced to seven, and the diatonic nature of the scale was ensured (see ex. 1).

Ex. 1
The hexachords

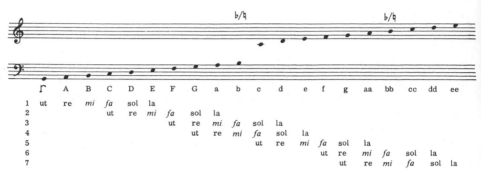

	Γ	A	B	C	D	E	F	G	a	b	c	d	e	f	g	aa	bb	cc	dd	ee
1	ut	re	mi	fa	sol	la														
2				ut	re	mi	fa	sol	la											
3							ut	re	mi	fa	sol	la								
4								ut	re	mi	fa	sol	la							
5											ut	re	mi	fa	sol	la				
6														ut	re	mi	fa	sol	la	
7															ut	re	mi	fa	sol	la

It was this particular 'Guidonian' conjunction of twenty letters with seven interlocking hexachords that was called the Hand. Each step was identified both by its relative position (serial letter) and its intervallic context (solmization syllable). For instance, the step 'aa *la–mi–re*' could relate functionally to its neighbours in three different ways: as *la* in a hexachord starting on c, as *mi* in a hexachord on f, and as *re* in a hexachord on g. By definition, then, a step was a *contextual* element, not an absolute entity: to name it was to define its functional position in a broader melodic context. For didactic and mnemonic purposes, the twenty steps were often represented visually on the tips and joints of the fingers of the left hand, hence the name of the system as a whole.

Ambiguities arose only in the case of the B, since this step could be either *mi* or *fa*, depending on the hexachord to which it belonged. The B could be *fa* in a hexachord starting on F (in which case it was separated by a semitone from A, and hence identical to our B♭), but in a hexachord on G it could be *mi* (in which case it was separated by a semitone from C, and hence identical to our B♮). Theorists distinguished two signs to specify (if necessary) the actual syllable carried by a step: ♭ = *fa*, and ♮ = *mi*. The latter sign was in practice more or less synonymous with the so-called *diesis* (⨉) (later formalized to ♯). It should be stressed that these three signs did not by definition require the changing of a pitch by a semitone up or down: they had that effect in many cases, but their primary function was to clarify the intervallic contexts of the notes they accompanied. The signs would assume their present-day meanings only in the course of the sixteenth century (see below).

To pronounce the appropriate hexachord syllables while singing a melody was called 'to solmize' (see ex. 2). Choirboys were rigorously trained in this practice from the very beginning of their musical education. They thus acquired the ability to recognize immediately the inherent hexachord patterns of any given tune. Medieval staff notation presumed that ability, and could therefore afford to be unspecific about the pitches of individual steps: these would be self-evident if their melodic contexts were properly understood. (An important consequence of this is that it is wrong to assume that each notated step in an early source is natural ('white key') unless it carries an accidental. The assumption is doubly wrong since accidentals in early sources do not necessarily mean what they mean today. One cannot, in fact, make any *a priori* statement about the pitch of such a step unless the

1 The Guidonian Hand from Amerus,
Practica artis musice (1271)

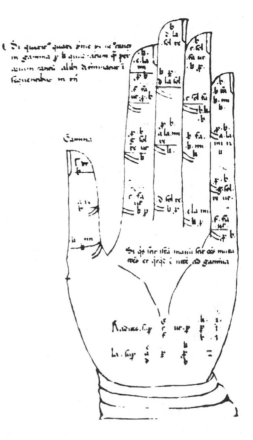

intervallic context is taken into account.) Thorough practical training in solmization was therefore a prerequisite for being able to read staff notation at all. To give an example, in many cases only the intervallic context could tell musicians whether the progression A–B should be sung as *mi–fa* (A–B♭) or *re–mi* (A–B♮) (see ex. 2).

Ex. 2

Solmization

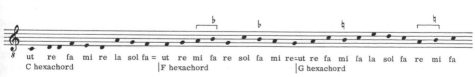

ut re fa mi re la sol fa = ut re mi fa re sol fa mi re=ut re fa mi fa la sol fa re mi fa
C hexachord |F hexachord |G hexachord

The term *ficta* applied to all steps not defined in the Hand. Thus, any step that involved the irregular placement of a hexachord along the serial letters was considered 'feigned'. D *fa*, for instance, would be a feigned step since it implies a hexachord, starting on A, in spite of the fact that the step is identical, in terms of pitch, to its 'true' counterpart, D *sol–re*:

	Γ	A	B	C	D	E	F	G	a	b	c	etc
feigned		ut	re	mi	**fa**	sol	la					
true		ut	re	mi	fa	**sol**	la					
				ut	**re**	mi	fa	sol	la			

The standard way of indicating the placement of an irregular hexachord was to locate its central *mi–fa* progression. In the case of a hexachord on A, for instance, the C should be marked *mi*, through either of the signs ♮ or ♯ (which tend to mean exactly the same thing; see ex. 3a). The intervallic context then dictated that C and F be sung as C♯ and F♯. Note that in ex. 3a, the performance of F as F♯ is implicit (from our point of view), and cannot be specified by a *mi* sign. Only if the F is also *mi*, in a different hexachord, can it carry the sign ♮ or ♯ (ex. 3b).

Ex. 3
Location of the *mi–fa* progression

Other *ficta* steps were those outside the range Γ *ut–ee la* (G – *e''*). The first step to exceed the Hand at the upper end was *f''*, which step was conceived (and frequently indicated) as *fa* in a feigned hexachord on *c''* (see ex. 4a). At the lower end, a feigned F below Γ *ut* could be implied by notating a *fa* signature in the bass clef (see ex. 4b).

Ex. 4
Ficta steps outside the Hand

The concept of musica ficta was defined in negative terms (that is, *ficta* = not *recta*), and its meaning depended on the definition of its counterpart, *recta*. The latter definition, as we have seen, was comparatively narrow (*recta* = anything in the Guidonian Hand, that is, in effect, the diatonic scale but with B♭ and B♮ as equal partners). This may explain why the practical relevance of the *recta/ficta* distinction gradually diminished in the course of the period 1300–1600. Around 1300, a division between 'Guidonian' and 'non-Guidonian' steps may well have been useful to distinguish irregular melodic progressions from orthodox ones, but as composers explored and expanded the musical idiom in the course of the

268

fourteenth and fifteenth centuries, it was inevitable that they would transgress the narrow boundaries of *musica recta* more and more. Consequently, the criteria for 'irregular' and those for *ficta* began to diverge.

By the fifteenth century, musica ficta covered a large number of widely-employed practices, most of them accepted and approved by theorists: inflections of cadential leading tones; modal transpositions involving key signatures with more than one flat; 'emergency' inflections to avoid inadmissible harmonic or melodic intervals; steps outside the range G–*e''*; and so on. If theorists discussed these

Ex. 5

Johannes Tinctoris, *Missa sine nomine* I, Kyrie I

© W.E. Melin, *Johannes Tinctoris Opera Omnia*, Corpus Mensurabilis Musicae (1976)

practices, they did so primarily in treatises dealing with counterpoint and modality rather than the Guidonian Hand: feigned steps had now become so commonplace that they hardly deserved special mention. This indicates that the criterion on which the *ficta/recta* distinction was based, the Guidonian Hand, was increasingly becoming an anachronism in the Renaissance – at least in polyphonic music. Composers were entirely free to move within and without the Hand: it made no qualitative difference to the music they wrote. Although the Hand remained a cornerstone in music education, its practical use as a conceptual tool diminished.

An example of a composition which moves almost entirely outside the realm of *musica recta* is Johannes Tinctoris's three-voice *Missa sine nomine* no.1 (see the beginning of the Kyrie I in ex. 5). Its key signatures, and several internal accidentals, indicate that this Mass is conceived in terms of seven interlocking hexachords starting on the pitches $B\flat$, $E\flat$, F, $B\flat$, $e\flat$, f, and $b\flat$. All but the sixth of these hexachords are feigned. Besides, the bass part comprises four feigned steps below Γ. It is clear that *ficta* has here become the rule, *recta* the exception. Yet to all appearances this is a perfectly conventional fifteenth-century composition, in the C Dorian mode. So what is the relevance of knowing that the piece is almost entirely *ficta*?

The answer must be that it tells us how contemporary musicians conceived 'tonal space'. If a composition is entirely *ficta*, it means that the system of the Hand is permanently suspended, and that the diatonic 'sphere' that *is* in force constitutes an essentially different order. By implication it is to say that different diatonic spheres are conceptually disjunct. Music cannot move in two diatonic spheres at the same time; at the most it can 'jump' from one sphere to another. But as modal transpositions such as the one illustrated here became more and more frequent (from the mid-fifteenth century onwards), it was inevitable that a different outlook on the tonal space would emerge. By the late sixteenth century that space was no longer seen as an assembly of segregated diatonic spheres (one *recta*, the others *ficta*), but as a continuum in which all diatonic spheres were integrated, and simultaneously present.

Typically, the earliest attempts to write what we would call 'chromatic' passages were simply quick traversals through several diatonic spheres in a row, and thus they never called the diatonic nature of the tonal space in question. One of the most famous examples is Adrian Willaert's four-part motet *Quid non ebrietas* (c.1519), the most spectacular feature of which is that it ends on a notated seventh which sounds as an octave ($\it eb\flat$ in the tenor against d' in the discantus). The fundamental novelty of this piece is that by searching for the limits of the tonal space, it discovers that this space is spiral: there are no limits. The tonal propeller of the motet is the tenor which runs with dazzling speed through twelve hexachords starting successively on the pitches f, c', $b\flat$, $e\flat$, $a\flat$, $d\flat$, $g\flat$, $f\flat$, $B\flat\flat$, $e\flat\flat$, $d\flat\flat$, and $g\flat\flat$ (see ex. 6). In terms of how each note relates to its immediate neighbours, however, the voice is strictly diatonic. The trick of the piece is that if one moves away far enough from the Hand, one eventually comes back into the Hand. For when, after an extended *ficta* passage (notes 23–55), Willaert marks C as *fa* (note 59), we are dealing with a *recta* step again (c *fa*), despite the fact that the step is to be performed as $c\flat$: the tenor has come full circle, at least nominally. In the same paradoxical way, the pitches $a\flat$, $f\flat$, $g\flat$, and $b\flat\flat$ (notes 60–5) are *recta* steps (namely, *a mi*, *f ut*, *g re*, and *b fa*). But the tenor passes even beyond this 'second Hand', and it ends up moving in hexachords on *e♭♭* and *d♭♭*.

As a tonal propeller, the tenor draws the other voice-parts round the spiral as well, for the rules of counterpoint demand that these keep adjusting to the tenor in order to avoid diminished and augmented harmonic intervals. But Willaert has written the latter voices in such a way that they can jump back to the 'first Hand' at the last moment, when the tenor has to go forward to complete its rotation. This explains the final *e♭♭–d'* juxtaposition: the tenor and the other voices are more than a full rotation apart (see ex. 6).

Ex. 6
Adrian Willaert, *Quid non ebrietas (c.*1519)

In spite of its 'floating tonality', Willaert's motet is not genuinely chromatic. All it does is to jump from one diatonic sphere to the next, duly respecting the 'white-key' nature of each individual sphere. At the same time, however, *Quid non ebrietas* is iconoclastic in that it discovers the *spiral* nature of the tonal space. If two diatonic spheres that are conceptually disjunct can vertically coexist (as the *e–d'* juxtaposition in the motet proves), and if pitches like *a♭*, *f♭*, *g♭*, *c'♭*, and *b♭♭* can be explained, in certain contexts, as *recta* steps (see above), the whole diatonic system collapses. In these circumstances, it is not surprising that musicians eventually came to think of the tonal space as a chromatic continuum.

The most powerful image of that new continuum was the keyboard. The Guidonian Hand can be seen as a keyboard with all the black keys taken out. The Guidonian system did not acknowledge the existence of a semitone step between, for instance, C and D: there was simply no key in that place. One needed to 'feign' an entirely different keyboard (likewise consisting of white keys only) to conceptualise our pitch *C♯*. Now all the independent diatonic keyboards that could be 'feigned' had wonderfully merged in the one chromatic keyboard. Here, the realms of *ficta* and *recta* were simultaneously present, without any qualitative distinction. As a visual representation, the chromatic keyboard was so compelling that pitches like *C♯* gradually came to be regarded as steps in their own right: they were there all the time, not just under 'feigned' conditions.

A corollary of these developments is the changed meaning of the signs ♯ and ♭. Traditionally these signs were used to clarify the intervallic context, but in the course of the sixteenth century they came to prescribe inflections by a semitone, independent of context (as they do now). This development presupposes the recognition that every step in the gamut is permanently surrounded by semitone steps, to which one can move directly, without having to invoke complex mental constructions. It thus provides clear proof that 'Guidonian' thinking was finally giving way to modern 'keyboard' thinking.

The difference between the early and modern meanings of accidental signs is a fundamental one, and should be kept in mind in discussions of the problem of unspecified inflections. Naturally, fourteenth- to sixteenth-century sources cannot be expected to provide 'accidentals' in the modern sense. This immediately raises the question whether we are justified to phrase the problem in terms of 'inflections' and 'unspecified'. The word 'inflection' implies the existence of a step *from which* to inflect; hence it betrays thinking in terms of the chromatic keyboard. The word 'unspecified' implies that the hexachord to which a note belongs does not specify its pitch, whereas an accidental – if it were provided – would. Both premises are anachronistic. Let us briefly return to ex. 3a to illustrate this. In the example, the note on the F-line represents, in keyboard terms, the *pitch f*, and the 'inflection' from that pitch to *f♯* is therefore considered unspecified. In terms of the Hand, however, the pitch *f* is non-existent in this context: with the introduction of a hexachord on A the music has moved into a different realm, where the *step* F cannot but represent our *pitch f♯*. There is no note to inflect, and hence there is no inflection to specify.

The problem, then, is not so much that the notation of early music is 'incomplete', but that modern notation cannot presume hexachord thinking on the part of its users, and therefore needs to be a lot more explicit. Medieval and Renaissance singers, without exception, had spent years and years of their youth practising solmization in plainsong. As a consequence, hexachord thinking had become so firmly ingrained that pitches could not possibly be in doubt as long as the intervallic contexts were unambiguous. The ideal notation, in their terms, was one that left no doubt about the hexachords, not one that spelled out each individual 'inflection'. Although surviving sources do not always live up to this ideal, the fact remains that the problem of 'unspecified inflections' is largely our own.

It is this problem that is nowadays described as musica ficta, and it should be stressed at once that this modern meaning of musica ficta has little to do with the original meaning. Two examples may illustrate this. In ex. 3a, all four steps are *ficta* in the original definition. According to the modern definition, however, three of these – C *mi*, D *fa* and E *sol* – are not *ficta*, since they do not involve unspecified inflections. Conversely, the following unspecified inflection of a cadential leading tone (in Tinctoris's *Missa sine nomine* no.1; see ex. 7) is *ficta* in the modern sense, but *recta* in the original sense, since the inflection restores the feigned step E *fa* (= E♭) to the realm of the Hand (E *mi* − E♮).

Ex. 7
Johannes Tinctoris, *Missa sine nomine* 1, Kyrie II

Strictly speaking, then, it is incorrect to speak of either musica ficta or 'unspecified inflections'. The real problem, for us no more than for the men who used the original sources, is that of 'singing properly'. To sing properly, the theorists tell us, is to read, understand, and interpret music consistently in terms of hexachord patterns, using whatever clues the melodic structure and notation provide, and applying standard rules for problematic situations. It is, in other words, to master the art of solmization.

Rules of solmization which involve unspecified inflections (from our point of view) are mostly motivated by laws of counterpoint. The most important of these laws are: (1) intervals should be perfect in direct melodic leaps of a fourth or fifth, or in melodically outlined fourths and fifths; (2) harmonic intervals of the fourth, fifth, and octave should be perfect; (3) the sixth immediately preceding the octave in a cadence should be major; and so on. The practical application of these rules is not without difficulties. There are many cases in which obeying one rule means the violation of another. Situations which allow more than one interpretation are legion, and accidentals in sources are often confusing rather than elucidating. Even so, these are primarily problems of solmization, not of musica ficta (in either sense). The proper place to discuss them is in studies of the theory and practice of this underestimated art.

Most present-day editors of pre-1600 music consider it their responsibility to indicate implied inflections in published scores, usually by placing editorial accidentals over the inflected notes. Others object that editors should not give the impression of knowing more than they do know, and draw analogies with practices that are open to interpretation (realizations of thoroughbasses, fingerings in keyboard music, etc.). These objections are surely unjustified. Early notation *did* aim to be unambiguous about pitches (or rather intervals, which amounts to the same thing), even though the surviving sources are often not. Only if one ignores one of the essential tools for interpreting early notation can one accuse it of being 'incomplete'. And if early notation was in principle meant to be unambiguous, there is no reason for modern notation to represent it as ambiguous. What medieval and Renaissance composers specified by assuming knowledge of solmization on the part of singers, modern notation should specify in its way.

That is not to say that there is no room for more initiative on the part of present-day musicians. Modern performance practice of pre-1600 music could benefit substantially from the restoration of solmization as a living practice. It would increase understanding of the structure and notation of medieval and Renaissance music, and would stimulate a more critical attitude towards editions. Both editor and performer need to think in the concepts and categories of medieval and Renaissance musicians, difficult though that is. Only then will we be able to distinguish our limitations and strengths from those of the men whose music we wish to revive.

Select bibliography

M. BENT, 'Musica recta and Musica ficta', *Musica Disciplina*, xxvi (1972), pp. 73–100; and 'Diatonic *ficta*', *Early Music History*, iv (1984), pp. 1–48

K. BERGER, *Musica ficta. Theories of accidental inflections in vocal polyphony from Marchetto da Padova to Gioseffo Zarlino* (Cambridge, 1987)

39 Renaissance pitch

Kenneth Kreitner

The modern pitch standard of $a' = 440$ (that is, the custom among Western performers and instrument makers of placing the A above middle C at a pitch corresponding to 440 hertz or cycles per second) is the result of an international conference held in London in 1939. Before that time, various pitch standards prevailed in various cities and institutions, and before precise measurement of pitch became possible in the nineteenth century, these local standards varied a great deal: eighteenth-century flutes, for example, survive with a half dozen or more interchangeable middle joints of different lengths to accommodate the tuning notes a travelling flautist might encounter. The adoption of an international pitch standard today is thus an enormous convenience.

There are, of course, variations: some orchestras, for example, have adopted a slightly higher pitch for a more brilliant sound. But perhaps the most significant system of alternative pitch standards over the last few decades has been that adopted by performers of Baroque music on historical instruments. In the pursuit of historical authenticity, many of these players have taken a pitch standard slightly lower than our $a' = 440$ – most often an alternative convention of $a' = 415$ (a semi-tone below modern pitch) – but sometimes adopt other standards to conform with the supposed pitch of a particular time and place or to fit a particular historical wind instrument.

The success of this 'Baroque pitch', both in musical terms and as a source of snob appeal, has led performers and scholars of Renaissance music to wonder about their own pitch standards. However, the question is much more difficult for the fifteenth and sixteenth centuries than for the eighteenth: clues corresponding to those that gave us Baroque pitch are just not there. Wind instruments from the Renaissance (recorders, flutes, cornetts, and organ pipes are the most useful indicators) are scarcer and more likely to have been damaged or altered; the original key of an instrument or pitch-name for an organ pipe is often not known (it is hard, for example, to distinguish a recorder in F at high pitch from one in G at low); and Renaissance theorists are uniformly silent or ambiguous on the matter. Besides, much of the music that concerns us is vocal rather than instrumental, and estimating the vocal ranges of Renaissance choirs is a slippery calculation at best – all the more so in the cases of boys, falsettists, and castratos, whose vocal techniques, and thus ranges, in the Renaissance remain more or less conjectural.

In short, whatever the historical validity of modern Baroque pitch may be, we cannot provide anything nearly as precise for music before 1600. The best we can do is to examine what role pitch standards played in the musical life of the Renaissance, and establish the implications of that role for historically-informed performance today. This article will focus mostly on the sacred polyphony of the later fifteenth and sixteenth centuries because the performing forces and conditions for this music are relatively well understood; but many of these observations must have applied to earlier repertories as well as to secular music.

Fixed and flexible pitch standards

The crucial question here concerns the relationship between written and sounding pitch in the music of the Renaissance. Was this relationship more or less consistent, at least locally, like ours today (and if so, how did the various local pitch standards differ from our $a' = 440$)? Or was it much more flexible, a function of each individual performance and its particular forces? This proves an exceptionally difficult question, not susceptible to easy answers or direct proof: no recordings survive from the Renaissance to compare with the notation, nor, for lack of an intelligible vocabulary to describe pitch standards, is there any unequivocal evidence from contemporary commentators. Modern scholarly opinion has tended to swing back and forth between fixed and flexible pitch, and the time may have come to find a course between them.

First of all, it should be established that local pitch standards did exist in the Middle Ages and Renaissance, at the very least among instrumentalists, for whom precise and consistent tuning was essential: most woodwinds and cornetts of this period were made in one piece, and thus their pitch was established by the maker and could not be much altered by the player. Any group of instrumentalists that included woodwinds or cornetts and played together regularly must perforce have adopted a single pitch standard, and this standard must in effect have become the dominant pitch for the entire musical institution: in 1420, for example, Alfonso V of Aragon ordered a small organ for his chapel, 'tuned to the minstrels'. Assuming that this organ was used with the singers of the royal chapel, the singers, the instrumentalists, and the organist of the Aragonese court must all have been subject, at least sometimes, to a single standard of pitch. This must have been true, even if undocumented, just about everywhere.

Yet just as clearly, for most European choirs, especially before 1500, performance with instrumentalists was the exception rather than the rule for liturgical monophony and polyphony alike; and this dominant tradition of un-accompanied singing makes the notion of flexible pitch much more plausible. When singing a cappella, singers would take a pitch from their chapelmaster or a tenorista, who, so far as we know, found this starting pitch without recourse to a musical instrument. For these choirs, the pitch level of a performance was completely at the whim of the director, who would have known the vocal limits of his choir and the ranges of the repertory, but who could rely on memory and judgment rather than on fidelity to an outside standard. The notated pitch and the performing pitch of a piece would thus have been quite independent, their relation flexible according to the capability and preference of the individual choir. In other words, the highness or lowness of the notes on the staff indi-cated, in effect, not their absolute highness or lowness in performance, but their position relative to one another and the position of the semitones and tones in their scale.

This point is often a difficult one for modern musicians to accept. The idea that an A on the treble-clef staff means approximately 440Hz in the ear and never, except by prearrangement (as in transposing instruments) 256Hz, is so basic to our musical experience and our understanding of what musical notation means, that it is hard fully to imagine a world in which such a custom had not yet developed. Yet one such world, and a most significant one, has existed even within recent memory:

flexible pitch governed the performance of Gregorian chant at the time of Vatican II just as it surely did in the Middle Ages.

Although chant in the various modes is written at various pitch levels, all the chant in a particular institution tends to be sung at roughly the same average pitch. If the choir is singing alone, this 'transposition' need not even be conscious: it is easy, with a bit of experience, for its director to eyeball the general range of a piece and place its sung pitch at a comfortable level; or if an organ is accompanying (either playing along with the choir or playing versets between the verses), the organist can apply a fairly simple set of transpositions to bring all the modes to a practical level. (Arnolt Schlick, in his *Spiegel der Orgelmacher und Organisten* (1511), provided instructions for this and showed the approximate sizes of pipes needed to make an organ suitable for accompanying chant with these various transpositions.) Since chant was after all the bread and butter of even the best polyphonic singers of the Renaissance, this sort of flexible pitch must have been a fundamental part of their training and daily life.

Polyphony complicates the issue: it is much harder to spot and remember the general ranges of four or more parts at once and place them all in a comfortable range for everybody. But again, this is a matter of training and experience, and the lesson of advanced *a cappella* polyphonic traditions today shows that it can surely be done: traditional black American gospel quartets, for example, are known to sing entire concerts of complex music without reference to any outside pitch standard (and with remarkable consistency from night to night), just through intimate familiarity with their repertory and with the limits and comfortable sections of their own voices.

Flexible pitch is a simple and elegant idea. It fits in well with what we know about the musical life of singers in the Renaissance, and it seems to provide neat solutions to the pitch difficulties the polyphonic repertory sometimes presents. Suddenly pieces notated in uncomfortably high or low registers, and disturbing differences in written pitch within the surviving repertory of a particular choir, are no problem: if performing pitch was at the choir director's discretion, then all the repertory of a given choir could be sung at the same pitch level. Only pieces with exceptionally wide ranges, pieces that could not be moved up or down without causing trouble for the sopranos or basses, remain problematic; and these, for most of the Renaissance, are gratifyingly rare.

We may have yielded, however, to this temptation a little too quickly and too completely. A number of pieces of evidence suggest that, especially in the sixteenth century, the pitch of sacred polyphony was not quite so flexible as that of chant.

First, beginning in the later fifteenth century, instruments – particularly organs, shawms, trombones, trumpets, cornetts, and recorders – performed with singers on polyphonic pieces more and more often. The presence of such instruments, in the days before equal temperament and Boehm keywork, would have made certain transpositions much more practical than others (a number of tutors for various instruments explain how to do this), but would effectively have rendered *free* transposition impossible. The greater technical complexity of polyphony, and the challenge of tuning vertical sonorities, make it a very different story from chant.

Second, composers in the Renaissance did see some need to adjust, or at least control, the written pitch of their music. Tinctoris, in the *Liber de natura et proprietate tonorum* (1476), devoted six chapters to describing and illustrating what he called 'irregular modes', which amount to nothing more than transpositions down by fifths or up by fourths (adding a flat with each successive transposition); these written-out transpositions would be quite unnecessary in a world where notated and sung pitch were completely independent. Indeed, in such a world we might not expect to find key signatures at all – a simple set of staves, clefs, and notes, with written pitch varying as it might, would have been enough to show the semitones and tones.

Third, the effect of these key signatures and regular and irregular modes was to bring a great deal of the Renaissance repertory into a similar and generally comfortable range; for example, as David Fallows calculated in 1985, of the sixty-three motets secure in the Josquin canon of that time, at least fifty-six are within a tone of being comfortable at $a' = 440$ for a modern choir of falsettists, tenors, and basses. Even if we accept the principle of flexible pitch, then, Josquin's choirs would not have had to vary the relation between written and sounding pitch very much.

Fourth, individual compositions are sometimes preserved at one pitch level in one source and another in another. The motet *Absalon fili mi*, long attributed to Josquin but possibly by La Rue, is the most famous example of this, but it remains also the most puzzling. As Fallows points out, its two versions, a ninth apart, are both uncomfortable at modern pitch (the bass of the one descends to B♭ below the bass-clef staff, the superius of the other ascends to B♭ above the treble), and a much more practical version could easily have been written halfway in between. But there are plenty of clearer and less problematic cases: Arthur Mendel observed in 1948 that the two printed editions of Carpentras's Lamentations, dated 1532 and 1557, are pitched a fourth apart; Iain Fenlon and James Haar have noted this phenomenon a number of times among early Italian madrigals (Costanzo Festa's *Il vero libro di madrigali a tre voci* (1543), for example, contains two pieces that appear elsewhere a fourth higher, and four that appear elsewhere a full octave higher); and David Wulstan has described similar pieces among the works of Tomkins, White, and Fayrfax. Whatever the exact implications of this practice might be in each case, the examples at least show that some singers found the notated pitch level significant enough to benefit from a written-out transposition.

Fifth, several composers from the fifteenth and early sixteenth centuries – most prominently Tinctoris, Okeghem and La Rue – have left sacred works written in exceptionally low ranges, descending to C and B♭ below the bass-clef staff. Virtually all of these pieces could have been transposed up to a comfortable level within the notational conventions of the time, and thus their low written pitch seems to be a deliberate choice. In at least some of these pieces (not only *Absalon fili mi*, but also Okeghem's *Intemerata Dei mater* and La Rue's Requiem) the low pitch is matched with a sombre or imploring text in a way that modern ears, at least, find most moving; and it is difficult to avoid the conclusion that the composers wrote them in this low range because they wanted to hear them down there for a special musical effect.

Finally, at least for the late sixteenth century, there is evidence that certain clef combinations implied certain codes of transposition. We shall examine this principle more closely in the next section, but for the moment it need only be observed that such transpositions would be needless and meaningless if pitch standards were completely flexible anyway.

The dearth and dispersion of hard evidence has obliged us to cast the net wide, and this, as with so many of the broader questions of Renaissance performance practice, has doubtless tended to obscure variations over time and from place to place. The answer may, then, be simply that variable pitch standards were necessary for chant and sufficient for medieval polyphony, but that as the Renaissance developed and sacred polyphony became more common, its ranges wider, and its manner of performance more stereotyped within a given choir, the original flexibility gradually stiffened. Pitch may have remained flexible in theory throughout the Renaissance, and no doubt pitch standards did vary somewhat between choirs; but from around 1500 onwards, within a given choir, the relation between written and sung pitch may not have had to flex as much as we might suppose.

Clef-codes and transpositions

Standing somewhere between fixed and flexible pitch, and a nice refinement of both, at least for the late sixteenth century and after, is the theory of clef-codes: the notion that certain combinations of clefs were understood to imply particular transpositions. The theory has taken various forms over the years, but in its simplest state it runs something like this.

Musicians in the Renaissance were disinclined to use leger lines as extensively as we do today; instead, they employed a much wider variety of G, C, and F clefs, adjusting the clef of a particular vocal line rather meticulously to fit its range. A soprano (or C1) clef at the beginning of a voice part, then, was generally a pretty good indication that it would not go below B or above E (see ex. 1).

Ex. 1
Soprano (C1) clef: range

In the fifteenth century, these clefs varied a good deal from piece to piece; by the late sixteenth century, however, they had crystallized into a few stereotyped combinations. The basic clef combination, often called 'normal clefs' or *chiavi naturali*, was soprano-alto-tenor-bass, and it outlined a set of ranges that a modern male choir, with falsettists or boys on the top line, finds quite practical (see ex. 2).

Ex. 2
'Chiavi naturali': ranges

But there was also a second very common clef combination, called high clefs or *chiavette*, typically treble-mezzo-alto-baritone, outlining ranges a third higher (see ex. 3).

Ex. 3
'Chiavette': ranges

Both clef combinations are routinely found side-by-side in the repertory of a single choir, and if taken literally, the high clefs would tend to put every voice into a shrill and uncomfortable register. This is the main source for the clef-code theory: if music in the high clefs is transposed down by a minor third, its ranges match those of music in the low clefs, and it becomes much easier to sing. The stereotyped clef combinations, then, could have acted as a signal to the choir director, telling whether the starting pitch should be intoned where it lies or a minor third down. (The reason music in high clefs was not originally written a third down is that this would have required the addition of three sharps to the key signature, and sharp key signatures were not used in the Renaissance.)

This notion of transposition down by a third was widely believed throughout the nineteenth century and well into the twentieth, but Mendel in 1948 suggested that transposition down by a fourth (adding a sharp or deleting a flat) had a much better claim: no less an authority than Praetorius, in the third volume of the *Syntagma musicum* (1619), says that when music in the high clefs is put into score or tablature for an accompanying instrument, it should usually be transposed down a fourth (but in a few cases down a fifth). Mendel went on to cite a few confirming examples from the prints of Schütz in which choral parts in the low clefs are given an organ accompaniment that matches their written pitch, but the accompaniments to pieces in high clefs are written or implied by rubric a fourth down. (The apparent concern with organ accompaniment here means only that this kind of transposition becomes a problem needing a conscious solution only when the music is accompanied; when performing *a cappella*, choirs would just take the lower starting pitch and sing.)

Mendel makes a persuasive case, but two cautions are worth observing. First, Praetorius and Schütz were Baroque and not Renaissance musicians; the practices they illustrated were surely part of a long tradition and not innovations, and we must remember that no authentic Renaissance theorist mentions this sort of transposition at all. So it is difficult to know exactly when and where these clef-codes began to be used and how wide-spread they were at any given time in the sixteenth century. Second, even if we know that one piece was sung at organ pitch as written, and another only after being transposed down, we still do not know the standard of organ pitch in any musical institution of the Renaissance and thus cannot precisely reconstruct the pitch of any of the music.

Since Mendel's time, various attempts have been made to refine Praetorius's system further. More elaborate clef-codes, based on subtler distinctions in the clef combinations, have been proposed, notably by H. K. Andrews and David Wulstan. And indeed, there are some arguments against a too thorough application of the principle to late-sixteenth-century polyphony. A Victoria print from 1600, for example, provides 'organum' parts (actually keyboard scores to some or all of the vocal parts) for a number of sacred works that had previously appeared unaccompanied: unlike Schütz's organ accompaniments, none of these, even for pieces in high clefs, is transposed. The whole question of contemporary written accompaniments to Renaissance polyphony needs to be examined more fully in this light.

Still, the basic principle that, at least at the end of the Renaissance, music in high clefs was sometimes transposed down a third or fourth in performance seems unassailable; and it should be considered for any late-sixteenth-century piece for which no indication exists to the contrary.

Renaissance pitch today

Renaissance pitch is today a matter of practical concern for three groups: editors, who seek to translate early music into modern notation without misrepresenting its original meaning; instrument builders, who try to make new instruments that will approach the sound and feel of those played in the Renaissance; and performers, who, at their best, want to sing and play this music in a manner as faithful as possible to what they know about its original performance conditions. Ideally, of course, the three should all work together, and indeed they generally do; but their methods and purposes, their possibilities and constraints, are often quite separate.

Editors of Renaissance music have approached the problem of notated pitch in various ways over the years. Earlier in this century it was common, especially in editions designed for performance by choirs and accompanists more accustomed to music from the eighteenth and nineteenth centuries, to publish musical editions in transpositions to suit a typical SATB choir (which most often meant moving music up to fit choirs with women on the alto line). The old Byrd edition and some early issues of *Das Chorwerk* are familiar examples of this tradition, which, if it resulted in more performances of the music, did much good, and probably no real harm as long as the editors indicated the original pitch level somewhere (as most did). Transposition does, however, tend to clutter up the page with unwieldy key signatures and to make study, especially quick comparison of pieces, rather more cumbersome.

Perhaps for this reason, and because of the growing familiarity of this music to so many singers, more recent editors of scholarly and performing editions alike (if indeed that distinction is still meaningful) have tended instead to reproduce the original written pitch of a piece and allow the individual choir to transpose as it wishes. A few scholarly editions (some volumes of the new Byrd and Senfl editions, for example) have attempted to incorporate clef-codes, transposing the pieces in high clefs down and adding sharps; but on the whole, considering the questions that surround any particular clef-code, such a practice seems potentially regrettable. A happier solution, perhaps the happiest of all, has been adopted by Alan Brown in his volumes of the new Byrd edition. Brown transcribes the music at the pitch notated in the sources, but then adds a footnote to each piece suggesting, on historical grounds, a likely configuration of voices and a transposition that might bring it to something like its original sung pitch.

Makers of Renaissance instruments – or, more accurately, makers of Renaissance winds and organs, since strings can of course be tuned to various standards (within certain limits) by the player – have generally stuck to $a' = 440$. Their motive is largely economic: Renaissance players have not yet created the kind of demand for alternative pitches that Baroque players have; but beyond this, alternative pitch standards for Renaissance winds are much harder to come by and agree on. Even for a single time and place, evidence of pitch standards can conflict and baffle: Edward Tarr, for example, has measured the pitch of more than fifty curved, mute, and tenor cornetts from sixteenth-century Venice, finding As as low as 430Hz (about a quarter-tone below $a' = 440$) and as high as 496 (between B-natural and C at $a' = 440$).

There are, however, at least initial signs that the convention of tuning Renaissance instruments to $a' = 440$ may be weakening. Professional-quality cornetts and sackbuts are increasingly being made at $a' = 466$ or thereabouts (that is, a semitone above modern pitch), partly to reflect the number of surviving sixteenth- and seventeenth-century brasswinds at a slightly higher pitch, and partly because instruments at 466 can be played with Baroque instruments at 415 just by transposing down a tone. Lutenists, guitarists, harpsichordists, viol players, and so on also often have to make one instrument do for Renaissance and early Baroque music, and thus many prefer to keep their instruments at $a' = 415$ when they can. Perhaps most significantly, some builders are beginning to make exact copies, at original pitch, of surviving sixteenth-century instruments; surely this trend will continue as builders and players become more and more serious about performing pre-1600 music. The day of alternative pitch standards for Renaissance instruments is probably not far off; at the moment, however, it is hard to know exactly what those standards will be or how widely they will be applied.

Most school, church, and amateur choirs singing Renaissance polyphony today use $a' = 440$ as a starting point, if only for the convenience of using a piano or other instrument in rehearsal. Inevitably some pieces end up being transposed from there, but it is probably fair to say that most often this transposition is made not in the conscious pursuit of historical accuracy, but as a practical compromise necessary to sing the repertory comfortably with performing forces very different from those in the Renaissance (again, the most conspicuous difference is the use of mixed rather than all-male choirs). Professional vocal ensembles, many of whom have specialized in Renaissance music, tend to be constituted more with the repertory in mind, but even they sometimes transpose up or down on historical grounds, or to fit the music to the singers in the group, or in pursuit of an aesthetic ideal. The most scrupulous conductors rightly explain their approach to pitch in programme or sleeve notes.

The importance of pitch promises only to increase as our understanding and performance of Renaissance music continue to grow and improve. At the moment, however, there is no obvious choice for an alternative pitch standard paralleling the one that has developed for Baroque music, nor any easy answer to the more fundamental question of fixed and flexible pitch. So perhaps the best advice for now is caution. Flexible pitch and clef-codes have been widely accepted, and indeed both have much to recommend them in a good many cases, but they must be applied cautiously: they are all too effective as a scholarly cloak over compromise and lazy thinking.

Select bibliography

H. K. ANDREWS, 'Transposition of Byrd's vocal polyphony', *Music & Letters*, xliii (1962), pp. 25–37

R. BOWERS, 'The performing pitch of English 15th-century church polyphony', *Early Music*, viii (1980), pp. 21–8

R. BRAY, 'More light on early Tudor pitch', *Early Music*, viii (1980), pp. 35–42

H. M. BROWN, 'Notes (and transposing notes) on the viol in the early sixteenth century', in I. Fenlon (ed.) *Music in medieval and early modern Europe: patronage, sources and texts* (Cambridge, 1981), pp. 61–78; and 'Notes (and transposing notes) on the transverse flute in the early sixteenth century', *Journal of the American Musical Instrument Society*, xii (1986), pp. 5–39

D. FALLOWS, 'Specific information on the ensembles for composed polyphony, 1400–1474', in S. Boorman (ed.), *Studies in the performance of late mediaeval music* (Cambridge, 1983), pp. 109–59; and 'The performing ensembles in Josquin's sacred music', *Tijdschrift van de Vereniging voor Nederlandse Muziekgeschiedenis*, xxxv (1985), pp. 32–64

K. KREITNER, 'Very low ranges in the sacred music of Ockeghem and Tinctoris', *Early Music*, xiv (1986), pp. 467–79

A. MENDEL, 'Pitch in the 16th and early 17th centuries', *Musical Quarterly*, xxxiv (1948), pp. 28–45, 199–221, 336–57, 575–93; repr. in A. J. Ellis and A. Mendel, *Studies in the history of musical pitch* (Amsterdam, 1968), pp. 88–169; and 'Pitch in Western music since 1500: a re-examination', *Acta Musicologica*, l (1978), pp. 1–93

E. H. TARR, 'Ein Katalog erhaltener Zinken', *Basler Jahrbuch für historische Musikpraxis*, v (1981), pp. 11–262

R. WEBER, 'Some researches into pitch in the 16th century with particular reference to the instruments in the Accademia Filarmonica of Verona', *Galpin Society Journal*, xxviii (1975), pp. 7–10

D. WULSTAN, 'The problem of pitch in sixteenth-century English vocal music', *Proceedings of the Royal Musical Association*, xciii (1967), pp. 97–112

40 Is underlay necessary?

Honey Meconi

Text underlay is one of the biggest problems facing performers and editors of music before 1600. Manuscripts and prints contain texts that are often inaccurate, incomplete, or inconsistent in the different voices. More frustrating is the seeming casualness with which syllables are often aligned to pitches, especially during the fifteenth and early sixteenth centuries. Performer and editor must somehow choose a solution out of a mass of unhelpful source information, making decisions that often have a high degree of arbitrariness behind them. This essay discusses elements of that problem. Because music prior to 1400 has engendered less gnashing of teeth – music overlay is more prevalent than text underlay during this period – and because the sources are clearest in the latter half of the sixteenth century, I will concentrate on the fifteenth and early sixteenth centuries.

The modern literature on underlay is extensive. There are significant writings on each of the major early theoretical discussions; these include the anonymous Venice manuscript from the fifteenth century, Lanfranco and Vicentino (articles by Don Harrán), Zarlino (translation and commentary by Vered Cohen), Stocker (article by Edward Lowinsky; translation and commentary by Albert C. Rotola), and Luchini (article by Allan Atlas). Thoughtful discussions on general issues and specific sources have been written by numerous scholars; those by Howard Mayer Brown are particularly noteworthy. A concise summary of major precepts as well as some new ideas can be found in Timothy McGee's guide to performing early music.

Unquestionably, though, the major treatment is Don Harrán's recent book, *Word-tone relations in musical thought*. Harrán examines writings on the word-tone relationship from antiquity to the early seventeenth century, demonstrating that there was a consistent concern with proper text expression throughout this time. The book contains a huge appendix listing all the statements on word-tone relation for early music that he was able to uncover. This final appendix is subdivided into twenty-one different topic headings under which 116 rules and exceptions are listed.

The following is a culling of Harrán's appendix, and provides the twelve most frequently cited statements concerning word-tone relations.

1 Music must be accommodated to the words (30 citations: from Plato to Magone, 1615)

2 Music should follow the verbal accentuation, with stressed syllables adapted to long notes and unstressed ones to short notes (29 citations: from Augustine to Cerone, 1613)

3 Music should be ordered according to the structure of its text (27 citations: from *Commemoratio brevis*, tenth century, to Cerone, 1613)

4 One syllable should be assigned to a ligature of two or more notes (22 citations: from Amerus, 1271, to Zacconi, 1622)

5 The singer should see to articulating the text by careful breathing (13 citations: from Guido to Cerone, 1613)

6 The composer should strive for a careful alignment of pitches and syllables (12 citations: from Odington, *c.* 1300, to Magone, 1615)

7 The singer should strive for a clear and correct pronunciation (10 citations: from Rutgerus, *c.* 1500, to Praetorius, 1614/15)

8 In mensural music, all unligated notes should carry their own syllable (7 citations: from Jacques de Liège, *c.* 1340, to Tigrini, 1588)

9 The first larger note that follows a series of semiminims or smaller values ought not to carry a syllable (7 citations: from Lanfranco, 1533, to Burmeister, 1606)

10 Syllables should never be repeated in plainsong or mensural music (7 citations: from Rossetti, 1529, to Cerone, 1613)

11 Sometimes the semiminim and white note that follow a dotted minim carry their own syllables (6 citations: from Lanfranco, 1533, to Tigrini, 1588)

12 Repeats of words are forbidden in plainsong (6 citations: from *Instituta patrum,* ? twelfth century, to Cerone, 1613)

As this selection shows, statements about underlay occur over the centuries, but the most specific rules date from 1533, being found in the treatises of Lanfranco, Vicentino, Zarlino and Stocker. Paradoxically, this period of greatest information about setting words to music (or vice-versa) is also the period for which we least need such information. Music from this time was usually written with concern for textual clarity in mind, text setting is frequently syllabic, repeated notes occur often, proper accentuation is found. Though problems still exist, they are of a smaller dimension than those encountered in music of the fifteenth and early sixteenth centuries. The question then arises: are these sixteenth-century rules applicable to music from an earlier time? Can they also serve as guidelines when we perform and edit works before 1533?

Scholars have suggested a cautious 'yes' for several reasons. Sixteenth-century theorists are largely in agreement as to underlay rules, suggesting a strong tradition. It is unlikely, too, that Lanfranco was creating rules from nothing when he wrote in 1533; again, a tradition is presumed. Also, though Stocker writes of generational differences with composers and underlay rules, he states rules that are obligatory no matter what, and these go for the Josquin generation as well (and by extension, possibly earlier still). Stocker even goes so far as to say that one must improve upon the composer if the composer has been negligent in following the rules, but it is a rare editor who would accept that responsibility these days.

However, the application of sixteenth-century rules to fifteenth-century music works only up to a point. There are too many places where they simply cannot be applied. And if the theorists are of no help, assumptions that some other system must be involved are stymied by the sources. Although some are clear, most are not, and this includes sources that would have been used for performance. It also includes some of the very few items we have that seem to be autographs – several Pietrequin pieces and the Isaac 'de manu sua' compositions in Berlin, Staatsbibliothek Preußischer Kulturbesitz, Mus. MS 40021. Nor do sources whose scribes must have had considerable musical knowledge fare any better. Indeed, manuscripts sent throughout Europe from the scriptorium used by the Habsburg-Burgundian court show considerable variety in their texting and underlay practices, suggesting either, again, considerable leeway in what was acceptable, or, perhaps more intriguing, the possibility of differing practices in different parts of Europe. This last suggestion is one that well deserves exploring; indeed, Stocker implies the existence of a wide variety of texting practices in the objections he presumes would be raised against his rules.

The lack of consistency in the underlay practices of early manuscripts, combined with the problems of applying sixteenth-century rules, would suggest that there was a wide variety of acceptable practices, brought to fruition by the individual performers. The switch from music overlay to text underlay may have hastened the advent of the singer's responsibility. With text underlay, extra care would be needed to ensure a word-tone match, and most scribes did not take the trouble. We have probably also underestimated the abilities of early singers. Trained from childhood in, relatively speaking, a small number of musical styles, they must have been the most phenomenal sight-readers the vocal profession has ever known. Texts such as the Mass Ordinary, Magnificat, Marian antiphons and dozens of others would have been learnt by heart at an early age. Various types of secular music, especially chansons based on repetition schemes, were probably performed from memory since so little music is actually involved (iconography depicting people playing from music may reflect amateur rather than professional performance). Their minds must have been free to encounter and handle easily the 'problems' of text underlay, and the sources reflect a prevailing confidence that the performers could do it on their own.

The point is sometimes raised that the inherent problems of imitative counterpoint prevented composers from solving problems of text declamation, and that it remained for later generations (specifically that of Willaert) to deal with declamation (with its concurrent ease of underlay), counterpoint having been mastered. This surely does earlier composers a considerable disservice. First, there are several areas of composition where homophony and syllabic texting are the norm; these include certain secular genres as well as rather less important sacred ones. Clearly composers were capable of writing in a style where underlay would present no problem; for the most part during this period they chose not to.

Second, theorists are silent about the fine points of underlay prior to 1533, indicating that it was not of great importance to them, at least as far as composition was concerned. They wrote about what concerned them; we must conclude that underlay did not. In addition we must remember that theorists also functioned to some extent as critics at that time. They named names, they praised specific pieces of music, they slapped composers on the wrist for perceived infractions of the rules. But it is the writers of the sixteenth century who complain about underlay, not those of the fifteenth.

Composers must have been happy with the underlay options available to them or they would have done something about it. Imprecise underlay is not the result of a notational system that cannot express it, in the way that, say, duple metre was before the fourteenth century. But this is not to say that composers were unconcerned with text; rather it is that their concern manifested itself not in 'proper' text underlay and declamation, but in ways different from those valued by the sixteenth century. One only has to look at *forme-fixe* chansons to see overall formal structure – and usually phrasing as well – completely dominated by the text. And one should point out that changes in what was acceptable regarding word-tone relations also occurred throughout the sixteenth century. Josquin, originally hailed as the master in this respect, was soon considered old school, displaced by Willaert and others more 'sensitive'. Eventually anything that smacked of polyphony at all was intolerable to the late sixteenth-century textual avant-garde.

What were the reasons for the increasing concern with text underlay? The intellectual and educational trend of humanism has long been cited in this regard. The concern with Greek *ethos* and the remarkable powers of music was linked with the idea that only with proper text declamation could these powers unfold. There was an enormous interest in all aspects of language, beginning with the restoration of pure classical Latin and extending to the vernacular as well (it is the sixteenth century, after all, that sees the institution of the Académie Française). The rediscovery of Aristotle's *Poetics* made the doctrine of *imitazione della natura*, with its resulting musical stress on the representation of speech, of great importance.

But other factors figured as well. Words – and their musical settings – played a role in the religious battles that scarred the sixteenth century, and both sides became greatly concerned with delivery of their message. In the secular realm at least, the fifteenth-century practice of incorporating popular melodies (always textually more representative of speech) into art works helped lead to a new musical syntax. At the same time composers were moving towards exerting more control over their products, establishing to a greater degree than ever before invariable elements of their music – in anticipation, conscious or not, of times when they might no longer be involved in its performance. The underlay of text became one of these elements.

It is important to realize that in our investigations of underlay we have, to a large extent, been labouring under two assumptions. First, we have generally accepted the sixteenth-century textual polemic about precise underlay being better than imprecise underlay: that music is indeed the servant of the text. This is an age-old battle, but deciding in favour of text over music is not much use if we are dealing with a time when either music was more important to the composers or they felt that text was being handled adequately with the methods they used. We should not adopt without question the idea that texting that conforms to humanistic ideas about declamation is somehow better or more musical. Looking at the music written before Lanfranco, we must conclude that composers often preferred melismatic to syllabic settings, moving melodies to repeated notes, polyphony to homophony. We must remember that we are dealing with an art, not a science, and that the eradication of imprecise text underlay is not the equivalent of the eradication of smallpox. There are many ways to convey the meaning of the text, precise underlay being only one of them. Music has its own powers; it is not necessarily dependent on text to move the emotions. Text at times must surely have functioned only as a foil for musical interplay.

Tied in with this first assumption is the one that there is a single solution to the problem of text underlay in any given piece, if only we could find it. Naturally, as performers and editors we are forced to make a single solution, but this does not mean that we should acquiesce in this assumption. Instead of asking what the 'correct' underlay for a piece might be, we should ask what options the performer would have had. We would probably be better off to consider underlay – especially in music performed by soloists, which may have been most of it – as one of the factors least capable of being pinned down in contemporary performance, and hence more akin to tempo, articulation, performing pitch, and dynamics than to musica ficta. In short, it was an element that was likely to vary with each performance.

With this in mind, let us consider the list of questions that a twentieth-century performer might ask when determining underlay for a piece:

1 How many lines of the piece are to be performed? (We cannot assume that all available parts were always performed in pre-1600 music, and we should experiment with smaller combinations.)

2 Which lines will be performed vocally? instrumentally? both?

3 If using instruments, which ones (and how many) will be used?

4 Will lines be sung by men, women, or boys?

5 How many voices will sing each line?

6 What will be sung: vowel sound? If so, which? solmization syllables? text? text of pre-existent material?

7 Will any portions of music be repeated with different text?

8 How will the text be pronounced? Will Latin be performed with a regional accent? What region? That of the composer's birth, the place of residence when the work was written, or the origin or destination of the source?

9 At what pitch will the piece be performed?

10 How will the underlay sound with the voice characteristics of the individual performers being used?

11 Will simultaneity of vowel sound be sought? (This vastly aids intonation; its possibility or even desirability must be determined.)

12 Where will the piece be performed? In what acoustic?

This list may seem excessive, but all of these factors can affect vocal timbre, volume, and clarity, and thus underlay. Such a list in effect undermines the authority of the editor, for it is impossible for any editor other than one working with a single specific performance in mind to be able to foresee the answers to the above questions. In a way, these questions are those that would have informed contemporary performances of this music, though the options available to early performers – or perhaps one should say the options acceptable to early performers – may well have been more restricted or more apparent to them than our options today.

All of this suggests that we should retain great flexibility in our approach to underlay, since it is likely that contemporary performers did so as well. It also suggests we should adopt a greater sense of experimentation. The criteria most often cited for acceptability of underlay – the matching of declamation and musicality – are rather too restrictive. We have already discussed how declamation was apparently less of a concern pre-Lanfranco than afterwards, and 'the most musical solution' to a given problem is a matter of great subjectivity. In addition, it is far from clear that composers were always striving for the greatest musicality (whatever that would mean) in any given piece. Many pieces must have been written as experiments, as curiosities, to solve problems, to be amusing or intentionally different. Many composers – and 'audiences' of the time – must have found the intellectual, the cerebral, to be very stimulating and emotionally exciting, just as many of us do now. In short, the degree of experimentation in applying underlay should match that of the fifteenth century. This is not to say that anarchy should prevail – sixteenth-century rules do make a good starting place – but rather to conclude that for many pieces a variety of different underlays would have been acceptable.

In addition to flexibility in the placement of underlay, flexibility in what goes under the notes is worth investigating. The current practice of vocalizing many parts previously assumed to be instrumental has taken its impetus from iconographical and archival evidence, but there is perhaps some theoretical evidence as well, specifically that provided in Gaffurius's treatise *Practica musicae* (1496). Here he divides vocal music into three types: singing with solmization syllables (the preferred way for instructing children), singing without text (easily done by skilled singers) and singing with words, the desired goal of the best singers. These divisions are quoted by Stocker late in the next century. There is no particular need to mention the second style unless it was used; hence, we should assume some practice of vocalizing in performances of music.

It might also be worth while to experiment with the use of solmization syllables. Singers certainly used them to learn music, and Stocker even says that some musicians (imperfect ones) are content with solmization. Indeed, there is a rather tangential instance of the use of solmization in the twentieth century that suggests that it might be satisfying in earlier music as well: the American tradition of 'shape-note' singing, alive today in parts of the rural south and mid-west of the United States.

The term 'shape-note' singing (sometimes called 'Sacred Harp' singing) refers to the use of other shapes in addition to ovals as noteheads; the choice of shape determines what solmization syllable (and hence pitch) will be sung for that note. The system originated at the very close of the eighteenth century as a means of spreading musical literacy and was very successful to this end. The music for which this system is used is non-denominational, non-liturgical, Christian devotional music, performed entirely *a cappella*. Texted performances of these pieces are normally preceded by a rendition using the solmization syllables only. Perhaps surprisingly, it is a very appealing practice.

Although this system is not directly connected with European music before 1600, there are some curious parallels between the two systems, as well as one significant chronological tie. An early version of the shape-note system simply used the syllables themselves rather than notes, reminiscent of early medieval notational practices. This was followed by a diastematic version of the shape notes, and then by use of a staff. Much of the repertory originated with a three-voice texture (STB) that was then modernized by the addition of an alto voice, thus repeating the historical procedure of the fifteenth-century chanson. Texts are spread out among the four parts (in other words, to perform the text singers must look at both their own and others' parts). Pitch is given by an elder male singer without reference to any instrument or pitch standard.

The chronological tie to earlier music is perhaps a significant one. Although the particular solmization practice associated with 'shape-note' singing was not connected to it until just before 1800, the practice itself is derived from European systems as is, to some extent, the repertory. This is because the repertory sung today is built on a foundation of eighteenth-century American music from New

England, which in turn grew from music brought over with the earliest settlers as well as music imported while America was still a British colony. In other words, some of this music was being sung more than two hundred years ago, and there is a real possibility that aspects of its performance practice, including vocal traditions, may be unchanged since that time or even earlier. This music, though dominant in New England in the eighteenth century, was chased into the backwoods with the beginnings of America's cultural inferiority complex and concurrent importation of Handel, Haydn, and other European art composers. Consequently the music represents an art music requiring musical literacy preserved in an essentially rural culture of probably significant performance stability. It is possible, then, that study of its practices may suggest ideas about the performance of pre-1600 European art music.

One last thought. I have tried to argue that in what is considered the most problematic period, the problems lie more with our desire for finality than with the nature of the music and the underlay itself. Though a certain type of underlay can be notated with great precision, underlay that was flexible in its original conception cannot be. In that sense, early sources were technologically deficient, and our notational system remains so today. Overcoming this deficiency would probably have to involve both the third and the fourth dimensions, so it may be a while before this problem is solved. Yet we currently have almost everything we need to liberate ourselves from the tyranny of editing. Computer music programmes exist today that, in addition to creating beautiful scores of pre-1600 music, can change underlay (and musica ficta, and performing pitch, and so on) with great ease. What is needed now is for music intended for performance to be disseminated on disk, which could then be experimented with and altered with little effort, generating performances where underlay can be fitted to as many different variables as possible. And this, one suspects, is not so very far in the future.

Select bibliography

Specific theorists

Anonymous, c. 1440: D. HARRÁN, 'In pursuit of origins: the earliest writing on text underlay (*c.* 1440)', *Acta Musicologica*, l (1978), pp. 217–40

Gaffurius, 1496: F. GAFFURIUS, *Practica musicae*, trans. C. A. Miller (American Institute of Musicology, 1968)

Lanfranco, 1533: D. HARRÁN, 'New light on the question of text underlay prior to Zarlino', *Acta Musicologica*, xlv (1973), pp. 24–56

Del Lago, 1541: D. HARRÁN, 'The theorist Giovanni del Lago: a new view of the man and his writings', *Musica Disciplina*, xxvii (1973), pp. 107–51

Vicentino, 1555: D. HARRÁN, 'Vicentino and his rules of text underlay', *Musical Quarterly*, lix (1973), pp. 620–32

Zarlino, 1558: G. ZARLINO, 'On the modes': Part Four of *Le Istitutioni Harmoniche*, trans. V. Cohen (New Haven, 1983)

Stocker, c. 1570–80: G. STOQUERUS, *De musica verbali libri duo: two books on verbal music*, trans. A. C. Rotola (Lincoln, Nebraska, 1988); and E. E. LOWINSKY, 'A treatise on text underlay by a German disciple of Francisco de Salinas', in *Festschrift Heinrich Besseler zum Sechzigsten Geburtstag* (Leipzig, 1961), pp. 231–51

Luchini, c. 1588–98: A. ATLAS, 'Paolo Luchini's *Della Musica*: a little-known source for text underlay from the late sixteenth century', *Journal of Musicology*, ii (1983), pp. 62–80

General

H. M. BROWN, *A Florentine chansonnier from the time of Lorenzo the Magnificent* (Chicago, 1983), I, pp. 168–80; and 'Words and music in early sixteenth-century chansons: text underlay in Florence, Biblioteca del Conservatorio, Ms Basevi 2442', in L. Finscher (ed.), *Formen und Probleme der Überlieferung mehrstimmiger Musik im Zeitalter Josquins Desprez* (Munich, 1981), pp. 97–141

D. HARRÁN, *Word-tone relations in musical thought from antiquity to the seventeenth century* (American Institute of Musicology, 1986)

E. E. LOWINSKY, *The Medici Codex of 1518* (Chicago, 1968), I, pp. 90–107

T. J. MCGEE, *Medieval and Renaissance music: a performer's guide* (Toronto, 1985)

L. L. PERKINS, *The Mellon Chansonnier* (New Haven, 1979), I, pp. 137–48; and 'Toward a rational approach to text placement in the secular music of Dufay's time', in A. Atlas (ed.), *Papers read at the Dufay Quincentenary Conference, Brooklyn College, December 6–7, 1974* (Brooklyn, NY, 1976), pp. 102–14

J. RAHN, 'Text underlay in French monophonic song', *Current Musicology*, xxiv (1977), pp. 63–79

F. TIRRO, 'La stesura del testo nei manoscritti di Giovanni Spataro', *Rivista Italiana di Musicologia*, xv (1980), pp. 31–70

41 Restored pronunciation for the performance of vocal music

Alison Wray

Many a Pandora's box has been opened in the pursuit of an approach to music performance that is sensitive to the origins of the piece. The one labelled 'reconstructed pronunciation' has been conveniently ignored by most until recently, and even now its lid is being lifted only very cautiously. Most people recognize that once you commit yourself to some new facet of the art, you cannot easily justify going back, and reconstructed pronunciation is arguably one of the heaviest burdens that a group of singers could take up, both because of the inherent complexity of the whole subject and because they must rely on others to provide the information they need. Pronunciation is not simply the extension of some area covered in a general musical education, such as ornamentation and bowing technique are, but is a speciality within an entirely separate discipline. Or rather, it is a whole set of specialities, for a scholar of the history of English pronunciation will not necessarily be a specialist in the history of German or Italian.

In the following account a brief overview of the history of English pronunciation will be used to provide a background against which arguments for and against reconstruction can be explored.

Languages change . . .

It seems to be a characteristic of all human languages that they change across time. There does not appear to be a single and simple explanation for why they change, though certain things are known to contribute. One of the most important is the fact that language plays a significant role in our social identity. We modify our speech, particularly our pronunciation, but also our vocabulary and grammar, to match that of the group to which we wish to belong. In Britain, where accent is a major indicator of class, there are many situations in which your pronunciation may let you down and isolate you, whether because it is considered too common or too posh.

Usually languages change slowly. But sometimes a small change can trigger others in quick succession, until the sum effect is a very large alteration to the language in a relatively short space of time. This is what happened to the pronunciation of the English language in the period from about 1400 to 1650 in a linguistic event normally referred to as the Great Vowel Shift. There were also changes to English grammar and vocabulary, but these are not central to this discussion. Some linguists have suggested that the Great Vowel Shift was triggered by the emergence of the middle class as a powerful force in politics and commerce. The way to get on would be to speak like a merchant from East Anglia, whereas before it was to speak like an earl at the royal court.

Once the equilibrium is upset, change occurs naturally in the next generation. Adults often are not entirely successful in picking up new accents and so their children grow up hearing a hybrid of two sets of sounds, which do not necessarily fit together properly. In the course of acquiring the language the child's brain will edit the sounds into one set, thus producing a version of the language subtly different from anything spoken by the parents.

The Great Vowel Shift in English (*c.* 1400–1650)

The Great Vowel Shift affected the long vowels and the diphthongs of English in stressed position. The changes to the short vowels and the unstressed ones were minimal. During and after the period of the Shift there were also some small but noticeable alterations to a few consonants. For example, r ceased to be pronounced in some positions – it used to be sounded twice in 'FARMER'; -gh in words like 'THOUGH' and 'BOUGH' which used to be pronounced like the -ch in 'LOCH' became silent, as did, later, the g on the front of 'GNAW' and the k on the front of 'KNIGHT'.

The Great Vowel Shift was precisely what it says – a shift around the mouth by the vowels. According to one theory, some time during the fifteenth century just two of the vowels, [i:] (as in a careful pronunciation of our modern word 'BLEED') and [u:] (as in a careful pronunciation of our modern word 'SOON'), moved from their positions by turning into the diphthongs [əi] and [əu]. [əi] is approximately the sound you get if you take the 'p' and the 'c' out of 'PERCY'. [əu] is the sound in the current standard (southern) English pronunciation of 'KNOW' and 'STONE'.

This change affected words like 'SIDE' and 'HOUSE': 'SIDE' had been pronounced like our modern word 'SEED' but now it became [səid]. 'HOUSE', which had rhymed with our modern pronunciation of 'MOOSE' became [həus]. This meant that the sounds [i:] and [u:] now occurred in few, if any, words. When sounds as useful as these two are not being used very much, there is a tendency for other sounds to modify towards them. At the time when 'SIDE' was pronounced [si:d], the word 'SEED' was pronounced [se:d] (with a vowel like French é, or to put it another way, rhyming with the modern Scottish pronunciation of 'STAYED'). But when 'SIDE' changed from [si:d] to [səid] there was no longer any reason to stop 'SEED' drifting into the space it left behind, sounding more and more like [si:d] (as indeed it does today) – there was no danger of misunderstanding, because [si:d] no longer had any other meaning.

So the next thing that happened after [i:] and [u:] became [əi] and [əu] was that [e:] became [i:], and [o:], the corresponding vowel made at the back of the mouth (pronounced like the sound in the French word 'BEAU' or the Scottish pronunciation of 'ROPE'), became [u:]. By this process 'MOVE' changed to its present pronunciation from one in which it had approximately rhymed with modern Scottish 'STOVE'. This in its turn left spaces where [e:] and [o:] had been, and into those spaces eventually moved the next vowels down, [ɛ:] and [ɔ:], so that 'STEAM', which had had a vowel rather like the one in modern 'STARE', developed the one in Scottish 'STAYED', and 'BOAT' changed from sounding rather like modern 'BOUGHT' to having the vowel of French 'BEAU' and Scottish 'STOVE'. And so it went on.

Working across that basic pattern were various other forces that caused groups of words to break away from their main category, either not moving so far, or moving further, or in a different direction. Most often the determining factor in this was some preceding or following consonant that prevented the normal moves and maybe instigated others. For example, whilst the pronunciation of the short vowel in 'HAT' and 'MAN' changed very little, where an L plus another consonant followed, it became, ultimately, [ɔ:] (e.g. 'CHALK,' 'MALT', 'ALL'), or [ɑ:] (e.g. 'CALM', 'HALF'). Where a nasal vowel followed, it developed to modern [ei] (e.g. 'ANCIENT, 'FLAME') or [ɑ:] (e.g. 'CHANT', 'EXAMPLE'). A preceding W or QU changed it to [ʋ] (e.g. 'WARRANT', 'SWAN', 'QUARREL', 'QUALITY') unless a G, (C)K, NG or X followed the vowel (e.g. 'QUACK', 'WAX', 'WAG', 'TWANG'), and so on.

'The' pronunciation

The Great Vowel Shift was complex, that is clear; but it may seem that a reasonable amount of diligent work could access the pronunciation for a given date. However, there is a considerable problem in searching for 'the' pronunciation. If languages change according to the mechanisms described earlier, then it is evident that on any one day during the period of the Great Vowel Shift you could have heard different pronunciations of a word even amongst 'standard' English speakers, according to whether you talked to an adult or to his grandchild, to a merchant, a baron or a farm labourer, to a lawyer educated at Eton and Cambridge or his clerk who had been educated locally, to a native of Sussex, Herefordshire or Yorkshire, and so on. Writers of the time, who composed rhyming poetry, lists of homophones, commentaries on the pronunciation of the language (for various purposes) and other works of considerable use to us today, demonstrate by their failure to agree with one another just how differently from each other people were speaking across the length and breadth of Britain and from one generation to the next. The 'orthoepists', that is, those writers whose interest was in the 'Art of Pronunciation', attempted to contrast the 'degenerate' speech of those around them with what they considered to be more correct; but their own speech too was a mixture of old and new forms, and their target, 'correct English', was a moving one.

Whose pronunciation is it?

The question we need to ask in relation to reconstructing pronunciation for a song text is, therefore, whose pronunciation is it to be? We might aim for the pronunciation used by the first singer or group of singers. Perhaps it is recorded that they came from Devon, or from Northumberland. If so, we could aim to include aspects of the appropriate regionalisms for that time. But supposing the composer did not intend his work to be given its first performance by those singers, and shuddered every time they pronounced a word in their regional way? Should not the desires and intentions of the composer be taken into account? Arguably, the pronunciation to which a composer sets his music is the one he uses himself, the one he mutters under his breath as he constructs the piece. So, would it not be valid to aim for his speech, including his own Northamptonshire or Kentish twang? This too can cause problems if taken to its logical conclusion. Handel must have muttered the words of *Messiah* to himself as he composed it, but he surely did not intend his singers to reproduce his German accent. The middle road is to hypothesize about what range of pronunciations the composer would have considered acceptable. Insofar as a composer had fairly average pronunciation for his age and place of residence, that range should comprise of a selection of sounds that co-existed at the given date and which, in certain combinations, would provide plausible pronunciations for ordinary, reasonably educated individuals. That is, pronunciations that *could* have existed at the time, and which, had they been heard, would have seemed quite unremarkable because they fell within the range of what people heard around them every day.

Plausibility

The key to reconstruction, then, if we are to be practical about it, is *plausibility*, and the key to plausibility is the correct *selection* of sound combinations from the range we know to have existed at any given time. To make that selection, it is necessary to understand the structure of the English sound system as a whole, the way in which the Great Vowel Shift operated within it, which sound changes caused which new ones, the mechanisms by which alien sounds such as regionalisms infiltrated the standard language and became popular, and the reaction that the brain of the child and adult has to a set of sounds that do not fit together properly. To whatever extent our knowledge of these things is still incomplete, our reconstructions run the risk of missing being entirely plausible.

Where do we get the information from?

We are fortunate that during the period from about 1500 onwards many people wrote about the pronunciation of English. The Scolar Press has reissued a considerable number of these texts in facsimile. However, these books are rather difficult to follow and tend not to agree with one another, each author reflecting a slightly different experience of and attitude towards the changing language. Nevertheless, they are the most valuable resource we have. A number of modern scholars have studied the works closely and written detailed commentaries upon them. It is from these books that we can most easily see the range of sounds that appear to have been current at any given time. The work that is generally considered the most detailed and authoritative is Dobson's *English pronunciation 1500–1700*. Even from this, though, it is not easy to deduce plausible pronunciation sets, as it so carefully details what is very complex information. For the foreseeable future, the reconstruction of pronunciation in a less than haphazard way must remain the domain of the linguistic expert.

Other languages

Although English is unusual in having changed quite so much since the fourteenth century, all languages have changed to some extent. Besides the overall tendency of the sounds, grammar and vocabulary of any language to alter gradually over an extended period of time, we see, in many cases, one dialect gain, in the course of political changes, a high status in relation to others. Where this has happened, it may be inappropriate to reconstruct earlier versions of the modern standard language. This is the case with Italian. The states of Italy were not united into one kingdom until 1861; 'standard' Italian dates only from this time, when one dialect, that of the educated in Tuscany, was selected for that purpose. It was, admittedly, already of high status as the preferred literary language, but only two *per cent* of the population actually spoke it! The rest spoke other dialects, some quite unintelligible to a Tuscan speaker. In Monteverdi's day, some 250 years earlier, Tuscan Italian, though already admired as the language of the great writer Dante, would not have held any real sway amongst the singers in Mantua and Venice. To reconstruct pronunciation for cities other than the Tuscan capital Florence, then, requires an understanding of the history of what are now considered 'non-standard' dialects.

The most complicated story, however, relates to the pronunciation of Latin. Ever since the days of the extended Roman Empire the pronunciation of the Latin language has been subject to considerable variation from one location to another. Latin had been around so long and was so central to the administration and religion of the European countries that it took on, in its pronunciation, the characteristics of the native language around it. The effect of this is most marked in England, for the Great Vowel Shift changed not only the vowels of English but of English Latin too. This is how the word 'PISCES', to take one example, changed from [piːseːs] to modern [paisiːz]: as described earlier, [iː] diphthongized to [əi] and later to [ai], and [eː] moved up into the space of [iː]. In France, Italy, Spain and Germany Latin was also pronounced according to the rules of its host language, or rather, the rules of the appropriate local dialects of these languages.

Superimposed upon the so-called 'vernacular pronunciations' of Latin was an increasing body of knowledge about the way Latin had been pronounced in the Classical period, and various scholars tried to replace the use of the first with the second. In Britain this ultimately succeeded in the classroom in the late nineteenth century, and around the same time the Italianate pronunciation of Latin began to gain popularity in church contexts. The effect of these changes was that the old vernacular pronunciation of Latin all but died out. When we seek to reconstruct the pronunciation of, say, Byrd's Latin texts, then, we need to recognize that we are not looking for some earlier version of Italianate Latin, nor yet anything related to the Classical pronunciation. Rather, we have to contend with a system to which most of us today are totally unaccustomed. Being based on the vernacular, the rules of that system in their own right must be combined with what we know about the changing vowels of English itself at that time.

Singing the speech

A number of issues arise in relation to the differences between singing and speech. Firstly, the information that we have about pronunciation in the past is almost always a commentary on speech, not singing. The sounds used in singing may have been different both for reasons of vocal production and acoustics and because of fashions and traditions. Not only have those fashions changed over the years, but so also have approaches to singing technique. Because of these factors we cannot be sure that even the most plausible of reconstructions for speech is accurate for the sung medium, nor that if we modify the vowels according to modern technical practices in singing, that we shall automatically imitate the singers of previous centuries.

Any new language will require some getting used to, if it has sounds that do not occur in the singer's native language. Vowels which the singers have never had to use before have to be fitted somehow into their production technique – in the English of Dowland and Tomkins a way has to be found of singing the first element of the diphthongs [əi] and [əu], perhaps for a minim, so that it both sounds convincing and does not compromise the timbre of the voice anywhere in its range. When you are singing in a new modern foreign language you can at least ask native speakers for their opinion of how to sing the sounds and, even better, listen to native speaker singers doing it themselves. But where extinct pronunciations are concerned we must rely on our own ears much more. At their first encounter with reconstructed pronunciation singers often find that the tuning suffers, particularly if the language demands a very forward, bright production, as with Spanish Latin.

Sometimes the use of a plausible system of sounds for speech is undermined by the texts of the songs and it is necessary to permit a little variation. In a madrigal by Thomas Tomkins, published in 1622, we find the rhyming of the two words 'eyes' and 'contraries'. We know that 'eyes' was pronounced with the diphthong [əi] that had developed from [i:] in Middle English, and so we can be sure that the last syllable of 'contraries' had the same sound. However, in another madrigal by Tomkins published in the same year the two words 'harmony' and 'agree' are rhymed. We know that 'agree' had the sound [i:], regularly developed from the [e:] of Middle English, so 'harmony' must also end with [i:], as it does today. What could cause the final syllable of 'contrary' (to switch to the singular) to be different to that of 'harmony'? Both have three syllables and both had stress on the first syllable and (here at least) secondary stress on the third. The answer is, most probably, that they were *not* different, but both had two quite acceptable pronunciations, with [əi] or [i:]. Simply, in one madrigal one pronunciation has been used and in the other text the other pronunciation. What is at fault, then, is a reconstruction that picks, for the sake of consistency, only one pronunciation or the other, working on the basis that any given individual would have a tendency to prefer one of them in speech. It is not this assumption that is necessarily false, but the attempt to transfer a plausible norm for everyday speech into a medium which uses non-spontaneous language.

Is it valid to use old pronunciations?

Reconstructed pronunciation is still novel and in many ways contentious. The issue of its validity is a complex one, and each person will come to different conclusions, but it is perhaps worth exploring some of the arguments that can be put forward on each side.

Firstly, the purpose of reconstruction is to bring us into closer touch with the original intentions of the composer and to give us an insight into what he may have heard when the piece was first performed. But as we have seen, we have no means of recreating the pronunciation of any given individual (unless it be one of the contemporary writers who has described his own speech). There was far too much variation in pronunciation for us to home in accurately on one person, even if we know his age, class, birthplace and attitudes.

However, we can recreate what is *plausible*, and that is surely enough. It aligns with what a hypothetical singer might have done without anyone thinking his pronunciation was in the least bit odd. This is no less than what we aim for when performing in a modern foreign language: we do not aim to sound exactly like some other person, just to pronounce the language in such a way that we fall within the range of variation covered by native speakers. If all the sounds we make fit into a single system, then no single one will stand out and make the whole of it sound implausible.

Nevertheless, the very aim of reconstructing pronunciation for vocal music can be challenged, with a dimension to the argument that does not exist for instrumental music. Words are not like crotchets and quavers, even though the pursuit of information about how to pronounce them is comparable to that of how to attack a note and how long to hold it. Words convey meaning in a much narrower and pre-determined sense than music does. The text of a song not only creates an auditory effect, but is made up of meaningful words which link to convey specific ideas. Instrumental music, while it may convey one emotion to one person and another to another, is accessible to all. Words, on the other hand, express ideas with far less scope for variation and mean nothing at all if we cannot recognize and make sense of them. If you use a reconstructed pronunciation that is so unlike the modern language as to be incomprehensible, the meaning conveyed by the words is lost. Thus, in the attempt to recreate the sounds that the first audience heard we may sacrifice a significant aspect of the impact that the work had on them, namely the ideas that the words conveyed. The same is, of course, true of singing in modern foreign languages. Unless we have considerable ability in a language, listening to the original texts separates us from the meaning. On the other hand, listening to a translation destroys the relationship between the words and music, often so intrinsic to the composition.

Of course, some song texts are little more than vehicles for the music, and are not full of profound ideas. It is, perhaps, easier to justify using a reconstructed pronunciation for these than for works the text of which is of important religious significance, is humorous or expresses complex ideas of some other kind. Much depends upon whether a given modern performance of the music is intended to communicate at the text level with the audience, or to give them a live demonstration of the piece as it may have sounded originally.

But, one might argue, the question of total incomprehensibility does not apply, in the most part, to music of only three or four hundred years ago. Once one's ear has become accustomed to it, it is, even in the case of English, no more alien than a reasonably strong regional accent. However, this may be the most alienating aspect of all for the audience. In order to take in ideas efficiently when we listen to speech, we must avoid getting distracted by the 'packaging' they come in. Once you start listening to how a Brummie's accent actually operates, you will be considerably less efficient at taking in what he is saying. There is a danger that a listener will focus on the sounds of the reconstructed pronunciation and fail to decode the words into the ideas they convey. On the other hand, it is not at all clear whether audiences usually bother to decode songwords anyway.

It is clear, then, that there is not only no single reliable way of reconstructing pronunciation for music from earlier centuries, but also that some people may not even consider it a valid thing to be doing. But there is no need for polarization. Few of those who choose not to use reconstructed pronunciation themselves would be short-sighted enough to claim that there is nothing to learn about the music by knowing about it. And those who do use it would, one hopes, do so only when there are good reasons to justify it and when it is not going to be detrimental to the audience's ability to appreciate the music. Ideally, then, research into old pronunciations should open doors, making more options available to the singers, without cornering them into the 'trap' of authenticity at any cost.

Select bibliography

Interested readers are referred to the considerable body of general and specific texts by linguists on language change and the history of European languages, a few examples of which are listed below. Dobson is by far the most detailed account of Early Modern English pronunciation; Copeman is unique both in the breadth of its coverage and in being written with musicians in mind.

Language change

J. AITCHISON, *Language change – progress or decay?* (London, 1981)
C. BARBER, *The story of language*, 2nd edn (London, 1972)

History of English pronunciation

C. BARBER, *Early modern English* (London, 1976)
A. C. BAUGH and T. CABLE, *A history of the English language*, 3rd edn (New York, 1989)
E. J. DOBSON, *English pronunciation 1500–1700*, 2nd edn (Oxford, 1968)
E. EKWALL, *A history of modern English sounds and morphology*, trans. & ed. A. Ward (Oxford, 1975)

The pronunciation of Latin

H. COPEMAN, *Singing in Latin* (Oxford, 1990)
F. BRITTAIN, *Latin in church* (London, 1955)

42 Finding the right context: where to perform early music

Jan Nuchelmans

It is usually through reproductions of paintings that we become familiar with them. The originals can often still be seen in museums and collections, and even if it requires a considerable amount of travel, we can, if we really want to, see the original painting. We hear music only through 'reproduction': the original piece exists in the composer's head alone. Music is given to us in a mute, non-sounding format through notation – itself a kind of reproduction. As many an art-lover will know, the quality of art reproductions is sometimes very poor, but this is something we can establish only if we have the opportunity to compare the reproduction with the original. As far as music – and particularly music from before 1600 – is concerned, the situation is much worse: so many decisions have to be taken before we can reproduce what we believe to have been the composer's intentions that the risk of distortion or discolouration is considerable.

With the increasing interaction between organologists, instrument makers, scholars and performers, all weighing the evidence, evolving and evaluating, we draw ever nearer to the supposed truth. A persistent search for the truth will undoubtedly bring us gradually closer to it: sounds and colours from the past are awoken from an apparently eternal sleep, the details of the Middle Ages and Renaissance begin to fill out. With the ever-increasing amount of information gathered over the last few decades, certain distortions have been corrected. Medieval music is unlikely to be played on 'modern' instruments, and the Renaissance violin is gradually being used more and more in music from around 1600, but how many Renaissance instruments are still used to perform medieval music? What happens in such cases is comparable to the restoration of a fresco with the aid of oil-paint: using the wrong raw material changes the colour of the original.

Although we have already travelled some way down the road of period performance practice, there is one respect in which we seem to have become stuck. In the same concert hall we hear one day Machaut's Mass, the next Stravinsky's *Le Sacre du Printemps*, and we seldom question whether such uniform treatment in terms of acoustic and ambiance is desirable. Of course, we often have no choice. But it cannot be denied that the influence of the physical setting is one of the decisive factors in the final result. Here, too, colours are changed. (The acoustic problem is not limited to medieval and Renaissance music: to perform a Monteverdi opera in a church will make it difficult to hear the words; to listen to his Vespers of 1610 in the concert hall will iron out many of its most powerful sound effects.)

This brief article can consider only a few aspects of the question of performing space; it would be impossible in this context to give directions for the whole of the vast and multi-coloured repertory of the Middle Ages and Renaissance. I shall concentrate on the questions raised by music performed in church, in private houses and palaces, leaving to one side, for the present, music played outside or in the theatre.

In many cases, a concert location cannot be chosen: it is simply there. But sometimes, as happens at the larger festivals, it is possible to choose between several locations. When public interest is likely to be limited (for example, in remote areas, when several concerts are being given simultaneously or with very specialist repertory), a small space will be sufficient. If public attendance is high (for instance, at a festival where 'festival fever' tends to attract bigger audiences than for isolated concerts), a larger location will be needed. In this case, that will usually be a nineteenth- or twentieth-century concert hall.

Modern halls have many advantages, for they are built to offer the audience an ideal environment for listening to music: the chairs are comfortable; the musicians can be clearly seen and heard; food and drinks can be bought; access for the disabled may be guaranteed; heating, air-conditioning, toilet facilities are all provided; and they can hold large, ticket-holding audiences. Historical buildings, on the other hand, often lack most of these advantages. Think, for example, of an old castle, deep in the country. Access is poor, staircases are built to suit our smaller ancestors, the temperature is below our norm, or the fire in the grate disturbs the sound of the lutes and viols – and maybe our concentration.

The atmosphere of an old building is certainly not to be despised, but how far can we be sure that the repertory performed corresponds to what was originally heard there? Do medieval motets sound better in a seventeenth-century house on a Dutch canal than in a modern concert hall? Does Bach sound better in a medieval castle or a nineteenth-century building? In short, should we look for historically correct locations for every single repertory? What do we do with a programme that combines Ars subtilior motets before the interval with sixteenth-century songs after it? Or perhaps such programming should be considered old-fashioned and no longer acceptable.

But is there a town that can boast a variety of locations from all these different periods? Shall we ever be 'authentic' to such a degree that we play thirteenth-century music exclusively in thirteenth-century buildings? If we follow this idea through to its logical end, in future Bach's Passions could only be performed in Leipzig, Perotinus's organa in Paris and Landini would not be heard anywhere outside Florence. The experience could, of course, be recorded on video. Or, following on from the reconstruction of old instruments and the reproduction of facsimiles, will we endeavour in future to reconstruct original locations? In Japan you can already find Holland Village where small sections of Dutch towns have been reconstructed. One of Holland Village's most recent attractions is the Utrecht Dom Tower, only a few metres less high than the 112 metres of the original. Will there ever be a similar tourist attraction where the history of music is revived, perhaps with repeat performances of Machaut's *Messe de Nostre Dame* in a copy of Rheims Cathedral or of Dufay's motet *Nuper rosarum flores* in a reconstruction of Brunelleschi's dome? Or perhaps dances in period costume to music from the Susato collections in a pub modelled on a Brueghel painting.

This is clearly going beyond the realm of feasibility. Yet should we not try to observe some considerations? A song recital in the main hall of the Amsterdam Concertgebouw, where the subtleties and intimacies of the art of solo singing can be projected only by over-emphasis, is surely wrong. Recordings might serve us better in this regard, but even these sometimes suffer the negative influences of performers having become used to the unnaturally large-scale venue. Surely it is one of the aims of the 'early music' movement to approach as closely as possible the original even with all the possible variety of history?

Various aspects of the music itself are dependent on the location in which it is to be performed, notably tempo. To what extent was the tempo of plainchant or early polyphony influenced by the resonant acoustics of Romanesque churches? If a location that resembles that of the original circumstances of performance is used, the answer can be reached quickly and fairly conclusively. In a modern concert hall with virtually no acoustic, it is tempting to speed up the tempo. Ought we to adjust our tempo to suit an unsuitable acoustic? It would be like suggesting that a Mozart piano concerto should be played slower in a reverberant church than in a dry hall. The ideal is clear: don't play Mozart piano concertos in a church and bear in mind the acoustic of the original setting for an indication of what might have been the original tempo.

Comprehensibility does not seem to have been an issue in most of the sacred music of the Middle Ages, although already in the Renaissance, Erasmus often complains on this very score. A resonant acoustic is quite acceptable for much of the earlier repertory. On the other hand, there is a large part of the medieval repertory in which comprehensibility does play an essential role. There is no point in singing of one's love for someone in verse after verse (as the troubadours did) or to tell a long story about a miracle (as in the *Cantigas de Santa María*), if the words are inaudible because of an over-resonant acoustic. It may solve part of the problem to slow down the tempo, but that does not always present the ideal solution. In addition, there is the question whether this kind of story-telling was intended for large audiences or for performance in much smaller, more intimate settings.

The solution is far from easy. At the Holland Festival of Early Music in Utrecht, only a small part of a very extensive repertory can be performed in a really appropriate location, but we do attempt to find the most suitable space possible. We are lucky in that we have at our disposal a number of medieval churches that afford nearly ideal settings for sacred music up to about 1600. But problems always crop up with regard to the secular repertory of the period. The rough outline of the old city of Utrecht has been preserved, but there are very few secular buildings from before the seventeenth century still standing. Even if they are still there, their interiors have been completely changed over the years. A town like Regensburg fares slightly better with its 'Tage der alten Musik', because besides the old churches there are a number of historic secular buildings. York, too, is in a good position to hold an early music festival, but the WDR festival in Herne, on the contrary, holds all its concerts in modern halls. The situation in the United States – where in most towns a house from the end of the nineteenth century is the earliest historic building – is naturally less than ideal. The First San Antonio Early Music Festival in Texas was relatively lucky in having at its disposal two eighteenth-century mission posts in the gardens of the Alamo and the Spanish Governor's Palace. So the road to 'authentic' locations or environments is often blocked, but we must try where we can.

Another factor that has, unfortunately, to be taken into consideration, is the size of audience a location can hold. The multi-functional, modern Centre Vredenburg offers an alternative in Utrecht, but although lutes and other 'soft' instruments can be heard in all its corners, we generally use it only for larger-scale, orchestral productions. Groups like the Hilliard Ensemble and the Tallis Scholars have also sung there: the results are acceptable, but it is clear that much of the sacred repertory suffers from not having a church acoustic. But then the decision to have a larger audience in a less appropriate space is often dictated by economics. This compromise is often necessary, not least because it enables us to locate other concerts in often smaller – if more suitable – places and still bear the financial loss. Only with considerably more sponsorship or subsidy could these smaller venues be viable, but, then, sponsors are not usually so keen on smaller audiences. Potential concert-goers might also have to be disappointed.

A specific problem is about to beset us in Utrecht. The relevant authorities have decided that Roman Catholic churches are no longer to be used indiscriminately for concerts. Only sacred music is to be allowed, and no entrance fees can be charged. This alone would create various logistical problems as regards financial considerations, and it seems that it will no longer be possible to use these churches. The irony is that these measures conform to the argument for performing sacred music in church yet at the same time deprive us of the appropriate setting.

That setting is essential if an attempt is made to recreate the original function of music: say, for example, the reconstruction of the Office of Vespers or some other liturgical service, perhaps sung at the appropriate time of day (or night). To attempt such a reconstruction in a modern concert hall would simply be anachronistic. Convincingly 'authentic' surroundings can help the audience to relive something of the original 'performance' context. A visitor to the Belgian castle of Alden Biesen can almost imagine that he is in the Renaissance during the annual 'Day of Early Music' held there. He or she can enjoy the appropriate music in the castle itself, the church and the open air. The modern dress of the audience, the snack-bar and the car park are the only distractions.

By way of conclusion, I would like briefly to consider the importance of the appropriate acoustical ambiance in recordings. A good example of an attempt to reconstruct a sense of the appropriate setting is the recording of Machaut's *Messe de Nostre Dame* by the Taverner Consort directed by Andrew Parrott. Here the various kinds of music in the reconstruction (chant and polyphony) are sung from different places, following a conjectural reconstruction of the original positioning. It helps to create the impression that the listener is witnessing the original performance in the original circumstances. Equally interesting is the BBC recording in which Soriano's double-choir arrangement of Palestrina's *Missa Papae Marcelli* is sung in the Sistine Chapel by the William Byrd Choir directed by Gavin Turner. Here the actual process of recording proved to be highly problematic because of the extraordinary acoustical properties of the Chapel. Technology already enables us to select different artificial acoustics – why not develop a specialized version for the early music lover with options on the Sistine Chapel, St Mark's, Notre Dame, a room in a medieval castle and so on? At least we would be more aware of the enormous differences in individual acoustical circumstances. If this were then linked to a video recording, with period instruments and costumes, it would give some impression of the spaces in which musical repertories were originally heard and would demonstrate the influence of the environment on performance. Clearly – and even supposing such a development was really desirable – it would in many cases be simply impossible. The hall in which the musicians of the Munich court chapel played and were immortalized by

Hans Mielich in the codex of Lassus's Penitential Psalms, was burned to the ground in 1750. The last traces of the great Romanesque church of St Mary in Utrecht disappeared in the nineteenth century. All we have left are manuscripts of the chant that was sung there, and a number of painstakingly detailed paintings and drawings by the seventeenth-century Dutch artist Pieter Saenredam. In such cases, reconstruction of the original contexts for these great musical repertories is no longer an option.

Even within local limitations concert organizers can at least think about the choice of location for a given concert: a suitable acoustic and ambiance cannot but help to enhance the listener's appreciation of whatever music. There is one source of consolation where the appropriate setting is just not feasible: true musicians will perhaps in any case make the concert-goer oblivious to the surroundings.

VI Performance techniques

43　Framing the life of the words

Paul Hillier

There are fashions in the performance of early music that make our renderings as much a thing of the moment as the clothes we wear. Even so, we cannot turn the clock back or wilfully ignore the burgeoning fruits of scholarship. The use of historical pronunciation in the performance of early music is still a relatively new and untried development, but one that is now definitely on the move. My own experiences in this direction began with work on medieval English lyrics, where clearly some knowledge of Middle English is necessary, as the words are substantially different from those of the modern language. I later worked on Elizabethan English, first for lute songs, and subsequently for vocal polyphony (which is when things begin to get more complicated in performance), where it can perhaps be argued that the words are so similar to their modern counterparts that no revival of earlier pronunciation is really necessary. Finally, I turned to the question of how to pronounce Tudor Latin, which again might be deemed a luxury or superfluity by those more concerned with 'musical expression', not to mention the impatience of singers who may not share my amateur interest in philology and phonetics.

So what is the purpose behind these attempts to perform medieval and Renaissance music with 'original' pronunciation? I cannot answer for others, but for me it has very little to do with gaining a seal of 'authenticity'. It does, however, reflect a more than passing interest in the history of the English language and in the actual sounds of Chaucer and Shakespeare as it might originally have been spoken, though this by itself would not be sufficient reason to inflict my interest upon others through the medium of song. The whole activity only becomes fully worthwhile if our enjoyment of the music is enhanced; if, indeed, 'musical expression' is served by science and not the other way around. The purpose, therefore, is to stir up fresh ideas about the music, to help us listen to it in a new way, to realize its rhetorical powers in as invigorating a manner as possible, and also to understand more deeply the nature of its beauty.

The singing of early music has come a long way in the past forty years, but it still has a way to go (and always will do, fortunately). The present situation is one of abundance, especially in Britain, where there is a whole generation of singers, schooled and adept in the performance of vocal polyphony, with often wonderful results; and that same generation has also yielded many gifted soloists, not to mention their counterparts in the instrumental world. Other countries have followed suit, especially France and Spain, whose important song repertories can only properly be served by native singers or long-term residents in that cultural environment. We are also witnessing a confabulation between the early music world and the more traditional proponents of our classical heritage, and this is clearly to be welcomed. But there is also a suspicion that we have only scratched the surface of vocal performance and its potential for fresh developments. And if we have any doubts about this, they can be silenced by briefly exploring the worlds of contemporary and non-Western vocal music, both readily available on disc.

Here I must make a general observation about modern singing of early music: singers have largely learned to minimalize vibrato, yet still sing with a basically modern production whose main characteristic is a stream of sound in which the words are largely undifferentiated. The text may be clamorously clear, fully coloured by the changing vowels and consonants, but the physical properties of the language do not seem to be felt, either physically or emotionally, by the singers, at least not as they are when the language is spoken. Instead there is a barrier of produced sound, a continual deposit of 'expressive' sonority, between the singer and the words. The main reason for this is that in modern vocal production the placing of the voice is significantly different for singing than for speech, and this is primarily caused by received ideals of vocal tone, and the need for sustaining the sound for quite long periods and often at considerable volume. (To get an idea of the other possible mixtures available we need only listen to jazz and folk singers to realize that a large difference between these two aspects of vocal production, the sung and the spoken, is neither inevitable nor necessarily better.) To what extent this difference was present in sixteenth-century singing, we cannot know absolutely. But we can at least get some ideas by exploring historical pronunciation; and in turn this may touch off our own imaginative responses, with interesting results.

It is not enough merely for the words to be pronounced differently. A language or dialect, at any given period, is not just a random collection of sounds. It has a recognizable identity arising from the general placing of the voice needed for the sounds used. French is placed differently from English, German from Italian and so on. The intonation patterns within a language can be revealing too, distinguishing American and British English from each other, for example, or reminding us of historical links – coastal Dutch (especially in the Friesian Islands) overheard from a short distance can sound just like the rise and fall of English, more so than Australian or American English. We need to develop an instinctive feel for the language (that is, dialect, historical pronunciation) so that it can become second nature. We need, like actors, to get behind the message of the text and inside the formal patterns of the language so that it can become a vehicle for expressing the whole gamut of emotions and meanings.

We should be very cautious about linking the use of historical pronunciation to claims of 'authenticity'. Authentic it may be, but I doubt if this is a matter that the original composers would have set much store by. For example: should we use a northern French pronunciation of Latin for the motets of Josquin Desprez? Quite apart from his many works written in Italy and sung there by choirs that drew their singers from Flanders, France, Germany, Spain, England and Italy, we should remember that Josquin's music was very widely disseminated, and presumably sung with differing Latin pronunciations. So we are not on the trail of some authentic beast known as 'the correct historical pronunciation for a particular piece of music'. We seek rather to apply the evidence about historical pronunciation to generate ideas for use in singing the music today. In particular, I propose getting away from modern vocal production with its largely undifferentiated sound, to a more vernacular, speech-based idiom and style of production.

It could perhaps be argued that any pronunciation would fit this purpose, but in practice it does not work out like that. You need a *reason* for changing things and, more specifically, you need a frame of reference beyond personal intuition. A little knowledge can cause problems – it would be easy to imagine that singers exposed to an initial bout of Tudor speech might decide that an all-purpose, rural inflection would suffice, and that no further effort was needed. This would lead to a diffuse and generalized effect, about as useful to music as ham-acting is to Shakespeare. An objective framework would clarify everyone's efforts, bring the sound into particular focus and permit true freedom of expression by specifying limits.

There is a further consideration here: by taking our modern voices (and modern training) and attempting to build a style for sixteenth-century music, we can all too easily engage in a series of negative activities. The singer is told not to use vibrato, not to do this or that with regard to dynamics, tempos, tone-colour, contrast and other expressive devices. Thus, the natural connection between emotion and voice, thought and its expression, words and music, is inhibited and enveloped in a set of cautionary restrictions. Something has to fill the gap created by unlearning part or all of a modern singing technique and its attendant assumptions. The search for a style based on historical pronunciation offers a specific direction and can establish a positive mental attitude, with a supporting framework in the shape of philological evidence – to fall back on.

It is important to recognize that we must fully assimilate the information that is available to us and the implications of what we find ourselves doing with it. In other words, it has to become natural; and this takes time. Is it worth the trouble?

My own experience leads me to assert that historical pronunciation *does* make a difference and that it is a difference well worth having. Tudor English has vivid colours of its own which are woven into Tudor music in much the same way that the sound of French is woven into a *mélodie* by Debussy or Poulenc. I discovered the startling difference when I started to sing Dowland's ayres with an Elizabethan pronunciation: 'problems' of style and interpretation simply disappeared. These were no longer English Lieder without vibrato, but wonderful marriages of Tudor poetry and Tudor music. The voice seemed of itself to find a new placement (closer to speech production as it happens), lost a little in overall power, relinquished the sostenuto-legato phrasing that had been bred into it, felt a gain in the subtlety of rhetoric available, and sang in a way that felt surprisingly natural. The question of vibrato had somehow become irrelevant.

A soloist can set his own pace, but for an ensemble or choir the process is more complex. When this approach is applied to choral music, it quickly becomes apparent that the results are potentially *more* interesting and vivid, although greater expenditure of time and effort will be needed to obtain anything worth while. Above all, a more vernacular-based vocal production breaks up the familiar choral legato, encouraging a more rhythmic, even 'instrumental' definition to the musical fabric. This thinner, more abrasive, less sumptuous sound, potentially dramatic, however, through articulation and fresh contrasts of verbal colour, goes along with the general trend of early music as it uncovers the sounds of the past: at first there is an apparent loss of the warmth of familiar textures, but then we recognize new sounds emerging to enrich our experience of the music. For many of us it soon becomes difficult, if not impossible, to return to the sound palette we knew before.

Finally, some kind of rapprochement may be possible. Modern vernacular English could serve as the basis for singing Tudor music – having put myself through the experience described, I can see that it is possible; but equally, the experience is necessary before the conclusion can be acted upon.

Some people have responded to this process by regretting the threatened loss of 'objective' (floating, remote) sound, saying that they liked the style our choirs have developed for this music precisely for its meditative, unassertive qualities. I believe that a reappraisal of the sound and style of Renaissance music (especially vocal polyphony) is no bad thing – and if the result has tougher sinews, starker colours, and encourages greater rhythmic articulation, then that need not signify a loss of inner poise or tender beauty of sound, but rather an intensification of the whole experience which, I agree, holds these qualities at its core. For me it would, I imagine, be like hearing John Donne or Lancelot Andrewes read one of their own sermons, rather than hearing them in the suave, comfortable tones of a modern actor; more like, I can only imagine, hearing Evensong celebrated by the early Anglicans with their newly written book of prayer, than hearing this week's Choral Evensong on the radio.

44 Reconstructing lost voices

John Potter

Of the vast corpus of pieces written before the period we call Baroque, by far the greater part is vocal music. To get an idea of what this repertory might have sounded like, we have to strip away generations of accumulated information about what singing is, using only what can be deduced from written sources (with all the ambiguities and pitfalls that this implies). There is an additional pain threshold that singers have to cross: singing is a visceral activity, the voice is the only instrument which is directly expressive of mind and body. Singing is a personal and physical statement which is firmly rooted in the here and now, making the re-creation of historical styles something of a compromise, especially as some repertories (Tudor polyphony, for example) have never entirely disappeared from sight. In-strumentalists have had the luxury of re-inventing a sound world from scratch, and the radical fervour of the 'early music' movement has been largely fired by the possibilities offered by this blank slate. The direct acoustic relationship between an instrument and its appearance has meant that makers can provide players with the physical means to recreate older styles and techniques, giving players an authority that singers have to do without.

For singers, academic research, geared as it is to the quantifiable, is inevitably inconclusive and more than usually speculative. There has been no revolution in singing to compare with that in instrumental playing. In England the very musical, Oxbridge-trained light voices adjusted to the new requirements with the minimum of change in their existing techniques: the 'Reservata holler', as Howard Mayer Brown called it, proved much less enduring than the relatively conventional singing preferred by David Munrow. The ease with which good musicians with small voices can find a niche in the profession has tended to mean a lack of curiosity and experiment among singers, to the extent that musicians and audiences alike often take for granted the sometimes bizarre mix of ultra-authentic band and 'unreconstructed' singers that can characterize modern performances.

It is possible, with a little detective work, to trace the history of singing teaching and technique backwards and, bearing in mind that we now know a great deal about how the voice actually works, we can arrive at a number of generalizations about what earlier singing may have been like. In the first place, without twentieth-century social mobility and the universality of recording, there must have been greater individuality: no clones of one's favourite singer, endlessly replicated on plastic. We should also bear in mind that until relatively recently very few singers were specialized professionals in the sense that we understand the term today. During the nineteenth century, the growth of the market economy, the breaching of many class protocols and the development of communications had the paradoxical effect of bringing together musicians and public as never before, while reducing the expectations that each had of the other: the narrow pursuit of excellence took over from the enjoyment of variety. By about the middle of the century it is possible to distinguish two broad schools of singing technique, which might be termed the 'scientific' and the 'pragmatic'. The former sought to devise a pedagogy based on how the voice was thought to work according to the latest 'scientific' information, while those unwilling to accept the science advocated a 'natural' technique derived from the 'lost' art of *bel canto* which they claimed to have re-discovered. Traces of this division can be heard in the earliest gramophone recordings before the LP further narrowed the acceptable definition of good singing.

Among the 'scientists', Manuel García stands out as an important observer of the workings of the voice. He witnessed the first tenor high C sung in chest voice, and he realized that the singers of the 1830s were using a lower larynx position than those of previous generations. There is some controversy over García's abilities as a singer and teacher, but he was undoubtedly a remarkable observer of the human voice. He considered, among other things, what we now know as Tibetan chant as well as singing on the inhaled breath, processes for which he naturally found no application but which are standard features of today's extended vocal technique repertory; he also invented the laryngoscope so he could speak with some authority about what actually happens in the throat. It seems likely that García was witness to a change in technique that was occurring during his lifetime, a change appropriate to the music dramas of Verdi in which the old-style virtuosity of Rossini (and before him Mozart and the late Baroque) had no place.

Similar vocal shifts have occurred when a previous technique or style has become unable to express the text in a way appropriate to the prevailing aesthetic. There are obvious points at which we can see this kind of change happening: around 1600 with the development of the new monodic style and the conscious reduction of polyphonic artifice; in the early twentieth century with Futurist and Dadaist declamation reacting against the excesses of late Romantic opera; and post-World War II in extended vocal techniques and 'early music' itself. Each of these new styles would seem to have occurred because the mainstream has become in some way decadent, and a similar event, perhaps a more significant and radical development, happened during the nineteenth century with the change from the simple virtuosity of late Baroque technique to the darker, richer and less mobile singing of nineteenth-century opera.

The richness of the modern voice derives largely from singing with the lower larynx position first observed by García. Modern research tells us that lowering the larynx increases the length of the vocal tract (the space between the teeth and the larynx) and gives the singer access to an additional formant, or resonance, which enables the voice to project over a large orchestra without any extra effort. In order to achieve this quite a wide mouth position is required, with the jaw dropped further than would be the case in speech. There is a price to be paid for this efficiency: clarity of vowels is sacrificed to purity of tone, hence the old cliché that you cannot tell what language opera singers are singing in. There are also muscular restrictions on agility and a reduction of potential range in a highly cultivated voice. We can now begin to see that the voices of earlier generations were probably lighter and more agile, smaller and less able to project but with a more speech-like clarity of vowels. This gives us quite a lot to go on when looking at earlier written sources.

There is one further aspect of the modern technique to be considered: most teachers insist on systematized breathing, usually controlled by the muscles of the diaphragm, as the foundation of a good technique. There is no conclusive evidence for modern efficient breathing until late in the eighteenth century, after the demise of the castratos. These extraordinary singers developed barrel-shaped chests while retaining a child-sized larynx, enabling them to achieve enormous feats of breath control. It was only after castration came to be considered unethical that there was any need for anything approaching a modern breathing technique. There are plenty of references to the need for a good pair of lungs to avoid having to breathe too frequently, but the attention paid to breathing just does not have the rigour that we might expect from our experience of modern singing.

Vocal music until the early twentieth century pre-supposes the reproduction and communication of a literary text which has its origin in the language variety spoken by the author. England has been a plurality of linguistic communities since pre-historic times. The Norman invasion in the eleventh century resulted in French joining Latin as the official and artistic language for several hundred years, until the increasing national consciousness of the English court eventually saw the return of English as a high-status language. It was a language of many varieties, that of the South in general and the court in particular having the highest status. By the sixteenth century, English had made inroads into religious music, previously only set to Latin texts, and in the madrigal there existed a vernacular secular music form which was widespread among the upper and emerging middle classes. Madrigals were sung by both professional and amateur musicians and, naturally enough, the singers used the pronunciation they had been born with. Alan Durant has pointed out that this variety in accent is not reflected in current recordings and performances of madrigals which use Received Pronunciation (RP) as a kind of cultural absolute. The accent of today's singers, in other words, differs from those used in earlier times on grounds of class rather than geography. For specifically musical reasons a great deal is lost by ignoring the plurality of accent and the rich variety of tone colour that this implies. Elizabethan singers presumably sang with a relatively high larynx position and a relatively forward jaw position, which would have made it fairly easy for them to enunciate the texts and still retain an accent similar to that used in their speech, which would have been the dialect appropriate to them as individuals. Whether or not singers take the decision to re-create an old pronunciation (and there are many arguments on both sides), it is important to realize the effect of speech-related singing on the music. Actors' voice coaches look for the 'phonetic set' that makes the language or accent work, and this colours the whole timbre just as it does when learning a foreign language.

The colour and shape of the language become the main determinants of vocal colour, rather than the notions of 'beautiful' tone quality which are at the heart of modern 'classical' singing. When you remove the two basic elements of a modern technique (namely the low-larynx tone colour and its accompanying breathing technique), what you are left with is language. Without the sustained lines produced by well-supported breathing but with the speech-like tone quality that is a consequence of a higher larynx position, the phrasing of a line will derive its energy directly from the text. Diphthongs, so rich in earlier varieties of English, mean that the text is always in motion at the level of the syllable. At the level of the phrase the shape of the music will be influenced by the rise and fall of the spoken literary phrase with its innate rhythms and stresses. The effect of this in many pieces will be to replace conventional ideas of tempo with a pacing derived from the rhetoric of the text. The frequency spectrum of a diphthong is often extremely complex and this will have implications for tuning. One of the curious by-products of the current 'early music' fashion for singing in RP and using very little vibrato has been the ability to tune very precisely by using pure vowels. It is hard to imagine dialect singers doing this. It may be that from our vantage point of 'pure' vowels and the dreaded Equal Temperament we are now over-emphasizing the importance of 'pure' tuning. If one has a sufficiently rich spectrum of overtones, it may not be possible to determine thirds and fifths with any consistency, and the tuning of cadences in particular is likely to be governed by the exigencies of vowel colour rather than strict but abstract notions of temperament. The net effect of all these factors is to integrate the musical and the literary texts, which is perhaps what we should expect when composer, poet and performer would often be one and the same person.

We have now to ask whether there is any evidence from the written sources to back up the idea of a speech-related singing which I have so far proposed solely by extrapolating from what we know about language and vocal mechanisms. Using written sources to unravel an oral/aural process is at best unsatisfactory, and an objective review of the literature is virtually impossible, given the large number of imponderables inherent in the texts.

Although there is a considerable amount of material from the sixteenth century onwards, the information curve slopes rapidly downwards into the medieval period. Perhaps the best we can hope for is a kind of a dialogue with these long-dead performers and composers, trying to match our expectations with the many possible interpretations of their writings: no source should be accepted without question. The lack of early evidence may just mean that nothing has survived, but quite a lot of musical material has come down to us and a more likely hypothesis is that singing was valued differently, with perhaps many aspects universally assumed or taken for granted. The earliest surviving singing treatise is by Conrad von Zabern and dates from 1474. Much of what Conrad says would be regarded by modern singers as common sense – sing together and in time, don't strain, and so on. He mentions the importance of the natural articulation of words and that high notes are to be sung in the head register. The same precepts appear in 1515 in the work of Andreas Vogelsang (or Andreas Ornithoparcus, as he preferred to be called) which John Dowland translated into English in 1606. Dowland even quotes a joke found in Conrad about 'unlearned singers' who sing *aremus* ('let us plough') instead of *oremus* ('let us pray'). There is nothing about breathing technique, and the most common adjective used to describe tone-colour is 'sweet', a description that recurs for several centuries in the literature. The general picture appears to be of singing as a refinement of speech, which accords well with what we would expect from the phonetic hypotheses.

Evidence of a more sophisticated kind survives in the Italian sources. There are tantalizing glimpses of an earlier tradition of improvised music which dates back beyond the fourteenth century, and this comes into focus with the ornamentation handbooks of the sixteenth and seventeeth centuries. Ornamentation is often a problem for singers today: when and where and how much are questions to which there never seem to be satisfactory answers. The creative balance between performer and composer has swung so much in favour of the latter that we now consider the printed score to have the status of an icon, which makes it hard for modern singers to be spontaneous. The sixteenth-century virtuosos probably did not work from a score at all, but improvised on tunes that they already knew.

Modern jazz works in exactly the same way and has similar characteristics; the music can be abstractly virtuoso or the ornamentation can heighten the expressiveness of the text (and there are a thousand possibilities in between). One of the great joys of singing 'early music' is having the jazz singer's freedom to create and re-create, not just to interpret.

The answer to the problem of ornamentation depends on what you are trying to achieve: if you want to show how fast you can sing, then there is a lot that you can do; if your main concern is to express the text, you may find that there are better ways than sheer speed. Most of the treatises from this period consist of examples of divisions or new and improved ornaments, with occasional instruction in how to execute them. A common observation (from Maffei, Zacconi and others) is that fast *passaggi* originate in the throat. This is not quite the truism it seems to be, but implies relatively little pressure on the larynx. Many of the scale-like runs are extremely quick, pre-supposing a virtuosity that comes from light, agile and quiet singing with the energy concentrated in the throat and leaving the breath to look after itself. A modern well-supported technique finds this kind of singing very difficult to cope with, and the repertory has now been largely lost to instrumentalists who (not having the subtleties of text to worry about) tend to play the pieces in a very dogmatically virtuoso manner. The difference is like that between a jazz singer and a saxophonist: the former uses improvisation to enhance the text, while the latter has no text to impede his virtuosity. Significantly, Caccini and many other writers condemn ornamentation for its own sake.

The idea of a speech-like singing is never very far away from most of the sources. Maffei's famous letter of 1562 says that the virtuoso voice is soft, with the mouth opening no further than in conversational speech. Interestingly, he also says that singers should be able to sing in all ranges. There is a repertory of 'tenor-bass' songs from the period which calls for a range of more than three octaves. This is rarely performed today because the modern highly cultivated voice usually assumes a much narrower compass. Singers who have not been 'trained' in the modern way (such as most rock singers) are more likely to have the extremes of their registers intact, in much the same way as a Renaissance performer. Zarlino (1558) and Zacconi (1592) also say that chamber singing is quiet (as opposed to the louder and more primitive church singing). Caccini, in his preface to *Le Nuove Musiche* (1602), talks of a way of singing where one would 'speak in tones'. He links this to the concept of *sprezzatura*, a subtle elasticity of tempo which has the effect of creating an illusion of speech. Although Caccini claimed to be the originator of this concept, the idea is fundamental to rhetoric and oratory, the disciplines of literature and public speaking which many writers call on when trying to explain how song works. Vicentino (1555) draws an exact parallel between oratory and singing, with tempo and dynamics changing at will to suit the text. His remarks on tempo are essential reading for anyone who wants to understand pre-Romantic singing: strict tempos are essentially alien to the proper expression of the words. The influence of these attitudes permeated much of Europe, and some of the most interesting descriptions of Italian singing are by foreigners. Praetorius (1619) acknowledges the writings of Caccini and Bovicelli and refers to oratory and the expression of the text. He talks of the basic requirement of a good natural voice, and the impression given by his writings, as with those of so many of his contemporaries, is of singing as a kind of heightened speech. Mersenne (1636–7), similarly well-versed in Caccini, describes Italian singers as almost living the very emotions that they are singing about – a far cry from the dispassionate renderings often heard in modern performances.

Using the deconstructed 'technique' that the sources suggest and the phonetic detective work implies, we can gain access to a means of performing the music that is not only historically appropriate but makes the music live in the present. The development of modern technique has restricted singing to a small number of highly trained specialists, and this exclusivity has tended to perpetuate itself in 'early music'. This is not what sixteenth-century singing is about; if you can speak you can sing. There is no reason why text-orientated early music singing should not find a much wider relevance in the plurality of contemporary musics. Unfortunately we are too often taught that a good technique is an end in itself: to make a beautiful sound based on a well-supported breathing technique. This separation of technique from text is a key factor in inhibiting any comprehensive re-evaluation of singing technique and has prevented singers from acquiring an organic relationship with their music. The integrity of the poetic text, the sound-world of the poet, is too often ignored because of technical demands.

Instrumentalists have long accepted the consequences of reconstructed instruments: the sound of the viol, for example, derives partly from the physical factors of materials and construction, and partly from the stylistic implications that flow from these. The two elements together make the chemistry of phrasing and tone colour that are so characteristic of modern viol playing. The equivalent point for a singer – the level at which phrasing and tone colour interact – is in the pronunciation of words, since what is left when you take away the props of a modern technique is the raw material of language itself. The shape and sound of a word is very much the equivalent of horse-hair on gut. It is also much more than that: it is that point where, as Barthes put it, 'the melody really works at the language – not at what it says, but the voluptuousness of its sound-signifiers, of its letters – where melody explores how the language works and identifies with that work'.

Select bibliography

R. BARTHES, 'The grain of the voice', in *Image, music, text* (London, 1984)

H. M. BROWN, 'Choral music in the English Renaissance', *Early Music*, vi/2 (1978), pp. 164–9; and *Embellishing 16th-century music* (Oxford, 1974)

A. DURANT, *Conditions of music* (London, 1984)

J. DYER, 'Singing with proper refinement', *Early Music*, vi/2 (1978), pp. 207–19

M. GARCÍA, *Traité complet de l'art du chant*, trans. D. V. Paschke, *A complete treatise on the art of singing* (New York, 1975 & 1984)

R. GREENLEE, 'Dispositione di voce: passage to florid singing', *Early Music*, xv/1 (1987), pp. 47–56

C. MACCLINTOCK, *Readings in the history of music in performance* (Bloomington, 1982)

J. SUNDBERG, *The science of the singing voice* (Illinois, 1987)

M. UMBERTI, 'Vocal techniques in Italy in the second half of the sixteenth century', *Early Music*, ix/4 (1981), pp. 486–98

45 Pythagoras at the forge: tuning in early music

Rogers Covey-Crump

Preliminary considerations

Much work has been done in rediscovering the forces, timbres and styles appropriate to the performance of pre-Classical musical repertory. Integral to this has been the readoption of documented tuning systems for instruments of fixed tuning such as the organ, clavichord, harpsichord and lute. Perhaps the most recent development in this field lies with the viol consort, where the best groups have rediscovered the possibility of achieving a proportion of Just or Perfect major thirds. (Throughout this article the words Just and Perfect are synonymous.)

For players of instruments that permit flexibility of tuning, and for unaccompanied singers, intonation is far harder to define than other parameters of performance since it is at best a blend of good aural training, sound technique and a knowledge of temperament, and, at worst, a total lack of blend, resulting from poor technique and ignorance of tuning systems. In practice a keyboard temperament can only be a reference standard since no performer can possibly temper intervals in the precise way demanded by fixed tuning. Indeed, any attempt at tempering will interfere with rather than help a good performance. The instincts of the best performers will produce tuning that is closer to Just or to Mean Tone tuning than to modern Equal Temperament. However, all performers need special guidance in achieving satisfactory tuning in what I will label 'Pythagorean' repertory.

Solo performers have the opportunity to be self-critical through the medium of commercial or studio recording. They can monitor their own level of achievement and take or reject the advice of their producer, and with luck the tuning will approximate to what feels right for that particular repertory. For a group of singers or instrumentalists the question of tuning becomes much more complex as each line may be in or out of tune with itself or the other lines.

The perception and taste of the performer is usually determined by early experience or by professional training. Players whose experience has been primarily in nineteenth- or twentieth-century chamber music or in orchestras are aware and may be suspicious of the narrow, flat Just major third used by period instrumentalists. After the physical differences of their instruments, the most obvious feature of historically-aware performance is the much reduced use of vibrato and a tuning closer to Just or Mean Tone than to Equal Temperament. String players are likely to produce Just major thirds even if a continuo keyboard is in a Classical or Baroque temperament such as Vallotti in which the third is a little wider than Just.

If tuning could be isolated from all the other parameters, what would tell the performer or listener that it was good or bad? Octaves, fifths and fourths are very basic to the structure of musical texture. If they sound sour, then there is little hope for any of the smaller intervals. Defective technique often results in inconsistency of intonation, but an added hazard for singers is vowel colour, and in any case singers do not always hear accurately the pitch that they think they are producing. The listener can perceive that some vowels flatten the pitch while others sharpen it. Take the word 'Alleluia'. A cruel test is to ask a singer to sing the word slowly on one note without any vibrato, dividing it into five syllables. It is likely that 'Al-' and '-le-' will sound flat on the note given; '-lu-' will probably sound in tune, '-i-' will sound sharper; and the final '-a-' flat. *A cappella* singing is particularly vulnerable to bad vowels. A trained singer can find the right placing of the vowel to correct such pitch deviations, but one badly placed vowel can sour the effect of an otherwise Justly tuned triad.

Since vocal music is more important than instrumental music before 1600, I shall concentrate on the issues of tuning in vocal performance where, in theory at least, greater subtlety is possible.

Fine shadings of tuning can best be heard between paired voices or instruments that share a very similar harmonic or overtone spectrum, because our ears identify the quality of intervals between voices by the interaction of the overtones. The beauty of an unaccompanied melodic line is determined by the consistency of pitch so that each note of the melody has precisely one 'slot'. In polyphony some notes of the scale or mode will have two or even three 'slots' depending on the harmonic context. The addition of a third and fourth line to a two-part texture gives greater responsibility to everyone since at any one time one note of the basic triad is likely to be doubled. Good tuning in polyphony demands accurate melodic movement as a starting point, but the vertical relationship of harmony must be accommodated simultaneously. Trained choirs and vocal consorts tend towards Mean Tone tuning, but the best performers, when thoroughly rehearsed, are capable of Just or Pythagorean tuning.

So, in what directions must pitch be 'bent' to achieve good tuning, and what tuning is 'right' for a particular period and a particular European country? We shall find that geography is indeed important, and that the 'right' tuning varies with the repertory: it is not, unfortunately, carved in stone for each century.

A brief historical survey

In addition to the performing instinct that seems to get the tuning 'right', I believe that the approach of the performer should be determined by a desire to appreciate the attitude of medieval and Renaissance composers and performers to their craft. Broadly speaking, Western harmony developed from the parallel fourths and fifths of organum, through the discovery of the consonant version of the major third to the concept of ways of tuning that would allow the development of chromatic harmony towards enharmonicity. Total enharmonic freedom occurs only with Equal Temperament. In all other temperaments each accidental has its own discrete identity so that an enharmonic shift involves a tuning adjustment on a held note. At this point I should mention that Just tuning makes similar demands, if and when it is attempted, in order to achieve the smoothest possible tuning of two adjacent harmonies.

For many centuries the ideas of Greek philosophers, in particular those of Pythagoras, permeated the teaching of the sciences, of which music was one. For all practical purposes octaves, fifths and fourths were considered perfect consonant intervals; thirds, sixths and sevenths dissonances. (Seconds, whether major or minor, are best left out of this discussion for the moment.) On the European continent, the development of two- and three-part polyphony up to and including Machaut and his contemporaries shows increasingly complex linear elaboration, but it also reveals a distinct harmonic hierarchy. The most common static intervals, as opposed to passing harmonics, are octave, fifth and fourth. If a major third occurs on a long note, then it almost without exception demands outward resolution to an open fifth. Composers knew that the thirds resulting from tuning instruments of fixed pitches like organ and harp with pure octaves, fifths and fourths were the wide, rough Pythagorean major thirds, and the correspondingly dull Pythagorean minor third. Lutes, with several strings and, usually, adjustable frets, seem to have been tuned from quite early times in something approximating to Equal Temperament. The mellow harmonic content and the inability to sustain allowed a degree of tolerance in tuning matters that was not granted on the organ nor later the harmonically bright-toned harpsichord. (Indeed, much evidence of late medieval tuning has been adduced in recent years from research into the clavichord.)

When one examines the stylistic innovations of the fifteenth century, the most obvious harmonic development is the increasing use of the major third and a corresponding shift towards its function as a consonant interval: fifths begin to resolve inwards to major thirds, and final cadences with the fifths filled in by a major third become more common. The documentation of keyboard tuning seems to be in step with this aspect of stylistic change. Early keyboard anthologies such as the Buxheim Organ Book eschew the third, but when thirds do occur they do so predominantly as Schismatic thirds. (A Schismatic third occurs on a keyboard when three thirds are nearly pure but the remainder are wide, rough Pythagorean thirds. An octave, for example, is the sum of two Pythagorean thirds and a Schismatic or nearly pure third.) It was realized that appropriate transposition of the tuning would place the Schismatic thirds in 'usable' keys. If the Wolf fifth is placed between B and F♯ (or technically G♭), then these nearly pure thirds occur between A and C♯ (D♭), D and F♯ (G♭) and E and G♯ (A♭). These approximations to pure thirds are a mathematical coincidence. The sequence of tuning involved is actually: C upwards to G, G downwards to D, D up to A, A down to E, E up to B; then (starting from the C above the first C) C down to F, F up to B♭, B♭ down to E♭, E♭ up to A♭, A♭ down to D♭ and finally D♭ up to G♭ in which every fifth and fourth is tuned perfect. The point is that the D♭, G♭ and the A♭ sound like pure-tuned C♯, F♯ and G♯. (If you are puzzled, but sufficiently motivated to explore, then you might try tuning the octave between middle and treble C on a harpsichord.)

The next and more far-reaching development was Mean Tone tuning. The essence of this system is to accommodate as many Just major thirds as possible on a standard keyboard. Europe became obsessed with thirds. This may sound like an exaggeration, but it is abundantly clear from a study of fifteenth-century harmonic procedures and of keyboard tuning evidence. It is not fanciful to suppose that this change was triggered by the work of English composers and performers. A prominent element in the 'Contenance angloise' observed by French medieval writers must have been the way in which the English singers tuned their music (questions of tone colour and expressivity can only be conjectural). A study of the English repertory demonstrates an early awareness of the possibilities of harmonic expression allowed by consonant, pure thirds compared to the more arid climate of fifths and fourths. Dufay, Josquin and succeeding continental composers appear to have taken note of the work of John Dunstable and probably of the English carol and its increasingly modern harmonic feel. A very apt and well-known example of this genre is 'There is no rose of such virtue', with its definite 'major key' feel; consistently perfect, Just tuning of its component harmonies can be achieved without undue difficulty.

This last point leads directly to a consideration of the instincts of late-twentieth-century professional singers when confronted by repertory from between 1150 and 1600. Some years of experience in this field have convinced me of a number of shortcomings in British vocal training, and ignorance of the basic anatomy of tuning is one. Even the most experienced ensemble singers have received little or no tuition. Only those singers who graduated in music or who happen to have a knowledge of keyboard temperaments are likely to have received any guidance in the theory of tuning. Even so, it is difficult to relate the theory to the practice: the simple truth is that good intonation is largely done by feel. In my experience, the hardest tuning to achieve in unaccompanied vocal music is that demanded by the Pythagorean régime, that is, medieval repertory up to and including Machaut. During the initial stages of rehearsal or with singers less experienced in the early repertory, they usually fail to stretch the major third and to make the minor second (diatonic semitone) sufficiently small. Also, they fail to give the major second its full, Just width. As rehearsal proceeds, the tuning will tend towards Pythagorean as singers progressively perfect their fifths and fourths: in the early stages the pitch can suffer badly.

With post-Machaut and most English fifteenth-century repertory, the 'right' tuning is something between the keyboard compromise of Mean Tone and the perfection of Just Tuning. Music students may read about Just Intonation and understand the theory of simple whole number ratios of pitch frequencies, or they may have approached the subject via the harmonic series, but they often do not know that there is a sizeable body of repertory that can be sung in true Just intonation.

Renaissance polyphony achieves its aural perfection through many parameters. Blend, balance and intonation are probably the main considerations, and they link up to each other in an indivisible way. The blend of an individual voice part within a choir is determined principally by uniformity of vowel colour: one singer producing the wrong vowel upsets the unison and 'sticks out'. Good tuning between two or more vocal parts is achieved by good balance of dynamic and, again, uniformity of vowel colour. On this topic there are many instances of modern editions where the editor has failed to rationalize word underlay and presents melismas with interacting lines on different vowels when there is no definite evidence for such a discrepancy. Discrepancies of this kind can be a hindrance to a satisfactory performance. Then there is the question of vocal vibrato which was used, according to historical evidence, only as an expressive device. Before modern times it was not considered desirable as an ever-present quality. Good tuning is audible only when vibrato is virtually absent or perfectly matched between the voices, both in width and in speed, and this applies to all repertories. The best players and singers are capable of hitting notes in the middle, and the best performers instinctively clarify lush polyphony or highlight poignant harmony by passages or brief moments of vibratoless Just intonation.

Some practical advice

If my analysis of performance practice is correct, and my conscious application of tuning theory appears to fit in with the predominantly unconscious application of the principles by fellow performers, how, then, does theory intermingle with practice?

A superficial examination of the repertory to be performed will reveal the function of the major third. If few thirds are present, and those that are occur as passing harmonies and not as the result of a harmonic resolution, then the composer clearly had the Pythagorean aesthetic as his starting point. Where thirds are abundant and perceptible points of repose, then it is likely that the composer expected to hear Just thirds. The compositional style of English composers demonstrates the latter as a distinct shift away from the harmonic language of Landini, Machaut and the Mannerists, although there is a large repertory of Anglo-French conductus that pose the possibility of alternative or mixed tunings of thirds without compromising the trueness of octaves, fifths and fourths. The progressive erosion of the Pythagorean tuning system by the adoption of Mean Tone tuning demonstrates the increasing importance that was becoming attached to thirds at the expense of pure fifths and fourths. It is arguable that singers always tended towards Just, pure thirds and naturally sang perfect fifths and fourths anyway. Machaut and the Mannerists were not conservative in the notes that they wrote, but their harmonies feel most convincing if some attempt is made to tune to the Pythagorean rather than a Just or Mean Tone scale. A distinct feature of Dunstable and his contemporaries is that the music works in predominantly Just intonation. Let us look at these tuning systems in a little more detail.

A perfectly-tuned triad demands a root, a fifth and a third. The frequency of vibration of the fifth must be precisely half as fast again as that of the root. Expressed more scientifically they are in the ratio $3:2$. The major third in the triad has a vibration frequency with the ratio $5:4$ to the root, while a minor third has the frequency ratio $6:5$ with respect to the root. Thus, the notes of the major triad are in the relationship $4:5:6$. They are in fact adjacent notes in the harmonic or overtone series counting the fundamental as 1 (one). These simple ratios define Just or perfect tuning. The actual ratio of a major third in Equal Temperament is the mathematically irrational (twelfth root of two to the power four):1 which comes to $1.259921:1$. The Just third is $1.25:1$ precisely. Why do perfectly tuned triads not automatically produce perfectly tuned harmony in the course of a harmonic progression or indeed the course of a piece? The answer is that the Just third is not 'structural' to the vast majority of repertory since the Just Intonation scale allows of only three major and two minor triads. Additional triads require additional tuning slots.

The essence of the Pythagorean system of tuning is that all fifths and fourths are perfect except for one of each. All major seconds are the pure major tone with a ratio of $9:8$. All minor seconds (diatonic semitones) are the very small Limma ($256:243$), and the major third is the discordant irrational interval of $81:64$.

The essence of the Just Intonation scale is that the three degrees of the scale that form major thirds above a root are flattened from their Pythagorean slots to form Just thirds. The remaining 'white notes' fall into their Pythagorean slots. Similarly, the Just minor scale requires the raising of those degrees that form minor thirds above a root.

How much of a compromise is the Mean Tone system? The fifth is narrowed by a twentieth of a semitone in Equal Temperament; the fourth is stretched by the same amount. The major second is narrowed by nearly a tenth of a semitone from its Just/Pythagorean dimension. The minor second and the chromatic semitone are wider than Just. These two varieties of semitone are wider than their Just counterparts, but all four are distinctly different from their single counterpart in Equal Temperament. In the context of a major scale or mode, the most noticeable deviation is in the fourth and the seventh degrees, or in modern parlance the subdominant and the leading note. Melodically, the fourth sounds sharp and the seventh sounds flat. The receptive ear soon accommodates to these slightly strange scales because the many Just thirds more than compensate. (Indeed, the use of chromaticism in late sixteenth-century keyboard repertory often exploits the two sizes of semitone to great effect.) Gesualdo's apparently tortuous chromaticism actually conforms to a Mean Tone structure. He will appear to modulate

Ex. 1

Carlo Gesualdo, Tenebrae Responsory for Holy Saturday

Nam et ille

© W. Weismann and G.E. Watkins (eds.) *C.Gesualdo: Sämtliche Werke* (Hamburg, 1957 – 67)

sharpwards or flatwards, but rarely in both directions within the same piece. As an example of this in the Versus section of the Fourth Responsory for the Tenebrae for Holy Saturday, he employs an E♯ in the final chord, the last F♮ occurring five bars earlier. This separation allows ample time for singers to accommodate the E♯ (see Ex. 1). The actual triadic sequence of this passage, set to the words '. . . et subvertit potentias diaboli', is B♭ major → F major, 1st inversion → A minor, 1st inversion → E major → minor → B major, 1st inversion → E major → C♯ minor, 1st inversion → C♯ major. The reprise ('Nam et ille captus est . . .') takes the key back to an F major triad at the end of the second bar. True modulation occurs since the pitch of the E♯ is unlikely to coincide with that of the F♮ s cited.

Performers of pre-1600 music can quite easily accustom themselves to lower leading notes, but the raising of the subdominant in Mean Tone is quite at odds with the function of that note as a dominant seventh. A Just-tuned seventh above the dominant, possible in unaccompanied singing, is pitched distinctly lower than a Just subdominant and a lot lower than a Mean Tone subdominant, and this partly explains the late arrival of the seventh chord as a usable entity. Significantly, it appears to be the English madrigal composers who first exploited sevenths and even ninths to artistic effect in the late-sixteenth century.

Professor Easley Blackwood's remarkable account of tuning systems ought to be required reading for all professional musicians with any interest in tuning. The most significant aspect of his book is the introduction of a simple method of notating tuning by suffixing simple fractional numbers to notes printed on staves or simply giving their names by upper-case letters. Blackwood's starting point is the 'white note' Pythagorean major scale:

C D E F G A B (C) which he notates as C_o D_o E_o F_o G_o A_o B_o (C_o).
The tiny interval between a Pythagorean E above C and a Just E above C is the Syntonic Comma (ratio 81:80). Blackwood simply defines the Just E as E_{-1}, that is to say, one comma less (lower or flatter) than E_o. Since a Just major second added to a Just minor third make a perfect fifth, it follows that a Just minor third is a comma wider than its Pythagorean counterpart, so that a Just minor third above D_o is F_{+1}. Alternatively, a Just minor third below F_o is D_{-1}. Thus it is clear that small adjustments can produce Just intervals as required. Blackwood notates the Natural or Just Intonation scale as C_o D_o E_{-1} F_o G_o A_{-1} B_{-1} (C_o). To avoid confusion, it is worth noting that all notes sharing the same subscript, if used in combination as in a chord, stand in a Pythagorean relationship. If that combination produces octaves, fifths, fourths and major seconds, then these intervals are identical with Just intervals; Pythagorean sevenths, thirds and minor seconds are most definitely not Just intervals. The bugbear of the Just scale is that it contains a Pythagorean minor third between the second and fourth degrees (D_o F_o) and a sour, narrow fifth between the second and the sixth degrees (D_o A_{-1}). This presents a serious problem in the Dorian mode, and it would seem clear, therefore, that medieval theorists did not recognize the possibility that performers might tend towards Just intonation – or did they? Marchetto da Padova insisted upon sharpened major thirds and very narrow leading notes to tonic intervals as in the standard double leading note cadence, but it is reasonable to presume that singers in the fourteenth century sang closer to Pythagorean since all instruments of fixed tuning, particularly organs, were in that tuning. These technicalities serve to hint at some of the problems which performers ought to be

aware of: if intractable problems arise in the preparation of a performance, they often involve tuning difficulties. Some of the repertory works only if someone in a group knows something about the ambient tuning system. A work as late as the Requiem Mass of Lassus has a harmonic structure that can catch out the unwary. It starts innocently in C major, but soon switches to a Dorian D minor and then oscillates between the two. The result of this oscillation is usually a fall in pitch by the end of the first Kyrie. The clue here is that the ambient system for Lassus was Mean Tone. Whether a keyboard is present or not, the knowledge that the second degree is a little dull and the fourth degree distinctly high should help the tuning and the pitch stability.

Technically there is only one Mean Tone system: it divides the Just major third into two equal tones. This is achieved by narrowing eleven fifths by a quarter of a Syntonic Comma. The results are easily visible in Blackwood's notation: $C_0\ D_{-\frac{1}{2}}\ E_{-1}\ F_{+\frac{1}{4}}\ G_{-\frac{1}{4}}\ A_{-\frac{3}{4}}\ B_{-1\frac{1}{4}}\ C_0$ (remembering that the + and − are the degree of bending away from Pythagorean tuning slots). C major is the most convenient scale for the purposes of this account, but the principles apply to any key or mode or to any 'harmonic cell' – the tonality or chord structure of a single moment in a piece. This last point is of vital importance to a singer since tuning is an instinctive response to each chord or harmony as it occurs. In the Just scale, A_{-1} is the pure tuning for a third above F_0, but it is not the right pitch for A in relation to a G triad. A_0 is the A that relates to $G_0\ B_{-1}\ D_0$ just as D_0 relates to $C_0\ E_{-1}\ G_0$. A_0 becomes the local supertonic to G_0. Singers readily take account of the two different versions of A, and that is what good tuning is about. (I have talked of the 'tendency' towards a particular tuning because it is clear that no group of musicians can ever achieve total allegiance to any of the tuning systems outlined. Some thirds in a performance of Landini or Machaut will – and probably should – come closer to Just than to Pythagorean. For those seeking to recreate a medieval performance style, whatever that might be, it is likely that little has changed in this particular area.)

I will conclude this account by mentioning some of the practical problems encountered generally by performers, but particularly by unaccompanied singers when preparing unfamiliar repertory. Singers accustomed to the feel of English and continental polyphony of the late fifteenth and early to mid-sixteenth centuries tend towards a tuning that is somewhere between Just and Mean Tone. Such singers will encounter problems if they have to cope with any essentially Pythagorean textures since they are unlikely to appreciate the mental adjustment required. Sound advice to them is: stretch the major second to its full Just/Pythagorean width, narrow the minor second and stretch the major third well beyond what is comfortable. This applies to every single interval in the piece. Concentration on these principles should assist in producing really pure fifths and fourths and excitingly abrasive harmonies, a quality that is a distinctive feature of Anglo-French conductus of the twelfth and thirteenth centuries. Singers who are skilled enough to give convincing accounts of the tortuous textures of Gesualdo are in fact closer to Just tuning than to Mean Tone. Should the director of a group feel that the singers will be aided by the presence of a keyboard, then it should not be assumed that Mean Tone will help. Allowing for the fine tuning of thirds that singers can achieve, overall pitch stability may be aided by a very discreet background of Equal Temperament or even a Baroque temperament such as Werckmeister or Vallotti.

Performance of polyphony from the mid- and later sixteenth century is usually aided by an awareness of the principles of Mean Tone tuning, and, if a keyboard is used in performance, then singers and keyboard will be in far closer agreement

Table 1: Interval sizes

Interval	Frequency ratio	Size in cents	Nearest equivalent Equal Temperament interval
Just intervals			
Octave	2:1	1200.00	1200.00
Fifth	3:2	701.96	700.00
Fourth	4:3	498.04	500.00
Major third	5:4	386.31	400.00
Minor third	6:5	315.64	300.00
Major second or Major tone	9:8	203.91	200.00
Minor tone	10:9	182.40	200.00
Minor second or Diatonic semitone	16:15	111.73	100.00
Chromatic semitone	25:24	70.67	100.00
Pythagorean intervals			
Major third	81:64	407.82	400.00
Minor third	32:27	294.13	300.00
Minor second or Limma	256:243	90.22	100.00
Syntonic Comma	81:80	21.51	—
Mean tone intervals			
Fifth	$(3:2)(80:81)^{\frac{1}{4}}$	696.58	700.00
Fourth	$(4:3)(81:80)^{\frac{1}{4}}$	503.42	500.00
Major second or Mean tone	$(5:4)^{\frac{1}{2}}$	193.16	200.00
Minor second	$(256:243)(81:80)^{1\frac{1}{4}}$	117.11	100.00
Chromatic semitone	(Major second): (minor second)	76.05	100.00

325

than if an anachronistic temperament is employed. This advice applies to the mainstream repertory and not to highly-chromatic works.

Since tuning is mainly about vertical chording and not about solo melodic lines, I have concentrated upon that and said little about what makes good melodic tuning. Earlier I mentioned consistency of interval size: this is a feature of the best western European singers, and that consistency tends towards Pythagorean. However, eastern European folk-singing, for example, is a very different genre, one strongly characterized by Just melodic tuning.

Select bibliography

E. BLACKWOOD, *The structure of recognizable diatonic tunings* (Princeton, 1985)

J. W. HERLINGER, 'Marchetto's division of the whole tone', *Journal of the American Musicological Society*, xxxiv (1981), pp. 193–216

M. LINDLEY, 'Temperament', *New Grove* (London, 1980)

A. PADGHAM, *The well-tempered organ* (Oxford, 1986)

46 Tempo to 1500

Richard Sherr

Tempo, that is, 'the rate per unit of time of metrical pulses in performance' (*The New Harvard Dictionary of Music*), in particular the speed to be chosen at the beginning of a piece of music, is something about which musicians in the fourteenth and fifteenth centuries either agreed totally or in which they had no interest whatsoever. Nobody, with the exception of one theorist who tried to relate the speed of notes to divisions of the hour (a remarkable feat considering that no one had watches or even clocks with second hands), seemed to think that it was a matter worth discussing. We, unfortunately, want to know about such things, and the lack of guidance from the period itself is a bit frustrating. We can only assume that, in determining tempo, they, like us, responded to the cues of the notation itself. For instance, anybody wishing to play ex. 1 on the piano would realize first that the 'beat' of the measure has to consist of three crotchets; given that, the performer would then realize that he or she has to take a tempo in which the crotchet of 3/4 moved rather slowly in order to play the extremely small note values.

Ex. 1

Likewise a modern performer confronted with a transcription of fourteenth-century French secular music as in ex. 2 might very well decide that this was in 'compound metre' consisting of a fairly fast beat on the dotted crotchet. But a fourteenth-century French musician would have seen a notation of ex. 2 that looked like ex. 3. It would have told him that the time signature was C or *tempus imperfectum, prolatio maior*, and that meant that the note shape called the semibreve (◆) might be worth two or three of the note shapes called minims (♩) depending on context, and (again depending on context) a single minim might have the value of one minim or two; furthermore, he would not have had the concept of 'strong' and

Ex. 2
Guillaume de Machaut, beginning of the rondeau 'Quant ma dame' (Rondeau no. 19)

Ex. 3

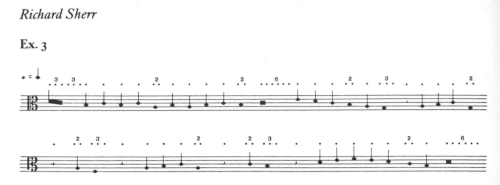

(Paris, Bibliothèque Nationale, fonds français 1584 (A in the Machaut complex), f. 480v)

'weak' beats, nor would he have the orientation system provided by bar lines. In short, the rules of the notational system would force the fourteenth-century musician into counting equal beats at the level of the minim as indicated by the dots above the notes in ex. 3 (something that is even more necessary in this piece, as the tenor is actually written in *tempus imperfectum, prolatio minor*, or 2/4: the two voices will work together only if we assume a minim/quaver beat).

In other words, although compound metre might exist at a structural level (the division of the measure into two semibreves of three minims each), it probably did not exist at the practical performing level, where the performer had to think of the piece by counting minims as beats. It follows from this that a tempo cannot be chosen that is too fast to allow minims/quavers to be so counted (chances are that the tempo that the modern performer would pick would be too fast). This is true of all mensurations in the French system of notation, and explains how mensurations that were different at the semibreve-breve level could be written simultaneously (as the minims were exactly equivalent), and also how melodic phrases could so often switch from what we would call 3/4 to what we would call 6/8 (merely different organizations of the basic minim beat) without changing mensurations. Indeed, if we count minims/quavers instead of semibreves/dotted crotchets, the following example of 'difficult' music of the late fourteenth century which looks so formidable in our notation because it is not easily reducible to compound metre, (especially a fast one), becomes much easier to perform (although it still presents some difficulties: see ex. 4).

Ex. 4
Anthonello de Caserta, beginning of the ballade 'Dame gentil'

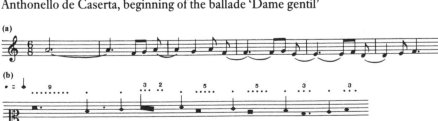

(Modena, Biblioteca Estense, L. 568, f.38v)

Italian music of the fourteenth century was written under a different system of notation, which we transcribe in a different way. When confronted with an example of Italian music in modern notation (see ex. 5), a modern performer might pick a fairly fast crotchet beat to make the semiquavers move at a good clip. An Italian musician would have seen ex. 6 and recognized it as *octonaria*, a mensuration in which the breve could be divided into two, four or eight parts, of which the smallest were minims. This would also have suggested a tempo related to the practicalities of reading the notation. Italian notation was 'bar/breve oriented'; accordingly, it was possible to conceive of the beat as a division of the bar/breve rather than the bar/breve as a sum of beats (as in French notation). In fact, the Italian mensurations were actually called 'divisiones'. In this notation, the minim remains constant, but the semibreve could be worth from two to four minims depending on how many semibreves appeared within the dots that marked the breve/bar. The basic beat would seem to be a duple division of the breve itself (hence our 2/4 measure). Performance of this piece seems not to have been dependent on counting minims; therefore, the tempo could be faster than in the French example.

Ex. 5
Jacopo da Bologna, beginning of the madrigal 'Aquil'altera'

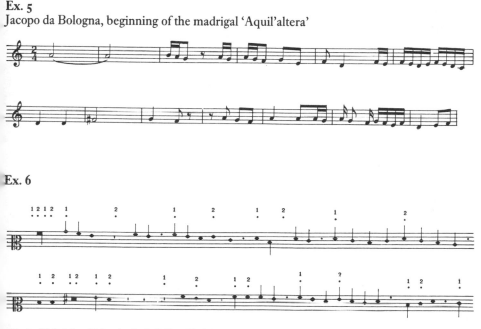

Ex. 6

(Paris, Bibliothèque Nationale, fonds italien 568, f. 2v)

But what should these tempos be? As I mentioned, nobody talks about it much, but that does not mean that it cannot be approximated. By careful analysis of theoretical discussions of 'tempus' (which did not mean tempo) in French and Italian music, combined with empirical experiment, Salvatore Gullo has come up with the following suggestions for the speed of the minims of the notational system of French and Italian music (see table 1):

Table 1

Speed of the minim (adapted from Gullo, pp. 68 and 85; 240 MM = four beats a second)

ITALIAN NOTATION

Mensuration	Speed of the minim
duodenaria	280–320 MM (transcribed in modern editions as 3/4: minim = semiquaver)
novenaria	210–240 MM (transcribed in modern editions as 9/8: minim = quaver). A breve of *duodenaria* lasts as long as a breve of *novenaria*; hence the minims are in a 4:3 relationship.
octonaria	280–320 MM (transcribed in modern editions as 2/4: minim = semiquaver)
senaria imperfecta	210–240 MM (transcribed in modern editions as 6/8: minim = quaver). A breve of *octonaria* lasts ⅔ as long as the breve of *duodenaria* (2 beats out of the 3/4 measure) and is equal to the breve of the *senaria imperfecta*, the minims being in a 4:3 relationship.
senaria perfecta	280–320 MM (transcribed in modern editions as 3/4: minim = quaver). A breve of *senaria perfecta* lasts as long as ½ breve of *duodenaria*.
quaternaria	280–320 MM (transcribed in modern editions as 2/4: minim = quaver). A breve of *quaternaria* lasts ⅓ as long as the breve of *duodenaria*, and ½ as long as the breve of *octonaria* (1 beat of the 3/4), and its minims move at the same speed as in those mensurations, even though we transcribe them as quavers instead of semiquavers.
ternaria	210–240 MM
binaria	280–320 MM

FRENCH NOTATION

Mensuration	Speed of the minim*
tempus perfectum, prolatio maior	210–240 MM (⊙, transcribed in modern editions as 9/8: minim = quaver)
tempus perfectum, prolatio minor	210–240 MM (○, transcribed in modern editions as 3/4: minim = quaver)
tempus imperfectum, prolatio maior	210–240 MM (𝄴, transcribed in modern editions as 6/8: minim = quaver)
tempus imperfectum, prolatio minor	210–240 MM (𝄵, transcribed in modern editions as 2/4: minim = quaver)

*The minim is equal in all French mensurations

Gullo's suggestions can be confirmed through the testimony of Michaele Savanarola, a fifteenth-century Italian doctor, and apparently the only person ever specifically to relate the speed of the pulse to the tempo of the music of his day. Doctors may have thought the pulse was 'musical', but they seemed to have been interested mainly in the musical proportions, and, contrary to what may be popular belief, the music theorists who mention pulse (Ramos, Gaffurius, Zarlino), do not, in fact, relate it to tempo, but instead present it as analogous to the tactus or beat because it, like the tactus, was believed to be divided into two equal parts.

As Kümmel has explained, Savanarola basically says that he has found that the normal pulse is somewhat slower than the division he knew as *quaternaria*, yet faster than the division he knew as *senaria imperfecta* (which was analogous to the French *tempus imperfectum, prolatio maior* (Ȼ), and was even called *senaria gallica*). He is referring to the 'beat' of the breve/bar in each division, and he clearly believes that *quaternaria* and *senaria imperfecta* denoted absolute tempos that could be easily remembered (he says that anybody can learn the tempos from a good musician 'in eight hours'); otherwise, they would be useless as a measure of the pulse. In *quaternaria*, the breve could be divided into two semibreves and four minims (2 + 2), while in *senaria imperfecta* the breve was divided into two semibreves and six minims (3 + 3); furthermore, in the Italian system, the breve of *senaria imperfecta* was twice as long as the breve of *quaternaria*, thus creating a 4:3 proportion at the level of the minim (see table 1).

The practical effect of this is difficult to put into words, but can be resolved by a simple experiment: (1) take your pulse, then speed up slightly; (2) divide that beat into four – you now have the speed of the minim in *quaternaria*, *octonaria*, and *duodenaria*:

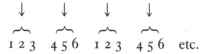

1 2 3 4   1 2 3 4   1 2 3 4   etc.;

(3) take the same beat and divide it into three (two beats = six) – you now have the speed of the minim of *senaria imperfecta* and *novenaria*, and also the speed of the minim in the French *tempus imperfectum, prolatio maior*, hence the speed of minims in all French mensurations:

↓   ↓   ↓   ↓

1 2 3   4 5 6   1 2 3   4 5 6   etc.

Now, let us convert this to metronome markings. Say your pulse is equal to 72 beats a minute and you speed it up to 76; this will give you 304 MM (76 × 4) for the minim of *quaternaria*, and 228 MM (76 × 3) for the minim of *senaria imperfecta*, speeds which fall perfectly within those suggested by Gullo (see table 1). You will also have arrived at a perfectly decent tempo (which, of course, could go somewhat faster or slower depending on the performer) at which to perform exx. 3, 4, and 6. It will, however, probably be a tempo slower than the one you might have chosen if you were presented simply with the modern notation. I would argue, then, that our decision to transcribe the mensurations ⊙ and Ȼ of fourteenth-century French music and the Italian *senaria* and *novenaria* as compound metres, and even to transcribe ○ and C as 3/4 and 2/4, invites performers to sing the music at tempos faster than the original performers would reasonably have chosen, while our decision to transcribe the minims of *duodenaria* and *octonaria* as semiquavers gives a better indication of tempo, but again implies one that is too fast. Yet, it still seems that the accepted level of transcription is correct for this music (transcribing ₵ as 6/4, for instance, would almost certainly produce a tempo that was too slow). The best advice is to consider: (1) the quaver to be the basic beat in French music of the fourteenth century; (2) 6/8 and 3/4 are made up of six quavers, not two dotted crotchets or three crotchets; and (3) semiquavers in Italian music do not go as fast as they look. Better yet, perform everything from the original notation (this last a dream, alas).

Tempo in fifteenth-century music

Around 1430, as Besseler and others have noted, the mensurations which most directly required minim counting because they created semibreves of unequal length (⊙ and ₵) dropped out of general use, and became reserved for special situations, leaving *tempus perfectum* and *tempus imperfectum* (O and C) as the basic mensurations. In these mensurations, the semibreve is always equal to two minims, and it is only after they have been well established that we get the first discussions of

1 Josquin Desprez, 'Et in terra' from the Mass *L'homme armé super voces musicales*

'tactus' (beat), defined as a duply divided beat inscribed by a down- up motion of the hand, normally designating the semibreve (many pictures of singing groups show one of the singers with his hand raised, presumably beginning to beat the tactus). The notation also shows minims divided into two semiminims (♩) and even into four fusae (♪). These are used so frequently that the common sense reasoning illustrated in ex. 1 (that, in the absence of any other indications, a tempo chosen to allow small note values to be performed at a reasonable speed will be slower than one chosen if they are not present), can probably be invoked to show that the tempo of the minim had slowed down and with it the tempo of the semibreve (see illus. 1). And while theorists may not in fact equate the speed of the tactus with the heartbeat, experience shows that it (70 MM–80 MM) is in fact a good indication of the tempo of the semibreve for the music of the mid to late fifteenth century.

Now, however, a different kind of tempo problem arises concerning the tempo relationships among sections of a multi-sectioned work. For instance, a common series of time signatures in two contiguous but self-contained sections of a piece in the later fifteenth century is ○ – all voices, ¢ – all voices. Theorists (most of them from the sixteenth century) tell us that in ○ the tactus is placed on the semibreve, in ¢ the tactus was placed on the breve, implying the tactus equation shown in ex. 7.

Ex. 7

If the beat remains constant, then this will cause semibreves in ¢ to move twice as fast as those in ○ (that is why it is also called 'diminution by half'). If the general level of note values increases in ¢, that is if breves really do replace semibreves as the carrier of the tactus, then it is easy to perform this equation, and in fact, there will be no perception of an increase in tempo, as in this example from Dufay's motet *Nuper rosarum flores* (see ex. 8).

Ex. 8
Guillaume Dufay, from the motet *Nuper rosarum flores*

(a)

(Trent, Museo Provinciale d'Arte, Castello del Buon Consiglio MS92, f. 21 v)

(b) Transcription indicating diminution

But quite often this does not happen, and sections in ₵ seem to employ as many minims and semiminims as sections in ○ (as in illus. 1). Applying the equation in ex. 7 to the performance of illus. 1 will illustrate the problem: a tempo that will work for the semibreves of ○ may seem too fast to allow performance of the semibreves, minims, semiminims of ₵, yet a tempo that will allow for easy performance of those notes in ₵ may be too slow for a reasonable performance of the section in ○ (see ex. 9).

Ex. 9
Excerpt from illus. 1, considering the tactus to be unchanging and to be on the semibreve in ○ and on the breve in ₵

Performers and editors have tended to respond to this by increasing the semibreve beat/tactus only slightly in ₵ (and not by slowing up the tactus in ○). Recently, Berger has shown that there is theoretical support for the idea put forth by Bent, Planchart and others that the semibreve tactus could speed up by a ratio of 4:3 when moving from ○ to ₵, and that it was the great influence of Johannes Tinctoris, writing in the 1470s, that eventually destroyed this option (but even Tinctoris says that under ₵ the tactus speeds up). Thus, ex. 9 might have been performed as in ex. 10.

The matter is by no means settled, however (see the article by Rob C. Wegman in the bibliography), and even more controversy surrounds the interpretations of the signatures ○2 and Ø when they follow ○. Technically, these should always require 'diminution by half' (speeding up semibreves by a factor of two while keeping the tempo/beat the same), but such an interpretation seems on occasion to create speeds that are much too fast. (This problem becomes acute in those pieces where sections are to be sung first in ○ and then repeated in Ø; can the composer really have intended an exact repeat to zip along at twice the tempo of the first rendition? The resolution of these arguments is not yet in sight; Hamm's suggestion that ₵ indicated only a slight speeding up of the semibreve beat has been attacked, and

Ex. 10

The same passage, considering the tactus to change in the proportion 4 semibreves of ₵ = 3 semibreves of ○

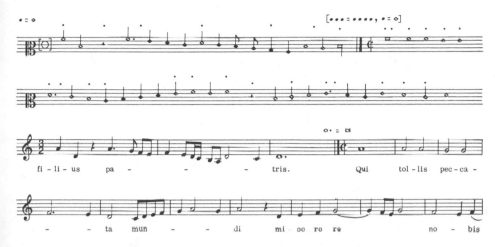

whirlpool of controversy has begun to swirl around the meaning of ○2. Unfortunately, a mass of theoretical evidence from the sixteenth century is not of much help because concepts of tactus may have changed by then. For now, I can only echo for the fifteenth century the advice of Salvatore Gullo, given after his discussions of tempo in the thirteenth and fourteenth centuries: 'Choose your tempo so that you can still perform the smallest note values at a comfortable speed' (p. 88).

The reader will perhaps have noticed by now an assumption that runs through this chapter, mainly that there was a 'tempo giusto' (a commonly-recognized tempo norm) employed in the period *c.* 1300–1500, even though that tempo might itself change over time. This is a common belief among scholars, and it seems to be supported by the evidence, although it flies in the face of modern musical experience in which pieces can have tempos that are fast or slow or in between. In fact, there was recognition of tempo differences in this period. There was an old tradition of varying the tempo of chants depending on the importance of the feast (the most solemn feasts were to have the slowest tempo), and the practicalities of the liturgy might also influence tempo; papal masters of ceremonies occasionally instruct the papal choir to speed up or slow down depending on the length of liturgical action. Should we consider these things when we perform sacred music of the fourteenth and fifteenth centuries? Should there not be a difference in the tempos of sacred and secular pieces? My fourteenth-century examples are all drawn from secular works. Isorhythmic motets may appear too slow when minims are beaten at the tempo giusto I suggest for the other pieces. Secular music of the fifteenth century may appear too slow if the semibreve tempo giusto of sacred music is applied to it. And certainly, dances were performed at different tempos.

Richard Sherr

Select bibliography

W. APEL, *The notation of polyphonic music 900–1600* (Cambridge, Mass., 1953)

A. M. BUSSE BERGER, 'The origin and early history of proportion signs', *Journal of the American Musicological Society*, xli (1988), pp. 403–33

D. BONGE, 'Gaffurius on pulse and tempo: a reinterpretation', *Musica Disciplina*, xxxvi (1982), pp. 167–90

S. GULLO, *Das Tempo in der Musik des XIII. und XIV. Jahrhunderts* (Berne, 1964)

C. HAMM, *A chronology of the works of Guillaume Dufay based on a study of mensural practice* (Princeton, 1964)

W. F. KÜMMEL, 'Zum Tempo in der italienischen Mensuralmusik des 15. Jahrhunderts', *Acta Musicologica*, xlii (1970), pp. 150–63

A. PLANCHART, 'The relative speed of *tempora* in the period of Dufay', *Royal Musical Association Research Chronicle*, xvii (1981), pp. 33–51

C. SACHS, *Rhythm and tempo: a study in music history* (New York, 1953)

E. SCHROEDER, 'The stroke comes full circle: ○ and ℂ in writings on music, ca. 1450–1540', *Musica Disciplina*, xxxvi (1982), pp. 119–66

N. G. SIRAISI, 'The music of pulse in the writings of Italian academic physicians (fourteenth and fifteenth centuries)', *Speculum*, l (1975), pp. 689–710

R. C. WEGMAN, 'Concerning tempo in the English Polyphonic Mass *c.* 1420–70', *Acta Musicologica*, lxi (1989), pp. 40–65; and 'Communication', *Journal of the American Musicological Society*, xlii (1989), pp. 437–43, with a response from Richard Taruskin on pp. 443–52

47 Tempo and tactus after 1500

Ephraim Segerman

This article considers how tempo was written about in the sixteenth century, and attempts to estimate the speed of the standard tempo that musicians thought of as unexceptional. The sources are more than somewhat ambiguous on this matter, so recourse is made to examining seventeenth-century sources, which are much more explicit. Analysis of the latter indicates that tempos in earlier music seem to have been rather slower than those felt appropriate by modern scholars and performers, and gives a better perspective on what sixteenth century tempos might have been.

Fundamental to the question of tempo is how it was thought of by the musicians themselves. Sources from the late fifteenth to the eighteenth centuries usually related tempo to an up and down movement of the hand. The word 'tactus' applied to the tempo as governed by this motion as well as its indication by the time signature. Other words for tactus were measure, full stroke, *mensura*, *compás*, *misura*, *battuta*, *Schlag*, *ictus*, *percussio* and *praescriptum*. Tactus related only to tempo and not to rhythm. It included both up and down motions, a full cycle. The relationship between the tactus and the reciprocating hand movements was likened to that between the pulse and (their concept of) the reciprocating beats of the heart, called individually 'diastole' and 'systole' or 'arsis' and 'thesis'. Neither up nor down hand movement was stressed more than the other; the sources are divided between those starting with an up motion and those starting with a down. The up and down motions were even (of equal duration) in common time and in triple time with three beats in each motion, or they were uneven in triple time with one motion twice the duration of the other.

It was usual in common time to notate the full time of a tactus with a semibreve ('alla semibreve' or 'integer valor notarum'). Alternatives were to notate it with a breve ('alla breve' or 'proportio dupla', also called 'diminution') or with a minim ('alla minima', also called 'augmentation'). The 'alla breve' notation was preferred when one wanted to avoid having to write too many short notes when the music was fast, or to impart an aura of learning. With these alternatives, the time duration of each hand motion, if equal, was fixed, and the differences were whether it was notated by one minim, semibreve or crotchet in common time (or three of these in triple time) in 'alla semibreve', 'alla breve' or 'alla minima' respectively. In triple time when the hand motions were of unequal duration, the quicker of the motions corresponded to one of these, the slower to two, and the total time of the tactus (both motions) was the same as when the motions were equal. There were time signature notations and fancy Latin names for each of these possibilities.

This was the simplest theoretical position, with one standard tactus for all notated music. It was followed when different voices in a polyphonic composition used different notation. It could also be followed in successive sections of a composition, but there were alternatives. One was that the notation and tempo remained constant, but the rate of hand movement could be doubled or halved. This created ambiguity in how the time signature related the notation to the hand movements. The other was that one could take the tactus somewhat faster than that which was considered to be the standard. A faster tactus for fast divisions was recommended by Luis Milán (1536), and this was mentioned by Mace (1676) as a common fault amongst most performers, including master musicians. So for situations other than different voices performing simultaneously, the time signature sign ₵ often did not mean its usual 'alla minima', but meant either the same as, or a somewhat faster version of, the standard 'alla semibreve' tactus (which had the time signature C). This was the practical situation, but musicians did recognize an 'official' way of beating the tactus of a standard 'official' tempo 'alla semibreve' when they wrote about it. The concern here is what that 'official' tempo was.

There is a psychological reason for tempo not to be completely arbitrary but to tend towards being related to the pulse. Hearing is the earliest sense developed in a person, and at birth one has already had the powerful experience of the sounds in the womb, which are dominated by the heartbeat. So we would expect a standard tempo to be close to a simple relationship with the heartbeat and thus the pulse. The question addressed is whether the pulse (usually in the range of 60–80 MM) corresponded to crotchets, minims or semibreves in the standard tempo notated in the standard 'alla semibreve' common time.

What the early sources wrote about the time duration of the standard tactus was occasionally quite explicit, was usually to some extent ambiguous, but was never, to my knowledge, inconsistent with other sources. Modern interpretations have often been explicit, but not necessarily consistent with the early sources, or each other. Modern writers have assumed that the semibreve or the minim corresponded to the pulse beat. These opinions have been based on interpretations of early sources which are ambiguous in the information they offer.

There is less ambiguous seventeenth-century information favouring the crotchet. The most precise early writer on tempo was Praetorius (1619). He wrote that at a good moderate speed ('wenn man einem rechten mittelmassigen Tact helt') there were 160 'tempora' in a quarter of an hour. Sachs (1953) calculated this to be crotchet = 85 MM since early theorists associated 'tempus' with a breve. Praetorius wrote much about tactus as a governor of tempo and how it related to time signatures, but the above relationship between tempo and the breve did not relate to tactus. It is likely that Praetorius did not feel that tactus needed mentioning because it was ordinary, *i.e.* 'alla semibreve'.

Another seventeenth-century theorist who related tempo directly to time measurement was Mersenne (1636). He was a scientist intent on exploring possibilities, and was not interested in the popularity or dignity of one practice as compared to another. He wrote that musicians 'make the measure [tactus] last more or less as they wish', and for convenience in illustration assumed a one-second tactus in 'alla semibreve', (also mentioning that musicians took two seconds and four seconds). In the one-second semibreve tactus, he associated the hand movements with the diastole and systole beats of the heart, with a second being a rather slow pulse beat. This is the origin of Arnold Dolmetsch's comment (1946) that 'Mersenne in his *Harmonie universelle* published in 1636 first gave the time value of a minim as that of a beat of the heart'. We must not confuse this beat of the heart (as Dolmetsch may have) with the pulse, which is half as fast.

Dolmetsch quoted Simpson (1668): 'Some speak of having recourse to the motion of a lively pulse for the measure of Crotchets; or to the little Minutes of a

338

steddy going Watch for Quavers . . .', adding that an average beat of the pulse was considered to be 72 beats per minute. He then concluded that since a watch of that period ticked at 300 times a minute, minim = 75 MM, ignoring or misunderstanding the first part of the Simpson quote indicating that it would be the crotchet. Donington (1963) quoted the same Simpson passage and Dolmetsch's conclusion, accepting it for an ordinary allegro.

The scholar's job is not to choose the information he prefers from a source where there is either ambiguity or apparent self-contradiction. When, in this case, there is an apparent self-contradiction, a choice should be made only when he can present a reasonable case for resolving the contradiction. So a minim = 75 MM solution of the contradiction requires a reasonable way of interpreting Simpson's apparently saying crotchet = pulse so that he meant two crotchets = pulse, and a crotchet solution requires a reasonable way of interpreting his apparently saying quaver = watch tick so that he meant quaver = two watch ticks.

The most uncertain element here is Simpson's term 'little Minutes'. If he meant 'ticks' he could have said so, or used the words 'beats' or 'strokes'. In a very similar context Playford/Purcell (1694) used 'regular Motions of a Watch'. Regular motions are repeating and usually reciprocating like the tactus, breathing or a swinging pendulum, where the full motion of the regularity includes two equal and opposite individual motions. So if the watch's mechanism was thought of as like that of a pendulum clock, Simpson and Playford/Purcell could have considered that a 'little Minute' or a 'regular Motion' of a watch included two ticks. This argument for the crotchet solution does not have compelling force, but it is quite possible. For the minim solution to be taken seriously, it needs an argument for two crotchets = pulse that makes as much sense as this one. One can cite two heartbeats = pulse (which could have been Dolmetch's confusion), but this is not acceptable because Simpson wrote 'pulse', and an hypothesis that does not assume a mistake in a source is preferred if there is no additional evidence for the mistake.

The passage in Playford/Purcell which mentioned 'regular Motions of a Watch' said that crotchets were almost as fast as these 'regular Motions' at a very fast tempo stated to be twice as fast as the normal one in earlier editions. (By this time there were three standard tempos: the normal one notated by C, a somewhat faster one notated by ₵, and this one notated by 𝄵). In the normal tempo, two of the four crotchet beats in a measure (tactus) corresponded to 'the slow Motions of the Pendulum' of 'a large Chamber-Clock'. The pendulum of such a clock is about a metre long, which has a full oscillation every two seconds. The minim solution above to the apparent contradiction in Simpson would be supported if a 'slow Motion of the Pendulum' was one swing, and the crotchet solution if it was a full oscillation. The word 'slow' implies a choice between slow and fast. A full oscillation versus a single swing provides this choice, so the crotchet solution is favoured here as well.

However, the strongest evidence for the crotchet solution comes from Mace's ceiling-to-floor pendulum (see illus. 1). The frequency of vibration of a pendulum only depends on its length, and the length here is the height of the ceiling. That height was higher than Mace could reach. The reach of a short man is about two metres, so the ceiling was at least that high. Mace's music room was a square with sides six yards long, with galleries for auditors extending three yards from the square's sides. There were small balconies on the far edges of the galleries. The

Chap. XI.

1 Thomas Mace,
Musick's monument
(London, 1676),
p. 80: 'How to
keep time well'

An Infallib'e Rule. how to keep Time well.

NOw I will proceed to the enabling of you to *perform your Time*, and by a moſt *Exact*, *Eaſe*, and *Infallible Way*; which ſhall be as a *Touch-ſtone*, to try whomſoever ſhall pretend to *keep Time, the moſt Exactly*; and it is *Thus*.

Take a *Bullet*, or any *Round Piece*, of what *weighty thing you pleaſe*, to the weight of *half a Pound*, or a *Pound*, (more or leſs) and *faſten It*, to the *End* of a *Pack-thread*, or any other *String*, long enough to reach the *Top of the Seiling of the Room*, in which you intend to *Practice*.

Then faſten the *End* of the *String* upon ſome *Hook*, or *Nail*, to the *Top of the Seiling*, ſo, as the *Weight* may well-nigh *touch the bottom of the Floor*; and when this is done, ſet It to *work*, after *this manner*, viz.

Take the *Weight* in your *Hand*, and carry It to *one ſide of the Room*, lifting It ſo *high* as you can *reach*; then let it *fall out of your Hand*; and you ſhall obſerve, ' That *This Weight, will keep* ' an *Exact True Motion of Time, forwards, and backwards, for an* ' *Hour or Two together*.

A ſtrange Secret of the Pendent.

' And that although, at every *Return*, It ſtrikes a *ſhorter Com-* ' *paſs*, than It did the *Time before*; yet it keeps the former *Exact* ' *Proportion*, (for *Length*, or *Quantity* of *Time*) *Infallibly*: Yea, ' when It makes ſo *little a Motion*, as you can *ſcarcely perceive It* ' *move*, It *Then gives the ſelf-ſame Meaſure*, (for *Quantity*) as It did ' *at firſt*: The which is *a pritty ſtrange thing*, yet moſt *Certain*; And ' *Eaſily prov'd*, by any.

' Now I ſay, having found out, ſuch an *Aſſur'd Time-keeper*, as ' *This* is, Let it be your *Director*, in all your *Curious Private Pra-* ' *ctices*.

How to make uſe of This Perfect Time-keeper.

' And thus, I would have you make uſe of It, *viz.* when you ' have ſet it to Work; Firſt, *Sit, and Obſerve It in Its Motion*, ' *Well*; and *take good Notice, of the Proportion of Time It ſtrikes*: ' And here you muſt know, That according to the *Length*, or *Shortneſs*

galleries were one step lower than the music room, which was like a slightly raised stage. What Mace wrote about the height of the music room was that it was 'not too High', with good acoustics being the main consideration. The ceiling was arched. This makes sense of Mace's phrase 'Top of the Seiling'. I suggest that for good acoustics the height of the ceiling for a room of such a large area would more likely be close to four than to two metres.

The frequency of a pendulum equals 0.50 divided by the square root of the length (given in metres). Since the full cycle for the pendulum corresponds to a semibreve, the MM for crotchets equals 240 times the frequency, or 120 divided by the square root of the length. For the length equal to two, three and four metres, crotchet equals 85, 69 and 60 MM respectively. For minim = 75 MM as Dolmetsch suggested, Mace's pendulum would need to be 0.64 metres long, a very unlikely possibility.

Mace suggested that the maximum length of the pendulum should be used for practising, implying that in performance it was likely to be shorter. My estimate is that for the long pendulum the tempo was in the region of crotchet equals 60–70 MM, and when it was shorter it was raised by about a metre so that crotchet equals 70–85 MM.

Mace instructed each crotchet beat to be counted 'One, Two, Three, Four' 'with Deliberation'. The passage of Simpson's quoted above had the same instruction, with these words pronounced 'as you would (leisurely) read them'. Playford/Purcell wrote 'telling one, two, three, four, distinctly'. Purcell (1696) wrote 'moderately tell four, by saying one, two, three, four', apparently for the two faster tempos as well as the normal one.

Sachs (1953) quoted the Simpson version of this and wrote 'Such counting yields about MM = 64'. If he meant this for each number, it agrees with Mace's pendulum information, implying that the crotchet corresponded to the pulse. But that is unlikely because he subsequently wrote that 'each two of these syllables formed a motor unit [pulse] – a fact that the reader will fully understand on reading the section on tactus'. The Simpson book does not have a section on tactus, so Sachs was referring to the section in his own book called 'Binary Tactus', starting on p. 217. There he made many assertions about tempo, citing no new evidence on this matter. It appears that he was relying on it being self-evident that each hand movement of the tactus corresponded with the pulse, which he called the 'motor unit' since he believed that it related to many repeating body movements.

An example of a modern author who assumed that the semibreve approximated the pulse was Apel (1953), who wrote that the tactus in the period discussed (up to 1600) was semibreve = 50–60 MM without citing any evidence. Another example is Howard Mayer Brown in his 'Tactus' entry in the *New Grove Dictionary of Instruments* (1984). He concluded that semibreve = *c.* 60–70 MM in *integer valor* ('alla semibreve'), citing Gaffurius's statement (1496) that 'one tactus equalled the pulse of a man breathing normally'. The original is rather more ambiguous than this translation.

Dale Bonge (1982) has convincingly shown that Gaffurius did not equate the time of the tactus with the pulse, but just considered them to be related by diastole–systole analogy, as did Ramos de Pareja (1482). There remains a problem, though, about what was intended by Gaffurius mentioning 'breathing' in the passage quoted by Brown. In Bonge's translation: 'For a regular semibreve equalling a full measure of time, namely, in the manner of the pulse of [someone] breathing evenly, . . .'. If Gaffurius was referring to the heartbeat pulse, breathing evenly does not perform its apparent function of avoiding an anomalous pulse, since exertion or emotion raises both pulse and breathing rates without causing particular unevenness. This argues for the possibility that Gaffurius was referring to the pulsation of even breathing, as mentioned in the 'Tempo and Expression Marks' entry by Fallows in the *New Grove Dictionary of Instruments*. If this was the case, and the in and out of breathing directly corresponded to the up and down of the tactus, then one tactus approximated four heartbeat pulses.

Stronger evidence supporting the hypothesis that the standard tempo and its standard notation did not change markedly during the sixteenth and seventeenth centuries is from Neusidler (1536) who indicated that the four crotchets in the semibreve tactus should be counted 'gently' ('fein gemach') 'eins, zwei, drei, vier', which is similar to the recommendations of Mace and Simpson. Lanfranco (1533) indicated that the hand movement of the tactus was governed by a healthy pulse. This is ambiguous as to whether one or two pulse beats were in each movement. Johannes Buchner (*c.* 1520) related the tactus to a man's leisurely stride. If the left and right steps of the stride corresponded to the up and down of the tactus, then one tactus equalled either two or four pulse beats, depending on how slow 'leisurely' meant and how fast Buchner's pulse was.

Determining what the standard tempo was says nothing about musical genres that have different tempos, such as dances. For these genres, tempos can sometimes be estimated by looking at sources that use the fastest notes then recognized, which were demisemiquavers, and noting their occurrence. For this one needs to know the fastest that musicians could play before high speed became an essential component of good technique. Mersenne (1636) wrote that this was sixteen notes per second for divisions or graces ('aux passages & aux fredons') for 'those who are esteemed to have a very fast and light hand, when they use all the speed possible for them'. Quantz (1752) indicated that it was 10.7 notes per second (8 notes per pulse beat, which he defined as 80 beats per minute) for articulated notes ('with double tonguing or with bowing') played by competent musicians. A competent keyboard player who is not especially esteemed for speed would have had an intermediate fastest speed, say thirteen notes per second.

For sources I pick the Fitzwilliam Virginal Book (*c.* 1614) and Robert Dowland's *Varietie of Lute Lessons* (1610), and I count the numbers of pavins, almaines, galliards and corantos that have demisemiquavers. This order of listing the dances is of expected increasing tempos, as can be inferred from Morley's (1597) discussion of them. In the harpischord book I ignore the few pieces having hemidemisemiquavers, assuming them to be vehicles of the type of players Mersenne mentioned. For the four dances, I find thirty-five, eight, four and no pieces respectively. From this I conclude that the tempo of a coranto was too fast for demisemiquavers, and that demisemiquavers in galliards were played at approximately thirteen notes per second, or crotchet = 96 MM. For the lute book I find five, three, one and one pieces respectively, with the demisemiquavers in the galliard and the coranto, being on the final cadence, to be ignored because of the rallentando there. From this I conclude that at the almaine tempo demisemiquavers were played about as fast as they could be, or at 10.7 notes per second, so crotchet = 80 MM. We would expect a sesquialtera relationship between pavin and galliard tempos, so I estimate that for the pavin, crotchet = 64 MM. If the same was the case for almaine and coranto tempos, crotchet = 120 MM for the coranto. Charles Butler (1636) wrote 'The triple is oft called Galliard-time, and the duple Pavin-time'. He was apparently referring to standard tempos. The pavin tempo deduced in the above analysis endorses the crotchet = pulse conclusion for the standard tempo arrived at earlier.

Dance specialists will not be happy with the tempos deduced here, but I am not aware of any reason why the dances could not be done at these tempos, most of which are considerably slower than those normally taken today. Singers and instrumentalists will be equally surprised. Slower tempos in music and dance afford greater opportunities for division and other ornamentation.

In conclusion, there is evidence from early and late in the seventeenth century that clearly favours crotchet = pulse beat as the standard tempo for music in common time. There is evidence for such a standard tempo associated with the pulse beat from early in the sixteenth century, but it is not clear whether the pulse beat was notated by crotchets or minims. From the way that modern scholars and musicians have ignored or misinterpreted the seventeenth-century information, it appears that the standard tempos of modern musicianship are faster than those preferred then, and this most probably applies to the sixteenth century as well.

Table 1: Summary of late seventeenth-century English evidence on duple tempos

Author	Date	Notation	Time signature	Source of tempo for comparison	Estimated number/min. in source	Assumed units	MM: crotchets per minute in C or ₵
Simpson	1668	crotchets	[C or ₵]	the motions of a lively pulse	70–85	pulses	70–85
Simpson	1668	quavers	[C or ₵]	the little Minutes of a Steddy going watch	(a) 300*	ticks	150
Playford/Purcell	1694	crotchets	♪	almost as fast as the regular motions of a watch	(b) 150	balance returns	75
Playford/Purcell	1694	minims	C	the slow motions of the pendulum of a large chamber clock	(a) 60* (b) 30	swings returns	120 60
Mace	1676	semibreves	[C]	[pendulum] Top of the Seiling [to] the bottom of the Floor [4 metres long]	15	returns	60

*Ambiguity in the watch and clock pendulum interpretations is shown in the (a) and (b) alternatives. Since we expect early sources of information to be consistent, and sources 1 and 5 are unambiguous, it is clear that the (b) alternatives are to be preferred, leading to estimated tempos of crotchet = 60–70 MM in C, 70–85 MM in ₵ and 120–140 MM in ♪

Select bibliography

Primary sources

J. BUCHNER, *Fundamentbuch* (*c.* 1520)
C. BUTLER, *The principles of musick* (London, 1636)
R. DOWLAND, *A varietie of lute lessons* (London, 1610)
F. GAFFURIUS, *Practica musice* (Milan, 1496)
G. M. LANFRANCO, *Scintille di musica* (Brescia, 1533)

T. MACE, *Musick's monument* (London, 1676)

L. MILÁN, *El maestro* (1536)

M. MERSENNE, *Harmonie universelle* (Paris, 1636); trans. R. E. Chapman (The Hague, 1957)

T. MORLEY, *A plaine and easie introduction to practicall musicke* (London, 1597); ed. R. A. Harman (London, 1952)

H. NEWSIDLER, *Ein newgeordnet Künstlich Lautenbuch* (Nuremberg, 1536)

J. PLAYFORD, *Introduction to the Skill of Musick*, ed. 'Corrected and Amended by Mr. Henry Purcell' (London, 1694), p. 25; quoted in Donington (1963), p. 344

M. PRAETORIUS, *Syntagma musicum* (Wolfenbüttel, 1619)

H. PURCELL, *A choice collection of lessons* (London, 1696), p. 4; quoted in Donington (1963), p. 344

J. J. QUANTZ, *Versuch einer Anweisung die Flote traversiere zu spielen* (Berlin, 1752), Chap. XVII, Sect. VII, para. 51, 55; trans. E. R. Reilly (New York, 1966)

B. RAMOS DE PAREJA, *Musica practica* (Bologna, 1482)

C. SIMPSON, *A compendium of practical musick* (London, 1668:); ed. P. J. Lord (Oxford, 1970)

General

W. APEL, *The Notation of Polyphonic Music 900–1600* (Cambridge, Mass, 1953; 1st edn. 1942), p. 147

D. BONGE, 'Gaffurius on Pulse and Tempo', *Musica Disciplina*, xxxvi (1982), pp. 167–74

R. DONINGTON, *The interpretation of early music* (London, 1963) (especially pp. 344–5)

C. SACHS, *Rhythm and Tempo* (New York, 1953), pp. 201–3

48 Divisions in Renaissance music

Bernard Thomas

The subject of divisions in sixteenth-century music has a rather theoretical feeling to many of us today. We all know that they were frequently used (though in theory banned from certain kinds of liturgical music), but we really understand remarkably little about how they were used. And in practice very few performers of pre-Baroque music today pay much attention to this question, apart from a handful (mostly North Americans) who studied at Basle. In Britain the use of divisions is still comparatively rare, especially among the more established 'serious' performers of early music – curiously those who work in the more informal end of the spectrum are frequently a lot more adventurous in this respect.

Clearly this has a lot to do with education. In fact, Basle is still almost the only place where it is possible to get any training in this area. In Britain there is no institution offering anything more than an occasional token workshop. To be fair to the institutions, they are confronted by genuine problems, the chief one being that the majority of gifted early music students at conservatoires are primarily interested in Baroque music, in which much of the technical vocabulary is integrated into the music; the Baroque flautist can study examples such as Telemann's *Methodische Sonaten*, thoroughly digest them, and get a real understanding of the central place of ornamentation in Baroque music, but there is no equivalent in pre-Baroque music. There are, of course, examples of complete pieces with divisions (which I will discuss below), but the extent to which material taken from one situation can be applied to another is highly questionable. Essentially, a student of Renaissance ornamentation has to piece together a style in a jigsaw-like process of adding together bits of information from many sources; with much late Baroque music the information is more immediate, and the technique-building part of the repertory is easily available. So it is not surprising that the young student, when faced with the decision of how to spend his few precious years at college, chooses the Baroque option, in which he has some idea of the end result, rather than the Renaissance (or earlier) option, which requires much work of a more experimental nature.

The basic problem is that we are talking about reconstructing a whole style of performance from a very motley (and frequently unrepresentative) collection of source materials. To place the problem in some sort of context, it is as if in four hundred years' time someone wanted to reconstruct Oscar Peterson's performing style, not by means of listening to whole performances, but only by reference to lists of riffs from some kind of teach-yourself-jazz book or computer programme.

Analogies with jazz are useful, because they remind us that the Renaissance tradition of diminution was part of an organic musical style that musicians – both professional and dilettante – would have absorbed from an early age. Jazz grew over much of the present century in a similar organic fashion, and also developed similar virtuoso styles of improvisation.

To learn Renaissance ornamentation today, the student needs to acquire a vocabulary of division motifs suitable for different musical situations. Learning to apply these motifs is more difficult, and depends to some extent on a rudimentary practical knowledge of counterpoint (that is, actually improvising counterpoints to given melodies, not doing exercises on paper). The tendency for music colleges to treat such things as 'theory', quite separate from performance, does not help the situation. The process of learning divisions is very like that of learning to speak a language (rather than simply reading it), in which a new word or phrase has to be used several times before it becomes firmly lodged in the speaker's active vocabulary. Without the repetition and consolidation that form the basis for this vocabulary, the student is like a tourist who has constantly to refer to his phrase book.

Sources

I The diminution manuals

There are, of course, a number of treatises on divisions, or diminution manuals, as musicologists like to call them. Apart from Ganassi (1535) and Ortiz (1553), these are all clustered in the forty or so years from 1584 onwards (the date of Dalla Casa's *Il vero modo di diminuir*), and all appeared in northern Italy. While they differ in emphasis (Ganassi focused on the recorder, Ortiz on the viol, and Dalla Casa on the cornetto, while Bovicelli concentrated on the human voice), most of the books have one important characteristic in common; the core of each volume is a table of divisions organized according to interval (that is, you are presented with twenty ways of decorating a note that rises by a tone, followed by a set of different figures for rising a third, and so on); there are normally separate tables of cadential decorations in the most common modes. Most also have some examples of decorated top parts, or in some cases of *viola bastarda* music, which represents the pinnacle of the whole development.

So if it is just a question of buying the facsimiles and studying the repertory, why is the whole subject beset with problems? One reason is clear from the dates of these collections, most of which are a manifestation of the hot-house atmosphere of Italian mannerism, rather than a retrospective look at Renaissance traditions. If we leave aside Ganassi and Ortiz for the moment, two very interesting features of the remaining books emerge:

1 A dramatic change in style over a few years. While Dalla Casa essentially presents figures of fast – sometimes very fast – notes in runs of apparently equal semi- and demisemiquavers, and this pattern is continued, rather more tastefully by Bassano (1591), from Riccardo Rognoni (1592) onwards we find many irregular rhythms, and in general a mannered, almost erratic style that contrasts dramatically with the smooth flow of typical Renaissance divisions. So we are dealing with a very rapidly changing style, which is after all what one would expect from northern Italy as the then centre of the avant-garde in many arts. To use the material in these widely-varying books, we have to be very sure of the musical context in which we employ them.

2 The complete pieces chosen by the authors of these treatises were not current works of their own generation, but pieces from at least two generations back: a small group of Franco-Flemish chansons of the 1540s, and madrigals from Cipriano de Rore's first book, probably written about the same time, dominate the

collections. This trend continues right up to Vincenzo Bonizzi's *viola bastarda* collection of 1626, which contains the most outrageously extreme settings of music, of anything up to a hundred years old (Sandrin's 'Douce memoire'). So it is important to establish what these complete examples are not: they are not examples of how to decorate works composed in the 1580s or 1590s (or whenever), nor are they examples of how to perform the chansons of Clemens non Papa or the early madrigals of Cipriano de Rore according to mid-century standards. The original undecorated pieces are nothing more than springboards; they provide a nice safe structure over which the mannerist performers could create their personal improvisations, which could range from the elegant to the bizarre. I think we have to assume that the potential audience knew the models; much of the charm of this repertory is to do with interaction between new material and model.

There is a precedent in the early Renaissance for this use of older material as a starting-point for fresh invention and caprice. A whole repertory exists of late-fifteenth-century instrumental elaborations of material from earlier in that century; again most of these pieces are based on a handful of melodies, either chanson tenors ('De tous biens playne', 'J'ay pris amours', 'Fors seulement', etc.) or basse-danse melodies ('La Spagna'). This last is possibly a useful reminder that material can survive over generations in different forms, and how at this distance we can misinterpret the function of a particular link in this chain (in the 1970s Renaissance specialists were regularly performing a three-part *La Spagna* as if it was a unique example of notated dance music; more recently it has become known that this piece was a movement from a Mass by Heinrich Isaac).

I certainly do not want to discourage anyone from studying the material in the mannerist diminution manuals. It is a question of taking them for what they are: manifestations of the avant-garde of their time, a time in which the art of diminution had been taken to such a height that it developed its own special process. If one were to choose a text-book for what we might call High Renaissance improvisation (that is, pre-mannerist), I would suggest Ortiz. His *Tratado de glosas* of 1553 has been rather neglected; it has been largely ignored by players of wind instruments because it has been regarded as viol-player's territory, and string-players have concentrated on the ricercare at the expense of his very useful repertory of decorative figures. This tendency for modern instrumentalists to develop largely without reference to players of other instruments is one of the main obstacles to understanding many aspects of Renaissance music; it was obviously not a characteristic of musical life in the Renaissance, given that Ganassi wrote treatises both for the recorder and the viol, and that Dalla Casa, supposedly a virtuoso cornetto player, arranged ten pieces for the *viola bastarda*.

To return to Ortiz, there are a number of reasons – quite apart from the timing of his publication right in the middle of the century – to take his material very seriously indeed in any study of Renaissance improvisation:

1 The high quality of his finished pieces, especially the recercadas on ground basses. Perhaps the most outstanding characteristic of these is his use of what Virgiliano calls 'perfidie'. This is where a figure is apparently repeated, but changed by its context: for instance, with an initial appearance beginning after the beat, and the second beginning on the beat, or alternatively the use of a figure played first over one chord, then over another. We have to respect any musician who can produce material like this. Even his little pieces over the *La Spagna* melody

are effortless and unpretentious masterpieces of improvised counterpoint. He is not at all interested in fast notes for their own sake, but rather in achieving balance, grace and elegance.

2 His tables of divisions are useful in several ways: they are not particularly difficult technically, and yet they are more varied and less mechanical than Dalla Casa's. A nice feature is the inclusion of triplets, which many of the other sources ignore.

3 His material can be – with reasonable safety – applied to music of roughly his own time. It is true that the two models he chooses for complete examples (Sandrin's 'Douce memoire' and Arcadelt's 'O felici occhi miei') are from one generation back, but what he does with them does not necessarily involve slowing them down dramatically.

4 Especially interesting are his examples of 'fifth-part' writing. This may seem academic, but it is far from being so. Study of much four-part sixteenth-century music shows a surprisingly fixed approach to the division of the material between the parts, especially at cadences; until well after the middle of the century the early Renaissance convention by which the top part normally had the leading note and the tenor the note above the final at cadences continued in force, at least in the majority of cases. This convention may seem boring, until we examine the question of fifth parts. The very predictably of the voice-leading in the basic four parts allows a remarkable degree of freedom in the fifth part, as well as forcing it into certain melodic behaviour that would be unthinkable in any of the basic four parts. From the middle of the sixteenth century onwards, a definite tradition of fifth parts can be found in simple dance music (for example, the Hessen books of 1555, but also in the occasional piece in the Attaingnant dance books of 1530–57); the progressions forced on these parts by the desire to avoid consecutives can often seem bizarre, but their very eccentricity can, in the right hands, become a virtue. Ortiz's fifth parts on 'O felici occhi miei' and 'Douce memoire' should be studied and committed to memory by every serious student of Renaissance music.

However, Ortiz is not the only useful source for late Renaissance divisions. Giovanni Bassano's print of 1591, though coming only a year before Riccardo Rognoni's very manneristic examples, contains some beautifully paced and elegant divisions, particularly those on chansons such as Lassus's 'Susanne un jour' and Crécquillon's 'Un gay bergier' and 'Oncques amour'. They represent the high point of traditional Renaissance divisions, just before the turn to mannerism, and many of the texted pieces, while unspectacular in terms of the quantity of divisions, are perhaps especially useful precisely because they are not artifically elaborate, but are relatively close to the kind of thing a gifted performer of the time would have had, literally, at his fingertips. Particularly effective is Bassano's *bastarda* version of Rore's 'Ancor che col partire', which uses both the bass and the tenor part, but is fully texted.

II Other sources

It is clear that the mannerist manuals have to be used with discretion, and that whatever the virtues of Ortiz, we have to search more widely for material on ornamentation. In Howard Mayer Brown's book on this subject, there is a list of a few examples of decorated pieces from sources other than the manuals. Leaving aside for the moment the question of lute and keyboard music, it is possible to find isolated examples of written-out divisions included in normal collections of music:

1 Petrucci's *Frottole libro sexto* (1505), contains a few decorated pieces, in one case, 'Aime sospiri', a version of a piece that has survived undecorated.

2 British Library, Royal Appendix 74–6 contains some decorated pavans (some for lost pieces, some for pieces elsewhere in the manuscript). A useful example is a piece called the 'Pavan of Albart', which is a simply but nicely decorated version of a popular French *pavane*, 'Si je m'en vois'.

3 Other dance sources included divisions, notably Praetorius's *Terpsichore*, which ends with four pieces called *Reprisen*, in which sequences of four-bar sections in a slow galliard rhythm are decorated in the top part. As well as these rather substantial examples, *Terpsichore* contains a handful of other pieces with divisions, scattered through the collection. Pieces with simple divisions occur in the books of Susato, Phalèse, Mainerio and others, and also Antonio Brunelli's *Scherzi, arie e canzonette* of 1616.

4 Certain ricercars in the Italian collection *Musica nova* of 1540 have few cadential and other flourishes which are not in themselves particularly significant or original, but which are special simply because they appear in a normal context, and are not part of some didactic work.

It seems clear that, given the ability to distinguish decoration from basic progression, one will find little examples in many different places, albeit very widely scattered. Perhaps the problem is that present-day musicians are not necessarily trained to make the above distinction, but only to play the notes put in front of them. What is required is a practical, analytical approach to the music, an ability to spot and assimilate examples that can be used effectively.

Lute and keyboard music

A rich source of ornamentation of all kinds – if one knows what to do with it – is tablature, both for fretted instruments, and for keyboard. Obviously tablature, which in its purest form is a set of instructions about where the player puts his fingers, relates much more directly to actual performance than does mensural notation; so it is not surprising to find that written-out divisions are much more common in lute and keyboard music than in music written in parts.

The lute-player today is in a unique position compared to his colleagues playing wind and bowed instruments. He has a large repertory in which melodic ornamentation is often completely integrated into the music, though there is much evidence to suggest that additional graces such as mordents and short trills, were assumed at times. He even has division parts designed for ensemble use, as in the solo lute parts of the English mixed consort repertory, and there are many examples in music for two or more lutes of single-line divisions of a contrapuntal kind, as in the 'La Spagna' settings in the Siena lute book.

The keyboard-player is not so well off, especially as far as music before around 1580 is concerned. Of course, the whole English virginal repertory abounds with elegant ornamentation, as a typical pavan with repeats will show. Again, however, we get the feeling that this repertory is the tip of an iceberg, the climax of a long development. Much of the ornamentation in this repertory sounds quite ridiculous when applied to other instruments. If we go back half a century, we find already quite well-developed and idiomatic keyboard divisions in the very Italianate

Attaingnant dances for keyboard (1530), the Gardane *Intabolatura* of 1551, and in the music from the Castell' Arquato MSS. Once again, this has to be treated very circumspectly if we are to use the material for other instruments. The divisions in these collections often involve a great deal of passing dissonance, which is not in itself a problem in music with a clear chordal structure (see below), but it also involves irrational leaps from one register to another, as in ex. 1. If we were to transfer the moving passage to a melody instrument such as a cornetto or recorder, the leaps would sound quite bizarre, but when the whole is played on one or more plucked instruments, the ear smooths out the melodic progressions. Even bowed instruments can get away with a little of this, but not wind instruments. The difference between lutes at one extreme, and wind at the other, can be summed up in the fact that lutes often had their lower courses doubled at the octave. If we imagine a recorder consort, or indeed any wind consort, in which every note below middle C was doubled an octave higher, the differences become clear.

Ex. 1

(a) Pavana (Castell' Arquato, no.1)

(b) Ripresa (Castell' Arquato, no.2)

To some extent we have to assume that every instrument had its own idiom: flue instruments may well have been played with a lot of finger vibrato, as they are in traditional music in many parts of the world (eastern Europe, China, Ireland, etc.). It is reasonable to assume, however, that instruments capable of playing both chords and melodies would have had a radically different approach to divisions from those confined to a single line, which would presumably have had essentially the same approach to musical intervals, and a roughly comparable range, as has the human voice.

So singers and players of sustaining instruments have to be very selective in adapting material from lute and keyboard divisions. Perhaps ornate intabulations are more useful as a general guide to the way a decorated piece is shaped and paced, than as a specific model to be actually transferred to another instrument.

Ornamentation and harmonic rhythm

Many surviving lute and keyboard pieces with divisions are based on quite slow-moving harmonies, sometimes in the form of regular changes every three or four beats, as in the passamezzo antico, passamezzo moderno and other ground bass patterns. It is striking that in such pieces the diminutions are less inclined to follow normal rules about dissonance than in other intabulations. It seems clear that the ear tolerates irregularities much more easily when the harmonics are very clear and predictable. We can see this in many of the cadential divisions found in the diminution manuals, and they are often much freer than the interval divisions, for a similar reason: Renaissance cadences are stereotyped, and because the ear does not have to learn anything new, it can cope with a somewhat wild-sounding division.

Ornamentation and climax

The best examples of decorated pieces usually conform to the general aesthetic that underlies much abstract instrumental music (and a great deal of vocal music) of the Renaissance, by which the pacing is carefully controlled. Bassano's outstanding versions of chansons such as 'Un gay bergier', 'Susanne un jour' and so on, fastidiously control the degree of rhythmic excitement: each phrase of the song has slightly more ornamentation than its predecessor, leading to an impressive roulade at the end. This is exactly what the theorist Zacconi advises when discussing diminutions. However, this principle of progression works on two levels; that of the piece as a whole, and that of the individual phrase, in which again the greatest amount of ornamentation should come at the cadence. This sounds like common sense, but in my experience it takes musicians of today quite a long time to acquire a sense of this structural aspect, presumably because they are brought up to assume that structure is entirely the responsibility of the composer.

Ornamentation and personal style

The use of divisions brings up a paradox in the revival of early music. All the use of historical evidence almost presupposes that the whole function of the player today is to reconstruct, to get as close to what musicians 'then' would have done. And yet the best musicians of the time, while working within a clearly understood tradition, would have each had their own personal style, just as the best jazz and rock performers have today. I would argue that even when engaged in the somewhat artificial process of trying to reconstruct diminution practice at this distance in time, the development of a personal style should be regarded as a positive help, provided the performer does not become locked into it, and that the style continues to develop.

The bastarda style

This is an endlessly fascinating subject, which I cannot take very far here. It was associated particularly with the viol, but there are examples for the human voice, for

351

Ex. 2
Diego Ortiz, Recercada 'Doulce memoire'

the violin, and even one for the trombone. Basically, it is a style of arrangement in which a solo performer does not simply take a cantus or bassus part and decorates that, but rather moves from part to part, and even goes into the fifth-part mode found in Ortiz (see ex. 2), and at times into extremely virtuoso runs across the whole range of the instrument (to accommodate the aspirations of *bastarda* players, new ways of tuning the viol were devised, taking the bottom string down a fourth). A great deal of musical invention went into the best *bastarda* pieces, and it is clear that it was in this music that the Renaissance and mannerist traditions reached their highest point. The difficulty in reviving it is that much of the subtlety of this music – however impressive it may sound technically – is lost if the listener does not have some working knowledge of the model.

Select bibliography

H. M. BROWN, *Embellishing sixteenth-century music* (London, 1976)
R. DONINGTON, *The interpretation of early music* (London, 1963)

49 'Perfect' instruments

Andrew Lawrence-King

In 1577 the Venetian printer Gardane published an edition of madrigals in score: 'Tutti Madrigali di Cipriano de Rore a 4 voci spartiti et accommodati per sonar d'ogni sorte d'instrumento perfetto'. While madrigals were more normally sung from partbooks, this score advertised itself as suitable material for any kind of 'perfect' instrument (that is, any instrument that could play chords and polyphony rather than just a single melodic line); such a publication saved lutenists, harpists and keyboard players the trouble of intabulating works from the individual parts. It could be used to accompany a group of singers, to perform a madrigal as a solo song with instrumental accompaniment, to play a four-part madrigal as an instrumental solo, or simply as a study score for students of composition: the concept of 'accompaniment' in Renaissance music embraces all of these functions.

The essence of good accompaniment in any style of music is the ability to react sympathetically. This always involves some element of improvisation, which may be on the level of the actual notes played – as in continuo realization – or on the level of rhythmic and dynamic change; in either case it requires a thorough understanding of the music. Seventeenth-century treatises on continuo accompaniment emphasize the need for an accompanist to have a good grasp of counterpoint, so that he can not only construct his own part, but also guide the whole performance from the inside (as opposed to the modern conductor, who directs from outside). Of course, the early writers of continuo music did not invent the idea of solo song, nor of chordal accompaniment: their achievement was to develop a notation that gave the accompanist the necessary information in the simplest possible form. (Thus Caccini entitled his 1614 book *Nuove musiche e nuova maniera di scriverle* – New pieces and a new way of writing them.) By minimizing the notation, they maximized the accompanist's freedom to react spontaneously to the music around him.

Improvisatory performance practices are particularly resistant to musicological investigation, although a number of scholars (notably Nino Pirrotta) have made successful studies of unwritten music. Continuo playing clearly derives from unwritten styles developed during the sixteenth century, but continuo treatises give more hard information on content than on style. Nevertheless, for an accompanist as for any musician, it is just these elusive and intangible subtleties that are the most interesting: they are the stuff of which music is made. This article does not pretend to be a survey of the available evidence; rather it is an attempt to understand the role of the Renaissance tenorista. My practical suggestions are accordingly based first on my own experience of accompanying Renaissance music, and second on written sources. I also seek to draw reasonable inferences from the first continuo treatises of the early seventeenth century.

Polyphonic styles

The idea of a solo song with instrumental accompaniment is so familiar to us that we take it for granted, as indeed most Renaissance listeners would have done. But in polyphonic music, the idea of 'accompaniment' is misleading: the lute, harp or keyboard is actually a replacement for a missing voice, possibly for several voices. The ideal that the accompanist strives for is the perfect imitation of the human voice on each of the individual polyphonic lines of his part. He is a partner to the soloist, 'holding' the tenor for him.

Burgundian three-part chansons from the fifteenth century often sound like a solo with accompaniment even when performed by three singers, because the upper voice has a different tessitura and more 'vocal' style. They can be effectively performed as solos to a harp or lute, and there survives a transcription of the lower two voices of a Dufay chanson on to a single stave: a part for a tenorista, made by combining two missing voices. In 1507 Petrucci printed a book of lute pieces by Spinacino which contained a number of transcriptions of Burgundian chansons for two lutes. The lower two parts, which are little altered from the original, are played by the second lute, while the first plays an elaborate solo part that ranges across the whole compass of the instrument. In Dalza's lutebook (also printed by Petrucci the following year), the accompanying part in some duets is labelled 'tenor e contra', even when the part is not consistently in two voices.

Petrucci's printing of the Bossinensis lute-book is evidence of the popularity of solo song arrangements, for it consists of arrangements for singer and lute of four-part frottolas. The singer takes the top line of the original, the lute plays the bass and one of the inner parts. The frottola (simpler, lighter and more harmonically directional than the madrigal) is well suited to this treatment, and the texture of the lute part is ideal for the instrument. The bass moves in fourths and fifths (making good use of the open strings), while the tenor has interesting cross-rhythms and melodic fragments. The loss of the (usually uninteresting) alto is more than compensated for by the gain in polyphonic clarity.

In *The book of the courtier* (1528), Castiglione mentions the performance of madrigals by a solo singer, and in 1536 Willaert published madrigals by Verdelot in lute-song transcriptions, with the lute playing all three lower parts. The fashion for solo song even allowed the occasional interruption to the text. In Verdelot's 'Quanto sia lieto il giorno', the line 'Io ninfa e voi pastori', set in dialogue between high and low voices, loses the 'pastori' to the lute in Willaert's arrangement.

The concept of an accompaniment as the sum of polyphonic voices remained popular and can be seen in many English lute songs, such as Dowland's 'Flow my tears' or (a late and extreme example) John Danyel's 'Can dolefull notes', a polyphonic chromatic fantasia for voice and lute. The role of the lute was even emulated by the viola da gamba. In the lyra-viol style, composers such as Tobias Hume sought to create an illusion of polyphony on a bowed instrument (as J. S. Bach was to do later in the Suites for unaccompanied cello).

If a 'perfect' instrument could replace voices in an accompanying role, it could even take over the whole piece and play it as an instrumental solo. For many instruments, this was probably a more important source of repertory than specifically instrumental compositions. A fifteenth-century French romance, *Cleriadus et Meliadice*, tells how the hero, Cleriadus, wrote music for a poem by

Meliadice and spent some time 'putting it on the harp'. As he reports to Meliadice by letter: 'J'ay mis vostre chanson en chant . . . et si est desia mise sur le harpe'. In addition to finding the right notes, he was presumably also experimenting with different ways to re-create the effect of his two-part vocal original on a plucked instrument.

Many such instrumental arrangements are collected together in the early fifteenth-century Faenza Codex, where they are presented in two-part score, even if the vocal original is in three or four parts. The tenor is preserved almost unchanged, but the upper part is swathed in ornamentation, however florid the original. If this is what is entailed in 'putting a piece on the harp' (or keyboard, lute etc.), we should ask ourselves what is the purpose of such complex ornamentation (which is also found in many later transcriptions of vocal pieces).

Ex. 1
Ornamentation as an aid to phrasing

(a) Paul Hofheimer, Lied 'Nach Willen dein'

(b) In a version for organ by Hans Kotter (1513)

(c) In an anonymous version for organ (1530)

(d) In a version for lute by Hans Neusidler (1536)

On one level, it is simply decoration for its own sake and represents an ideal of the kind of ornamentation that could, with taste and discretion, be applied to any piece. But in the context of instrumental performance of a vocal piece, ornamentation takes on an extra role. Not only can fine divisions preserve interest in a piece that lacks any text; they can also produce the effect of subtle articulations or of the development of long notes, and so help the instrumentalist realize his desire to emulate the perfect expressivity of the human voice. Thus a note that could not be sustained on the harp, say, is replaced by a group of shorter notes; even a keyboard instrument can be made to sound expressive if a 'dead' long note is replaced by flickering rhythms, giving an illusion of crescendo and diminuendo (see ex. 1). In bar 1, for example, a singer could phrase this with a crescendo through the bar; an instrument needs extra notes to create the same effect.

Musicological opinion is still divided on the question of whether the Faenza transcriptions were intended for any particular 'perfect' instrument and, if so,

which one. In any case, there are later collections of transcriptions for lute, harp and keyboard, and also of the 'ogni sorte' kind. Henestrosa's *Libro de cifra nueva* (1557) contains a number of chansons by Crécquillon, Clemens non Papa and similar figures in straightforward transcriptions for 'arpa, tecla y vihuela'.

Chordal styles

Replacing voices is, however, only one aspect of Renaissance accompaniment. Another arises when the accompanist is asked to play along with a piece that is already complete in itself. The accompaniment needs a considerable degree of improvisation (even if sometimes on the level of tactful silences) in order to respond to the music being created by the soloists: since the polyphony is already

Ex. 1 contd

there, the accompanist's first concern is to avoid getting in the way. This sounds like negative, or at least very elementary, counsel; but if one accepts the principle, it has profound implications. In this style, the accompanist should allow the soloists to set the tempo at each new beginning: in other words, he should play on the main beats to begin with, and not play any tempo-determining rhythm until the tempo is clear. He should not double the details of ornamental figuration, lest he obscure its rhythm or intonation. Most of all, his role is now definitely secondary, so he should not be over-concerned with being heard. (It is always tempting when playing a soft instrument in an ensemble to wait for the quietest moment and make yourself heard during it, at great cost to the dynamic shape of the whole.)

The idea of using an accompanying instrument to add texture pre-dates written polyphony: the ancient Celtic harpists who assisted a reciter in his performance; knights who, like the hero of the *Roman de Horn*, sang lais to the harp; the two fiddle players who performed the *estampida* that became the song 'Kalenda maya'; the pairs of instruments that are depicted in the book of *Cantigas* of Alfonso el Sabio; the Renaissance tenorista who accompanied a *cantastorie*'s declamation of epic verses in the market square: in all these duos an instrument was adding lustre to a performance that was essentially already complete.

The purpose of this background accompaniment in these many different styles of music is to add harmonic texture and to define the rhythmic structure. The simplest way to do this is with a drone bass, and several medieval instruments are ideal for this purpose. The drone tuning of the medieval fiddle and the naming of its bass string (and those of the harp) as 'bordun' suggest that these instruments could have added rich sonority to a melody by means of plucked or bowed drones. The need to commit oneself to some kind of rhythm (since the drone has to be reiterated with each pluck or bow stroke) helps explain why these instruments are more suitable for the lighter genres than for the rhapsodic freedom of the troubadour *canso*.

Christopher Page has shown that when monophonic song was accompanied, the instrument of accompaniment was usually a fiddle. As he points out, re-entrant and drone tunings produce a fascinating kaleidoscope of texture, even though the player feels he is just playing the tune; he is able to provide an accompaniment to a singer, or a fascinating self-accompanied solo. Since the music exists only as a single melodic line, the accompanist should not feel he is adding an element of contrast or tension against the melody; rather, he is doubling the melody in heterophony. Even if the 'doubling' consists only of playing drones, the feeling is that one is playing the tune on the drone note. Unison or octave doubling, 'fifthing' (adding a parallel part mostly in fifths with the tune), varied drones that follow the contours of the melody: all create the impression of a single melody seen through an ever changing filter of instrumental texture.

Jerome of Moravia's treatise on fiddle playing also describes how an advanced player could improvise a more complicated accompaniment, by 'harmonizing' the melody with bass notes: 'that which is most difficult, serious and excellent in this art: to know how to reply with the *borduni* in the first harmonies to any note from which any melody is woven . . .' (following Christopher Page's translation). Page has suggested this means improvising a second part to a singer, perhaps by fifthing: but perhaps the fiddle player is 'replying' on the bass strings to the notes he himself is playing on the melody string. This is indeed an advanced technique, in the sense

359

of being difficult to execute. The results of such virtuoso improvisation would sound musically sophisticated, and could even point to an approximation of the sound of a polyphonic chanson (see ex. 2). It has been suggested (by Pirrotta and Haar) that the sound of the Italian trecento madrigal derives from improvisatory organ playing: perhaps the texture of the Burgundian chanson derives from improvised accompaniments to monodic song.

Ex. 2
From accompanied monody to Burgundian chanson

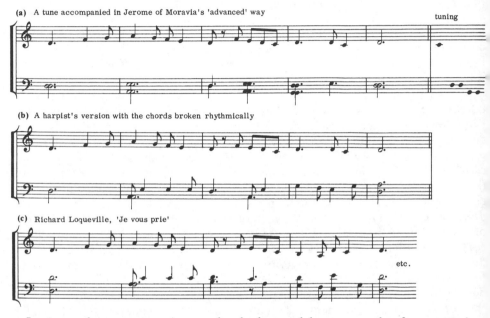

(a) A tune accompanied in Jerome of Moravia's 'advanced' way

tuning

(b) A harpist's version with the chords broken rhythmically

(c) Richard Loqueville, 'Je vous prie'

etc.

In sixteenth-century music, too, the rhythm-and-harmony style of accompaniment works best in lighter genres – frottolas and dances rather than madrigals. Dalza's 1508 lutebook contains some dance movements set as duets, in which the accompanying lute repeats a rhythmic pattern, sometimes in completely static harmony. The Renaissance 'tenor' represents the next level of harmonic sophistication, in which the repeated unit is a simple harmonic sequence – what was later called a ground bass. These Renaissance tenors (and the chord sequences and tunes associated with them) soon came to form a kind of musical *lingua franca* for both improvised and written music all over Europe: the descending tetrachord of passacaglia; the three chord trick of bergamasca ('In an English country garden'); the longer sequence, passamezzo ('Greensleeves'), and very many more.

The Ap Huw MS, a seventeenth-century copy of a mid-sixteenth-century Welsh source, preserves simple settings and variations for harp on the twenty-four Welsh 'measures'. Although the Ap Huw notation is not yet fully understood, it is clear that these 'measures' correspond in function to the Italian tenors, and that they too were the starting point for both instrumental and vocal improvising: a student of music in Wales would be expected to learn the measures, starting with just one or two sequences and elementary variations, and progressing to the complete canon of twenty-four with complex ornamentation.

The popularity of Renaissance tenors was both a cause and a symptom of the increasing tendency of improvising musicians to think chordally rather than polyphonically. Instruments with only a limited capacity to play true polyphony could still be accepted as 'perfect', if they could provide effective chordal accompaniment, and the Spanish guitar, cittern, and *arpanetta* grew in popularity, especially in lighter music. The two notation systems for the guitar show clearly the dichotomy between chordal and polyphonic thinking: there was a tablature for polyphonic writing and a system of chord symbols and rhythm signs known as *alfabeto* for strummed passages. The tuning of the cittern favoured simple left-hand fingerings for the most commonly used harmonies, so that even unsophisticated musicians could strum the chords of a ground. No written music survives for the *arpanetta* (a large psaltery with strings on both sides of the soundbox), but the instrument was played throughout Europe for domestic entertainment. Its set-up with treble strings on one side and bass strings on the other encourages a tune-and-chords style, which no doubt drew in part on the tenor repertory.

The *lira da braccio*, a violin-like instrument with a flattened bridge to allow chordal playing, was particularly associated with the performance of epic verse to *arie*, melodic formulae related to the harmonic patterns of the tenors. Seventeenth-century publications contain highly developed compositions in this form (Frescobaldi's *Aria di passacaglia* and *Aria di romanesca*; Monteverdi's 'Zefiro torna' over the *ciacona* bass), but the Petrucci prints of the early sixteenth century present a number of simple frottolas without texts, as music which could be used for any set of verses (written or improvised) in the appropriate metre. Music like this, which continued to be published throughout the sixteenth century, and certain declamatory songs, such as Tromboncino's 'Voi che passate qui' (in Petrucci's *Frottole libro settimo*, 1507), are clearly courtly versions of the improvised performances to be heard in any square. The whole frottola style, with its forthright rhythms and simple harmony, is closely connected to the improvisations of the tenoristas, if not actually derived from them.

When accompanying a piece that is already polyphonically complete, a player of a chordal instrument is free to concentrate on the structural elements of rhythm and harmony, and can adapt his part to the exigencies of the moment. Indeed, the very fact that he is in a certain way 'unnecessary' means that he is in a unique position to guide the whole ensemble. Early continuo sources suggest ways in which this could be done; for example, by playing an impulse-giving chord on the down-beat before an entry. Whereas the polyphonic accompanist tries to become an equal partner by imitating the voice, the chordal player complements the voices by being different: he may lend support in the background or lead with clear gestures.

This principle of direction from the accompanist obtained particularly in church music. From early in the sixteenth century, organists would have accompanied Masses and motets from a score or *intavolatura* prepared from the individual parts. This could have been anything from a rough sketch based on the lowest parts (*basso seguente*) to a fully worked-out accompaniment. The figured bass of Viadana's first continuo motets (written in the 1590s) was intended as the basis for the preparation of such an *intavolatura*, rather than as a part to play from. Conversely, some English lute songs with intabulated accompaniments are stylistically closer to continuo song than to the old polyphonic style: it is important to separate the sound world of a piece of music (which may depend crucially on improvisation) from its presentation in a written source.

Viadana's pieces also offered a more organized way of performing with a reduced number of singers: the practice until then had been to leave the organ to cover any missing parts, even if that left gaps in the text. English verse anthems also exploit the contrast between sections for a solo voice or voices, where the organ completes the polyphonic texture by playing the lines not sung, and tuttis, where the organ part gives a sketch – usually little more than treble and bass – of the vocal polyphony. Presumably the organist should fill out this sketch with the appropriate harmonies, and thus accompany the choir in quite a different way from that adopted for the polyphonic verse sections. Viadana suggests this full texture for the tutti sections of his motets: 'When the tutti sections are played on the organ, they are to be played with both hands and the pedals but without the addition of other registers [stops]'.

Ornamental styles

Where the music is already complete, another way of adding interest is to play a decorative part, ornamenting one of the polyphonic lines or ranging freely through the texture. Ortiz (1553), taking strictly polyphonic madrigals as his starting point, shows how this can be done on the viola da gamba. That some instruments are more suitable for this style than others is a theme taken up by continuo writers such as Agazzari (*Del sonare sopra 'l basso con tutti li stromenti e dell' uso loro nel conserto*).

Agazzari distinguishes between 'instruments of fundament' (those which can play both bass line and harmony, and can therefore provide a complete accompaniment), and 'instruments of ornament' (those which add to the texture with divisions or exotic colour). Structural accompaniment is allotted to organ, harpsichord and, in the case of small ensembles, lute, theorbo, and harp. Decorative playing – 'mingling with the voices in various ways' – is the preserve of lute, theorbo, harp, lirone, cittern, spinet, guitar, etc. It is important for the accompanist to observe the difference in function by playing either structurally and chordally or soloistically, as appropriate. The early continuo literature contains many warnings against throwing confusing decorations into a basic accompaniment, which should be simple, confined to a narrow compass and low in register (it may often double the bass at the octave). When one does decide to ornament, it is important to play with the panache (and sheer volume) of a soloist.

'Perfect' instruments played in each of these roles in the music for the Florentine *Intermedi* (1589). *Lira da braccio*, lirone (its tenor equivalent), harpsichord, organ and chitarrone provided chordal support; viola da gamba and sackbut played polyphonic lines; lute, harp and psaltery could have adopted chordal or decorative styles (these quiet instruments could play alone as the foundation for a small ensemble, or add ornamentation in the tuttis).

Since Agazzari's instruments of ornamentation include the lirone (which only plays chords), it is clear that the concept of 'ornamentation' includes the possibility of playing a sonorous chordal part to add colour. Agazzari's phrase is 'scherzando e contrapontegiando' (having fun and playing counterpoints ... to make the harmony more agreeable and sonorous). The idea that the thirteen lutes in the *Intermedi* simultaneously played melodic lines against an ensemble of nearly two hundred singers and instruments (including a choir of sackbuts) is impracticable as they would have been inaudible. As in the English masques, massed lutes and harps must have played chordal accompaniments: a continuo section in all but name.

Combining the style

Certain instruments were recognized as 'perfect', not only in the sense that they were apt for the task of accompaniment, but also in a symbolic and mysterious way as emblems of the musical aesthetic of the age. In fifteenth-century France, the harp was associated with Celtic folk-lore and chivalric romances. As the instrument of Tristan, the harper-knight, it symbolized a self-conscious delight in the intricacy of counterpoint, an evocative amalgam of science and magic.

In sixteenth-century Italy, the harp's position was usurped by the lute, which became by far the most important instrument for the accompaniment of written songs. Improvised singing, on the other hand, was especially associated with the *lira da braccio*, symbol of the humanists' fascination with classical culture. The philosopher Marsilio Ficino regarded his lyre as a therapeutic instrument: it calmed his spirit and dispelled melancholy. The poet Poliziano, a fellow member of the Platonic Academy, said of him that 'his *lira*, far more successful than the lyre of Thracian Orpheus, has brought back from the underworld what is (if I am not mistaken) the true Euridyce – that is, Platonic wisdom'. The chordal playing of the *lira* not only reflected a new harmonic awareness, but also symbolized the Renaissance view of music as an earthly imitation of the harmony of the spheres.

These elements of polyphonic and harmonic accompaniment combined to form *basso continuo* in a process that was audibly complete by the time of the Florentine *Intermedi*, even though the figured bass notation came later. The role of the tenorista evolved into that of the continuo player; sixteenth century tenors became seventeenth century ground basses; the instruments themselves were made larger, louder and lower in compass.

As chordal instruments came to be associated with the new reciting style of Caccini, Peri and the Florentine Academy, new ideals emerged. The new instruments – chitarrone, lirone, *arpa doppia*, etc. – were cultivated in imitation of the ancient Greek *cetra*. The various 'perfect' instruments could each express certain emotions and evoke certain feelings. Each was now seen as representing one facet of the *cetra*, the mythical instrument of Orpheus, with its divine power 'to calm the troubled breast, to inflame even the coldest heart to righteous anger or to love': the 'perfect' instrument.

Select bibliography

A. AGAZZARI, *Del sonare sopra 'l basso con tutti li stromenti e dell' uso loro nel conserto* (1607), trans. O. Strunk, *Source readings in Music History* (New York, 1950)

F. T. ARNOLD, *The art of accompaniment from a thorough-bass as practised in the 17th and 18th centuries* (London, 1931; repr. New York, 1965)

G. CACCINI, *Nuove musiche e nuova maniera di scriverle* (1614), ed. in *Recent Researches in the Music of the Baroque Era*, xxviii (1978)

B. CASTIGLIONE, *The book of the courtier* (1528), trans. Hoby, 1561 (London, 1928)

J. HAAR, *Italian poetry and music in the Renaissance* (London, 1986)

L. LOCKWOOD, 'Pietrobono and the instrumental tradition at Ferrara in the fifteenth century', *Rivista italiana di musicologia*, x (1975), pp. 115–33

G. MOORE, *Am I too loud? Memoirs of an accompanist* (London, 1962)

C. PAGE, 'The performance of songs in late medieval France', *Early Music*, x/4 (1982), pp. 441–50

N. PIRROTTA, 'Tradizione orale e tradizione scritta nella musica', in *L'ars nova italiana del trecento*, ii (Certaldo, 1969)

D. PLAMENAC (ed.), *Keyboard music of the late Middle Ages in Codex Faenza 117*, in *Corpus mensurabilis musicae*, lvii (1972)

Chronology and Glossary

Chronology

Dates	Historical events	Musical figures	Main sources	Musical developments
312	Edict of Milan grants freedom of worship to all Christians. Emperor Constantine (312–37).			
325	Council of Nicaea (Nicene creed).	St Ambrose c. 340–97.		Ambrosian chant, hymns, *Te Deum*. Development of Roman liturgy.
410	Fall of the Roman Empire.	Boethius c. 480–524.	*De institutione musica.*	
c. 530	Founding of monastic orders. St Benedict 480–543.	Cassiodorus c. 485–c. 580.	*Institutiones divinarum et humanarum litterarum.*	Monastic hours.
	Gregory the Great, Pope 590–604.	Isidore of Seville c. 559–636.	*Etymologiae.*	'Gregorian' chant. Regularization of liturgical ritual, including chant, for the Mass (gradual) and Office (anti-

Date	Historical events	People	Treatises / Works	Musical developments
711	Moslem invasion of Spain.			Church modes.
800	Charlemagne (768–814) crowned Emperor of the Romans.	Alcuin c. 735–804.		
816–	Benedictine monastery of St Gall reaches height of creativity.	Notker Balbulus c. 840–912. Hucbald c. 840–930.	*Liber hymnorum* (884). *De harmonica institutione* (?c. 880).	Sequence. Tropes.
848	Foundation of monastery of St Martial, Limoges.		*Musica enchiriadis* and *Scholica enchiriadis* (c. 900).	Organum (parallel).
909	Foundation of monastery of Cluny.			Liturgical drama.
		Guido of Arezzo c. 991/2–after 1033.	*Regularis concordia* (c. 970). Winchester Troper (c. 980). *Micrologus*.	Organum (free). Guidonian Hand, solmization, hexachords.
			The Cambridge Songbook (c. 1000).	
1017	Suppression of Mozarabic rite.	John of (?Affligem/Cotton) fl. c. 1100.	*De musica*. *Ad organum faciendum* (anon.). Fleury Playbook (late 12c.).	The Play of Daniel.

Dates	Historical events	Musical figures	Main sources	Musical developments
–1130	Debate over apostolicity of St Martial.		School of Aquitaine: 25 MSS.	Florid organum (sustained-note style). Discant. Voice exchange.
1120	Santiago de Compostela becomes archiepiscopal see.		Codex Calixtinus (c. 1140).	
1137	Marriage of Eleanor of Aquitaine (c. 1120–80) (1) to Louis VII	William IX, Duke of Aquitaine (1071–1127), Marcabru, Jaufre Rudel,		Troubadour songs: vers, canso, sirventes, tenso, alba.
1152	(2) to Henry of Anjou.	Bernart de Ventadorn, Peire Vidal, Arnaut Daniel, Giraut de Bornelh.		
1160	Maurice de Sully becomes Bishop of Paris and from 1163 rebuilds Notre Dame.	Leoninus c. 1163–90.	Magnus liber organi (1160–80).	Florid organum duplum and organum triplum, conductus, motet.
c. 1200	Notre Dame completed.	Perotinus fl. c. 1200.	Notre Dame School MSS.	
1209	First Albigensian crusade, troubadours dispersed.	Minnesingers: Walther von der Vogelweide d. 1228, Neidhart von Reuenthal d. after 1236.		Spruch. Bar form (aab).

Year	Events	Theorists	Treatises	Concepts
		Johannes de Garlandia fl. c. 1240.	*De plana musica* and *De mensurabili musica.*	Rhythmic modes.
1253	Thibaut de Champagne, King of Navarre, dies.	Trouvères: Blondel (1180–1220), Jehan Bretel, Gace Brulé, Adam de la Halle fl. 1280.		Grande chanson courtoise: lai, descort, etc. Rondeau, ballade, virelai.
1254	Alfonso the Wise founds a chair of music at Salamanca University.		*Cantigas de Santa María.*	
			Carmina Burana.	

FROM THE OLD TO THE NEW ART: 1250–1400

Year	Events	Theorists	Treatises	Concepts
		Anonymous IV c. 1285. Franco of Cologne fl. 1280. Petrus de Cruce fl. c. 1290. Johannes de Grocheio fl. c. 1300. Walter Odington fl. 1298–1316.	*De mensuris et discantu. Ars cantus mensurabilis. Tractatus de tonis. De musica.*	Franconian notation.
			Summa de speculatione musice.	
			Worcester Fragments c. 1330.	Organum, motet, conductus.
1305–78	Papacy in Avignon leading to the Great Schism (1378–1417).	Johannes de Muris c. 1300–c. 1350. Jacques de Liège, after 1300.	*Ars nove musice* (c. 1320).	Mensural notation, coloration.
			Speculum musice. Roman de Fauvel (1310–16).	Polyphonic song: *formes fixes* (virelai, ballade, rondeau), chace.

Dates	Historical events	Musical figures	Main sources	Musical developments
		Philippe de Vitry 1291–1361.	*Ars nova* (c. 1320).	French Ars nova: isorhythmic motet.
		Marchetto da Padova *fl.* 1305–26.	*Lucidarium in arte musicae planae/Pomerium artis musicae mensuratae.* Apt MS (c. 1400). Ivrea Codex (c. 1365). Rossi Codex (1330–45).	Italian notation.
		Jacopo da Bologna *fl. c.* 1350, Gherardello da Firenze d. *c.* 1363.		Italian Ars nova: ballata, madrigal, caccia.
			Robertsbridge Codex (c. 1365).	Keyboard music: *estampie.*
		Guillaume de Machaut *c.* 1300–77.	*Remède de Fortune* (1342/9) and *Livre du Voir Dit* (c. 1365).	Lai; polyphonic chanson (*formes fixes*). Polyphonic Mass movements, *Messe de Nostre Dame* (cycle).
		Francesco Landini *c.* 1325–97, Andrea da Firenze d. 1415.	Squarcialupi Codex (1410–15).	Madrigals, ballate.
		Jacob Senleches *fl.* 1378–95; Solage *fl.* 1370–90, Baude Cordier *fl.* 1380.	Chantilly MS (c. 1400).	Mannered notation, Ars subtilior.
		Matteo da Perugia d. 1418. Johannes Ciconia *c.* 1365–	Modena MS (c. 1410).	Fusion of Italian and French techniques: motets, ballate,

Date	Event	Composers	Sources	Style / Techniques
		Leonel Power d. 1445, John Dunstable d. 1453.	Old Hall MS (c. 1410–30).	English discant style, isorhythmic and canonic Mass movements.
c. 1441	Martin le Franc, *Le Champion des Dames*.	Binchois c. 1400–60, Guillaume Dufay c. 1398–1474.	Aosta MS, Bologna MS Q15, Canonici MS (Bodleian, Oxford), Trent Codices (1440–80).	'La contenance angloise'. Cyclic Masses, cantus firmus, isorhythmic motet dies out, polyphonic Requiem.
1453	Fall of Constantinople.	Johannes Okeghem c. 1420–97, Antoine Busnois c. 1430–92, Heyne van Ghizeghem *fl.* 1475. Johannes Tinctoris c. 1435–1511. Franchinus Gaffurius 1451–1522	Chansonniers: Laborde, Cordiforme, Copenhagen, Pixérécourt, Medici, Mellon. *De inventione et usu musicae* (c. 1487). *Practica musicae* (1496).	Polyphonic chanson: (*formes fixes*, shift from ballade to rondeau).
	Cultural hegemony of the dukes of Burgundy from Philip the Bold (d. 1404) to Charles the Bold (d. 1477).			

Date	Event	Composers	Sources	Style / Techniques
1501	Advent of music printing.	Josquin Desprez c. 1440–1521, Alexander Agricola 1446–1506, Jacob Obrecht c. 1458–1505, Loyset Compère c. 1450–1518.	Chigi Codex (c. 1497). Petrucci prints 1501– and Andrea Antico 1510–.	Cantus firmus techniques developed: paraphrase, canonic and parody Masses, devotional motets.

Dates	Historical events	Musical figures	Main sources	Musical developments
1517	Martin Luther nails his 95 theses to the door of Wittenberg Church.	Heinrich Isaac c. 1450–1517.	*Choralis constantinus* (publ. 1550–5).	Mass propers.
1518	Henry VIII and François I meet at the Field of Cloth of Gold; Charles V crowned Holy Roman Emperor.	Pierre de La Rue c. 1460–1518, Antoine Brumel c. 1460–c. 1520, Jean Mouton c. 1459–1522. Bartolomeo Tromboncino d. c. 1535, Marco Cara d. c. 1530.		Through-composed chanson, move towards more homophonic textures. Canti carnascialeschi, frottola, lauda.
1527	Sack of Rome.	Francisco de Peñalosa d. 1528, Juan del Encina 1468/9–c. 1529 Claudin de Sermisy c. 1485–1562, Clément Janequin c. 1485–1560. Ludwig Senfl c. 1486–1542/3. William Cornysh d. 1523, Robert Fayrfax 1464–1521, John Taverner c. 1495–1545.	*Cancionero de Palacio*, Elvas, Sevilla etc. Printed collections of Pierre Attaingnant 1528– . Printed Liederbuch 1512– . Eton Choirbook (1490–1502), Henry VIII Songbook.	Villancico. Parisian chanson.
1534	Henry VIII breaks with Rome.	Thomas Tallis c. 1505–1585.		English anthem.

1538	League of Nuremberg.	Costanzo Festa d. 1545, Philippe Verdelot d. by 1552, Jacques Arcadelt d. 1568, Cipriano de Rore 1516–65.		Madrigal.
		Francesco Spinacino. Joan Ambrosio Dalza. Francesco da Milano 1497–1543.	*Intabulatura di lauto* (1507). *Intabolatura de lauto* (1508).	Instrumental intabulations, lute dances.
		Luis Milán c. 1500–61.	*El Maestro* (1536)	Vihuela accompanied solo song.
		Sebastian Virdung b. c. 1465. Arnolt Schlick c. 1460–by 1521.	*Musica Getutscht* (1511). *Tabulaturen* (1512).	Keyboard music.
		Marco Antonio Cavazzoni c. 1490–c. 1560.	*Recerchari*, etc. (1523).	Free compositions: fantasia, ricercar.
		Antonio de Cabezón 1510–66. Juan Bermudo c. 1510–65.	*Obras de música para tecla* (1578). *Declaración de instrumentos* (1555).	Tiento.
		Cristóbal de Morales c. 1500–53.		Lamentations.
1545	Council of Trent convened.	Nicholas Gombert c. 1500–56.	Printed collections of Susato 1543–.	Parody Mass.

Dates	Historical events	Musical figures	Main sources	Musical developments
1552	Treaty of Passau grants freedom of worship to Lutherans.	Adrian Willaert c. 1490–1562. Clemens non Papa c. 1510–56/8, Andrea Gabrieli c. 1510–86.	*Musica nova* (1559).	Cori spezzati.
		Heinrich Glarean 1488–1563.	*Dodecachordon* (1547).	Modal theory.
		Gioseffo Zarlino d. 1590.	*Istitutioni harmoniche* (1558).	
1562	Discussions on music open at the Council of Trent.	Giovanni Pierluigi da Palestrina c. 1525–94. Orlande de Lassus 1532–94.	First published collection 1554. First published collection 1555.	Psalm-settings.
		Tomás Luis de Victoria c. 1548–1611. Giovanni Gabrieli d. 1612.	*Sacrae symphoniae* (1597).	Concerted music for voices and instruments.
		William Byrd 1543–1623.	*Cantiones sacrae* (1575) (with Tallis), *Gradualia* (1605). *My Ladye Nevelle's Booke* (1591).	Mass propers. Keyboard variations.
		Orlando Gibbons 1583–1625, John Bull d. 1628. Thomas Morley d. 1602.	*Fitzwilliam Virginal Book* (1609–19). *Consort Lessons* (1599).	Viol and mixed consort music.
		John Dowland 1563–1626.	*First Booke of Songes* (1597).	Lute song.

1589	Intermedi for *La Pellegrina* performed in Florence at the wedding festivities of Grand Duke Ferdinando de' Medici.	Thoinot Arbeau 1520–95. Giaches de Wert 1535–96.	*Orchésographie* (1589).	Dance. Virtuoso madrigal.
		Luca Marenzio 1553–99. Carlo Gesualdo c. 1560–1613.	Madrigal books 1580–	
		Giulio Caccini c. 1545–1618. Jacopo Peri (1561–1633). Claudio Monteverdi 1567–1643.	*Le nuove musiche* (1602). *Euridice* (1600). Madrigal books 1587– , Vespers 1610, *L'Orfeo* 1607.	Monody. Opera.

For a more detailed survey of the period, the reader might wish to consult the general music histories of Donald Jay Grout, Richard Crocker and Gerald Abraham or the more specialized studies: those of Richard Hoppin and Jeremy Yudkin for the years up to 1400; that of Reinhard Strohm (in press) for the fifteenth century; and those of Gustave Reese and Howard Mayer Brown for the fifteenth and sixteenth centuries. For easy reference on names and dates the reader can go to *The Concise Grove* (1988), *The New Everyman Dictionary of Music* (1988), ed. David Cummings, and *A Dictionary of Early Music from the Troubadours to Monteverdi* (1981) by Jerome and Elizabeth Roche. Those who can read German will appreciate the *dtv-Atlas zur Musik*, vol. 1 (1977) by Ulrich Michels. For authoritative and compact definitions of terms and concepts, all musicians turn to *The New Harvard Dictionary of Music* (1986); for fuller reference most large public and institutional libraries have the twenty-volume *New Grove Dictionary of Music and Musicians* (1980) and the three-volume *New Grove Dictionary of Musical Instruments* (1984).

Glossary

Aaron, Pietro (*c.* 1480–*c.* 1550). Italian music theorist and composer who published at least five treatises dealing, in a practical yet forward-looking way, with such matters as modes, counterpoint and tuning. *De institutitione harmonica* (Bologna, 1516) and *Toscanello* (Venice, 1523) are probably the most important; his correspondence with other theorists is also of interest.

Adam de la Halle (1245/50–?1285/8 or after 1306). Trouvère. Many of the details of his life are still shrouded in mystery, but he probably studied in Paris, subsequently serving at various French courts. His death is mentioned in a poem of 1288, but his presence is apparently reported in England in 1306. An important musical figure, he composed monophonic chansons, polyphonic rondeaux and music for three plays, the most famous of which is *Le jeu de Robin et de Marion*.

Agazzari, Agostino (1578–1640). Italian composer and writer responsible for one of the earliest treatises on the art of continuo (*Del sonare sopra 'l basso con tutti li stromenti e dell' uso loro nel conserto*, 1607). A *dramma pastorale* entitled *Eumelio* (1606) is attributed to him.

Agricola, Alexander (?1446–1506). Composer of the Franco-Flemish school who worked at a number of courts in Italy, France and Spain and who achieved considerable renown. His works, stylistically not dissimilar to those of Okeghem, include eight Masses, about twenty motets and in the region of fifty chansons as well as some instrumental pieces.

Alba [Fr.: aube]. A troubadour poem that is based on the theme of lovers who part at dawn ('alba') after a night of secret passion. The most famous example is Giraut de Bornelh's *Reis glorios*.

Alba [Alva], **Alonso de** (d. 1528). Spanish composer who served as a royal chaplain in the chapels of Isabella and her daughter Juana. A three-voice Mass and a number of other liturgical settings as well as one four-voice villancico are attributed to him in Hispanic sources.

Alberti, Gasparo (*c.* 1480–*c.* 1560). Italian composer who spent most of his working life in Bergamo. He wrote exclusively music for the liturgy, much of it in *falsobordone* style, though his five Masses (three of which were printed in Venice in 1549) are more contrapuntal. He was an influential figure in the development of North Italian sacred music.

Alcuin (*c.* 735–804). Counsellor and cultural adviser to Charlemagne for much of the latter part of his life, Alcuin was renowned as a scholar and poet. There is evidence to suggest that he wrote on music, though the specific works (such as the brief work on the modes entitled *Musica*) attributed to him in more recent times cannot be proved to be by him.

Alfonso el Sabio [Alfonso X] (1221–84). King of Castile who earned the epithet of 'the Wise' for his organization of the Spanish legal system. An enlightened patron of the arts, he founded the chair of music at Salamanca University (1254) and supervised the compilation of the vast collection of songs known as the *Cantigas de Santa Maria*.

Almain [alman, allemande]. A dance that would appear to have originated in Germany, probably as a development of the basse danse. The earliest known reference to it under this name dates from 1521. During the sixteenth century it generally indicated a dance in duple time with three repeated strains.

Alta [capella]. The Latin term given for the standard fifteenth-century instrumental combination of two or three shawms and sackbut, described by Tinctoris in his *De inventione et usu musicae* of *c.* 1485.

Alteration. A principle of early notational practice in mensural music (first used in modal notation of the second half of the twelfth century) whereby the value of the second of two equal notes (at first usually applied to the breve, later to the semibreve and minim) is doubled.

Alternatim. Latin term used to describe

the performance of alternate sections of the liturgy with different forces. The alternating of polyphony with plainchant was first practised in responsories, but subsequently spread to psalms, hymns, sequences and even the Ordinary of the Mass. Alternation of fauxbourdon with chant, or of the choir with organ, is also common.

Amerus (*fl.* 1271). English theorist who travelled to Italy where he is thought to have written his didactic treatise *Practica artis musice*, possibly in 1271. After a full discussion of plainchant (including a tonary), there is a chapter dedicated to the composition of polyphony, the earliest example known to have been written in Italy.

Anchieta, Juan de (1462–1523). Important Spanish composer who served in the Castilian and Aragonese royal chapels from 1489 until his death. He travelled to Flanders in the service of Juana, daughter of Ferdinand and Isabella. His sacred works (including Mass and Magnificat settings and motets) are, however, largely free of the complex contrapuntal devices favoured by his northern colleagues.

Anonymous. Many surviving works, especially from the earlier part of the period, bear no composer ascription. Thus, a large proportion of the music composed before 1600 is anonymous and until recently has received relatively little critical or analytical attention, sometimes creating a considerable distortion of the 'facts'.

Anonymous IV. Appellation used for the anonymous author of perhaps the most important treatise of the thirteenth century on mensural music, the *De mensuris et discantu*. This would appear to have been written by an Englishman, probably between 1270 and 1280, and is strongly influenced by the writings of Johannes de Garlandia. Its importance lies in the light it sheds on the development of the Notre Dame school.

Anthonello de Caserta (*fl.* late 14th–early 15th centuries). Italian composer who may have been active in northern Italy or Naples. He composed songs in both Italian and French; six or seven ballate, a

madrigal, and eight more contrapuntally complex *forme-fixe* chansons are attributed to him.

Antico, Andrea (*c.* 1480–after 1539). Italian music publisher, active first in Rome (1510–18) and subsequently in Venice (1520–1 and 1533–9). The first known music publisher in Rome, he developed a method different from that evolved by Petrucci in Venice: music and text were printed together from engraved blocks. Apart from volumes of frottolas, madrigals and sacred works, he also published the first collection of Italian keyboard music.

Antiphon. A term used in the Roman rite from about the fourth century for a liturgical chant with a prose text commonly associated with psalmody, usually as a refrain to psalm or canticle verses. During the thirteenth century rhymed antiphons developed, while processional, Marian and other devotional antiphons outside psalmody became increasingly important as a genre within their own right. Polyphonic settings of such votive antiphons abound throughout the fifteenth and sixteenth centuries. See also VOTIVE MASS.

Apt MS. French manuscript dating from the beginning of the fifteenth century, now in St Anne's Cathedral, Apt. Its forty-five folios contain forty-eight pieces from the repertory of the papal court in Avignon during the Great Schism (1378–1417) including works by such composers as Tapissier and Philippe de Vitry.

Arcadelt, Jacques (?1505–1568). Composer of either French or Flemish origin who worked in France and Italy, in Venice and Rome. He composed a number of sacred works, much in the manner of Josquin, but the most prolific and important part of his output was secular music: about 120 chansons and over 200 madrigals.

Arnaut de Zwolle, Henri (d. 1466). Netherlands scientist and writer. Having probably studied in Paris, he entered the service of Philip the Good, Duke of Burgundy, as 'medical professor and astronomer'. He subsequently served at the French royal court. He is particularly important for his treatise on musical instruments, probably written about 1440, which gives the earliest extant technical descriptions for instruments in use during the period.

Arpa doppia. See HARP.

Ars nova. Latin term used broadly to describe the music of the fourteenth century as opposed to that of the thirteenth (the Ars antiqua). The basis for this 'new art' lies with the new notational techniques described in Philippe de Vitry's *Ars nova* of about 1322. The Ars nova is the generally accepted term for French music from this time to the death of Machaut in 1377, the main musical forms being the isorhythmic motet and polyphonic chanson.

Ars subtilior. A term used to describe the 'more subtle art' that found expression in the works of the generation of French composers after Machaut: Jacob de Senleches, Philippus de Caserta, Cuvelier, etc. Their music is often extremely complex rhythmically, stretching to their limits the notational principles established by the Ars nova.

Artusi, Giovanni Maria (*c.* 1540–1613). Italian theorist and composer, a staunch defender of the conservative theories of his teacher Zarlino and who entered into polemical discussions with more progressive musical thinkers such as Vincenzo Galilei. In his *L'Artusi, overo Delle imperfettioni della moderna musica* (1600–3) he criticized the counterpoint of an unnamed composer who turned out to be Monteverdi.

Attaingnant, Pierre (*c.* 1494–1551/2). French music publisher active in Paris from 1525. His new and highly efficient method of printing by single impression quickly swept through Europe, making him the single most important music publisher of the 1530s and 40s. Masses, motets and psalm settings rolled off his presses, but he was particularly influential in the diffusion of the Parisian chanson which reached its apogee at this time.

Aube. See ALBA.

Augustine of Hippo (354–430). Saint and Father of the Church. By his own account, St Augustine loved music almost too well,

being much concerned with psalm and hymn singing in his ministry. His treatise (begun in 387 and completed in 391) survives incomplete as the *De musica libri sex* which is concerned primarily with the philosophical and theological ramifications of musical study. It was extremely influential throughout the Middle Ages.

Aulos. Perhaps the most important instrument of ancient Greece, the aulos was a reed instrument, though it is often mistranslated as 'flute'. It generally took the form of paired pipes, but whether it had single or double reeds is a matter of controversy.

Ballade. With the rondeau and virelai, one of the three musico-poetic fixed forms dominating French song composition in the fourteenth and fifteenth centuries. In its most developed form it consists of three stanzas with the musical scheme *AAB*.

Ballata. Italian poetico-musical form cultivated from the second half of the thirteenth century to the fifteenth. Originally a dance-song based on an oral monophonic tradition, only the texts have survived for the earliest ballate; polyphonic settings date from the 1360s. It was especially favoured in northern Italy by such composers as Bartolino da Padova, Ciconia and others. Ballate by Dufay and Hugo de Lantins are among the last examples of the genre.

Banchieri, Adriano (1568–1634). Italian composer and theorist remembered primarily for his six books of canzonettas and his treatises on performance practice. In *L'organo suonarino* (1605) he gives instructions for accompanying chant, while the *Cartella musicale* (1614) discusses harmony, rhythm and vocal ornamentation.

Bartolino da Padova (*fl. c.* 1365–1405). Italian composer and contemporary of Landini who probably worked in Florence 1388–90. His extant ballate (27) and madrigals (11) expand on the style initiated by Jacopo da Bologna.

Bartolomeo degli Organi (1474–1539). Italian composer, organist and singer who worked for most of his life in Florence. His surviving works include ten secular pieces, a lauda and some instrumental music.

Bassano, Giovanni (*c.* 1558–1617). Italian composer and cornett player who was at one time head of the instrumental ensemble at St Mark's, Venice. His works include polychoral motets and canzonettas, while his treatise on ornamentation (*Ricercate, passaggi et cadentie*, 1585) was highly influential.

Basse danse [bassadanza]. A court dance common in the fifteenth and sixteenth centuries that tended to be less athletic and more graceful than the 'alta danza'. In the fifteenth century, the music was written down as a simple line of long notes, apparently used as a basis for improvisation.

Bauldeweyn, Noel (*c.* 1480–1530). Flemish composer who served as choirmaster in churches in Mechelen and Antwerp. His seven Masses, about ten motets and a few songs combine features of the Netherlandish school of the late fifteenth century with elements of the new style cultivated by Josquin.

Bedyngham, Johannes (d. 1459/60). English composer whose works were relatively widely disseminated. These include two Mass cycles, three motets and a number of songs, one of which, 'O rosa bella', is also ascribed to Dunstable.

Bergamasca. A dance of the sixteenth and seventeenth centuries that may have originated in Bergamo, Italy. Based on a recurrent harmonic sequence, it was often used as a basis for instrumental variations.

Bergerette. A word sometimes used for virelais with a single stanza composed in the second half of the fifteenth century. In the sixteenth century it was also used for some pastoral songs and for some triple-time dances.

Bernart de Ventadorn (*c.* 1130/40–*c.* 1190/1200). Troubadour poet and composer. He served at various courts, including those of Eleanor of Aquitaine and Raimon V, Count of Toulouse. An unusually high percentage of his works (eighteen out of forty-five) survive with complete melodies. He may have been important in stimulating the trouvère tradition in northern France through working there.

Binchois [Gilles de Bins] (*c.* 1400–1460).

Franco-Flemish composer who, along with Dufay and Dunstable, was a leading musical figure of the first half of the fifteenth century. He served in the Burgundian court chapel from the late 1420s. Much of his music is thought to have been lost, but eight Mass movement pairs and a further twelve single movements survive, together with some thirty other sacred works. Nearly sixty songs are attributed to him; some also survive in keyboard arrangements, while tenor lines from others were used for basses danses and Mass cycles.

Boen, Johannes (d. 1367). Dutch priest and music theorist who studied at Oxford and possibly Paris and wrote two treatises. The earlier of the two, *Ars [Musicae]* from the mid-fourteenth century deals with Ars nova mensural music, while the *Musica* (1357) puts forward what amounts to a fairly original doctrine of consonance.

Boethius, Ancius Manlius Severinus (*c.* 480–*c.* 524). Roman statesman and author whose writings on music were highly influential throughout the medieval period. His *De institutione musica*, in which he discusses the mathematical basis of music and its relationship to the universe, became the most widespread treatise of the Middle Ages.

Boluda, Gines de (*c.* 1550–1592). Spanish composer who was chapelmaster at Toledo Cathedral from 1580. All his surviving works are liturgical, and include two Mass settings.

Bombarde. See SHAWM.

Bonizzi, Vincenzo (d. 1630). Italian composer and player of the viol and harpsichord. He held posts in Ferrara and Parma, and was most famous for his skill as a performer, his interest in ornamentation being clear from his collection of instrumental music published in 1626.

Book of Hours. Devotional book enormously popular in the Middle Ages. Essentially a prayerbook compiled for the lay person wishing to follow the daily canonical hours of the liturgy, a Book of Hours often became a symbol of individual piety. Highly ornate and costly, illuminated Books of Hours were often presented as diplomatic gifts, and these can be important as sources for iconographical evidence for medieval performance practice.

Borrono, Pietro Paolo (*fl.* 1531–49). Italian composer and lutenist who published three volumes of lute music (1536, 1546, 1548). Fantasias, dances, intabulations and toccatas feature amongst his works.

Bossinensis, Franciscus (*fl.* 1510). Italian composer who had two volumes of lute music published by Petrucci (1509, 1511). These comprise over 120 arrangements of frottolas by other composers as well as almost fifty ricercars.

Bovicelli, Giovanni Battista (*fl.* 1592–4). Italian music theorist whose treatise *Regole, passaggi di musica* (1594) is a significant source of information on vocal ornamentation.

Bruhier, Antoine (*fl.* early sixteenth century). Singer and composer, possibly of Provençal origin, who served in the papal chapel in the first two decades of the sixteenth century. Various works may have been written by him (including a Mass and two motets as well as a number of secular pieces), although there is possible confusion with a later composer by the name of Jean de la Bruguière.

Brumel, Antoine (*c.* 1460–*c.* 1515). French composer who held various appointments in France (Chartres, Laon and Paris) and Italy (the court of Alfonso I d'Este, 1506–10). Primarily a composer of sacred music. Fifteen Masses by him survive as well as a number of motets and secular pieces. His later works display a tendency towards concentration and rhythmic regularity. He was one of Josquin's most eminent contemporaries.

Brunelli, Antonio (*c.* 1575–before 1630). Italian composer and theorist and an important figure in the stylistic transition from the Renaissance to the Baroque. He wrote in both the monodic idiom developed by the Florentines and the polyphonic tradition of sacred vocal music.

Brussels, Bibliothèque Royale, MS 215–216. A formal choirbook from the Netherlands court scribal workshop and copied partly by Petrus Alamire *c.*

1512–16. It contains works by Josquin, La Rue and Pipelare.

Buccina. A curved instrument dating from Roman times, originally made from an animal's horn which came to be covered with and sometimes formed completely from brass. Limited to only a few notes, it is mainly referred to in Roman literature as a signalling instrument in pastoral or military contexts.

Buchner, Hans [Johannes] (1483–1538). German organist and composer best known for his didactic treatise *Fundamentum* of about 1520. This is a guide to organ playing including sections on how to arrange vocal pieces and to improvise around a cantus firmus. The theoretical part is followed by a substantial collection of musical examples.

Burmeister, Joachim (1564–1629). German theorist who developed an analytical system based on musico-rhetorical figures. His most influential work was the *Musica autoschedastike* of 1601. He also wrote a large number of simple hymn-tune compositions.

Busnois, Antoine (*c.* 1430–1492). French composer who may have studied with Okeghem in Tours and who served in the Burgundian chapel. His compositional output (which includes some sixty songs – mostly rondeaux – as well as two cantus firmus Mass settings and a number of other sacred works) represents the generation between Dufay and Josquin at its best.

Buxheim Organ Book. German manuscript (169 folios), mostly written about 1460 and now in the Bavarian State Library, Munich. It contains over 250 compositions for organ, including liturgical pieces based on cantus firmi, song arrangements and dances as well as Conrad Paumann's *Fundamentum organisandi*.

Byrd, William (1543–1623). English composer of astonishing versatility who enjoyed royal patronage (despite his adherence to the Catholic faith) before retiring to Essex in 1593. In 1575 he and Thomas Tallis were granted a patent by Elizabeth I to print music. This resulted in the *Cantiones sacrae* (1575, 1589–91) and the two volumes of the *Gradualia* (1605–7). He also composed Anglican service music as well as many secular pieces including polyphonic and consort songs, fantasias and In nomines for viol consort, and a large amount of keyboard music.

Caccia [It.: 'chase', 'hunt']. An Italian poetico-musical form of the fourteenth and fifteenth centuries, the caccia, as the name would imply, takes the hunt, whether in realistic or allegorical (the pursuit of love) terms, as its theme.

Caccini, Francesca (1587–?1640). Singer and composer; eldest daughter of Giulio Caccini. She worked and performed for most of her life in Florence, the Medici family refusing to allow her to accept a position at the French court. As a composer she is best known for her opera *La liberazione di Ruggiero* (first performed in 1625), but she also made a significant contribution to the development of solo song with *Il primo libro delle musiche* of 1618.

Caccini, Giulio (*c.* 1545–1618). Italian singer and composer who served for most of his career at the Medici court in Florence. An important contributor to the development of monody, he wrote several of the earliest operas as well as *Le nuove musiche* (1602) and *Nuove musiche e nuova maniera di scriverle* (1614).

Canción. Spanish term for a refrain song similar to the French virelai, it being the preferred form of the older generations of composers represented in the *Cancionero Musical de Palacio* (second half of the fifteenth century).

Cancionero Musical de Palacio. See MADRID, PALACIO REAL, BIBLIOTECA, MS 1335.

Candido, Serafino (*fl.* 1570–80). Italian composer who may have worked in Augsburg and who certainly visited Venice at least once. His *Delle mascherate musicali*, a collection of nine masking songs, villanellas and madrigals with a dedication signed by the composer, was published there in 1571.

Canso. Provençal term used by troubadours during the twelfth and thirteenth centuries denoting a song, in particular a strophic song on a courtly love theme.

Cantigas de Santa María. The collection of over four hundred monophonic songs in Gallego-Portuguese compiled from about 1250 to 1280 at the instigation and under the supervision of Alfonso X 'the Wise'. The songs recount the miracles of the Virgin Mary, every tenth cantiga being a simple song of praise to her. Many of the melodies may be popular in origin. The illustrations and texts of the four surviving copies provide important information on musical practice of the time at the Castilian court.

Cantilena. Latin term used in the Middle Ages to denote a song or simply a melody, and employed variously to describe both chant and secular monophony.

Cantor. A term which originated in Jewish and early Christian worship to denote the singer who sang the solo sections of the liturgy. In medieval cathedrals the cantor was also the director of the choir.

Cantus. Literally the Latin word for 'song', it was used in a general sense throughout the Middle Ages and Renaissance to mean melody. It also had the specific meaning of the upper voice part in a polyphonic composition.

Cantus firmus. Latin term (literal meaning 'fixed song') describing a plainchant or other pre-existing melody used as a basis for polyphonic composition throughout the fourteenth to the sixteenth centuries.

Canzona [It.: 'song']. Term most commonly used to denote an instrumental composition of the sixteenth to seventeenth centuries and probably originating from arrangements of French chansons. Keyboard and ensemble canzonas were composed, Merulo being a key figure in the early development of the genre. It was also used by frottola and madrigal composers for settings of lyric poems in a particular form by or in the style of Petrarch.

Capirola, Vicenzo (1474–after 1548). Italian lutenist and composer of noble lineage. A manuscript of over forty of his lute pieces (including intabulations, dances and ricercars) is preceded by a short preface with practical remarks on lute playing. It dates from around 1517 and is now in the Newberry Library, Chicago.

Cara, Marchetto (*c.* 1470–?1525). Italian composer, singer and lutenist. He served at the Mantuan court from at least 1494 and was appointed *maestro di cappella* in 1511. With Tromboncino he was one of the most important composers of frottolas in the early sixteenth century: over a hundred works by him survive.

Carol/Carole. The French carole, together with its English counterpart the carol, developed as a dance-song from at least the twelfth century. The carole was probably a round or processional dance, and enjoyed enormous popularity in French courtly circles until about the middle of the fourteenth century when it was superseded by the basse danse. The English carol of the fifteenth century was a strophic refrain song (in English or Latin), often in association with certain feasts or occasions, notably Christmas.

Caron, Firminius (*fl. c.* 1460–90). French composer, about whom no documentation has been found, though he was praised by Tinctoris and his works were widely copied. Five Masses are attributed to him (including one on the *L'homme armé* melody), as well as about twenty songs.

Carpentras [Elzear Genet] (*c.* 1470–1548). French singer and composer who served in Avignon and Rome for most of his career. The four volumes of his works (prepared by him after his retirement to Avignon in 1526) include five Masses, hymn and Magnificat settings and a set of Lamentations which continued to be performed in the Sistine Chapel for much of the sixteenth century. A few secular works are also attributed to him.

Casanatense MS. See ROME, BIBLIOTECA CASANATENSE MS 2856

Cassiodorus (*c.* 485–*c.* 580). Roman statesman and writer whose works include several passages dedicated to music and the arts. The chapter entitled *De musica* in his *Institutiones divinarum et humanarum litterarum*, in which he considers the power

of music, was extremely influential in monastic circles in the seventh, eighth and ninth centuries and was used by Isidore as a source for his *Etymologiae*.

Castiglione, Baldassare (1478–1529). Italian writer whose main work, *Il libro del cortegiano* (1528), gives valuable insight into attitudes towards music and the practice of it in aristocratic circles in Italy in the first decades of the sixteenth century.

Ceballos, Rodrigo de (*c.* 1530–1581). Spanish composer who served principally in the cathedrals of Seville (1553–6) and Toledo (1556–61) and subsequently Granada. Three Masses and some forty motets, all in highly polished polyphony, are attributed to him.

Cerone, Pietro (1566–1625). Italian theorist and singer who served at the Madrid court. His controversial treatise *El melopeo y maestro* of 1613 is important for its emphasis on practical music-making and for the influence it exerted on Spanish musical thought well into the eighteenth century.

Cetra. See CITTERN.

Chace. French fourteenth-century term for a canon and one used, for example, by Machaut to describe the canonic section of his lai 'Je ne cesse de prier'. It was also used for a small surviving repertory from the same period of canonic works of an onomatopeic nature which imitated, for example, birdsong.

Chanson [Fr.: 'song']. A term used generally for any lyric poem in French and more specifically for a French polyphonic song throughout the fourteenth to sixteenth centuries. Machaut was largely responsible for the early cultivation of the French polyphonic song in courtly circles, but it found fullest and widest expression with the fifteenth-century composers Dufay and Binchois and their Franco-Flemish successors. The so-called Parisian chanson, far simpler in musical style, thrived in the 1530s and 40s with the numerous published collections of Pierre Attaingnant.

Chanson de geste. An epic poem cultivated in the early Middle Ages which commonly concerned heroic exploits. *The Song of Roland* (*c.* 1080) is the most famous example. These poems may well have been performed to a simple melody which was repeated for each line of verse.

Chanson de toile. A term found in French thirteenth-century sources to denote a spinning or weaving song in which a lady, in the absence of her lover, spins while she awaits his return. Of the twenty extant examples, only half survive with their melodies.

Chansonnier. A manuscript or printed book containing chansons, with or without music, from the thirteenth to the sixteenth centuries. See also DIJON, BIBLIO-THÈQUE MUNICIPALE, 517 and NEW HAVEN, YALE UNIVERSITY.

Chant [plainchant, plainsong]. A term used to describe, in the broadest sense, the monophonic melodies of the early Christian liturgies and, more specifically, those of the Roman Catholic Church ('Gregorian' chant). The various repertories (Ambrosian, Gallican, Mozarabic, etc.) were distinguished by their own modal idioms and (from the ninth century) notation: from this time, too, the 'Gregorian' tradition developed tonaries in which melodies were listed by mode. The chant repertory was divided early on into psalmodic and non-psalmodic (hymns, sequence and Mass Ordinary). Three basic melodic styles emerged, defined by the number of notes to a syllable and dependent on the liturgical function of the individual chant: syllabic (one syllable), neumatic (up to about twelve) and melismatic (more than twelve). Chant formed the basis for the composition of most sacred polyphony throughout the Middle Ages and Renaissance.

Chantilly MS. Southern French manuscript of the late fourteenth century (or possibly an Italian copy of the early fifteenth) of sixty-four folios now preserved in the Musée Condé at Chantilly near Paris under the callmark 564 (*olim* 1047). It contains repertory of the papal court at Avignon and of the Aragonese and Navarrese courts dating from the second half of the fourteenth century, including motets, ballades, rondeaux and virelais, some in the complex Ars subtilior idiom.

Chiavette. Italian term indicating (with the *chiavi naturali*) the two combinations of clefs that dominated most *a cappella* polyphonic music of the High Renaissance. Their use can provide clues as to the pitch of a given piece of polyphony.

Chigi Codex. See ROME, BIBLIOTECA APOSTOLICA VATICANA, CHIGI C.VIII.234.

Chipre. Fourteenth-century composer, perhaps from Cyprus and possibly connected with the papal court in Avignon. A three-voice Kyrie, interesting for its rhythmic patterns, is attributed to him.

Chitarrone. See THEORBO.

Chordophone. A generic term used to describe instruments that produce sound by strings stretched across fixed points.

Chrétien de Troyes (*fl. c.* 1160–90). French trouvère. The earliest lyric poet in French, he wrote the Arthurian romances *Perceval* and *Lancelot*, and five lyric poems are attributed to him (three with music).

Ciconia, Johannes (*c.* 1335/73–1412). Composer and theorist who could be one of two men by this name both connected with Liège. Recent opinion has inclined towards the younger of the two (who obtained a post in Padua Cathedral in the first years of the fifteenth century) on the stylistic evidence of the music. His songs, motets and Mass movements combine elements from the French Ars nova and the Italian trecento idiom in a startlingly original way that was to exert considerable influence over musical developments at that time.

Cittern [It.: cetra]. A plucked instrument with wire strings, not dissimilar to but lower in status than the lute, that was particularly popular in the sixteenth and seventeenth centuries, though it can be traced back to the sixth century. Unlike the lute, however, it was usually played with a plectrum. The name derives from the Greek kithara with which it can be linked. See also LYRE.

Clausula. Latin term used with regard to Notre Dame polyphony to describe short passages of chant set in discant (note-against-note) style as more modern substitutes for organum. It contributed, with new words added to the upper parts, to the development of the motet in about 1200.

Clavichord. A keyboard instrument that dates from at least the early fifteenth century, although fourteenth-century references to a mysterious instrument known as the chekker may indicate the existence of the clavichord from much earlier. Usually in the form of a rectangular box, it is probably the earliest keyboard instrument in which the sound is produced by strings being struck when the keys are depressed. It was widely used throughout Europe during the Renaissance, and in Germany until the nineteenth century.

Clemens non Papa [Jacob Clement] (*c.* 1510/15–1555/6). Flemish composer based for most of his life in Flanders, although he may have served in the itinerant court of Charles V. His output was prolific, including fifteen Masses, well over two hundred motets, Dutch three-voice settings of the psalms and about eighty chansons. The origin of the epithet 'non Papa' is not clear, but perhaps made reference to Pope Clement VII who died in 1534.

Codex Calixtinus. Manuscript of about the mid-twelfth century which, according to legend, was compiled by Pope Calixtus II (1119–24), but probably originally from central France and now in the cathedral library of Santiago de Compostela. Written in Aquitanian notation, it is one of the earliest manuscripts of liturgical polyphony and the conductus.

Color. See ISORYTHM.

Compère, Loyset (*c.* 1445–1518). French composer and singer who served in Milan as well as at the French court. Three Mass cycles, sixteen motets, six Magnificat settings and a number of chansons, all in the prevailing Franco-Netherlandish style of the turn of the fifteenth century, are attributed to him.

Conductus. Latin term for a song in Latin verse, usually of a serious or religious nature. It would appear to have originated in southern France and flourished until the latter part of the mid-thirteenth century among the composers of the Notre Dame school. It was subsequently ousted by the motet.

Conrad von Zabern (d. 1476/81). German theorist who taught at a number of German universities during the fifteenth century. Four treatises by him survive, all thought to date from the 1460s and 70s, all didactic in tone and reflecting his belief that elementary music training was essential for all clerics and teachers.

Consort. A term used to denote a small instrumental ensemble throughout the sixteenth and seventeenth centuries. It was sometimes used for a group of a variety of instruments, today termed the 'mixed' consort, as opposed to the 'whole' consort in which all the instruments are of the same family but at different pitches (e.g. viol consort).

Consort song. Term used to describe works for solo voice or voices and instruments in England from the last quarter of the sixteenth century to about 1625.

Contenance angloise, La [Fr.: 'English manner']. Expression used by Martin Le Franc in his poem *Le Champion des dames* (1441–2) with reference to the English style of Dunstable in a passage on the state of the arts in France.

Contra. Prefix commonly used in the designation of voice parts: e.g. 'contra-tenor' or 'contrabassus'.

Contrafactum. Term used to describe the substitution of one text for another in a piece of music that otherwise remains essentially the same. In medieval song it usually refers to the addition of new words to an existing melody, while in the sixteenth century it is used mainly to indicate the substitution of a sacred for a secular text.

Copla. Hispanic verse form, usually sung, of four lines rhymed *abcb*.

Coprario [Coperario], **John** (*c.* 1570/80–1626). English composer who served mainly at court, and who apparently Italianicized his name (Cooper) after a visit to Italy. He published two sets of songs (1606, 1613) and composed a great deal of music for viol consort. He also wrote a practical guide to composition entitled *Rules how to compose*.

Coranto [Fr.: courante]. Dance and instrumental form that seems to have emerged as a recognized genre in the mid-sixteenth century in printed collections such as those of Phalèse (1549) and manuscript sources such as the Philidor Collection (*c.* 1570).

Cordiforme Chansonnier. One of the most beautifully illuminated of fifteenth-century songbooks and, as its name would suggest, shaped in the form of a heart. It was copied in Savoy by a single scribe before 1477 and its repertory includes secular works by composers such as Dufay, Busnois, Okeghem and Binchois.

Cornett. A wooden wind instrument widely used throughout Europe from the fifteenth to the seventeenth centuries. Its name, 'little horn', would suggest that it derived in some way from animal horns although medieval iconography reveals that both straight and curved instruments were used. It is not known from what date the cornett began to provide support for choral music, but this became its main function by the end of the Renaissance, notably in the Venetian polychoral music of Andrea and Giovanni Gabrieli.

Council of Constance. Church council (1414–18) at which Martin V was elected pope to bring an end to the Great Schism (1378–1417). It is thought that Dufay may have been among the thousands of clerics who attended the Council and that he may have come across English music there.

Council of Trent. Council convened by Pope Paul III (1534–49) in 1542 in response to the Reformation and in order to clarify points of doctrine and promulgate certain disciplinary reforms. These included long discussions on the role of music in the Church in the later sessions of the Council held in the early 1560s before it ended in December 1563. Intelligibility of the sung word and the banning of any musical elements that might be considered 'impure' (e.g. secular cantus firmi) were two of the main concerns.

Crécquillon, Thomas (*c.* 1480/1500–?1557). Flemish composer who served for at least part of his career in the chapel of Charles V. He composed almost two hundred chansons, two Lamentations cycles, Masses and motets. Published collections of his music (one of chansons, 1544, and two of motets, 1559 and 1576) ensured that it was widely known throughout Europe.

Crumhorn. A wind-cap instrument (with its double reed enclosed in a cap) with a crook-shaped bottom. Its origins are somewhat confused, but it would seem to have emerged towards the end of the fifteenth century and quickly gained in popularity. As with the recorder and viol, the sixteenth-century crumhorn came in various sizes encompassing a wide range and forming a consort that provided another highly distinctive and contrasted instrumental sonority. Its popularity waned in the 1600s, and it fell out of use until its revival earlier this century.

Cutting, Francis (*fl.* 1583–*c.* 1603). English composer and lutenist active in London in the 1580s. Many dances and character pieces for lute by him survive in manuscript sources.

Dalla Casa, Girolamo (d. 1601). Italian composer and instrumentalist who served (with his brothers Giovanni and Nicolò) at St Mark's, Venice, in the second half of the sixteenth century. He composed motets and madrigals and wrote an influential treatise on ornamentation (1584).

Dalza, Joan Ambrosio (*fl.* 1508). Italian lutenist and composer whose *Intabolatura de lauto libro quarto* was published by Petrucci in 1508. The collection is remarkable in that it contains only four intabulations of vocal pieces, the rest (including forty-two dances and nine ricercars) being originally conceived for the lute.

Danyel, John (1564–*c.* 1626). English lutenist and composer who was held in high esteem in his own day, his name being linked to that of Dowland in a madrigal by Tomkins. He published a collection of lute songs in 1606; several solo lute pieces by him survive.

Descort [derived from Lat.: 'discordia']. The standard Provençal word for lai (an extended song form of the thirteenth and fourteenth centuries) from which, at least musically, it cannot be distinguished. Confusion and dispute have, however, arisen since it was also used to designate a poem in which the verses differ one from the other.

Diastematic [Gr.: 'interval']. A term used to describe notation in which the relative pitch of the notes of a melody are indicated by their vertical placing on the page but without reference to ruled lines.

Dijon, Bibliothèque municipale, 517 (olim 204) [Dijon Chansonnier]. Important chansonnier of the period *c.* 1470–75, probably compiled in the Loire valley. It consists of 204 folios and includes over 160 chansons by composers such as Busnois (30), Okeghem (10), Hayne van Ghizeghem, Compère, Binchois, Dufay, Robert Morton and many others.

Diminution. A term used to describe a technique of ornamentation, common throughout the Renaissance, whereby long notes are broken down into a number of faster notes by way of melodic variation.

Discant. Type of note-against-note polyphony, based on a plainchant tenor, and originally improvised. In English discant the cantus firmus was sometimes presented in the upper or middle voice.

Discantus [Lat.: 'singing a part']. A term with a variety of closely-connected meanings in the medieval period, from polyphony in general to the voice part added to the tenor to create polyphony and, by extrapolation, the highest voice in polyphony (equivalent to cantus or superius).

Division. A seventeenth-century English term for a variation technique in which the notes of a cantus firmus or ground bass are improvised into shorter notes.

Doni, Giovanni Battista (1595–1647). Italian philologist and music theorist with a strong interest in Greek music theory.

Dot of division (punctum divisionis). First used by Petrus de Cruce in his modifications of the notational system developed by Franco of Cologne in the later thirteenth century to alter the notated rhythm of a small group of notes by marking off the perfections.

Dowland, John (1563–1626). English composer and virtuoso lutenist who travelled widely through Europe before eventually securing a post at court in 1612. He published four volumes of ayres for voice and lute (1597, 1600, 1603, 1612), and composed about seventy pieces for solo lute (fantasias, dances and variations) as well as the *Lachrimae* for viol consort.

Dowland, Robert (*c.* 1591–1641). English composer, lutenist and editor, son of John Dowland. He was perhaps most important for his publication of two collections in 1610 (*A musicall banquet* and *Varietie of lute-lessons*) with works by the leading English and continental composers.

Dufay, Guillaume (*c.* 1398–1474). French composer recognized as the leading figure of his generation. He was a choirboy at Cambrai Cathedral, to which he returned in 1439–51 and from 1458 to his death. From not later than 1419 to 1439 he worked in Italy, at Rimini, Bologna, Rome, Florence and elsewhere. Connections established then with the Dukes of Savoy were renewed when he returned in the 1450s; and he seems to have been on cordial terms with Lorenzo, Piero and Giovanni de' Medici, King René of Anjou and both Dukes of Burgundy as well as Brunelleschi, Donatello and Martin le Franc. He was one of the last composers to cultivate the isorhythmic motet (thirteen, including the famous *Nuper rosarum flores* for the dedication of Florence Cathedral) and among the earliest to write four-voice tenor-based Mass cycles (four, including perhaps the first *Missa L'homme armé*). Many other sacred pieces and over eighty songs also survive.

Dunstable [Dunstaple], **John** (*c.* 1390–1453). English composer who is reputed to have had a substantial influence on the new style used by Dufay and Binchois. The prominent representation of his works in continental sources attests that he was considered by far the leading English composer of his time and one of the most significant composers in Europe. He was associated with John, Duke of Bedford, spent some time in France, and was praised on his tombstone also as a mathematician and astronomer. Among some seventy works ascribed to him – several of them certainly by other composers – there are early Mass cycles and a series of important isorhythmic motets, alongside elaborate settings of service music.

Dux [Lat.: 'leader']. The antecedent of a canon, followed by the consequent 'comes' (lit: 'follower').

Encina [Enzina], **Juan del** [Fermoselle, Juan de] (1468–1529/30). Spanish poet, dramatist and composer. The foremost song composer of his day in Spain, he served the Duke of Alba before going to Rome to find favour with the papacy. On the death of Leo X in 1521 he returned to Spain and spent the last years of his life as prior of León Cathedral. Most of his plays, of which music is an integral part, were written before he left for Rome and were published in his *Cancionero* of 1496. Over sixty of his songs, mostly villancicos in a strikingly homophonic idiom, are preserved in manuscripts associated with the royal courts.

Envoi. Term used to describe the addition to the regular stanzas of a troubadour song or ballade of three or four lines by way of conclusion, usually in the form of an address to a loved one or patron.

Erasmus, Desiderius (1469–1536). Netherlands humanist and writer who may have known Okeghem and was apparently a choirboy under Obrecht. His views on music were influenced both by his studies of ancient writers and by his theological leanings and reforming zeal. It has been said that the spirit of his ideas is reflected in the reforms promulgated by the Council of Trent.

Escobar, Pedro de (*c.* 1465–after 1535). Portuguese composer active in Spain at the royal court and Seville Cathedral. His works include two Masses, seven motets, a number of songs and the earliest polyphonic Requiem found in Spanish sources.

Escobedo, Bartolomé de (*c.* 1500–1563). Spanish composer who sang in the papal choir in Rome for most of his career. He composed at least two Masses and several motets.

Estampie [estampida, istampite]. A medieval term used to describe a type of instrumental dance (or textless melody) divided into repeated sections. Some songs also follow a similar structure.

Eton Choirbook. English manuscript compiled during the years 1490 to 1502 for use at Eton College chapel. The original index lists ninety-three pieces, but only sixty-four survive. These are mostly motets and votive antiphons, many of them in honour of the Virgin, by composers such as William Cornysh, John Browne and Richard Davy. The distinctive style of many of the pieces – with florid, high treble parts – is not found elsewhere in Europe.

Fabri, Martinus (*fl. c.* 1400). Composer, probably of Dutch or Flemish origin. Two French ballades and two Dutch songs are attributed to him.

Faburden/fauxbourdon. Terms used in the fifteenth century for improvised polyphony, usually around a chant. Normally two voices were written down and the third was either in fourths below the upper voice or in thirds above the lower voice. Sometimes, however, particularly in England, only the middle voice was written, and the other voices were improvised according to certain rules. By the sixteenth century the term was being used for any homophonic setting of a simple chant, such as a psalm.

Faenza, Biblioteca Comunale, MS 117 [Faenza MS]. An important manuscript of Italian music of the fifteenth century. The original layer, containing keyboard intabulations, was copied in northern Italy in the first decades of the century. Later, in 1473–4, Johannes Bonadies added twenty-two short polyphonic pieces, including Mass movements, Magnificat settings, motets and some secular works, along with several treatises.

Fantasia. Term for an instrumental piece which generally involves idiomatic instrumental writing and an imaginative freedom of form on the part of the composer. Lute fantasias were first cultivated at the beginning of the sixteenth century by Francesco da Milano in Italy and Luis Milán in Spain. The keyboard fantasia developed rather later in the century with William Byrd as its chief exponent.

Faugues, Guillaume (*fl. c.* 1460–70). French or Flemish composer, documented at the Sainte-Chapelle at Bourges in 1462 and 1471, and mentioned several times by Tinctoris. Four Mass cycles (one based on the *L'homme armé* melody) are attributed to him in late fifteenth-century sources and are unusual in their use of musical repetition.

Fauxbourdon. See FABURDEN.

Fayrfax, Robert (1464–1521). English composer who served in the Chapel Royal from 1497 and received degrees from Cambridge (MusD, 1504) and Oxford (DMus, 1511). His extant works include six Mass cycles, two Magnificat settings, ten votive antiphons and a number of secular pieces.

Festa, Costanzo (*c.* 1490–1545). Italian composer and singer who served at the French court (*c.* 1514) and subsequently in the papal chapel. His four Masses, over sixty motets and a number of madrigals reveal him to be a master of the polyphonic idiom developed by Josquin and as such he was an important figure in Italy's musical predominance in the sixteenth century.

Févin, Antoine de (*c.* 1470–1511/12). French composer, who from at least 1507 worked at the French court. His works, characterized by formal clarity, include ten Masses, three Magnificat settings, over twelve motets and numerous chansons, usually in three voices with a borrowed secular melody in the tenor.

Fibonacci series. Numerical system, occurring naturally in the structure of fir cones, whereby the sum of the previous two numbers provides the next in the series, e.g.: 0, 1, 1, 2, 3, 5, 8, 13, 21, 34, etc. Each number also represents the nearest whole number to the Golden Section of the two numbers surrounding it. It has been argued that such number systems and proportions can be detected behind musical works from the Middle Ages to the present day. See also GOLDEN SECTION.

Fiddle. Term used during the Middle Ages and Renaissance to denote any string instrument played with a bow, but also used for a specific example now commonly referred to as the medieval fiddle. It could take various shapes but invariably had gut strings. During the Middle Ages it was used to accompany songs, sometimes on special occasions in church.

Finck, Hermann (1527–1558). German theorist, composer and organist and the great-nephew of the composer Heinrich Finck (1444/5–1527). His treatise, *Practica musica* (1556), was intended as a comprehensive guide to the rudiments of music.

Fitzwilliam Virginal Book. English manuscript (220 folios) of keyboard music now in the Fitzwilliam Museum, Cambridge. It is thought to have been copied by Francis Tregian in the years 1606–19, and contains almost 300 pieces by composers such as William Byrd, John Bull and Giles Farnaby.

Flauto dolce. See RECORDER.

Flute. Flutes of various kinds are known from ancient times, but after the Fall of Rome they do not reappear in Western art until the tenth and eleventh centuries. The typical transverse flute is often represented from 1500 onwards as part of consorts of various instruments.

Formes fixes [Fr.: 'fixed forms']. Poetic forms, usually involving a refrain structure, that dictated the musical form of chansons during the fourteenth and fifteenth centuries. The main 'fixed forms' were the ballade, rondeau and virelai.

Franchois, Johannes (*fl.* 1410–30). Composer of four Mass movements, an isorhythmic motet and three rondeaux. His identity is in dispute.

Frottola. A type of polyphonic song cultivated in northern Italy in the period *c.* 1470–*c.* 1530, the main centre being the Mantuan court where the most important composers of the frottola, Tromboncino and Cara, were employed. The frottola is distinguished by having the melody in the top voice, simple rhythms and essentially homophonic textures.

Frye, Walter (*fl. c.* 1450–75). English composer who may have worked in Ely Cathedral and London. His works, including three cantus firmus-based Mass cycles as well as a number of other sacred pieces and songs, were well known on the continent.

Gabrieli, Andrea (1533–85). Italian composer who worked in Munich (where he met Lassus) before becoming organist at St Mark's, Venice, in 1566. A prolific composer, he made an important contribution to the *cori spezzati* tradition, contrasting voices and instruments on ceremonial occasions.

Gabrieli, Giovanni (*c.* 1553/6–1612). Italian composer and nephew of Andrea Gabrieli, in the footsteps of whose career he followed closely, taking over his position at St Mark's in 1585. Apart from his collections of sacred music (*Symphoniae sacrae*, 1597, 1615), he composed a considerable amount of instrumental ensemble music.

Gaffurius, Franchinus (1451–1522). Italian theorist and composer who served in various Italian centres before becoming *maestro di cappella* of Milan Cathedral in 1484. Most of his music was composed there. He had met Tinctoris in Naples before publishing his three most important treatises: *Theorica musicae* (1492); *Practica musicae* (1496); and *De harmonia musicorum instrumentorum opus* (1518). These reveal a mixture of progressive and conservative tendencies.

Galilei, Vincenzo (late 1520s–1591). Italian theorist and composer who studied with Zarlino in Venice; father of Galileo Galilei. From 1572 he settled in Florence where he was a leading member of the Florentine Camerata. In his *Dialogo* (1591), he gave his full support to the 'revival' of monody. He also composed madrigals and lute pieces as well as a treatise on the lute entitled *Fronimo* (1568).

Galliard. A lively, triple-metre dance that is thought to have originated in northern Italy. The earliest existing examples were published by Attaingnant in 1529–30; it enjoyed great popularity as an instrumental genre among English composers of the late sixteenth century.

Ganassi dal Fontego, Sylvestro di (1492–*c.* 1550). Italian instrumentalist who wrote two important treatises on instrumental performance: *Opera intitulata Fontegara* (1535): and *Regola rubertina* (two volumes, 1542/3). These discuss practical techniques of the recorder and viol respectively and thus shed valuable light on sixteenth-century performance practice.

Gardane, Antonio (1509–69). First in an important family of music publishers: his two sons, Alessandro (*c.* 1539–*c.* 1591) and Angelo (1540–1611) taking the business into the seventeenth century. From 1538, Antonio issued volumes of all kinds of music, but especially madrigals by such composers as Arcadelt, Willaert and Lassus and, from 1546, much lute tablature.

Gerle, Hans (*c.* 1500–70). German lute maker and instrumentalist, probably the son of the lute maker Conrad Gerle. He compiled several volumes of instrumental music, some with introductory essays on playing technique, which were published between 1532 and 1552.

Gesualdo, Carlo, Prince of Venosa (*c.* 1561–1613). Italian nobleman and composer who achieved professional standing at the court in Ferrara where he was much influenced by the music of Luzzaschi. His six books of madrigals (1594–1611) and three collections of sacred music (1603–11) reveal an unusually dissonant style.

Giovanelli, Ruggiero (*c.* 1560–1625). Italian composer who worked at various musical institutions in Rome (including the Sistine Chapel, 1583–91) and who may have been a pupil of Palestrina. He published six books of madrigals (1585–1606) and two of motets (1593, 1604) and four Masses.

Giraut de Bornelh (*c.* 1140–*c.* 1200). Troubadour, poet and composer. He travelled widely throughout southern France and northern Spain, and he may have participated in the crusades. Of the almost eighty poems attributed to Giraut, only four survive with music, among them the well-known alba *Reis glorios*.

Gittern. A form of medieval lute, smaller and with a shorter neck than the Renaissance lute, and which probably came to

Europe in the late thirteenth century from Arab countries. Usually with three or four courses of strings plucked with a quill, it was ousted during the fifteenth century by the lute.

Glarean, Heinrich (1488–1563). Swiss theorist and humanist much influenced by Erasmus whom he met in Basle in 1514. In turn, his treatise *Dodecachordon* (1547), in which he developed a new modal theory, was one of the most influential of the Renaissance. It is also an important anthology of music of the Josquin period.

Golden Section. Numerical proportion recognized since antiquity as important in natural and man-made structures. The Golden Section divides a fixed length into two so that the ratio of the shorter portion to the longer portion is the same as that of the longer portion to the whole (0.618034 . . .). Composers would seem to have been aware of the structural importance of this proportion from at least the Middle Ages.

Gombert, Nicholas (*c.* 1495–*c.* 1560). Flemish composer who may have been a pupil of Josquin and who served for most of his career in the chapel of Charles V. Ten Masses, over one hundred and sixty motets and other sacred works survive, mostly in the equal-voiced polyphony that was the hallmark of his style. He also composed over seventy chansons, not stylistically dissimilar to his motets.

'Gregorian' chant. See CHANT.

Grenon, Nicolas (*c.* 1380–1456). French composer and teacher. From at least 1399 a clerk at Notre Dame, Paris, he also served at Laon and Cambrai Cathedrals before entering the service of John the Fearless, Duke of Burgundy, in 1412 as master of the choirboys of the ducal chapel. After the Duke's death in 1419, he returned to Cambrai, apart from two years (1425–7) as master of the boys of the papal chapel. He composed polyphonic chansons (five extant) and isorhythmic motets (four), while his only Mass movement, a Gloria, survives incomplete.

Grossin, Estienne (*fl. c.* 1420). French composer who held various church posts in Paris. Several Mass movements (including a four-movement setting linked by a 'trombetta' part), two motets and two chansons are attributed to him.

Guerrero, Francisco (1528–99). Spanish composer and pupil of Morales who from 1574–99 was *maestro de capilla* at Seville Cathedral. He also travelled to Rome, Venice and the Holy Land. He composed eighteen Masses and about 150 motets, most of which appeared in print between 1555 and 1539, as well as a collection of spiritual songs (1589).

Guido of Arezzo (*c.* 991–after 1033). Theorist based for much of his life at a Benedictine monastery near Arezzo. In about 1028 he was called to Rome by Pope John XIX to teach his new method of notation. His treatise, *Micrologus* was probably the most influential after Boethius throughout the Middle Ages.

Guidonian Hand, The. A technique developed by Guido of Arezzo to help singers to read music by allotting the different notes (represented by solmization syllables) of the gamut (or scalic system derived from the hexachords) to various parts of the hand. When the choirmaster pointed to a particular joint or section of a finger, the singer would know which note to sing: it would appear to have been an important teaching method throughout the Middle Ages.

Guillaume IX, Duke of Aquitaine (1071–1137). Generally held to be the earliest of the troubadours, at least the first whose works have survived. His adventurous life included the composition of at least eleven poems, of which only one survives with music.

Guitar. The origins of the guitar remain obscure; it may have originated in Europe or have been introduced there from Arab countries. In any case, it appears to have emerged in European culture during the fifteenth century (still earlier literary references are difficult to distinguish from the gittern), at which time the four-course instrument retained much in common with the lute and vihuela. The five-course *viola da mano* was popular in Italy from the late fifteenth century.

Harp. One of the most important instruments of the Middle Ages, although even in the sixteenth century there seems to have been some confusion between the terms harp and lyre. Its importance in medieval culture was reinforced by its association with King David and this is reflected in the iconography of the Psalmist, a valuable source of information on the instrument. The number of strings generally increased during the period so that by the Renaissance twenty-four or more gut strings were common. The double-strung harp (arpa doppia), allowing for a fully chromatic range, was developed and became increasingly popular during the second half of the sixteenth century.

Hayne van Ghizeghem (*c.* 1445–1477/*c.* 1490). Franco-Flemish composer, documented at the Burgundian court 1457–77, though he surely lived until at least 1490. Some twenty chansons are attributed to him in various sources of the late fifteenth and early sixteenth centuries. At least two of these, 'De tous biens plaine' and 'Allez regrets', were enormously popular during that period.

Head motif. A musical idea, or motto, used to link a sequence of pieces or movements. It was a device often used throughout the fifteenth and sixteenth centuries as a unifying factor in the cyclic Mass.

Henestrosa. See VENEGAS DE HENE-STROSA, LUIS DE.

Hexachord. A scale of six notes [*ut, re, mi, fa, sol, la*] with a semitone between the third and fourth notes. It was first described by Guido of Arezzo (*c.* 991–after 1033), and from at least that time formed the basis for composing and singing polyphony. The three main hexachords are: *hexachordum durum* on G (with B natural); *hexachordum molle* on F (with B flat); and *hexachordum naturale* on C.

Hocket. A medieval term for a compositional device used in the thirteenth and fourteenth centuries whereby the individual voices of a polyphonic piece alternated sounding notes and rests in rapid succession to achieve a special effect. The best known and most extended example is Machaut's *Hoquetus David.*

Hofhaimer, Paul (1459–1537). Austrian organist and composer. He held various posts as organist, from 1489 serving Maximilian I and in 1519 becoming organist at Salzburg Cathedral. He was renowned for his skills as an improviser and also as a teacher, and he was an expert on organ-building. Apart from the German songs and his *Harmoniae poeticae* (Nuremberg, 1539), few of his works have survived.

Holborne, Antony (d. 1602). English composer about whom little is known except that he left an important collection of instrumental pieces entitled *The cittharn Schoole* (1597), as well as several other volumes published between 1596 and 1612.

Horn. Horns of various shapes and sizes are depicted in a great variety of medieval iconographical sources, often, as would be expected, in the context of the hunt. By the end of the sixteenth century two basic types of horn – the crescent-shaped hunting horn and the coiled helical horn – had emerged and these were to lead eventually to the development of the orchestral or French horn of later centuries.

Hucbald (*c.* 840–930). Theorist and composer. A monk at Tournai, his *De harmonica institutione* (*c.* 880) is the earliest known work to describe in a systematic way the principles of Western music theory. Each theoretical point is illustrated by an example of chant. He also composed some Offices for saints' days.

Hurdy-gurdy [organistrum]. A medieval string instrument in which the encased strings (melody and drone) are bowed mechanically by a resin-coated wooden wheel (turned by a handle) and which also has a simple keyboard mechanism bearing on the melody strings. In the Middle Ages the hurdy-gurdy was used for teaching purposes and for accompanying songs. Always popular amongst minstrels, it has remained in use in certain areas as a street or folk instrument to this day.

Idiophone. The generic term for an instrument that produces sound from its own substance, as in the case of cymbals or rattles.

Ileborgh, Adam (*fl. c.* 1448). German composer important for composing or at least compiling one of the earliest books of music for organ (the 'Ileborgh tablature'). It comprises five preludes and three cantus firmus settings.

Imperfection. A term used to describe the process in the notation of early mensural music whereby the relationship between two notes is 2:1, rather than the perfect ratio of 3:1.

Intabulation [It.: intavolatura]. Term used to describe the arrangement of a vocal piece for keyboard, lute or other plucked instrument in music of the fourteenth to the sixteenth centuries written in tablature (a system of notation using letters or numbers instead of note-heads on a staff). Intabulations tended to become more elaborate and more freely based on their models – and so more idiomatically instrumental – towards the end of the period.

Integer valor [Lat.: 'whole value']. Term often used of a cantus firmus to refer to its presentation in its basic note values when it is then subject to proportional changes, sometimes indicated by verbal instructions.

Intermedio [It.; Fr.: intermede]. A musico-dramatic entertainment performed between the acts of plays during the Renaissance. It would appear to have originated towards the end of the fifteenth century and to have become more widespread in the course of the first half of the sixteenth century, but the most famous example dates from the Medici wedding of 1589 (known as the Florentine Intermedi). Various aspects of the intermedio tradition were influential in the development of opera.

Isaac, Heinrich (*c.* 1450–1517). Flemish composer who worked at various musical centres, but principally in Florence (1485–93 and 1514–17) and, from 1496, at the court of Maximilian I. A prolific, not to say comprehensive composer, he published almost a hundred settings of the Proper of the Mass which were published after his death in the three-volume collection entitled the *Choralis Constantinus*. He also composed about forty settings of the Ordinary as well as numerous secular works in a variety of local styles: chansons, Tenorlieder and frottolas.

Isorhythm. Term invented by Friedrich Ludwig for motets of the fourteenth and fifteenth centuries to describe the repetition of rhythmic patterns. Recurring rhythmic patterns, usually but not exclusively, in the tenor became an important principle of composition in the motets of Vitry and Machaut (giving rise to the isorhythmic motet that continued to be cultivated well into the fifteenth century by Dufay and his contemporaries). Isorhythm is also found in Mass movements by English composers of the turn of the fourteenth century. Repetitions of pitch content were termed the color, while those of rhythm the talea: the two did not necessarily coincide.

Ivrea MS. French manuscript (64 folios) dating from the years around 1365–80, preserved in the Biblioteca Capitolare, Ivrea. It may have been compiled in the papal court in Avignon, and contains over eighty works from the period of Philippe de Vitry and Guillaume de Machaut. Most are sacred pieces (Mass movements and motets), but there are also a few chansons.

Jacopo da Bologna (*fl.* 1340–60). Italian composer and theorist who worked at various north Italian courts; he may also have been a university teacher. Apart from writing a treatise (*L'arte del biscanto misurato*), he composed about thirty two- and three-voice madrigals and caccias, and at least one motet.

Jacques de Liège (*c.* 1260–after 1330). French theorist whose *Speculum musice*, is the most extensive surviving treatise from the Ars nova period. In his discussion of the nature of music he follows Boethius, but the chapters dedicated to chant and mensural music refer to current practice, revealing a strong preference for traditional procedures.

Janequin, Clément (*c.* 1485–1558). French composer who held various positions in Bordeaux before moving to Angers Cathedral by the early 1530s, by which time some of his chansons had been published by Attaingnant. In 1549 he settled in Paris as a student at the university, but it was not until the last years of his life that he finally held the position of *compositeur ordinaire du roi*. He concentrated on the composition of psalm-settings and chansons, of which more than 150 survive. He was, and is, best known for the extended songs imitating sounds such as birdsong and those of hunting or battles, but he composed in a wide range of styles, from lyrical, melancholic pieces to bawdy narratives, all of which reveal his concern for rhythmic declamation.

Jehannot de l'Escurel [Jehan de Lescurel] (d. 1304). French composer. Born in Paris, he served as a cleric at Notre Dame until he was hanged for debauchery. Thirty-four works are attributed to him, all of them monophonic except for one three-voice rondeau.

Jerome of Moravia (*fl.* 1271–1304). Dominican monk and music theorist. His treatise is largely derived from Boethius and other early medieval writers, but there are original chapters on composing chants and singing styles.

Johannes de Grocheio (*fl. c.* 1300). French theorist who was active in Paris in the late thirteenth century. His treatise entitled *De musica* displays considerable awareness of contemporary practical concerns and is also important for its discussion of secular monophonic forms.

Johannes de Lymburgia (*fl.* 1400–40). Composer, probably from Limbourg (now in Belgium). He worked in Liège and Vicenza before being appointed a canon of Notre Dame in 1436. His works include Mass movements (and one – probably composite – cycle), Magnificats, hymns and laude.

Josquin Desprez [Près, Josquin des] (*c.* 1440–1521). French composer of unchallenged pre-eminence around 1500 and arguably the greatest single influence on composers throughout the sixteenth century. Many details of his life remain tantalizingly elusive though he seems to have been mainly in Milan from 1459 to 1479, was in the papal chapel 1486–95,

was chapelmaster to the Duke of Ferrara 1503–4, and then spent his remaining years as provost of Notre Dame, Condé. Similarly, the full extent of his output is considerably in question, because a very large number of plainly or demonstrably spurious works were ascribed to him, particularly in later German prints: even the seventeen Masses published in three volumes by Petrucci (1502–14 and later editions) include several works now thought to be of dubious authorship.

Jota. Spanish song and dance, originating in Aragonese folk tradition, and usually in fast triple time.

Kerle, Jacobus de (1531/2–1591). Netherlands composer. He held various posts, among them organist of Augsburg Cathedral (1568–74), and he also served at the imperial court in Vienna (1582) and Prague (1583). Fifteen volumes of his Masses and motets were published between 1557 and 1585.

Kettledrums [Eng.: nakers; It.: nacchere]. Hemispherical drums are known from at least the second and third centuries BC. Usually paired, they were adopted throughout thirteenth-century Europe as a result of the Crusades. Their role during the Middle Ages and Renaissance remained primarily military and ceremonial.

Kithara. See LYRE.

Kleber, Leonhard (*c.* 1495–1556). German organist who studied at Heidelberg before holding several teaching posts at German universities. He compiled an extensive and important collection of organ music in tablature in the early 1520s.

Kotter, Hans (*c.* 1485–1541). German organist and composer. A pupil of Hofheimer, he held various posts in Germany. He helped to compile three books of organ music, including some of his own pieces. These display considerable inventiveness and a sure sense of idiomatic keyboard writing.

Lai. An extended song form (usually monophonic) cultivated during the thirteenth and fourteenth centuries. It consisted of a number of stanzas (by the fourteenth century, normally twelve), the form and musical content of each being different. Machaut was the chief exponent of the most highly developed examples, including four settings that include polyphony.

Lamentations. Polyphonic settings of verses from the Lamentations of the prophet Jeremiah date from the turn of the fifteenth century, a collection of such compositions by La Rue, Isaac and their contemporaries being published by Petrucci in 1506. Later contributors to the genre included Morales, Lassus, Palestrina, Byrd and Tallis. Each verse is typically preceded by a melismatic setting of one of the Hebrew letters (Aleph, Beth, etc.).

Landini, Francesco (*c.* 1325–97). Florentine composer and organist, the leading Italian composer of the fourteenth century. About 140 ballate are attributed to him, as well as some madrigals, a caccia and one virelai. He is important for his assimilation of various French influences into the Italian style he inherited from his predecessors.

Lanfranco, Giovanni Maria (*c.* 1490–1545). Italian theorist who worked at several north Italian centres before becoming *maestro di cappella* in Parma in 1540. His treatise *Scintille di musica* (1533) presents the basics of Renaissance musical theory in clear, didactic terms, with unusually unambiguous treatment of matters such as the tactus in mensural music, tuning and underlay.

Lantins, Arnold de (d. 1432). Composer from the diocese of Liège, who was at the court of Pesaro in 1423, at Venice in 1428, and in the papal chapel 1431–2. His works, which include a Mass cycle and several Mass movements and other sacred works and about fifteen chansons, are preserved in north Italian sources.

Lantins, Hugo de (*fl.* 1420–30). Composer from the diocese of Liège, possibly brother of Arnold. He was at the court of Pesaro in 1423, perhaps in Venice soon after, and seems to have had a close association with Dufay. He, too, composed Mass movements, motets and chansons (mostly rondeaux), but his works are characterized by his extensive use of imitation.

La Rue, Pierre de (*c.* 1460–1518). Flemish composer who sang in cathedral choirs in Siena and 's-Hertogenbosch before joining the Burgundian chapel for Philip the Fair's first journey to Spain in 1501–3, returning there in 1506–8. He later served at the court of Marguerite of Austria. One of the leading composers of his time, he composed over thirty Mass cycles, twenty-six motets, a set of Lamentations, seven Magnificats and about thirty chansons.

Lassus, Orlande de [Lasso, Orlando di] (1530/2–1594). Franco-Flemish composer who spent the early part of his career in Italy (Mantua, Naples, Rome). In 1556 he was appointed a singer in the chapel of Duke Albrecht V of Bavaria, becoming master of the Munich court chapel in 1563 and serving there till his death. He was an extremely prolific composer who contributed with consummate mastery to every compositional genre he touched. His sacred works include about seventy Masses, four Passions, about a hundred Magnificats, Lamentations settings and many other liturgical pieces, while his secular output features hundreds of madrigals, villanelle, chansons and Lieder. His music was published in enormous quantities throughout Europe during his lifetime and in the years after his death, though much remained in manuscript.

La Torre, Francisco de (*fl.* 1483–1504). Spanish composer who served in the Aragonese royal chapel choir from 1483 until 1503 when he took charge of the choirboys of Seville Cathedral. A setting of the *Libera me* from the Office of the Dead apparently continued to be sung in Spain for several centuries. He also composed a number of songs and a three-part instrumental 'Alta'.

Lauda spirituale. The main form of religious song cultivated in Italy during the period. It developed in the thirteenth century during a wave of religious fervour that swept through north Italy, Germany and southern France. Polyphonic laude date from the fifteenth century, often written in a simple, chordal style.

Le Jeune, Claude [Claudin] (1528/30–1600). Prolific French composer, one of the main exponents of *musique mesurée à l'antique*. Little is known of his early life, his name first appearing in an anthology of chansons printed in Louvain in 1552. By 1564 he had settled in Paris, some years later, after 1579, becoming 'maistre des enfans de musicque' at the court of François of Anjou. In Paris he was an active member of the Académie de Poésie et de Musique (1570) and it was in that context that he developed the theory of *musique mesurée*, resulting in homophonic settings of the quantitative metres prescribed by the Académie. An ardent Protestant, his output includes almost 350 psalm-settings, as well as many secular and sacred chansons, Italian madrigals and three instrumental fantasias.

Leoninus [Leonin] (*fl. c.* 1163–1201). 'Magister Leoninus' whom the theorist Anonymous IV referred to as the 'best composer of organum', and as compiler of a *Magnus liber* of two-voice organa for the solo sections of graduals, alleluias and responsories for the whole liturgical year which were subsequently modified and added to by Perotinus. His *Magnus liber* appears to survive as a unit in the famous Notre Dame manuscripts.

Lescurel. See JEHANNOT DE L'ES-CUREL.

Liber Usualis [Lat.]. Literally 'the book of common practice', the Liber Usualis was first published by the monks of Solesmes in 1896. It contains prayers, lessons and chant for the Mass and Office of the major feasts of the liturgical year, thus selecting and combining the relevant passages from the various liturgical books – the missal, gradual, antiphoner and breviary – that had previously been used separately.

Ligature. A symbol used in the notation of music from the twelfth to the sixteenth centuries to link two or more notes. The rhythmic values of those notes are determined by the shape of the ligature. Codified in the mid-thirteenth century by the theorist Franco of Cologne, the use of ligatures died out during the sixteenth century.

Lira da braccio. Renaissance bowed string instrument with a violin-shaped body, but a wide fingerboard and relatively flat bridge to accommodate five stoppable strings and two drones. It was much favoured by poet-musicians in fifteenth-century Italy for the accompaniment of their improvised recitations. Often associated with mythological characters such as Apollo and Orpheus, it was also used in the intermedio. The lirone was the lira da braccio's larger, bass counterpart (played between the knees rather than under the chin); its fingerboard could accommodate nine to fourteen strings plus two to four drones. Both instruments fell out of use early in the seventeenth century.

Lirone. See LIRA DA BRACCIO.

Liturgical drama. A type of religious play in which a Latin text (usually developed from the liturgy) is sung monophonically. The important early centres for liturgical drama were St Martial, St Gall, Winchester and Fleury. Plays developed from the dialogues of Christmas (*Officium pastorum* and *Officium stelle*) and Easter (*Visitatio sepulchri*) are the most numerous and important types of liturgical drama. Other plays with Biblical subjects (for example, the *Play of Daniel*), saints' plays (Miracles) and Passion plays also exist, though these fall rather into the category of vernacular medieval drama.

Lobo, Alonso (*c.* 1555–1617). Spanish composer who trained as a choirboy at Seville Cathedral, assisted Guerrero there in 1593 and took over as chapelmaster in 1604. His many Mass settings and motets were much admired by Victoria.

Loqueville, Richard (d. 1418). French composer who in 1410 served the Duke of Bar as harp tutor to his son and teacher of chant to the ducal chapel choirboys. From 1413 he was master of the choristers at Cambrai Cathedral and is thought to have taught the young Dufay. Several Mass movements, an isorhythmic motet, four rondeaux and a ballade are attributed to him.

Luchini, Paolo (*c.* 1535–98). Italian theorist and singer. An Augustinian friar, he spent most of his life at the monastery of Valmanente where he taught Lodovico

Zacconi. He compiled the three books of his *Musica theorica e practica*, a compendium of musical theory drawing on many writers of the earlier part of the Renaissance, in about 1591–2. Essentially a traditionalist, he shows some appreciation of the musical developments of his own time, notably as regards word setting.

Lute. Plucked string instrument descended from the Arabic 'ud and introduced into Europe through the Moorish occupation of Spain from 711. It retained a central position in Western music-making until the eighteenth century. The earliest surviving music for the lute dates from the late fifteenth century, and important collections of the early repertory were published by Petrucci in 1507–11. The lute gained in stature as a solo and an accompanying instrument during the sixteenth century and featured prominently in the works of John Dowland.

Luther, Martin (1483–1546). German reformer. Musically trained and inclined, he was consistently concerned with the role of music in the Reformation and the relationship between words and music. He collaborated with Walter to write chant suited to the German language, and he also composed and arranged numerous hymn melodies.

Luzzaschi, Luzzasco (?1545–1607). Italian composer who served at the Este court in Ferrara as singer and organist. He achieved considerable fame as a keyboard player (Frescobaldi was one of his pupils), but few keyboard works by him have survived, and he is better known for his seven books of five-part madrigals (1571–1604), as well as one for three sopranos and keyboard (1601) written for the celebrated 'singing ladies' of Ferrara.

Lyre. Ancient string instrument. Together with the kithara it was the most important string instrument of ancient Greece and Rome. In the Middle Ages it was commonly associated with King David and appears with increasing frequency in illustrations from the late seventh century onwards.

Machaut, Guillaume de (c. 1300–1377). French composer and poet; the most important figure of the Ars nova. He served various members of the aristocracy, including John of Luxembourg, King of Bohemia (c. 1323–46) and John, Duke of Berry, and was highly regarded in his own day. In his many motets and songs, he followed the compositional principles outlined in Philippe de Vitry's *Ars nova*. He made an enormous contribution to the development of isorhythmic technique; all but three of his twenty-three motets employ isorhythm, which is also used in his *Messe de Nostre Dame*, the earliest known Mass cycle. He also composed monophonic and polyphonic secular music, including nineteen lais, over forty ballades, twenty-two rondeaux, thirty-three virelais, and was thus an important figure in the development of the polyphonic *forme-fixe* chanson.

Madrid, Palacio Real, Biblioteca, MS 1335 [Cancionero Musical de Palacio]. This vast collection of songs from the time of Ferdinand and Isabella (1474–1516) may have originally contained as many as 550 pieces, though only 463 survive. Many of the songs are anonymous, but there are attributions to Juan del Encina, Francisco de La Torre, Juan Urrede, Madrid, Francisco de Peñalosa, Juan de Anchieta, Millan and many others.

Madrigal. [It.: madrigale]. The term refers to two distinct and unrelated musical genres: (1) a poetico-musical form cultivated in Italy during the fourteenth century; and (2) a setting of secular verse from the sixteenth and early seventeenth centuries. Only about two hundred examples of (1) survive, mostly from the period c. 1320 to c. 1360 when it would seem to have gone into decline, and almost all of these are for two voices. The sixteenth-century madrigal developed in the 1520s as a serious and refined musical setting of Petrarch-style verse in which the music often strove to reflect the poetic imagery (word-painting). Early exponents were Arcadelt, Festa and Verdelot who were in turn succeeded by Willaert, Rore and de Wert: their settings could range from three to six voices, though by the middle of the century five was the norm.

Bold experimentation with madrigalian effects occurred towards the end of the sixteenth century with composers such as Marenzio, Luzzaschi, Gesualdo and Monteverdi, whose later books of madrigals employed Baroque techniques. The Italian madrigal found another late flowering in England with the publication in 1588 of Yonge's *Musica transalpina*.

Maffei, Giovanni Camillo (*fl.* 1562–73). Italian singer and lutenist who was also a physician and served for the last part of his career in Naples. A letter to his master Giovanni di Capua, count of Altavilla (published in 1562), goes into some detail about the art of singing and vocal embellishment.

Magnificat. A Vespers canticle the text of which is taken from *Luke* i, 46–55. The earliest polyphonic settings date from the fourteenth century, but it was during the fifteenth and sixteenth centuries that it was most cultivated by composers such as Dufay (5), Lassus (about 100) and Palestrina (over 30). Many settings from this period were performed in alternatim, that is with alternative verses only set to polyphony, the intervening verses being chanted or set instrumentally.

Mainerio, Giorgio (*c.* 1535–82). Italian composer who sang and taught for most of his life at the cathedrals of Udine and Aquileia. Though a priest and a composer of sacred music, he is best known today for his important collection of ensemble dance music entitled *Il primo libro di balli* (1578).

Mandora. [Fr.: Mandore]. A sixteenth-century term for a plucked string instrument with a rounded body, similar to the mandolin. Repertory for the instrument survives from the late sixteenth century.

Marchetto da Padova (?1274; *fl.* 1305–26). Italian theorist and composer who worked at Padua cathedral for at least part of his life. He composed motets, but is best known for his treatises: *Lucidarium* (1309–18); *Pomerium* (1318–26); and a summary of the *Pomerium* entitled *Brevis compilacio*. The material of the *Lucidarium* is mostly based on other authors, although Marchetto at one point refutes Pythagoras

and proposes the division of the tone into five equal parts. The *Pomerium* deals with mensural music.

Marenzio, Luca (1533/4–1599). Italian composer active for most of his career in Rome, although he also visited Verona, Florence (where he contributed to the 1589 intermedi) and even Poland (1595–6). He published twenty-three books of madrigals (over 400) and villanellas (about 80) between 1580 and 1599, and he also composed about seventy-five motets. His madrigals remained popular for many years.

Martinelli, Caterina (*c.* 1589–1608). Italian singer. She served at the Mantuan court at the same time as Monteverdi who composed the title role of *L'Arianna* for her. She died before the first performance, but Monteverdi paid her further tribute with the madrigal cycle *Lagrime d'amante al sepolcro dell'amata* (Book VI, 1614).

Martini, Johannes (*c.* 1440–97/8). Flemish composer who worked for most of his carrer in the chapel of Ercole I d'Este in Ferrara, although he also served for a short time at the Sforza court in Milan (1474). Ten Masses by him survive, as well as motets and many other sacred works, including a large number of homophonic psalm settings. He also composed secular pieces with French and Italian titles possibly intended as instrumental ensemble music.

Mass. With the celebration of the Eucharist at the centre of the Christian liturgy, the Mass has given rise to musical settings from at least the seventh century. The chants for the Proper (the Introit, Gradual, Alleluia (or Tract), Sequence, Offertory and Communion) and the Ordinary (Kyrie, Gloria, Credo, Sanctus, Agnus Dei, Ite missa est) of the Mass were mostly composed by the eleventh century. Chants for the Proper formed the basis for organum as early as the tenth century, while organum settings of the Ordinary date from at least the twelfth century. From the fourteenth century, polyphonic settings tended to concentrate on the five main texts (the Ite missa est was often not set) of the Ordinary, although Propers continued to be set throughout the period. From this time, too, date the earliest cyclic Masses in which these five movements were linked musically by the use of recurring head motifs, or a common cantus firmus (sometimes referred to as the 'tenor' Mass, the cantus firmus usually being presented in that voice) or, by the sixteenth century, polyphonic model whether secular chanson or sacred motet (parody Mass). Mass settings could also be based on canonic or paraphrase (free allusion to chant) techniques.

Mass of Barcelona. Mass setting from the late fourteenth century, probably connected with the repertory of the papal court in Avignon. It is a compilation of settings of the five movements of the Ordinary (copied successively at the beginning of the manuscript in which it is preserved) rather than a true cyclic Mass.

Mass of Notre Dame. See MESSE DE NOSTRE DAME.

Mass of Sorbonne. Early (and incomplete) example of an attempt to unify the Ordinary of the Mass into a cyclic whole. Sections from the Kyrie and the Sanctus are quoted in the Agnus Dei, apparently for this purpose. The Sorbonne Mass has been rather dubiously attributed to Johannes Lambuleti.

Mass of Toulouse. An anonymous late fourteenth-century polyphonic setting of the Mass (minus the Gloria) in which the surviving movements would appear to be linked together for performance by the same forces rather than by any deliberate attempt at musical unification.

Mass of Tournai. An anonymous three-voice setting of the Mass from the first half of the fourteenth century. It would not, however, appear to be by one composer, and is a compilation of individual settings of the five movements of the Mass which are written in different styles.

Matteo da Perugia (d. by 1418). Italian composer who worked for most of his career in Milan. He was a prolific composer who, like Ciconia, drew on both French and Italian traditions, writing isorhythmic motets, Mass movements and chansons as well as Italian ballate.

Matins. See OFFICE.

Melisma [Gr.: 'song']. A term most commonly used in chant or monophony where one syllable of text carries an unspecified number of notes. Certain 'Gregorian' chants – such as graduals, tracts, responsories and alleluias – are characteristically melismatic. Chant melismas were particularly important for the development of polyphony in that it was initially these sections that formed the basis for organum. The adjective melismatic is often used to describe any florid vocal line in music from the period.

Mellon Chansonnier. See NEW HAVEN, YALE UNIVERSITY, BEINECKE RARE BOOK AND MANUSCRIPT LIBRARY, 91.

Mensuration. System, established in about 1250 by Franco of Cologne, devised to measure the exact rhythmic relationships between the different note values: long, breve and semibreve, etc. It formed the basis for music and its notation until the end of the sixteenth century. The relationships were: *modus* (long to breve); *tempus* (breve to semibreve); and *prolatio* (semibreve to minim). These could be 3:1 (perfect) or 2:1 (imperfect) according to context, although *modus* was generally imperfect. Mensural music or mensural notation describes music measured in this way.

Mersenne, Marin (1588–1648). French philosopher and theorist who considerably influenced ideas in music in the first half of the seventeenth century through his treatise *Harmonie universelle* (1636–7).

Messe de Nostre Dame. Setting for four voices by Machaut of the Ordinary of the Mass in which the movements are linked musically and thus form the earliest known example of a cyclic Mass. The Gloria and Credo are freely constructed, the other movements (including a setting of the Ite missa est) being isorhythmic.

Milán, Luis (*c.* 1500–*c.* 1561). Spanish vihuelist and composer, active for most of his career in Valencia where until at least 1538 he was associated with the ducal court. His *Libro de música de vihuela de mano intitulado El maestro* (1536) was the first published collection of instrumental music in Spain. It includes freely-composed fantasias as well as intabulations, and gives verbal indications of tempo for many of the pieces.

Milano, Francesco da (1497–1543). Italian composer and lutenist who served in Rome. He was an extremely prolific composer (more than forty volumes of his lute music were published between 1536 and 1603 in addition to twenty-five extant manuscript sources), and enjoyed a considerable reputation. His works include freely-composed ricercares and fantasias as well as intabulations of vocal pieces by such composers as Josquin, Sermisy and Janequin.

Minnesang. The courtly lyric tradition that flourished in Germany from the twelfth to the fourteenth centuries: the Minnesingers being the German equivalent to the troubadours. As in the Provençal tradition, the Minnesang was cultivated in noble circles and spread by itinerant musicians. The main topic was also love, particularly the service of love without necessarily any prospect of a reward. The Minnesang reached its height in the second half of the thirteenth century, but the surviving melodies are preserved in manuscripts from the fourteenth and fifteenth centuries. Walter von der Vogelweide and Neidhart von Reuental were important figures in the development of the Minnesang: its influence is still apparent in the works of Oswald von Wolkenstein who died in 1445.

Mode. Term most commonly used to describe the sequence of notes or scales that formed the basis for music of this period. According to the theorists, the choice of mode dictated on which note a melody might begin and end, the overall shape of the melody and even its emotional or expressive content. This clearly had important ramifications for the modes of particular chants and for the polyphony based on those chants. In 'Gregorian' chant there were eight modes (generally known as the 'church modes') drawn from the four Greek modes in authentic and plagal versions, or according to the way the notes were grouped around the so-called

'final', the note of greatest importance in the hierarchy. Mode was also used in the Middle Ages with respect to certain rhythmic patterns: see RHYTHMIC MODES.

Modena MS. An important source for the French repertory of the second half of the fourteenth century and beginning of the fifteenth century, now in the Biblioteca Estense in Modena (callmark alpha M.5.24). Three of the gatherings were probably copied in Bologna in about 1410, the other two, containing works by Matteo da Perugia, may have been written in Milan, probably before his death in 1418. It contains a hundred pieces of all kinds, including Mass movements, motets, ballades, rondeaux, virelais, madrigals and ballate, by composers such as Matteo da Perugia, Machaut, Anthonello de Caserta, Philippus da Caserta, Jacob de Senleches and many others.

Moderne, Jacques (*c.* 1495/1500–*c.* 1562). French music printer. He began to publish music in 1532 using Pierre Attaingnant's method of printing by single impression; he became that publisher's main rival in France. About fifty volumes of all kinds of music came from his presses, including Masses, motets, chansons and instrumental music of the period by composers such as Arcadelt, Willaert and Gombert.

Molins, P. des (*fl.* mid-fourteenth century). French composer, possibly the Philippe des Moulins who was in the service of the Duke of Berry in 1368. His two surviving works – a ballade and a rondeau, both in three voices – were widely disseminated, the former also in a two-voice keyboard version.

Mondéjar, Alonso de (*fl.* beginning of the sixteenth century). Spanish composer who served in the royal chapels of Ferdinand and Isabella (1474–1516). Eleven songs by him are included in the *Cancionero Musical de Palacio*, and further works (another song, a setting of the Magnificat and three motets) are in other Hispanic sources of the period.

Monochord. An ancient instrument with only one string, said to have been invented by Pythagoras in the fifth century BC. In ancient Greece it would appear to have been played as a solo and an ensemble instrument. It is often cited in treatises of the Middle Ages and Renaissance, and was apparently a valuable teaching aid throughout the period.

Monody. An early form of accompanied solo song developed towards the very end of the sixteenth century principally in Florentine musical circles in their attempts to emulate the music of the Ancients. The first collection of monodies is found in Caccini's *Le nuove musiche* (1601/2).

Monteverdi, Claudio (1567–1643). Italian composer. He worked at the Mantuan court (*c.* 1591–1612) before being appointed *maestro di cappella* at St Mark's, Venice, a position he held until his death. His nine books of madrigals (1587–1651) reveal most completely the transformation of musical style from the contrapuntal idiom of other late-Renaissance madrigalists such as Giaches de Wert to the new monodic idiom which found greatest expression in his operas.

Montpellier MS. An important source for the early motet now in the Faculté de Médicine in Montpellier as manuscript H196. With 336 polyphonic pieces it is the largest single source for motets from the thirteenth century and the very beginning of the fourteenth, and represents most of the early forms of the genre.

Morales, Cristóbal de (*c.* 1500–1553). Spanish composer who received his musical education in Seville before serving at Ávila Cathedral (1526–31) and in the papal chapel (1535–45). He then held various positions in Spain before becoming *maestro de capilla* at Málaga Cathedral in 1551. His compositional output consists almost entirely of sacred music, including more than twenty Masses (of which two are Requiems), sixteen settings of the Magnificat, two of the Lamentations and over one hundred motets.

Morley, Thomas (1557/8–1602). English composer and a pupil of William Byrd. He became organist of St Paul's by 1589 and a Gentleman of the Chapel Royal in 1592.

In 1598 he took over the royal music printing patent acquired by Byrd; his editions of Italian madrigals (some in translation) were largely responsible for the vogue that genre enjoyed in England at the end of the sixteenth century. He also edited *The triumphes of Oriana* (1601) and published a practical treatise (*Plaine and easie introduction*, 1597) that enjoyed enormous popularity. He composed much service music, but is best remembered for his secular output, including about a hundred madrigals and canzonets.

Morton, Robert (*c.* 1430–after 1476). English composer who served in the Burgundian chapel (1457–76). At least eight songs by him survive, some of them in widely-disseminated sources; four other songs have doubtful attributions. It is clear, none the less, that he was representative of the Burgundian chanson at its height.

Motet. A term used widely and loosely for many kinds of music, including the polytextual, tenor-based works of the thirteenth century, any fourteenth-century works based on a repeated (often permutated) tenor, and any work from the fifteenth and sixteenth centuries with Latin text (apart from Mass cycles and smaller Office pieces such as hymns).

Mouton, Jean (before 1459–1522). French composer who held various church positions before becoming associated with the French royal court in 1502. About fifteen Masses and over twenty chansons are attributed to him, but he was a particularly prolific composer of motets (over 100). Many of these display great skill and draw on the wide variety of compositional techniques of the Josquin era.

Mudarra, Alonso (*c.*1510–1580). Spanish vihuelist and composer who had connections with the court of Charles V and became a canon of Seville Cathedral in 1546. His *Tres libros de música* (1546) contains over seventy works for the vihuela and related instruments.

Musica ficta [Lat.: 'feigned music']. Originally used to describe pitches not found on the Guidonian Hand, and therefore, by implication, any pitches that were sharpened or flattened, the term came in the course of the fourteenth century to mean accidental inflections that were not written down but were to be assumed by the performer. These are a major topic of contention for both editors and performers.

Narváez, Luys de (*fl.* 1530–50). Spanish composer and vihuelist who from the 1540s taught the royal children. His collection of vihuela music *Los seys libros del delphin* (1538) includes fantasias, sets of variations and intabulations of vocal pieces. He also composed at least two motets.

Navarro, Juan (*c.* 1530–1580). Spanish composer who held the position of *maestro de capilla* at the cathedrals of Ávila (1563–6), Salamanca (1566–74), Ciudad Rodrigo (1574–8) and Palencia. He composed a large number of Magnificat and psalm-settings and hymns which were also popular in the New World.

Neume. A notational sign used in the Middle Ages, primarily for chant. Each sign may represent from one to four notes, but there were a number of different neumatic systems and methods of notation in use in Europe at different times: for example, those found in the tenth-century sources preserved at St Gall, the twelfth-century Beneventan neumes in Italy and those of the Aquitanian notation used in southern France.

Neusidler, Hans (*c.* 1508/9–1563). German composer and lutenist. From 1530 he was based in Nuremberg as a lute teacher and maker. His treatise on the lute formed part of the first of his eight lutebooks (1536–49) which also included ricercares, dances and vocal intabulations. His sons, Melchior (1531–90) and Conrad (1541–*c.* 1604), were also lutenists and composers.

New Haven, Yale University, Beinecke Rare Book and Manuscript Library, 91 [Mellon Chansonnier]. Important chansonnier copied in about 1476 and probably connected with the Neapolitan court. It contains fifty-seven songs with texts in Latin, Italian, Spanish, English, but mainly in French. Composers include:

Dufay, Okeghem, Busnois, Vincenet, Frye, Tinctoris, Regis, Hayne van Ghizeghem and others.

Notation. The written representation of music underwent many radical changes during the Middle Ages: from the earliest neume system of St Gall, Switzerland, which gave only the relative pitch between notes, through the staff notation (pitches represented on a four-line stave) and solmization syllables of Guido of Arezzo (*c.* 991–after 1033) (which were used alongside neumatic notations), to the rhythmic modes and ligatures (groupings of notes) of Franco of Cologne (*fl.* mid-thirteenth century) and the development of mensural notation in which the rhythmic duration of each note was clearly defined. Further modifications to this were made by Philippe de Vitry (1291–1361) and Petrus de Cruce (*fl.* *c.* 1290) who developed the complex system of 'mannered notation'. The basic principles established by Vitry held good for mensural music of the fourteenth to the sixteenth centuries, although during the fifteenth century black note heads gave way to white, and there was a general trend in the sixteenth century towards simplification, the ligature being used less and less. Other systems of notation for instrumental music were developed during the fifteenth century: see TABLATURE. See also RED NOTATION.

Notker of St Gall [Notker Balbulus ('the Stammerer')] (*c.* 840–912). Monk at the Benedictine Abbey of St Gall in Switzerland. His *Liber hymnorum* (884) contains a number of texts for sequences.

Notre Dame organum. See ORGANUM.

Obrecht, Jacob (*c.* 1458–1505). Netherlands composer who worked at various important musical centres in the Low Countries including Cambrai, Bruges and Antwerp. He also visited Italy more than once, dying during a sojourn in Ferrara. He composed at least twenty-eight Masses and the same number of motets, making much and varied use of borrowed material. Over thirty songs and instrumental pieces are also attributed to him.

Odington, Walter (*fl.* 1298–1316). English music theorist. His treatise entitled *Summa de speculatione musice* is one of the most important of the period, the first four sections being concerned with theoretical questions, the last two with musical practice.

Offertory. A chant of the Proper of the Mass introduced by St Augustine (d. 430) to accompany the offering of the bread and wine. It is usually preceded by an antiphon, part of which may form a closing refrain. Polyphonic settings of the Offertory date from the fifteenth century onwards.

Office. Divine Office comprises the eight daily services of the Roman Church (excluding the Mass), beginning (usually at 3am) with Matins, followed by Lauds (at dawn), and at three-hourly intervals by Prime, Terce, and None (the 'Little Hours'). Vespers then follows at twilight and Compline before retiring. Each service consists of a number of psalms and canticles with antiphons, followed by responsories, hymns, versicles with responsories and prayers, all of which are selected according to the pattern of the liturgical year, and chanted or sung in polyphony depending on the importance of the feast. The Office of the Dead was the service of burial.

Okeghem, Johannes (*c.* 1420–1497). Franco-Flemish composer who sang at Antwerp and the Bourbon court before joining the French royal chapel in 1451, becoming first chaplain there by 1454. He retained that position for the rest of his life, being also treasurer of the church of St Martin, Tours. His fourteen known Mass cycles show an extraordinary variety of unusual formal and technical devices; and they mark him as one of the most individual composers of his generation. A small number of motets and over twenty songs also survive. His Requiem Mass is the earliest surviving polyphonic setting.

Old Hall MS. An English MS collection, dating from the beginning of the fifteenth century, containing sacred music by such composers as Leonel Power, John Dunstable, Pycard, Qweldryk, Roy Henry and many others. The identity of Roy Henry and the exact history of the MS remain unresolved. The contents are organized according to liturgical category based on the movements of the Ordinary of the Mass. It is now thought that a gathering of Kyries may have been lost.

Organ. The invention of the organ dates from the third century BC and the instrument features prominently in medieval musical life. Small portative organs, with bellows operated by one of the player's hands, are commonly depicted in the iconography of the period. By the fifteenth century, larger organs, placed in churches in at least a semi-permanent position near the singers and with the bellows operated by a second person, were distinguished by the term 'positive'. The earliest surviving organ pieces date from the fourteenth century; by the sixteenth century distinctive regional schools of organ building and compositional style were already emerging.

Organum. In general terms 'consonant music', but more specifically a type of early medieval polyphony. The word was also used to refer to the organ or any musical instrument. In the twelfth century, it usually took the form of a sustained-note tenor (*vox principalis*), which was almost always based on existing material, with a faster-moving upper part (or parts) added (*vox organalis*). As the century progressed, a distinction was made between melismatic organum, in which the *vox organalis* developed in melismas over the *vox principalis*, and note-against-note organum. Both kinds are found in the repertory of the Notre Dame school as represented in the *Magnus liber*. By the end of the twelfth century Perotinus was using modal rhythms to compose organum in three or four voices.

Ornithoparchus, Andreas (b. *c.* 1490). German theorist. A university graduate and follower of Erasmus, he published his *Musicae activae micrologus*, an essentially practical guide to composition and music-making, in 1517. It went through several editions, and was translated into English in 1609 by John Dowland.

Ortiz, Diego (*c.* 1510–*c.* 1570). Spanish

theorist and composer who served the Spanish viceroy in Naples from 1558 until at least 1565. His *Tratado de glosas* was published in 1553 and is the earliest surviving guide to ornamentation in bowed string music. It includes over twenty pieces for the viol.

Oswald von Wolkenstein (*c.* 1377–1445). South-German poet-composer of aristocratic birth. Events from his active political and diplomatic career are recounted in his songs. Sometimes classified as a Meistersinger, his highly individual approach to composition, especially as regards his text-setting and fondness for through-composed songs, sets him apart from Meistergesang. He also drew on a much wider range of compositional techniques, including canon, organum, hocket and conductus, while his texting of the tenor anticipates the Tenorlied.

Palestrina, Giovanni Pierluigi da (1525/6–94). Italian composer who spent his working career in Rome serving as *maestro di cappella* of the Capella Giulia (1551–5 and from 1571) and meanwhile at two of the main churches there: S Giovanni in Laterano (1555–60) and S Maria Maggiore (1561–6). One of the greatest masters of the Renaissance, his reputation and influence were enormous. Numerous collections of his music (over a hundred Masses, almost four hundred motets, much other sacred music and nearly a hundred madrigals survive) were published during the 1560s and 70s. In 1577 he was appointed to rework the chant books following the Council of Trent.

Paolo da Firenze [Paolo tenorista] (c. 1436). Italian composer and theorist who served various members of the nobility in Florence and Rome. He may have been involved with the compilation of the Squarcialupi MS; he almost certainly moved in the same circles as Landini. His thirteen surviving madrigals and over forty ballate reveal a mixture of progressive and conservative elements and some French influence. He also composed two liturgical pieces which combine an upper melodic line in the Italian manner with a cantus firmus, and wrote at least one treatise.

Paraphrase. Term used to describe the quotation of a chant melody in one or more voices of a polyphonic piece of the Renaissance. The chant is modified or only alluded to rather than quoted in full.

Parody. Term used to describe the Renaissance technique of using an existing piece (perhaps a motet or chanson) as a basis for composition of another piece, usually a Mass. All the voices of the model are quoted and assimilated in the new work.

Passamezzo. An Italian dance in duple metre that flourished from the mid-sixteenth century. It is based on a simple chordal sequence that varies slightly according to whether it follows the *passamezzo antico* or *passamezzo moderno* pattern. Sets of variations were often developed over these harmonic schemes.

Pastourelle. A French (Provençal) medieval lyric associated with a pastoral theme such as a knight wooing a shepherdess and popular with troubadours and trouvères during the twelfth and thirteenth centuries.

Pastrana, Pedro de (*c.* 1480–after 1559). Spanish composer who served Charles V and was appointed *maestro de capilla* to Prince Philip in 1547. A six-part Mass, four Magnificats, some psalm settings, and several villancicos are attributed to him.

Paumann, Conrad (*c.* 1410–73). German composer and organist. Blind from birth, he held a number of positions as organist before being appointed as organist at the Bavarian court. He nevertheless travelled widely and his reputation spread throughout most of Europe. Few of his works survive, but his one polyphonic song and his settings for organ of secular melodies reveal that he was aware of the latest developments in the Burgundian chanson. His influence can be seen in the Buxheim Organ Book.

Pavan. A stately, duple-metre court dance, probably of Italian origin, that became popular during the sixteenth century. It often preceded a group of faster, triple-time dances, and was commonly paired with the saltarello or, in northern Europe, the galliard.

Peñalosa, Francisco de (*c.* 1470–1528).

Spanish composer who served at the Aragonese court until the death of Ferdinand the Catholic in 1516 and later in the papal chapel and Seville Cathedral. He was the leading Spanish composer of the Josquin era, combining local traditions with Franco-Flemish techniques of composition. Seven Masses, about thirty motets and other sacred works (including a set of Lamentations) as well as some songs are attributed to him.

Perotinus (*fl. c.* 1200). French composer of organum, perhaps the Petrus Succentor at Notre Dame who died in 1226. The only clear information about him comes from the rather later English theorist known as Anonymous IV, who says that he revised Leoninus's *Magnus liber organi* and names seven of his works, including the four-voice organa *Viderunt* and *Sederunt*. These grand pieces occur at the beginning of two of the great Notre Dame manuscripts and are probably the ones mentioned in decrees of 1198 and 1199.

Petrarca, Francesco [Petrarch] (1304–74). Italian poet. Only one musical setting of his poetry survives from his own lifetime, but an important and long-lived Petrarch revival began in 1501 with the publication of the *Canzionere* by Benedetto Gareth and Pietro Bembo. His verse, which was set by almost all the Italian madrigalists, also inspired other Italian poets of the period such as Sannazaro and Tasso, whose poems were in turn to provide the inspiration for countless musical settings.

Petrucci, Ottaviano (dei) (1466–1539). Italian music printer who moved to Venice in about 1490 and whose *Harmonice musices odhecaton A* (1501) was the first printed collection of polyphonic music. Collections of songs were followed by volumes of Masses and motets, and in 1507 he also published the first printed book of lute tablature. His miraculously elegant publications present a wide and remarkably comprehensive selection of the music in circulation during the first decades of the sixteenth century.

Petrus frater dictus Palma ociosa (*fl.* 1336). French theorist and monk of the Cistercian order at Cherchamps (Amiens). His treatise, *Compendium de discantu mensurabili* (1336), divides music into *mensurabilis* and *immensurabilis*, roughly speaking polyphony and plainchant respectively. He draws on the authority of such writers as Boethius and Isidore, but also reveals that he is well versed in the 'new art' of the fourteenth century.

Peverara, Laura (*c.* 1545–1601). Italian singer who was born in Mantua and became one of the virtuoso lady performers at the Ferrarese court (1580–98). Her extraordinary singing ability and her charm inspired the dedication of three major musical anthologies in the 1580s.

Phalèse. Family of music printers active in the Low Countries during the sixteenth century. Pierre (*c.* 1510–1573/6) published a wide variety of music, including lute tablature, and notably the works of Clemens non Papa. His son, also Pierre (*c.* 1550–1629), took over the business in about 1575 and transferred from Louvain to Antwerp, publishing volumes of Italian madrigals.

Philippus de Caserta (*fl. c.* 1379). French theorist and composer. It is possible that the *Tractatus de diversis figuris* sometimes attributed to Edigius de Murino may in fact be by Philippus. He certainly used some of the notational and rhythmic devices described there in his own works which include a Credo and six ballades.

Pietrequin Bonnel (*fl.* late fifteenth century). French singer and composer who worked at a number of musical centres throughout Europe, including the court of Savoy, Florence and the French royal court in the chapel of Anne of Brittany. Six chansons (all but one, rondeaux) are attributed to him.

Pietrobono (*c.* 1417–97). Italian lutenist and singer who worked for most of his career at the Este court in Ferrara, although he also visited the Hungarian court in the 1480s. His reputation as a lutenist in his own day was sufficient for a medal to be struck in his honour.

Pipelare, Mattaeus (*c.* 1450–*c.* 1515). Flemish composer who worked in

Antwerp and s'Hertogenbosch. He composed eleven Masses, motets and chansons in French and Flemish in a wide variety of styles.

Plainchant, plainsong. See CHANT.

Planctus. [Provençal: planh; Fr.: plaint, complainte]. A song of lamentation popular throughout the Middle Ages in Latin and in the vernacular. Various types of planctus date from the ninth century, but by about the twelfth century two kinds predominated: laments of the Virgin Mary and the songs of the lamenting lover. The former held an important place in liturgical drama, notably in the lamenting of the three Marys at the Cross in the *Visitatio sepulchri*. Planctus melodies are often overtly emotional.

Plato (*c.* 429–347 BC). Greek philosopher whose comments on music are of great interest in themselves and because of their influence on writers of the medieval period and again in the Italian Renaissance. Platonic thought was reflected in the idea of the 'harmony of the spheres' or a cosmic, inaudible harmonic system based on numerical proportions (*musica mundana*), a belief only brought into question towards the end of the Middle Ages. Plato's musical writings were examined with renewed interest in the second half of the sixteenth century amongst the members of the Florentine Camerata who wished to gain insight into ancient musical practice.

Play of Daniel. Medieval drama from twelfth-century Beauvais. It is unusual in that all but two (the hymn and *Te Deum* sung by way of conclusion) of its texts and melodies are non-liturgical and draw on a wide range of forms and styles.

Plectrum. A small piece of material, probably a quill or slither of bone or wood, used to pluck string instruments such as the lute. It seems to have been the usual means of playing lute-type instruments until at least the mid-fifteenth century; it is unsuitable for the polyphonic intabulations and other solo pieces of the sixteenth century.

Ponce, Juan (*c.* 1480-after 1521). Spanish composer who served in the royal Aragonese chapel of Ferdinand the Catholic (d. 1516). Twelve songs are attributed to Ponce in the *Cancionero Musical de Palacio* including a student drinking-song *Ave color vini clari*. A three-voice *Salve regina* also survives.

Porta, Costanzo (1528/9–1601). Italian composer. He was a pupil of Willaert's at St Mark's, Venice, and subsequently held the position of *maestro di cappella* at a number of Italian cathedrals. He was a prolific composer of sacred music, including over two hundred motets, fifteen Masses and a vesper hymn cycle: twelve volumes of this output were published (1555–1605). Five books of madrigals also appeared (1555–86).

Power, Leonel (?1370/85–1445). English composer who, with John Dunstable, was a leading figure in the development of an English style at the beginning of the fifteenth century. He served Thomas, Duke of Clarence (d. 1421), and at Canterbury. He may have been a teacher: an elementary treatise on discant is attributed to him. Many of his works are included in the oldest layer of the Old Hall MS. At least one cyclic Mass (one of the earliest examples of the genre) can be definitely attributed to him, as well as paired and single Mass movements.

Praetorius, Michael (?1571–1621). German composer and theorist. He worked in various German centres, including Wolfenbüttel where he was court organist from 1595 and Kapellmeister from 1604. He was a very prolific composer, but is best known today for his collection of instrumental dances entitled *Terpsichore* (1612) and his detailed and extended treatise *Syntagma musicum* (3 vols., 1614–20).

Prioris, Johannes (*c.* 1460–*c.* 1514). Franco-Netherlandish composer who served at the French court. His extant works, including five Masses, a Requiem Mass, six Magnificats, motets and chansons, reveal a wide grasp of contemporary compositional styles and techniques.

Prosdocimus de Beldemandis (d. 1428). Italian theorist. He studied at the universities of Bologna and Padua and later taught there. His *Exposiciones* (1404) is a commentary on the writings of the French theorist Johannes de Muris, but his later works cover every aspect of late medieval music theory, including the fourteenth-century Italian notational system.

Prosula. Term used to describe a text, usually syllabic, added to chant melismas. Chants for the Proper and Ordinary of the Mass (especially the Kyrie and the Offertory) as well as the Office (principally the responsories for Vespers and Matins) were subjected to this treatment, reportedly in order to help memorize the melodies, and resulting in an enrichment of the liturgy.

Psalter. Book containing the psalms and the biblical canticles, often put together according to local practice for the weekly chanting or reading of the psalms that forms the basis of the Office. It may form a separate book or be incorporated into the breviary. Early manuscript psalters were often richly illuminated.

Psaltery [Lat.: psalterium]. A string instrument related to the zither family. The name is derived from the Latin which originally denoted any plucked instrument associated with King David and the singing of the psalms. In the twelfth century the Middle Eastern psaltery decisively influenced the shape of the European instrument. It remained in regular use until the late fifteenth century.

Pythagoras. Greek philosopher active about 530 BC. He is said to have discovered the numerical proportions that relate to the intervals of the musical scale, and this emphasis on numbers together with the doctrine of the harmony of the spheres were the most influential aspects of Greek musical theory during the medieval period. Pythagorean intonation – a temperament based on pure fifths (tuned in the ratio 3:2) – appears to have been particularly important during the Middle Ages.

Quadratic notation. Term for the notation developed in northern France in the twelfth century in which pitches were represented by small squares, either individually or in ligatures. It was used in the Notre Dame repertory and became the

universally-accepted form for the notation of plainchant.

Quevedo, Bartolomé de (*c.* 1510–69). Spanish theorist and composer whose career brought him into contact with the royal court and Toledo Cathedral. A few works by him survive, but he is perhaps most important for his commentary on the section concerning musicians and musical practice in Pope John XXII's *De vita et honestate clericorum.*

Qweldryk (*fl. c.* 1400). English composer, possibly associated with the estate of Fountains Abbey of that name near York. He is represented in the Old Hall MS by a four-voice Gloria and a three-voice Credo, both of which are isorhythmic.

Rabāb. String instrument of the bowed fiddle type, possibly related to the European rebec.

Rabel. See REBEC.

Ramos de Pareja, Bartolomé (*c.* 1440–*c.* 1491). Spanish theorist and composer who was active as a teacher at the universities of Salamanca, Bologna (from *c.* 1472) and Rome (*c.* 1484–91). An original thinker who often adopted the performer's viewpoint, with his controversial *Musica Practica* (1482) he influenced many later theorists.

Rastrum. A type of pen with a number of nibs used to draw one or more staves at a time. Study of the rastrum, and the way in which it was used, can provide clues to the physical study of a given manuscript.

Rebec [Sp.: rabel]. Bowed string instrument believed to have originated in the tenth century and used throughout Europe during most of the Middle Ages and Renaissance. It could be pear-shaped or straight and narrow, have anything from one to five strings and be played on the lap or the shoulder.

Recorder [It.: flauto dolce]. A woodwind instrument distinguished from the transverse flute by being end-blown. It would seem to have originated in Italy in the fourteenth century and became important as a consort instrument during the Renaissance. Like the viol, the recorder came in a family of sizes (as many as eight according to Praetorius).

Red notation. The earliest known examples of red notes are to be found in the early fourteenth-century *Roman de Fauvel* where they are used in tenor parts to signify transition from *modus perfectus* to *modus imperfectus* (from ternary to binary). The red notes in black notation thus had a similar relationship to blackened notes in white notation of the fifteenth century (coloration): that is, three red notes are equal to two black ones.

Refrain [Fr.]. In medieval song a passage of a melody (with words) that is introduced into another work (monophonic song or polyphonic motet).

Regis, Johannes (*c.* 1425–*c.* 1496). Netherlands composer who worked mainly in Soignies, though he had earlier been Dufay's *clerc* in Cambrai. His extant works include two cantus firmus Masses and eight motets.

Requiem Mass. The Mass for the Dead, deriving its name from the opening words of the introit: 'Requiem aeternam dona eis, Domine'. Similar to the Proper of the Mass, it comprises an Introit, Kyrie, Gradual, Tract, Sequence, Offertory, Sanctus and Benedictus, Agnus Dei and Communion texts. In the earliest polyphonic settings by Okeghem, Richafort, La Rue, Escobar, Morales and Palestrina the texts varied slightly, and the Sequence was not usually included.

Responsory. Chants used from at least the eleventh century as musical postludes to the lessons. Great responsories were sung at Matins and monastic Vespers, while short responsories followed the readings in the lesser Hours. A soloist sings the verse, in alternation with the chorus singing a refrain or 'respond'. It was these solo sections that were first set polyphonically in the Notre Dame repertory.

Rhymed office. Term used to denote a liturgical text drawn from the historical books of the Bible. Usually dedicated to the lives of saints, the musical items were usually antiphons or responsories with rhymed or metrical texts.

Rhythmic modes. Term used to describe the organization of rhythmic patterns (all in triple metre) during the medieval period. Johannes de Garlandia (*c.* 1240) defined and listed six modes, and these formed the basis for much of the music of the twelfth and thirteenth centuries.

Ribera, Bernardino de (d. 1570/71). Spanish composer who was chapelmaster at the cathedrals of Ávila (1559–62), where he taught Victoria, and Toledo (1563–71). Various sacred works by him survive, including two Masses and some motets.

Ricercare [ricercar] [It.: 'to search out']. An instrumental piece (usually for lute or keyboard), at first in the manner of a prelude and later an imitative or quasi-fugal work. The term is used by Spinacino in his *Intabulatura de lauto* of 1507 and for keyboard pieces with imitative passages in Cavazzoni's *Recherchari, motetti, canzoni* of 1523. Ensemble ricercars in imitative style date from the first half of the sixteenth century.

Ripa, Albertus da [Albert de Rippe] (*c.* 1500–51). Italian lutenist and composer who served first in Mantua and then at the French court. Renowned as a performer, he was also a prolific composer and arranger.

Riquier, Guiraut (*c.* 1230–*c.* 1300). Provençal poet and composer usually considered the last of the troubadours. Some of his 89 extant poems reveal details of his life and he is known to have served at the courts of Navarre and Castile. Over half of his poems have survived with their melodies, most falling into the *canso* or *vers* categories.

Robertsbridge Codex. English MS from the second quarter of the fourteenth century containing the earliest known examples of keyboard music. Three *estampies* and three arrangements of motets are copied on its two folios.

Rognoni, Riccardo (d. 1619/20). Italian composer, theorist and instrumentalist who worked in Milan. His treatise on diminutions (*Passaggi per potersi essercitare nel diminuire terminatamente con ogni sorte di instromenti*, 1592) contains examples of figurations in order of increasing technical difficulty. He makes an important distinction between the techniques required for wind and string instruments.

Romance [Sp.] Term used to denote a ballad or narrative song form. It was particularly popular in Spain during the period 1450–1550 where it flourished alongside the villancico. By the beginning of the seventeenth century, however, it had acquired a refrain and was largely indistinguishable from its rival.

Roman de Fauvel. An early fourteenth-century satirical allegory on the Church in narrative form by Gervais de Bus. In one source 167 musical items (some by Philippe de Vitry), both monophonic and polyphonic, are inserted, thus forming an important compendium of musical forms (34 polyphonic motets, 30 *prosae* and lais, 25 rondeaux, 26 refrains and 52 alleluias, responses, etc.). from the beginning of the Ars nova period.

Rome, Biblioteca Apostolica Vaticana, Chigi C.VIII.234. The 'Chigi Codex', a presentation manuscript probably originally prepared for Philippe Bouton, possibly by the scribe Martin Bourgeois. It probably reached Spain in the early years of the sixteenth century and subsequently came into the possession of Alexander VI. It contains forty pieces by composers such as Okeghem, Regis, Compère, Josquin, La Rue, Agricola, Busnois and many others.

Rome, Biblioteca Casanatense, MS 2856. Known as the Chansonnier of Isabella d'Este and believed to have been compiled around 1481, this source is important for the large number of textless – and therefore possibly instrumental – pieces it contains.

Rondeau. One of the three *formes fixes* (together with the ballade and virelai) that would appear to have originated as a dance-song in the thirteenth century but which by the fourteenth was an independent song form with a refrain. (These refrains sometimes took on a life of their own in the *motet ente*.) The first polyphonic examples of the rondeau are attributed to Adam de la Halle, its form becoming more clearly defined in the Machaut period prior to its flowering in the fifteenth century.

Rondellus. A style of composition popular in England in the thirteenth century, notable for the use of voice-exchange. Phrases could be exchanged between the two upper voices (supported by a tenor or *pes*) or between all three. The rondellus was described by Walter Odington in about 1300, and was recognized on the continent as a peculiarly English practice.

Rore, Cipriano de (1515/6–65). Flemish composer who was also active in Italy in the 1540s and 50s at Ferrara and Parma and who was briefly *maestro di cappella* at St Mark's, Venice, in 1563. His ten books of madrigals (1542–66) were especially influential for their successful fusion of northern and Italian styles and for their controlled use of imagery. He also produced five books of motets (1544–63, 1595), Masses, chansons and other works.

Rossetti, Biagio (d. after 1547). Italian theorist and organist. Born in Verona, he spent most of his career there as cathedral organist. His treatise *Libellus de rudimentis musices* (1529) was intended for the training of choirboys and cathedral singers and apart from the conventional approach to the theoretical side, is of interest for its emphasis on vocal technique and the importance of understanding and conveying the meaning of the text.

Ructis, Ar. de [Ruttis] (*fl.* 1420). Composer, about whom nothing is known, of a three-voice piece *Prevalet simplicitas* in the important early fifteenth-century MS Oxford, Can. Misc. 213.

Ruffo, Vincenzo (*c.* 1508–1587). Italian composer who was trained at Verona Cathedral and held posts there, in Milan (1563–72), where he came under the influence of Cardinal Borromeo and the Counter-Reformation, and in Pistoia before returning to Verona. A prolific composer, he had written about 260 madrigals before he abandoned secular music in 1563. After this time, he dedicated himself to the composition of sacred works, heavily influenced by the concerns of the Counter-Reformation regarding intelligibility of the text.

Sackbut. See TROMBONE.

St Martial MSS. At least three important manuscripts of twelfth-century polyphony from the library of the Abbey of St Martial of Limoges survive in the Bibliothèque Nationale in Paris. They contain strophic poems (versus and conductus), tropes of the 'Benedicamus Domino' and sequences in melismatic organum and note-against-note discant.

Sandrin, Pierre (*c.* 1490–after 1561). French composer. He served at the French royal chapel and as *maestro di cappella* at the Ferrarese court. He composed chansons in a wide range of styles and many of them were used in parody Masses and in lute and keyboard intabulations.

Santa María, Tomás de (d. 1570). Spanish theorist and composer. He held the position of organist in various Dominican monasteries in Castile, notably at San Pablo, Valladolid. There he may have met the Cabezons whom he would appear to have consulted in the preparation of his *Arte de tañer fantasia* (1565).

Schlick, Arnolt (*c.* 1460–1521). German organist and composer. He worked all over Germany and the Netherlands as an organist and organ consultant. The earliest printed collection of organ tablature in Germany (*Tabulaturen etlicher Lobgesang*, 1512) includes works by him, while his treatise on organ building and playing, *Spiegel der Orgelmacher und Organisten*, dates from 1511.

Schütz, Heinrich (1585–1672). The most important German composer of the seventeenth century, he contributed prolifically to almost all forms of sacred music, and even composed an opera (*Dafne*, 1627), now lost.

Senfl, Ludwig (*c.* 1486–1542/3). Swiss composer who probably studied with Isaac at the Imperial court in Vienna; certainly in 1513 he succeeded Isaac as court composer. By 1523 he was in the service of the Duke of Bavaria in Munich, and in the 1530s he corresponded with Martin Luther. The most important composer active in Germany during the Reformation, he composed seven Masses, a large number of motets and German Lieder, some satirical in tone, others based on folksong.

Sequence. A medieval Latin chant, wide-ranging and syllabic in style, that reached the height of its importance *c.* 850–1150. The texts were normally in double-versicle structure, with new music for each pair of versicles; later they conformed to regular verse patterns. Generally associated with particular feasts, they were normally sung at Mass, after the Alleluia. The variety of the earlier repertory is represented in the *Liber hymnorum* of Notker of St Gall (*c.* 840–912). The earliest polyphonic settings of sequences date from as early as the tenth century (some are included in the *Musica enchiriadis*), and are found throughout the period until after the Council of Trent's banning of all but four sequence texts.

Sermisy, Claudin de (*c.* 1490–1562). French composer who worked for most of his life in the French royal chapel. His sacred works, which include twelve Masses, a rare early polyphonic setting of the Passion, and numerous motets and Magnificats, are stylistically similar to those of Josquin. He was particularly important, however, as a composer of chansons and from the late 1520s led the way with the four-voice Parisian chanson.

Shawm. A double-reed instrument of various sizes that was widely used throughout Europe from at least the late thirteenth century: it has various counterparts in other cultures. By the sixteenth century the standard shawm family consisted of the treble, alto (generally known as the bombarde), tenor and bass. Its main function in the medieval period was as a ceremonial instrument, often for outdoor events, and usually played together with the sackbut. From at least the mid-fifteenth century such groups of so-called 'loud' musicians (the alta capella) also accompanied the basse-danse.

Slide-trumpet. See TRUMPET.

Solmization. The system in Western music, dating from the early part of the eleventh century and closely associated with Guido of Arezzo (*c.* 991–after 1033), by which certain syllables (*ut, re, mi, fa, sol, la*) are used as mnemonics for the melodic pitches of the hexachord. The decisive interval in each hexachord is the interval *mi-fa* which denotes the semitone, and the aligning of syllable to pitch within the hexachord allowed the singer to identify where the semitones would occur.

Soriano, Francesco (1548/9–1621). Italian composer, possibly a pupil of Palestrina. He worked at a number of churches in Rome, as well as in the Cappella Giulia (1603–20). In 1612, he completed Palestrina's revision of the chant books, and, a master of the polychoral style, he published books of motets (1597, 1616), Masses (1609) and madrigals (1581–1602).

Spinacino, Francesco (*fl.* 1507). Italian lutenist and composer. Highly regarded as a performer, in 1507 he published two books of *Intabulatura de lauto* in Venice. These comprise prelude-like ricercars as well as intabulations or arrangements of polyphonic motets and chansons.

Spinet. Small keyboard instrument of the harpsichord family, the earliest known and rather primitive examples of which, of German origin, date from the late sixteenth century. Its use during the seventeenth century was primarily for domestic music-making.

Squarcialupi MS; Florence Biblioteca Medicea Laurenziana, Pal. 87. An important source of Italian trecento music, compiled in Florence between 1410 and 1415, but containing repertory from as early as the mid-fourteenth century. The pieces are organized in chronological order by composer, with the largest section being devoted to the works of Francesco Landini. The anthology also includes works by Jacopo da Bologna, Gherardello da Firenze and many others.

Stocker, Gaspar [Stoquerus] (*fl. c.* 1570). German theorist who travelled and worked in Italy and Spain, where he studied at Salamanca University with Francisco de Salinas. His *De musica verbali libri duo* of about 1570 gives considerable space to the question of text underlay. His discussion is based to a large extent on the writings of Zarlino, but he also established fixed rules which he derived from Zarlino

as well as from a consideration of the works of the Josquin generation (whom he termed the 'ancients') and that of Willaert (the 'moderns').

Strambotto. Italian poetic form of eight eleven-syllable lines. The *strambotto toscano*, with the rhyme scheme *ababbcc*, and the *strambotto siciliano* (*abababab*) were often set to music in the Renaissance.

Strasbourg MS 222.c.22. A mixed manuscript copied in stages in the first half of the fifteenth century, destroyed by fire in 1870, but known from an incomplete copy made by Coussemaker.

Susato, Tylman (*c.* 1500–61/4). Music publisher and composer active in Antwerp. He established the first important music press in the Low Countries, publishing 25 books of chansons, three of Masses and nineteen of motets as well as eleven volumes of *Musyck boexken* including Flemish songs and metrical psalm settings in Dutch. He composed chansons, Flemish songs, motets and dance music.

Tablature. Notational system using letters or numbers (as opposed to note-heads) placed on a stave to denote pitches, and additional signs (usually above the stave) for durational or rhythmic values. Various local systems (in France, Germany, Italy and Spain) developed toward the end of the Middle Ages. Most keyboard and all lute music of the Renaissance is notated in tablature.

Tabor. A small side-drum with snares, commonly paired from the thirteenth century with a simple end-blown pipe, both instruments being played by one person to accompany dancing.

Tactus. The term used during the fifteenth and sixteenth centuries for a beat or the unit of time indicated by a hand movement. Generally speaking the tactus (the movement of the hand up and down once) was held to be more or less equal to the normal pulse rate of a man (60–70 times per minute).

Talea. See ISORYTHM.

Tallis, Thomas (*c.* 1505–85). English composer. Having held a number of posts as organist and singer in London and Kent, he became a Gentleman of the

Glossary

Chapel Royal in 1543. He was organist of the royal household until his death. In 1575 he and William Byrd were granted a royal licence to publish music, and their volume of Latin motets (*Cantiones sacrae*) appeared later that year. His Latin church music also includes Mass settings, a Magnificat, responsories and hymns as well as the extraordinary forty-voice motet *Spem in alium*. He was one of the first composers to write for the Anglican liturgy, and he also contributed two In Nomines to the viol consort repertory.

Tambourine. Instrument of ancient and undetermined origin that became popular throughout Europe during the Middle Ages. At first associated primarily with wandering minstrels, it was subsequently to be found in a wide variety of contexts and tambourinists were often employed at court.

Tapissier, Johannes (*c.* 1370–1410). French composer. He had entered the service of Philip the Bold, Duke of Burgundy, by 1391, and he travelled widely with the court. He also had an 'escole de chant' in Paris where he trained choirboys. He composed some Mass movements as well as a four-voice isorhythmic motet lamenting the Great Schism.

Taverner, John (*c.* 1490–1545). English composer, one of the most important of his day. He worked as a singer and lay clerk at a number of churches, and in 1526 became teacher of the choristers at Christ Church, Oxford. His extant works include eight Masses (the most famous being the 'Western Wynde' and the 'Gloria tibi trinitas'), three Magnificat settings and many motets and votive antiphons. A few partsongs also survive.

Tenor [after Lat. tenere, 'to hold']. In music of the late Middle Ages and Renaissance the tenor was usually – though not always – the cantus firmus-bearing and therefore the structural voice. Examples include the tenor Mass (in which the movements are based on the cantus firmus in the tenor) and the German Tenorlied in which a pre-existing tune was used as a cantus firmus in the tenor. It only gradually became equated with the range suitable for the high male voice.

Tenorista. Term used in the late Middle Ages and Renaissance to denote the singer or instrumentalist trained in taking the tenor part in a polyphonic composition (see TENOR). He was therefore not necessarily a tenor in the modern sense.

Tenorlied. The main type of German polyphonic song in the period about 1450–1550. A pre-existing Lied melody, used as a cantus firmus in the tenor, is accompanied contrapuntally by two or three more voices.

Tetrachord. A term used to denote four notes contained within a perfect fourth. Important in ancient Greek theory for the structure of melodies, the combination of intervals could vary according to type: diatonic, chromatic and enharmonic. In the Middle Ages, the most common grouping was tone, semitone, tone.

Theorbo. A member of the Western lute family, particularly popular during the seventeenth century as an accompanying instrument. It is distinguished from the lute by its long neck allowing for the addition of lower-pitched, unstopped bass strings, and is thus very similar to the chitarrone, the term first adopted in Italy to describe a theorbo-like instrument from about 1590 until the mid-seventeenth century.

Tibia. An ancient Roman wind instrument very similar in shape and function to the Greek aulos.

Tigrini, Orazio (*c.* 1535–91). Italian theorist and composer. He worked for most of his life at Arezzo Cathedral where he became *maestro di cappella* and *maestro di canto* from 1587. His *Il compendio della musica nel quale si tratta dell'arte del contrapunto* (1588) is an important guide to practical composition in the late Renaissance. He displays his own contrapuntal mastery in his six-voice madrigals (two books: 1582, 1591).

Tinctoris, Johannes (*c.* 1435–?1511). Franco-Flemish theorist and composer. He may have been a singer at Cambrai before becoming master of the choirboys at Orleans Cathedral in 1463. From about

1472 he served at the Neapolitan court. One of the most important theorists of his time, he wrote at least twelve treatises, probably mostly during the 1470s, including the earliest known dictionary of terms, the *Terminorum musicae deffinitorium*. Five Masses, a Lamentations setting and several motets and chansons are attributed to him.

Tomkins, Thomas (1572–1656). Welsh composer who may have been a pupil of Byrd's. He was appointed organist of Worcester Cathedral in 1596 and Gentleman of the Chapel Royal by 1620 where he was also organist from 1625, though he continued to hold his position at Worcester until 1654. He composed over a hundred anthems, his *Musica Deo sacra* being published posthumously in 1668, as well as madrigals, keyboard pieces and works for viol consort.

Tordesillas, Pedro/Alfonso Hernández de (*fl.* 1500). Spanish singers. It is not clear which of the Tordesillas brothers, both of whom served in the royal chapels of Ferdinand and Isabella, was the composer of the Lamentation and Magnificat settings as well as one villancico in the Palace Songbook ascribed to 'Tordesillas'. Both had the mysterious soubriquet of 'el ojo' ['the eye'].

Torrentes, Andrés de (*c.* 1510–80). Spanish composer who was appointed *maestro de capilla* of Toledo Cathedral in December 1539, a post he held intermittently until his death. He composed Masses, settings of the Magnificat and the Lamentations, hymns and psalms.

Trent Codices. Seven MSS now in Trent, containing music (almost 2000 pieces) of the period 1400 to 1475. The two earliest were copied in the second quarter of the fifteenth century in various locations in northern Italy and elsewhere; the other five were compiled in Trent between 1445 and 1475. They contain works by Dufay, Binchois, Busnois and other Franco-Flemish masters, as well as pieces by German, Italian and English (Dunstable, Power, etc.) composers.

Troiano, Massimo (d. after 1570). Italian composer. He served in the Munich Hofkapelle under Lassus in the late 1560s, and in 1568 published an admirably detailed account of the wedding celebrations of Duke Wilhelm V. He also published four books of *canzoni alla napolitana* (1567–9).

Tromboncino, Bartolomeo (*c.* 1470–*c.* 1535). Italian composer. He worked for most of his life for the Marquis of Mantua, though he also visited Ferrara (1502–8, possibly till 1521) and Venice. A prolific composer of frottolas, he experimented with various forms and styles of text, and he also wrote sacred *laude*, a set of Lamentations and a motet.

Trombone. Usually referred to as the sackbut (from the old English term), the trombone emerged during the fifteenth century when it was an important constituent of the court and town band. In the sixteenth century it came to be used, together with the cornett, in vocal church music, notably in the polychoral works of Andrea and Giovanni Gabrieli.

Trope. In the Middle Ages, a piece that complements an existing chant, either by serving as an introduction to that chant or forming interpolations within it. It can even replace the chant. Troping would appear to be almost as old as some of the chants they were designed to complement; the sequence can be considered an alleluia trope, though it quickly enjoyed an independent existence. Introductory tropes highlight aspects of the texts of the chants they introduce, often borrowing phrases from the Bible. Interpolated tropes are most commonly found in the Gloria. Melismatic tropes – purely musical melismas introduced into the chant – are also found from at least the twelfth century, though the practice may date from much earlier.

Troubadour, trouvère. Poet-composers working in France in the twelfth and thirteenth centuries: the troubadours being based in the south and writing in Provençal (*langue d'oc*), the trouvères in the north and writing in early French (*langue d'oil*). The troubadours apparently originated in Poitiers, spreading through southern France, Catalonia and northern Italy.

They were often, but not always, of noble origin or moved in high social circles; courtly love was the main topic of their songs, though these adopted highly varied and sophisticated forms. The trouvère tradition related quite closely to that of the troubadours in subject matter and forms, though a distinctive feature was the gathering of literary groups or *puys*. Only a small proportion of extant troubadour verse survives with music, though there is music for most of the trouvère repertory.

Trumpet. Trumpets have existed since ancient times, originally as short, straight instruments of wood, brass or silver. In the course of the Middle Ages the trumpeter gained in importance and status as a court musician who performed as a herald and at all major court events. By the Renaissance every self-respecting court boasted a corps of trumpeters and drummers usually dressed in the livery of the royal or noble employer. During this period the slide-trumpet with a slide-mechanism (similar in principle to the trombone) to alter the length of the instrument and fill in the gaps in the harmonic series was also developed.

'ud. Arab short-necked lute, the direct ancestor of the European lute. It would appear to date from as early as the seventh or eighth century.

Ugolino of Orvieto (*c.* 1380–1457). Italian theorist and composer. He worked for most of his life in Forlì until, as a strong Guelph supporter, he was forced to leave the city in 1430 and take refuge in Ferrara. He served at Ferrara Cathedral until his death. His speculative treatise *Declaratio musice discipline* (1430–5) was well known throughout the fifteenth century and was later cited by Ramos de Pareja and Gaffurius. Three two-voice pieces by him also survive.

Vecchi, Orazio (1550–1605). Italian composer. He held the post of *maestro di cappella* at various cathedrals – Salò (1581–4), Modena (1584–6) and Reggio Emilia (1586) – before settling at Modena (1593), where he was also connected with the court from 1598. Though a priest, he was actively involved in dramatic music, his madrigal-comedy *L'Amfiparnaso* dating

from 1597. He was also a prolific composer of canzonettas (six books: 1580–97), madrigals (two books: 1583, 1589) and sacred works (five books: 1587–1607).

Velut, Gilet (*fl.* early fifteenth century). French composer who sang at Cambrai in 1409 and at the court of Cyprus two years later. Two Mass movements, two motets and four chansons are attributed to him.

Venegas de Henestrosa, Luis (*c.* 1510–*c.* 1557). Spanish composer. He seems to have been based in Toledo as a priest. In 1557 he published his *Libro de cifra nueva*, a collection of instrumental fantasias, tientos and arrangements of vocal music from hymns to chansons.

Verdelot [Deslouges], **Philippe** (?1470/80–before 1552). French composer. He may have left France early in his career; later he held posts in Florence (1523–7) and Rome. Almost sixty motets and two Masses survive by him, displaying a shift in style that possibly reflects his move to Italy. Similarly, he composed very few chansons, but a great many madrigals. These, and his motets, were widely known.

Versus. A term with various uses in the Middle Ages, but specifically, from the eleventh century onwards, a type of Latin sacred song with both rhyme and metrical scansion. In the context of plainchant, it can refer to the verse of the introit, gradual, tract, alleluia or responsory, i.e. the unit of text within a chant, but without any indication of a metrical structure. In other contexts, however, it could also have the specific meaning of a line of metric poetry.

Vespers. See OFFICE.

Viadana, Lodovico (*c.* 1560–1627). Italian composer. His career took him to Padua, Rome and Mantua (at least 1594–7) among other places. Possibly a pupil of Costanzo Porta, he was himself an influential teacher. His prolific output includes twenty-three books of sacred works (1588–1619), notably the *Concerti ecclesiastici* of 1602, as well as two volumes of canzonettas (1590, 1594) and one of instrumental ensemble pieces (1610).

Vicentino, Nicola (1511–*c.* 1576). Italian

composer and theorist. Possibly a pupil of Willaert in Venice, he worked in Ferrara, Rome and Siena before becoming *maestro di cappella* of Vicenza Cathedral by 1563. His *L'antica musica ridotta alla moderna prattica* (1555) reveals his important contribution to the experimental harmonic advances of the early seventeenth century. He also produced at least two volumes of madrigals and one of motets.

Victoria, Tomás Luis de (1548–1611). Spanish composer. Trained as a choirboy at Ávila Cathedral, he spent most of his career in Rome, returning to Spain only in the 1580s. Apart from a further visit to Rome (1592–5), he remained at the Descalzas Reales convent in Madrid, in the service of the Dowager Empress Maria, until his death. He composed only sacred music (including some twenty Masses, an *Officium defunctorum* (1605), two Passions, Lamentations, eighteen settings of the Magnificat and about fifty motets) most of which was published in his own lifetime.

Vihuela [Sp.]. Term originally used in Spanish-speaking regions for various string instruments but which by the sixteenth century had come to refer to a flat-backed, plucked instrument (the *vihuela de mano*) closely linked to the guitar and the viol. Literary references to the vihuela date from as early as the thirteenth century, but it was during the sixteenth that it reached its apogee, with important publications by Milán, Narváez, Fuenllana and others. In Spain it was generally preferred to the lute, but by the end of the sixteenth century it would appear to have been superseded by the guitar in popularity.

Villancico. Musico-poetic form cultivated in Spanish-speaking countries in the late fifteenth and sixteenth centuries. Its origins lie in a medieval dance lyric with strong rustic or popular themes, but formally it is not dissimilar to the virelai. Usually the melody in the top voice is accompanied by two or three other voices in simple counterpoint. During the sixteenth century features of the Italian madrigal were assimilated, though relig-

ious themes became more and more prevalent.

Villanella [villanesca]. A light vocal form that first became popular in Italy in the 1530s. It would seem to have originated in Naples and developed from the frottola, with essentially homophonic textures and the melody in the top voice. The first published collection of villanellas was the *Canzone villanesche alla napolitana* of 1537. The form spread to Venice where it was cultivated, in a more sophisticated way, by Willaert and subsequently by Lassus who published two volumes in 1555 and 1581.

Viol [It.: viola da gamba]. A bowed string instrument with frets that first appeared in Europe in the fifteenth century, probably in Spain via North Africa, although the exact nature of its origin remains a matter of debate. It rapidly became one of the most popular of Renaissance instruments, being made in various sizes; evidence of viol consorts dates from the early sixteenth century.

Viola bastarda. An Italian term used in the sixteenth and seventeenth centuries for a small bass viol.

Virelai. One of the three French *formes fixes* (together with the rondeau and ballade) cultivated in the fourteenth and fifteenth centuries. Also originally a dance song, its musical form is essentially *ABBAA*.

Virginal. A term first used in an English treatise of *c.* 1460 (and still in currency until well into the seventeenth century) for a type of small harpsichord. Early examples are rectangular in shape but they could take a variety of forms, with harp-shaped or even polygonal designs being found in Italy.

Vitry, Philippe de (1291–1361). French theorist and composer. Having studied at the Sorbonne, he spent most of his career in royal service as secretary and diplomat. He was made Bishop of Meaux in 1351. His treatise entitled *Ars nova* (*c.* 1322–3) pioneered new developments in rhythm and notation that marked the 'new art' in Western musical history. Twelve motets are ascribed to him (the earliest of them being included in the *Roman de Fauvel*), in which the use of isorhythm as a structural principle was to prove especially influential on subsequent generations.

Voice-exchange. A technique employed in medieval polyphony whereby two voices of equal range exchange short musical phrases. It is found in the Notre Dame repertory, but was particularly cultivated by thirteenth-century English composers.

Votive Mass. Votive Masses are quite separate from those of the regular Church calendar. In the Middle Ages they were often endowed to benefit the souls of the dead, though there was also a growing tendency to add regular votive Masses to specific days of the week, such as the Mass in honour of the Virgin (or 'Lady Mass') usually celebrated on Saturdays. Alongside this development came that of the 'votive antiphon', again dedicated to the Virgin and sung at the end of Compline. Both provided further and very specific opportunities for the composition and performance of polyphony.

Walther von der Vogelweide (*c.* 1170–*c.* 1230). German Minnesinger. Probably of Austrian origin, he was at the Viennese court by about 1190, and later visited a number of European musical centres. He was renowned for his politically trenchant *Spruch* and perfected the form and content of that and the Minnelied. Despite a prolific output in both genres, only one complete surviving melody can be attributed to him with any certainty.

Weerbecke [Werbeck], **Gaspar van** (*c.* 1445–after 1517). Netherlands composer who may have been connected with the court of Charles the Bold of Burgundy before serving at the Sforza court in Milan from the early 1470s. He subsequently served in the papal choir and in the chapel of Philip the Fair. Most of his surviving works are sacred, and many of them, including Masses and motets, were published by Petrucci in the first decade of the sixteenth century. Five chansons are also attributed to him. His works reveal his mastery of the Netherlandish polyphonic idiom, but also the simpler, homophonic style of native Italian composers.

Wert, Giaches de (1535–96). Flemish composer active in Italy. From at least 1565 until 1592 he was *maestro di capella* to the Gonzaga family in Mantua, but he was also involved with poets and musicians of the Este court in Ferrara. A prolific and versatile composer (sixteen books of madrigals and secular vocal works were published between 1558 and 1608, as well as three books of sacred pieces, 1566–81), he exerted considerable influence over the young Monteverdi.

White, Robert (*c.* 1538–74). English composer. Having studied at Cambridge (1555–62), he became Master of the Choristers at Ely Cathedral (1562–6), Chester and Westminster Abbey (from 1570). He composed a considerable amount of sacred music (including two sets of Lamentations, other Latin liturgical works and anthems), as well as six viol fantasias.

Willaert, Adrian (*c.* 1490–1562). Flemish composer. He studied in Paris (under Mouton) before travelling to Italy where he was appointed *maestro di cappella* of St Mark's, Venice, in 1527. A prolific composer (eight Masses, over fifty hymns and psalms, almost two hundred motets, as well as about sixty chansons and some seventy madrigals), he was also an influential teacher: Porta, Rore, Zarlino and Andrea Gabrieli were among his pupils.

Winchester Troper. English MS, preserved at Corpus Christi, Cambridge, but originally from Winchester. Dating from *c.* 996–*c.* 1050, and containing 174 organa, it is one of the very earliest sources of polyphony.

Zacconi, Lodovico (1555–1627). Italian theorist. From 1577 to 1583 he studied in Venice under Andrea Gabrieli, subsequently being appointed a singer of the court chapel in Graz and later, from 1590 to 1596, at the Munich Hofkapelle under Lassus. He then returned to Italy. His *Prattica di musica*, published in two parts in 1592 and 1622, is an invaluable source for the light it sheds on contemporary performance practice.

Zacharius, Antonius [Antonio Zacar] (*fl.* 1391–1413). Italian composer, easily confused with Nicola Zacharie of Brindisi. Antonio would appear to have been the older of the two, and to have been the composer of the Mass movements attributed to 'Zacar', since some of them are based on secular songs ascribed with greater certainty to him. Nine secular pieces by him (mostly ballate) survive.

Zarlino, Gioseffo (1517–90). Italian theorist and composer. In 1541 he settled in Venice where he studied with Willaert, becoming *maestro di cappella* of St Mark's in 1565. His major contribution to the history of music theory, *Le istitutioni harmoniche* (1558), combined speculation on the musical traditions of the Ancients with contemporary compositional practice. He also composed motets (two books: 1549, 1566) and some madrigals.

Index

427